DATE DUE			

Mass Communication Review Yearbook

Editorial Board

Mass Communication Review Yearbook

Volume 3

1982

D. Charles Whitney
Ellen Wartella
Editors

Sven Windahl
Associate Editor

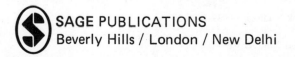
SAGE PUBLICATIONS
Beverly Hills / London / New Delhi

302.23
M 38
144152
May 1988

For information address:

SAGE Publications, Inc.
275 South Beverly Drive
Beverly Hills, California 90212

SAGE Publications India Pvt. Ltd.
C-236 Defence Colony
New Delhi 110 024, India

SAGE Publications Ltd
28 Banner Street
London EC1Y 8QE, England

Printed in the United States of America

International Standard Book Number 0-8039-1828-3

International Standard Series Number 0196-8017

FIRST PRINTING

Contents

Mass Communication Review Yearbook

About the Editors

D. CHARLES WHITNEY is research assistant professor in the Institute of Communications Research and assistant professor of journalism at the University of Illinois at Urbana-Champaign. He is a member of the Association for Education in Journalism, the International Association for Mass Communication Research, the International Communication Association, and the executive board of the Midwest Association for Public Opinion Research. His research has focused on sociological approaches to the study of mass communicators and on mass communication and public opinion. He is coeditor, with James S. Ettema, of *Individuals in Mass Media Organizations: Creativity and Constraint,* Volume 10 of the Sage Annual Reviews of Communication Research.

ELLEN WARTELLA is research assistant professor in the Institute of Communications Research and assistant professor of journalism at the University of Illinois at Urbana-Champaign. Her research on children and television has been published in a variety of communication journals and edited collections. She is coauthor of *How Children Learn to Buy* and editor of *Children Communicating,* Volume 7 of the Sage Annual Reviews of Communication Research. She is on the editorial board of the *Journal of Broadcasting* and is a member of the Broadcast Educators Association, the International Communication Association, the International Association for Mass Communication Research, and the Society for Research in Child Development. She is head of the Communication Theory and Methodology Division of the Association for Education in Journalism, and has been a consultant to the Federal Trade Commission and the Federal Communications Commission.

SVEN WINDAHL is senior lecturer in sociology and information techniques at the University College of Växjoe and the University of Lund. He has published in a number of communication journals and is coauthor, with Denis McQuail, of *Communication Models for the Study of Mass Communication.* Since 1976 he has been a principal investigator on a media panel research program at the University of Lund, and in 1981-1982 was visiting professor in the School of Journalism and Mass Communication at the University of Minnesota.

Preface

As new editors of the Sage *Mass Communication Review Yearbook* series, we are fortunate to follow the model established by our predecessors G. Cleveland Wilhoit and Harold de Bock. They have established this series as a collection of mass communication scholarship that is truly international in scope and diverse in theoretical and methodological orientation: Their work marks an excellent beginning to the series. We will both adopt and necessarily adapt their concept in this and future volumes.

As with the earlier volumes, Volume 3 has been aided by the members of our editorial board, whose names are listed in the front matter of the *Yearbook*. Thirty-eight scholars from around the world have recommended material for inclusion in this volume. Their assistance has been invaluable.

Of the hundreds of manuscripts and articles we evaluated, those selected were chosen for their diversity of critical and empirical theoretical approaches and variety of methodologies. Also, we were particularly interested in including major writings about the New World Information Order and the MacBride Commission.

Our associate editor, Sven Windahl, has aided us admirably in selecting materials for the *Yearbook* and in suggesting the kind of focus that would be most valuable to European researchers. We look forward to continuing to work with him on the next volume.

We wish to thank G. Cleveland Wilhoit and F. Gerald Kline for recommending us as editors of this series. We very much appreciate their advice and counsel. Doctoral students Ginny Bishoff and Linda Maguire of the Institute of Communications Research, University of Illinois, have provided bibliographic and administrative assistance; Marvene Blackmore and Anita Specht have helped with clerical matters.

Our colleagues of the Institute of Communications Research here at Illinois, and in particular Thomas Guback, have provided us with assistance in finding articles and manuscripts, suggestions for inclusion, and administrative support for the book. We wish to thank them.

—D. Charles Whitney
Ellen Wartella

INTRODUCTION

D. Charles Whitney and Ellen Wartella

By now, this series has achieved some stability. A reader who has followed the *Mass Communication Review Yearbook* through the past years can expect to find, and will find, familiar themes and a familiar structure in these pages. This volume, like the others, contains an amalgam of approaches to mass communication; it attempts, like the others, to represent the best thought and scholarship on the topic in recent years and makes a conscious effort to represent the work of established and young scholars from around the globe.

New editors, however, necessarily place different foci on the task of compiling a collection. We believe it is important to outline briefly our orientation to the field, as it underlies our approach to this task. While certainly it complements that of our predecessors, there are variations. We are less concerned, perhaps, with establishing a dialogue between Europeans and Americans than Wilhoit and de Bock were. In part that is because we believe such a dialogue has been established, to the benefit surely of both but particularly of the latter. We believe it is fair to say that those in the United States, in part because of the previous volumes in this series, are more aware of the criticisms of American-style communications research than was true even three years ago. There is, therefore, less emphasis in this volume on the "what's wrong with your kind of research" sort of arguments that have been made in various quarters in the recent past. Instead, we view it as our task to present studies from diverse places, which scholars of diverse orientations can evaluate on their own merits.

Nonetheless, the critiques from the recent past, including a few in this volume, have affected both our own work and our values as researchers. We have tried to avoid including pieces of research that are craftsmanlike and in some cases very skillfully executed, but which offer little substance. Such research still abounds. However, as our discussion below should indicate, neither do we believe that methodological sophistication and reliance on receiver-oriented views of communication effects necessarily disqualify a piece of research as interesting or important. By the same token, as Americans particularly have come to recognize recently, neither does lack of these elements prejudice a piece of work.

It would appear that we are endorsing a hodgepodge view of the field, a continuation of what Roberts and Bachen, in Chapter 1, below, describe as a characterization of mass communication research as a "potpourri, a borrowing area, lacking in unifying theory, a collection of suburbs in search of a city." Perhaps so.

But while this diversity of approach, theoretically and methodologically, has troubled mass communication researchers, particularly those who attempt to integrate the field and those who for good theoretical reasons wish to dismiss much of it, we view it otherwise: To us it suggests (a) that no scholar or school has convincingly demonstrated closure; none has a complete answer; (b) the current refraction of the field amply demonstrates that multiple perspectives produce varied results, and any future attempt at integration can be called into account if it does not reconcile them; and (c) that clearly the field of mass communication research will never regress to any of the formulations of its scope that might have seemed plausible a decade ago.

SCOPE OF THE YEARBOOK

Collected within this volume are forty chapters by authors from thirteen countries. In reviewing the several hundred pieces of work considered for this volume, we had a number of different purposes: The first was to expose to an American audience the work, and in some cases the names, of scholars of whom many might not be aware; moreover, for that audience, we also leaned heavily on selections from journals beyond its routine reading habits. However, on advice of our associate editor, Professor Windahl, we hope to serve an international audience by including some of the better American work which might be routinely available in the United States but less accessible elsewhere.

The volume is organized into six sections; of these, three have counterparts in previous volumes: Theoretical Perspectives on Communication Effects, International Communication, and Political Communication. The first of these, Theoretical Perspectives, likely will remain first in all numbers of this series. The second, International Communication (previously called International and Comparative Research), has been modified substantially from past volumes, because events have dictated it, as we note below. The third, Political Communication, is included in part because a substantial amount of energy and skill within the mass communication research community continues to be focused on this topic.

New sections are entitled On Television, Leisure and Media Use: Time and Money, and Dialogue. The first of these, a section on television, renders this volume the first in the series to focus on a medium. The articles themselves do this in various ways, and approaches from the most microscopic to the most macroscopic are included. The articles in the second of the new sections, on media use and leisure, are likewise diverse, but the range is different; here the spread is from the abstract-empirical to the cultural-historical. The final section, entitled Dialogue, might well be called Unfinished Business. Collected here are continuations of and responses to debates begun in the second volume of the series.

PART I: THEORETICAL PERSPECTIVES
ON COMMUNICATION EFFECTS

The past two volumes in this series have focused rather clearly on critiques of research perspectives, and two of the five chapters in this section, those by Thomas and Halloran, do that here. As might be expected, few of the authors here, or anywhere else, for that matter, clearly lay out what their full-blown theoretical perspectives are. What we have are five representatives of differing approaches to theorizing.

In their article on mass communication effects, which we have selected from the *Annual Review of Psychology*, Donald Roberts and Christine Bachen update previous reviews of the effects literature (Weiss, 1969, 1971) and find the field "resurgent," as it casts off a "limited effects" model. The review is dominated by citation to American empirical research, but to a lesser extent than the Weiss reviews on which it builds: Here we see references to American and British cultural writing, to the uses and gratifications literature, and to several sorts of structural approaches. The approach to theorizing is to lay out and review the approaches adopted by a number of researchers and to examine the progress made in defined areas in the 1970s; their overall conclusion is that the past ten years have seen the emergence of the formulation of higher-level statements about communication effects, statements grounded in empirical findings, more than was evident a decade ago.

Sari Thomas's review of what she considers mechanistic paradigms in the social and communication sciences concludes that models derived from such paradigms lack force; her purpose in her review is to argue for a "sociogenic, culturalist perspective" in communication research, one she finds applicable to various realms of inquiry about communication. Her review, however, is more a criticism of previous research than a specification of direction for future efforts, though clearly some such specification is derivable from the article.

Very different from either of these is David Phillips's work on air crashes and the mass media, which argues that multiple-death airline "accidents" in the United States can be viewed as possible imitative mass murders. Using available data including news-content analyses and air-crash records as a backdrop and confirmation, Philips explores the possibility for a modern theory of sociological imitation based on nineteenth-century writings by Tarde, LeBon, and others. Thus, while Roberts and Bachen approach theory from what the field of communication effects has been doing in the past decade, and Thomas wishes, by examining its assumptions and directions, to redirect it radically, Phillips is offering an account for a novel if still somewhat mechanical formulation of a direct media effect.

James Lemert's ambition in his chapter is somewhat different. His goal is to rescue scholars of communication and public opinion from a reductionist model; in doing so, however, Lemert remains clearly within the tradition of American-style political communication research (and this section should be read with those chapters in Part V). Lemert's project is to raise as a concern the levels-of-analysis problem and to remind researchers that failure to recognize some long-known conceptual problems has masked important findings in the past.

A final contribution in this section is James Halloran's discussion of the context of mass communication research. It may be viewed as a continuation of arguments Professor Halloran began to make in the second of this series. Again he reminds us that context always influences the content of research and that pressing problems remain internationally on the use and impact of emerging communication technologies. His discussion of ideology here, however, is new and of considerable import, and this chapter should be read with those in Part II on international communication.

PART II: INTERNATIONAL COMMUNICATION

Arguably the most important document on mass communication of a generation became available in 1981. The UNESCO International Commission for the Study of Communication Problems, presided over by Sean MacBride of the Republic of Ireland, made its report in late 1980, to the apparent satisfaction of virtually no one. That the stir raised by the MacBride Commission Report has been great should be of no surprise, as the orientations of the participants, and the commission's critics, differ profoundly, and the stakes in this debate are high. As MacBride notes in the preface to the report, international debates on world communication reached a level of stridency in the 1970s and the mandate to the commission was quite broad. While MacBride writes with optimism that some level of consensus was reached in the report, a number of its critics, including many of those whose comments are included here, argue otherwise. MacBride suggests the "New World Information and Communication Order" may be "more accurately defined as a process than any given set of conditions and practices," but other commentators argue that this commission has not defined that order at all. Moreover, as some of these critics note, the report almost by necessity represents a set of geopolitical compromises; hence it gives rise to contradictions, vaguenesses, and points of future conflict. As MacBride himself has noted publicly, however, this report may be the most criticized unread document in recent history; our abstract here is necessarily brief, and the report merits a full reading.

In addition to the sections of the report and commentaries on it, we have included the "Declaration of Talloires," a statement of principles issued by a group of Western journalists in the wake of the report, and two articles on the theory of media imperalism and cultural dependency. The latter two, and the notion of dependency, are clearly important to the debate on world communication and the MacBride Report. In this section, Professor C. C. Lee lays out what he believes to be problems inherent in the analysis of media, economic and cultural dependency theory. He suggests that most writers on the Left, in their articulation of problems in the world communication order, "are good at diagnosis but poor at therapy," in that they have pointed to a number of problems in that order, but their "suggestions for policy solutions tend to be unrealistic and always stop short of enough specification and elaboration to be empirically testable."

Professor Fejes's article on the theory of media imperialism differs considerably from Professor Lee's. While Lee would like to rationalize the study of dependency by making it empirically testable, Fejes suggests that this is currently beyond the capabilities of the social sciences; if this is so, then to render the concepts so narrowly will necessarily kill the theory aborning.

It should go without saying that the articles collected here hardly represent the last word on the topic. Volume 4 in this series certainly will continue the dialogue on the world information order.

PART III: ON TELEVISION

The five articles we have chosen for this section were not selected explicitly because they deal with a particular medium. Rather they were included because they represent important approaches and directions in the field of mass commu nication research. They range from the relatively microscopic level of experimental study of children's attention to television to the macroscopic cultural-institutional analysis of this medium. What is truly interesting within levels, though, is what has happened along the way: No longer is the viewer in these studies considered a receptacle, on the one hand, or the institution viewed as monolith, on the other.

In the first of these articles, Daniel Anderson and his colleagues demonstrate that for young children of varying ages, TV program comprehensibility is a major determinant of attention to television, thus undermining the notions that children are eyes-glued-to-the-set viewers or are attuned primarily to production features of programming. The importance of this research should not be underestimated. In most approaches, attention is viewed as a necessary condition for comprehension. Here Anderson and his colleagues suggest clearly that the reverse may be true as well; hence the relationship may best be considered interactive.

Also of considerable importance is the next article, by Messaris and Sarett. The recent past has seen a decline in the importance ascribed to parent-child interactions concerning television, and this chapter seeks to reverse that trend. Messaris and Sarett argue that such interactions influence children's development of cognitive categories regarding the real world, their interpretations of television, their acquisition of behaviors from television, and their development of real-world social relationships. Moreover, Messaris and Sarett argue that examination of such consequences requires employment of qualitative research methods to supplement quantitative ones.

Lull's study of television employs a qualitative methodology, that of the ethnography, to examine the social uses to which television is put in families. Lull also argues, following a uses-and-gratifications model, that audience members "create specific and sometimes elaborate practical actions involving the mass media in order to gratify particular needs in the social context of family television viewing." His typology of such needs includes structural uses like environmental and regulative needs and relational uses, including communication facilitation, affiliation or avoidance, social learning and competence, or dominance display. His observational and interview data furnish rich evidence that these uses are derived from family viewing.

A rather different approach to the use of television is in the next article, by Csikszentmihalyi and Kubey. These authors persuaded adults to report activities and mood states when signaled at random intervals by an electronic paging "beeper" over the course of a week. They report television use to be detached, tied consistently to feelings of relaxation, passivity, and drowsiness. Moreover, a valuable feature of this study is the comparison of television attention with other realms of activity, such as work and public leisure. Reading the Lull study with this one offers a view of watching television that is richer than those usually available. Lull suggests that viewing serves as a context for social strategies and uses. Csikszentmihalyi and Kubey, on the other hand, find viewing to be passive and uninvolving. These stands are not necessarily in conflict. Both suggest, as do the previous two studies, that for the audience, watching television is more than simply watching television. It is a context in which things are done.

The final selection in Part III is a critical/institutional analysis of American network television as a monopoly business and as a cultural apparatus. Douglas Kellner attempts to develop a critical theory of television by focusing on the network, by which he means not simply ABC, NBC, or CBS, but the system of commercial broadcasting more generally. He departs from extant critical analyses of media institutions by focusing on a number of "contradictions" within the American system. Most analyses of television to date, he argues, have failed to account for many of these tensions, to the detriment of serious theorizing about the location of television in social thought. Clearly this article is in a different realm from the others in this section; it is, however, a lucid and provocative account of the American commercial television system.

Of considerable interest to television studies but not available at press time for this volume is the forthcoming update of the 1972 Surgeon General's report on television and social behavior (Pearl, Bouthilet, and Lazar, forthcoming). It is our hope to be able to include material from this report in the next volume of this series.

PART IV: LEISURE AND MEDIA USE:
TIME AND MONEY

In this section are five articles on use of mass media and leisure. The approaches vary. While each author is concerned with how people make use of cultural materials, the relevant evidence for each is different. It is possible, for example, when a researcher considers the use of media materials, to begin by attempting an index or measure of such usage: One builds a "culture scale" by attempting to look at the time or money spent on cultural products; in large part, this is Richard

Peterson's ambition in the first article in this section. This article is clearly administrative, as Professor Peterson rues the "untidy" state of data related to understanding how much and what kinds of leisure products people consume, and how much, if anything, people obtain by consuming them.

The next three articles can profitably be read together. Maxwell McCombs and Chaim Eyal, in studying aggregate economic expenditures for American media 1968-1977, and Jeremy Tunstall, in studying the British press in the "age of television," are concerned with alterations in the use of print media in a time of change in the media marketplace. McCombs and Eyal characterize U.S. print media expenditures as "resilient" in the face of economic and functional competition from audiovisual media. Tunstall's analysis of the British press, on the other hand, employs more diversified data, and his findings are somewhat richer. His principal assertion, that the British press has become more polarized along class lines with the advent of television, is the sort of conclusion that the aggregate economic data approach of McCombs and Eyal cannot be sensitive to: Within the institution of the British press, Tunstall's data show, economic health remains, but press organizations have had to modify their goals, ambitions, and content. The Sahin and Robinson article looks more directly at television. Here the authors' concern is with how men and women make use of time in modern society, and their reading of U.S. time diary studies that parallel the time points in the McCombs and Eyal data. And while the McCombs and Eyal data appear to indicate that the amount of spending on media declined in the decade, the Sahin and Robinson time data indicate a different trend in media use: The decade was marked by a decrease in time required for work, and this increase in available free time was "colonized," and more, by increased use of television.

Taken together, these studies appear to indicate that in the 1970s people were shifting slightly in how they allocated finite resources, time, and money in filling their lives. However, the four studies that lead this section, relying as they do on aggregate data, can say relatively little about *how* cultural products are used in making sense of one's life. Other approaches to the study of media as use of leisure, which focus less on what is "consumed" and more on how meaning is taken, or created, from cultural products, are necessary for that. The final paper in this section, by Simon Frith, is in that realm. Taking punk rock music as a case study, Frith reviews contrasting theoretical approaches to criticism of popular culture, notably those of the Frankfurt School and those of the followers of Walter Benjamin. His conclusion is that these contrasting approaches mirror a larger problem of contradiction in understanding the meaning of "consumption" in the study of popular culture. Two comments seem necessary here. First is that Frith's project is one that cannot be transferred directly to the sorts of research the previous authors have executed; he is dealing with a subculture, not the mass culture, if culture is implied at all in the preceding works. Second is that his work articulates an approach to the study of the meanings constructed in the use of media barely implied in the preceding studies, and therein lies its strength.

PART V: POLITICAL COMMUNICATION

Since empirical mass communication research began to grow up in the 1940s, there has been no shortage of interest in and research about the relationship between mass communication and politics, and particularly there has been no shortage of effort to demonstrate that the mass media impact on the way people reach political decisions. However, this road has been rocky, and parked beside it are the remains of a number of models.

This is not to say that interest in the field has declined. On the contrary, the emergence, ten years ago now, of the agenda-setting hypothesis breathed new life into the area. Although the two earlier volumes in this series have contained chapters on this hypothesis, and although this past year has marked the publication of a major review of this literature (McCombs, 1981), we have included several articles in this section dealing with it as well, homage to the dominance of this model in political communication research.

The first article, by Carlsson, Dahlberg, and Rosengren, examines relationships between social structure, aggregate public opinion, and mass media news and opinion across eight years in Sweden and finds that a measure of social structure, business demand for skilled labor, exerts a more direct and stronger influence on an opinion measure than does press information and opinion. This careful study, however, is at a grand aggregate level, and as other agenda-setting studies below suggest, the model demands tests at the individual level as well.

The chapter by Becker is a stern look at agenda-setting research to date. About agenda-setting, Becker might well have chosen the Scottish legal doctrine, "not proved." As Becker points out, the agenda-setting model as explored to date has oversimplified what is a complex phenomenon, in large part because of conceptual vagueness and methodological problems and because of a general failure to articulate assumptions underlying the models.

The following chapter by Weaver is in part an answer to Becker. Weaver finds himself more "optimistic" about the agenda-setting phenomenon than does Becker and discusses whether the existence of such a phenomenon is evidence of media manipulation. Here, he admits, a researcher is groping in gray conceptual areas, but his review suggests that in general there is little evidence to suggest such a relationship.

While Doris Graber is known for her agenda-setting research as well, her aim here is to suggest that much recent research on mass communication and public opinion has become mired because of a concern with what she labels "pseudo-opinion." Moreover, she argues, the research agenda should be shifted to include information-processing models not heretofore adopted in political communication research, and, at a higher level of analysis, to include further research on the "linkage" between public and press opinion and governmental political decision-making.

Steven H. Chaffee and Sun Yuel Choe introduce a new unit of analysis, that of time of reaching an election decision, to account for differences in media use and media influence. Inconsistencies in impact of the media on political decision-making, they argue, can in part be resolved by attention to varying times of decision: The media do not influence those who are committed to a candidate before a campaign begins, and they certainly do not influence those "late deciders" who pay no attention to them, but among those who decide during a campaign, media content can exert an influence.

What these five studies suggest is that while an earlier "limited effects" model of mass communication influence may be too narrow-gauge, it is absolutely necessary to stipulate a considerable amount of—to specify to a relatively high degree—the conditions under which political media exert political effects; these studies, in short, are arguments for a return to a "powerful effects" model not of media influence, but of moderate and demonstrable effects.

The final two selections in this section are less closely tied to the effects paradigm, though the chapter by Blumler borrows heavily from it. Blumler and Elliott in their respective chapters are more concerned with the producers of political messages, as is Weaver in part. Blumler's search is for a political philosophy of mass communication that would serve as a guide for political communicators, especially in television, and for the polity. His review draws the outline for such a philosophy by relying on recent Western thought on political democracy and takes issue with Marxist analyses of media.

Elliott's chapter is clearly outside the "mainstream" of political communication-effects research. It can, however, profitably be read with the Blumler article, for the assumptions each makes about the nature of media organizations are both parallel and distinct. Elliott's article is a fascinating exploration of the applicability of cultural studies' notions of ritual to press performance in situations where the social order is disrupted, and his findings are persuasive. Of particular interest, in addition, are his conclusions, which suggest use of an interactional model and qualitative approaches to the study of the relationship between audiences and political media, and in this context, this chapter should be compared with Weaver's comments on media manipulation.

In sum, these articles should suggest that the field of political communication is neither static nor monolithic. In terms of emphasis here, however, it would appear, and unfairly so, that it is largely effects-centered and quantitatively based, and it is our hope that future volumes will broaden that range somewhat.

PART VI: DIALOGUE

Perhaps nothing marks research and scholarship more clearly than debate and dissent. In past volumes of this series, the bulk of debate has focused primarily on the broad issues of perspective and traditions in research—European versus American, critical versus cultural versus administrative. An exception was the beginning of a critique of the cultivation research by George Gerbner and his colleagues at the University of Pennsylvania, by Paul Hirsch and others. Given the nature, quality, and breadth of the critique by Hirsch and the response by Gerbner and his associates, our decision to include these articles was without hesitation. The critique and response are particularly valuable for raising issues at several levels: Within these articles are issues of theory, method, validation, and procedure. They suggest as well that which is known but rarely articulated within the research community—that the process of doing research is more than the careful and dispassionate process of thinking and collecting evidence and thinking again; research is a social activity and open to question, to disagreement, to conflict.

The final paper in this section is also by way of response to an article in the last volume. In it, Graham Murdock replies to Anderson and Sharrock's contentions that studies of news bias have ignored problems of validation. While Murdock agrees with them that content-analytic studies cannot stand alone, his reply suggests that the earlier reading of the media-studies literature was too narrow.

CONCLUSIONS

That we have included a "dialogue" section is an indication of what we think is an important trend in the field: that it has begun to develop its own literature of criticism relatively independent of other disciplines but still at a fairly high level of conceptualization. Such criticism, moreover, may be found not only in the last section of this volume but elsewhere in it as well, as the Becker and Weaver and Fejes and Lee chapters testify.

Our review of the current literature of mass communication research over the past few months has led us to several other generalizations as well, and we hope the book reflects these. Chief among them is one Professor Wilhoit noted in the last volume, that citations to great social thinkers are on the increase. Moreover, citations in American work to European and British sources are increasing as well. There is substantial evidence that the flow of ideas about mass communication is becoming not only two-way but truly international, in many directions.

In addition, the field is seeing greater reliance on qualitative methodologies, and not just at macroscopic levels; included in this volume are several representatives of qualitative research at the individual and microsocial levels, and these were exceedingly rare just a few years ago. Why this is occurring is not simply answered; that it is occurring, however, we view as a favorable and healthy development.

This, however, should not be read as an indication that quantitative empirical approaches to the field are in retreat. On the contrary, development continues in these areas, particularly in regions where such approaches are already strong, such as in media-effects and political communication research. Moreover, these two areas are also moving toward genuine development by reliance on and augmentation of recent developments in cognitive psychology and cognitive social psychology, and there is no sign that such developments will wane.

Finally, we must note that there appears to be increasing interest in, and certainly a quickening urgency about, the development of the field of international mass communication research. The articles by Lee and Fejes, and the commentary on the MacBride Commission Report generally, signal this. The former especially are also evidence that serious consideration is being given to development of theoretical models in this area.

In all, our review of materials in the field indicates optimism for the future. Certainly there is no reason to believe that in the near future theory in the field will become unified or elegant. The concerns that the scholars here and others in the area have are too closely tied to the real world and its exigencies for one to expect that. However, under the penumbra of mass communication research, a generous amount of high-quality thought, energy, and experience is being applied to problems of complexity and substance, and this is a promising sign.

CONTENT OF FUTURE VOLUMES

Making forecasts about the contents of future numbers in any series is hazardous duty. Such contents are dependent upon the emergence of quality research within more specialized topic areas. However, it is certain that the next number in this series will allot space to continuing discussion of international communication, and we would hope that theoretical developments in this field especially will be featured. Other topics in which significant research can be expected to surface in the next year include two of special promise. These are economic and technological policy research and studies of mass communicators, and we would expect sections devoted to them. About the rest we are hopeful but not certain.

REFERENCES

McCOMBS, M. (1981) "The agenda-setting approach." In D. D. Nimmo and K. R. Sanders (eds.) Handbook of Political Communication. Beverly Hills, CA: Sage Publications.

PEARL, D., L. BOUTHILET, and D. LAZAR [eds.] (forthcoming) Television and Behavior: Ten Years of Scientific Progress and Implications for the Eighties. Washington, DC: Government Printing Office.

WEISS, W. (1971) "Mass communication." Annual Rev. of Psychology 22: 309-336.

——— (1969) "Effects of the mass media of communication." In G. Lindzey and E. Aronson (eds.) Handbook of Social Psychology. Reading, MA: Addison-Wesley

PART I

THEORETICAL PERSPECTIVES ON COMMUNICATION EFFECTS

Theory, certainly, is an enduring concern for all scholars of communication. The first two volumes in this series explored the interchange of theoretical perspectives between American and British and European scholars, and a principal concern in those volumes was the relationship between theorizing and the boundaries of the field. In this volume, however, the bulk of the section stresses summary, integration, and elaboration of what theory in mass communication is.

The first article in this section is a summary of recent research on the effects of mass communication. American empirical research is stressed. As Roberts and Bachen demonstrate, the recent past is marked by some features for which others have seen fit to criticize mass communication research, namely its diversity and relative lack of emphasis on theorizing. However, as they also note, the recent past is marked as well by an emphasis on cognition that may lead to genuine conceptual development.

The second article in this series, however, calls into question the paradigms of media effects generally employed in media research and in corollary areas. Sari Thomas's perspective, a cultural approach to understanding mass communication, is represented by other research included in this volume.

David Phillips, in the third article included here, argues for a modern theory of imitation and suggestion in media-effects studies. This article is included in large part because it represents a novel and disturbing departure from the usual range of inquiry into communication effects.

The contribution by James Lemert, arguing for a change of direction in studying public opinion, is, as the author himself suggests, not a novel contribution, as it draws directly on the work of others. But if Lemert's advice is heeded, the way media scholars attempt to study mass communication effects on public opinion would be altered considerably. This chapter can profitably be read with those in Part V, the section on political communication.

Finally, the contribution by James Halloran, which can serve as an introduction to Part II, International Communication, represents an extension of suggestions and criticisms Halloran first made in Volume 2. His discussion of ideology in communication research can benefit all.

This update of Walter Weiss's earlier reviews of mass communication effects covers the waterfront of recent research on the effects of mass communication. Roberts and Bachen note that the field of mass communication research in recent years has seen a broadening and deepening of understanding about effects, manifested in a growth of the field, attempts at synthesis, and especially in a widening of the domain. This, coupled with a growth of cognitive approaches to the area, according to the authors, leads to a conclusion of genuine conceptual development in the field. Donald F. Roberts is associate professor and Christine M. Bachen a doctoral student and research associate at the Institute for Communication Research, Stanford University.

1

MASS COMMUNICATION EFFECTS

Donald F. Roberts and Christine M. Bachen

INTRODUCTION AND OVERVIEW

It is appropriate to describe the state of mass communication research at the end of the 1970s as resurgent. By the end of the 1950s the field was limping along under the burden of the "law of minimal effects"—the generalization that the dominant influence of the mass media was reinforcement

Preparation of this review was aided by a grant from the John and Mary R. Markle Foundation.

of the status quo, an effect viewed by many as having little import (Katz 1977, Comstock et al 1978). The past decade, however, has witnessed a revival of the view that the mass media exert powerful influences on the way people perceive, think about, and ultimately act in their world.

The field's resurgence is manifested in various ways. One is the presence in our bibliography of a number of communication journals and annuals that simply did not exist when the decade began In addition, a number of major syntheses of the effects of mass media on different aspects of human behavior have appeared (Kraus & Davis 1976, Lerner & Nelson 1977, Comstock et al 1978, Murray & Kippax 1979). A third indicator of the field's revival is the emergence (in some cases reemergence) of an array of new and important dependent variables—a broadening of the meaning of the term "mass media effect." The earlier focus on persuasion and attitude change has given way to a belief that the media exert important influences on the consciousness and world view of the audience (Gerbner & Gross 1976a, Katz 1980). Concern with cognitive effects, with mass communication's influence on how people perceive and organize their world, is becoming more the rule than the exception. Moreover, "cognitive" effects are being conceptualized more broadly, extending beyond traditional knowledge indexes to include such outcomes as perceptions of reality, issue salience, information holding, message discrimination, and so forth (Clarke & Kline 1974, Chaffee 1977). Other healthy trends include increased attention to contingent conditions underlying media effects (McLeod & Reeves 1980), a return to a concern with entertainment fare and its impact on consciousness and cognitions (Gerbner et al 1979, Tannenbaum 1980), and growing attention to *processing* of mass mediated information including: examinations of how social and cognitive factors affect comprehension of narrative plots (Collins 1979a), of the role of cognitive development in children's comprehension of television messages (Wackman & Wartella 1977, Roberts et al 1978), and of whether "meaning" is extracted from print and television in the same way (Salomon 1979a). Finally, the field is beginning to spawn a number of lively theoretical and methodological debates. Special issues of journals, entire annuals, and a number of syntheses and "reconsiderations" debate whether "there is any there, there . . ." in terms of such issues as uses and gratifications research (Blumler & Katz 1974, Swanson 1979a), the impact of television violence (Comstock et al 1978, Eysenck & Nias 1978), the role of mass communication in economic and social development (Rogers 1976a, Schramm & Lerner 1976), and the significance for broadcasting of social research (Carey 1978, Halloran 1978, Katz 1978a,b).

All this is not to say that characterizations of mass communication research applied by earlier reviewers—descriptions of the field as a potpourri, a borrowing area, lacking in unifying theory, a collection of suburbs in search of a city (Schramm 1962, Tannebaum & Greenberg 1968, Weiss 1971, Liebert & Schwartzberg 1977)—are no longer accurate. They remain as valid today as they were then. But this should not be surprising given the sheer ubiquity of the mass media in everyday aspects of contemporary U.S. society, hence the "problem orientation" of the field. Almost every dimension of social behavior is at least potentially influenced by mass communication (Weiss 1969, Comstock et al 1978, Chaffee 1979). Politics, health, prosocial and antisocial behavior, attitudes toward almost every definable group within society, occupational knowledge, education, consumer behavior, all these and more have been pointed to by parents, educators, policy makers, and the media themselves as being influenced, for better or ill, by mass communication. In the face of such an array of concerns, researchers from a variety of fields with a variety of theoretical orientations contribute to the mass communication research literature in order to "solve problems." Small wonder that so many of these contributions maintain an applied tenor, and that "communication variables" seem to proliferate faster than does our understanding (Foley 1979).

This problem orientation is one of the factors that for so long led researchers to concentrate on attitude and behavior change as *the* important media effect. At bottom, public concern with media portrayals of sex or violence, or with the role of television in political campaigns, is based on assumptions of direct effects of media content on behavior. And given the dominant view of the 1950s and 1960s that attitudes directly mediated behavior, it was reasonable to focus on the impact of media on behavior when convenient (e.g. votes, fights in the schoolyard) and on attitudes when less convenient (e.g. whom do you like or dislike?). It was only as the gradual accumulation of evidence made the causal linkages among knowledge, attitude, and behavior highly ambiguous that the media's impact on various cognitive indicators began to receive more attention (Chaffee 1977). Thus, current research and theorizing indicate that the cognitive outcomes of mass communication, whether from informational or entertainment content, are no longer taken for granted or deemed less important than attitudinal or behavioral outcomes (Chaffee 1977, Dennis 1978). Rather, various cognitive effects have gained at least conceptual equality, and in some areas, conceptual dominance.

This is not to imply that concern with how specific kinds of media content affect people's behavior or with how special groups of people might be affected is waning. Mass communication research continues to respond to problems articulated by various interest groups and/or funding sources because the media continue to impinge on most areas of social behavior. Thus, much of the literature organizes itself around various "problems" defined in terms of the particular kind of behavior mass communication content is presumed to influence (e.g. politics, violence, health) or in terms of special audiences presumed to be particularly vulnerable (e.g. children, the poor, women, the aging) (Comstock 1978, Comstock et al 1978).

To some extent this review reflects that problem orientation because it is convenient and it indicates the kinds of research that have been emphasized. For example, we continue to deal with children and youth as a special audience, a practice which certainly mirrors current literature. Nevertheless, organization of empirical findings in terms of special topics or groups can be dysfunctional to the development of more general, middle-range theories of the process and effects of mass communication. To the extent that studies of political campaigns, product campaigns, health campaigns, and so forth are conceptualized and dealt with separately, the benefits of comparison are lost. We give up the advantage of sharpened contrast between differences, we risk overlooking important similarities, and we sometimes assume nonexistent differences. Comstock et al (1978) provide an example of the benefits to be gained from handling the results of two types of campaign—political and product oriented—within the same framework. The following pages attempt to overlay the more common problem areas with a somewhat more general, process-oriented framework.

A few caveats are necessary. The literature search concentrated on work published between 1975 and early 1980, but some reference to earlier literature is made in order to provide a context for current research. The review does not pretend to be comprehensive. Given the eclectic nature of the field, our strategy was to emphasize work particularly relevant to psychologists. This we interpreted to mean primarily work concerned with the influence on individuals of exposure to media content. Hence, these pages contain little consideration of the various sociological and institutional studies that take a more macroscopic view of mass media processes and organizations. Finally, even in those topic areas that are covered, we make no claim to be all-inclusive. We attempted to provide a sense of the conceptual issues that have received research attention and to detail many, but not all, of the relevant empirical studies. We believe that the following pages fairly represent the mainstream of mass communication research over the past 5 years, at least insofar as the effects of mass communication on individuals are concerned.

PATTERNS OF USE

Exposure to the various media is a necessary precondition for any effect of content on people to occur. Exposure is a function of a number of environmental, social, and psychological conditions that influence the availability of various media and types of media content, the communication skills and information needs of people, and the psychosocial gratifications related to media use. The picture emerging from work reported during the past 5 years does not differ greatly from earlier findings. There has been a tendency for television use to increase; the evidence is that newspaper use is decreasing, patterns of radio and magazine use continue to receive short shrift in the academic literature; there is increasing attention to children's use of news media; there has been a great deal of activity in the area of uses and gratifications research.

Television

An extensive analysis of Nielsen data through 1976 indicates that the trend in amount of television viewing since the early 1960s has been upward. Although there are wide variations depending on which segment of the audience is surveyed, the trend holds across most demographic classifications but is most pronounced among groups which viewed less a decade ago. For example, from 1970 to 1976 the average hours per day that the household television set was on increased from 6.5 hours to over 6.8 hours. However, for that part of the sample in which the head of household had less than one year of college education the increase was only two tenths of an hour (from 6.8 to 7.0). But in households indexed by one or more years of college, the increase was almost eight tenths of an hour [from 5.6 to 6.39 (Comstock et al 1978)]. Moreover, over 25% of mothers in a recent national sample of families reported that the TV set was on for at least 9 hours per day (Newspaper Advertising Bureau 1978), and over 35% of a sample of California families were classified as "constant television households," households in which the set was on most of the afternoon, during dinner, and most of the evening (Medrich 1979). Amount of time the set is on, of course, is quite different from the amount of time that any particular individual views. Nevertheless, to the extent that an operating television set is a relatively constant feature of the environment, individuals tend to view more.

The most frequently examined predictors of individual television use continue to be gender, various socioeconomic status indicators, and age, with the latter receiving the greatest emphasis. Purposive television viewing begins between 2 and 3 years of age (Anderson et al 1979, von Feilitzen 1976). Several syntheses of a large number of U.S. studies describe the age progression in amount of viewing as one of gradual increase to a peak in early adolescence, followed by a sharp decline in late adolescence, relatively low amounts of viewing during adulthood, and then a gradual increase through later adulthood to the heaviest period of use after the age of 50 years (Bower 1973, Chaffee & Wilson 1975, Comstock et al 1978). A review of international studies of television viewing patterns generally accords with these findings (Murray & Kippax 1979).

The relationship between amount of television viewing and age can be largely attributed to variations in available time which occur as a function of competing activities located by different periods in the life cycle. This is illustrated by such phenomena as the temporary decrease in children's amount of viewing at about 5 or 6 years of age, when school begins to compete for their time (Comstock et al 1978), and by the dramatic increase in all media use among older people who, subsequent to retirement, have a good deal of time to view, listen, and read (Chaffee & Wilson 1975, Danowski 1975, Atkin 1976).

Studies continue to indicate that adult women view more than men (again, probably due to available time) and that amount of viewing is inversely related to education, income, and occupational status, although all of these relationships tend to be somewhat weaker than they were some years ago (Bower 1973, Comstock et al 1978). The data are also relatively consistent in the finding that blacks view more than whites even after controls for socioeconomic status and education are applied. More interesting is the evidence that patterns of television use among blacks depart rather dramatically from patterns revealed by whites. Younger black adults view more than do older blacks, and better educated blacks view more than do lesser educated blacks (Comstock et al 1978). Allen & Bielby (1979) point to the dangers in comparative studies that conceive of blacks as a relatively homogeneous group, and demonstrate wide variations in media behavior within a black sample.

The role ascribed to television in our society is that of light entertainer; hence, most people are content to "watch television" as opposed to watching particular programs (Comstock et al 1978). Probably the best indicator of what types of television content are viewed, then, is inherent in the distribution of programs in any TV log. Of course, various demographic and personality variables have been shown to relate to viewing of different types of television content. However, with the exception of a number of studies of children's exposure to news programming examined below, little has appeared to change the general patterns reported in earlier reviews (Liebert & Schwartzberg 1977, Comstock et al 1978).

Newspapers

Recent evidence suggests that daily newspaper readership is in a period of real decline. According to National Opinion Research Center surveys, the proportion of adults who claimed to read a newspaper every day declined from 73% in 1967, to 66% in 1975, to only 57% in 1978 (Robinson & Jeffres 1979).

Attempts to explain the decrease have ranged from examinations of increased television news programming (Bogart 1975a) to sociological phenomena such as the decline in home ownership, the increase in single person households, the increase of women in the labor force, changes in amount of available time, and fractionation of the cities (Bogart 1975b, Denbow 1975, Robinson & Jeffres 1979), to such psychological constructs as "traditional values," "satisfaction with life" (Bryant et al 1976), and various civic attitudes (McCombs & Poindexter 1978). Stamm & Fortini-Campbell (1977) report strong positive correlations between individuals' sense of belonging to a community and newspaper subscriptions and readership.

Most of the same demographic variables that predict television use also predict newspaper readership. However, several of the relationships are reversed. Two recent, large-scale studies (Newspaper Advertising Bureau 1978, 1980a,b,c, Robinson & Jeffres 1979) continue to find that daily newspaper reading is positively related to income and education, that whites read more than blacks, and that there is less newspaper availability in single parent households and in households with younger children.

Newspaper readership is directly related to age (Robinson & Jeffres 1979), the relationship appearing as early as the elementary school years (Newspaper Advertising Bureau 1980a). Large proportions of younger people, however, do not have the newspaper habit. Robinson & Jeffres (1979) found that over 85% of a national sample of people over 60 years reported "using a newspaper yesterday," but just 51% of adults under the age of 29 years did so. A particularly noteworthy dimension of this finding is that it represents an increase in the age differences found a decade earlier. That is, there is a striking trend toward decreasing newspaper use across age cohorts; young adults who do not manifest a newspaper habit are less likely than earlier generations to develop that habit as they grow older (Jennings & Niemi 1975, Robinson & Jeffres 1979). Conversely, each succeeding generation is more likely than its predecessor to cite television over newspapers as its major news source (Roper Organization 1977). These findings take on particular significance in light of research (reported later) on the relationship between media use and public affairs knowledge.

Children and the News Media

Interest in the role of the mass media in the political socialization of children has sparked increased attention to children's exposure to news and public affairs media. Not surprisingly, most children's introduction to the world of politics and public affairs comes through television. Although much of the evidence is based on nonrandom samples of children, and it is often difficult to determine just what "news viewing" consists of, several studies converge in their finding that children are exposed to television news at much younger ages than had been previously assumed (Hawkins et al 1975, Roberts et al 1975, Rubin 1978, Prisuta 1979). Indeed, news viewing occurs among significant numbers of early elementary school and even kindergarten children (Atkin 1978, Egan 1978). Most studies find that news viewing increases with age throughout the childhood and adolescent years to the point that almost all adolescents report at least minimal television news exposure. Atkin (1978) found that over half of a sample of elementary school children watched Saturday morning children's news programming "a lot." There is also evidence that self-reported liking for news programs predicts amount of news viewing even among young children (Atkin 1978, Prisuta 1979), although these data suffer from problems of correlated response error.

Newspaper use, of course, depends on the development of reading skills. The newspaper, as well as other print media, begins to be relatively comprehensible after the age of 9 years, which is also about the time that school-related newspaper use begins. By late adolescence half of the 15- to 17-year-olds responding reported regular newspaper reading (Newspaper Advertising Bureau 1980a). The importance of the newspaper as a source of information increases throughout the school years (Conway et al 1975, Newspaper Advertising Bureau 1980a,b). In spite of the increase in newspaper use, however, the data are quite clear that children continue to prefer television over newspapers as a source of information during both the elementary school years (Egan 1978) and the high school years (Atkins & Elwood 1978), a trend which we have already noted now continues into adulthood. High school students also label television as the most believable news medium (Atkins & Elwood 1978).

Attention has also focused on how the family context influences children's use of the news media. There is evidence for a modeling effect in that children whose parents view television news are more likely to view, and for an effect of direct stimulation in that children whose parents discuss the news with them are more likely to view (Atkin 1978, Egan 1978). Similarly, the availability of a daily newspaper in the household, parental newspaper behavior, and parental discussion of newspaper content all predict children's newspaper use (Newspaper Advertising Bureau 1980a,c). Finally, the family communication system typology described by Chaffee et al (1977) indicates how the norms inherent in a family interactions influence children's public affairs media use. Children from homes stressing independent thinking and self-expression on potentially controversial topics continue to report more exposure to the news media (Jackson-Beeck & Chaffee 1975, Roberts et al 1975).

Given the evidence that parents and the environment they create are important mediators of children's future news media behavior, and that successive cohorts of young adults use newspapers less and television news more, the decline in newspaper readership and increased dependence on television for news and information seems likely to continue at an increasing pace.

Uses and Gratifications

Although recent claims that uses and gratifications research has become the most popular and important approach to the study of mass communication (Swanson 1979a,b) seem a bit overstated, the amount of empirical activity and theoretical debate focusing on the uses and gratifications approach certainly supports Blumler & Katz's (1974) contention that "it is well and truly launched on a third major phase of its development . . ." (p. 13). Uses and gratifications research is audience centered, asking what people do with media rather than what the media do to people. It has been summarized as "concerned with 1. the social and psychological origins of 2. needs, which generate 3. expectations of 4. the mass media or other sources, which lead to 5. differential patterns of media exposure (or engagement in other activities), resulting in 6. need gratifications and 7. other consequences, perhaps mostly unintended ones" (Katz et al 1974, p. 20). Blumler & Katz (1974) characterize early uses and gratifications studies (1940s and 50s) as primarily descriptive, and the second phase (1960s) as mainly concerned with operationalizing the needs presumed to mediate different patterns of media consumption. Current work they see as more explanatory in nature—concerned with relating media consumption to systematic formulations of social and psychological needs and, ultimately, with understanding the relationship between patterns of gratifications sought and obtained and media effects. Palmgreen & Rayburn (1979) argue that it is just this emphasis on the "active" audience and concern with how need-related gratification activities mediate effects that underlies the burgeoning popularity of the approach. Certainly current work expresses these concerns, but empirical demonstrations of the genesis of basic needs presumed to underlie consumption, or of how gratifications sought and/or obtained mediate more "traditional" effects, or that the audience is indeed active, are more the exception than the rule.

Not surprisingly, increased interest in uses and gratifications research has spawned critical voices. Several point to the tautological shortcomings of functional theories in general (Carey & Kreiling 1974, Elliott 1974, Anderson & Meyer 1975), and comment on the problems inherent in uses and gratifications' concentration on the individual-as-system rather than the individual-within-a-system (Elliot 1974, Messaris 1977). The approach is also taken to task as fundamentally "atheoretical," as being more a research strategy or hueristic than a theory (Elliot 1974, Weiss 1976, Swanson 1977, Becker 1979), and as failing to provide any systematic linkages between media gratifications and their social and psychological origins (Katz et al 1974, Levy 1977). Swanson (1976, 1977, 1979b) scores the approach for lack of conceptual clarity, noting that terms such as "function," "use," "gratification," "need," and "motive" are rarely defined, let alone explicated. Similarly, Blumler (1979) notes a number of problems with the notion of the "active" audience, including a great deal of variance in meaning for the term, a tendency to treat activity as an either/or matter, and failure to recognize that activity might vary across both media and time. Swanson (1979b) argues that audience activity should be defined only in terms of the assignment of meaning—selectivity during interpretation as opposed to selective exposure or selective attention (Katz 1979)—and contends that the typical research strategy of relating exposure patterns to gratifications precludes the possibility of demonstrating an active audience.

Critics have also focused on the approach's reliance on self-report data. This method, it is argued, forces respondents to treat all exposure as the result of deliberate choice (ignoring possible roles of habit, social expectations, casual encounters, etc), risks eliciting conventional beliefs about media use because it demands a degree of awareness and analytical ability that respondents may not have, is subject to distortion because of its retrospective nature, and provides no independent evidence for the existence or importance of respondent-identified needs or gratifications (Elliot 1974, Messaris 1977, Becker 1979).

Recent empirical work reveals that although much of the criticism is deserved, issues raised by the critics are being addressed (Katz 1979). For example, consider the extensive list of needs that adults report they seek to gratify through the mass media: surveillance, excitement, reinforcement, guidance, anticipated communication, relaxation, alienation, information acquisition, interpretation, tension reduction, social integration, social and parasocial interaction, entertainment, affective guidance, behavioral guidance, social contact, self and personal identity, reassurance, escape, and so on (McLeod & Becker 1974, Peled & Katz 1974, Canadian Broadcasting Corporation 1975, Kippax & Murray 1977, Levy 1977, Wenner 1977, Nordlund 1978, Becker 1979). Needs articulated by children and adolescents show some differences, but many more similarities (Brown et al 1974, Greenberg 1974, Johnstone 1974, von Feilitzen 1976, Lometti et al 1977, Rubin 1979). And needs articulated by a sample of elderly people look very much the same (Danowski 1975, Wenner 1976). Such profusion can be frustrating, but may be due more to the kind of looseness of terminology noted earlier than to any legitimate proliferation of needs. That is, just as Murray & Kippax (1979) found in a survey of cross-national studies, a general picture of four basic clusters of needs into which most of the foregoing can be fitted tends to emerge: self and personal identity, social contact, diversion and entertainment, and information and knowledge about the world. Blumler (1979) argues for reduction to three fundamental orientations toward the media: cognitive, diversion, and personal. But regardless of whether one settles on three, four, or five clusters of needs, the point is that there is a high degree of similarity in the various lists, a convincing convergence for the very reason that it emerges from such profusion (Katz 1979).

Other trends in current uses and gratifications research also speak to some of the criticisms. Studies have been concerned with validating various gratifications measures and with examining the notion of communication avoidances—reasons for not reading, viewing, or listening (McLeod & Becker 1974, Levy 1977, Becker 1979). Research has tested the assumption that individuals differentiate among channels on the basis of expected gratifications and that different media do indeed fulfill different needs (Lometti et al 1977, Stroman & Becker 1978, Adoni 1979). Palmgreen and his associates (Palmgreen & Rayburn 1979; Palmgreen et al 1980) have begun to examine the relationship between gratifications sought from the media and gratifications obtained. They find important differences between the two dimensions which argues against the teleological criticism that any gratification sought must be obtained, and raises several new theoretical issues. Finally, following the lead of Blumler & McQuail (1969) and attempting to support the active audience assumption, a few studies report evidence linking gratifications (or avoidances) to such traditional "effects" measures as political information, political attitudes, and perceptions of issue salience (McLeod & Becker 1974, McLeod et al 1974, Becker 1976).

The predominant "cognitive" or "instrumental" flavor of most of the studies cited above bears comment. There is a striking tendency for uses and gratifications researchers to concentrate on the utilitarian aspects of media consumption. They concentrate on political communication (Becker 1979) or news (Levy 1977, 1978) or on public television (Palmgreen & Rayburn 1979). They ask where adolescents obtain useful family planning information (Kline et al 1974) and political values (Adoni 1979). They focus on media use during significant sociopolitical events such as wars (Dotan & Cohen 1976) or political scandals (Becker 1976). Of course, even studies of the news generate mention of entertainment, of diversion, of escape, but it is striking how seldom uses and gratifications researchers examine the entertainment function in and of itself. When one considers that most people use most media most of the time for entertainment (Comstock et al 1978, Tannenbaum 1980), the relative absence of research on this central function of mass communication is disconcerting to say the least. It is to be hoped that Tannenbaum's (1980) recent volume signals the emergence of more concern with the entertainment function per se.

EFFECTS ON ADULTS

To the extent that concern focuses on how individuals respond to media content, the fundamental effects of mass communication are cognitive. Regardless of whether influence is direct or indirect, immediate or delayed, short-term or long-term, regardless of whether ultimate concern is with emotions, attitudes, or behavior, any "effect" of media content on individuals originates with whether and how people interpret and incorporate information transmitted by the media into their existing conceptualizations of the world (Roberts 1971). Thus, the basic link between media content and human social behavior is forged in the interaction between information transmitted by the media on the one hand and human information processing on the other. This implies that differences in responses to mass communication may derive from variations in exposure to media or types of media content—the kinds of variations touched on in preceding paragraphs. Or, more important to the present section, differences in response may derive from variations in how similar messages are interpreted by different people or by similar people under differing conditions. Hence, one trend of recent mass communication research has been to specify the various conditions under which people respond to mass-mediated information (McLeod & Reeves 1980).

Recent work has also begun to assess the cognitive effects of media in more audience-centered terms. Attention has been focused on the media's role in determining what issues people think about—the public's agenda—quite independent of how much they might know about any one of those issues. Measures of information "holding" as distinct from knowledge have been used. Other work takes what can be called a cultural perspective, attempting to assess the relationship between media use and the cultivation of major dimensions of belief systems—how people conceive of power or roles or norms within a given society. And, of course, there is continued fascination with communication campaigns, with the role of the mass media in planned change programs. The following pages review those areas that have received more than passing research attention over the past 5 years.

Transmission of Knowledge and Information
Typically the media's ability to transmit information is examined in the context of news and public affairs content. This practice reflects the view, articulated by communication scholars (Schramm 1971) and media practitioners (Halberstam 1979) alike, that the primary function of the news media is to provide information. Clearly the effects of public affairs content, the avowed purpose of which is to inform, deserve close scrutiny. Nevertheless, it is also clear that content designed to fulfill other functions (e.g. entertainment) also conveys a great deal of information.

People perceive themselves as acquiring a great deal of information from the mass media. When the Roper Organization (1977) asked a national sample of adults where they get most of their information about "what's going on in the world," over 95% answered in terms of the mass media.

Often such self-perceptions are tested by relating media exposure to scores on various knowledge indices, usually comprised of specific questions about current political figures or issues. Work in this vein conducted prior to 1975 is reviewed by Becker et al (1975) and by Kraus & Davis (1976). More recent studies using respondents ranging from black adolescents (Tan & Vaughn 1976), to adults from various different nations (Chaffee & Izcaray 1975, Feigert 1976), to a variety of U.S. samples continue to find moderate positive relationships between public affairs media use and current affairs knowledge (Atkin et al 1976, Atkin & Heald 1976, Patterson & McClure 1976, Palmgreen 1979, Quarles 1979, Becker & Whitney 1980). In many of these studies the relationship has withstood controls for education, although education itself is more often than not found to be a stronger predictor of knowledge than is media use.

Partly in response to what they feel may be a premature acceptance of the generalization that education is vastly more important than media use for current affairs knowledge acquisition, Clarke & Kline (1974) have called for new approaches to measuring both media exposure and knowledge. Their reconsideration of media effects argues against the normative, intrusive nature of knowledge items based on the kinds of "textbook" information that, although salient to educators and researchers, may not be at all relevant knowledge to the public. They advocate more audience centered measures of "information holding," based on "problems" articulated by respondents and the number of solutions and actors that are mentioned in relation to those problems. Similarly, they propose to abandon media use indices for measures of "message discrimination" based on asking people whether they have seen, read, or heard anything about the self-nominated problems, and obtaining descriptions of the content and channel of these "discriminated" messages. A trend toward employing measures of information holding and message discrimination has begun to emerge in the literature. As with the traditional approaches, studies using such audience-centered measures also find positive relationships between levels of information and both media exposure and message discrimination (Edlestein 1974, Palmgreen et al 1974, Clarke & Fredin 1978, Becker et al 1979a). Moreover, at least under some conditions message discrimination has been found to be more strongly related to information holding than is either media use (Palmgreen 1979) or education (Clarke & Kline 1974).

A number of findings elaborate and modify these first-order relationships between media use and information. Perhaps most striking among them is that the term "media use" is too general. Contrary to popular conceptions of the dominance of television news, much of this work indicates that it is more accurate to talk about a relationship between print use and knowledge. In those studies where newspaper vs television comparisons were made, only two instances of even moderate positive relationships between television use and knowledge appeared (Atkin et al 1976, Atkin & Heald 1976); in most studies the television-knowledge relationship hovered near zero (Patterson & McClure 1976, Tan & Vaughn 1976, Clarke & Fredin 1978, Becker et al 1979b, Quarles 1979, Becker & Whitney 1980). These findings are somewhat disturbing given the evidence reviewed earlier indicating a general decline in regular newspaper use with each succeeding generation.

One explanation offered for the superior power of newspaper use vs television exposure to predict knowledge levels is based on differences between the media in format and content. That television's search for exciting visuals often leads to a focus on peripheral aspects of the news, on action and events rather than issues and policies, is well documented (Robinson 1975, Carey 1976, Hofstetter & Zukin 1979). Hence, it is argued, people who depend on television for their news obtain a fragmented, nonrepresentative view of the world which mediates against the acquisition of substantive current events information. Patterson & McClure (1976) write: "Network news may be fascinating. It may be highly entertaining. But it is simply not informative" (p. 54). The implicit value judgment in this argument, of course, is that the corpus of information found in newspapers is more substantive, more "central" than that found in television. A second explanation posits that the superiority of print for imparting knowledge stems from differences in people's skill at processing information from the two media which, in turn, stems from differences in training. This argument notes that in our society both the current educational system and norms developed prior to the advent of broadcasting emphasize and train people to deal with print for information acquisition. Hence the obtained differences in predictive power are hypothesized to reflect differences in training or other information processing variables (Becker & Whitney 1980). But in at least one experiment literate adults acquired far more information from television news than did adult nonreaders, indicating that the skills necessary for reading also enhance the ability to decode audiovisual information (Stauffer et al 1978).

All this, of course, is not to say that people do not acquire information from television. Indeed they do, as is demonstrated when the measure of information acquisition is specific to observed television content and viewers and nonviewers are compared. Recent examples of this approach in the area of current events information are found in studies of the impact of the Carter-Ford debates. These found that debate viewing led to increased information about the candidates, the differences between them, and their stands on various issues (Morrison et al 1977, Bishop et al 1978, Wald &

Lupfer 1978, Dennis et al 1979, Miller & MacKuen 1979). Results of these and other studies of the debates are fully discussed in several overview papers (Chaffee 1978, Chaffee & Dennis 1979, Sears & Chaffee 1979). In addition, studies report that exposure to televised political commercials is related to increased information about issues and candidates (Atkin & Heald 1976, Patterson & McClure 1976).

The studies cited above have examined a number of other variables that, depending on conditions, influence the media use-information level relationship. These include consideration of such factors as whether concern is with local or national affairs and amount and quality of media coverage (Clarke & Fredin 1978, Palmgreen 1979, Becker & Whitney 1980), and of such social and psychological factors as group membership, number of coorientation peers and discussion partners, interest in politics, motivations for using news media, degree of black nationalism, age, education, and so on (Chaffee & Izcaray 1975, Atkin et al 1976, Tan & Vaughn 1976, Genova & Greenberg 1979, Palmgreen 1979, Quarles 1979). The relationships are anything but simple, and recent work makes it abundantly clear that one of the more important tasks facing the field is careful specification of the conditions under which various media effects do and do not occur.

The Gap Hypothesis

Work concerned with the knowledge gap hypothesis exemplifies why such elaboration of contingent conditions is necessary. As initially formulated in communication research, the gap hypothesis simply states that higher socioeconomic segments of a population acquire information from the mass media faster than do lower socioeconomic segments, thus increasing the difference in the amount of knowledge held by the two segments (Tichenor et al 1970). Stated thus, the hypothesis implies that any attempt to use media to equalize the distribution of knowledge within a social system seems doomed not just to fail, but to increase inequities. Moreover, the initial hypothesis fails to specify any factors mediating the knowledge gap. However, several recent studies find conditions under which knowledge gaps (as well as other communication effects gaps) narrow (Tichenor et al 1973, Donohue et al 1975, Shingi & Mody 1976, Maccoby et al 1977, McLeod et al 1979), calling the initial implication of the hypothesis into question and emphasizing the need to construct and elaborate a theoretical model to explain knowledge gap phenomena.

Several recent papers have attempted the latter task. Ettema & Kline (1977) list a number of factors that have been posited, usually as post hoc explanations, to account for widening and narrowing of the knowledge gap. These, they argue, can be reduced to three categories of causal factors that may account for knowledge gap phenomena: 1. transituational deficits (lack of communication skills) on the part of one of the population segments under consideration; 2. between-group differences in perceived relevance and/or motivation to acquire the information under study; 3. ceiling effects imposed either by message content or by the information of concern. Although there have been no direct tests of the three models, the tenor of the Ettema and Kline paper tends to favor a difference interpretation because in most instances in which a widening of the gap has been demonstrated, factors that might reduce the motivation of lower socioeconomic segments of the population to acquire information seem to have been operating. Moreover, findings that the knowledge gap narrowed when concern focused on local community issues about which there was conflict also points to a motivational interpretation (Donohue et al 1975). Conflict, it is argued, increases both information salience and the likelihood of interpersonal discussion among various population segments, as well as the functionality of acquiring such information. Genova & Greenberg (1979) also argue that interest in an issue is a better predictor of a knowledge gap than is socioeconomic status.

Additional evidence that motivational differences are important mediators of gap phenomena comes from an imaginative study of "equivalences" in use of and response to the Carter-Ford debates and communication about the debates (McLeod et al 1979). This work moves the gap literature forward on several fronts: it is based on a longitudinal design permitting examination of change; it includes exposure to several different information sources; it measures involvement, decision making, participation, and attachment to system values as well as knowledge; it divides the sample not only in terms of education but also on the basis of age and interest in politics. Moreover, the study makes an important distinction between "equivalence of exposure" and "equivalence of effect" and examines whether obtained differences on a given criterion are more strongly related to differences in exposure or to predictive strength given equal exposure (the latter indicating differences in communication skills). Their finding that less educated, younger, and less interested people were less exposed to the debates and to information about them, but gained as much as did better educated, older, and more interested people per *unit of exposure,* supports a motivational as opposed to a deficit interpretation of gap phenomena. Their finding that a gap was more likely to occur on measures other than knowledge is also important, given that most "gap" research has focused on knowledge.

Agenda Setting

Research on the agenda-setting hypothesis has increased dramatically. We suspect that some of the popularity of the approach stems from its assertion of the power of the media in conjunction with its simultaneous affirmation of the independence of the individual—a promise of both cake and consumption.

Agenda setting refers to the ability of the mass media to influence the level of the public's awareness of issues as opposed to their specific knowledge about those issues—in Cohen's (1963) terms, what to think about as opposed to what to think. As initially put forth, the hypothesis deals with aggregate phenomena and proposes a main effect. It states that the degree to which the media attend to a given issue determines the degree to which the public ascribes importance to that issue. The strength of the causal hypothesis varies from a weak version that predicts simply an overlap between media and public agendas with little regard to their respective ordering of issues, to a moderate version that predicts similar rankings of issues, to a strong version that posits similar weightings of issues across the two agendas (McCombs 1977). Adequate tests of the hypothesis, then, depend on careful conceptualization and measurement of both the media and the public agenda and the execution of research designs that allow causal inferences. Unfortunately, the literature in this area is not marked by consistency in either area.

Media agendas have been measured via straightforward counts of the number of articles concerning various issues appearing in major news magazines (Funkhouser 1973, MacKuen 1979), enumeration of issues covered by newspapers and TV and then identified as salient by respondents (Palmgreen & Clarke 1977), counts of issue categories weighted by airtime or column inches over some specific period of time (Williams & Semlak 1978), and counts of stories referring to specific problems or controversies that were covered on the front page or editorial page of at least four of five selected newspapers (Gormley 1975). Similarly, there is variation in terms of whether the media agenda is examined in terms of a single, short-term event such as a presidential visit to a local city (Kaid et al 1977) or the presidential debates (Becker et al 1979b), a longer-term event such as a presidential campaign (McCombs & Shaw 1972), a single issue such as Watergate (Weaver et al 1975b), or an array of major issues that captured media attention across several decades (MacKuen 1979). Other variations in the operationalization of the media agenda which make comparisons difficult include the duration of the interval across which the index is constructed (Eyal et al 1979), the use of local vs national issues (Palmgreen & Clarke 1977) and other variations in the nature of issues (Eyal 1979), and the level of generality at which an "issue" is defined (Gormley 1975). The ease with which the agenda-setting effect is demonstrated increases the more broadly an issue area is defined.

Similar diversity is found in operationalizations of the public agenda. Measurement strategies have included importance ratings of a list of issues on closed-ended scales (Gormley 1975) and nominations of important problems in response to open-ended questions. The latter approach requests nominations of problems perceived to be personally important (McCombs & Shaw 1972), important to the community or country (MacKuen 1979), or issues most often talked about, or some combination of the preceding (Becker et al 1975, Williams & Semlak 1978, Becker et al 1979b).

Some investigators have been content to assume that the direction of causality is from media to public, making no attempt to eliminate the alternative possibilities that either the media respond to the public's agenda, or that both media and public agenda are simply reflections of an environment in which events set the agenda. Nevertheless, in spite of the lack of consistency across studies and the various methodological weaknesses in some of the research, there has been enough activity to permit some tentative generalizations and to indicate that the agenda-setting function of the media deserves close attention.

Fortunately, some work has introduced at least some of the controls necessary to permit causal inferences. Time-lagged correlational designs have been used to eliminate the possibility that the public agenda establishes the media agenda (Tipton et al 1975, McCombs 1977, Sohn 1978). And although for certain economic issues the public does seem to respond to the environment independently of media treatment (MacKuen 1979), there is mounting evidence that media emphasis on certain issues fluctuates from "objective" indicators of those issues in the environment and that public concern follows media emphases (Funkhouser 1973, MacKuen 1979). Overall, evidence supporting a causal influence of the media on the public's agenda, at least under some conditions, is beginning to accumulate.

Some work has attempted to go beyond the main effect prediction to specify both media related and audience related factors conditioning the agenda-setting effect. One of the most frequently examined conditioning factors is the nature of the medium. Both print and television have been shown to influence the public agenda. McCombs & Shaw's (1972) seminal work found effects for both media and no difference between them, several studies based exclusively on broadcast news have demonstrated the phenomenon (Siune & Borre 1975, Zucker 1978), and there is evidence that televised political commercials can raise the salience of issues (Patterson & McClure 1976). However, the many studies which compare the agenda setting function of TV and newspapers generally give the nod to print (Tipton et al 1975, Benton & Frazier 1976, McClure & Patterson 1976, McCombs 1977, McCombs & Weaver 1977, Mullins 1977, Weaver 1977, Williams & Larsen 1977). McClure & Patterson (1976) contend that television's role as an agenda setter improves for certain dramatic, highly pictorial events which are uncomplicated and which sustain intense and extended coverage, but Becker et al (1979b) found no agenda-setting impact of the televised presidential debates. On the other hand, Palmgreen & Clarke (1977) report that although newspapers exercised a stronger agenda-setting influence in terms of local issues, network television news was dominant for national issues. Two studies also report at least a minimal agenda-setting impact of radio (Siune & Borre 1975, Williams & Larsen 1977). There is also evidence that the agenda-setting impact of each medium may differ over time. McCombs (1977) found that television's influence increased over the course of an election campaign, although it never surpassed that of local newspapers. Eyal ct al (1979) discuss the importance of the time frame within which the agenda-setting function of each medium might occur and be measured, and Eyal (1979) considers a variety of additional possible theoretical and methodological factors that might explain the apparent superiority of newspapers over television as agenda setters.

Among the various audience attributes that have been examined, fairly consistent results concern amount of media exposure. The strength of the agenda-setting phenomenon is directly related to amount of news exposure (Weaver et al 1975a,b, McClure & Patterson 1976). Weaver et al (1976) found that the agenda people held differed as a function of whether they reported relying primarily on television, on newspapers, or on both for political information, a result that Winter (1979) cites in his call for future work examining the nature as well as quantity of media exposure. Chaffee & Wilson's (1977) imaginative study of diversity in public agenda as a function of the number of newspapers available in a given community also supports the exposure agenda relationship.

There have been few consistent findings on other audience related characteristics. Several studies have employed a measure of "need for orientation" —an index of "inherent curiosity about the environment" (Weaver et al 1975b)—as a predictor of agenda holding. This index has included measures of interest in or perceived relevance of a campaign, degree of certainty about a candidate or issue, party affiliation, and political participation. Work employing such indexes finds that higher levels of need for orientation locate greater acceptance of the media agenda (Weaver et al 1975a,b, Weaver 1977). However, it is difficult to determine just what the mediating factor is. Interest in the campaign is an important part of the index, but studies measuring interest alone have found positive relationships (MacKuen 1979) and negative relationships (McLeod et al 1974). Moreover, there has been enough variety in the way that various components of the need for orientation index have been operationalized to lead to some confusion. Williams & Semlak (1978), for example, listed eight variables that might be used in such an index and obtained different results depending on whether the media agenda was defined in terms of newspapers or television.

Other audience attributes examined in relation to the agenda-setting phenomenon include age (McLeod et al 1974), education (Mullins 1977, MacKuen 1979), respondents' amount of political information (Williams & Larsen 1977), and respondents' preference for one medium over another as a source of news (Williams & Larsen 1977, Williams & Semlak 1978).

Finally, there has been attention to the relationship between interpersonal communication and the agenda-setting effect, but the matter remains in dispute. Recent work has shown that interpersonal communication reduces the agenda-setting impact of the media (Weaver et al 1975a) and that it facilitates the impact (Atwood et al 1976). Winter (1979) examines these and earlier studies in terms of methodological differences that may account for the conflicting results. Given the evidence for a reciprocal relationship between mass communication behavior and interpersonal communication behavior, and Chaffee's (1979) convincing analysis of the futility of thinking in terms of competition between mass media and interpersonal channels, the role of interpersonal communication in agenda setting demands further investigation.

Cultivation of Beliefs

Ironically, several proponents of a return to the view that mass communications exert powerful influences argue for a return to the idea that the dominant effect is reinforcement. However, the rather innocent tone of Klapper's (1960) conclusion that the media serve primarily to reinforce existing attitudes has changed to "excursions and alarums" about the media's cultivation of a consciousness that seldom differs from an establishment view of the status quo. Klapper's work, of course, must be seen in an historical context of fear that the media had immense power to manipulate people immediately and directly—to change the status quo. More recent concern with the power of the media to affect belief systems derives from the revival of conflict theory and social criticism during the 1960s (Katz 1980). Katz calls what has emerged theories of "ideological effects" based on a view that the latent structure of mass media messages distorts (or selectively presents) reality in ways that perpetuate the interests of the existing power structure. These theories view media as the handmaidens of the establishment, arguing that news programming legitimizes managerial power (Glasgow group 1976), that current affairs programs advocate parlimentarianism (Hall 1977), that routine news practices perpetuate existing norms, conventions, and sociopolitical relationships (Tuchman 1977), that the fundamental message of television drama is the definition of the nature of power—a power that tends to reside in white, middle-class males who operate within established norms and conventions (Gerbner et al 1978, 1979).

Whether and how such latent messages are perceived by mass media audiences, and how they are responded to if they are perceived, are the critical questions to be asked if the validity of such theories is to be tested. Katz (1978b, 1980) voices optimism when he notes a progression in this work from surface to "deep" content analysis, to comparisons of media reality with independent measures of reality, and finally to recent attempts to operationalize measures of "consciousness" in order to examine how the audience might be affected. This move toward empirical tests of the powerful effects hypothesis is exemplified in the work of Noelle-Neumann and Gerbner.

Noelle-Neumann (1973, 1974) contends that because people avoid social isolation, they tend to voice opinions that support what they perceive to be dominant opinions and to suppress perceived "unpopular" opinions. This, in turn, changes the "opinion environment" such that it reinforces the perceived dominance of the majority opinion, which leads to further suppression of minority opinion, and so on, creating a "spiral of silence." She also notes that the mass media play a large role in defining the opinion environment. Because of their ubiquity, the repetitiveness of their messages, and the relative unanimity among journalists in how they view and report the world (a unanimity that tends to support the establishment), the media are viewed as operating to limit individual selective perception, hence to limit independent judgment. Thus, the opinion environment created by the mass media cannot but help to create a spiral of silence for all but the establishment opinion. A combination of rigorous content analyses and measures of public opinion compared *over time* has provided a method for testing the spiral of silence theory (Noelle-Neumann 1977). The results indicate that the media may restrict individual selective perception, and that the more they do so the more silent minority voices become and the more the dominant voice of the status quo is reinforced. In short, Noelle-Neumann appears to be developing a solid empirical basis for her call to return to a concept of at least one powerful media effect.

Reinforcement is also the dominant effect of television in the view of George Gerbner and his colleagues, but reinforcement of the most fundamental kind in that it is synonomous with enculturation. They assert that "television is the central cultural arm of American Society," and argue that the medium socializes people into standardized roles and behaviors not so much by affecting specific opinions and attitudes as through the "cultivation" of more basic assumptions about the nature of social reality (Gerbner & Gross 1976a,b). The ability of television to do this derives from: (*a*) the uniformity of its message system which acts to maintain and reinforce conventional values and behaviors, (*b*) the reach and scope of the medium and the nonselective use made of it, and (*c*) the realism with which it presents its view of the world, a realism that hides the synthetic, selective nature of television drama (Gerbner & Gross 1976a, Gerbner et al 1979).

The basic procedure for testing the cultivation model requires periodic analyses of large aggregates of programming in order to obtain comprehensive descriptions of the symbolic world of television. Among other things, these analyses reveal dimensions on which television's world differs from the real world. This, in turn, allows comparison of heavy and light television viewers' conceptions of reality on those dimensions where the real and symbolic worlds differ. Comparisons of this type have consistently demonstrated a stable relationship between patterns of television content and heavy viewers' conceptions of reality. For example, adults averaging four or more hours of televiewing per day were more likely than adults averaging two or less hours per day to overestimate both the proportion of people in the U.S. employed in law enforcement occupations and their own chances of being involved in a violent incident. Heavy viewers were also less likely to feel that most people can be trusted. In all cases, the responses of heavy viewers revealed a conception of the world that differs from reality but that is characteristic of television's world. Moreover, the responses withstood controls for age, education, gender, and amount of newspaper reading (Gerbner & Gross 1976a,b). Similar findings have been reported with samples of children (Gerbner et al 1978) and adolescents (Gerbner et al 1979). The 1979 article concludes: "The most significant and recurring conclusion of our long-range study is that one correlate of television viewing is a heightened and unequal sense of danger and risk in a mean and selfish world" (p. 196). Although interesting, the conclusion fails to satisfy the promise of the model. Given that these studies have extended over several years, it is disappointing that time-lagged procedures or some other form of causal analysis has not been applied to the data. The obtained synchronous relationships appear strong, but the critical test of the causal implication of the cultivation model remains to be conducted. Moreover, several recent studies raise doubts about some of the synchronous relationships used to support the model. Doob & Macdonald (1979) found no relationship between amount of television viewing and fear of the environment when the actual incidence of crime in respondents' neighborhoods was controlled. Even more fundamental questions are raised by Hirsch's (1980) extensive reanalysis of the National Opinion Research Center data set which Gerbner and his colleagues used to support much of the cultivation model. Hirsch finds "remarkably little support" for a cultivation effect, and warns that acceptance of the hypothesis at this time is premature and unwarranted. We suspect that the next few years will witness a healthy debate over the cultivation hypothesis.

Other studies have demonstrated television's impact on cultural images. Caron (1979) controlled Eskimo children's first experience with television and found that exposure to a TV series devoted to the portrayal of a variety of cultures had a significant impact on their images and evaluations of other cultural groups, particularly those close to them. Coldevin (1979) reports that the introduction of television into a previously isolated area of northern Canada accelerated adolescents' acculturation to Euro-Canadian structures and values, and increased the culture replacement gap between them and their more traditional parents.

Campaigns and Development

A long-standing debate in communication research concerns the ability of mass communication campaigns to produce change. The "minimal effects" position was largely based on early studies that found little change following campaigns conducted in the U.S. (Weiss 1969). On the other hand, an extensive literature on the role of communication in economic and social development, particularly in third world countries, presented a rather optimistic view of what mass media could do (Lerner & Schramm 1967, Rogers & Shoemaker 1971). Over the past decade, however, positions have changed. Development communication scholars have become much less sanguine about the potential of mass communication, acting alone, to engender meaningful change directly, at least in the third world (Rogers 1976a,b), while several health related campaigns have encouraged optimism among some U.S. researchers (Farquhar et al 1977, McAlister et al 1980).

The Stanford Heart Disease Prevention Program's (SHDPP) three community study exemplifies a successful U.S. campaign (Farquhar et al 1977, Maccoby et al 1977). This project used a community-based quasi-experimental field design (Farquhar 1978) to examine the potential of media to influence people's dietary, smoking, and exercise habits in order to reduce the risk of heart disease. Two communities received a two-year campaign using television, radio, newspapers, direct mail, billboards, and posters. In one of these communities, media were augmented with intensive face-to-face instruction of a subsample of "high risk" individuals. A third community served as a no-treatment control. At the end of a year, individuals in the treatment communities showed dramatic increases in knowledge about risk factors associated with heart disease. Moreover, there were significant decreases in saturated fat intake, numbers of cigarettes smoked, plasma-cholesterol levels, and systolic blood pressure. Overall, the probability of heart disease was reduced within campaign community samples while it actually increased in the control community. Finally, by the end of the second year of the campaign, the community receiving the media-only treatment manifested as much change as did the community augmented by face-to-face instruction

Several other health related media campaigns have also achieved significant change. Rogers (1976b) describes several successful radio-based public health and nutrition projects in Tanzania. In spite of its reputation as a failure, the televised experimental health program "Feeling Good" engendered a number of behavior changes among the few who saw it (Mielke & Swinehart 1976). A small-scale study in New York (Dubren 1977) and a nationwide program in Finland (McAlister et al 1980) successfully used television to counsel smokers on cessation procedures. Not all such health related projects are as effective, however (Atkin 1979).

Maccoby & Alexander (1979, 1980) describe several key features of the three-community project, many of which appear to have operated in other successful campaigns. Some, such as extensive use of formative evaluation in message design and utilization of creative media scheduling, pertain primarily to the campaign's communication components. However, others such as development of specific objectives for each component of the campaign and stimulation of interpersonal networks, recognize that a change campaign requires more than communication. Indeed, an important feature of this study is that it conceptualized communication as necessary but not sufficient to engender meaningful change. The project's emphasis on "community-based" intervention reflects the belief that change occurs within a social structure and that characteristics of that structure facilitate or impede change independent of the communication aspects of the campaign. Thus, a critical dimension of this project was its concern with elements of the social structure. Both the goals and the communication components of the campaign were designed with that structure in mind, and there were a number of attempts to use the structure to facilitate and maintain both communication and change.

The need to adapt the communication components of change efforts to the realities of the social structure in which change is to be achieved is a central issue in the current reassessment of the role of communication in economic and social development. Many of the "failures" pointed to in recent criticisms of both the general role of mass communication and the specific role of diffusion models in development attempts articulate the position that "Western" communication paradigms failed to account for the realities of non-Western social structures (Beltran S. 1975, 1976; Diaz Bordenave 1976; Roling et al 1976). And indeed, numerous examples of the benefits of various communication and change campaigns accruing to the already more advantaged segments of the population (Rogers 1976b, Roling et al 1976) certainly point to a failure of many campaigns to account for structural factors. However, given our preceding discussion of the gap hypothesis and the evidence that various U.S. campaigns (presumably conducted using Western paradigms) have also increased inequities in the distribution of knowledge and goods, it seems reasonable to wonder whether the fault lies as much with the communication models as with the way in which the models are put into practice. Rogers' (1976a) insightful examination of the history of development efforts and the suggestions for future research it leads to, as well as the new directions suggested by such critics as Diaz Bordenave (1976), strike us more as remedies for ethnocentric operationalizations of fundamentally sound theoretical concepts than as lethal blows to either the diffusion model or our fundamental belief that mass communication has an important role to play in development.

Indeed, recent attempts to respond to one form of structural constraints by merging network analysis with the diffusion model (Rogers 1976c, 1977) and to use findings from earlier diffusion studies for formative and predictive purposes (Roling et al 1976, Shingi & Mody 1976) indicate that researchers are beginning to respond to the complexities of development in third world countries with appropriately more complex methodologies. Similarly, Whiting's (1976) analysis of communication as it both facilitates and impedes change, and the various alternative conceptions of the role of communication in change emerging in China (Chu 1976) and elsewhere (Rogers 1976b), lead us to view future research on development communication with a good deal of anticipation. Finally, several scholars (Nordenstreng & Schiller 1979) have begun to develop yet another paradigm for national development which calls for examination of dimensions of individual action and intranational structure within an international economic framework that influences both.

Space precludes fuller consideration of the current debate over just what development means, let alone how it can be achieved. However, the philosophical and scientific issues being raised in that debate appear to be having a profound and healthy impact on the entire field of mass communication research.

EFFECTS ON CHILDREN AND ADOLESCENTS

Given the "special status" accorded children in the U.S. (Roberts et al 1980), it would be surprising if attention to how children use and respond to television had not remained one of the liveliest areas of mass communication research, or if many of the "problems" addressed did not continue to reflect current social issues. The impact of violent programming on children continues to be of concern, but at a reduced level from 10 years ago. There has been a moderate increase in work on the prosocial effects of the medium. Concern with the effects of advertising and with political socialization has burgeoned, and research on the potential role of the medium in sex-role stereotyping has begun to appear.

More interesting than the ebb and flow of categories of "effects" are changes in the way various problems are being addressed. Ten years ago questions tended to be posed in terms of main effects (Does TV violence facilitate aggressive behavior?) and to be guided by social learning theory (Liebert & Schwartzberg 1977). Currently there is movement toward considering television as just one element, albeit an important one, in a larger system of influences acting on the developing child (Comstock et al 1978). This has led to less concern with main effects and more attempts to identify and elaborate contingent conditions. Social learning remains a primary theoretical framework for much of the work, but it has begun to share the spotlight with other approaches, including information processing, social scripts, attribution theory, and so on. Finally, much recent work on children and television has adopted a long overdue developmental perspective. Recognition of both the policy-related and the scientific importance of ontogenetic changes in the child/television/social-system relationship has brought a heretofore missing richness to the area. Attempts to examine age-related change in attention to and comprehension of television content in terms of various approaches to cognitive and social development have begun to produce findings related to children's *processing* of television-mediated information, a promising extension of emphases on effects.

Attention and Comprehension

Pragmatic questions raised during the initial production stages of *Sesame Street* (Lesser 1974) as well as recent more theoretical attempts to understand children's information processing have engendered a rapidly growing body of work on the development of attention to television content. Hollenbeck & Slaby (1979) report that infants begin to respond differentially to various sound-picture conditions as early as 6 months. However, most studies find that age-related changes in attentional strategies occur somewhat later, paralleling changes in children's cognitive abilities.

Comstock et al's (1978) interpretation of earlier work on children's attention to TV in terms of cognitive development receives support from recent studies. Purposive viewing begins as early as 2½ years (Anderson & Levin 1976, Levin & Anderson 1976), along with attentional strategies foreshadowing those of adults. For example, changes in concrete symbolic content begin to mediate changes in attention. This is about the age at which children move from sensorimotor operations to concrete operations, and marks the beginning of attempts to internalize events symbolically. Hence, attentional variations linked to changes in concrete stimulus characteristics suggest that attention to television content is closely tied to cognitive abilities necessary to engage in symbolic activities (Anderson et al 1979). Similarly, several studies have varied the complexity and/or comprehensibility of program content in order to look at differences in attention (Krull & Husson 1979, Lorch et al 1979, Anderson et al 1980). Results of this work indicate that, among older children, program comprehensibility and visual attention conform to an inverted U curve where attention is optimal if content is neither too simple nor too complex. Failure to find strong differences as a function of content complexity among the youngest children provides another indicator of the importance of cognitive capacities in mediating attention.

The development of a continuous rating procedure that enables researchers to match the onset and termination of any number of program attributes to the onset and termination of children's visual attention (Levin & Anderson 1976) has added to information about how different program attributes elicit, maintain, and terminate attention. Among preschool children, "bit changes," transition points from one segment of programming to another, continue to be strong predictors of changes in attention, both in terms of elicitation and termination (Wartella & Ettema 1974, Anderson et al 1979, Alwitt et al 1980). Other program factors found to elicit and maintain attention within this age group include the visual and auditory presence of women, children's voices, and sound effects such as laughter and applause. Indeed, the data emphasize the importance of sound in attentional behavior to the point that certain visual attributes seem compelling only to the extent that they are associated with sound. Attributes negatively related to attention include male voices, animals, slow music, extended zooms and pans, and still photos (Anderson et al 1979). All of this fits nicely with Wartella & Ettema's (1974) findings that younger children's attention is highly responsive to perceptual variations in content but less so to conceptual variations, while conceptual changes are more important to older children. Unfortunately, recent work has not been extended to older children, precluding a more complete developmental examination of the results.

Anderson et al (1979) have also located a phenomenon they call "attentional inertia." This is the tendency for viewers to continue looking at the TV screen as a function of the preceding amount of time that attention has been maintained, irrespective of content or formal attributes. They speculate that such inertia is a result of processing information at progressively higher conceptual units of content. That is, the longer a look continues, the higher the probability that a viewer treats content in successively larger units, thus reducing the number of opportunities to break out of the attentional sequence. The phenomenon has been found with children and adults, but controlled age comparisons have not been reported. Nevertheless, earlier findings of continual increases across age in the duration of attention

(Levin & Anderson 1976) indicate that attentional inertia may also be a function of cognitive development insofar as changes in cognitive capabilities locate the capacity to process increasingly larger conceptual units.

The few early studies of television's influence on social behavior which included children of several ages uncovered striking differences in magnitude of effect as a function of age, leading to conjecture that there were age differences in processing the same content (Roberts 1973, Collins 1975). Collins (1979a) conceptualizes "mature" comprehension in terms of *selection* of essential information from the program, *ordering* the essential scenes according to some organizational scheme, and making *inferences* that go beyond what is explicitly presented to relate discrete units of information into a meaningful whole. He proceeds from the assumption that age-related differences in cognitive capabilities and accumulated experiences locate differences in how children comprehend a television program.

In order to test these notions, dramatic television programs were "parsed" to identify units of information as central or peripheral and explicit or implicit; entire programs were then edited into simple or complex versions in which scenes were presented in an ordered or randomized sequence. Subsequent to viewing a version of these programs, second, fifth and eighth graders were tested for recall of implicit and explicit content and ability to make inferences regarding that content (Collins et al 1978). This kind of approach has produced evidence that younger children select different information from dramatic presentations than do their older counterparts, fail to use the dramatic framework to organize and understand the narrative scenes, and make fewer inferences about implicit content and relationships among program elements, be they the linkage among the motives, acts, and consequences, or the simple insight that two scenes are temporally related (Collins et al 1974, Collins et al 1978, Collins 1979a,b). Newcomb & Collins (1979) also found that children understand programs as a function of the degree to which the portrayed context is similar to or different from their own backgrounds, but that the influence is greater among younger children. Collins (1979b) interprets these findings in terms of Schank & Abelson's (1977) notion of scripts. He argues that younger children's comprehension is dominated by personal scripts while older children are more able to apply a wider variety of scripts which depart from their personal social circumstances. This explanation dovetails nicely with several other discussions of children's comprehension of television content (Worth & Gross 1974, Comstock et al 1978).

Concern with how model characteristics influence children's observational learning has led to work on how children perceive television characters. Several studies explore the attributes children use to differentiate among TV characters and the bases on which they would choose to be like TV characters. The important judgmental dimensions appear to be humor, attractiveness, activity, and some kind of strength-dominated sex difference. Boys and girls use the same dimensions to distinguish among TV characters, but there are large sex differences in the criteria they use to determine whom they would most like to be like. Girls rely on the attractiveness dimension, boys use the activity and strength dimensions (Reeves & Greenberg 1977, Reeves & Miller 1978, Reeves & Lometti 1979). Reeves (1979) examines these and earlier findings in a developmentally based person perception framework and notes that the findings for TV characters differ from those for real people in terms of both the dimensions employed by children and the way that those dimensions are organized. He speculates that a model of TV character perception will have to differ from one of person perception.

Empirical work on the development and role of perceived reality in children's comprehension of and response to television has also begun to accumulate. Younger children, children with lower IQ scores, children who view a great deal of television, and children who manifest little understanding of the medium or its production techniques attribute more reality to television content, with the phenomenon increasing the more specifically the questions regarding the "realness" of television content are worded (Leifer et al 1974, Greenberg & Reeves 1976, Quarfoth 1979). Several studies have demonstrated that reality-fantasy distinctions are multidimensional, that various developmental trends may depend on the particular dimension the child is using when making a judgment, and that the spontaneous application of the ability to make reality-fantasy distinctions comes somewhat later than the ability itself (Hawkins 1977, Morison et al 1979). Assumptions that perceived reality would be a straightforward mediator of subsequent behavior are also being questioned. Reeves (1978) found that the degree to which portrayed prosocial behavior was perceived to be real predicted subsequent prosocial and antisocial behavior, but that the perceived reality of portrayed antisocial behavior had no effect.

Finally, in a reversal of much of the developmental work on children's comprehension of television, work on how different media influence the development of different cognitive behaviors is being reported. Salomon (1979a,b) argues that different media employ different symbol systems, that different symbol systems structure the world differently, and that different types of symbols not only require the use of different age-related cognitive skills, but also that they cultivate different cognitive skills. We expect the next decade to witness a great deal of work in this area.

Responses to Advertising

Over the past 5 years, questions about children's special vulnerability to television advertising raised by the Federal Communications Commission (1974) and the Federal Trade Commission (1978) brought the "problem" of television advertising and children to the center of the research arena. Much of the work is highly applied in that it is designed to address questions concerning the potentially misleading or unfair influence of specific advertising practices such as premium offers, separation of commercial and programs, and disclaimers (Adler 1977). However, the FTC decision to consider whether young children even understand the nature of commercials and the degree to which any lack of understanding might render all commercials unfair or misleading to children gave research a more theoretical tone, if only because it addressed the question in terms of various developmental models of cognition, information processing, and social behavior (Dorr 1978, Roberts et al 1978, Wackman et al 1978).

Children are exposed to a great many commercials—over 20,000 per year (Adler 1977). Those explicitly designed for children, the Saturday morning ads, dramatically over-represent toys and sugared food products (Council on Children, Media, and Merchandising 1977) and employ techniques usually appealing, sometimes confusing, and often not very informative to young children (Adler 1977, FTC 1978). For example, Atkin & Heald (1977) found that toy ads seldom present relevant substantive attributes of the products.

There is also evidence that children are influenced by commercials. Comstock et al (1978) review various studies which indicate that young children often request advertised products, that such requests tend to decrease as the child grows older, that there are some signs of a relationship between amount of exposure to commercials and purchase requests, and that teenagers report being at least somewhat influenced by commercials. Adler (1977) also cites evidence that commercials are moderately successful at fostering positive attitudes toward products. Galst & White (1976) demonstrated that young children's willingness to expend effort to see television commercials in an experimental situation was positively related to subsequent attempts to influence mothers' purchases in a supermarket. Goldberg & Gorn (1977) found that exposure to toy commercials influenced preschool children to make more "materialistic" as opposed to "social" choices in a test situation. Robertson & Rossiter (1974) report that the barrage of toy commercials antecedent to the Christmas holidays overcame the defenses of even initially skeptical children.

The important question, however, is not so much whether children are influenced by commercials, as whether whatever influence there is occurs because of failure to comprehend the commercial appeal. For example, there is little evidence that children comprehend typical commercial disclaimers much before the age of 7 (D. E. Liebert et al 1977, Roberts & Bachen 1978). However, rewording disclaimers into language appropriate to young children dramatically increases comprehension. Clearly ads can be designed so that even very young children understand their discrete elements in the same way that they understand discrete elements of dramatic narratives (Collins 1979a). Certainly the *Sesame Street* experience supports this (Lesser 1974).

A more fundamental question concerns children's understanding of the nature of commercials per se—that they differ from informational and entertainment messages, that they are intended to persuade and they use biased appeals, that they require different information processing strategies than other types of messages (Roberts et al 1978). The bulk of evidence indicates that understanding of this type does not occur much before the age of 7 years. An indirect approach to comprehension is found in several early studies that noted a lack of differentiation in visual attention across the transition from program to commercial, and little decline in attention to clustered commercials much before the age of 7 or 8 years, and interpreted this as indicating a failure to understand that commercials are different from program material (Ward et al 1972, Ward & Wackman 1973). However, more recent work finds attentional variations among younger as well as older children (Zuckerman et al 1978), and the evidence is mounting that perceptual as opposed to conceptual attributes mediate young children's attentional shifts as they relate to commercials (Wartella & Ettema 1974, Anderson et al 1979). Moreover, the connection between visual attention patterns and comprehension of complex concepts remains to be established (Dorr 1978).

A more direct approach is to interview children concerning the difference between commercials and programs or the purpose of commercials. Some early work found that children under 7 or 8 years of age expressed confusion regarding the program-commercial distinction (Ward et al 1977), but much of this confusion could be attributed to age differences in verbal ability. Similarly, data derived from interviews concerned with children's ability to explain the selling intent of commercials is open to such criticism. Nevertheless, there is rather consistent agreement that before the age of 7 fewer than half of the children interviewed comprehend the intent of commercials (Robertson & Rossiter 1974, Ward et al 1977). Moreover, Dorr (1978) reports preliminary data from a three-item multiple choice test, demanding less sophisticated language skills, that indicates the majority of a sample of 8- and 9-year-olds did not understand commercials' selling intent. Roberts et al (1978) go further to raise the question of whether comprehension of selling intent is sufficient, on the grounds that it is possible to understand that a commercial intends to sell a product but be totally oblivious to the fact that this implies that biased informational strategies may be used to achieve such intent.

There is also general agreement across studies that children's understanding of the nature of commercials increases with age. Similarly, recall of the content of commercials and the ability to integrate message elements into a meaningful and integrated framework increases with age (Ward et al 1977) although here, too, recognition as opposed to verbal measures indicate better memory at earlier ages (Wartella et al 1979). There is also a good deal of evidence that trust in commercials is negatively related to age (Robertson & Rossiter 1974, Adler 1977, Ward et al 1977, Comstock et al 1978, Roberts et al 1980). Whether age-related distrust is due to more sophisticated understanding of the nature of commercials, or to past experience with advertised products, or to peer pressures, or to some other factor remains to be established.

Underlying concern with whether children comprehend the nature of commercials is the assumption that the better children understand them the less susceptible to manipulation they will be (Christenson 1980). However, the relationship between comprehension of intent to persuade and resistance to persuasive appeals remains uncertain. Several recent studies have demonstrated that it is possible to increase even very young children's understanding of the selling intent of commercials. Dorr (1978) reports that training children about the production process and economic basis of the television industry dramatically increased kindergarten and second and third grade children's understanding of the selling intent of commercials. Roberts et al (1980) found that an instructional film concerned with teaching children about commercials and persuasive techniques engendered significant increases in skepticism toward commercials, particularly among the initially less skeptical viewers. Several other studies have found that television shows or public service announcements concerned with either commercials or products advertised on commercials can influence children's product choices and expressed attitudes toward products (Goldberg et al 1978, Roberts & Bachen 1978, Christenson 1980). Nevertheless, questions remain. Rossiter & Robertson (1974) found that even older children with relatively strong defenses against commercial appeals eventually succumbed to a barrage of toy commercials, and Adler (1977) notes a number of studies that indicate older children—those presumed to better understand commercial appeals—are frequently more influenced than their younger counterparts.

Finally, as with so many other areas of communication research, a good deal of work on contingent conditions has begun to appear. Such factors as peer and parent influences as well as a number of family context variables have been shown to condition or mediate children's responsiveness to commercials (Robertson & Rossiter 1977, Sheikh & Moleski 1977, Wackman et al 1977, Ward et al 1977).

Political Socialization

If an informed citizenry is important to the functioning of a participatory democracy, then how children learn to acquire the appropriate information is a critical outcome in the political socialization process. Hence, the development of patterns of exposure to mass-mediated political information—patterns such as those covered earlier—has recently become a legitimate political socialization criterion variable in and of itself (Chaffee et al 1977). More typically, however, communication researchers have concerned themselves with the degree to which media use is related to such outcomes as political and civic knowledge and attitudes on the assumption that these form the foundation of adult political behavior. Several reviews detail work conducted prior to 1975 (Kraus & Davis 1976, Chaffee et al 1977, Comstock et al 1978).

Evidence continues to mount that, relative to such other socialization agents as parents, schools, and peers, the mass media play an important role in the acquisition of political information. When asked to name the "best" source of information on a variety of political topics or to state where they get most of their political information, children ranging from 7 years upward give the media a lion's share of the nominations. Television is preferred overall, but reliance on newspapers increases as the child enters adolescence (Chaffee et al 1977, Atkins & Elwood 1978, Egan 1978, Rubin 1978, Newspaper Advertising Bureau 1980a). One sample of seventh graders simultaneously voiced reliance on the media and skepticism about the wisdom of such a choice (Rubin 1976).

The degree to which exposure to the media is related to children's level of political knowledge depends on both the age of the children and the way in which media use is operationalized. Among both elementary school children and adolescents there is a negative relationship between overall television viewing and political knowledge. When measures of television news viewing are used, however, the relationships tend to become relatively strong, at least among the younger children (Conway et al 1975, Atkin 1977, Atkin & Gantz 1978). Among adolescents the picture is somewhat clouded; studies find political information to be positively (Rubin 1978) and negatively (Chaffee et al 1977, Jackson-Beeck 1979) associated with public affairs news viewing. As with adults, the evidence is relatively consistent that newspaper use is strongly and positively related to various measures of political information regardless of age (Conway et al 1975, Chaffee et al 1977, Jackson-Beeck 1979, Newspaper Advertising Bureau 1980a). The importance of age in specifying any relationship between mass media use and political knowledge is further illustrated by the consistent finding that the strength of association between public affairs media use and political knowledge tends to increase with age (Roberts et al 1975, Hawkins et al 1975, Atkin & Gantz 1978, Rubin 1978). This, along with the age-related switch in predictive power from television use to print use, probably indicates an increase in the kinds of skills necessary to integrate politically relevant media content into a developing structure of political knowledge.

The question of causality, of course, underlies most examinations of the relationship between public affairs media use and political knowledge. Several studies have addressed this question using time-lagged correlation techniques with samples of both elementary school children (Atkin & Gantz 1978) and adolescents (Chaffee et al 1977). In both cases the evidence indicates that use of public affairs media causes subsequent increases in levels of political knowledge. Similarly, Hawkins et al (1975) found that preadolescents high in public affairs media use during the 1972 presidential campaign knew substantially more about Watergate the following spring than did those low in such media use.

Other indicators of political socialization have also been considered. Rubin (1978) reports that younger children high in public affairs viewing have more favorable attitudes toward government, and Atkin (1977) found that exposure to campaign advertisements predicted both liking for and information about presidential candidates among third through sixth graders. Chaffee et al (1977) found that adolescents who engaged in little print use were low in political efficacy while the reverse was true for high print users. Several studies have also reported positive relationships between public affairs media use and interpersonal discussion about politics (Hawkins et al 1975, Roberts et al 1975, Atkin & Gantz 1978, Jackson-Beeck 1979). Other variables considered in the preceding studies include interest in politics, willingness to declare partisan identity, ability to name parents' political affiliation, and engaging in political activities at school.

In general, the thrust of recent work on the role of media in political socialization has been toward multivariate designs that conceive of the media as just one influence in a total system of political socialization agents. Multivariate models presented in path analysis form demonstrate both the importance of media to any complete understanding of political socialization and the necessity of examining the media in a context of other socialization agents and background variables. Chaffee et al (1977) provide a thoughtful discussion of the problems inherent in relating mass communication research to political socialization, and encourage optimism that inquiry in this particular problem area will flourish.

Antisocial Behavior

Research on television and children has been dominated by concern with the impact of viewing portrayals of violence. Empirical studies focusing on this "problem" outweigh work in all other problem areas by more than four to one (Comstock et al 1978). Studies continue to mount, although at a much reduced rate from that of the early 1970s.

Several recent correlational studies continue to examine various contingent conditions that mediate the violence viewing-aggression relationship.

For example, in one large sample of children ranging from 6 through 18 years, violence viewing was negatively related to various demographic indicators of family education and income and to the child's degree of isolation, and positively related to measures of aggression such as amount of conflict with parents, frequency of fighting, and delinquent behavior (McCarthy et al 1975). A panel survey of fourth, sixth, and eighth graders found evidence that aggressive attitudes are strong predictors of later violence viewing, but that parental restrictions on exposure to certain programs can moderate such selective exposure (Atkin et al 1979). Edgar (1977) found that Australian children low in self-esteem were less likely to understand film violence and less likely to take action to preclude real violence. She also reports that it is the context rather than the nature of the portrayed violence that is important, children being most disturbed by portrayals of contexts that could easily be related to their own lives. Haynes (1978) points out that children may perceive and evaluate violence differently than do adults and that differences in perceptions can be expected to mediate different responses. In this vein, Collins & Zimmerman (1975) showed that experimentally manipulated perceptions engendered different responses to an aggressive film. Children who saw violence portrayed in a context of consistently negative motives and consequences inhibited subsequent violent responses. Children who viewed the same violent portrayal surrounded by mixed cues, some positive and some negative, were subsequently more aggressive. The authors suggest that divergent cues resulted in perceptions of the portrayed aggression as relatively positive.

Several large-scale field experiments have addressed some of the criticisms concerning the lack of ecological validity of work in this area. A Canadian study (Joy et al 1977) took advantage of the introduction of television into a previously isolated community by observing the changes in aggressive behavior of children in three towns over a period of 2 years. At the beginning of the study one town had no television, one town had one channel, and one town had multiple channels, including the U.S. networks. Longitudinal data indicate no differences in the aggressive behavior of elementary school children across the three towns at the beginning of the study, but a significant increase in such behavior among children in the town into which television was introduced. Cross-sectional data also indicate a dramatic increase in aggressiveness among children just receiving television, an outcome interpreted by the authors as possibly due to a "disinhibiting" effect rather than to the cumulative impact of viewing.

Finally, three field experiments are reported by Parke et al (1977). The studies, conducted in the U.S. and Belgium, exposed groups of adolescent boys living in minimum security institutions to unedited, feature-length films that were either aggressive or nonaggressive. Measures of aggressive behavior were derived from naturalistic observations made in the institutional setting before, during, and after the exposure periods. Results indicate that exposure to films portraying violence increased aggressive behavior, and that the effect was greatest among boys who were initially predisposed to be more aggressive. One study also produced support for a cumulative effect, viewers of five movies over the course of a week manifesting more aggressive behavior than viewers of a single movie. Taken together, these field experiments, in conjunction with those conducted prior to 1975 (Comstock et al 1978), provide relatively convincing evidence that television violence can have an antisocial impact.

Although publication of the Surgeon General's Scientific Advisory Committee's (1972) report on television and social behavior appears to have marked the crest of the wave of television and aggression research, efforts to review and integrate an almost bewildering array of studies using different methodologies, testing different hypotheses, focusing on different age groups, and producing what often seem to be conflicting results, continue to appear (Kaplan & Singer 1976, Andison 1977, Murray & Kippax 1979). At least one review finds little or no effect of television on the "level of violence in society" (Howitt & Cumberbatch 1975). However, the general consensus seems to be that there is a positive, causal relationship between viewing television violence and subsequent aggressive behavior. Of course, the relationship is conditioned by a host of environmental, individual, and content-related variables. Moreover, the strength with which the relationship has been demonstrated varies with the general empirical method and the specific operationalizations used in the various studies. Nevertheless, it is just this multiplicity of approaches and findings that led one major review to characterize the area of violence viewing and aggression as the one problem in television research in which there is enough diversity to instill great confidence in a causal interpretation (Comstock et al 1978).

Prosocial Effects

Research in this area grew out of recognition that the same principles underlying learning and performance of television-mediated antisocial behavior should also operate for more positive behavior. Fortunately, the large theoretical literature on observational learning and the available empirical data on television and children's aggressive behavior has enabled research on the medium's prosocial effects to move rapidly away from laboratory studies conducted with specially prepared stimuli toward field experiments conducted with naturally occurring television programs.

Children have little trouble recognizing the prosocial themes in entertainment programs. Interviews with hundreds of elementary school children who had viewed episodes of various programs with prosocial themes revealed that, regardless of whether the children viewed the program in a captive situation or under natural viewing conditions, approximately 90% of all viewers recalled at least one prosocial message—up to 5 hours after viewing (Columbia Broadcasting System 1977). Similarly, several studies have found significant levels of understanding of prosocial messages among kindergarten children (Silverman 1977).

Prosocial programs also influence behavior. One study found that second and third grade children were more cooperative on verbal problem-solving measures and on a behavioral helping measure subsequent to viewing an episode of *The Waltons* which emphasized a problem-solving theme (Baran et al 1979). Another found that fourth through tenth grade children who viewed an action-adventure program in which the protagonist coped constructively with an interpersonal conflict were subsequently more likely to help a peer than were children who viewed an aggressive or neutral program (Collins & Getz 1976). Still other work found that an episode of *Lassie* which emphasized helping behavior encouraged first graders to help a dog perceived to be in trouble at a cost to themselves (Sprakfin et al 1975), and that segments of *Sesame Street* depicting nonwhite children as primary characters made 3- to 5-year-olds more willing to select nonwhite playmates (Gorn et al 1976).

Several researchers have examined the impact of extended viewing of series of either neutral or prosocial programs by coding subsequent behavior in school settings. Coates et al (1976) observed children's frequency of social contacts and of giving positive reinforcement and punishment to peers in the nursery school before, during, and after a week of exposure to either *Sesame Street* or *Mister Rogers' Neighborhood.* Murray & Ahammer (1977) showed preschool children either a prosocial or a neutral television diet over a 4-week period and examined changes in helping behavior. Both studies report increases in prosocial behavior as a function of prosocial program content.

Work on the effect of combining television and various kinds of supplemental treatment such as verbal labeling or role playing has also begun to appear (Friedrich & Stein 1975, Ahammer & Murray 1979). Results indicate that preschool children are influenced by prosocial television content and that the influence can be increased significantly with the kinds of supplementary training that could logically be carried out in the nursery school setting.

Not all results are quite so straightforward or positive, however. Silverman (1977) showed 3-, 5-, and 7-year-olds *Sesame Street* segments edited to emphasize either resolution of conflict via cooperation or just cooperation. The treatment films influenced the cognitions of 5- and 7-year-olds, but not their behavior. Among 3-year-olds the conflict-cooperation pro-

gram had a negative effect, reducing cooperative behavior to below that of
children who viewed a control film. In addition, some of the studies cited
above found that the impact of prosocial programs depends on characteristics of the child such as initial levels of prosocial behavior, age, the specific
type of behavior being examined, and so forth (Friedrich & Stein 1975,
Coates et al 1976, Baran et al 1979). Finally, Sprafkin & Rubinstein (1979)
report a correlational study that found second, third, and fourth graders'
viewing of prosocial television programs accounted for no more than 1%
of the variance in an index of prosocial behavior exhibited in school. They
speculate that some of this lack of effect can be attributed to early overlearn-
ing of prosocial behavior which implies that such content functions more
as a reinforcer than a source of new information, a possibility that fits nicely
with the idea that in controlled experimental and measurement situations
the effect of prosocial content can be explained in terms of its cueing or
eliciting function (Baran et al 1979).

Speculation that some of the differences among children in response to
prosocial content is due both to presentation factors and to the particular
prosocial behavior being portrayed (Coates et al 1976, Sprafkin & Rubinstein 1979) points to a major problem with work in this area. There is an
obvious need to be more precise about what "prosocial content" means.
Effects categorized under this rubric have ranged across helping, kindness,
altruism, empathy, friendliness, creativity, stereotyping—almost any behavior with positive social value seems fair game. Little attention has been
paid to conceptual differences among such "prosocial" effects. Yet it is quite
reasonable to expect qualitative differences in the way television would
portray helping or task persistence as opposed to creativity or lack of
prejudice. And given what we know about differences in comprehension as
a function of differences in both presentation factors and the child viewer,
differences in response are also predictable.

Sex-Role Socialization

Concern with the status of women, in combination with the pervasiveness
of sex-role stereotypes in mass media content (Butler & Paisley 1980), has
led to the emergence of the media's role in sex-role socialization as a
"problem" area in its own right. Five years ago, research consisted almost
entirely of content analyses and speculation concerning the potential impact
of stereotypic sex-role portrayals (Busby 1975). Today, empirical studies of
children's responses to sex-role content are appearing. Pingree & Hawkins
(1980) note that it is difficult to test the degree to which media content
affects children's sex-role attitudes or behavior because representative,
unexposed control groups are impossible to find and because nontraditional,

nonsexist portrayals of male/female roles are rare. Nevertheless, it is possible to establish partial answers by determining whether there is any relationship between viewing and sex-role attitudes, and by testing whether exposure to nonstereotypic portrayals influences children to change from some presumed stereotypic baseline.

There appears to be a relationship between amount of television viewing and stereotypic responses to sex-role questions. Among children between 3 and 12 years, those who view more television give more traditional responses on various sex-role measures (Beuf 1974, Freuh & McGhee 1975). The relationship survives controls for age and sex, although older children and boys tend to be more stereotyped in their responses. Moreover, grade school children who viewed more nonsex stereotyped programs were more likely to accept the nontraditional role as appropriate (Miller & Reeves 1976). Of course, a difficulty with these studies is that children we would expect to give more traditional responses on a variety of issues tend to be heavier viewers (Comstock et al 1978). Still, demonstrating a relationship is a necessary first step in determining whether media affect sex-role expectations.

Several experiments have explored the impact of commercials portraying more or less traditional sex-role behavior. Tan (1979) reports a "cultivation effect" in that adolescent girls exposed to an "artificially heavy dose" of beauty commercials were more likely than a control group to respond that beauty characteristics were necessary to be popular with men and were personally important characteristics. Atkin & Miller (1975) and Pingree (1978) obtained tentative evidence that, under some conditions, young children exposed to commercials portraying women in nontraditional occupations give less traditional responses to questions about appropriate sex-role behavior. The weakness of their findings might be attributable to the use of commercials as stimuli. When, for example, children were exposed to inherently more appealing cartoons selected for stereotypic, neutral, or nonstereotypic sex-role content, 5- and 6-year-old girls who saw the nontraditional cartoon produced significantly lower sex-role stereotype scores (Davidson et al 1979).

The most encouraging work on television and sex-role socialization is presented in an extensive evaluation of *Freestyle,* a television series designed to reduce sex-role stereotypes among 9- through 12-year-olds and to expand career awareness for girls within that age range (Johnston et al 1980). Although the program had little effect in altering individual interest patterns, relative to control groups, viewers from seven different U.S. sites became more approving of girls in nontraditional roles and less stereotypic in their perceptions of what was "real" concerning the nontraditional sex-

role behavior of both males and females. These effects were greatly facilitated when the program was viewed in a school setting and accompanied
by classroom discussion, a combination that led to persistence of over 60%
of the original effect up to 9 months after exposure (Johnston & Davidscn
1980).

As with so many studies in other problem areas, then, work on sex-role
socialization supports a cultivation effect interpretation. The media appear
to contribute to the continuance of sex-stereotyped perceptions, but are
capable of establishing new perceptual sets when nonstereotypic content is
introduced.

RETROSPECT

Our sense at the end of the search conducted for this review is that mass
communication research has entered its adolescence. On the one hand, the
field is experiencing a period of rapid growth marked by a tremendous
outpouring of empirical studies. Many of these have attempted to use new
techniques and to adopt new perspectives. We also found conscious—
indeed, self-conscious—efforts to assert independence from such parent
disciplines as psychology and sociology.

On the other hand, a kind of consolidation of what has gone before is also
beginning to emerge. The optimism of the early years and the pessimism
of the 1950s have given way to recognition that mass communication plays
an important role in our social system, but that it is just one element in that
system. Moreover, we found the beginning of a good deal of higher level
conceptual development. The field's problem orientation probably means
that it will always be marked by some degree of brute empiricism, and there
remains some truth to Nordenstreng's (1968) characterization of U.S. communication research as long on empirical technique and short on thinking.
Nevertheless, one of the more pleasant surprises connected with this review
was the discovery that a great deal of conceptual development has begun
to emerge. The straightforward listing of studies and results typical of many
reviews of several decades ago has begun to give way to critical syntheses
of research in the service of formulating higher level generalizations about
the communication process. Even more encouraging, many of the higher
level statements that have begun to appear are solidly grounded in empirical
data.[2] In short, we believe that the trends in the field will make the task of
the next reviewer of mass communication effects particularly exciting.

[2]Some of our thinking about this issue derives from discussions with E. M. Rogers, who
plans to discuss the importance to communication research of such "meta-research" in his
Presidential Address to the 1981 Conference of the International Communication Association.

Literature Cited

Adler, R., ed. 1977. *Research on the effects of television advertising on children.* Washington DC: GPO

Adoni, H. 1979. The functions of mass media in the political socialization of adolescents. *Commun. Res.* 6:84–106

Ahammer, I. M., Murray, J. P. 1979. Kindness in the kindergarten: the relative influence of role playing and prosocial television in facilitating altruism. *Int. J. Behav. Dev.* 2:133–57

Allen, R. L., Bielby, W. T. 1979. Blacks' attitudes and behaviors toward television. *Commun. Res.* 6:437–62

Alwitt, L. F., Anderson, D. R., Lorch, E. P., Levin, S. R. 1980. Preschool children's visual attention to attributes of television. *Hum. Commun. Res.* In press

Anderson, D. R., Alwitt, L. F., Lorch, E. P., Levin, S. R. 1979. Watching children watch television. In *Attention and Cognitive Development,* ed. G. A. Hale, M. Lewis, pp. 331–61. New York: Plenum. 366 pp.

Anderson, D. R., Levin, S. R. 1976. Young children's attention to "Sesame Street." *Child Dev.* 47:806–11

Anderson, D. R., Lorch, E. P., Field, D. E., Sanders, J. 1980. The effects of TV program comprehensibility on preschool children's visual attention to television. *Child Dev.* In press

Anderson, J. A., Meyer, T. P. 1975. Functionalism and the mass media. *J. Broadcast.* 19.11–22

Andison, F. S. 1977. TV violence and viewer aggression: a cumulation of study results. *Public Opin. Q.* 41:314–31

Atkin, C. K. 1975. Communication and political socialization. *Polit. Commun. Rev.* 1:2–7

Atkin, C. K. 1976. Mass media and the aging. In *Aging and Communication,* ed. H. J. Oyer, E. H. Oyer, pp. 99–118, Baltimore. Md: Univ. Park Press. 302 pp.

Atkin, C. K. 1977. Effects of campaign advertising and newscasts on children. *Journ. Q.* 54:503–8

Atkin, C. K. 1978. Broadcast news programming and the child audience. *J. Broadcast.* 22:47–61

Atkin, C. K. 1979. Research evidence on mass mediated health communication campaigns. In *Communication Yearbook,* ed. D. Nimmo, 3:655–68. New Brunswick, NJ: Int. Commun. Assoc. 704 pp.

Atkin, C. K., Galloway, J., Nayman, O. 1976. News media exposure, political knowledge, and campaign interest. *Journ. Q.* 53:231–37

Atkin, C. K., Gantz, W. 1978. Television news and political socialization. *Public Opin. Q.* 42:183–98

Atkin, C. K., Greenberg, B., Korzenny, F., McDermott, S. 1979. Selective exposure to televised violence. *J. Broadcast.* 23:5–13

Atkin, C. K., Heald, G. 1976. Effects of political advertising. *Public Opin. Q.* 40:216–28

Atkin, C. K., Heald, G. 1977. The content of children's toy and food commercials. *J. Commun.* 27(1):107–14

Atkin, C. K., Miller, M. 1975. *The effects of television advertising on children: experimental evidence.* Presented at Ann. Meet. Int. Commun. Assoc., Chicago

Atkins, P. A., Elwood, H. 1978. TV news is first choice in survey of high schools. *Journ. Q.* 55:596–99

Atwood, L. E., Sohn, A., Sohn, H. 1976. *Community discussion and newspaper content.* Presented at Ann. Meet. Assoc. Educ. Journ., College Park, Md.

Baran, S. J., Chase, L. J., Courtright, J. A. 1979. Television drama as a facilitator of prosocial behavior: "The Waltons." *J. Broadcast.* 23:277–85

Becker, L. B. 1976. Two tests of media gratifications: Watergate and the 1974 election. *Journ. Q.* 53:29–33, 87

Becker, L. B. 1979. Measurement of gratifications. *Commun. Res.* 6:54–73

Becker, L. B., McCombs, M. E., McLeod, J. M. 1975. The development of political cognitions. In *Political Communication: Issues and Strategies for Research,* ed. S. H. Chaffee, pp. 21–63. Beverly Hills: Sage. 319 pp.

Becker, L. B., Sobowale, I. A., Casey, W. E. 1979a. Newspaper and television dependencies: effects on evaluations of public officials. *J. Broadcast.* 23:465–75

Becker, L. B., Weaver, D. H., Graber, D. A., McCombs, M. E. 1979b. Influence on public agendas. In *The Great Debates: Carter vs. Ford, 1976,* ed. S. Kraus, pp. 418–28. Bloomington: Indiana Univ. Press. 553 pp.

Becker, L. B., Whitney, D. C. 1980. Effects of media dependencies: audience assessment of government. *Commun. Res.* 7:95–120

Beltran S., L. R. 1975. Research ideologies in conflict. *J. Commun.* 25(2):187–93

Beltran S., L. R. 1976. Alien premises, objects, and methods in Latin American communication research. *Commun. Res.* 3:107–34

Benton, M., Frazier, P. J. 1976. The agenda-setting function of mass media at three levels of information holding. *Commun. Res.* 3:261–74

Beuf, A. 1974. Doctor, lawyer, household drudge. *J. Commun.* 24(2):142–45

Bishop, G. F., Oldendick, R. W., Tuchfarber A. J. 1978. Debate watching and the acquisition of political knowledge. *J. Commun.* 28(4):99–113

Blumler, J. G. 1979. The role of theory in uses and gratifications studies. *Commun. Res.* 6:9–36

Blumler, J. G., Katz, E. 1974. Forward. In *The Uses of Mass Communications: Current Perspectives on Gratifications Research.* ed. J. G. Blumler, E Katz. Beverly Hills: Sage. 318 pp.

Blumler, J. G., McQuail, D. 1969. *Television in Politics: Its Uses and Influences.* Chicago: Univ. Chicago Press. 379 pp.

Bogart, L. 1975a. How the challenge of television news affects the prosperity of daily newspapers. *Journ. Q.* 52:403–10

Bogart, L. 1975b. The future of the metropolitan daily. *J. Commun.* 25(2):30–43

Bower, R. T. 1973. *Television and the Public.* New York: Holt, Rinehart & Winston. 205 pp.

Brown, J. R., Cramond, J. K., Wilde, R. J. 1974. Displacement effects of television and the child's functional orientation to media. See Blumler & Katz 1974, pp. 93–112

Bryant, B., Currier, F., Morrison, A. 1976. Relating life style factors of a person to his choice of newspaper. *Journ. Q.* 53:74–79

Busby, L. J. 1975. Sex-role research on the mass media. *J. Commun.* 25(4):107–31

Butler, M., Paisley, W. 1980. *Women and the Mass Media: Sourcebook for Research and Action.* New York: Hum. Sci. Press. 432 pp.

Canadian Broadcasting Corporation. 1975. *Dimensions of audience response to television programs in Canada.* Toronto: CBC

Carey, J. W. 1976. How media shape campaigns. *J. Commun.* 26(2):50–57

Carey, J. W. 1978. The ambiguity of policy research. *J. Commun.* 28(2):114–19

Carey, J. W., Kreiling, A. L. 1974. Popular culture and uses and gratifications: notes toward an accommodation. See Blumler & Katz 1974, pp. 225–48

Caron, A. H. 1979. First-time exposure to television: effects on Inuit children's cultural images. *Commun. Res.* 6: 135–54

Chaffee, S. H. 1977. Mass media effects: new research perspectives. See Lerner & Nelson 1977, pp. 210–41

Chaffee, S. H. 1978. Presidential debates— are they helpful to voters? *Commun. Monogr.* 45:330–53

Chaffee, S. H. 1979. *Mass media vs. interpersonal channels: The synthetic competition.* Presented at Ann. Meet. Speech Commun. Assoc., San Antonio

Chaffee, S. H., Dennis, J. 1979. Presidential debates: an empirical assessment. In *The Past and Future of Presidential Debates.* ed. A. Ranney, pp. 75–106. Washington DC: Am. Enterp. Inst. 236 pp.

Chaffee, S. H., Izcaray, F. 1975. Mass communication functions in a media rich developing society. *Commun. Res.* 2:367–95

Chaffee, S. H., Jackson-Beeck, M., Durall, J., Wilson, D. 1977. Mass communication in political communication. In *Handbook of Political Socialization: Theory and Research.* ed. S. A. Renshon, pp. 223–58. New York: Free Press. 547 pp.

Chaffee, S. H., Wilson, D. G. 1975. *Adult life cycle changes in mass media use.* Presented at Ann. Meet. Assoc. Educ. Journ., Ottawa, Ontario, Canada

Chaffee, S. H., Wilson, D. G. 1977. Media rich, media poor: two studies of diversity in agenda-holding. *Journ. Q.* 54:466–76

Christenson, P. G. 1980. *The effects of consumer information processing announcements on children's perceptions of commercials and products.* PhD thesis. Stanford Univ., Stanford, Calif. 107 pp.

Chu, G. C. 1976. Group communication and development in mainland China—the functions of social pressure. See Schramm & Lerner 1976, pp. 119–33

Clarke, P., Fredin, E. 1978. Newspapers, television and political reasoning. *Public Opin. Q.* 42:143–60

Clarke, P., Kline, F. G. 1974. Media effects reconsidered: some new strategies for communication research. *Commun. Res.* 1:224–40

Coates, B., Pusser, H. E., Goodman, I. 1976. The influence of "Sesame Street" and "Mister Rogers' Neighborhood" on children's social behavior in the preschool. *Child Dev.* 47:138–44

Cohen, B. C. 1963. *The Press and Foreign Policy.* Princeton: Princeton Univ. Press. 228 pp.

Coldevin, G. A. 1979. Satellite television and cultural replacement among Canadian Eskimos: adults and adolescents compared. *Commun. Res.* 6:115–34

Collins, W. A. 1975. The developing child as viewer. *J. Commun.* 25(4):35–44

Collins, W. A. 1979a. Children's comprehension of television content. In *Children Communicating: Media and Development of Thought. Speech. Understanding.* ed. E. Wartella, pp. 21 52. Beverly Hills: Sage. 286 pp.

Collins, W. A. 1979b. *Social antecedents, cognitive processing, and comprehension of social portrayals on television.* Presented at Soc. Sci. Res. Counc. Conf. on Soc. Cognit. Soc. Behav., London, Ont. Canada

Collins, W. A., Berndt, T., Hess, V. 1974. Observational learning of motives and consequences for television aggression: a developmental study. *Child Dev.* 45:799–802

Collins, W. A., Getz, S. K. 1976. Children's social responses following modeled reactions to provocation: prosocial effects of a television drama. *J. Pers.* 44:488–500

Collins, W. A., Wellman, H., Keniston, A. H., Westby, S. D. 1978. Age-related aspects of comprehension and inference from a televised dramatic narrative. *Child Dev.* 49:389–99

Collins, W. A., Zimmermann, S. A. 1975. Convergent and divergent social cues: effects of televised aggression on children. *Commun. Res.* 2:331–46

Columbia Broadcasting System. 1977. *Communicating With Children Through Television: Studies of Messages and Other Impressions Conveyed by Five Children's Programs.* New York: CBS Econ. Res. 534 pp.

Comstock, G. 1978. The impact of television on American institutions. *J. Commun.* 28(2):12–28

Comstock, G., Chaffee, S., Katzman, N., McCombs, M., Roberts, D. 1978. *Television and Human Behavior.* New York: Columbia Univ. Press. 581 pp.

Conway, M. M., Stevens, A. J., Smith, R. G. 1975. The relation between media use and children's civic awareness. *Journ. Q.* 52:531–38

Council on Children, Media and Merchandising. 1977. *Edible TV: Your Child and Food Commercials.* Prepared for Senate Select Comm. Hum. Needs, 95th Congr., 1st session. Washington DC: GPO. 105 pp.

Danowski, J. 1975. *Informational aging: interpersonal and mass communication patterns in a retirement community.* Presented at Gerontol. Soc. Conv., Louisville, Ky.

Davidson, E. S., Yasuna, A., Tower, A. 1979. The effects of television cartoons on sex-role stereotyping in young girls. *Child Dev.* 50:597–600

Denbow, C. 1975. A test of predictors of newspaper subscribing. *Journ. Q.* 52:744–48

Dennis, E. E. 1978. *The Media Society: Evidence about Mass Communication in America.* Dubuque, Iowa: Brown. 166 pp.

Dennis, J., Chaffee, S. H., Choe, S. Y. 1979. Impact on partisan, image, and issue voting. See Becker et al 1979b, pp. 314–30

Diaz Bordenave, J. 1976. Communication of agricultural innovations in Latin America: the need for new models. *Commun. Res.* 3:135–54

Donohue, G. A., Tichenor, P. J., Olien, C. N. 1975. Mass media and the knowledge gap: a hypothesis reconsidered. *Commun. Res.* 2:3–23

Doob, A. N., Macdonald, G. E. 1979. Television viewing and fear of victimization: is the relationship causal? *J. Pers. Soc. Psychol.* 37:170–79

Dorr, A. 1978. *Children's advertising rulemaking comment.* Testimony to the Federal Trade Commission's Rulemaking Hearings on Television Advertising and Children, San Francisco, Calif., Nov. 31 pp.

Dotan, J., Cohen, A. A. 1976. Mass media use in the family during war and peace. *Commun. Res.* 3:393–402

Dubren, R. 1977. Evaluation of a televised stop-smoking clinic. *Public Health Rep.* 92:81–84

Edelstein, A. S. 1974. *The Uses of Communication in Decision-Making: A Comparative Study of Yugoslavia and the United States.* New York: Praeger. 270 pp.

Edgar, P. 1977. *Children and Screen Violence.* St. Lucia, Queensland, Aust: Univ. Queensland Press. 275 pp.

Egan, L. M. 1978. Children's viewing patterns for television news. *Journ. Q.* 55:337–42

Elliot, P. 1974. Uses and gratifications research: a critique and a sociological alternative. See Blumler & Katz 1974, pp. 249–68

Ettema, J. S., Kline, F. G. 1977. Deficits, differences, and ceilings: contingent conditions for understanding the knowledge gap. *Commun. Res.* 4:179–202

Eyal, C. H. 1979. *The roles of newspapers and television in agenda-setting.* Presented at Ann. Meet. Am. Assoc. Public Opin. Res., Buck Hills Falls, Pa.

Eyal, C. H., Winter, J. P., DeGeorge, W. F. 1979. *Time frame for agenda-setting.*

Presented at Ann. Meet. Am. Assoc. Public Opin. Res., Buck Hills Falls, Pa.

Eysenck, H. J., Nias, D. K. B. 1978. *Sex, Violence and the Media.* New York: St. Martin's. 306 pp.

Farquhar, J. W. 1978. The community-based model of life style intervention trials. *Am. J. Epidemiol.* 108:103–11

Farquhar, J. W., Wood, P. D., Breitrose, H., Haskell, W. L., Meyer, A. J., Maccoby, N., Alexander, J. K., Brown, B. W., McAlister, A. L., Nash, J. D., Stern, M. 1977. Community education for cardiovascular health. *Lancet* 1:1192–95

Federal Communications Commission. Children's Television Programs: Report and Policy Statement, 39 Fed. Reg. 39396, 39401; 50 F.C.C. 2nd 1,11

Federal Trade Commission. 1978. *FTC staff report on television advertising to children.* Washington DC: Fed. Trade Comm. 346 pp.

Feigert, F. B. 1976. Political competence and mass media use. *Public Opin. Q.* 40:234–38

Foley, J. M. 1979. Mass communication theory and research: an overview. See Atkin 1979, pp. 263–70

Freuh, T., McGhee, P. E. 1975. Traditional sex role development and amount of time spent watching television. *Dev. Psychol.* 11:109

Friedrich, L. K., Stein, A. H. 1975, Prosocial television and young children: the effects of verbal labeling and role playing on learning and behavior. *Child Dev.* 46:27–38

Funkhouser, G. R. 1973. Trends in media coverage of the issues of the 60's. *Journ. Q.* 50:533–38

Galst, J. P., White, M. A. 1976. The unhealthy persuader: the reinforcing value of television and children's purchase-influencing attempts at the supermarket. *Child Dev.* 47:1089–96

Genova, B. K. L., Greenberg, B. S. 1979. Interests in news and the knowledge gap. *Public Opin. Q.* 43:79–91

Gerbner, G., Gross, L. 1976a. Living with television: the violence profile. *J. Commun.* 26(2):173–99

Gerbner, G., Gross, L. 1976b. The scary world of television. *Psychol. Today,* April: 41–45, 89

Gerbner, G., Gross, L., Jackson-Beeck, M., Jeffries-Fox, S., Signorielli, N. 1978. Cultural indicators: violence profile No. 9 *J. Commun.* 28(3):176–207

Gerbner, G., Gross, L., Signorielli, N., Morgan, M., Jackson-Beeck, M. 1979. The demonstration of power: violence profile No. 10. *J. Commun.* 29(3):177–96

Glasgow University Media Group. 1976. *Bad News.* London: Routledge

Goldberg, M. E., Gorn, G. 1977. *Material vs. social preferences, parent-child relations and the child's emotional responses: three dimensions of responses to children's TV advertising.* Presented at 5th Ann. Telecommun. Policy Res. Conf., Airlie House, Va.

Goldberg, M. E., Gorn, G., Gibson, W. 1978. TV messages for snack and breakfast foods: do they influence children's preferences? *J. Consum. Res.* 5:73–81

Gormley, W. T. Jr. 1975. Newspaper agendas and political elites. *Journ. Q.* 52:30–38

Gorn, G. J., Goldberg, M. E., Kanungo, R. N. 1976. The role of educational television in changing the intergroup attitudes of children. *Child Dev.* 47:277–80

Greenberg, B. S. 1974. Gratifications of television viewing and their correlates for British children. See Blumler & Katz 1974, pp. 71–92

Greenberg, B. S., Reeves, B. 1976. Children and the perceived reality of television. *J. Soc. Issues* 32:86–97

Halberstam, D. 1979. *The Powers That Be.* New York: Knopf. 771 pp.

Hall, S. 1977. Culture, the media and the 'ideological effect.' In *Mass Communication and Society,* ed. J. Curran, M. Gurevitch, J. Woollacott, pp. 315–48. London: Arnold. 479 pp.

Halloran, J. D. 1978. Further development— or turning the clock back. *J. Commun.* 28(2):120–32

Hawkins, R. P. 1977. The dimensional structure of children's perceptions of television reality. *Commun. Res.* 4:299–320

Hawkins, R. P., Pingree, S. H., Roberts, D. F. 1975. Watergate and political socialization: the inescapable event. *Am. Politics Q.* 3:406–22

Haynes, R. B. 1978. Children's perceptions of "comic" and "authentic" cartoon violence. *J. Broadcast.* 22:63–70

Hirsch, P. M. 1980. *The "scary world" of the nonviewer and other anomalies: a reanalysis of Gerbner et al's findings on cultivation analysis.* Presented at Ann. Meet. Am. Assoc. Public Opin. Res., King's Island, Ohio

Hirsch, P. M., Miller, P. V., Kline, F. G., eds. 1977. *Strategies for Communication Research.* Beverly Hills: Sage. 288 pp.

Hofstetter, C. R., Zukin, C. 1979. TV network political news and advertising in the Nixon and McGovern campaigns. *Journ. Q.* 56:106–15, 152

Hollenbeck, A. R., Slaby, R. G. 1979. Infant visual and vocal responses to television. *Child Dev.* 50:41–45

Howitt, D., Cumberbatch, G. 1975. *Mass Media, Violence and Society.* London: Elek. 167 pp.

Jackson-Beeck, M. 1979. Interpersonal and mass communication in children's political socialization. *Journ. Q.* 56:48–53

Jackson-Beeck, M., Chaffee, S. H. 1975. *Family communication, mass communication, and differential political socialization.* Presented at Ann. Meet. Int. Commun. Assoc., Chicago

Jennings, M. K., Niemi, R. G. 1975. Continuity and change in political orientations: a longitudinal study of two generations. *Am. Polit. Sci. Rev.* 69:1316–35

Johnston, J., Davidson, T. 1980. *The persistence of effects—a supplement to ":An evaluation of 'Freestyle': a television series to reduce sex role stereotypes."* Ann Arbor: Inst. Soc. Res., Univ. Mich. 29 pp.

Johnston, J., Ettema, J., Davidson, T. 1980. *An evaluation of "Freestyle": a television series to reduce sex role stereotypes.* Ann Arbor: Inst. Soc. Res., Univ. Mich. 297 pp.

Johnstone, J. W. C. 1974. Social integration and mass media use among adolescents: a case study. See Blumler & Katz 1974, pp. 35–47

Joy, L. A., Kimball, M., Zabrack, M. L. 1977. *Television exposure and children's aggressive behavior.* Presented at Ann. Meet. Can. Psychol. Assoc., Vancouver, BC

Kaid, L. L., Hale, K., Williams, J. A. 1977. Media agenda setting of a specific political event. *Journ. Q.* 54:584–87

Kaplan, R. M., Singer, R. D. 1976. Television violence and viewer aggression: a re-examination of the evidence. *J. Soc. Issues* 32:35–70

Katz, E. 1977. *Social Research on Broadcasting: Proposals for Further Development.* London: British Broadcast. Corp. 116 pp.

Katz, E. 1978a. Looking for trouble. *J. Commun.* 28(2):90–95

Katz, E. 1978b. Of mutual interest. *J. Commun.* 28(2):133–41

Katz, E. 1979. The uses of Becker, Blumler, and Swanson. *Commun. Res.* 6:74–83

Katz, E. 1980. On conceptualizing media effects. In *Communications Studies: Decade of Dissent,* ed. T. MacCormak. Greenwich, Conn: JAI Press. In press

Katz, E., Blumler, J. G., Gurevitch, M. 1974. Utilization of mass communication by the individual. See Blumler & Katz 1974, pp. 19–32

Kippax, S., Murray, J. P. 1977. Using televi-

sion: programme content and need gratification. *Politics* 12:56–69

Klapper, J. T. 1960. *The Effects of Mass Communication.* Glencoe, Ill: Free Press. 302 pp.

Kline, F. G., Miller, P. V., Morrison, A. J. 1974. Adolescents and family planning information: an exploration of audience needs and media effects. See Blumler & Katz 1964, pp. 113–36

Kraus, S., Davis, D. 1976. *The Effects of Mass Communication on Political Behavior.* University Park: Penn. State Univ. Press. 308 pp.

Krull, R., Husson, W. 1979. Children's attention: the case of TV viewing. See Collins 1979, pp. 83–114

Leifer, A. D., Gordon, N. J., Graves, S. B. 1974. Children's television: more than mere entertainment. *Harv. Educ. Rev.* 44:213–45

Lerner, D., Nelson, L. M., eds. 1977. *Communication Research—a Half Century Appraisal.* Honolulu: Univ. Press Hawaii. 348 pp.

Lerner, D., Schramm, W., eds. 1967. *Communication and Change in the Developing Countries.* Honolulu: East-West Center Press. 333 pp.

Lesser, G. S. 1974. *Children and Television: Lessons from Sesame Street.* New York: Random House. 290 pp.

Levin, S. R., Anderson, D. R. 1976. The development of attention. *J. Commun.* 26(2):126–35

Levy, M. R. 1977. Experiencing television news. *J. Commun.* 27:112–17

Levy, M. R. 1978. Opinion leadership and television news uses. *Public Opin. Q.* 42:402–6

Liebert, D. E., Sprafkin, J. N., Liebert, R. M., Rubinstein, E. A. 1977. Effects of television disclaimers on the product expectations of children. *J. Commun.* 27(1):118–24

Liebert, R. M., Schwartzberg, N. S. 1977. Effects of mass media. *Ann. Rev. Psychol.* 28:141–73

Lometti, G. E., Reeves, B., Bybee, C. R. 1977. Investigating the assumptions of uses and gratifications research. *Commun. Res.* 4:321–38

Lorch, E. P., Anderson, D. R., Levin, S. R. 1979. The relationship of visual attention to children's comprehension of television. *Child Dev.* 50:722–27

Maccoby, N., Alexander, J. 1979. Field experimentation in community intervention. In *Research in Social Contexts: Bringing About Change,* ed. R. F. Munoz, L. R. Snowden, J. G. Kelley, pp. 69 100. San Francisco: Jossey Bass. 394 pp.

Maccoby, N., Alexander, J. 1980. Use of media in lifestyle programs. In *Behavioral Medicine: Changing Health Lifestyles,* ed. P. O. Davidson, S. M. Davidson, pp. 351–70. New York: Brunner/Mazel. 474 pp.

Maccoby, N., Farquhar, J. W., Wood, P. D., Alexander, J. 1977. Reducing the risk of cardiovascular disease: effects of a community-based campaign on knowledge and behavior. *J. Community Health* 3:100–14

MacKuen, M. B. 1979. *Social communication and the mass policy agenda.* PhD thesis. Univ. Mich., Ann Arbor. 175 pp.

McAlister, A., Puskaa P., Koskele, K., Pallonen, U., Maccoby, N. 1980. Mass communication and community organization for public health education. *Am. Psychol.* 35:375–79

McCarthy, E. D., Langner, T. S., Gersten, J. C., Eisenberg, J. G., Orzeck, L. 1975. Violence and behavior disorders. *J. Commun.* 25(4):71–85

McClure, R. D., Patterson, T. E. 1976. Setting the political agenda: print vs. network news. *J. Commun.* 26(2):23–28

McCombs, M. E. 1977. Newspapers versus television: mass communication effects across time. In *The Emergence of American Political Issues: The Agenda-Setting Function of the Press,* ed. D. L. Shaw, M.E. McCombs, pp. 89–105. St. Paul: West. 208 pp.

McCombs, M. E., Poindexter, P. 1978. *Civic attitudes and newspaper readership.* Presented at Ann. Meet. Midwest Assoc. Public Opin Res., Chicago

McCombs, M. E., Shaw, D. L. 1972. The agenda-setting function of mass media. *Public Opin. Q.* 36:176–87

McCombs, M. E., Weaver, D. H. 1977. *Voters and the mass media: information seeking, political interest, and issue agendas.* Presented at Ann. Meet. Am. Assoc. Public Opin. Res., Buck Hills Falls, Pa.

McLeod, J. M., Becker, L. B. 1974. Testing the validity of gratification measures through political effects analysis. See Blumler & Katz 1974, pp. 137–64

McLeod, J. M., Becker, L. B., Byrnes, J. E. 1974. Another look at the agenda setting function of the press. *Commun. Res.* 1:131–66

McLeod, J. M., Bybee, C. R., Durall, J. A. 1979. Equivalence of informed political participation: the 1976 presidential debates as a source of influence. *Commun. Res.* 6:463–87

McLeod, J. M., Reeves, B. 1980. On the nature of mass media effects. In *Television and Social Behavior: Beyond Violence and Children,* ed. S. B. Withey, R. P. Ables, pp 17–54. Hillsdale, NJ: Erlbaum. 356 pp.

Medrich, E. A. 1979. Constant television: a background to daily life. *J. Commun.* 29(3):171–76

Messaris, P. 1977. Biases of self-reported functions and gratifications of mass media use. *Et cetera: A Review of General Semantics* 34:316–29

Mielke, K. W., Swinehart, J. W. 1976. *Evaluation of the "Feeling Good" Television Series.* New York: Child. Telev. Workshop. 362 pp.

Miller, A. H., MacKuen, M. 1979. Informing the electorate: a national study. See Becker et al 1979b, pp. 269–97

Miller, M. M., Reeves, B. 1976. Linking dramatic TV content to children's occupational sex-role stereotypes. *J. Broadcast.* 20:35–50

Morison, P., McCarthy, M., Gardner, M. 1979. Exploring the realities of television with children. *J. Broadcast.* 23:453–63

Morrison, A. J., Steeper, F., Greendale, S. C. 1977. *The first 1976 presidential debate: the voters win.* Presented at Ann. Meet. Am. Assoc. Public Opin. Res., Buck Hills Falls, Pa.

Mullins, M. E. 1977. Agenda-setting and the young voter. See McCombs 1977, pp. 133–48

Murray, J. P., Ahammer, I. M. 1977. *Kindness in the kindergarten: a multidimensional program for facilitating altruism.* Presented at Bienn. Meet. Soc. Res. Child Dev., New Orleans

Murray, J. P., Kippax, S. 1979. From the early window to the late night show: international trends in the study of television's impact on children and adults. *Adv. Exp. Soc. Psychol.* 12:253–320

Newcomb, A. F., Collins, W. A. 1979. Children's comprehension of family role portrayals in televised dramas: effects of socioeconomic status, ethnicity, and age. *Dev. Psychol.* 15:417–23

Newspaper Advertising Bureau. 1978. *Children, Mothers and Newspapers.* New York: Newspaper Advert. Bur. 13 pp.

Newspaper Advertising Bureau. 1980a. *Children and Newspapers: Changing Patterns of Readership and Their Effects.* New York: Newspaper Advert. Bur. 96 pp.

Newspaper Advertising Bureau. 1980b. *Daily Newspapers in American Classrooms: A National Study of Their Impacts on Stu-*

dent Attitudes. Readership and Political Awareness. New York: Newspaper Advert. Bur. 46 pp.

Newspaper Advertising Bureau. 1980c. Mass Media in the Family Setting: Social Patterns in Media Availability and Use by Parents. New York: Newspaper Advert. Bur. 60 pp.

Noelle-Neumann, E. 1973. Return to the concept of powerful mass media. In Studies of Broadcasting, ed. H. Eguchi, K. Sata, 9:67–112. Tokyo: Nippon Hoso Kyokai

Noelle-Neumann, E. 1974. The spiral of silence: a theory of public opinion. J. Commun. 24(2):43–51

Noelle-Neumann, E. 1977. Turbulences in the climate of opinion: methodological applications of the spiral of silence theory. Public Opin. Q. 41:143–58

Nordenstreng, K. 1968. Communications research in the United States. Gazette 14(3):207–16

Nordenstreng, K., Schiller, H. I., eds. 1979. National Sovereignty and International Communication. New Jersey: Ablex. 286 pp.

Nordlund, J. 1978. Media interaction. Commun. Res. 5:150–75

Palmgreen, P. 1979. Mass media use and political knowledge. Journ. Monogr. 61, 39 pp.

Palmgreen, P., Clarke, P. 1977. Agenda-setting with local and national issues. Commun. Res. 4:435–52

Palmgreen, P., Kline, F. G., Clarke, P. 1974. Message discrimination and information-holding about political affairs. Presented at Ann. Meet. Int. Commun. Assoc., New Orleans

Palmgreen, P., Rayburn, J. D. 1979. Uses and gratifications and exposure to public television: a discrepency approach. Commun. Res. 6:181–202

Palmgreen, P., Wenner, L. A., Rayburn, J. D. 1980. Relations between gratifications sought and gratifications obtained: a study of television news. Commun. Res. 7:161–92

Parke, R. D., Berkowitz, L., Leyens, J. P., West, S., Sebastian, R. J. 1977. Some effects of violent and nonviolent movies on the behavior of juvenile delinquents. Adv. Exp. Soc. Psychol. 10:135–72

Patterson, T. E., McClure, R. D. 1976. The Unseeing Eye: The Myth of Television Power in National Elections. New York: Putnam. 218 pp.

Peled, T., Katz, E. 1974. Media functions in wartime: the Israel home front in October 1973. See Blumler & Katz 1974, pp. 49–69

Pingree, S. 1978. The effects of nonsexist television commercials and perceptions of reality on children's attitudes about women. Psychol. Women Q. 2:262–77

Pingree, S., Hawkins, R. P. 1980. Children and media. See Butler & Paisley 1980, pp. 279–99

Prisuta, R. H. 1979. The adolescent and television news: a viewer profile. Journ. Q. 56:277–82

Quarfoth, J. M. 1979. Children's understanding of the nature of television characters. J. Commun. 29(3):210–18

Quarles, R. C. 1979. Mass media use and voting behavior: the accuracy of political perceptions among first-time and experienced voters. Commun. Res. 6: 407–36

Reeves, B. 1978. Perceived TV reality as a predictor of children's social behavior. Journ. Q. 55:682–95

Reeves, B. 1979. Children's understanding of television people. See Collins 1979, pp. 115–56

Reeves, B., Greenberg, B. S. 1977. Children's perceptions of television characters. Hum. Commun. Res. 3:113–27

Reeves, B., Lometti, G. E. 1979. The dimensional structure of children's perceptions of television characters: a replication. Hum. Commun. Res. 5:247–56

Reeves, B., Miller, M. M. 1978. A multidimensional measure of children's identification with television characters. J. Broadcast. 22:71–85

Roberts, D. F. 1971. The nature of communication effects. In The Process and Effects of Mass Communication, ed. W. Schramm, D. F. Roberts, pp. 349–87. Urbana: Univ. Ill. Press. 997 pp.

Roberts, D. F. 1973. Communication and children: a developmental approach. In Handbook of Communication, ed. I. de Sola Pool, W. Schramm, pp. 174–215. Chicago: Rand McNally. 1011 pp.

Roberts, D. F., Bachen, C. M. 1978. The impact of within-ad disclosures vs. supplemental nutrition messages on children's understanding of the concept of a "balanced breakfast." Testimony to the Federal Trade Commission's Rulemaking Hearings on Television Advertising and Children, San Francisco, Nov. 21 pp.

Roberts, D. F., Bachen, C. M., Christenson, P. 1978. Children's information processing: perceptions of and cognitions about television commercials and supplemental consumer information. Testimony to the Federal Trade Commission's Rulemaking Hearings on Television Advertising and Children. San Francisco, Nov. 123 pp.

Roberts, D. F., Christenson, P., Gibson, W. A., Mooser, L., Goldberg, M. E. 1980. Developing discriminating consumers. *J. Commun.* 30(3):94–105

Roberts, D. F., Hawkins, R. P., Pingree, S. P. 1975. Do the mass media play a role in political socialization? *Aust. NZ J. Sociol.* 11:37–43

Robertson, T. S., Rossiter, J. R. 1974. Children and commercial persuasion: an attribution theory analysis. *J. Consum. Res.* 1:13–20

Robertson, T. S., Rossiter, J. R. 1977. Children's responsiveness to commercials. *J. Commun.* 27(1):101–5

Robinson, J. P., Jeffres, L. W. 1979. The changing role of newspapers in the age of television. *Journ. Monogr.* 63, 31 pp.

Robinson, M. J. 1975. American political legitimacy in an era of electronic journalism: reflections on the evening news. In *Television as a Social Force: New Approaches to TV Criticism.* ed. D. Cater, R. Adler, pp. 97–139. New York: Praeger. 171 pp.

Rogers, E. M. 1976a. Communication and development: the passing of the dominant paradigm. *Commun. Res.* 3:213–40

Rogers, E. M. 1976b. New perspectives on communication and development: overview. *Commun. Res.* 3:99–106

Rogers, E. M. 1976c. Where are we in understanding the diffusion of innovations? See Schramm & Lerner 1976, pp. 204–22

Rogers, E. M. 1977. Network analysis of the diffusion of innovations: family planning in Korean villages. See Lerner & Nelson 1977, pp. 117–47

Rogers, E. M., Shoemaker, F. F. 1971. *Communication of Innovations: A Cross-Cultural Approach.* New York: Free Press. 476 pp.

Roling, N. G., Ashcroft, J., Chege, F. W. 1976. The diffusion of innovations and the issue of equity in rural development. *Commun. Res.* 3:155–70

Roper Organization. 1977. *Changing Public Attitudes toward Television and Other Media.* New York: Telev. Inf. Off.

Rossiter, J. R., Robertson, T. S. 1974. Children's TV commercials: testing the defenses. *J. Commun.* 24(4):137–44

Rubin, A. M. 1976. Television in children's political socialization. *J. Broadcast.* 20:51–60

Rubin, A. M. 1978. Child and adolescent television use and political socialization. *Journ. Q.* 55:125–29

Rubin, A. M. 1979. Television use by children and adolescents. *Hum. Commun. Res.* 5:109–20

Salomon, G. 1979a. *Interaction of Media, Cognition and Learning.* San Francisco: Jossey-Bass. 282 pp.

Salomon, G. 1979b. Shape, not only content: how media symbols partake in the development of abilities. See Collins 1979, pp. 53–82

Schank, R., Abelson, R. 1977. *Scripts, Plans, Goals and Understanding: An Inquiry into Human Knowledge Structures.* Hillsdale, NJ: Erlbaum. 248 pp.

Schramm, W. 1962. Mass communication. *Ann. Rev. Psychol.* 13:251–84

Schramm, W. 1971. The nature of communication between humans. See Roberts 1971, pp. 3–53

Schramm, W., Lerner, D., eds. 1976. *Communication and Change: The Last Ten Years—And the Next.* Honolulu: Univ. Press Hawaii. 372 pp.

Sears, D. O., Chaffee, S. H. 1979. Uses and effects of the 1976 debates: an overview of empirical studies. See Becker et al 1979b, pp. 223–61

Sheikh, A. A., Moleski, L. M. 1977. Conflict in the family over commericals. *J. Commun.* 27(1):152–57

Shingi, P. M., Mody, B. 1976. The communication effects gap: a field experiment on television and agricultural ignorance in India. *Commun. Res.* 3:171–90

Silverman, L. T. 1977. *Effects of "Sesame Street" programming on the cooperative behavior of preschoolers.* PhD thesis. Stanford Univ., Stanford, Calif. 140 pp.

Siune, K., Borre, O. 1975. Setting the agenda for a Danish election. *J. Commun.* 25(1):65–73

Sohn, A. B. 1978. A longitudinal analysis of local non-political agenda-setting effects. *Journ. Q.* 55:325–33

Sprafkin, J. N., Liebert, R. M., Poulos, R. W. 1975. Effects of a prosocial televised example on children's helping. *J. Exp. Child Psychol.* 20:119–26

Sprafkin, J. N., Rubinstein, E. A. 1979. Children's television viewing habits and prosocial behavior: a field correlational study. *J. Broadcast.* 23:265–76

Stamm, K. R., Fortini-Campbell, L. 1977. *Readership and community identification.* Presented at Ann. Meet. Assoc. Educ. Journ., Houston

Stauffer, J., Frost, R., Rybolt, W. 1978. Literacy, illiteracy, and learning from television news. *Commun. Res.* 5:221–32

Stroman, C. A., Becker, L. B. 1978. Racial differences in gratifications. *Journ. Q.* 55:767–71

Surgeon General's Scientific Advisory Committee. 1972. *Television and Growing Up: The Impact of Televised Violence.* Washington DC: GPO. 169 pp.

Swanson, D. L. 1976. *Some theoretic approaches to the emerging study of political communication: a critical assessment.* Presented at Ann. Meet. Int. Commun. Assoc., 26th, Portland, Ore.

Swanson, D. L. 1977. The uses and misuses of uses and gratifications. *Hum. Commun. Res.* 3:214–21

Swanson, D. L. 1979a. The continuing evolution of the uses and gratifications approach. *Commun. Res.* 6:3–7

Swanson, D. L. 1979b. Political communication research and the uses and gratifications model: a critique. *Commun. Res.* 6:37–53

Tan, A. S. 1979. TV beauty ads and role expectations of adolescent female viewers. *Journ. Q.* 56:283–88

Tan, A. S., Vaughn, P. 1976. Mass media exposure, public affairs knowledge, and black militancy. *Journ. Q.* 53:271–79

Tannenbaum, P. H. 1980. An unstructured introduction to an amorphous area. In *The Entertainment Functions of Television,* ed. P. H. Tannenbaum, pp. 1–12. Hillsdale, NJ: Erlbaum. 262 pp.

Tannenbaum, P. H., Greenberg, B. S. 1968. Mass communication. *Ann. Rev. Psychol.* 19:351–86

Tichenor, P. J., Donohue, G. A., Olien, C. N. 1970. Mass media and differential growth in knowledge. *Public Opin Q.* 34:158–70

Tichenor, P. J., Rodenkirchen, J. M., Olien, C. N., Donohue, G. A. 1973. Community issues, conflict and public affairs knowledge. In *New Models for Communication Research,* ed. P. Clarke, pp. 45–79. Beverly Hills: Sage. 307 pp.

Tipton, L. P., Haney, R. D., Baseheart, J. R. 1975. Media agenda-setting in city and state election campaigns. *Journ. Q.* 52:15–22

Tuchman, G. 1977. The exception proves the rule: the study of routine news practice. See Hirsch et al 1977, pp. 43–62

von Feilitzen, C. 1976. The functions served by the media. In *Children and Television,* ed. R. Brown, pp. 90–115. Beverly Hills: Sage. 368 pp.

Wackman, D. B., Ward, S., Wartella, E. 1978. *Comments on 'FTC staff report on television advertising to children.'* Testimony to the Federal Trade Commission's Rulemaking Hearings on Television Advertising and Children, Washington DC, Nov. 24 pp

Wackman, D. B., Wartella, E. 1977. A review of cognitive development theory and research and the implications for research on children's responses to television. *Commun. Res.* 4:203–24

Wackman, D. B., Wartella, E., Ward, S. 1977. Learning to be consumers: the role of the family. *J. Commun.* 27:138–51

Wald, K. D., Lupfer, M. B. 1978. The presidential debate as a civics lesson. *Public Opin. Q.* 42:342–53

Ward, S., Levinson, D., Wackman, D. 1972. Children's attention to television advertising. In *Television and Social Behavior. Vol 4: Television in Day-to-Day Life: Patterns of Use,* ed. E. A. Rubinstein, G. A. Comstock, J. P. Murray, pp. 432–51. Washington DC: GPO. 603 pp.

Ward, S., Wackman, D. B. 1973. Children's information processing of television advertising. See Tichenor et al 1973, pp. 119–46

Ward, S., Wackman, D., Wartella, E. 1977. *How Children Learn to Buy: The Development of Consumer Information-Processing Skills.* Beverly Hills: Sage. 271 pp.

Wartella, E., Ettema, J. S. 1974. A cognitive developmental study of children's attention to television commercials. *Commun. Res.* 1:69–88

Wartella, E., Wackman, D. B., Ward, S., Shamir, J., Alexander, A. 1979. The young child as consumer. See Collins 1979, pp. 251–79

Weaver, D. H. 1977. Political issues and voter need for orientation. See McCombs 1977, pp. 107–19

Weaver, D. H., Auh, T. S., Stehla, T., Wilhoit, C. 1975a. *A path analysis of individual agenda-setting during the 1974 Indiana senatorial campaign.* Presented at Ann. Meet. Assoc. Educ. Journ., Ottawa, Canada

Weaver, D. H., Becker, L. B., McCombs, M. E. 1976. *Influence of the mass media on issues images, and political interest: the agenda-setting function of mass communication during the 1976 campaign.* Presented at Ann. Meet. Midwest Assoc. Public Opin. Res., Chicago

Weaver, D. H., McCombs, M. E., Spellman, C. 1975b. Watergate and the media: a case study of agenda-setting. *Am. Politics Q.* 3:458–72

Weiss, W. 1969. Effects of the mass media of communication. In *The Handbook of Social Psychology,* ed. G. Lindzey, E. Aronson, 5:77–195. Reading, Mass: Addison Wesley, 786 pp.

Weiss, W. 1971. Mass communication. *Ann. Rev. Psychol.* 22:309–36

Weiss, W. 1976. Review of *The Uses of Mass Communications: Current Perspectives on Gratifications Research.* ed. J. G. Blumler, E. Katz. *Public Opin. Q.* 40:132–33

Wenner, L. A. 1976. Functional analysis of TV viewing for older adults. *J. Broadcast.* 20:77–88

Wenner, L. A. 1977. *Political news on television: a uses and gratifications study.* PhD thesis. Univ. Iowa, Iowa City

Whiting, G. C. 1976. How does communication interface with change? *Commun. Res.* 3:191–212

Williams, W. Jr., Larsen, D. C. 1977. Agenda-setting in an off-election year. *Journ. Q.* 54:744–49

Williams, W. Jr., Semlak, W. 1978. Campaign 76: agenda-setting during the New Hampshire primary. *J. Broadcast.* 22:531–40

Winter, J. P. 1979. *Contingent conditions and the agenda-setting function.* Presented at Ann. Meet. Am. Assoc. Public Opin. Res., Buck Hills Falls, Pa.

Worth, S., Gross, L. 1974. Symbolic strategies. *J. Commun.* 24(4):27–39

Zucker, H. G. 1978. The variable nature of news media influence. In *Communication Yearbook 2.* ed. B. D. Ruben, 225–40. New Brunswick, NJ: Transaction. 587 pp.

Zuckerman, P., Ziegler, M., Stevenson, H. W. 1978. Children's viewing of television and recognition memory of commercials. *Child Dev.* 48:96–104

In this essay, Sari Thomas argues for a "sociogenic, culturalist perspective" in communication research by noting problems in the application of a mechanistic behavioral paradigm in communication-effects research, speech communication, psychopathology, and the study of mass communication institutions and their relationship to messages and effects. Thomas is assistant professor of radio-television-film at Temple University.

2

SOME PROBLEMS OF THE PARADIGM IN COMMUNICATION THEORY[1]

Sari Thomas

The etic organization of a world-wide cross-cultural scheme may be created by the analyst. The emic structure of a particular system must, I hold, be discovered. (But here I am assuming a philosophy of science which grants that in the universe some structures occur other than in the mind of the analyst himself. If one adopts a view that no structure of language or culture is present in the universe, except as a theoretical construct created by the analyst, then the paragraph must be restated in a different way, to preserve its usefulness in such a context. Specifically, the linguist who denies structure to a naive sentence or to a sonnet must settle for having his own statements, descriptions, or rules about these phenomena as also being without a publically available structure or ordering. Linguistic statement comprises a subvariety of language utterance, and hence can have no structure if language has no structure.)[2]

Pike's distinction between *etic* and *emic* can be very useful when instructing students in the ways of conducting non-egotistical and non-ethnocentric investigation. Although precautions against the *etic* approach as advised by Pike are often taken when they apply to the collection and analysis of research *data*, social scientists seem to be considerably more lax when it comes to methodological issues pertaining to general theoretical work. More specifically, 'clean', 'untainted', or *emic* data always stand within an epistemologically *etic* frame of research reference. So, it is at the very least naive to assume that such frames of reference, theories, models, or paradigms can ever be entirely *emic*.[3] The notion of data collection for its own sake and without paradigmatic bias is no less than scientific romanticism.[4] Nonetheless, while it is true that, once applied, a conceptual model is external to the research event and hence *etic*, the actual discovery of that model (and thus the implications for its appropriate use) needn't have been conceived acontextually, i.e., without appropriately reflecting the social events to which it refers. Therefore, it is incumbent upon researchers or empirically-motivated theorists first, to be aware of and articulate the conceptual model under which their specific labours are undertaken, and, second, to maintain a continuing critical examination of the intrinsic legitimacy of that model in each instance of its application.

1 My thanks to Paul Messaris for his careful and thoughtful readings of this paper

2 Kenneth Pike, 'Etic and Emic Standpoints for the Description of Behavior', in Alfred Smith (ed.), *Communication and Culture: Readings in the Codes of Human Interaction*, New York 1966, p. 153.

3 Ibid., p. 157.

4 Thomas S. Kuhn, *The Structure of Scientific Revolutions, Second Edition*, Chicago 1970, p. 28.

Although the sense of the above sentiments has been expressed on many occasions in a variety of contexts, it still appears to be the case among the social sciences that methodological rigour in the formulation of these basic conceptual models—those which deal with the theoretical modelling (or creation) of interactional structures—is frequently abandoned in favour of methodological refinements within unquestioned, pre-existing models.[5] Hence, we may have at our disposal a dozen statistical scaling techniques to be applied to event X. However, if one quarries the literature in which 'successful' employment of such techniques has been reported, it often seems as if questions as to whether or not X is empirically capable of isolation or subjection to statistical scaling are beside the point. Obviously such questions are far from beside the point if one is concerned with either simple (or pure) accuracy, or the effects that social scientific research has—not only in terms of its explicit application in various forms of legislative policy-making, but also as it is diffused into lay culture and thus contributes to general wordview.

In this paper, attention will be directly focussed upon certain of the underlying conceptual schemata of communication theory. Given that this relatively new and certainly popular academic 'field' would seem to include in its subject matter all sorts of interactional phenomena from language acquisition among people with organic brain-dysfunctions to the effects of television violence, it may be worthy to investigate the basic premiss on which such labours are most frequently based. In general, it will be argued that 'communication theory', since its formal inception, has been dependent on mechanistic concepts (initially borrowed from the physical sciences) that irrevocably bias and frequently invalidate its subsequent application to social matters. The first portion of this paper will attempt to provide an integrated overview of existing positions with respect to this argument. In the latter part, I will attempt to designate how this mechanical bias has been diffused into concrete issues of social communication theory and research.

SOME HISTORY OF COMMUNICATION MODELS

It would seem appropriate to open a 'history of . . .' with some sort of definition of the area. However, as will be seen, a definition of 'communication' is totally subject to the theoretical framework that is to be placed on social interaction. More importantly, my concern at present is not with a prescriptive definition of what activities should be subsumed under the rubric of 'communication' but, rather, with the description of those ideas to which the label 'communication theory' has recurrently been applied.

Without yielding to the temptation of labelling each droplet of water that has spouted from the same fountainhead, it would be safe to suggest that anyone exploring the genesis of 'communication theory' would find essentially two basic paradigms: (1) the *mechanical* model and (2) the *organic* model. A qualification is necessary: with few exceptions, the *organic* concept of which I will speak has rarely been forcefully articulated with specific regard to communication.[6] Rather, it is the *mechanical* concept which has been consistently imposed on events labeled as 'communication' *per se*. Hence, if we for the moment

---

5 See Harold Garfinkel, 'Remarks on Ethnomethodology', in John J. Gumperz and Dell Hymes (eds.), *Directions in Sociolinguistics: The Ethnography of Communication*, New York 1972, pp. 309-24, for an interesting and broader perspective on 'methodology'.

6 As will be indicated throughout the first half of this paper, a few individuals, most notably Birdwhistell and Thayer have discussed the organic model with specific regard to 'communication'. Nonetheless, notions of organic unity are much more common within other disciplines—particularly anthropology.

assume a 'majority rules' stance, it is the *mechanical* framework and no other which is the spine of 'communication theory' as it presently and popularly exists.

In the late nineteen forties, two major developments occurred which can be seen as having had profound and long-lasting effects on a discipline to be known as 'communication(s)'. The first event, the 1948 publication of Norbert Wiener's *Cybernetics*, provided a model which essentially described the structure of information flow within and between systems.[7] Second, the 1949 emergence of Claude Shannon's and Warren Weaver's 'information theory' led to the conceptualization of information as a measurement of organization.[8] Without examining the specific details of each of these developments, it is important to mention that both models have their roots in physical/mathematical paradigms and that their original, practical application was in the interest of mechanical, telecommunicative and/or computerized systems. Given that these models were both centrally concerned with the transmission of 'information', it seemed only reasonable to extend them to other spheres in which 'information' flow was paramount to the structure and behaviour of a system. Coupled with the popular emergence of the mid-nineteen fifties General System approach—a programme aimed at academic economizing by promoting unification among various disciplines in which theoretical isomorphy could be detected—the cybernetic and information theory models were soon extended to the investigation of biological and social systems. The stumbling block, of course, in these applications and extensions has much to do with the assumption *of* isomorphy—that the processes of one type of event are congruent with those of another.

THE PROBLEMS IN GENERAL THEORY

With specific reference to human 'communication', Birdwhistell,[9] Thayer,[10] and even general system theorist Ludwig von Bertalanffy,[11] and others have warned that the structure of processes of human social systems is more complicated than those structures created strictly by humans (i.e., technology). Indeed, many theorists have endeavoured diagrammatically to demonstrate these complications. (See, for example Osgood[12] or Westley and McLean.[13]) However, as well-meaning and interesting as these attempts have been, it may be suggested that they are not totally successful in overcoming this issue of 'complexity'. Specifically, if it were simply a matter of 'complexity', in the sense of a requirement for additional variables, there would really be no 'modelling' problem of which to speak; given a basic mechanistic framework, one would only need to designate (by means of block and flow diagrams or some such details) all the additional possibilities. On paper, such a diagram might be confusing to say the

7 Norbert Wiener, *Cybernetics*, Cambridge, Mass. 1948.
8 Claude E. Shannon and Warren Weaver, *The Mathematical Theory of Communication*, Urbana, Ill. 1949.
9 Ray L. Birdwhistell, *Kinesics and Context: Essays on Body Motion Communication*, Philadelphia 1970.
10 Lee Thayer, 'Communication Systems', in Ervin Laszlo (ed.), *The Relevance of General Systems Theory*, New York 1972.
11 Ludwig Von Bertalanffy, *General System Theory*, New York 1968.
12 Charles E. Osgood and K. V. Wilson, 'Some Terms and Associated Measures for Talking About Human Communication', Urbana 1961.
13 Bruce Westley and Malcolm MacLean, Jr., 'A Conceptual Model for Communication Research', *Journalism Quarterly*, **34** (1957), 31-38.

least; nevertheless for the trained analyst, it would be an adequate representation of the anatomy of human communication. Unfortunately, the 'complexity' is not so simple a matter as to be accounted for by an extra arrow here, a feedback loop there.[14] In Bertalanffy's terms, there is a distinction between 'open' and 'closed' systems.[15] Simplistically speaking, the 'open' system (the one on which the organic model is based), unlike the 'closed' system, has the ability, among other things, continually to experience material and energy change, to move toward higher differentiation (decrease in entropy), and to maintain a structure of multiple levels of integration. Unfortunately, even those theorists, such as Bertalanffy, who acknowledge *in theory* the profound differences between the two types of systems, often interpret this inapplicability of the 'closed', mechanical model to organic systems as nothing but a temporary stumbling block. They appear to assume, in other words, that somehow with advanced theorizing and research, we should ultimately be able to formulate mathematical models which approximate the dynamics of the 'open' system.[16] Others who operate within this framework, but with less grand expectations, still contend that 'aspects' of organic, social systems can logically be analyzed according to mechanically-formulated models.[17]

On the other hand, the position introduced by Birdwhistell and Thayer and that to be advanced in this paper is one which requires that much more than lip service be paid to the entirely different character of open, organic systems as opposed to closed, mechanical operations. In other words, we should no more borrow an inappropriate model of one character, extend it (*in its own terms*), and thereby expect that it will miraculously transmute into a system of another character, than we should expect to breed goldfish selectively in the hope that, after many generations, they will begin evolving into humans. So, such a model as proposed above (the one with arrows and loops added to take into account the dynamics of organic systems) would not *simply* be reductionistic, as the most common arguments against it claim. Rather, such a model would fail to capture the 'anatomy of human communication' not only because the organs and tissue would be absent (reductionism) but also because the skeleton, itself, would be misshaped.

It might be helpful at this point to examine some of the most basic 'communication' notions derived from cybernetic and information theory models in order to illustrate precisely how these fundamental schemata, with or without modification, are inappropriate in the description of human interaction.

The skeleton provided by most mechanical models of communication invariably contains two elements: (1) the *sender*—an agent supposedly responsible for the creation and emission of information and (2) the *receiver*—the beneficiary of the emission. The fact that the abbreviation *S-R* may be used to represent the paradigm suggested by sender-receiver theories as well as the stimulus-response model common to behaviourism is quite convenient: both cases involve an assmption that human *social* behaviour can be adequately

---

14 As will be discussed more fully later in this essay, the position here is that the notion of feedback does not alter the basic mechanical nature of the model. See Thayer, op. cit. on this issue as well.

15 Bertalanffy, op. cit., and Florian Znaniecki, *Cultural Sciences: Their Origin and Development*, Urbana 1963, p. 163.

16 Thayer, op. cit., p. 99.

17 E.g. R. Wayne Cowart, 'Information and Communication: What Can We Learn about People from Communication Machines', in T. Steinfatt (ed.), *Readings in Human Communication*, Englewood Cliffs, N.J. 1977.

explained in terms of independent, environmentally-isolated, discrete causal chains.[18]

Certainly, *S-R* theory has had its antagonists from Agnew to Chomsky, but here I am not concerned with counter-positions which argue on the basis of *either* ideologically-motivated, reactionary theory *or* Cartesian assumptions. Rather, with specific regard to communication, it is most important to consider the position of those antagonists who invoke the term 'process' in their arguments against action-reaction formulas. And here, it must be mentioned that, with few exceptions, the notion of 'process' has too often been offered in a quite cavalier fashion. In particular, the assertion that human experience *is* derived from something more than $a + b = c$ equations is not adequately explained away by 'process' as the cover term. Similarly, arguments invoking 'dynamism' (as a substitute for 'process') still do not account for those non-static elements to which they, at least implicity, refer.

TRANSMISSION

S-R models of 'communication' regard transmission as the transference or 'passage' of information from a sender to a receiver. In other words, these models imagine a linear activity with a beginning and an end. Thus, this activity, transmission, essentially involves the behaviour *in sequence* of *A* (the source, the sender) and *B* (the destination, the receiver).

This concept of 'transmission', as detailed in mechanical information theory models, is very problematic when applied to human (organic) activity. In S-R models, 'communication' (the supposed product of transmission) is understood as an event entailing the action of entity *A* upon entity *B*, the possible reciprocal action of *B* upon *A* (feedback), and so on. As Thayer[19] and Berlo[20] have suggested, the problem is that such paradigms imply that the component elements in an 'act' of information transmission behave independently of one another—that *A* introduces '*A*' data and that *B* responds with '*B*' data. While in a technologically-engineered system (e.g., a computer) *A* (as programmed) can continuously be relied upon to respond in '*A*' fashion (*regardless* of a change in system input), human behaviour is not so context-free. In the case of human interaction, *A* has a *variety* of '*A*' behaviour which, most importantly, is *not* programmed externally of any particular social context in which *A* emerges. In other words in human interaction the context is an integral part of the programme, and *A* becomes a different component in each context. What this suggests is not simply a matter of *B* adjusting to, or accommodating, '*A*' input and so forth, for, if this were the case, feedback loops, in theory, would ameliorate the problem. Rather, what *S-R* models (even with feedback) fail to achieve is the understanding of an empirical reality in which *A* and *B* are part of an *environment* which regulates their interaction. In short, the 'cause' and 'effects' of behaviour cannot be located within the component elements as an *S-R* model suggests.

18 This is not to imply that behaviouristic research is 'fraudulent'. No one would argue that many organisms (including humans) do not conform to varieties of classical and operant conditioning. Rather, the argument here is that at the social (phylogenetic) level of experience, behaviourism, as an explanatory device, is not particularly useful.

19 Lee Thayer, 'Communication Systems', in Ervin Laszlo (ed.), *The Relevance of General Systems Theory*, New York 1972.

20 David K. Berlo, 'Modelling the Communication Process', in T. Steinfatt (ed.), op. cit., note 17.

Moreover, the *SR* transmission contingency is designed to be measured in such a way as to make information transmission identifiable by a cumulation of discrete pieces of data (i.e., the amount of communication equals amount of 'transmissions' between *A* and *B*). Again, the problem of such a mechanical model is that it fails to consider interdependency or more specifically in this case, that the organic whole is greater than the sum of its parts. Thus, *S-R* theory falls short in terms of behaviourism, for example, in that, while the *S-R* model may be able to identify a learning *situation*, it cannot account for what a person *knows*. In this sense, the shortcoming of the *S-R* model is a result of a conceptual bias which permits interrelated events to be isolated from one another in analysis. While such isolating techniques may make for simple and convenient models, it is unfortunately the case that a model, to be useful, should validly and reliably represent the event for which it purports to stand. Returning to the learning issue, for example, *interrelationships* among a myriad of different experiences ultimately 'create' knowledge/behaviour. Despite the simplicity of the *S-R* learning model, one recognizes that even the most complete and careful *addition* of all relevant learning contingencies will not account for their interrelationship—the end product. Similarly a communication event is not simply a problem in addition: action + reaction ≠ interaction.

It must be emphasized that the criticism of *S-R* models outlined above is meant to apply to all descriptions of human communication behaviour. In other words, the author would resist the claim that there are some situations to which the model applies better than it does to others. An apparent exception to this proscription of *S-R* models could occur in a situation in which the object of inquiry was *not* the objective aspects of a communicational process but, rather, the subjective representation of that process in the consciousness of its participants and in their utterances. Even if the investigator's final interest were actually in the objective aspects of the process, it is quite conceivable that a consideration of its subjective aspect might be thought to be a necessary component of the total range of explanatory principles brought to bear on the investigation. Since, moreover, the sender-receiver model is not the exclusive property of scholars and is, in fact, an implicit premiss of considerable currency in the conceptions of certain segments of the 'lay public', it is bound to occupy a place in the work of any investigator in the situation just described. However, it is important to emphasize that even in such circumstances the *S-R* model is not the framework but the *object* of inquiry.

In other words, for most situations in which communication is to be studied, the problem encountered with any sender-receiver model is much more fundamental than, say, the demand for defining a broader context for interaction between a transmitter and receptor and/or imposing a new calculus for determining the cumulation of transmissions between a sender and receiver. In short, for most situations in which communication is to be studied, the entire notion of a sender-receiver relationship may tend to *obscure* the process of information transmission as it occurs at the social level of behaviour.

In the kind of 'subjectively-oriented' phase of investigation described above, it may be convenient (and not all that distorting) to designate interacting participants in such terms as speaker/listener, performer/spectator, etc. However, as will be discussed more fully in a critique of institutional research, it is rather rare that the implementation of a sender-receiver paradigm is confined to this phase of investigation. Rather it is a much more frequent occurrence that those employing *S-R* models are oriented not simply to description 'from within' of the interaction they are studying, but to the explication of effects and/or implications of that interaction, once described, without any shift in analytical terminology. The problem in such cases is the inaccurate assumption (usually only implicit) that human activity may be explained solely on the basis of the subjective definitions available to specific 'actors'.

Such an assumption is embodied explicitly in the premisses of such schools of thought as the 'uses and gratifications' perspective in mass communications research.[21] From the 'organic' perspective, the argument against this assumption would be that it misplaces the final locus of determination of social behaviour from the properties of a social totality (system or subsystem, group or subgroup) to the *self-defined* properties of the component elements (persons) of that totality. In other words, this assumption does for communication what some versions of 'social contract' theory attempted to do for the social process as a whole: to create the whole out of the intentions of its constituents.

INFORMATION

Although it might be argued that the 'transmission-related' aspects of the S-R communication model are sufficiently problematic to render the paradigm inappropriate to the study of the human world, there is another major component of the sender-receiver model which warrants scrutiny—the mechanical model's treatment of 'information'. In most S-R models of 'communication' there is an event, usually situated equidistant between the sender and the receiver, which is generally understood as the 'message'—the material in which information is embedded or of which it is composed. This mediating event, the information or message, is typically understood as the essence of or purpose for whatever action occurs between the sender and the receiver (i.e., transmission). Consequently, mechanical models of communication have been designed to analytically and operationally isolate the 'message' so that it may be studied as a self-contained event. It follows, therefore, that a number of basic concepts deriving from cybernetic and information theory paradigms are those which relate to the nature and/or measurement of this most critical element.

Typically, 'organic-oriented' arguments rebutting the validity of isolating and measuring the 'message' rest upon the premiss that social context is eliminated in such isolating and measurement maneuvers. Essentially, organic-communication theory argues that S-R models invoke very arbitrary (i.e., socially acontextual) standards in defining that which constitutes 'information' and that, as a result of such arbitrary modeling, one once again distorts human interaction. This distortion has both methodological and theoretical implications. The methodological issue simply relates to the question of whether or not a researcher is justified in examining and evaluating message form or content separately from its perception and assessment[22]—a possibility made very attractive by any model which physically situates information separate from its creation and reception. With regard to this methodological issue, as has been argued in the case of conceptualizing sender and receiver components, the organic-oriented argument need not be invoked against analysis conducted

21 See Paul Messaris, 'Biases in Self-Reported "Functions" and "Gratifications" of Mass Media Use', *Et Cetera*, **34**, 1977, 316-29.

22 Thayer argues against this isolation, from a 'uses and gratifications' perspective— which will later be challenged in this paper. See Lee Thayer, 'On the Mass Media and Mass Communication: Notes Toward a Theory', in Richard W. Budd and Brent D. Ruben, *Beyond Media: New Approaches to Mass Communication*, Rochelle Park, N.J. 1979.

purely and explicitly to determine what 'lies within' (in this case textual analysis). For, in such cases, one limits one's conclusions to the data used.[23] However, methodological opposition to the S-R model arises when acontextual analysis of 'information' is then proposed as a final account of the 'meaning' of a communicational process.

From the theoretical perspective, the case against the S-R paradigm's notion of information is, of course, related to what is seen as a distorted picture of human interaction—one that satisfies quite elegantly the requirements of paradigmatic simplicity but has little or no relationship to the complexity of actions for which the paradigm stands. Various issues may be used to illustrate such claims, but a brief discussion of just a few common S-R information-related concepts should sufficiently indicate the scope of the problem.

Very crucial to the S-R concept of information is the element of 'newness', embodied in the common notion that *behaviour is just behaviour, but communication occurs when new, potentially change-producing input is entered into the transmitting system*. As Rapoport has suggested 'In *any* situation, information about something we already know is worthless as information'.[24] Such sentiments quite naturally yield to the notion of 'redundancy'. Simply put, redundancy, as postulated by information theorists, occurs whenever data are repeated. It is an easy enough concept—one which is probably employed daily by English teachers and editors when correcting copy. The problem, for those who are concerned with events as parts of human behaviour rather than as texts, is that the literal notion of repetition as advanced in mechanical models has little or no relationship to the virtual sense of 'previously provided' information. In other words, the notion is, at best, an imperfect guide to those situations in human interaction in which it is operationally possible to have redundant information. Take the following hypothetical dialogue as an illustration of the problem:

A: Hello. My name is Sender.
B: Nice to meet you. My name is Receiver.
A: What do you do for a living, Receiver?
B: My name is Receiver.

According to an S-R analysis of this interaction, one would conclude that person *B* has not provided person *A* with worthwhile information—*B* has been 'redundant' in terms of his/her second utterance. On the other hand, the organic approach, with its insistence upon empirical correspondence between a behavioural event and its analysis (in this case, the recognition of multiple levels of meanings) might find *B*'s second utterance highly 'informational', as it were. For instance, *A* might deduce from the conversation that *B* is hard of hearing and/or a trifle bizarre. In any case, the only redundancy in the dialogue is mathematical, *not* behavioural. The entire issue of redundancy in its application to human behaviour has been correctly epitomized in Heraclitus' poignant assertion: *All flows. A man can never step in the same river twice.*

Objections to the S-R model's concept of *noise* are not unlike those raised with respect to the redundancy issue. Noise is generally understood as any interference or distortion that arises during a transmission between sender and

23 See Hugh D. Duncan, 'Communication and Social Order' in Lloyd W. Matson and Ashley Montague (eds.), *The Human Dialogue: Perspectives on Communication,* New York 1967, p. 390.

24 Anatol Rapoport, 'What is Information?', in A. Smith (ed.), *Communication and Culture: Readings in the Codes of Human Interaction,* New York 1966, p. 42.

receiver and as having no relationship to the message itself—i.e., the message intended by the sender. Whereas redundancy (although useless *as* information *per se*) is viewed by mechanically-minded theorists as having a beneficial potential in the transmission process, noise is seen as negative interference. More specifically, since *S-R* theorists assume that complete fidelity in the transmission process is unlikely (i.e., the sender's intended message will at some point in the transmission experience some distortion or noise before reaching the receiver), the element of redundancy is seen as having the potential to compensate for this distortion. Repetition, in other words, is thought to clarify parts of a message that otherwise might have been made unintelligible by noise.

Unfortunately, as in the case of redundancy, we again have a socially acontextual assignment of message characteristics. Noise, *like silence*, will always have an informational capacity in human interactions—which is simply another way of saying that, as in the case of redundancy, noise (in the *S-R* sense) does not socially exist. Although it is a somewhat trivialized example, 'snow' (telecommunicative interference) on one's television set may be used to demonstrate this point. Snow certainly interferes with 'good' reception, but it similarly might 'inform' a viewer that someone in another part of the house is using an electrical appliance—just as the television set suddenly going 'dead' (silence) doesn't merely signify the closure of transmission but, rather, indicates that something may be wrong.

Much of the problem posed by the concept of noise is related to another common *S-R* element: the channel. Unlike redundancy and noise, the notion 'channel' is not a message characteristic *per se*. Rather, channels, in general, are the means by or through which messages are transmitted. Here again we find a concept which contributes to the mechanistic notion of communication as a discrete, discontinuous event. The simple assumption that information functional to a given interaction (which as noted is regulated by its social *context*) is characteristically siphoned through a single gateway is quite antithetical to any organic paradigm. Surely, if one chooses to consider arbitrarily only one channel of transmission in a given interaction, it is quite reasonable to further postulate the existence of noise, i.e., (in this case) all information from other channels present, but not considered in the analysis. However, if we regard 'silence' as informational, 'noise' as very real information on an as yet unanalyzed level, and 'redundancy' as a means of message *alteration*, we come away with a very different concept from that proposed by *S-R* chains—namely, that in human social contexts, information is continuously available and that *nothing never happens*.[25]

From the discussion of *S-R* concepts to this point, we have achieved sufficient basis to determine that which is at the core of such conceptual paradigms. In short, all mechanical models of communication, when imposed on human behaviour, completely eliminate all those characteristic of human interaction (e.g., ever-continuous activity, multiple levels of meaning, the use of multiple channels simultaneously, etc.) which distinguish it from the behaviour of machines.

In fairness, it must be said that many theorists working in the areas of cybernetics and information theory have made clear the inapplicability of their mechanical and stochastic schemes to human communication (e.g., Carnap's 'logical probabilities'[26]). Cherry, in his stage-setting book, *On Human Communication*, points out on several occasions how various *S-R* schemes are intentionally inattentive to issues involving either meaning or use of informa-

25 See Birdwhistell, op. cit., p. 4.
26 R. Carnap, *Logical Foundations of Probability*, Chicago 1950.

tion.[27] Indeed, arguments will not be made here that there is no value whatsoever in theoretically treating human interaction outside of its ecologically-given social context, which invariably *does* circumscribe questions of meaning and use. However, the willingness to forgo such arguments must be made on the condition that such approaches are kept entirely clear of *social* theory and research. Unfortunately, as the next section of this paper indicates, most social communication work to date relies most heavily on those models designed for machines.

THE PROBLEMS IN SPECIFIC CONTEXTS

Historically, the *S-R* model is not located exclusively in the province of either behaviourists, information theorists or cyberneticists. Particularly in more recent years (1960 and onward), an inordinate number of 'communication' theories have found their way into scholarly texts and journals. The models explicitly or implicitly proposed by these theories, often accompanied by precisely delineated and complicated diagrammatic representations of human communication, have often been assessed as new, and distinct from earlier formulations of Wiener or Shannon, etc. Yet, in the terms previously set forth for the description of 'mechanical' models, the vast majority of these 'newer' frameworks, despite their claims of originality, proceed to propose no more than variations on the original theme.[28] Indeed from the Aristotelian model set forth in *Rhetoric* to most contemporary mainstream approaches to human communication, the *S-R* paradigm reigns supreme.

In this section of the paper, I would like to call brief attention to the more practical outcome of this *S-R* reign, as it were—its diffusion into more specific areas of the study of human behaviour.[29]

LEARNING THEORY AND LABORATORY/EXPERIMENTAL RESEARCH

Although the issue of 'learning' is typically classified under psychology or 'behavioural science', it is noted here because of its particular relevance to the methodological development of communication research. As suggested earlier, learning theory is at the core of *S-R* formulations (and vice versa) in that the action-reaction, stimulus-response conceptualizations, in terms of the acquisition of skills or the ability to perform (i.e., learning) were the warp and woof of the research carried out by the founders of behaviourism (e.g., Wundt, Thorndike, Pavlov, Skinner). Traditionally, these research issues were and continue to be examined in laboratory situations in which careful manipulation of experimental variables is employed in order to measure subjects' learning of actions *new* to their behavioural repertoire. Because of the intentional, indeed, prototypical use of the *S-R* paradigm, the problematic elements are simple to identify. To name a few: (1) the conceptualization of behaviour as resulting from a series of discrete causal chains, (2) the emphasis on the 'new', change-invoked behaviour as the totality of the learning experience, and (3) the implementation

27 Colin Cherry, *On Human Communication*, Second Edition, Cambridge 1966.
28 There are some notable exceptions to this argument, e.g., the theories of Innis and McLuhan.
29 It might be noted here that the author would agree with Berger and Luckmann's general assertion that theory production is a *specific* industry in its own right, and hence, the separation between 'general theory' and 'specific applications' is not meant to indicate that the former is somehow less 'real', less meaningful, or less socially effective. See Peter Berger and Thomas Luckmann, *The Social Construction of Reality: A Treatise in the Sociology of Knowledge*, New York 1967.

of an imposed experimental design, conducted within a sterile laboratory thereby eliminating many elements (e.g., other 'channels', 'noise') which naturally occur in the generalizable subject's social environment. These problems have been transferred rather straightforwardly to issues of supposed specific 'communication' concern as will be explored in the discussion which follows.

COMMUNICATION 'EFFECTS'

If one examines two very major currents of mainstream 'communication' theory and research—(1) interpersonal persuasion and (2) mass media effects—one can see quite clearly the imprint of the mechanical, behaviouristic approach. Of major issue is the notion of 'communication' as something done to somebody—an idea that will be explored more fully in the discussion of institutional research. As a result of this most fundamental perspective, the analysis of 'change' (be it, for example, a function of face-to-face debate or television drama) becomes tantamount to the measurement of communication—or in short, effective communication. Similarly, it is not uncommon to communication research on 'effects' to first name arbitrarily the components of the interactions—e.g., the speech-maker, television programme; the audience—and to study their supposed actions and reactions in channel-, noise-, redundancy- and silence-delimited experimental contexts.

The critical assessment of this line of research is not meant to imply that those moments of obvious, measurable change-effects are not part of a normal social system or that they are uninteresting. Rather, it is first suggested that such effects may be a result of a complex set of issues and that the seeming S-R linearity of the effects obtained may well be a result of the paradigmatic research bias imposed on their study.[30] Second, while effects in the sense of measurable change are certainly one part of the story, so to speak, the function of most communicative interaction is not that of effects as change, but effects as maintenance, which, of course, is not analyzable by any approach which essentially is constructed to examine what somebody does to somebody else. Thus, to direct communication research to the study of those moments in the system where effect means newness and alteration, is not exploiting the full sense of how social information is processed and exchanged.

SPEECH COMMUNICATION

In the United States at least, one of the most conventional understandings of interpersonal communication is not in its alignment with disciplines traditionally associated with the study of social system and structure (e.g., anthropology, sociology) but, rather, with the area known as 'speech' (and sometimes extended to 'speech communication'). Although it may justifiably be argued that this common liaison is a result of academic bureaucracy, the development of this association seems far from arbitrary when one examines how such amalgamations reflect the paradigmatic bias to which this paper addresses itself. To begin with, given that human behaviour so greatly involves verbal interaction, it apparently made much sense to equate communicative behaviour with the use of language. Indeed, this equation is so implicitly ingrained in the popular body of communication theory and research (i.e., much work in communication seems to regard verbal interaction unquestioningly as *the* scope of inquiry) that the notion of 'speech communication', in terms of *textual* analysis, would seem redundant. Of course, the point here is that if we limit arbitrarily our investigations to but one channel or mode of interaction (e.g., speech) we necessarily fail

30 See Robert Rosenthal, *Experimenter Effects in Behavioral Research*, New York 1966.

to understand all the other components of interaction that are quite necessary to meaning and behaviour,[31] e.g., body motion, paralanguage, proxemics, silence, etc.[32]

An additional matter also works to make the speech/communication association quite appealing on *S-R* terms: the classic relationship between the study of speech, on one hand, and rhetoric and forensics, on the other. More specifically, mechanical models of communication are essentially concerned with 'fidelity' or the accuracy with which a message is transmitted from sender to receiver (and hence, the notions of noise and redundancy). In these terms, communication is seen solely as a matter of effect, i.e., one measures what noticeably (and one might add superficially) 'gets' to the receiver. Similarly, in the study of debate and persuasion, a fundamental concern rests upon how speech is effective. Clearly, in neither the general nor specific of these cases is communication viewed as a process which is not only a means to an immediate end, but an 'end', itself, in its very nature as a system of social integration.

PSYCHOPATHOLOGY AND HUMAN RELATIONS

It is an inevitable (and perhaps ironic) outgrowth of mechanical information theory that the notion of communication carries with it some classically unscientific baggage, i.e., value judgement. As noted above, the emphasis on 'talk' and especially that the talk 'reach' the intended receiver becomes not simply a matter of objective measurement, but one of evaluating the 'worth' of the whole business, i.e., if it gets 'across', it is good; if not, failure. This orientation to communication has an important effect on both (1) the theory and treatment of 'behavioural disorders', and (2) the popular (lay) understanding of the nature and regulation of interpersonal relationships.

If we begin with popular psychology, as it were, we see first of all the emphasis on talk as a means to 'healthy' relationships; revelation through speech is the current panacea for the maintenance of friendships, family harmony, love affairs, and so forth.[33] Conversely, faltering interpersonal relationships are typecast by their failure to 'communicate'—an emphasis not only on speech and the irrelevancy of silence, but on communication in terms of a value scale. This jargon, I think, is not merely a bastardization of scientific terminology (as is, say, 'Social Darwinism'), but a rather accurate, although perhaps primitive reflection of mainstream (mechanical) 'communication' theory.

When we move one level from these popular notions to the clinical treatment of behaviour, we find similar problems. Social abnormality is typically equated with behavioural pathology and, hence, even among supposedly trained scientists, abnormality is no longer meaningful in its objective sense of statistical deviation, but rather, its meaning becomes loaded with value concepts, e.g.,

31 For an interesting discussion of this verbal bias see Larry Gross, 'Modes of Communication and the Acquisition of Symbolic Competence', in David E. Olson, (ed.), *Media and Symbols: The Forms of Expression, Communication, and Education*, Chicago 1974, pp. 56-80.

32 This is not to say that all individuals studying interpersonal communication deliberately choose to ignore non-speech elements of interaction, but that often, attention to these other phenomena is cursory. Many approaches, for example, demonstrate a subjectivist inference that all non-speech behaviour is but modification of speech acts themselves. See Birdwhistell, op. cit., for a cogent rebuttal to such claims.

33 For an interesting mass culture example of this lesson, see Linda Riley, 'Conflict Strategies in the T.V. Soap Opera: A Descriptive Analysis', M.A. Thesis, Temple University, Philadelphia 1977, in which it is shown that 'concealment' of problems in soap operas usually leads to disastrous ends.

unhealthiness, illness, pathology, etc. This bears most directly on *S-R* modelling in terms of the common notion of insanity as the chaotic distorton of communicative behaviour—in other words, noise. In fact, recent study of abnormal behaviour indicates that much abnormality (e.g. schizophrenia[34]) is as socially patterned (i.e., demonstrating consistent communicational norms across those 'affected') as that of social behaviour falling within the sane or normal range. In short, we may simply be addressing a problem of difference rather than random chaos;[35] the 'noise' needs analysis on a different level.[36]

The conceptualization of insanity as noise is not surprising given the basic sender-receiver paradigm. More specifically, if we regard transmission as an act in which something created by one individual is sent to another, it is inevitable that many have similarly come to see communication systems as a whole as something 'invented' by the sender rather than *internalized* by him/her as a result of social processes.[37] In other words, the model which fundamentally designates independent, causal agents, likewise obligates its adherents to understand a behaver's 'emissions' as self-formulated.[38] Hence, behaviour may be viewed as incidentally noisy or chaotic ('bad' senders) rather than socially patterned. It might also be noted that an additional outcome of this mechanical bias involves not only conceptual orientation, but applied theory as well—namely, many forms of psychotherapy. Not only do many clinical practitioners regard 'psychiatric' or 'psychological' disturbance as a result of what Birdwhistell has labeled 'isolated traumatic effects'[39] (reflecting the mechanical notion of communication as an additive process involving discrete units) but the treatment context itself—a 'one on one' intentionally external to the patient's social environment—similarly reflects the asocial or anti-organic bias.

MASS COMMUNICATION INSTITUTIONS AND THEIR RELATIONSHIP TO MESSAGES AND EFFECTS

One of the more problematic areas of communication research and one which receives relatively little criticism on the basis of paradigm[40] is that which studies

34 See Birdwhistell, op. cit., p. 15; Gregory Bateson, *Steps to an Ecology of Mind*, New York 1972, pp. 194-270, and J. Reusch and G. Bateson, *Communication: The Social Matrix of Society*, New York, 1968, for a more complete analysis of this issue.

35 This is not arbitrarily to prescribe that we either disregard or refuse to treat behavioural abnormality. Rather, it suggests that the need and method of treatment hinge quite importantly on our definition of the problem. In short, our entire approach to deviance will be quite different if we see it as something 'gone wrong' *in* the behaver/sender, on one hand, or as an outgrowth of a socialization that differs from the, statistically speaking, normal range of socialized patterns.

36 See Thomas Szasz, 'The Myth of Mental Illness', *American Psychologist*, 15 (1960), 113-18, and Reusch and Bateson, op. cit.

37 Birdwhistell, op. cit., p. 15.

38 The classic distinction in psychology between the 'psychopathic' and 'sociopathic' personalities attests to this distinction. Coleman, in his text on 'abnormal psychology', defines the 'psychopathic' disorder as characterized by such traits as 'impulsivity, inability to profit from experience, and unethical behavior' (p. 657), whereas the 'sociopathic' disorder is defined by 'inability to conform to prevailing social standards; lack of social responsibility' (p. 670). The implications, of course, suggest that psychopathological behaviour is somehow not rooted in sociocultural conditions. James C. Coleman, *Abnormal Psychology and Modern Life*, Glenview, Ill. 1964.

39 Birdwhistell, op. cit., p. 15.

40 Here the issue of paradigm refers to the general epistemological slant rather than very

the institutions of the mass media—the 'senders' of mass-communicated messages. In their supposed role of creators and disseminators of information, members of the television, film, radio, publishing and recording industries have been damned (or, less frequently, praised) for what they are assumed to have 'sent' to their audiences (receivers). Organizational, 'gatekeeping', policymaking, regulational and assorted other varieties of 'institutional' research have emerged in order to gain a better understanding of the processes of these potentially powerful industries. While one certainly cannot argue that the study of cultural institutions is unenlightening, we·must be reminded that the most traditional 'communicational' study of mass-media institutions is not frequently constructed to be conceptually equivalent to anthropological-institutional study (e.g., research on kinship or religion). Rather, the traditional communication interest has been that of examining a collection of senders who at least implicitly are assumed to be consciously formulating and creating information to be mass dispensed, and who are clearly distinct from the recipients of the 'messages'. This, of course, is clearly in line with the linear, causal, S-R chain.

As a result of this way of thinking about 'mass communication' we attack the popular media, for example, for their shallow and/or prurient presentations on the grounds that 'we', the receivers, are made subject to such indignities because 'they', the senders, are only interested in capital and merchandising. On what superficially seems like the other side of the fence, arguments claiming that the at-best mediocrity of these mass-mediated presentations is a result of receiver dispositions (i.e., 'they get what they want') do not remove the locus of assessed control from the institutions—the senders either benevolently or greedily *choose* to accomodate their receivers with the requisite messages.

If we accept the notion that the mass media are one of the main, if not *the* main embodiment of the folklore and myth of the culture, and that such folklore and myth are crucially related to the development and maintenace of cultural values and interactional rules, then it would seem terribly important to know as much as we can about those institutions that create and distribute this information. Unfortunately, the S-R bias may be misdirecting our attention in *this* regard. As I have argued more extensively elsewhere,[41] those in the roles of 'creating' our mass-media messages (a 'from-within' assessment) are hardly more responsible for the nature of the information they dispense than those on the seemingly receiving end of the process. In short, ultimately we are *all* receivers—the recipients of cultural values, codes, norms and so forth that exist well before and beyond the life spans of any particular individuals who happen to be located in one social role or another in the larger industry of the production of culture. This argument is not meant to imply that the study of those individuals or groups formally situated in the mass communication industries would be uninteresting from an ethnographic perspective, but that *as institutions*, it may be only the anthropological perspective, which hierarchically situates the smaller structure within the larger cultural framework, that will permit the kinds of questions we traditionally pose in mass-communication institutional research to be accurately answered. Hence, as long as we persist in conceptually isolating our scope of inquiry to senders and receivers, we may, at best, get a 'from within' analysis that will ultimately be confirmed by our model, but not necessarily by social reality.

Finally, it might be noted that if a change in our orientation to 'institutions' (as detailed above) is important, then a (not as yet discussed) corresponding altera-

specific approaches within the same epistemological framework. Certainly, 'institutional' research has been involved in much controversy in terms of the latter issue.
41 Sari Thomas, 'Why Television Is Not Art' (forthcoming).

tion to our 'mass communication effects' models might likewise be in order. Historically, controversy between the 'hypodermic' and 'uses and gratifications' models has, respectively, presented the mass media as either (1) uniformly injecting and, hence, affecting a relatively passive audience, or (2) involving an active audience of individuals in which each person, according to his/her own needs, selectively becomes exposed and attends to the presentations. Mass media 'messages', therefore, are viewed either as being pumped out by senders, or constructed in the minds or by the behaviour of receivers. However, as explained above, it is ultimately hard to view the 'industry' as a collection of omnipotent creators. On the other hand, it is equally problematic to assume that the 'selectivity' (in terms of perception, exposure, attention, etc.) manifested in people's behaviour can take priority to the larger social context. More specifically, it can be argued that mass-media 'messages' demonstrate such a high degree of folkoric/mythological uniformity across media, genre, and so forth (a uniformity which is culturally, rather than specifically media-industry induced) that their differential exploitation by consumers is ultimately of little consequence.[42]

Therefore, in summary, the whole S-R paradigm when applied to mass communication is distorting when any of the model's components, (1) institutions (2) presentations/messages (3) effects, is examined in the isolation and linearity imposed by the model.

THE POLITICS OF THE MECHANICAL MODEL: POPULAR IDEOLOGY

Birdwhistell has indicated a number of reasons which may account for the popularity of the mechanical model and its application to communication: (1) its simplicity, (2) its structure as essentially dyadic (sender-receiver), which familiarly corresponds to the general dichotomous nature of Western language and thought, and (3) its correspondence to the literary model of interaction most clearly found in the structure of drama.[43]

While all of these possibilities seem likely contributors to the model's wide acceptance, there exists at least one additional consideration: the ideological nature of a model which postulates sociobehavioural autonomy. Despite the mechanical nature of sender-receiver models, there still exists within the general paradigm the implication of independent, causal agents. If, for example, we take the 'mental illness' or 'insanity' model described earlier, we see that the locus of deviance, as it were, is to be found in the individual behaver/sender. Similarly, the S R orientation to mass-media institutions (i.e., as 'senders') gives us cause to turn to specific individuals or groups of individuals as those agents responsible for that with which we are confronted. Even the 'uses and gratifications' position, also discussed, ultimately permits us to look upon consumers as autonomous individuals who do what they will with that with which they are presented. Clearly, in terms of the maintenance of our existing social structure, any model which postulates this sort of autonomy is of considerable convenience in terms of its homeostatic function: it stands to reason that it *would* be the dominant or mainstream paradigm. Let me be more specific.

To the extent that we can articulate problems, anger, misgivings, and so forth, in terms of 'bad' senders, 'malfunctioning' or 'irresponsible' receivers, etc., our

---

42 A more complex discussion of the uniformity of myth and its interpretation is presented in Sari Thomas, 'Some Methodological Implications of Interviewing about Media Use', presented at the Conference on Text and Context: The Analysis of Oral Discourse, May 2, 1980, Philadelphia, and in *Mass. Comm. Review* (in press).
43 Birdwhistell, op. cit., p. 12.

only commitment to social change and reorganization need be in either replacing or exchanging individuals in roles within the already existing social structure and/or prescribing and subsequently compelling individuals to assume existing parts. Hence, it is assumed, for example, that changes among television network executives might change the character rather than the titles of programmes, and much popular press is given to, say, Fred Silverman's move from ABC to NBC. Ironically, when it is subsequently discovered that ABC's programming does not undergo radical change upon Silverman's departure, the press informs us that, 'in reality', it was Fred Quinn (Silverman's former boss at ABC) who must have been and continues to be either the 'brains' or the 'villain' behind the network's operations. In short, the S-R model is most conservative; it tends not to give us reason to call for structural/systemic alterations that are larger than and beyond the scope of the behaviour of given individuals—functionaries of the social system.

Now, there is one glaring inconsistency which emerges in terms of the above analysis: If sender-receiver models can be likened to the stimulus-response paradigms of behaviourism, why is it that conservatives (like former U.S. Vice-President Spiro Agnew) rail against Skinnerian principles? Does not the S-R learning model indicate that individuals are a product of 'conditioning' rather than autonomous forces? Does not such a model call for shifting the locus of responsibility away from the individual, and hence, question the overriding system which provides the reinforcement contingencies?

The answer to such questions is an undeniable 'yes'. In other words, as Skinner quite elegantly tries to point out in *Beyond Freedom and Dignity*, behaviour is not a matter of autonomous will.[44] However, it is at this point where the distinction between the S-R of sender-receiver models and the S-R of stimulus-response frameworks must be drawn. While it is quite true that the sender-receiver models reflect the mechanical bias of stimulus-response models in terms of their reliance on independent, linear, socially acontextual activity chains, the classical behaviourist models can either be viewed (benevolently) as not attempting to account for social phenomena, or seen as simply going about the analysis of social behaviour from the wrong end, so to speak. In other words, as discussed earlier, S-R contingencies cannot be additively tallied for an account of social interaction. Hence, results obtained through behaviourist experiments are not wrong, they simply lack explanatory value at the social level of behaviour, which unfortunately, is the level at which most questions are posed. (See note 18). The sender-receiver models, when applied to human interaction, on the other hand, *enter* the scope of inquiry *at the social level*. Human communication, by virtue of its reliance on shared codes, *is* a social phenomenon. Hence, the application of any model which strips human communication of its social essence, as it were, is not studying the interactional phenomenon which it purports to analyze.

Therefore, *ideologically*-speaking, the social-organic and behaviourist positions are considerably similar in that neither places the locus of control within the individual, and hence, by logical extension, both positions require that social change be mandated at the social level, i.e., change in social *structure*. Given this, it is no wonder that neither approach enjoys great popularity. On the other hand, the sender-receiver model, when applied to matters of policy, does not require basic systemic reorganization. It is a model which implicitly reinforces social structure.

44 B. F. Skinner, *Beyond Freedom and Dignity*, New York 1971, passim.

THE POLITICS OF THE MECHANICAL MODEL: ACADEMIC IDEOLOGY

Before closing this essay, I would like to suggest that academic adherence to the sender-receiver model cannot be attributed to the notion that most communication scholars are politically conservative and hence, subscribe to a model which ultimately is incapable of prescribing substantial social change. Indeed, a major point of this essay and, in fact, a premiss of the organic paradigm as a whole, is to require that a sociogenic, culturalist perspective be assumed in the description and interpretation of behaviour. Hence, the previous section on 'popular' ideology and its relationship to the mechanical model of communication was not meant to indicate that autonomous, conscious effort is 'behind' the *S-R* model's popularity.

In this final section, however, I would like to address one issue which seems to contribute quite largely to the model's widespread popularity among scholars in particular. Essentially, the weight of the mechanical communication model among academics rests most heavily on its seemingly scientific character. As previously discussed, the *S-R* model lends itself quite conveniently to experimental analysis, high-level quantification, and so forth—in short, methods of research control and description most notably identified with the physical sciences. To the extent that academic respectability in the study of social behaviour was (and is) seen as coextant with its 'scientific' nature, it apparently seemed only too natural to want to approximate, and therefore, 'borrow', the tools of already established (physical) *sciences*.[45]

Now, it must be made clear that the author is in *no* way prepared to launch a 'humanistic' (which has almost come to mean anti-science[46]) tirade against this kind of mentality. Rather, it is suggested that 'approximations' and 'borrowing' of this order were achieved with some degree of facileness. For example, as Thayer points out with respect to the cause-effect approach to mass communication:

[This approach] was (mistakenly) assumed by most social and behavioral scientists of that day to be the guiding paradigm of the physical sciences, to whom they looked for model and legitimacy. The assumption was wrong on two counts: physicists had never been constrained by so simplistic and naive a version of the cause→effect paradigm ... and, even in the less constraining form held by physicists of that earlier day, the cause→effect paradigm was giving way rapidly to a much different kind of basic orientation....

In the physical sciences, it [cause→effect approach] had the status of an hypothesis. Its status in the social and behavioral sciences has been, for the most part, that of an ideology ... what cannot be studied by cause→effect methods [in social science] is, by default, considered largely irrelevant.[47]

We may argue that there are certain characteristics to which inquiry must conform in order to be scientific, e.g., a public (non-introspective) character, replicability, systematization, falsifiability, and so forth, but just as one is theoretically mistaken in demanding isomorphy between one type of system and another (see discussion of General System approach, pp. 429ff, above), one is likewise in error in assuming that descriptive methods and techniques must be isomorphic—even among 'sciences'. In short, failure to conduct research in a

45 See Jurgen Habermas, *Communication and the Evolution of Society*, Boston 1979, p. 96.

46 Sari Thomas, 'Film, Science and Reality', in A. Wiener (ed.), *Reality and the Camera: Essays in Ethnographic Film Theory, Criticism and Practice*, Berkeley and Los Angeles (forthcoming).

47 Thayer, op. cit., p. 43.

laboratory (or according to experimental design), and/or to obtain statistically-derived analyses is *not* that which causes an event to be *non*-scientific or *quasi*-scientific. Indeed, one could claim that the inappropriate employment of investigatory techniques is far more cardinal a sin against scientific validity.

These issues return us full circle to the notions of paradigm and model. Although the terms 'model' and 'paradigm' are often used interchangeably (as I have done throughout this paper), it might be helpful to regard 'model' as a subset of 'paradigm'. Essentially, if we take Kuhn's notion of paradigm—a fundamental abstraction of the conceptual schemata underlying and maintaining a particular research/scientific tradition[48]—a 'model' may be defined as a more-abbreviated and more-specifically derived articulation of that paradigm (i.e., a meta-abstraction). Keeping this admittedly tentative distinction in mind, it can be noted that while Kuhn persuasively demonstrates the need for *paradigms* in scientific communities,[49] the necessity of a model accompanying *every* paradigm remains highly questionable.

It may be argued that, to the extent that a conceptual schema is forced to be articulated in abbreviated and/or graphic form (the notion of a model proposed above), it is inevitable that the paradigm to which it belongs will be mechanically prescribed. This 'mechanization', as it were, need not be reductionistic or incongruous with the paradigm *if* that paradigm is justifiably mechanistic in its original abstraction. However, to the extent that a mechanical bias is inappropriate to the original paradigm, modelling may not only be unnecessary, but incorrect and misleading. Therefore, for those who might wish for a 'model' of the organic communication paradigm (in order to complement the elegance of a sender-message-receiver model) there may be some disappointment. It may simply be the case that the organic paradigm must be sufficiently forceful in its own, non-mechanical, yet scientific, terms.

48 Kuhn, op. cit. pp. 10-12.
49 Ibid., pp. 63-65.

David Phillips marshals evidence in this article that media accounts of murder-suicides stimulate imitative murder-suicides disguised as airplane crashes, and that the greater the publicity of original murder-suicides, the greater the increase in such plane crashes. The article then reviews nineteenth-century sociological writing on imitation and suggestion and posits an updated theory of imitation and suggestion as it affects social behavior consistent with these findings. David P. Phillips is associate professor of sociology at the University of California, San Diego.

3

AIRPLANE ACCIDENTS, MURDER, AND THE MASS MEDIA

Towards a Theory of Imitation and Suggestion*

David P. Phillips

Despite the classic contributions of Tarde, LeBon, and Mead, modern sociology has very largely neglected the concepts of imitation and suggestion. Sociologists' neglect of these concepts is somewhat surprising, because there has been widespread interest in imitation, suggestion, and modeling outside of sociology, particularly in the fields of psychology and economics.[1] The effect of imitation has been extensively documented by psy

*I thank M. Murphy, City Editor of the *Los Angeles Times*; J. Pilkington and M. Pritchard of the Vanderbilt Television News Archives; J. Coolman and L. Cruse, Documents Department, University Library, University of California at San Diego; D. O'Hagan, J. Fitzsimmons, S. Stuart, and A. Wood, Computer Center, U.C.S.D.; C. Broderick, B. Dance, H. Field, R. Kuever, S. Newcomb, S. Ostroff, R. Rafalovich, R. Schultz, and L. Seegmiller for helping me collect and analyze large amounts of data; and my colleagues B. Berger, F. Davis, M. Davis, G. Hall, R. Madsen, C. Mukerji, and J. Wiseman for criticisms and comments.

chologists studying the impact of the mass media (especially television) on violence (Berkowitz; Comstock; Comstock and Fisher; Comstock and Lindsey; Flanders; Goranson; Klapper; Liebert and Schwartzberg; Singer; Surgeon General's Scientific Advisory Committee on Television and Social Behavior). To date, there have been more than 2,300 studies on this topic.

Most psychological studies on the impact of the mass media have examined the effect of imitation *in the laboratory.* In contrast, economic studies of imitation have focused on the effect of imitation *in the market place.* Much economic research has shown that consumer behavior is affected by advertising built on the processes of imitation and suggestion. In an effort to use these processes to shape consumer behavior, U.S. industries spend more than $23,000,000,000 each year on advertising. (For information on the amount spent on advertising, see Sandage and Fryburger; for reviews documenting the effects of advertising, see Dirksen and Kroeger; Michman and Jugenheimer; Sandage and Fryburger; for general reviews of factors affecting consumer behavior, see Britt; Cohen; Engel et al.; Jacoby.) The literature on these topics is estimated to include at least 5,000 articles and books (Jacoby).

Despite the many psychological and economic studies on this topic, there has been almost no modern sociological work on imitation and suggestion. To my knowledge, the only sociological research documenting the effects of imitation in large geographic areas is by Phillips (a, b, d). I presented evidence indicating that (a) publicized suicide stories trigger additional, imitative suicides, and that (b) some of these imitative suicides are disguised as automobile accidents. In support of these claims, I presented the following evidence: (1) suicides increase significantly just after suicide stories are publicized in the newspapers; (2) fatal automobile accidents also increase just after publicized suicide stories; (3) single-car accidents increase more than other types of accidents just after suicide stories; (4) the age of drivers crashing in single-car accidents after the suicide story is correlated with the age of the person described in the suicide story; (5) the more publicity given to the suicide story, the greater the increase in suicides and the greater the increase in motor vehicle accidents; (6) the increase in suicides and in motor vehicle accidents occurs primarily in the geographic areas where the suicide story is publicized.

I noted that these findings persist after one corrects for the effects of random, seasonal, and yearly fluctuations in the data. After testing several other explanations of the findings, I concluded that suicide stories trigger additional, imitative suicides, some of which are disguised as automobile accidents.

In the studies just cited, I did not propose a sociological theory of imitation and suggestion. I believed that such a theory would be premature until one could show that the earlier work could be generalized to new bodies of data. In this paper I will show that my earlier findings can indeed be generalized. I will show that publicized stories trigger not only suicides, but murders as well, not only automobile accidents, but also airplane accidents (both commercial and noncommercial). In short, I will show that the impact of suggestion is at once more general and more grave than was previously suspected. In view of the findings to be presented, I believe it would now be useful to propose a sociological theory of imitation and suggestion. Such a theory will be described after presentation of the findings.

Description of Study

In this report I will examine the impact of murder–suicide stories. These are stories about a person who first commits murder, then suicide. I will present what I believe to be the first systematic, empirical, quantitative evidence for a large geographic area suggesting that murder–suicide stories trigger additional, imitative murder–suicides.

Many murderers may try to disguise murder–suicides as accidents to protect their survivors from insurance problems and from social stigma. One type of disguised murder–suicide may occur when a pilot deliberately crashes an airplane with passengers on board. If murder–suicide stories trigger additional murder–suicides, then fatal airplane accidents should increase abruptly and briefly just after murder–suicide stories are publicized. In addition, the more publicity given to these murder–suicide stories, the more airplane accidents should increase. In the rest of this paper I will show that fatal airplane accidents do indeed behave as predicted. In the first half of this report I will examine *non*commercial plane crashes; in the second half of the report, *commercial* plane crashes will be studied.

ANALYSIS OF NONCOMMERCIAL PLANE CRASHES

An exhaustive list of U.S. noncommercial plane accidents is provided by the U.S. National Transportation Safety Board (a).[2] The murder–suicide stories to be studied consist of all stories meeting five criteria. It was assumed that stories meeting these criteria would be the most likely to trigger airplane crashes. In general, the criteria were designed to maximize the chances that a pilot would identify his circumstances with those described in the murder–suicide story. In addition, the criteria were designed to ensure that the murder–suicide story was highly publicized. The five criteria are as follows: (1) The story must concern deaths occurring in the United States, not elsewhere. This criterion was established because a U.S. pilot is more likely to identify with American deaths than with foreign ones. (2) The story must concern one murderer acting alone. This criterion was established because a pilot bent on murder–suicide is more likely to identify with a *single* murderer than with several murderers acting together. (3) The story must concern a murderer and victims who die within a very short space of time.[3] This type of murder–suicide story is the most likely to affect a pilot bent on murder–suicide, because a pilot who deliberately crashes his plane is likely to kill himself and his passengers nearly simultaneously. (4) The story must concern a murderer who kills two or more victims. This type of story is likely to be very heavily publicized, in contrast to the more routine murder–suicide story, in which only one victim is killed. (5) The story must be carried on the front page of the *New York Times* or the *Los Angeles Times* or appear on the ABC, CBS, or NBC network evening news programs, 1968–73. The period under study ends in 1973 because that is the last year before the Arab Oil Embargo markedly changed aircraft traffic patterns. The study period begins on August 5, 1968, because systematic recording of network television news coverage began on this date. In all, eighteen stories meet the five criteria listed above; these stories are identified later in this paper.[4]

Nonsystematic, exploratory study of the period prior to 1968 suggested that noncommercial airplane fatalities behave like motor vehicle fatalities (Phillips, b, d) and rise to a sharp peak on the third day after a publicized death. On the basis of these exploratory results it was predicted that a third-day peak should also be found in the study period, 1968–73. Figure 1 [line (1)] shows the daily fluctuation of all U.S. noncommercial airplane accident fatalities before and after the above-mentioned murder–suicide stories. It is evident that airplane fatalities behave as predicted and increase very sharply on the third day after publicized murder–suicides.[5]

Figure 1 [line (3)] shows the fluctuation of fatalities from *single-fatality* plane crashes. A single-fatality crash cannot imply *both* murder *and* suicide. Hence, this type of plane crash should not be triggered by murder–suicide stories. As expected, fatalities from this type of crash do not increase after publicized murder–suicides. In contrast, however, fatalities from *multi*-fatality crashes do increase very steeply, as expected [Figure 1, line (2)].

These multi-fatality crashes resulted in 461 fatalities in the 14-day period under study. One-fourteenth of these ($461/14 = 32.93$) would be expected on the third day, given the null hypothesis of no relationship between the publicized murder–suicide and airplane fatalities. The observed number of deaths on the third day (63) is almost twice the number expected ($63/32.93 = 1.91$). This third-day peak in fatalities is significant at .0160 [this figure was determined by methods described in (6)].

Relationship between Amount of Publicity Devoted to the Murder–Suicide Story and the Number of Fatal Noncommercial Crashes Thereafter
If murder–suicide stories do indeed help to trigger some fatal airplane accidents, then the more publicity given to a murder–suicide, the more

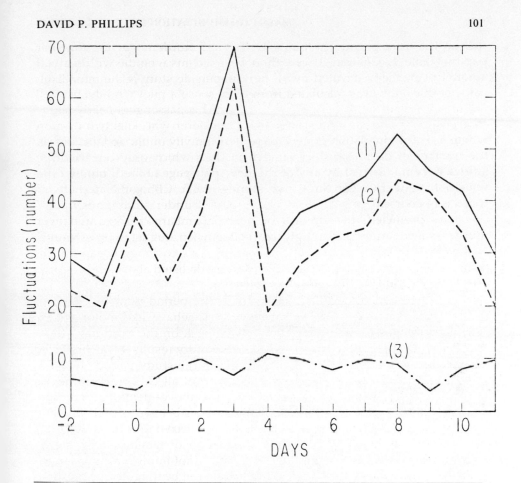

Figure 1. DAILY FLUCTUATION OF U. S. NONCOMMERCIAL PLANE FATALITIES FOR A TWO-WEEK PERIOD BEFORE, DURING (DAY 0), AND AFTER PUBLICIZED MURDER-SUICIDES (U. S., 1968-73) Note: Line (1) indicates the fluctuation of fatalities for all noncommercial plane crashes, line (2) indicates the fluctuation of fatalities for multi-fatality noncommercial plane crashes, line (3) indicates the fluctuation of fatalities for single-fatality noncommercial plane crashes. For sources of data, see text and note 4.

airplane accidents should increase just after the murder-suicide. This hypothesis will be tested after the development of an index of newspaper publicity.

In the midpoint of the period under study, there were 1,838 daily newspapers in the U.S. and thus it is not easy to measure the total amount of newspaper publicity devoted nationwide to a murder-suicide story. The measurement procedure adopted here seems plausible and is convenient. Almost half of all the operative civilian aircraft in the United States are concentrated in only nine states. The largest newspaper from each of these states was examined to determine which murder-suicide stories were car-

ried on the front page.[7] The publicity devoted to a story by these newspapers (Table 1, Column 3) can then be used as an index of the total
amount of publicity devoted by all newspapers. For any given story, the
value of this index was calculated from

$$\sum_{i=1}^{9} X_i Y_i$$

where X_i is the circulation of newspaper i at the time of the story and Y_i is
the number of days that story stayed on the front page. Note that five
stories were not carried by any of the newspapers examined, only by the
television networks. For these five stories, the value of the newspaper
index is of course 0.

As predicted, the amount of newspaper publicity devoted to a
murder–suicide story is strongly correlated with the number of multi-

Table 1. RELATIONSHIP BETWEEN PUBLICITY DEVOTED TO A MURDER–SUICIDE STORY AND
NUMBER OF FATAL U. S. NONCOMMERCIAL PLANE CRASHES AFTER THAT STORY. 1968–73

Name of Reported Murderer in Murder-Suicide Story	Date of Murder-Suicide	Total Known Front Page Newspaper Circulation Devoted to Story	Number of Networks Carrying Story on Network Evening Television News	Number of Multi-Fatality Plane Crashes in the Week After the Murder-Suicide
F. Chegwin	08/07/68	856,621	0	6
S. Kline ⎫	12/18/68			
C. Bray ⎬	12/19/68	1,032,655	1	6
R. McLachlan	01/01/69	3,470,925	0	5
C. Stein	02/10/69	0	1	3
T. Walton	02/21/69	0	3	3
C. Gish	05/14/70	0	1	4
J. White	09/23/70	440,570	1	7
E. Pruyn	01/26/71	634,371	1	2
R. Putnam	07/13/71	1,044,660	2	4
G. Giffe	10/04/71	3,220,174	0	8
G. Logan	11/26/71	966,293	0	8
R. Cowden	12/13/71	404,957	1	4
J. Van Praag	03/07/72	981,661	0	4
H. McLeod	05/29/72	3,764,339	3	8
D. Tolstet	10/06/72	0	2	2
R. Jordan	01/23/73	0	1	2
S. Cloud	10/18/73	823,935	0	4

*The bracketed murder-suicide stories occur within a day of each other and are
treated as one story. Information on total network coverage of the first, second,
and fourth stories is unavailable (see note 11). The dates used in this table and
throughout the study of noncommercial crashes indicate the times when the murder-
suicides actually occurred, rather than the times when these crimes were first
publicized.

fatality crashes after that story (Pearson $r = .637$); $P = .003$, one-tailed test).[8]

In contrast to these findings, television publicity does not seem to be significantly correlated with the occurrence of multi-fatality crashes. The number of networks covering a murder–suicide story on the network evening news programs (Table 1, Column 4) can be taken as an index of the amount of network television publicity devoted to the story. This index was nonsignificantly correlated ($r = .379$; $P = .082$; one-tailed test; $n = 14$) with the number of multi-fatality plane crashes occurring after each story.[9] For the fourteen stories for which information on both television and newspaper coverage is available (Table 1), the correlation between newspaper coverage and crashes ($r = .734$) is almost as high as the multiple correlation between newspaper–television coverage and crashes ($R = .737$). Evidently, newspaper coverage alone predicts multi-fatality crashes almost as well as newspaper and television coverage combined.[10]

Thus far I have shown that (1) multi-fatality crashes increase after murder–suicide stories, and (2) the more newspaper publicity devoted to a story, the more plane crashes occur just after that story. I will now show that (3) the increase in multi-fatality plane crashes occurs mainly in the states where the murder–suicide story is publicized. This finding would be expected if multi-fatality plane crashes are triggered by publicized murder–suicides.

Relationship between Location of Publicity Devoted to the Murder–Suicide Story and the Location of Noncommercial Crashes Occurring Thereafter

Before we can proceed further, some definitions must be supplied. The "experimental period" consists of the seven days 0–6 days after the publicized murder–suicide. The "control period" consists of the remaining seven days designated in Figure 1. For any given story, the publicity area is defined as the state or states known to be receiving newspaper publicity about the story.[11] The nonpublicity area consists of all the remaining states.

If plane crashes increase mainly in the area where the murder–suicide story is publicized, then there should be a disproportionately large number of crashes in the publicity area in the experimental period. On the other hand, given the null hypothesis, the publicity area should not differ from the entire United States with respect to the probability of a crash occurring in the experimental period. In the 14 day interval under study, there were $N = 121$ multi-fatality crashes in the U.S.; $p = .52$ ($= 63/121$) of these crashes were in the experimental period. In the publicity area there were $N = 20$ multi-fatality crashes; $x = 15$ of these were in the experimental period. Given the null hypothesis, the probability of 15 or more crashes in the experimental period in the publicity area can be evaluated with the hypergeometric distribution, one tailed.[12]

$$P(x \geq 15) = \sum_{x=15}^{20} \left[\binom{N_p}{x} \binom{N - N_p}{n - x} \Big/ \binom{N}{n} \right]$$

$$P(x \geq 15) = \sum_{x=15}^{20} \left[\binom{63}{x} \binom{58}{20 - x} \Big/ \binom{121}{20} \right]$$

$$= .0213$$

Hence, multi-fatality plane crashes increase disproportionately in the areas where the murder–suicide stories are known to be publicized.

In this section I have presented evidence indicating that (1) publicized murder–suicide stories trigger some fatal noncommercial plane crashes and that (2) some noncommercial plane crashes are murder–suicides in disguise.[13] The policy implications of this evidence are disturbing but not necessarily grave. Relatively few people fly in noncommercial planes; hence, relatively few people run the risk of falling victim to a noncommercial pilot bent on murder–suicide. Furthermore, the average noncommercial plane crash involves only a small number of passengers. Hence a noncommercial pilot bent on murder–suicide can kill only a very small number of people.

In strong contrast, a *commercial* pilot bent on murder–suicide can kill a very large number of people. Thus, if some *commercial* plane crashes are murder–suicides in disguise, the policy implications would be very serious indeed.

In the next section I will present data indicating that *commercial* plane crash fatalities increase very considerably just after publicized murder–suicides. I will also show that the more publicity given to the murder–suicide story, the more commercial plane crash fatalities occur.

ANALYSIS OF COMMERCIAL PLANE CRASHES

If publicized murder–suicide stories trigger some fatal commercial air crashes, then there should be more commercial air crash fatalities just after the stories than just before.[14] This hypothesis will be tested after some terms and procedures are defined.

Definition of Terms
The term "experimental period" will be defined as the period 0–7 days after the murder–suicide is publicized in the *New York Times* or *Los Angeles Times*.[15] The term "control period" is defined as a period of duration equal to the "experimental period" but occurring just prior to the murder–suicide story, that is, −1 to −8 days before the story is publicized by the newspapers.

Determination of Time Period to Be Examined

The commercial plane crashes to be studied occur in the period 1950–73. This study period ends in 1973 (as in the noncommercial plane study) for reasons outlined earlier in this paper. The study period starts in 1950 (rather than 1968 as in the noncommercial plane study) for the following reasons. At the beginning of the noncommercial plane study it was assumed that television publicity might trigger some plane crashes. For this reason the starting point of the noncommercial plane study was chosen as August 5, 1968—the date on which systematic information on television coverage began. The findings in the noncommercial plane study contradicted the assumption that television publicity might trigger some plane crashes. Hence, it seems unnecessary to continue to use August 5, 1968 as a starting point for the investigation of commercial plane crashes. Instead, it seems more appropriate to use an earlier starting point so as to allow the examination of as many commercial plane crashes as possible. The earliest possible starting point is January 1, 1950—on this date the United States government first began to collect systematic information on commercial plane fatalities.[16] Thus, for the reasons outlined above, the starting point, January 1, 1950, will be adopted for the commercial plane study.

Determination of murder–suicide stories to be examined, 1950–73

A set of publicized stories meeting five criteria had already been generated for 1968–73, the period examined in the earlier study of noncommercial plane crashes. These stories will be used once again in the current investigation of commercial plane crashes.[17] In addition, a new set of stories will be generated according to the same five criteria for the period which was not examined in the noncommercial plane study (1950–67).[18]

Determination of the Hypothesis to Be Tested

Nonsystematic, exploratory research for the period before 1950 suggested a general increase in commercial plane fatalities in the experimental period 0–7 days after the publicized murder–suicide story. However, this exploratory research did not suggest a sharp, third-day peak in commercial plane fatalities analogous to the third-day peak observed in noncommercial plane fatalities. Consequently, a third-day peak was not predicted for the study period, 1950–73. Instead, the following, more conservative prediction was made: the number of U.S. commercial air crash fatalities in the experimental period 0–7 days after the story should be greater than the number of U.S. commercial air crash fatalities in the control period −1 to −8 days before the story. This prediction is tested below.

RESULTS OF COMMERCIAL PLANE CRASH INVESTIGATION

Table 2 provides a list of 39 publicized murder–suicide stories, together with the dates of fatal commercial air crashes occurring around the time of these stories and the number of persons killed in each crash. The bottom rows of this table indicate the total number of commercial air crash fatalities occurring in the experimental period just after the story and the total number of commercial air crash fatalities occurring in the control period just before the story.[19] It is evident that commercial airplane crash fatalities behave as predicted: the number of deaths just after the story (324) is more than *ten times* the number of deaths just before the story (31).

For reasons noted earlier in this paper, the statistical significance of a finding like this one must be assessed in terms of *crashes* rather than *fatalities*. (See note 6 for a detailed discussion of this point.)

In all, there are 16 fatal air crashes in the experimental and control periods combined. Given the null hypothesis that murder–suicide stories have no effect on airplane crashes, one-half of these crashes are expected to fall in the experimental period and one-half in the control period. In fact, however, 12 of the 16 crashes occur in the experimental period. Given the null hypothesis, the probability of 12 or more crashes in the experimental period is .038 (binomial test; $p = .5$; $n = 16$; $x \geq 12$). Hence, there are significantly more fatal commercial airplane crashes just after murder–suicide stories than just before.

Comparative Deadlines of Plane Crashes Occurring
Just Before and Just After Murder–Suicide Stories
It is interesting to note that the average crash in the experimental period is significantly more lethal than the average crash in the control period. On the average, there are 27 deaths per crash in the experimental period ($324/12 = 27$) in contrast to 7.75 deaths per crash in the control period ($31/4 = 7.75$). The difference between these two averages (27 versus 7.75) is statistically significant at .039 (randomization test, one-tailed).[20]

These results would be expected if murder–suicide stories do indeed trigger some commercial airplane fatalities, for two reasons: (1) A pilot who is bent on murder–suicide is trying to achieve a fatal crash, whether consciously or unconsciously. In such circumstances, any crash that occurs may well be a severe one, killing a large fraction of the persons on board. In contrast, a pilot who is trying to *save* the persons on board is trying to avoid a crash. A crash that occurs under these circumstances may be expected to kill a smaller fraction of the persons on board. (2) A pilot who is bent on murder–suicide may be more tempted to crash an airplane if that airplane has many persons on board.[21]

I have now shown that (1) there are significantly more fatal commercial air crashes just after the murder–suicide story than just before; and (2) on the average, crashes occurring just after the murder–suicide

Table 2. RELATIONSHIP BETWEEN PUBLICATION OF MURDER–SUICIDE STORIES AND OCCURRENCE OF FATAL U.S. AIR CARRIER CRASHES, 1950–73

Name of Reported Murderer in Murder-Suicide Story	Date of Publication of Story	U.S. Air Carrier Crashes Occurring in Control Period (with date of crash and number killed in crash)	U.S. Air Carrier Crashes Occurring in Experimental Period (with date and number killed in crash)	Total Known Front Page Newspaper Circulation Devoted to Story
Baker	04/26/50			1,572,570
Emeny	03/16/51			1,942,820
Yasiewicz	08/19/51		08/24/51 (50 dead)	794,163
Morgenthaler	10/20/52			399,393
Weigold	12/31/52		01/07/53 (7 dead) 01/07/53 (40 dead)	507,281
Conner	04/04/53			396,882
Felix } Boyd }	07/22/53 07/23/53		07/26/53 (3 dead)	783,684
Carroll	05/21/54			591,396
Losser	10/04/54			1,289,914
Rahner	12/04/54	11/30/54 (2 dead)		404,992
Alexander	06/29/55			1,144,361
Sanger	11/14/55		11/17/55 (28 dead)	600,769
Carter	12/02/55			412,167
Holland	12/30/55			412,167
Bauer	01/29/56			3,416,949
Hughes	12/05/56			428,323
Rawlings	11/27/57			440,394
Murphy	11/07/58			464,453
Wiener	12/02/58			570,717
Gardner	11/12/59		11/16/59 (42 dead)	1,407,743
Dotti } Frank }	01/15/60 01/15,16,17/60		01/18/60 (50 dead)	12,186,385
Cozzens	03/03/60			703,890
Clark	09/01/62			2,109,821
Whitman	08/02,03/66		08/06/66 (42 dead)	8,999,240
Rubertone	08/26/66	08/21/66 (9 dead)		635,619
Held	10/24/67			3,232,976
Chegwin	08/08/68	08/04/68 (3 dead)	08/10/68 (35 dead) 08/14/68 (21 dead)	856,621
Gish	05/15/70			0
White	09/24/70			440,570
Pruyn	01/27/71			634,371
Putnam	07/14/71			1,044,660
Giffe	10/04,05/71			3,220,174
Logan	11/27/71		12/04/71 (2 dead)	966,293
Cowden	12/14/71			404,957
Van Praag	03/08/72	03/03/72 (17 dead)		981,661
McLeod	05/30/72		05/30/72 (4 dead)	3,764,339
Tolstet	10/07/72			0
Jordan	01/24/73			0
Cloud	10/19/73			823,935
		Total dead in Control Period = 31	Total dead in Experimental Period = 324	

*The bracketed murder-suicide stories occur within one day of each other and are treated as one story.

story are significantly more lethal than crashes occurring just before the
murder–suicide story.

Daily Fluctuation of Commercial Airplane
Fatalities Before and After Murder–Suicide Stories
Figure 2 displays the daily fluctuations of U.S. commercial air crash fatalities before and after murder–suicide stories. The particular, two-week
period examined in this graph was chosen so as to make Figure 2 comparable with earlier graphs for noncommercial plane fatalities (Figure 1) and
motor vehicle fatalities (Phillips, b, Figure 1). There is a strong family
resemblance between these three graphs. In all three graphs the following
features are evident: (1) Fatalities increase just after the 0-date, not before;
(2) the increase in fatalities persists for seven to nine days; and (3) fatalities
rise to a sharp primary peak three or four days after the 0-date and a
smaller, secondary peak seven or eight days after the 0-date. The similarity between these three graphs presumably occurs because similar imitative processes trigger some motor vehicle crashes, noncommercial plane
crashes, and commercial plane crashes just after publicized stories about
suicide or murder–suicide.

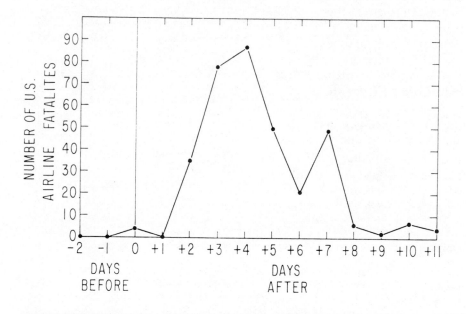

Figure 2. DAILY FLUCTUATION OF U. S. AIR CARRIER FATALITIES FOR A TWO-WEEK PERIOD BEFORE.
DURING (DAY 0). AND AFTER NEWSPAPER STORIES ABOUT MURDER–SUICIDES (U. S. 1950–73)
Note: The term "air carrier" is defined in note 16. which also gives the source of the air carrier crash fatality
data.

*Relationship Between Amount of Publicity Devoted to the Murder–Suicide Story
and the Number of Commercial Airplane Fatalities Occurring Just Afterwards*

If murder–suicide stories do indeed trigger some commercial airplane fatalities, then the greater the publicity devoted to the story, the greater the
number of fatalities that should occur just after the story is publicized. This
hypothesis will be tested after an index of newspaper publicity is described.

As noted earlier, there are more than 1,800 daily newspapers in the
U.S., and thus it is not easy to measure the total amount of publicity
devoted nationwide to a murder–suicide story. In practice, only a small
sample of newspapers can be studied. It seems appropriate to use the same
sample of newspapers as was used previously in the study of noncommercial plane crashes (see note 7). The publicity devoted to a story by these
newspapers (Table 2, column 4) can then be used as an index of the total
amount of newspaper publicity devoted nationwide to a murder–suicide
story. For any given story the value of this index was calculated from

$$\sum_{i=1}^{n} X_i Y_i$$

where X_i is the circulation of newspaper i at the time of the story, and Y_i is
the number of days that story stayed on the front page.[22] Note that the
index formula given above is identical to the index formula used in the
study of noncommercial plane crashes.

As predicted, the amount of newspaper publicity devoted to a
murder–suicide story is positively correlated with the number of commercial air crash fatalities in the experimental period just after the story
($r = .441$; $P - .002$; one tailed test)[23]

Earlier in this paper I presented findings suggesting that murder-
suicide stories trigger some *noncommercial* plane crashes. I have now presented findings suggesting that some *commercial* plane crashes may also be
triggered by murder–suicide stories. The evidence concerning commercial
plane crashes indicates that (1) these crashes increase significantly just
after murder–suicide stories; (2) these crashes are significantly more lethal
than crashes in a matched control period; and (3) the more publicity devoted to a murder–suicide story, the more commercial air crash fatalities
occur just afterwards.[24]

Summary of Results in All Investigations to Date

It has been shown in this and in previous investigations (Phillips, a, b, c, d)
that suicides, motor vehicle fatalities, noncommercial plane fatalities, and
commercial plane fatalities all increase significantly after stories about suicide or murder–suicide. In all the studies, the more publicity devoted to
the story, the more fatalities increase thereafter. In general, the fatalities
under study rise to a primary peak on the third or fourth day after the

publicized suicide or murder–suicide, followed by a secondary peak on the seventh or eighth day. In general, the rise in fatalities persists for about seven to nine days.

The only explanation that seems to account for all of these findings is that publicized suicides and murder–suicides trigger some imitative suicides and murder–suicides, some of which are disguised as motor vehicle accidents or plane crashes.

A Brief Theory of Imitation and Suggestion

In the beginning of this paper I noted that there is no modern sociological theory of imitation. I noted earlier that such a theory would be premature until one could generalize the findings to new bodies of data. In this paper I have now shown that my earlier findings can indeed be generalized. Consequently, I believe it is now appropriate to present a sociological theory of imitation; such a theory will be outlined in the remainder of this paper. It should be stressed that the theory to be presented is brief, tentative, and incomplete. A full-scale theory must await future research.

It is sometimes helpful to conceive of imitation as a kind of cultural contagion.[25] There may be certain analogies between cultural and biological contagion, and these analogies suggest some potentially fruitful lines of research. It may be valuable to explore six of these analogies, so long as we approach them, not with deference, but with caution. Like many analogies, that between biological and cultural contagion is useful but not perfect. Some of these imperfections will be discussed at the end of this paper, after we have explored six of the similarities between biological and cultural contagion.

First Analogy–Incubation Period
In biological contagion, the symptoms of the disease typically appear some time after a person has been infected with a microorganism. Is there a similar incubation period in *cultural* contagion? Support for this idea is provided in the present and in previous papers (Phillips, b, d). Automobile and airplane accidents do *not* increase immediately after front-page stories; instead, they increase after a three or four day lag. This lag in response may reflect the existence of an incubation period.[26]

In future research, it would be interesting to investigate the processes that result in the apparent incubation period. Does every type of front page story (including types not yet examined) display the same three or four day lag? Is there a difference between the type of person who dies three or four days after the story and persons who die a few days later? Perhaps persons who respond very rapidly to front page suicide stories are primed for suicide—they may have a past history of unsuccessful suicide attempts. In contrast, persons who respond more slowly to the front page story may not have thought of suicide until the appearance of the front page story. In general, does the idea of copying the front page event begin as an implicit, obscure notion which gradually becomes more explicit and less obscure over time?

Second Analogy—Immunization

Sometimes it is possible to immunize a person against a specific microorganism by exposing him to weakened strains of that microorganism. Can one similarly immunize a person against *cultural* contagion? Perhaps repeated exposure to minor suicide stories builds up one's resistance to the idea of suicide, so that eventually one becomes immune even to a major suicide story. Perhaps the cultural equivalent of biological immunization is boredom or indifference to what once would have been a virulent, powerful idea.

Sometimes it is possible to immunize a person against one microorganism by infecting him with mild doses of another. For example, one can immunize a person against smallpox by infecting him with cowpox. Is a similar kind of nonspecific immunization also possible in cultural contagion? Can one become immune to one idea after exposure to another, related idea? (See McGuire for a review of psychological experiments on factors capable of immunizing a person against new ideas.)

Third Analogy—Specific Versus Diffuse Contagion

In biological contagion, there is a specific connection between a particular microorganism and a particular disease. For example, the diphtheria bacterium causes only diphtheria, and not some other illnesses as well. Is *cultural* contagion similarly specific? The evidence in this and in previous papers indicates that cultural contagion is in some ways quite specific and in other ways diffuse.

Evidence for specificity of cultural contagion. / Phillips (d) showed that stories about a person who committed suicide triggered single-car, single-person accidents, *not* multiple-car, multiple-person crashes. This suggests that a particular type of story triggers one type of accident and not another— evidence for the specificity of cultural contagion. Further evidence appears in the present paper, which shows that murder—suicide stories trigger one type of plane crash and not another—*multiple*-fatality noncommercial crashes, rather than *single*-fatality crashes.

Evidence for diffuseness of cultural contagion. / On the other hand, there is also evidence of diffuse contagion as well. Phillips (a, b, d) showed that in some cases the *same* suicide stories may trigger not only suicides but also automobile accidents. Thus, a single stimulus apparently provokes two different types of imitative response simultaneously; this is evidence for diffuse, nonspecific cultural contagion.

In sum, there seems to be evidence for both specific and diffuse contagion. The relative importance of each type of contagion is not presently known and needs to be assessed in future research.

Fourth Analogy—Susceptibility to Contagion

Persons in poor biological health are known to be particularly susceptible to biological contagion. Is there a parallel process for those susceptible to cultural contagion? Persons who are anomic, have low self-esteem and a past history of failure may be said to be in poor cultural and psychological health. Are these people particularly susceptible to cultural contagion? Research on social movements (Toch) and on imitation (reviewed in Comstock; Comstock and Fisher; Flanders; Liebert and Schwartzberg) indicates that these persons are indeed more susceptible than others to suggestion and imitation. Presumably, these people are particularly susceptible to new ideas and suggestions because they are detached to some extent from the old ideas and suggestions of their society.

Fifth Analogy—Channels of Infection

Some biological illnesses are spread more efficiently through one medium than another. For example, cholera is transmitted more effectively through water than through air, while the opposite is true for pneumonia. Similarly, is cultural contagion more effectively conveyed through one channel than another? In this paper I have examined two channels of cultural contagion—television and newspapers. The evidence suggests that newspapers provide the most effective channel. Perhaps this is so because an individual can spend a great deal of time reading and rereading a newspaper story, whereas the same individual cannot repeatedly view and review a television story on the topic.[27] Thus, the individual can remain longer in contact with the contagious influence of a newspaper story and therefore can perhaps be more readily affected by it.

In future research, it would be interesting to examine a third channel of cultural contagion—word of mouth. Studies of word-of-mouth advertising (Dirksen and Kroeger; Engel et al.; Sandage and Fryburger) suggest that this may be the most effective channel of all.

Sixth Analogy—Quarantine

Centuries of experience have shown that the spread of biological contagion can be slowed or stopped through a quarantine of the infected individuals. The present and previous papers suggest that *cultural* quarantine may similarly reduce the spread of cultural contagion. Phillips (a, b, d) and the present paper show that (1) the less publicity given to the page one story, the smaller the increase in deaths thereafter; (2) there tends to be no increase in deaths in geographic areas where the newspaper stories are not publicized. Phillips (unpublished data) also showed that *inside* page suicide stories apparently have no effect whatever on subsequent mortality. All these findings together suggest that the less publicity given to an act like suicide or murder–suicide, the smaller the contagious effect of this act on others. In the extreme case a news "quarantine" on the story would presumably trigger the minimum number of additional deaths.[28]

IMPERFECTIONS IN THE ANALOGY BETWEEN BIOLOGICAL AND CULTURAL CONTAGION

As previously stated, the analogy between biological and cultural contagion is useful but imperfect. Several features of cultural contagion seem to have no parallel in biological contagion. For example, I will show in a future study that *fictional individuals* like movie heroes trigger imitation by real people in the U.S. population. No parallel process exists in biological contagion: in this type of contagion it is not possible for a fictional individual to infect a real person with a biological disease.

There is an additional aspect of cultural contagion which has no precise analogue in biological contagion. Individuals seem to vary much more in their response to cultural contagion than in their response to biological contagion. Almost every person who is inoculated with a 25 cc. culture of anthrax will contract that disease. But not everyone exposed to an intensely publicized suicide will thereupon harbor thoughts of self-destruction. This raises an obvious question for future research. What makes some people more susceptible than others to cultural contagion? A partial answer to this question was suggested in the discussion of the Fourth Analogy above. But a complete answer to this question must await further research.

THE IMITATION OF NONPATHOLOGICAL BEHAVIOR—AN ADDITIONAL AREA FOR FUTURE RESEARCH

In this paper I have restricted the empirical and theoretical discussion to *pathological* behaviors like suicide and murder–suicide. It seems evident that *non*pathological behavior is also very widely imitated. The child who copies his older brother, the junior faculty member who copies a senior colleague, the teenager who imitates Farrah Fawcett-Majors's hairstyle, the housewife who buys "Mr. Coffee" because Joe DiMaggio modeled that behavior, all of these people are imitating nonpathological, every-day behaviors. Future sociological research on imitation should focus on nonpathological as well as pathological behaviors.

Summary

In this paper I have tried to achieve two major goals. First, I have tried to show that the social impact of suggestion is more general and more grave than was previously suspected. I have presented evidence indicating that front page stories trigger not only suicides but murders as well, not only automobile accidents but also airplane accidents. My data suggest that some commercial airplane accidents may have been triggered by front page murder–suicide stories. If this is so, then the implications of this paper are very grave indeed.

Second, I have tried to move from my empirical findings towards a modern, sociological theory of imitation. Some nineteenth century sociologists began to theorize on this topic, but modern sociologists have virtually ignored it. Both the empirical evidence and the theoretical discussion presented in this paper suggest that it may be worth reestablishing a line of research which was open in the nineteenth century and has been closed ever since.

Notes

1. A small part of this paper (the evidence on noncommercial plane crashes) has been briefly reported in a two-page paper in *Science* (Phillips, c). The terms "imitate" and "suggest" will be defined throughout this paper as they are in *Webster's Unabridged Dictionary*: (1) imitate: to follow as a pattern . . . or example; (2) suggest: to mention as a possibility; to offer as an idea for consideration.
2. Noncommercial flying refers to "the use of an aircraft for purposes of pleasure, personal transportation, . . . private business, in corporate executive operations, and in other operations, wherein there is no direct monetary fee charged" (U.S. National Transportation Safety Board, a). Planes owned in the U.S. but crashing outside the fifty states are excluded from the analysis. I know of no large-scale, quantitative studies suggesting that noncommercial planes are sometimes used as instruments of both murder and suicide. There are some case studies suggesting a suicidal (but not a homicidal) component in some noncommercial plane crashes (Gibbons et al.; Stevens; Yanowitch et al.) Jones reviewed earlier work and also provided a case study. In addition, indirect evidence of a suicidal component in some crashes might perhaps be inferred from toxicological findings (Lacefield et al.) and possibly from personality tests of pilots involved in accidents (Sanders and Hofmann; Sanders et al.). However, the two last-named studies present mutually contradictory evidence.
3. A "short space of time" has been arbitrarily defined as 48 hours. In almost all cases the murderer shot himself but in a few cases (McLachlan, Stein, Putnam, and Cloud) the murderer was shot by the police after refusing to surrender. These cases were treated as suicide, because the murderer could have avoided death had he so desired. A well-known study by Wolfgang argues strongly that these cases, in which the victim precipitates his own death, should be treated as a type of suicide.
4. Two of these stories (Kline and Bray) occurred at almost the same time. In accord with previous procedure (Phillips, a, b, d) the two stories are treated as one to avoid problems arising from statistical dependence. Information on television network news coverage is provided by Vanderbilt Television News Archives (periodical issues). Weekend stories before July, 1970 are excluded from the analysis because until then weekend broadcasts were not recorded in the archives.
5. The particular two-week period studied in Figure 1 was chosen so as to make Figure 1 comparable with earlier results for automobiles (Phillips, b, d).
6. One cannot test the statistical significance of this peak in terms of *fatalities* because the

appropriate significance test requires the assumption that the timing of each fatality is independent of the timing of every other fatality. This assumption is obviously untenable for multiple-fatality crashes, in which several people may die nearly simultaneously. However, the statistical significance of the third-day peak can be assessed in terms of crashes rather than fatalities. These can be treated as independent of one another, provided one counts a midair collision between two planes as one crash. In the 14-day period under observation, there were 156 multi-fatality crashes. Under the null hypothesis, 1 14 of these (11.14) are expected to occur on the third day, while 19 crashes actually occur at this time. The binomial distribution can be used to evaluate the probability of 19 or more crashes, given the null hypothesis, and $p = 1$ 14, $n = 156$. This probability is .0160. Hence, there is a statistically significant third-day peak in multi-fatality plane crashes. An alternative approach to testing the statistical significance of the third-day peak would be to use one or another variant of the t-test. Unfortunately, this approach is probably not valid, because the t-test requires a number of assumptions that may not hold for these data. For the reader who wishes, nonetheless, to use the t-test, the following data are supplied:

Day of Cycle: $-2 \ -1 \ 0 \ 1 \ 2 \ 3 \ 4 \ 5 \ 6 \ 7 \ 8 \ 9 \ 10 \ 11$
No. of multi-fatality crashes: 7   8 12 6 10 19 9 10 13 12 14 15 12 9

7. The top nine states with respect to ownership of operative U.S. civil aircraft are, in order: California, Texas, Ohio, Illinois, Florida, Michigan, New York, Pennsylvania, and Washington (U.S. Department of Transportation, Table 7). The nine newspapers examined are: *Los Angeles Times, Dallas News, Cleveland Plain Dealer, Chicago Tribune, Miami Herald, Detroit News, New York Times, Philadelphia Bulletin,* and *Seattle Press Intelligencer.* For three states (Texas, New York, and Washington) the largest newspaper was not easily available; for these states, the second largest paper was used. Newspaper circulation figures come from Ayer Press (yearly volumes).

8. The observed correlation is significant at .003 if one uses the conventional significance test for r

$$t = \setminus (n - 2) (1 - r^2)$$

However, this test requires stringent assumptions that very probably do not hold for the data under study. In place of this test one can substitute a randomization test for the statistical significance of the observed correlation ($r = .637$). This test (which indicates that r is significant at .005) makes almost no assumptions about the data and is designed for use with interval-scale data (Pitman).

9. Because of the failure of recording equipment and other factors, the Vanderbilt Television News Archives does not have information on the total number of networks covering the stories about Chegwin, Kline, or McLachlan. Consequently, these stories were excluded in the calculation of the correlation between the television publicity devoted to a story and the number of crashes after that story. The weak correlation with television publicity may possibly occur because the television networks very seldom reported the murder–suicide stories as lead stories. Hence, these stories might be relatively invisible to a television viewer. In contrast, the newspapers did treat the murder–suicides under examination as lead stories page one.

10. For the fourteen stories for which information on both television and newspaper coverage is available, the partial correlation between newspaper coverage and the number of multi-fatality crashes (correcting for television coverage) is .683. As was noted earlier, *single-fatality crashes should not be triggered* by murder–suicide stories. Hence, the fluctuation of single-fatality crashes after a story should not be correlated with the amount of newspaper publicity devoted to that story. This prediction is consistent with the data ($r = .050$).

11. Because television publicity seems to be unrelated to plane crashes, television news coverage has been ignored in this analysis, and stories receiving no newspaper coverage (only television publicity) have been excluded from the analysis.

12. This application of the hypergeometric distribution is discussed in Mosteller et al., Table 3–3). $N = 121$ in the above analysis [and not 156 as in note 6] because the above analysis omits crashes associated with five stories publicized only on television and three missing planes which crashed in unknown locations. One would prefer to code crashes by location of take-off rather than by location of crash, but unfortunately the information necessary for this type of coding is often not available in the brief descriptions of accidents used in this paper.

13. One might argue that the third-day peak results from a fortuitous association between a day-of-the-week cycle in murder–suicide stories and a day-of-the-week cycle in multi-fatality crashes. For example, if most murder–suicides occur on Wednesday and most plane crashes occur on Saturday, then this would result in a peak in crashes three days after murder–suicides, even if murder–suicides have no effect on plane crashes. There are three pieces of evidence against this argument. (1) If the third-day peak is due to a day-of-the-week cycle in plane crashes, then the peak in crashes on the third day should be followed by an equally large peak one week later (on day 10), two weeks later, and so on. There is no evidence of a peak on day 10 (see note 6). In fact the number of crashes on this day (12) is almost precisely equal to $156/14 = 11.14$, the number to be expected if crashes are uniformly distributed from day -2 to day $+11$. (2) More generally, if the "day-of-the-week" argument is correct, there should be a strong, positive correlation, $r(x, x + 7)$ between the number of multi-fatality crashes on day x and the number of multi-fatality crashes on day $x + 7$. On the other hand, if this argument is not correct, then $r(x, x + 7)$ should be approximately 0. For the data displayed in note 8, $r(x, x + 7) = -.0206$. This does not support the "day-of-the-week" argument. (3) If the "day-of-the-week" argument is correct, then there is no causal connection between publicized murder–suicides and plane crashes; hence, there should be no correlation between the amount of publicity given to a murder–suicide story and the number of crashes thereafter. In addition, there should be no correlation between the location of the publicity devoted to the murder–suicide and the location of the plane crashes occurring thereafter. Both of these predictions are inconsistent with the data reported in this paper. In sum, the "day-of-theweek" argument does not seem to explain adequately the findings of this paper.
14. The general class of planes to be studied here is defined by the National Transportation Safety Board as "U.S. Air Carriers." These comprise U.S. commercial flight operators who have been issued a Certificate of Convenience and Necessity by the Civil Aeronautics Board, authorizing the carrier to engage in air transportation. These "Certificated Route Carriers" are often referred to as "Scheduled Airlines." For a more detailed and precise definition of "air carrier," see National Transportation Safety Board (b). The great bulk of studies on fatal air carrier accidents have been conducted by the Civil Aeronautics Board and by the National Transportation Safety Board, which publish a separate, extensive *Aircraft Accident Report* for each individual air carrier accident. For more general studies, see Beaty; Corkindale; and some of the studies cited in note 2.
15. Because of the findings in the noncommercial plane study, the definition of the term "experimental period" has been modified slightly for use in the present analysis of commercial airplane crashes. In the noncommercial plane study the starting point of the experimental period was taken as the date *when the murder–suicide actually occurred*. It was on this date that TV publicity was generally accorded to the murder–suicide. This starting point was adopted in the noncommercial plane study because it was assumed at the beginning of that study that TV publicity might trigger some crashes. However, the findings in the noncommercial plane study suggest that this assumption is incorrect: the findings suggest that TV stories do *not* trigger crashes. Hence, because of the findings in the noncommercial plane study, it seems appropriate to start the experimental period in the commercial plane study with the date of the newspaper story, rather than the date when the murder–suicide actually occurred.

The definition of the term "experimental period" used in the noncommercial plane study has been modified in one other way for use in the present analysis of commercial plane crashes. At the beginning of the noncommercial plane study it was assumed that plane crash fatalities would rise for a period of one week; a seven-day experimental period was arbitrarily assumed, in the absence of any firm evidence suggesting a different duration for the experimental period. However, the findings in the noncommercial plane study suggest that this "seven-day assumption" be modified slightly for use in the analysis of commercial air crashes. The findings in the noncommercial plane study suggest that plane crash fatalities rise for a period of *eight* days after the newspaper story. Hence, at the beginning of the present analysis of commercial plane crashes, an eight-day experimental period was adopted, extending 0–7 days after the date of the newspaper story about the murder–suicide.
16. Information on U.S. Air Carrier Accidents (1950–65) comes from the Office of Public Affairs, National Transportation Safety Board. For 1966–73 this information comes from *Annual Review of U.S. Air Carrier Accidents* (b).
17. Sometimes the "control period" for one story overlaps with the "experimental period" for

another story. When this happens, the statistical analysis is confounded. Hence, all such overlapping stories have been omitted from this analysis of commercial plane crashes. Because of this problem of "overlapping stories," four stories from the previous study of noncommercial plane crashes could no longer be used in the present analysis: the stories about (1) Kline and Bray; (2) McLachlan; (3) Stein; and (4) Walton. These stories could be used in the earlier study of noncommercial crashes, because that study employed a very restricted control period which extended only two days before the publicized murder–suicide. When such a restricted control period was used, the above four stories did not overlap.

18. For the period 1968–73 the term "publicized story" was defined as a story carried on (1) the front page of the *New York Times*, or (2) carried on the front page of the *Los Angeles Times*, or (3) appearing on the ABC, CBS, or NBC network evening news programs. Information on TV coverage is not available for the period prior to 1968; consequently, for this earlier period, a modified definition of "publicized story" must be used. For this earlier period a publicized story is defined as one carried on (1) the front page of the *New York Times*, or (2) the front page of the *Los Angeles Times*. These stories were found through a search of the *New York Times Index* under the headings "murder," "suicide," and "shootings." The *Los Angeles Times* stories were found through a search of the *Los Angeles Times* reference library (morgue) under the heading "murder–suicide." No attempt was made to search under other headings, such as "kidnappings," "hijackings," or "sabotage," which might have revealed additional stories about murder–suicide. However, one such story (about Frank) was found and used, because it occurred on the same day as another murder–suicide story (about Dotti), found through the conventional search procedure described above. As will be noted later, the statistical analysis to be used for commercial crashes requires examination of commercial crashes occurring before and after murder–suicide stories. Systematic information on plane crashes before one story was not available because this story occurred at the very beginning of the period (January 1, 1950) when the U.S. government began to publish systematic information on plane crashes. Hence, this story could not be used in the present study.

19. There is a very small number of "propeller to person" accidents in which a person is killed on the ground, typically as a result of walking into a spinning propeller. It is virtually certain that these accidents are not disguised murder–suicides; hence, these accidents were not examined in the present study.

20. This particular application of the randomization test has been suggested in a well-known text (Siegel, 152 56). Siegel notes that this randomization test requires very few assumptions about the data and is the most powerful available nonparametric interval scale test. The data used in this test consist of a list of the number of fatalities in each of the twelve plane crashes occurring in the experimental period (Table 2, col. 3) and an equivalent list for the control period (Table 2, col. 2). The analysis then proceeded as outlined by Siegel, except that a computer was used to facilitate calculations. The Mann–Whitney test, also nonparametric, might have been used in the present analysis, but this test is less powerful than the one employed and is more appropriate for use with ordinal-scale data.

21. Unfortunately, the number of cases in this study is too small to allow testing of the relative merits of points (1) and (2) mentioned in the text.

22. Note that three stories (examined here because they were in the earlier analysis of noncommercial plane crashes) were carried only by the television networks, not by any of the newspapers examined. If these three stories received publicity from newspapers other than those under study, this publicity was assumed to occur one day after the occurrence of the murder–suicide. This "assumed newspaper publicity date" is the date that has been recorded in Table 2, col. 1, for the three stories under discussion. All other dates in this column are of course actual rather than assumed newspaper publicity dates. Figures on newspaper circulation come from Ayer Press (yearly issues).

23. The observed correlation ($r = .441$) is significant at .002 if one uses the conventional significance test for r (described earlier in note 8). However, as was noted in that note, the conventional significance test requires stringent assumptions that probably do not hold for the data under analysis. Substituting the randomization test of significance described in note 8, one finds that the observed correlation, $r = .441$, is statistically significant at .014.

    One might argue that the observed positive correlation between newspaper circulation and the number of plane fatalities occurs because (1) the papers under study have increased their circulation over time, while (2) plane fatalities in the experimental period have also increased over time. The coexistence of these two positive secular trends would then imply that one should find a positive correlation between newspaper publicity and plane fatalities, even if newspaper publicity does not affect plane fatalities. This argument does not have merit because plane fatalities in the experimental period do *not* increase over time, as assumed in the above argument, but decrease instead. Hence, a negative correlation between newspaper publicity and plane fatalities would be expected if newspaper publicity has no effect on plane fatalities. Thus, the positive correlation actually observed ($r = .441$) is even more surprising than one would at first assume.

24. One might wish to see whether there is a relationship between the location of the publicity devoted to a murder–suicide and the location of commercial plane crashes occurring thereafter. However, such an analysis is probably rendered meaningless by the fact that commercial pilots travel to many cities and have the opportunity to read newspapers from all over the country. In consequence, one would not necessarily expect a correlation between the location of the publicity devoted to a murder–suicide story and the location of commercial plane crashes occuring thereafter.

As noted earlier in the paper, a detailed report of each commercial plane crash in the experimental and control periods is provided in individual *Aircraft Accident Reports*. Space does not permit an analysis of these detailed reports in the present paper; such an analysis will be presented in a future study.

25. In recent years, the term "cultural contagion" seems to have fallen into disfavor in the literature on collective behavior.

26. It should be stressed that, at present, one can only conjecture about the precise mechanisms causing the three or four day lag. This lag may result for many reasons, some of which are listed below: (1) the imitator of the publicized murder–suicide may not hear about that event until several days have elapsed; (2) the imitator of the publicized murder–suicide may need several days to come to a definite, explicit decision; (3) the imitator of the murder–suicide may need several days to make plans and to gain access to a plane. The concept of an "incubation period" can be plausibly applied only to some of the mechanisms just listed.

27. In the future, when videotape recorders become increasingly available, many people may be able to view and review television stories about murder–suicide. When this occurs, television might become a more effective channel of cultural contagion, if the argument proposed in the text is correct.

28. Of course, the First Amendment to the Constitution protects the right of the news media to publicize a suicide or murder–suicide story. The publicity accorded to such stories could be reduced only by the voluntary actions of the news media.

References

Ayer Press. 1950–1973. *Ayer Directory of Publications*. Philadelphia: Ayer Press.

Beaty, D. 1969. *The Human Factor in Aircraft Accidents*. London: Secker & Warburg.

Berkowitz, L. 1962. *Aggression: A Social Psychological Analysis*. New York: McGraw-Hill.

Britt, S. H. (ed.). 1970. *Psychological Experiments in Consumer Behavior*. New York: Wiley.

Cohen, J. B. (ed.). 1972. *Behavioral Science Foundations of Consumer Behavior*. New York: Free Press.

Comstock, G. 1975. *Television and Human Behavior: The Key Studies*. Santa Monica: Rand Corporation.

Comstock, G., and M. Fisher. 1975. *Television and Human Behavior: A Guide to the Pertinent Scientific Literature*. Santa Monica: Rand Corporation.

Comstock, G., and G. Lindsey. 1975. *Television and Human Behavior: The Research Horizon, Future and Present*. Santa Monica: Rand Corporation.

Corkindale, K. (ed.). 1973. *Behavioral Aspects of Aircraft Accidents*. Papers presented at the AGARD Aerospace Medical Panel Specialists' Meeting at Soesterberg, Netherlands.

Dirksen, C. J., and A. Kroeger. 1973. *Advertising Principles and Problems*. Homewood, Ill.: Irwin.

Engle, J. F., D. T. Kollat, and R. D. Blackwell. 1973. *Consumer Behavior*. New York: Holt, Rinehart & Winston.

Flanders, J. P. 1968. "A Review of Research on Imitative Behavior." *Psychological Bulletin* 69:316–37.

Gibbons, H. L., J. L. Plechus, and S. R. Mohler. 1967. "Consideration of Volitional Acts in Aircraft Accident Investigation." *Aerospace Medicine* 38:1057–59.

Goranson, R. E. 1969. "A Review of Recent Literature on Psychological Effects of Media Portrayals of Violence." In R. K. Baker and S. J. Ball (eds.), *Violence and the Media: A Staff Report to the National Commission on the Causes and Prevention of Violence*. Washington: Government Printing Office.

Jacoby, J. 1976. "Consumer Psychology: An Octennium." In M. R. Rosenzweig and L. W. Porter (eds.), *Annual Review of Psychology*. Palo Alto: Annual Reviews, Inc.

Jones, D. R. 1977. "Suicide by Aircraft: A Case Report." *Aviation Space Environmental Medicine* 48:454–59.

Klapper, J. T. 1960. *The Effects of Mass Communication*. New York: Free Press.

Lacefield, D. L., P. A. Roberts, and C. W. Blossom. 1975. "Toxicological Findings in Fatal Civil Aviation Accidents, Fiscal Years 1968–1974." *Aviation Space Environmental Medicine* 46:1030–32.

LeBon, G. 1895. *The Crowd*. London: Fisher Unwin.

Liebert, R. M., and N. S. Schwartzberg. 1977. "Effects of Mass Media." In M. R. Rosenzweig and L. W. Porter (eds.), *Annual Review of Psychology*. Palo Alto: Annual Reviews, Inc.

McGuire, W. J. 1968. "The Nature of Attitudes and Attitude Change." In G. Lindzey and E. Aronson (eds.), *The Handbook of Social Psychology*. Vol. 3. Reading: Addison-Wesley.

Mead, G. H. 1934. *Mind, Self, and Society: From the Standpoint of a Social Behaviorist*. Chicago: University of Chicago Press.

Michman, R. D., and D. W. Jugenheimer (eds.). 1976. *Strategic Advertising Decisions: Selected Readings*. Columbus, Ohio: Grid.

Mosteller, F., R. E. K. Rourke, and G. B. Thomas. 1970. *Probability with Statistical Applications*. Reading: Addison-Wesley.

Phillips, D. P. a:1974. "The Influence of Suggestion on Suicide: Substantive and Theoretical Implications of the Werther Effect." *American Sociological Review* 39:340–54.

————. b:1977. "Motor Vehicle Fatalities Increase Just After Publicized Suicide Stories." *Science* 196:1464–65.

————. c.1978. "Airplane Accident Fatalities Increase Just After Newspaper Stories About Murder and Suicide." *Science* 201:748–50.

————. d:1979. "Suicide, Motor Vehicle Fatalities, and the Mass Media: Evidence toward a Theory of Suggestion." *American Journal of Sociology* 84:1150–74.

Pitman, E. J. G. 1937. "Significance Tests Which May Be Applied to Samples from any Populations. II. The Correlation Coefficient Test." *Journal of the Royal Statistical Society* Series B 4:225–32.

Sandage, C. H., and V. Fryburger. 1975. *Advertising Theory and Practice*. Homewood, Ill.: Irwin.

Sanders, M. G., and M. A. Hofmann. 1975. "Personality Aspects of Involvement in Pilot-Error Accidents." *Aviation Space Environmental Medicine* 46:186–90.

Sanders, M. G., M. A. Hofmann, and T. A. Neese. 1976. "Cross-Validation Study of the Personality Aspects of Involvement in Pilot-Error Accidents." *Aviation Space Environmental Medicine* 47:177–79.

Siegel, S. 1956. *Nonparametric Statistics for the Behavioral Sciences.* New York: McGraw-Hill.

Singer, J. L. 1971. "The Influence of Violence Portrayed in Television or Motion Pictures upon Overt Aggressive Behavior." In J. L. Singer (ed.), *The Control of Aggression and Violence: Cognitive and Social Factors.* New York: Academic Press.

Stevens, P. J. 1970. *Fatal Civil Aircraft Accidents.* Bristol: Wright & Sons.

Surgeon General's Scientific Advisory Committee on Television and Social Behavior. 1972. *Television and Growing Up: The Impact of Televised Violence.* Washington: Government Printing Office.

Tarde, G. 1903. *The Laws of Imitation.* New York: Holt.

U.S. Department of Transportation. Periodic Volumes. *Airport Activity Statistics of Certificated Route Air Carriers.* Washington: Government Printing Office.

U.S. National Transportation Safety Board. a:1968–1973. *Briefs of Accidents U.S. Civil Aviation.* Washington: Government Printing Office.

U.S. National Transportation Safety Board. b:1966–1973. *Annual Review of U.S. Air Carrier Accidents.* Washington: Government Printing Office.

Vanderbilt University. Periodic Volumes. *Vanderbilt Television News Archives.* Nashville: Joint University Libraries.

Wolfgang, M. E. 1968. "Suicide by Means of Victim-Precipitated Homicide." In H. L. P. Resnick (ed.), *Suicidal Behaviors.* Boston: Little, Brown.

Yanowitch, R. E., J. R. Bergin, and E. A. Yanowitch. 1973. "Aircraft as an Instrument of Self-Destruction." *Aerospace Medicine* 44:675–78.

In these chapters from a recent book on public opinion and mass communication, James Lemert argues that theoretical "simple reductionism" has obscured the true relationship between communication and opinion, that elaborating election and influence frameworks for potential mass communication effects on public opinion enhances findings of communication influence, and that understanding the communication-opinion relationship requires specification and understanding of object as well as attitude change and participation as well as power. James B. Lemert is professor of journalism at the University of Oregon.

4

DOES MASS COMMUNICATION CHANGE PUBLIC OPINION AFTER ALL?

James B. Lemert

1
THE NEED FOR A NEW MODEL OF HOW THE MEDIA CHANGE PUBLIC OPINION

The mass media can, and probably do, change public opinion in the United States. But usually they don't do it in the way we think they have to. Common sense, the polls, and the accumulated mental habits of decades of social research all have led us to single out individual attitude change as both the necessary and the sufficient means of creating change in public opinion on an issue.

Mass media change the outcome of public opinion processes in a number of other ways, however—sometimes as much by what they don't do as by what they do. This book will explore a number of these other ways. Unfortunately, the evidence about these other ways often will be an amalgam of anecdotes and a few more carefully gathered research findings. This evidence is necessary at this time because theorists and mass media researchers often have neglected to study these media effects, have speculated about them without gathering evidence, or have investigated them in ways that seemed to foredoom finding very much. One purpose of this book will be to suggest some more productive areas of study.

From James B. Lemert, *Does Mass Communication Change Public Opinion After All? A New Approach to Effects Analysis*, pp. 1-37, 219-225. Chicago: Nelson-Hall, Inc., 1981. Reprinted by permission of the publisher and author.

As for the attitude-changing effects of mass media, an enormous collection of research findings is available, and we shall use it. But as we shall see later, even highly uniform and widespread changes in people's attitudes toward an issue are neither sufficient nor necessary to create a corresponding change in public opinion.

The Simple Reductionist Model

Ever since the brilliant work of Lazarsfeld and others at Columbia University in the 1940s, mass communication researchers have been living with an implicit, unarticulated set of assumptions about the relationship between the effects of the media on attitudes and on public opinion. These assumptions stimulated the gathering of a great deal of valuable evidence about media attitude effects, but they also tended toward a simple reductionist position that public opinion is a more-or-less straightforward sum of everybody's attitudes.

For our purposes, we can formulate at least three crucial corollaries of this simple reductionist view of the media and public opinion: First, if mass communication does produce massive attitude change toward an issue, that change is *sufficient* to have produced a change in public opinion. Second—and this is by no means the same as the first—if mass communication has *not* produced attitude change among its audience, public opinion change cannot have occurred. (In other words, attitude change is *necessary* for public opinion change.) Third, the attitudes of all members of media audiences count the same—that is, they are equally important in affecting the outcome of a public opinion process.

This simple reductionist approach, while never formally articulated, became the dominant tradition in mass media research. Other trends also contributed to this tradition. The developing social sciences consciously attempted to copy the data-gathering and testing methods used in the physical and biological sciences.

In the 1940s social psychology successfully applied these methods to the study of individual attitudes and attitude change, but the cost was high. Social psychologist Milton Rokeach suggests, for example, that the much more rapid progress made in the development of attitude measures helped lead the field away from other social psychological concepts, for which convenient

measurement devices were slower in developing.[1] For our purposes, then, the early development of social psychology rested
largely on the development of convenient operational definitions
of attitudes and thereby influenced the direction taken by public
opinion researchers.

In the late 1940s and early 1950s, political scientists borrowed
from social psychology and produced a series of important survey analyses of individual citizens' attitudes and voting behavior.[2]
In the mid-1950s, communication research began to develop as a
separate academic discipline influenced heavily by the concepts and
foci of social psychology and of one of its own applied fields,
speech. In those years, most active speech communication scholars
had a background in rhetoric, so they tended to concern themselves
with how and whether a communication (often by a source with
varying "ethos" or credibility) could change audience attitudes.

The developing mass media research tradition, then, sought to
explain media effects on public opinion by means of attitude
change. Even today, the single most frequently cited review of the
evidence about media effects is Joseph Klapper's *The Effects of
Mass Communication,* published in 1960. Klapper's book well
represents the implicit, simple reductionist assumptions of the
time. In his influential summary, Klapper concluded that "regardless of whether the effect in question be social or individual, the
media are more likely to reinforce than to change."[3] In mentioning
social and individual effects separately, Klapper's summary was
fairly unusual for its time, but the research findings he reviewed
concerned only individual-level effects. Therefore, it is hard to
see how a summary generalization about the book could have
mentioned social-level effects, without qualification or explanation,
unless some simple reductionist assumptions had been made.

For our purposes, we will treat any kind of reductionism as the
attempt to explain and reconstruct social-level phenomena from
individual-level data. The limits of reductionism remain an un-
solved and controversial problem today among social scientists—
controversial, that is, on those rare occasions when reductionism
is still discussed as a problem.[4] Political scientists Campbell, Converse, Miller, and Stokes concede that reconstructing collective
events from individual acts has not met with much success.[5] His-
torian Arnold Toynbee put it a little more strongly, saying that

our "ignorance" of how to relate collective and individual phenomena has characterized all scholarly efforts since Aristotle.[6]

A major key to relating individual and social levels appears to be, as Ernest Nagel and others put it, the development of "suitable correspondence rules" linking individual and collective concepts.[7] Most often, media researchers have embedded simple reductionist assumptions in their problem selection and analysis and have transmitted their assumptions to their students without even articulating them. We are entitled to the suspicion that, while many social scientists would have been a little uncomfortable with their simple reductionist "correspondence rules" if they had been required to make them explicit, the obvious successes of research in this tradition have rarely made it seem necessary to articulate and then to examine these rules. The three corollaries listed earlier—that attitude change is sufficient and necessary for public opinion change and that everybody's attitudes count the same—in effect are three such correspondence rules.

The reductionist effort to relate individual and social levels is not necessarily questioned here. In the field of public opinion, at least, this book will try to suggest some possible correspondence rules for converting individual attitude effects into public opinion effects. It will become obvious as we proceed that much more work remains to be done on these new "rules." But, as this book will show, rejecting simple reductionism is not at all incompatible with empirical research. In fact, using the approach to generate hypotheses is one of my chief aims.

In addition to the mental habits of media researchers, the simultaneous (but not entirely coincidental) development of the polling business helped promote a simple reductionist model of public opinion. For commercial reasons, preelection polls became a "loss leader" for pollsters in the 1940s. Today, polls have such a long record of generally successful prediction of elections that they form a key part of quite profitable businesses specializing in political campaigns. The model of public opinion implicit in polls is a simple reductionist one that now also goes well beyond election results to nonelectoral issues and trends: Public Opinion is treated as a set of percentages projected to a population.

A generation of social scientists now has grown to professional maturity without ever seeing a modern critic of polls focus on much besides the quality and representativeness of poll projections; the underlying model itself has not been seriously questioned since the late 1940s.[8] In his 1967 presidential address to the American Association for Public Opinion Research, Leo Bogart hinted at such criticism, but the book he later published as an expansion of these remarks seemed to back away from such a complaint: ". . . our understanding of public opinion is inseparable today . . . from the findings of public opinion surveys. . . ."[9]

Never mind, for the moment, that polls are vulnerable whenever we try to apply them to nonelectoral political life. Never mind also that their election predictions are notoriously vulnerable to changes in historical conditions. It is possible to accept poll results (1) as an indicator of public opinion under certain conditions and (2) as an indicator of population attitudes—*without in either case accepting the underlying simple reductionist model of public opinion*. We shall see how these things can be done in Chapters 2 and 9.

At the same time that new media research traditions and polling techniques were being developed and legitimized, the ranks of competent critics of the underlying simple reductionist model were thinned by age, career changes, and loss of confidence created by their inability to supply an alternative research strategy. Probably the last major criticism of the underlying public opinion model was provided in 1947 by Blumer, who felt forced to concede that he was hard pressed to suggest research techniques for the older model of public opinion he felt was realistic.[10] As long ago as 1937, Allport was flaying the "fictions" and "blind alleys" embedded in the older approach to public opinion that was then prevalent among journalists and scholars.[11]

In retrospect, then, we shouldn't have been surprised that the approach the polls embodied should have been regarded as a welcome, operationally viable alternative to the vague "group mind" tradition preceding it. Significantly, however, the single methodological suggestion Blumer was able to make was used two decades later by two political scientists, Warren Miller and Donald Stokes. The results of their study, and a succeeding one, can be interpreted as supporting some of the arguments made by Blumer.[12] But there was no sign that the political scientists involved had heard or read Blumer's argument.

Symptoms of the Model's Inadequacy

It would be both misleading and unfair to ignore several recent signs of dissatisfaction with what the prevailing research tradition has delivered to us.

Nimmo notes that the prevailing media effects tradition assumes that attitude change is necessary to produce voting change. He argues that, since researchers find that the media are unlikely to change attitudes, their results do not adequately account for those voting changes that do occur during a campaign. He believes that elections are won by breaking through the "weak perceptual barriers" of relatively uninvolved and uninformed voting blocs and getting them to view the alternative candidate as a better representative of their own basic values than the candidate of their own party.[13] Nimmo argues that the resulting "image" campaigns, which rely heavily on superficial television exposure of candidates and feedback from polls, have the effect of altering voting behavior *without* altering attitudes. It is often difficult to see how Nimmo's "perceptual" effects of mass communications would differ from an attitude effect, but that is beside the point.

My purpose here is to show that social scientists are beginning to reflect dissatisfaction with the ability of the traditional media effects approach to account for the social impact of mass media.

Blumler and McLeod explicitly criticized what they termed the " 'limited effects' model" of mass media impact, a model they attribute to Lazarsfeld et al.[14] Their panel study of 1970 voter turnout in Leeds, Great Britain, suggests that mass communication both increased and decreased turnout among young voters.

Another symptom of dissatisfaction is provided by the developing research field concerned with the "agenda-setting" function of the media. Like Nimmo, agenda-setting researchers seem to start by accepting the premise that the media aren't likely to change attitudes; but then they look for some other things that the media do change. In their original agenda-setting study, McCombs and Shaw found the issues given prominence by the media in the 1968 presidential campaign also were the issues that uncommitted voters thought were the most important in that campaign.[15] Shortly there-

after, McLeod, Becker, and Byrnes disputed some of these findings,[16] but this relatively new line of research has shown no signs
of ending with the earlier findings cited here.

A dramatic rediscovery among media researchers has been the
"new" interest area of "political communication." In the early
1970s, both the Association of Education in Journalism and the
International Communication Association formed political communication interest groups in their organizations. What these researchers seem to have most in common is the desire to look for
additional political effects to add to the list of attitude effects produced by the mass media. Political communication researchers who
are members of these two organizations have produced a notice-
able increase in references to Walter Lippmann's ideas about how
the media construct "fictions,"—that is, constructed versions of
political events, issues, and personalities.[17] These representatives of
reality are said to be the stimuli to which political actors respond
(see Chapter 3).

Political scientists also appear to have an increasing interest in
the mass media. Patterson and McClure have examined whether
television could change voters' minds.[18] Until recently, those few
political scientists who were concentrating on studies of mass communication published their results in journals outside of political
science, such as *Public Opinion Quarterly*. Now, however, several
major political science journals seem actively to be seeking media-
oriented research papers. Recently, for example, Miller, Goldenberg and Erbring matched newspaper content differences with
survey response differences in an effort to test newspaper effects
on trust/efficacy feelings.[19]

It seems fair to say that the signs of dissatisfaction cited so far
probably reflect unhappiness with the failure of the simple reductionist research strategy to test all the media effects it should have
tested; the dissatisfaction does not seem to have been with the
underlying assumptions themselves. For example, Blumler and
McLeod, in disputing what they (and others) term the "limited
effects" model of media impact, seem not to be disputing the underlying simple reductionist model itself. Their concern seems to be
whether researchers have prematurely closed the book on the list
of media effects, and they want to add some effects to the list.
And, in a tightly reasoned and elegant attack on the "limited

effects model" Chaffee and Choe recently showed that previous researchers had prematurely excluded the possibility that the mass media can help important numbers of people to make up their minds about who to vote for, during the campaign itself. (One of the findings regularly reported had been that almost everybody makes up their mind about their candidate either long before the fall campaign starts or on a last-minute whim.) What Blumler-McLeod and Chaffee-Choe apparently have in common is a challenge to the list of effects allowed by Klapper, but implicit agreement with Klapper about what to do with that list, once determined.[20]

Even the uses and gratifications approach illustrates the same point. A principal concern seems to have been to *locate* people who will be most susceptible to attitude change. These persons then are segregated and studied separately. Presumably the reason previous research failed to find strong media effects was that these "susceptibles" were mixed together with people who were using the mass media for other purposes. Again, it is the statements about media effects on individuals that are challenged, not the model underlying both new and old statements.

Similarly, a renewed interest in the way the media may help provide political socialization[21] *adds* evidence about an "extra" effect (i.e., attitude formation) to what we think we already know. But it does not change the way we translate individual-level effects into social ones. In Chapter 4, the reader will encounter some additional results suggesting that the mass media *can* have dramatic attitude formation/change effects. But in the case of this book, it is not *necessary* that the media have these effects. And, again, it is not even sufficient for public opinion change that such effects be produced (see Chapter 5).

However, a few stirrings of restlessness may concern the underlying simple reductionist model itself, though it is sometimes hard to tell.

In his recent presidential address to the American Political Science Association, Wahlke asserted that political behavior research had, among its other failings, consistently ignored level-of-analysis concerns. However, the remedies suggested concerned the other failings and, if anything, might worsen reductionist difficulties by concentrating on using bio-physiological concepts.[22]

Political communications researcher Maxwell E. McCombs wrote that traditional effects studies "typically . . . fragmented the ongoing process of communication. . . . What has passed for . . . theory has been, in reality, a loose collection of orientations toward data and a few empirical generalizations."[23] Unfortunately, the examples of promising new approaches cited were on the "let's add this one to the list" type.

British political scientist Colin Seymour-Ure has explicitly criticized our narrow focus on individual attitude change and has added a number of elite effects to the list. More importantly, he argues that a number of social-level effects have been ignored. In this connection, he lists individual-level and social-level effects.[24] His list even attempts to take both levels into account at the same time (for example, media effects on the relationship between individuals and bureaucracy).

But I hesitate for at least two reasons to say for certain that he is trying to do more than add to a list which may be incomplete, but which itself is unchallenged. First, despite the fact that the list of effects has been broken down into individual-individual, individual-political system, individual-group, group-group, and group-system categories, each effect has been treated as if it were a single effect. There appears to have been *no effort to construct new "correspondence rules" for the same effect at two different levels of analysis.* In that sense, Seymour Ure's approach might be regarded as still accepting a simple reductionist model. Second, most of the individual-level anecdotes he plugs into his list concern well-known political figures such as Richard Nixon and Edmund Muskie. Little attention is paid to effects on more ordinary members of the political system, so we are left to wonder how he would relate these individual effects to higher levels of analysis.

However, one relatively new approach may, in some of its applications and interpretations, represent an important departure from simple reductionism in the social sciences: "coorientation" research.

It would be misleading to say that a single data-gathering and conceptual approach characterizes coorientation research. But in very general terms, the coorientation school feels that mass media researchers, in their preoccupation with individual audience members' reactions to communications, have ignored higher-level units of analysis. These important higher-level units are created by comparing the *joint* attitudes and perceptions of two or more individuals who are *co*orienting themselves toward each other and toward some attitude object. For example, does each perceive accurately how the other feels about the object? Does each think the other agrees with him or her? If the answer to both questions is yes, does each know that the other knows he knows, and so on? It is possible to generate an enormous set of higher-level units in this way. The process creates variables that cannot be reconstituted from data provided by the individual respondent alone. Probably it will be a number of years before we can evaluate the usefulness of this approach.

So far, at least, the coorientation approach has been used somewhat more often for analysis of two-person groups than for analysis of the linkage between public opinion and decision-makers.[25] The latter analysis will be a major focus of this book.

Scheff and McLeod and Chaffee have pointed out some of the major conceptual and analytical problems involved in comparing the orientations of large aggregates of people (i.e., "public opinion") with those of an individual decision-maker.[26] Let me add some criticisms. For one thing, which people are compared with the decision-maker? Everybody—or what amounts to the same thing—a sample survey of everybody? Just the people who have expressed their attitudes to the decision-maker—in that sense, the only ones who have tried to *co*orient with him? For another thing, how do you determine the "dominant" orientation of this aggregate? The majority view? The plurality, if not a majority? On and on go the problems in coorientation research—problems that may have been settled much more often under pressure of having to define concepts operationally than in light of theoretical considerations. We will return briefly to consideration of the coorientation approach in Chapter 8.

Coorientation researchers and I have had to face many of the same conceptual problems in our separate approaches to the study of public opinion. In Chapter 2, I offer some of my own answers to some of these conceptual problems.

2
COMPONENTS OF THE PUBLIC OPINION MODEL

Our knowledge of the microscopic aspects of public opinion must remain of little avail until the relation of these bits of information to the operation of the political system in the large can be shown.
V. O. Key, Jr.

This chapter defines some components that are basic to an analysis of the role of the mass media in the public opinion process. Some ideas presented here are not new, having appeared in one form or another in widely scattered and often unappreciated works.

I have tried to resist the temptation to dwell on aspects of the public opinion process that are not of any particular use in developing the role of mass media. At times, though, it will be necessary to consider basic problems with what we think we know about certain nonmedia aspects of the public opinion processes.

Almost of necessity, this chapter runs the risk of disjointedness. It is composed of a series of definitions, each with a defense and an explanation. So perhaps a brief overview will be in order before we begin.

Public opinion will be given a definition that seems unusual at first glance. The most obvious objections to this definition will be considered and countered, and an attempt will be made to show that the definition does indeed encompass the kinds of things we usually think of as public opinion, while also having some unique advantages.

Then a distinction will be made between two public opinion situations; they will be termed the *influence framework* and the *election framework*.

Attitudes will be distinguished from public opinion; then attitudes toward issues will be distinguished from attitudes toward political participation. A series of attitude effects will be presented, with special emphasis on a concept called attitude object change.

Two other key elements—participation and power—will also be introduced and defined, with the suggestion that changes in participation and power can easily produce changes in public opinion.

PUBLIC OPINION

Public opinion is a perception imposed by the perceiver on information about citizen attitudes toward a publicly debated issue, personality, candidate, practice, or outcome.

A perception? Is public opinion a subjective phenomenon, then? Yes, it is, in the sense that the perceiver uses a more or less subjective process (1) to try to construct an impression of the current state of public opinion or (2) to try to anticipate a public reaction to a move then being considered. As Turner put it:

> Assessments of public opinion are continuously being made. . . . Since public opinion in an objective sense is a myth, an important aspect of public decision-making consists of accepting or repudiating the various assessments of opinion.[1]

But if the process of perceiving public opinion is indeed subjective, aren't we forced into an impossible research situation, with as many different versions of public opinion as there are people perceiving "it"?

While the process of perceiving public opinion may be subjective, it does not follow that it is idiosyncratic. A large number of political forces act to modify, "correct," or at least set limits to discrepancies among versions of public opinion that may be held by *key decision-makers.* Not least of these forces is pressure from the news media on decision-makers to define their current perception of public opinion on a controversial issue. And when relatively standardized national poll results are printed and broadcast, they will usually comprise part of the information about attitudes that is taken into account by decision-makers in forming their perceptions. Furthermore, serious misjudgments of public opinion may cost the decision-maker dearly.

In a valuable and neglected study of letter-writing to President Franklin D. Roosevelt, Sussmann reported many cases in which FDR's perception of public opinion on an issue did not coincide with perceptions held by members of Congress. In many cases, FDR pressured recalcitrant legislators by stimulating letter-writing to them by their own constituents:

> Reading this mail, the members of Congress became aware that even in their home districts it was the President, rather than they, who was coming to have first claim on the voters' allegiance. . . . Nor could the congressmen any longer claim a monopoly of knowledge of what the folks back home had on their minds. Roosevelt had new ways of assessing public opinion, including the polls and the mail [to FDR].[2]

But at least twice it was FDR, not the legislators, whose perception of public opinion was too idiosyncratic. His two misperceptions resulted in (1) a "colossal blunder . . . from the standpoint of legislative strategy" and (2) one of his two most notable failures to mobilize public support for a policy he wanted.[3]

Perhaps the ultimate "corrective" for an idiosyncratic perception of public opinion is when a major candidate goes down to ignominious defeat because his election strategy was based on that misperception. Converse, Clausen, and Miller interpret Goldwater's landslide defeat in 1964 as resulting largely from a misperception ". . . of that political reality which becomes important in winning votes and elections."[4] Goldwater's campaign decision-makers were misled by waves of enthusiastic mail, and Goldwater failed to move toward the center of the political spectrum in order to attract more votes.

So idiosyncratic assessments of what public opinion is can be very costly, politically, for key decision-makers.

Note that the political pressures exerted toward consistency are most likely to affect key decision-makers, who will often be elected or unelected government officials or legislators, political party officials, lobbyists, journalists, corporation public relations executives and so on. In cases where it seems necessary to gather and assess information about citizen attitudes, then, the penalty for idiosyncratic perceptions usually is greater for those decision-makers who ought to be most aware of public opinion. It is no accident, then, that the several studies of "pluralistic ignorance" almost uniformily show that the typical "man on the street" has perceptions of public opinion that are grossly discrepant from the information gathered by the researchers.[5] Presumably, key decision-makers' perceptions would have been closer to the mark, but to the best of my knowledge none of the "pluralistic ignorance" research has compared decision-makers' perceptions with those held by citizens under less pressure to be "correct."

In any event, though, my emphasis on key decision-makers means that the number of persons whose public opinion perceptions are critical to the political outcome is greatly reduced most of the time. Therefore, the subjectivity problem—the problem of getting inside the head of the perceiver—begins to shrink to more manageable size.

Nevertheless, it *is* possible to ask many people about their public opinion perceptions, such as in the "pluralistic ignorance" studies cited above. And under some conditions it seems *necessary* to do so. Such conditions came together in the November 1978 statewide tax election in Oregon. On the ballot were two competing property tax relief measures. If both passed, a provision in one of them required that the one receiving the greater majority would be the only one adopted. Voters therefore were placed in the position of having to guess what other voters would do. Based on our interviews with voters leaving the polls, it appears that as many as half the votes one of the two measures got came from people who were more afraid of the other measure's getting a majority than in favor of the one they voted for.[6] Since both measures failed, this was another case of "pluralistic ignorance." In such cases, the ballot itself invites voters to base their decisions on their perceptions of what others would do. The 1980 Carter-Reagan-Anderson race may boil down to the same kind of perceptual situation: Do anti-Reagan voters think Anderson has a chance to win?

Except in unusual circumstances, then, only the perceptions of relatively small numbers of key decision-makers matter much when we consider the linkage between public opinion and public policy. But how do we get at public opinion even if "it" is inside fewer heads? The job has already been done—and several times, at that.

▶ Remember Herbert Blumer? In Chapter 1, we saw that his tentative, relatively diffident suggestion about how researchers could study public opinion was later independently used by a succession of political scientists—including Miller and Stokes and, using the same data, Cnudde and McCrone. Neither pair of researchers referred to Blumer or to the specific problem of measuring a concept called public opinion. As part of a larger study, Miller and Stokes had asked more than one-hundred congressmen for their perceptions of constituency opinion on three broad issues and then tried to see how much influence these perceptions had on the way each legislator voted. Roughly similar kinds of studies have been done with state legislators—obviously influenced by Miller and Stokes' example, not Blumer's research suggestions.

▶ A number of coorientational studies have measured perceptions of public opinion and compared these perceptions with attitudes of members of the relevant public (see Grunig and Stamm[7] for a partial summary). In one study, for example, Martin et al. found that daily newspaper editors in Wisconsin wrote headlines for stories about a student demonstration that were more in accord with their perception of reader views than with their own attitudes toward the student protests.[8] Thus far at least, a number of the coorientational studies done by communication researchers have shown some conceptual difficulties in determining how best to define the "real" state of mind of the relevant public. Nevertheless, these studies clearly have attacked the subjectivity problem, with useful results.

▶ Both congressional and coorientational studies asked decision-makers to describe their perceptions, but other means of getting at subjective impressions of public opinion are available. Sussmann's study of letter-writing to FDR was done after Roosevelt's death. She drew large samples of the input—the letters themselves. She investigated the procedure Roosevelt established to have the letters summarized for him. She was able to reconstruct, from these summaries and from interviews with his associates, some of his perceptions. From the same sources, she was able to infer that Roosevelt placed greater reliance on letters as a source of constituent opinion than on polls, which were then relatively new. And in several cases, Roosevelt's speeches and decisions themselves seemed to have been in response to, or in anticipation of, a version of public opinion he had constructed for himself. In short, although asking decision-makers directly for their perceptions has some methodological advantages, it is not the only available technique.

Sussmann's approach is not the only indirect technique, either. Pressures from journalists and from political colleagues often lead decision-makers to articulate their perceptions of public opinion, whether they want to or not. For instance, the public outcry immediately after the firing of Special Prosecutor Archibald Cox in October 1973 led Presidential Assistant Alexander Haig to characterize public reaction as a "firestorm." Among his concessions (to "public opinion"?) following the "firestorm," President Nixon promised the Senate that he would give its leadership the ability to prevent a summary firing of the next special prosecutor.

Some writers, such as Bruce H. Westley, have asserted that terms "such . . . as 'public opinion' . . . have almost no scientific or intellectual standing today."[9] I would agree that the plethora of meanings given in the past to "public opinion" by different theorists and researchers has been less than helpful. But I would suggest that the pragmatism which seemed to bolster simple reductionist research efforts remains an important criterion to assess any conception of "public opinion." Simple reductionism, in my view, has failed several pragmatic tests. It doesn't explain old media effects findings very well and it hasn't generated much productive new research. So I shall be perfectly content to appeal to pragmatism: if productive new research ideas are not generated by my approach, and if my approach doesn't explain old anomalies and contradictions better, then my conception of public opinion will have failed the test. I hope that we shall see.

What we have seen so far is that empirical research *can* be done using the definition I am proposing. Further, many things we commonly regard as public opinion—polls and elections, for example —are *not* ruled out by this definition, as we shall see in the next section.

ELECTION AND INFLUENCE FRAMEWORKS

Perceptions are imposed on information about citizen attitudes within two general situational frameworks: (1) *elections* and (2) a less structured, much more frequent *influence framework*.

As recurrent ritual, elections help maintain the potency of public opinion as a factor to be considered in the political influence framework. Elections also help maintain the visibility and legitimacy of polls as a reflection of public opinion, a matter we shall discuss in more detail later.

But as an everyday political matter, public opinion perceptions occur in the political influence framework, not in the election framework. In the influence framework, decision-makers may receive information about citizen attitudes in a great variety of forms, either *directly* (e.g., from letters, telegrams, phone calls, feedback from crowds) or *indirectly* (e.g., from reports of informants, polls, editorial expressions, letters to the editor, news media definitions of the state of public opinion).

In the election framework, however, there are very few kinds of information: the voting outcomes, the turnout, and (when done) interviews with people who have just voted. Further, unlike the influence framework, there is broad agreement about the legitimacy of these three limited forms of information in the election framework. There still may be disagreement about what an election result means, but there is broad agreement on the information to be interpreted. The influence framework, however, leaves more room for variation because there is less consensus about what forms of information should be considered. In the influence framework decision-makers can (1) select only some of the diverse forms of information about citizen attitudes, rejecting the rich variety of others and/or (2) weight one form of information more heavily than another (polls versus letters from constituents, for example), while attending to both of them, and/or (3) pay more attention to

a poll done by Gallup than a poll done by Harris, or more attention to letters written by literate constituents than by less literate
ones—and so on.

Greater perceptual variability is possible in the influence framework than in the election framework for another reason, too. In
an election, the issues and the options are generally more simplified
than in the influence framework, where the matter may not yet have
even reached the formal agenda of the political system.[10] Furthermore, because of the much greater legitimacy attached to election
outcomes, decision-makers have a much greater tendency not to
dispute whether citizens acquiesce in a decision outcome. In the
more unstructured influence framework, however, citizen acquies-
cence will often be a central point of dispute between winners and
losers in a policy decision.

Despite all this, it is a mistake to assume that no variations will
occur in the way The Voice of the People is heard in elections. Almost invariably, the news media report alternative interpretations
of the meaning of election outcomes, some by contending interest-
group spokesmen and others by political reporters and presumably
nonpartisan pollsters and social scientists. Further, winning candidates often claim the vote "mandated" various policies they
espoused. Although a great deal of older evidence suggests that a
majority of voters don't usually make choices on the basis of specific policy alternatives, the mandate is an old political game. Even
after elections, then, observers often debate What Public Opinion
Was Saying, and especially *why*.

A consistent theme in this book will be that social scientists have
tended to regard elections (and their surrogate, the polls) as the
principal avenue by which public opinion is expressed. As a means
of expressing attitudes, voting has therefore also received much
more attention than other acts of participation, and our knowledge of how the media affect public opinion has suffered as a
result (see Chapter 5). The reason the influence framework should
have received far more attention from public opinion analysts was
stated well, ironically, by an election specialist:

> In the American institutional context, direct control [by elec-
> tions, of public policy] is difficult to imagine. The impact of any
> or many elections is limited by . . . the diverse checks and bal-

ances . . . the proliferation of nonelected public authorities, the powers of bureaucracies and courts, and the undisciplined party system. *However, the very dispersal of power which makes control unlikely also makes influences more probable.* In . . . conflicts and bargaining . . . some agency is likely to support the vital interests of any significant number of voters. (Emphasis added.) [11]

The term "influence framework" is used because, at best, public opinion is only one of many competing influences on decision-makers. Sometimes several competing influences all may act in roughly the same direction (e.g., Burstein and Freudenberg[12]). In such cases, we are talking primarily about "competition" in a variance-accounted-for sense. But probably more often we are talking about public opinion (and compatible "forces") competing *against* several other potential influences. A wide variety of factors other than public opinion may be aligned with, or opposed to, public opinion in the influence framework. Some of the other factors include advice from the decision-makers' colleagues, activities of lobbyists and interest groups, the decision-makers' own ambitions and policy preferences, advice from staff, and so on.

In our political culture, most decisions tend to be made in the influence framework while most of the political razzmatazz revolves around Election Day. While there may be such a thing as Influence Day, it doesn't seem to be scheduled far enough in advance to be printed on the calendars we get from our insurance agents.

The influence framework is *not* equivalent to what we usually think of as the period between elections. It includes, as well, information about citizen attitudes that may be coming in during an election campaign. Such information—letters, polls, donations, bumper stickers, the size and enthusiasm of crowds—is much more like influence framework information than like election framework information. In contrast with election results—where everybody knows the limited types of information to pay attention to—the information coming in during the campaign is much more variable and there are few ground rules determining which kinds of information about citizen attitudes are important. In short, the influence framework includes both campaign and noncampaign periods.[13] The judgmental situation is essentially the same.

One other thing before we go on to the next section: My distinction between influence and election frameworks is not intended to rule out the consideration of previous election results as one set of information about citizen attitudes in the influence framework. That is, decision-makers may very well refer to previous elections during their influence framework considerations. And, of course, they may very well try to anticipate how voters would react at the next election. The distinction between the two frameworks is based on major differences in the information available and in the complexity of the perceptual process.

ATTITUDES

An attitude is a state of affect felt by the individual toward what is, for that individual, a psychological object.

There are nearly as many definitions of this concept as there are writers in the field. For example, some distinguish between *opinion* (what the individual says or puts on a questionnaire) and *attitude* (what the individual *really* feels). We shall not use the vocabulary of that particular distinction, though it is obvious that attitude measures often get what the respondent wants to give. The term *opinion* will be reserved for use in the higher-level term *public opinion*.

As defined, the individual's attitude has two components: the feeling state (affect) and the object of that feeling state. Let's consider each in turn.

We shall follow traditional attitude theory in characterizing the affective component as having *direction* and *intensity*. Direction refers to whether the sign of the affect is positive (favorable), neutral, or negative. Intensity refers to how positive or negative the affect is. Does the individual like it a lot, or just a little?

What is a psychological object? Anything that the individual considers to be one: a song, the singer of that song (or maybe both the song and the singer together), a photo, a time of day, a job, a house, the idea of world peace, a flower, a poet, Edward Kennedy, all or some politicians, and so on.

In addition to direction and intensity, attitudes have *salience*. As used here, salience involves *both* the affective and the attitude object components. A salient attitude is one on which a large number of other attitudes depend and is usually a rather central attitude in the daily life of the individual. For example, attitudes toward oneself generally will be more salient than attitudes toward many public affairs issues discussed in mass media. A successful attack on a salient attitude probably would require a much greater amount of reorganization among dependent or related attitudes than a successful attack on a peripheral, isolated attitude object. It might be easier to produce change by reducing the connection between the object of the communication and the salient attitude.[14]

People may hold intense attitudes that are not salient, but the reverse probably is not true. One way to distinguish between salient and intense but peripheral attitudes was demonstrated by Stouffer. During the height of media coverage of the U.S.-USSR Cold War, Stouffer asked a national sample of Americans about what was worrying them. Worries about work, home, and family predominated. Less than 1 percent mentioned the communist threat. Even when the questions were more and more explicit about international political affairs, war, and so on, far less than 10 percent spontaneously mentioned the threat of communism. But when given an attitude intensity question that asked respondents to rate how great a danger American communists were to the country, more than 40 percent rated them a very great danger or a great danger.[15] For the less than 10 percent who spontaneously mentioned communism as worrying them, American communism was probably a salient attitude object. But many more people also rated it strongly as a threat, and we can conclude that these people held attitudes about communism that were roughly as intense, but not as salient.

ATTITUDE EFFECTS

Traditionally, attitude research has tended to concentrate on two kinds of changes in affect—*attitude change* and *attitude reinforcement*—and has tended to view them, at least conceptually, as mutually exclusive phenomena. Somewhat less attention has been paid to two changes that involve the attitude object component—*attitude formation* and *attitude object change*.

Types of Attitude Change

In common-sense terms, we generally think of attitude change only as complete *conversion* from one point of view to its opposite.

In research practice, however, attitude change has generally included much more than conversion. Figure 2.1 illustrates the many kinds of attitude change that researchers tend to treat as the same. Suppose a researcher has respondents rate some concept on an evaluative scale, then presents them with a communication about that concept and has them fill out the scale again.

Very often, the methods researchers use to score shifts in affect lump together into a composite attitude change score all the changes listed below the scale in Figure 2.1. It will be important for us to separate them *when we can*. To complicate the scoring of attitude change even more, researchers often count as attitude change only those shifts *toward* the direction advocated by the communication. When this happens, other shifts we might consider as attitude change are either subtracted from the attitude change score or are tallied separately in categories that may confuse attitude change with attitude reinforcement.

In general, where possible, we will specify the type of attitude change under consideration. Otherwise, the term "attitude change" will have to refer to the most general case—*the movement of affect toward a new sign.*

Attitude Reinforcement

The second general kind of affect shift is attitude reinforcement, defined as an increase in the intensity of affect felt toward an object without a change in sign.

Attitude Formation

The third effect mass communication can have is attitude formation. In principle, attitude formation involves both the recognition of an attitude object and the learning of an affective response to it. A good example of this process occurs when a mother tells a child, "That's a no-no!" Both the object and the affect presumably are communicated in that statement. But attitude formation is not limited to children even though we have surprisingly little clear evidence about the process with adults. For many of us, Rep. Peter Rodino was, in January 1973, a "new" attitude object. The ways in which we attached our own affective response probably

Figure 2.1
Five Types of Attitude Change

Good —:——:——:——:——:——:——:— Bad
extremely +3   quite +2   slightly +1   neither 0   slightly -1   quite -2   extremely -3

Type of Attitude Change	Does Sign Change?	Intensity Up?	Intensity Down?	Examples Before/After
Conversion	yes	no	no	+2 to -2
Super conversion	yes	yes	—	+2 to -3; -1 to +3
Ordinary change	yes	—	yes	+1 to 0; -2 to +1
Minor change	no	—	yes	+2 to +1; -3 to -2
Commitment	yes	yes	—	0 to +1

differed, but affect toward him was learned by millions of Americans as the House impeachment inquiry began. The same would be true of Howard Jarvis in 1978, a man known to relatively few Americans prior to the California "tax revolt."

One reason for ambiguities in evidence about adults' attitude formation is that *formation* may be scored and treated as if it were *change*. Attitude scoring tends to confuse commitment effects with attitude formation. (As we'll see later in this book, I've had to combine formation with change in the study of the "bandwagon" effects. But at least I don't claim the effects to be an attitude change.)

Another cluster of reasons for ambiguities resides in the fact that most of the relatively few studies of attitude formation have placed it within the framework of childhood socialization. Emphasis on socialization of young children, in turn, led to a deemphasis of media impact on attitude formation in two ways.

First, the effect of concentrating on the young has been to pit the mass media against powerful agents of socialization—parents, peers, and schools—at an age when these other agents were thought to be at their greatest power in attitude formation. For example, the prevailing consensus among students of political socialization has been that parents are critical in transmitting to their young children the basic political values that are thought to mold and pervade most of the political attitudes developed in later life.[16] There has been general agreement that, as the child enters school and then adolescence, peers and teachers begin to exert influence. Only fairly recently have researchers rediscovered the opportunity to study the role of mass media in socializing adolescents. Even now, slight attention has been paid to socialization processes among mature adults, and researchers who have concentrated on this group have tended to look at the acquisition of skills and habits rather than attitude formation.[17]

Second, attitude formation is not limited to the socialization process. People habitually recognize new attitude objects and attach an affective response to them whether or not they are being prepared for new social roles!

This brings us to the final general class of attitude effects, attitude object change. It is hard, sometimes, to distinguish attitude formation from object change.

Attitude Object Change

In a sense, attitude object change is the substitution of one attitude object for another. In its purest form, when attitude object change occurs, we would expect both the object and its associated affect to be replaced by an entirely new object and *its* associated affect. The importance of attitude object change is that it might therefore lead to changes in the way we react and behave *without any change in the affect felt toward either the old or the new object*.

Conceptually, both attitude formation and one kind of attitude object change involve the recognition of a new attitude object. It is generally more useful to distinguish between them by whether the affective response is new or whether it has been previously associated with the object. If the affect is also new, it is attitude formation; if old, it is object change.

Perhaps our tendency to create euphemisms represents what I mean by object change in a relatively clear and distilled form. We say an unmarried girl is "in trouble," a euphemism that tends to divert attention from her past behavior to her present predicament. The Nixon administration referred to "protective reaction strikes" in an effort to deemphasize the fact that the United States was still dropping bombs on North Vietnamese and Viet Cong targets after it had declared a bombing halt and to emphasize the defensive character of the air strikes. "Public power" is the term now used to refer to what conservatives bitterly attacked as "socialistic ownership of the means of production" during the Tennessee Valley Authority controversy many years ago. During the Cuban missile crisis, the United States imposed a "quarantine" on Russian ships, studiously avoiding the more warlike term "blockade." Advertising is full of euphemisms. Remember Lanolin (sheep grease)? Presumably people would rather buy the former than the latter. Similarly, it makes a difference whether journalists accept "sidewise waffling" or use the term "recession" when referring to a decline in our gross national product.

Some writers feel that what I am calling attitude object change is not the substitution of one object for another so much as it is a change in the attributes to which one reacts regarding a more or less constant attitude object.

These writers feel that the change in the object is only a substitution of a part (or aspect) for the whole, or of one part for another part. For example, in this view the euphemism "public power" substitutes a more favorable aspect (a utility operated for public benefit) for a less favorable one (ownership by the state). Both aspects are part of the whole. In this interpretation, the euphemism merely elevates the visibility and prominence of one aspect over another. Since most attitude objects in politics and in other kinds of social communication are complex and multidimensional, they are indeed susceptible to shifts in the criteria and dimensions used to judge them. As Newcomb, Turner, and Converse put it:

> We may perceive another person as being, among other things, a good conversationalist, a sloppy dresser, and a likely target when we need to borrow money. Although we may have attitudes toward each of these perceived characteristics separately, we also form attitudes toward the person as a whole, for we cognize him as a whole. . . . The fact that we may have such mixed reactions even to an object that we perceive as a whole at one level . . . means that we may express different attitudes when the cognitive context suggests a less inclusive aspect of the object.[15]

We just don't know enough yet about object change to settle the question whether (or when) object or attributes are exchanged. Prevailing attitude measurement techniques are insensitive to object change, because the only change they allow to show is a change in affect, and many object changes can take place *without* a change in expressed affect. Furthermore, even if object change did produce a change in the affect being expressed on attitude scales, it would be scored as "attitude change" because present attitude measurement devices implicitly assume that the object being asked about is a constant, while only affect is a variable. There is little question that students of attitudes and polling have tended to operate on what Bogart calls a "single opinion" model:

The prevailing model underlying our discipline is that of the single opinion. A person holds an opinion, which he communicates to an interviewer. When he is influenced to change his mind, he replaces his former opinion with another one. This model has the virtue of great simplicity, but it makes no sense, because conflicting and contradictory opinions may be held simultaneously and because they constantly jostle each other for dominance.[19]

Another unsettled question remains about object change. Some writers feel that object change is not really distinct from attitude change. In fact, Newcomb, Turner, and Converse feel that object change is really the primary method of producing attitude change.[20] In this view, new information about the object alters the criteria for evaluating it, leading in turn to changes in affect. Object change then would be a necessary way station on the road to attitude change, and thus always would be reflected indirectly by scales measuring changes in affect.

This would be a more convincing argument if it did not imply satisfaction with measurement practices that are not sensitive to object change except through affect change. What happens if the object changes—perhaps as part of a defensive reaction to a message—while the affect shows no sign of change? This result is quite possible without changes in affect. The implication is that traditional attitude measurement practices would be insensitive to these effects, and Guerrero and Hughes have shown that these effects can and do occur.[21] Rokeach also has cited results that, in my view, suggest that the failure to separate attitude object change from affect change will almost certainly lead us astray.[22]

Unless our methods allow object change to be expressed as easily as affect change, we probably never will be able to settle (1) when or whether objects or attributes change and (2) whether object change is just another way of talking about attitude change.

To detect object change, we need to give respondents the chance to tell us more about the objects they are rating. Edelstein has tried to apply such an approach to the study of how people choose their news media. He gave respondents the chance to express media preferences in relation to specific topics they themselves helped provide, and to say what attributes they were using in their choices.[23] A study by Grothe of "attitude change" among American tourists in the Soviet Union illustrates both how useful open-response items can be and how misleading standard fixed-response items can be. The open-response items allowed respondents to specify aspects of the USSR they liked least and most. For these items, it became apparent that they liked their contact with Russian people a lot, but they still did not like the Soviet government and political system. The scale measuring attitude change used a fixed concept—the USSR—and recorded only a slight net improvement in the favorability of attitudes toward the USSR.[24] This result almost certainly masked the extensive object differentiation shown by the open-ended items.

In summary, we don't yet know enough about attitude structure to settle many questions about object change. But unless we begin to try to isolate object change phenomena, we probably never will know enough.

Attitude object change may be an important effect of messages received through the mass media, especially among normally inactive and relatively unsophisticated persons. At the moment, object change seems the best available concept for explaining how certain changes in public opinion processes are produced. The reason for its importance is that most members of the population do not seem spontaneously to have worked out very many relationships among their political attitude objects.[25] Unlike political elites who consciously use the mass media to articulate issues for others, the great majority of our population may be vulnerable to attitude object change. However, I should point out quickly here that many researchers dispute this picture on nonelites. These researchers feel such a picture greatly underestimates the presence of ideology in the population.[26] Nevertheless, I'd suggest a relatively productive way of testing whether there be mass-elite differences in ideology would be through testing for object change differences.

The way elites and the mass media define issues can have important consequences for a population that seems relatively susceptible to messages directing their attention toward certain relations among attitude objects and away from others. For instance, McClosky, Hoffmann, and O'Hara reported that:

> ... followers of each [major U.S.] party, often ignorant of the issues and their consequences, find it difficult to distinguish their beliefs from those of the opposition and have little reason to be concerned with the consistency of their attitudes. . . . In short, if we mean by ideology a coherent body of informed social doctrine, it is possessed mainly by the articulate leadership, rarely by the masses.[27]

Attitude object change, then, is one of several possible effects of the way the mass media *define situations* (Chapter 3).

ISSUE ATTITUDES vs. PARTICIPATION ATTITUDES

To this point in our discussion of attitude effects you have probably been thinking mostly of attitudes toward objects such as political parties, candidates, issue proposals, the media, and so on. And why not? The topic of this book is public opinion, after all, and what could have more to do with public opinion processes than these kinds of attitude objects? If you agree that this is reasonable, you are in good company. In fact, attitude and attitude change studies historically have been preoccupied with this kind of *issue-centered* attitude.[28] However, the distinction between attitudes toward issues and attitudes toward the behavior of political participation is crucial to understanding how the mass media affect public opinion.

For purposes of this book, issue-centered attitudes are what we normally think of as attitudes in public affairs matters. Issue objects concern such general areas as policy proposals, political groups, candidates, government(s), the quality of life, the presidency and/or the current president, the economy, and so on. Attitudes toward behavior, on the other hand, may include such objects as the situation within which the behavior would have to take place, one's sense of adequacy in performing a given act or acts, the consequences of a given act if successfully completed, and so on. Often, attitudes toward *issues* are the focus of political communication in the media; attitudes toward *behavior* tend not to be, *especially when the behavior involved is participation in the influence framework.*

Judging from the history of thought about attitudes and public opinion, it has always been rather easy to ignore the problem of attitudes toward behavior. In fact, early in the history of social psychology, one of the major justifications for focusing on issue attitudes was the presumption that if one knew about attitudes, one knew about behavior. Attitudes were viewed as more or less decisive predispositions toward behavior. Therefore, what little early work was done on attitudes toward behavior tended to be outside the mainstream of social psychology. Rokeach believes that separating issue attitudes from behavioral attitudes has "severely retarded the growth not only of attitude theory but also of attitude-change theory."[29] In my view, this separation also helped for many years to hide the inadequacy of a simple reductionist approach to mass media and public opinion. It did this by directing our attention away from political participation as a means of communicating citizens' issue attitudes to decision-makers.

Nevertheless, it is now extremely difficult to pretend that issue-type attitudes predict behavior. In a major review of attitude-behavior studies, Wicker concluded: "Most socially significant questions involve overt behavior, rather than people's feelings, and the assumption that feelings are directly translated into action has not been demonstrated."[30]

Equally harsh things have been said by a number of other writers, including Schramm, who seems to have concluded that the discrepancy between attitudes and actions has been so great that it is better not to pay as much attention to attitude effects as to other kinds of media effects.[31]

Another sort of reaction does not deemphasize or dismiss the results of attitude studies. It does just the opposite, in perhaps an unintentionally ironic contrast to the way social psychology originally justified its preoccupation with issue attitudes. Instead of saying that we study attitudes because they predict behavior, this school of thought says, in effect, we study attitudes because they do *not* relate to behavior. A slight variant of this view has also been expressed by Chaffee and others in the communication theory literature.[32]

A number of other writers, however, are making and using the
distinction between attitudes toward issues and attitudes toward
behavior. Rokeach distinguishes between attitudes toward an "object" (his name for issue objects, as I've defined them) and attitudes toward the "situation." The situation generally is a social
context that may or may not be regarded as an appropriate opportunity for behavioral expression of issue attitudes. Thus, Rokeach
feels issue attitudes and situational attitudes "affect behavior in direct proportion to their perceived importance with respect to each
other."[33]

Fishbein also proposes that behavior is a joint function of issue
attitudes and situational factors, but his vocabulary and level of
analysis differ slightly from those of Rokeach. For Fishbein, behavior is a function of (1) attitude toward behavior, (2) "normative beliefs" (which include what I am calling issue attitudes) and
(3) motivation to comply with "normative beliefs."[34]

In a test of Fishbein's approach, Ajzen has reported results
which appear to show that there is not much difference between
Rokeach's formulation and Fishbein's more fully elaborated approach. The motivations aroused by the social situation appeared
to determine whether attitudes toward behavior or "normative beliefs" best predicted behavior.[35]

EFFICACY AS AN ATTITUDE TOWARD PARTICIPATION

A major focus of American political science almost from the
outset was a kind of behavior: the act of voting. Ironically, though,
it was not until the marriage of social psychological and survey
approaches to political science that scales were developed to measure attitudes toward voting and other acts of political participation. Since then, and for thirty years, political scientists have been
using a measure they call *political efficacy,* and probably it is still
the single most frequently used measure of attitudes toward participation. Political efficacy refers to the individual's feelings that
he or she can accomplish things through political participation.
Generally, efficacy feelings have been strongly related to the act
of voting and to even more active kinds of campaign activities.[36]
The relationship has been found so often and in so many different
elections that we can probably feel safe in saying that, if two

people have exactly the same strength of voting preferences, the one with the greater sense of efficacy will be more likely to vote.

Remember when I said that public opinion was a perception imposed on information about citizen attitudes? Voting is one way the citizen can communicate some information about his or her issue attitudes, but it is hardly the only way. Rarely—and only very recently—has political science extended its interest in efficacy and participation beyond election campaigns to the rest of the influence framework (see Chapter 5). And rarely has its interest in measuring attitudes toward participation gone beyond extremely general attitudes, such as feelings of efficacy, to measures that either incorporate the situation in which participation is to take place or specify the particular act of participation.

In Chapters 5 and 6, we shall look some more at how journalists and political communications influence participation by means of intermediary effects on issue attitudes, attitudes toward participation, or both.

PARTICIPATION

Participation in public opinion processes is the act of expressing issue-related attitudes, either by voting in the election framework or by a great variety of acts in the influence framework.

Most frequently, participation is necessary in order for the attitude to become visible to the decision-maker. But because of the way we have defined public opinion, information about citizen attitudes can come to a decision-maker *without* active *participation* by citizens on one occasion: *when and if the results of a survey are either made public or transmitted privately to some decision-maker.*

In the election framework, the basic form of participation is the act of voting. As mentioned earlier, other activities during the election campaign are not included in the election framework because the processes of imposing a perception on information about the extent and intensity of support are much more like those taking place in the influence framework. Further, voting participation seems to comprise a distinctly different mode of political participation, separable from several other distinct modes.[37]

Voting is probably the easiest and most routinized act of participation. Journalists routinely provide far more help to voting in elections than they do to any form of participation in the influence framework, probably because they feel it admirable and nonpartisan to facilitate voter turnout (see Chapter 6). Compared to many other countries, though, voting turnout is low in U.S. national elections, and even lower for state and local elections.

Even though voting participation is relatively low in the United States, other forms of participation occur even less often. While all their percentages may be too high because of social desirability factors, Verba and Nie estimate that more than five times as many people vote regularly as contact public officials to influence them concerning some issue.[38]

We are only beginning to get some careful evidence on participation outside of election campaigns. One estimate by Verba, Nie, and Kim is that about 20 percent of Americans have at some time contacted public officials, but Milbrath's 1977 book puts the figure at closer to 14 percent.[39] One of the major reasons for our lack of reliable information on such participation has been the fact that political science until recently examined participation primarily during relatively high-stimulus election campaigns. We shall return to this and other points about participation in Chapter 5.

In the late 1960s and early 1970s, evidence about participation outside of campaigns began slowly to accumulate. Verba and Brody reported that active participation regarding the war in Vietnam may have been visible, but it was not extensive. In their survey of 1,499 respondents in the spring of 1967, only eight people —one-half of 1 percent—said they had taken part in a demonstration.[40] This tiny percentage included acts of participation that may have occurred only once during a period of years.

How is it possible to believe that "the streets were filled with demonstrators," then, if they were such a small portion of the population? Even one-half of 1 percent is a lot of people when it is multiplied by the total number of adult Americans: Verba and Brody project it to 750,000 demonstrators. That number would be right up there with even the truly immense civil rights "March on Washington" in the heyday of Martin Luther King. It doesn't take nearly that many demonstrators to send nervous quivers through elected officials. And it would be a good hypothesis that extensive television coverage of demonstrations had the effect of inflating their visibility and extent.

It is rare for a commercial polling organization to ask about participation in the influence framework, but a Gallup poll seems to have been done several weeks after President Nixon's dismissal **of Special Prosecutor Archibald Cox. Some 3 percent said they** had written or telegraphed a congressman or senator about Watergate. While this isn't a large percentage of all Americans, it would project to 4.2 million American adults.[41] The Gallup survey did not make clear how much of the reported participation (messages to Congress) was in response to the Cox firing. Nevertheless, we do have some supplementary information. Western Union reported that more than 450,000 "Public-Opinion Mailgrams" were sent to Congress, Archibald Cox, and the White House in the period immediately after the firing.[42] Congressmen, according to news reports, reported being "swamped" by the flood of mail and telegraph messages. The White House was impressed enough to call it a "firestorm" and change its Watergate tactics for a time. Compared to the normal volume of public opinion messages, then, it does not take a large percentage of participating Americans to make a considerable impression in the influence framework.

One reason that even smaller amounts of participation often make devastating impressions on decision-makers is that, unlike elections, our political system is not well set up to cope with unstructured, unanticipated, and nonroutinized forms of participation. Thus, high participation incidents in the influence framework *exceed the capacity of decision-makers to cope routinely with the "flood" of information about citizen attitudes.*

POWER

We turn now from attitude and participation to power, a third component of public opinion. We have already seen that the act of participation means that some attitudes are visible to decision-makers while others are not. In this sense, participation gives these holders of visible attitudes more *power* than others. But we won't concentrate on this meaning of power. Instead, I'll mean by power the relative quality of the participation. Since we will often need to refer to the concept of participation quality, it will be convenient to use the label "power."

As Dreyer and Rosenbaum put it, "If opinion is to affect policy, it must make its way through the political system to decision-makers, and the system does not give equal weight to all opinion." They stress two distinct but related processes: (1) methods "by which opinion flows into the governmental structure . . . and affects the political decision-maker's assumptions or perceptions about the state of public opinion" and (2) "the way in which policy is made *within* the government structure and how public opinion is integrated into this policy."[43]

Largely because studies of public opinion and public policy have tended to concentrate primarily on the second process—see, for example, Luttbeg[44]—not enough attention has been paid to the first. And as for power research itself, many writers recently have criticized its almost exclusive preoccupation with whether the powerful succeed in getting decision-makers to do what they want them to do.[45] Power is just as crucial in determining whether issues become subject to debate (and popular participation) and in determining who participates. In my vocabulary, such determinations clearly are related to controlling the forms of information about citizen attitudes that may be available to decision-makers. The term "power," then, will be used merely as a convenient label for some important differences among actual or potential participants.

In the public opinion process, power is the relative ability of political actors (*a*) to block or initiate public discussion of potential issues, (*b*) to influence perceptions of public opinion held by key decision-makers once an issue "goes public," (*c*) to define issues and options under discussion, (*d*) to influence participation by others, and (*e*) to induce decision-makers to adopt a given policy. Abilities *a* through *d*, at least, greatly affect the kinds of incoming information about citizen attitudes. Obviously, though, there is some overlap between *e* and the others. For example, suppose you want decision-makers to keep the present policy by blocking discussion of a potential issue (*a*)? Or you want them to organize certain options out of the debate (*c*)?

Despite the fact that it is not always easy to separate power as control over public opinion information from more traditional senses of power, the effort will be helpful in our analysis of how the media affect public opinion. Both indirectly and directly, the mass media help control the flow of information about citizen attitudes. Indirectly, the media aid and/or interfere with the power of participants to control the flow of such information. And the mass media themselves directly affect the kinds of information reaching decision-makers about citizen attitudes.

Most writers agree that power is an idea whose time for misuse came a long while ago. Nevertheless, we shall try to follow two of the several suggestions made by Bachrach and Baratz: (1) Power is not the possession of political actors, but instead will be used as a convenient label to describe one or more of a number of *relationships* among actors, and (2) these relationships are not fixed; power can change.[46]

Chapter 7 will deal explicitly with how the mass media can alter these relationships, and Chapter 6 will deal indirectly with the same problem.

Journalists themselves benefit from the reputation for power (over public opinion, for example). Despite our tendency to equate power over public opinion with the power to change attitudes, and despite the publication of voluminous evidence that the media don't reliably change issue attitudes, plenty of people still believe in "the power of the media."

As this book attempts to explain, they probably are right, but for the wrong reasons.

OVERVIEW

We've seen that citizens' attitudes toward issues are not the only element in the public opinion process. If we hold constant the way decision-makers perceive public opinion, we are equipped by now to note three general kinds of changes in public opinion outcomes that can be brought about by mass communications: (1) changes in the amount, composition, and intensity of participation, (2) attitude change, attitude formation, and object change, and (3) changes in the relative power of participants.

Each of these three has been left deceptively incomplete. For example, if attitude change on an issue is to result in public opinion change on that issue, the change must ultimately be made visible. But if a person's attitude changes, *he may be less likely to participate and express his "new" attitude* (see Figure 3 in Chapter 5). We need to specify a number of intervening mechanisms before we know how these three kinds of changes can be produced by political communications in the mass media. The following chapters are devoted to this task.

NOTES

Chapter 1

1. Milton Rokeach, *Beliefs, Attitudes, and Values* (San Francisco: Jossey-Bass, 1968), pp. 156–59.

2. Robert A. Dahl, "The Behavioral Approach in Political Science: Epitaph for a Monument to a Successful Protest," *American Political Science Review* 55 (December 1961): 763–72.

3. Joseph T. Klapper, *The Effects of Mass Communication* (New York: Free Press, 1960), p. 8.

4. A good illustration of both the nature of the issue and an apparent reluctance to bring it up may be found in *Behavior Today,* 23 April 1973, pp. 1–3, including a note and a reprint of parts of a National Institute of Mental Health staff report. *Behavior Today* said the report "may never see the light of day," so reprinted excerpts of it. The report criticized NIMH funding of attempts to account for social problems by means of individual-level variables.

5. Angus Campbell, Philip E. Converse, Warren E. Miller, and Donald E. Stokes, *Elections and the Political Order* (New York: Wiley, 1966).

6. Quoted in Angus Campbell, "Voters and Elections: Past and Present," in *Political Opinion and Electoral Behavior*, ed. Edward C. Dreyer and Walter A. Rosenbaum (Belmont, Calif.: Wadsworth, 1966), p. 364.

7. Ernest Nagel, *The Structure of Science: Problems in the Logic of Scientific Explanation* (New York: Harcourt, Brace & World, 1961), p. 542.

8. Notably by Herbert Blumer, whose 1947 argument will be considered at length in Chapter 9.

9. Leo Bogart, *Silent Politics: Polls and the Awareness of Public Opinion* (New York: Wiley-Interscience, 1972), p. 152.

10. Herbert Blumer, "Public Opinion and Public Opinion Polling," *American Sociological Review* 13 (October 1948): 542–49. The article was prepared from his 1947 presentation to a group of public opinion scholars.

11. Floyd H. Allport, "Toward a Science of Public Opinion," *Public Opinion Quarterly* 1 (Spring 1937): 7–23.

12. Warren E. Miller and Donald E. Stokes, "Constituency Influence in Congress," *American Political Science Review* 57 (March 1963): 45–56; Charles F. Cnudde and Donald J. McCrone, "The Linkage Between Constituency Attitudes and Congressional Voting Behavior: A Causal Model," *American Political Science Review* 60 (March 1966): 66–72.

13. Dan Nimmo, *The Political Persuaders: The Techniques of Modern Election Campaigns* (Englewood Cliffs, N. J.: Prentice-Hall, 1970), pp. 180–81.

14. Jay G. Blumler and Jack M. McLeod, "Communication and Voter Turnout in Britain" (paper presented at the annual meeting of the Association for Education in Journalism, Ft. Collins, Colo., August 1973).

15. Maxwell E. McCombs and Donald L. Shaw, "The Agenda-Setting Function of Mass Media," *Public Opinion Quarterly* 36 (Summer 1972): 176–87.

16. Jack M. McLeod, Lee B. Becker, and James E. Byrnes, "Another Look at the Agenda Setting Function of the Press" (paper presented at the annual meeting of the Association for Education in Journalism, Ft. Collins, Colo., August 1973).

17. Walter Lippmann, *Public Opinion* (New York: Macmillan, 1922).

18. Thomas E. Patterson and Robert D. McClure, *The Unseeing Eye: The Myth of Television Power in National Elections* (New York: Putman's, 1976).

19. Arthur H. Miller, Edie N. Goldenberg, and Lutz Erbring, "Type-Set Politics: Impact of Newspapers on Public Confidence," *American Political Science Review* 73 (March 1979): 67–84.

20. Blumler and McLeod, "Communication and Voter Turnout"; Steven H. Chaffee and Sun Yuel Choe, "Time of Decision and Media Use During the Ford-Carter Campaign," *Public Opinion Quarterly* 44 (Spring 1980): 53–69.

21. For example, Steven H. Chaffee, L. Scott Ward, and Leonard P. Tipton, "Mass Communication and Political Socialization," *Journalism Quarterly* 47 (Winter 1970): 647–59.

22. John C. Wahlke, "Pre-Behavioralism in Political Science," *American Political Science Review* 73 (March 1979): 9–31.

23. Maxwell E. McCombs, "Mass Communication in Political Campaigns: Information, Gratification, and Persuasion," in *Current Perspectives in Mass Communication Research*, ed. F. Gerald Kline and Phillip J. Tichenor (Beverly Hills: Sage, 1972), pp. 187–88.

24. Colin Seymour-Ure, *The Political Impact of Mass Media* (London: Constable; Beverly Hills: Sage, 1974), p. 47.

25. Keith R. Stamm and John E. Bowes, both of the University of Washington, have perhaps been more active than most other co-orientation researchers in this area. I thank Keith Stamm for his helpful and open-minded consideration of some of the ideas expressed in this book.

26. Thomas J. Scheff, "Toward a Sociological Model of Consensus," *American Sociological Review* 32 (February 1967): 32–46; Jack M. McLeod and Steven H. Chaffee, "The Construction of Social Reality," *The Social Influence Process*, ed. James T. Tedeschi (Chicago: Aldine-Atherton, 1972).

CHAPTER 2

1. Ralph H. Turner, "Collective Behavior," in *Handbook of Modern Sociology*, ed. Robert E. L. Faris (Chicago: Rand McNally, 1964), p. 415.

2. Leila A. Sussmann, *Dear FDR: A Study of Political Letter-Writing* (Totowa, N. J.: Bedminster Press, 1963), p. 79. Perhaps because it was done under the auspices of Columbia University's Bureau of Applied Social Research, this book shares with Joseph Klapper's book (*The Effects of Mass Communication*) a simple reductionist view of public opinion. Nevertheless, the research methodology used seemed less affected by this reductionist conception than did the conclusions drawn by its author about the superiority of "scientific" polls over other forms of information about citizen attitudes.

3. Ibid., pp. 75–76.

4. Philip E. Converse, Aage R. Clausen, and Warren E. Miller, "Electoral Myth and Reality: The 1964 Election," in *Political Opinion*

and Electoral Behavior: Essays and Studies, ed. Edward C. Dreyer and Walter A. Rosenbaum (Belmont, Calif.: Wadsworth, 1966), p. 24.

5. For example, James M. Fields and Howard Schuman, "Public Beliefs about the Beliefs of the Public," *Public Opinion Quarterly* 40 (Winter 1976-77): 427-48; Hubert O'Gorman with Stephen L. Garry, "Pluralistic Ignorance—A Replication and Extension," *Public Opinion Quarterly* 40 (Winter 1976-77): 449-58; Elizabeth Noelle-Neumann, "Pluralistic Ignorance and the Spiral of Silence," *Public Opinion Quarterly* 41 (Summer 1977): 143-58.

6. This unpublished study was done by the author, his graduate assistant, Eric Belden, and members of his undergraduate public opinion class.

7. James E. Grunig and Keith R. Stamm, "Communication and Co-orientation of Collectivities," *American Behavioral Scientist* 16 (March-April 1973): 567-91.

8. Ralph K. Martin, Garrett J. O'Keefe, and Oguz B. Nayman, "Opinion, Agreement and Accuracy Between Editors and Their Readers," *Journalism Quarterly* 49 (Autumn 1972): 460-68.

9. Bruce H. Westley, "Part II: Communication Settings," *Human Communication Research* 1 (Winter 1975): 186-89.

10. Roger W. Cobb and Charles D. Elder, *Participation in American Politics: The Dynamics of Agenda-Building* (Boston: Allyn and Bacon, 1972).

11. Gerald M. Pomper, "Controls and Influence in American Elections (Even 1968)," *American Behavioral Scientist* 13 (November-December 1969): 216.

12. Paul Burstein and William Freudenberg, "Changing Public Policy. The Impact of Public Opinion, Antiwar Demonstrations, and War Costs on Senate Voting on Vietnam War Motions," *American Journal of Sociology* 84 (July 1978): 99-122.

13. James N. Rosenau has used a technique that is ideally suited to certain research purposes in the study of the influence framework: He drew large samples of actual participants rather than trying to sort out participants from general samples (see Chapter 5). However, the title of his work, *Citizenship Between Elections: An Inquiry Into the Mobilizable American* (New York: Free Press, 1974), may affirm the need to keep reminding people that the influence framework also includes campaigns. Nevertheless, Rosenau's book stands apart from most others in political science for its concern with participation in the influence framework.

14. E.g., Richard F. Carter, "Communication and Affective Relations," *Journalism Quarterly* 42 (Spring 1965): 203-12.

15. Samuel A. Stouffer, *Communism, Conformity and Civil Liberties* (New York: Doubleday, 1955).

16. See especially David Easton's work and that by Fred Greenstein. E.g., David Easton and Robert D. Hess, "The Child's Political

World," and Fred I. Greenstein, "The Significance of Party Identification," both in *Psychology and Politics*, ed. Leroy N. Rieselbach and George I. Balch. (New York: Holt, Rinehart & Winston, 1969), pp. 89–106, and p. 190, respectively.

17. See Jack M. McLeod and Garrett J. O'Keefe, "The Socialization Perspective and Communication Behavior," in *Current Perspectives in Mass Communication Research*, ed. F. Gerald Kline and Phillip J. Tichenor. (Beverly Hills: Sage, 1972), pp. 121–58.

18. Theodore M. Newcomb, Ralph H. Turner, and Philip E. Converse, *Social Psychology: The Study of Human Interaction* (New York: Holt, Rinehart & Winston, 1965), p. 54.

19. Leo Bogart, "No Opinion, Don't Know, and Maybe No Answer,"*Public Opinion Quarterly* 31 (Fall 1967): 344.

20. Newcomb, Turner, and Converse, *Social Psychology*, pp. 82–88.

21. José L. Guerrero and G. David Hughes, "An Empirical Test of the Fishbein Model," *Journalism Quarterly* 49 (Winter 1972): 684–91.

22. Milton Rokeach, "Attitude Change and Behavioral Change," *Public Opinion Quarterly* 30 (Winter 1966–67): 529–50. In Rokeach's vocabulary, an attitude toward the situation has been aroused and is being expressed, rather than the attitude toward the intended attitude object.

23. Alex S. Edelstein, "A Fresh Look at Some Stale Canards about Mass Communication" (paper presented at the annual convention of the Pacific chapter, American Association for Public Opinion Research, Asilomar, Calif., 4 March 1972).

24. Peter Grothe, "Attitude Change of American Tourists in the Soviet Union" (paper presented at the annual convention of the Pacific chapter, American Association for Public Opinion Research, Asilomar, Calif., 4 March 1972).

25. Probably the best-known evidence for this view may be found in Philip E. Converse, "The Nature of Belief Systems in Mass Publics," a 1964 report that was slightly edited and then reprinted in *Public Opinion and Politics: A Reader*, ed. William T. Crotty (New York: Holt, Rinehart & Winston, 1970), pp. 129–55.

26. For an insightful review of the debate, see W. Lance Bennett, "The Growth of Knowledge in Mass Belief Studies: An Epistemological Critique," *American Journal of Political Science* 21 (August 1977): 465–500.

27. Herbert McClosky, Paul J. Hoffmann, and Rosemary O'Hara, "Issue Conflict and Consensus among Party Leaders and Followers," *Public Opinion and Public Policy*, ed. Norman R. Luttbeg, rev. ed. (Homewood, Ill.: Dorsey Press, 1974), p. 367.

28. See, for example, an early review of the history of social psychology by Gordon W. Allport, "The Historical Background of Modern Social Psychology," in *Handbook of Social Psychology, Vol.*

1: Theory and Method, ed. Gardner Lindzey (Cambridge, Mass.: Addison-Wesley, 1954), pp. 3–54.

29. Rokeach, "Attitude Change," p. 531.

30. Allan W. Wicker, "Attitudes versus Actions: The Relationship of Verbal and Overt Behavioral Responses to Attitude Objects," *Journal of Social Issues* 25 (Autumn 1969): 75.

31. Wilbur Schramm, *Men, Messages and Media: A Look at Human Communication* (New York: Harper & Row, 1973), pp. 215–20.

32. E.g., Steven H. Chaffee and Joseph W. Lindner, "Three Processes of Value Change Without Behavioral Change," *Journal of Communication* 19 (March 1969): 30–40.

33. Rokeach, "Attitude Change," p. 533.

34. Martin Fishbein, "Attitude and the Prediction of Behavior," in *Readings in Attitude Theory and Measurement,* ed. Martin Fishbein (New York: Wiley, 1967).

35. Icek Ajzen, "Attitudinal vs. Normative Messages: An Investigation of the Differential Effects of Persuasive Communications on Behavior," *Sociometry* 34 (June 1971): 263–80.

36. On changes concerning efficacy, compare Lester W. Milbrath and M. L. Goel, *Political Participation: How and Why Do People Get Involved in Politics?* (Chicago: Rand McNally, 1977), pp. 57–61.

37. Sidney Verba, Norman H. Nie, and Jae-on Kim, *The Modes of Democratic Participation: A Cross-National Comparison* (Beverly Hills, Calif.: Sage, 1971); and Sidney Verba and Norman H. Nie, *Participation in America: Political Democracy and Social Equality* (New York: Harper & Row, 1972).

38. Sidney Verba and Norman H. Nie, "Political Participation," in Fred I. Greenstein and Nelson W. Polsby, eds., *Handbook of Political Science* (Reading, Mass.: Addison-Wesley, 1975), as cited in Milbrath and Goel, *Political Participation,* pp. 22–23.

39. Verba, Nie, and Kim, *Modes of Democratic Participation;* Milbrath and Goel, *Political Participation.*

40. Sidney Verba and Richard Brody, "Participation, Policy Preferences, and the War in Vietnam," *Public Opinion Quarterly* 34 (Fall 1970): 325–32.

41. Projected figure was adapted from data provided in the *Gallup Opinion Index,* December 1973, p. 5.

42. For $2.00, anyone can send a one-hundred word "Public-Opinion Mailgram" to a public official. A combination of telegraph with mail delivery, the service began in 1971. Western Union reported that the 450,000 messages easily set a record in their history for a single event. The service now is used extensively for lobbying purposes; source is a report by Paul E. Hood, "Dial-a-Lobby ... Buttonholing Congress pays off for Western Union," *National Observer,* 11 May 1974, p. 8.

43. Edward C. Dreyer and Walter A. Rosenbaum, *Political Opinions and Electoral Behavior: Essays and Studies* (Belmont, Calif.: Wadsworth, 1966), pp. 382–83.

44. Norman R. Luttbeg, ed., *Public Opinion and Public Policy,* rev. ed. (Homewood, Ill.: Dorsey Press, 1974), pp. 1–10.

45. E.g., Roger Cobb, Jennie Keith Ross, and Marc Howard Ross, "Agenda Building as a Comparative Political ᴾrocess," *American Political Science Review* 70 (March 1976): 126–38.

46. Peter Bachrach and Morton S. Baratz, "Decisions and Nondecisions: An Analytical Framework," *American Political Science Review* 57 (September 1963): 632–42.

Professor Halloran's emphasis on context in this essay is multifaceted. Researchers must be aware of the context in which their research is conducted; they must be aware to a greater extent than they have been of what precisely gives rise to the sorts of questions they ask, and for whom they are to be answered. Context is viewed more globally, however, as Professor Halloran reviews the comments of researchers from a number of countries. James D. Halloran is director of the Centre for Communication Research at the University of Leicester.

5

THE CONTEXT OF
MASS COMMUNICATION RESEARCH

James D. Halloran

Several years ago it was stated quite unequivocally in a UNESCO publication that intelligent communication policies depended on the availability of information that only research could provide. This statement was part of a plea for more research and for the development of communication policies and related research policies, and it seems reasonable to suggest that, together with many other forces and pressures, it played a part in the growth of mass communication research in recent years.

Despite these welcome developments, however, we are still very short on information — the sort of information that would provide a reliable base for policy formulation and decision making — and this becomes particularly evident when we are called upon to address ourselves to all aspects of the communication process within the wider international setting, such as the remit of the MacBride Commission requires.

It is not just a question of not having enough information, but that the information we have is partial and unbalanced.

What is more, because of the way research has been defined, initiated, supported and organized, and because of the tasks it has been called on to perform (say over the last fifty years) we find that it is not just a question of not having enough information, but that the information we have is partial and unbalanced. We know far more about some parts of the world than about others; we know far more about some aspects of the communication process than about others, and we have more analyses and interpretations from certain value positions than from others. An additional complication is that the implications of these imbalances are not properly understood, and as a result we

This is written in a purely personal capacity and should not be seen as representing the views of any institution, organization or association.

From James D. Halloran, *The Context of Mass Communication Research*, Occasional Papers 13, Asian Mass Communication Research and Information Centre, Singapore, January 1981. Reprinted by permission of the publisher.

not infrequently encounter universal generalizations and cross cultural applications which are just not valid.

Research is not initiated, organized, executed or applied in a social/political vacuum.

In this paper, then, I think it is essential to emphasize at the outset that research is not initiated, organized, executed or applied in a social/political vacuum. A true understanding of the nature of research and its application, calls for an understanding of the historical, economic, political, organizational, professional and personal factors which impinge on the research process in so many ways.

Put briefly, these are the factors that govern what research is carried out and, perhaps more importantly, what research is not carried out. In some way or other the questions we ask in research are indications of what we consider to be important or problematic. They reflect our priorities, our values, our concerns, as well as our compromises with regard to what is allowed or is otherwise possible.

Unfortunately, it would appear that many researchers, irrespective of their country of origin, do not recognize this situation. They accept as given, or take for granted as an unquestioned assumption, what ideally they should regard as problematic, and this, not surprisingly is reflected in their work, what they do, how they interpret it, and how they seek to apply it.

They accept as given, or take for granted as an unquestioned assumption, what ideally they should regard as problematic.

The situation outlined above is an important consideration for those of us who regard research as essentially a conditioned or circumscribed attempt to construct reality. It does this by the areas or topics that are selected and by the use of concepts, techniques, categories, systems of classification and categorization, and the positing of relationships within these areas. Again, these concepts, categories and relationships do not develop in a vacuum, they are not neutral, therefore we should know about the framework within which they have developed and are being applied. This is particularly important when comparisons are being made between different approaches.

I referred earlier to the unbalanced or uneven distribution of research internationally, and this is clearly a reflection of other areas of economic and informational imbalance which characterize the international scene. Certainly as far as quantity is concerned, there is no doubt that the mass communication research field is dominated by research from western, industrialized nations, and this also applies to research which deals with media and development and

Third World problems generally. Moreover, as we shall see later, it is dominated by a particular kind of research.

Research on media and development has been, and is currently being, carried out in the Third World where the development criteria used and the overall approach are totally inappropriate.

Over the years, many researchers have been accused of exporting western research concepts, models and methods which are not appropriate to Third World developmental problems. In general this is a valid point, but it is also an issue which is frequently characterized by false conceptualizations and confusion. There is a problem — make no mistake about this — but it is not always well defined and, as a result, the right lessons are not always learned. Research on media and development has been, and is currently being, carried out in the Third World where the developmental criteria used and the overall approach are totally inappropriate. But this is not primarily because it is "western research", whatever this may be; it is because it is *bad research, and bad social science.* As I hope to show, this research with its inadequate models of society and limited notions of the communication process is, and always has been, equally inapplicable and equally unsatisfactory in the industrialized nations where it was originally conceived. As we shall see, there are clear differences within "western research".

A further difficulty also arises because of these misconceptions. The understandable concern about what is seen as research imperialism often takes the form of a demand that research in the developing countries must be carried out by researchers from those countries. Up to a point, at practical and educational levels, there is something to be said for this. But it by no means solves the problem. In fact it may exacerbate it, if the native researchers have been trained (as they so often have) by those researchers from the industrialized nations who favour the inadequate approaches I have just mentioned. As Antonio Pasquali reminds us (although in another context), we need to beware of the "local collaborator" who tends to be more "obtuse", more "inflexible" and more "anti-nationalist" than his "principal".

The understandable concern about what is seen as research imperialism often takes the form of a demand that research in developing countries must be carried out by researchers from those countries.

Returning to our central theme, our point of departure must be with the main stream of mass communication research (mostly stemming from the USA although with widely scattered followers and advocates internationally) which for want of a better term I shall refer to as "conventional research". In broad, general terms by "conventional research" I mean that with a mainly value free, positivistic, empiricist, behaviouristic, psychological emphasis. However, in criticizing this approach in mass communication

Research was carried out with a view to improving the effectiveness of the media often regarded simply as objects of study.

research, I do not want to be seen as throwing the baby out with the bath water. It is essentially a matter of emphasis and balance. Of course, there is much useful work that might fall under the above-mentioned headings. I must also emphasize that my comments on this type of work should not be seen as an opposition to rigorous methods, experimental work, quantification, etc. There is a criticism however, of the primacy of this position, where "scientific" is defined solely or mainly in terms of method, and where little or no attention is given to theory, concepts or the nature of the relevant substantive issues and their relationship to wider societal concerns. It should also be noted that this problem is not confined to communication research — it is central to the whole of social science.

In the USA, mass communication research had developed, like other branches of social science, essentially as a response to the requirements of modern, industrial, urban society for empirical, quantitative, policy related information about its operations. Research was carried out with a view to improving the effectiveness of the media often regarded simply as objects of study or as "neutral tools" in achieving stated aims and objectives, often of a commercial nature. This was at the heart of administrative or service research where the emphasis was on improving methods to facilitate the achievement of specific goals rather than on refining concepts, developing theories or achieving social change.

In this way the research although often referred to as abstracted empiricism was certainly not abstracted from the society within which it operated and which it was geared to serve. With this in mind, we should ask about the questions which have not been asked as well as those questions which have. In what was a media rather than a societal centred approach, theory was neglected and the media were not seen in relation to other institutions. There were few if any questions about power, organization and control, little reference to structural considerations and rarely were attempts made to study the social meaning of the media in historical or contemporary contexts.

In what was a media rather than a societal centred approach, theory was neglected and the media were not seen in relation to other institutions.

The emphasis on answers seen to be useful in the short term, the concentration on methods, (particularly on what could be measured with its false notion of precision), the focus on the individual with the related confinement of media influence to attitude change and the accompanying tendencies to ignore the possible influence of the media on

Contained in these value free, positivistic, behaviouristic approaches is a view of man existent mainly for the instrumental purpose of studying him.

institutions, in defining social reality, in setting the social-political agenda, in legitimating certain forms of behaviour and institutional arrangements and on cultural change generally, has led to a completely inadequate understanding of the communication process and the notion of media influence. It must be remembered that these ideas were widely held, that they were exported and that they are still with us, although as we shall see, they are increasingly challenged.

It has also been argued that contained in these value free, positivistic, behaviouristic approaches is a view of man existent mainly for the instrumental purpose of studying him. Whether or not this is true, it is certainly important to have regard to the images of men and models of society implicit in this work.

Of course, sociology is based on ideas as well as on tasks and operations, and there is no doubt that the ideas of the founding fathers, as well as the social concerns of the time, played an important part in the development of social science in the USA. But mass communication research in the USA was more closely linked to social psychology and to professional and commercial interests than to sociology. Admittedly, scholars like Lazarsfeld grappled with the problems posed by the conflict between critical and theoretical interests on the one hand and empirical demands on the other, but the critical challenge and the theoretical concerns never really surfaced in sustained research programmes.

It would be unfair and inaccurate to suggest that over the years all mass communication and related research in the USA had been slavishly administrative.

Kurt Lang has argued that the incompatibility between the different streams of communication research was not nearly as sharp as those who mistake ideology for social science may want to believe. He has a point here, and it is possible that things need not have developed in the way they did. But today, as distinct from thirty years ago, the record speaks for itself in terms both of the amount and type of work that has been produced and of the questions that are currently being asked.

It would, of course, be quite unfair and indeed inaccurate, to suggest that over the years all mass communication and related research in the USA had been slavishly administrative. It is not as simple as that. There have been many strands to the work and critical messages, social concerns and certainly professional accomplishments have not been entirely lacking. Still, even today, it is difficult to detect,

*If it is dangerous
to generalize about
conventional mass
communication
research, then it is
even more dangerous
to do so about the
so-called critical
approach.*

in what is a vast body of work, any conscious underlying philosophy or purpose, or still less an overriding social or political concern.* Thousands of projects have been carried out, but there is little evidence of the systematic accumulation and development of a corpus of knowledge, and there have been few atter ,)ts to relate the work to an appropriate social theory. It is still mainly a matter of doing rather than of thinking, of serving rather than questioning or challenging.

What then of the "critical research" that has been mentioned in passing, as being opposed to the aforementioned conventional research? If it is dangerous to generalize about conventional mass communication research, then it is even more dangerous to do so about the so called critical approach, which although owing much more to European thought and scholarship than the conventional approach, nevertheless reflects the influence of American sociology.

It could be argued that the main unity of the critical approach — if in fact a unity can be identified — is in its opposition to conventional work rather than in any shared more positive approach. For, as we shall see, the critical umbrella covers a variety of positions, and in fact, there are those who would suggest that some of the more extreme ideological positions should not really be classified as social scientific research. There is also another problem about the use of the word "critical", which has to do with the fact that researchers who share the same theoretical position or research approach, are frequently selective in choosing their targets. Researchers from two different countries may confine their criticisms to only one of those countries as though there was nothing to criticise in the other.

*The main unity of the
critical approach is
in its opposition to
conventional work
rather than in any
shared more positive
approach.*

However, let me proceed (with a plea for tolerance), to write about critical, problem and policy-oriented research, primarily with a sociological perspective. It should be noted here that a distinction is made between policy-oriented research and policy research. The latter is frequently of the variety which seeks to bring about the efficient execution of policy and thereby make the existing system more efficient. On the whole, it is not concerned to ask questions about the validity of the system or to challenge predominant values or suggest alternatives. Policy-oriented research, on the other hand, ideally addresses itself to the major

---

*Unless, of course it may be seen in the attempts in recent years to counter critical and UNESCO related research — see below.

issues of our time, and is concerned, amongst other things, with questioning the values and claims of the system, applying independent criteria, suggesting alternatives with regard to both means and ends, exploring the possibility of new forms and structures, and so on. It is not necessary to make an either/or issue out of these different approaches. We are not talking about incompatibilities, but about the different implications for policy and society of approaches which prevailed in the past (and which, up to a point, are still with us) and those which are now emerging. Put crudely, and to repeat, the conventional approaches of the past which characterized so much communication research, explicitly or implicitly, served and supported rather than criticized or challenged.

> *The conventional approaches of the past which characterized so much communication research explicitly or implicitly served and supported rather than criticized or challenged.*

To emphasize the point made earlier, it is appreciated that to talk in terms of a critical, problem and policy-oriented, sociological approach may beg more questions than it answers. There are different sociological approaches, and it might be said for example that sociological functionalism may have more in common with psychological functionalism than it has with other, more critical sociological approaches. There is some truth in this, but even so I would still maintain, with the qualifications that follow later, that there is something meaningful and distinctive about the emerging critical sociological perspective referred to above, and most definitely something that marks it off from the approaches that prevailed in the past.

My decision to adopt this line is influenced by the fact that I see this developing, critical thrust not only as offering the greatest contrast and challenge to the older approaches, but also as providing the major contribution to the current international debate on vital communication issues. Its advocates and practitioners have played no small part in the development of mass communication research in Europe (particularly in Britain), and it has also been influential internationally, particularly through UNESCO publications, where some would say it had supplanted the earlier, conventional approach associated with the name of Wilbur Schramm and his colleagues. In fact, this is one of the main problem areas to which we shall shortly return in some detail.

> *I see this developing, critical thrust not only as offering the greatest contrast and challenge to the older approaches.*

Another point worth making is that on the whole critical research, although stemming from a wide range of positions and reflecting different values, is less likely than conventional research to be encumbered by historical and institutional relationships with journalism and broadcasting. More-ever, it is not as closely linked with markets, audiences and publics, and is less inclined to have a service, administrative or commercial character. Needless to say, it is not without its value implications, but it is definitely more independent of the institutions it is studying.

Critical research does not ignore problems central to the media, but ideally it never takes these problems as defined by media practitioners or politicians.

As far as media institutions are concerned, the approach is more likely to be from the outside, with a critical policy or problem orientation. Critical research does not ignore problems central to the media, but ideally it never takes these problems as defined by media practitioners or politicians. Its starting points are the major social issues of our time, not necessarily the major media issues as narrowly defined by the professionals, owners or controllers.

At the risk of over-simplification, let me attempt to summarize the main characteristics of this emerging approach. First, and foremost is that it deals with communication as a social process; secondly, that it studies media institutions not in isolation but as, and together with, other institutions, and within the wider social context (nationally and internationally); and thirdly, that it conceptualizes research in terms of structure, organization, professionalization, socialization, participation, and so on.

One of the clear implications of this is that all apsects of the communication process should be studied. The factors (historical, economic, political, organizational, technological, professional, personal, etc.) which impinge on the production process and determine what is produced demand close scrutiny as well as those which influence how what is produced is used. In the past, the emphasis in research was on use, reaction, effects, influence, etc., not on ownership, control, structure, organization and production relationships.

This approach also shows the futility of studying communication in isolation, or of studying communication policies without reference to other related policies.

The same basic principles and questions are relevant, *mutatis mutandis,* wherever the research is carried out, first, second, third or fourth world. Moreover, this approach also shows the futility of studying communication in isolation, or of studying communication policies without reference to other related policies (educational, cultural, economic, social, etc). The relationship between media policies and education policies and the implications and consequences of such relationships in different countries would in fact make an excellent subject for comparative international research.

In passing it is worth commenting, albeit briefly, on some of the problems of international comparative research. The subject is by its very nature difficult, but it has been rendered more difficult by the unthinking acceptance of some of the notions of conventional research referred to above.

At the heart of the problem is the failure to recognize that social research is embedded in cultural values and that the fundamental differences (culture, language, demographic structure, experience, expectations, etc.) which obtain in different societies preclude the use of carbon copy survey or interview methods which assume that genuine comparability can be achieved only by administering the same questions in the same way in all participating countries. One has only to take note of the relationship between language and culture to realise that this approach is patently absurd. Methods of data collection appropriate in one country may not be so in another. It is the essential response that we seek to compare and, given cultural differences, the same type of response will be evoked by different verbal/cultural stimuli in different countries.

At the heart of the problem is the failure to recognize that social research is embedded in cultural values.

Whilst on this matter of comparative research and research methods, it is also worth noting that simple categorizations or classifications in terms of media systems of institutions may tell us little beyond the superficial and the obvious, and may even obscure important differences at a more fundamental, cultural level. We should not make hasty inferences about the nature of the relationships between media and culture and the overall social implications of those relationships from superficial structural data. It used to be common (and it still happens in some fields) to infer effects from an analysis of media content. More recently there has been an equally erroneous tendency to make statements about content, influence, consciousness and social consequences, solely from studies of ownership and control. We need to be careful here, for there is nothing automatic or mechanical about these linking processes. This is another area calling for careful, systematic, disciplined, comparative research, and where we need to be on our guard lest we uncritically accept attractive slogans and ready-made, over-simplified formulae.

It is also worth noting that simple categorizations or classifications in terms of media systems of institutions may tell us little beyond the superficial and the obvious.

As I hope to illustrate later, critical research, or at least much of it in many countries, has to survive in what can be a hostile atmosphere. The questioning of basic assumptions, conventional wisdom, media myths and the accepted ways of doing things, together with the suggestions that the media should be demystified and the call for an exploration of alternatives are bound to be seen as a threat and a challenge by those who (nationally and internationally) own or control the media, who regulate the global flow of communication, who will benefit from the maintenance of the status quo, and who stand to lose from any changes. These people and institutions may control the research purse strings as well.

We need to remember that on the whole the medium is the system, that it tends to be elitist, primarily one-way, operating from the top downwards, and serving the interests of those in power. I suggest that although there are important differences from country to country, this basic pattern is well nigh universal, and that a similar pattern prevails internationally.

Systematic comparative research based on an agreed operationalization of such concepts as participation, access manipulation, etc. should give the correct answer, but this is easier said than done.

If this is disputed, then systematic comparative research based on an agreed operationalization of such concepts as participation, access, manipulation, etc., should give the correct answer, but this is easier said than done. However, if we really wish to understand the full human and social implications of different forms and arrangements, if we wish to see what participation actually means in terms of human behaviour and involvement, and then explore the possibility of alternatives, this is the sort of research we must be prepared to do. Knowledge derived from such work might also help us to challenge the myths and false claims, and eliminate some of the cant and hypocrisy which all too frequently characterize the debate on these and related issues. The MacBride Commission have an important role to play in encouraging developments in this direction.

Mass communication research is not a game for remote academics engaged in research for the sake of research.

Granted the present international position, mass communication research is not a game for remote academics engaged in research for the sake of research. Once the critical stance is adopted and responsibilities as independent researchers, scholars and intellectuals accepted, the researchers almost inevitably will find himself in conflict with extremely powerful national and international forces who are convinced that they (and the world at large) have nothing whatsoever to gain from critical investigations. They are convinced that they know all they want to know about communication and the media. The current situation suits them fine and its maintenance or extension is what they seek. Alternative forms of thinking are not welcome because they might lead to alternative systems. What is more,

The critical researcher needs to ensure that he does not leave himself open to attack from the international media establishment because of a lack of balance in his own research activities.

they are most favourably placed to defend their position, because they set the agenda and control the discourse.

It is worth remembering in this connection (and I shall return to it later) the massive, well-orchestrated counter-attack mounted by the international media establishment against the UNESCO-supported and related research which had exposed the nature and inequity of the international information order and suggested, *inter alia,* how the imbalance might be redressed.

Amongst other things then, the critical researcher questions and seeks to change the lack of balance in the international information order, but in so doing he needs to ensure that he does not leave himself open to attack from the international media establishment because of the lack of balance in his own research activities, or because he has failed to define the problems or apply his critical criteria within a wider universal context. He is not always as careful here as he might be.

Of course, everything cannot be attempted at once. Selections have to be made from many areas of possible enquiry, and it is perfectly legitimate to establish research priorities and make choices accordingly. But it is neither legitimate nor responsible for the researcher to be partial, blind, or perhaps just simply naive, to such a degree that an outsider might assume that there were parts of the world so perfect that critical criteria, say with regard to access, participation and manipulation, need never be applied. We need balance in research as well as in other communication areas.

We need balance in research as well as in other communication areas.

Let us now look at a specific problem, central to the terms of reference of the MacBride Commission. I refer to the debate on such issues as free flow, balance, the right to communicate, new information order, the draft declaration, and so on.

Rosemary Righter in her IPI sponsored book, *Whose News? Politics, the Press and the Third World,* has quite a few things to say, not all of them accurate by any means, about UNESCO policy with regard to mass communication research. Righter refers to an extensive UNESCO research programme launched on the recommendation of a meeting of experts convened by UNESCO at Montreal in 1969 "to identify the ways in which the mass media can best serve the needs of present and future society". She refers to the Montreal Conference [for which I prepared the working

document*] as a watershed in UNESCO's approach to its
research programme. Perhaps it was a watershed — I would
like to think it was — but should this be the case, there is
far more to it than is suggested in the narrow, politically
focussed, line (completely lacking in historical and sociological perspective and betraying little understanding of the
nature and development of mass communication research)
developed by Ms Righter in her book.

*One of the main
criticisms raised by
communication scholars
and social scientists
about mass
communication research
has to do with its
theoretical paucity
in the fifties
and sixties.*

Quoting John Lee, one of the few UNESCO "consultants"
to meet with her approval, Ms Righter sees the Montreal meeting as marking a shift from "a theoretical
approach into an international action programme". Granted
Ms Righter's background, I presume this is an understandable interpretation for her, but for anyone familiar with
mass communication research it is bound to seem somewhat strange. One of the main criticisms raised by communications scholars and social scientists about mass communication research has to do with its theoretical paucity in
the fifties and sixties.

The research programmes, projects, reports etc., which are
seen as stemming from the post-Montreal approach, are
criticised, and at one level dismissed, by Righter because
she considers most of them as "wholly irrelevant to the
actual problems of communication in the societies
UNESCO exists to help". But Ms Righter would appear to
want it both ways. She regards the work as useless and
riddled with jargon but "to dismiss it for that reason would
be to ignore the purpose of UNESCO's new research programme" which, quoting Lee again, she sees (without any
obvious enthusiasm) as being essentially geared to informing policy-makers and as deliberately including "all aspects
of the communication process — as an integral total".
Admirable objectives I would have thought!

This new direction and emphasis is obviously not welcomed. That researchers should want to ask questions about
media ownership and control, the formulation of communication policy, decision making in policy formulation,
journalistic values, qualitative analyses of content, the
agenda setting function of the media, the role of the media
in the formation of social consciousness, the relationship
between the media and other institutions, and between the
communication process and other social processes, and

---

*Mass Media and Society: The Need of Research, Reports and
Papers in Communication No. 59.*

Righter believes that the changes are a clear indication that "Big Brother" is already on the march.

about international communication patterns, is treated with suspicion and reserve by Ms Righter. She grudgingly accepts that there could be legitimate reasons for these questions and for such kinds of research. But clearly her main concern is not with a disciplined, social scientific approach to media and communication questions or with genuine attempts to systematically study complex processes and institutions so that policy may be better informed. Her preoccupation is with her perceptions of the political/policy implications of recent research developments, particularly those associated with UNESCO and which question the accepted ways of doing things.

Unable to resist the well worn philistinian crack about more research meaning more jobs, Ms Righter eventually comes to her main point, namely that this new direction in research is essentially disturbing because it necessarily implies in the long run "regulation of content and the shaping of national values by governmental fiat". She believes that the changes are a clear indication that "Big Brother" is already on the march.

There is much more that could be said about this journalistic exercise with its lack of substantiation, amazing leaps and non sequiturs, its selective use of names and material, its frequent quoting of passages out of context and its general lack of understanding of the development, nature and scope of communication research. However, to review this book is not my task here and I refer to it at some length primarily to provide illustrative material in a contemporary and highly relevant setting. I do this to show that currently, and arguably for the first time, mass communication research is in the centre of the international political stage. Its planning, execution, interpretation, presentation, application etc. is increasingly being seen in this context and consequently it is likely to be judged with regard to its relevance, and even its competence, from different political standpoints.

For the first time, mass communication research is in the centre of the international political stage.

There is a widespread tendency among media professionals and politicians (now that they are forced to take notice of research from time to time) to write of a research project as "bad", incompetent, irrelevant, etc. simply if the results do not support their views. Rarely do they have the necessary knowledge and background which would enable them to use more objective, valid criteria. They know little about the communication process or about research, yet they are in a priviledged position with regard to the presentation and interpretation of research results. Up to a point they control the debate about themselves.

Admittedly mass communication research has not always been in the centre of the international political arena as it is today but even before the change it was never conceived, planned or carried out in a social-political vacuum.

In one way there is nothing new about this. Admittedly mass communication research has not always been in the centre of the international political arena as it is today but even before the aforementioned change it was never conceived, planned or carried out in a social-political vacuum. As we should know, research frequently tends, in some way or other, to reflect the values and reinforce the system within which it is conceived, supported and executed. In fact, in some countries it is deliberately intended that it should do this and it is important to look at research as a possible form of social control. It is arguable that in many western countries this was particularly the case before the advent of the critical, problem and policy-oriented research referred to above and that this is the norm in centrally planned societies.

However, unlike Righter, we must look at the development of the new direction in research quite apart from its relationship to UNESCO. The Montreal meeting was important as an international platform, but, as I see it, its prime achievement was to facilitate a pulling together and an articulation of the previously mentioned changes that were already taking place in certain academic research circles. Amongst other things, this development also reflected changes that were taking place in the various disciplinary streams that contribute to the reservoir of mass communication research. This was particularly true in sociology and in approaches to the nature of knowledge and concepts of reality. These changes are far more fundamental than those perceived by Righter and they cannot be adequately accounted for in terms of her obsessions with international, leftist, conspiracy theories.

This development also reflected changes that were taking place in the various disciplinary streams that contribute to the reservoir of mass communication research.

The international aspect is important, however, and so is the UNESCO Montreal meeting and subsequent UNESCO involvement in research. For these represent, together with many other related developments, a recognition by a number of prominent international scholars (of many different political colours and from several disciplines and countries) that the conventional, mainly North American, approach to mass communication research, described earlier in this paper, which had dominated the general field as well as the UNESCO programme over the previous twenty years had been theoretically, conceptually, methodologically and socially inadequate. There was a corresponding agreement that changes were long overdue.

*A glance at the full
list of participants
at this and subsequent
"panel" meetings will
show that the groups
were not as homogenous
as some would have us
believe.*

Not all the Montreal participants were motivated in the same way and not all wished to travel in the same direction. A glance at the full list of participants at this and subsequent "panel" meetings (as distinct from the selected list produced by Righter) will show that the groups were not as homogeneous as some would have us believe. However, despite the differences in background and interest, there was a high degree of consensus with regard to the inadequacies of the past and on the need for some sort of changes in research approaches. Moreover, this agreement stemmed mainly from social scientific considerations, although it was recognised that social scientific criteria are not formulated in a vacuum.

Returning once more to Righter's book, it is interesting to see, both explicitly and implicitly, directly and indirectly (e.g. via Lee), how the author apparently regards with approval (although perhaps without recognising the real nature of what she is approving) the conventional research approaches (and their advocates) that prevailed before Montreal. In fact, these approaches are still very much in evidence in some quarters, and are reflected in some of the activities that have recently been mounted as a counter to the UNESCO sponsored and related research. This counter-research is not accidental and it appears to have been conceived as an integral part of a well orchestrated attack on UNESCO and anyone associated with research, which, it is feared, might produce results critical of the prevailing international media system. In fact, some would argue that it represents a good example of the direct relationship between ideology and research.

*This counter-research
is not accidental and
it appears to have
been conceived as an
integral part of a
well-orchestrated
attack on UNESCO and
anyone associated
with research, which
might produce results
critical of the
prevailing
international media
system.*

As I see it, the main hope of quite a number of researchers at that time (as expressed in the Montreal working paper, conference report and other publications) was that some form of critical approach (along the lines referred to elsewhere in this paper) — not homogeneous, not representing any given ideological position, but diverse and pluralistic — would take over from the conventional research which up to that time had characterised both the field in general and UNESCO's research policies and programmes.

As indicated earlier, this type of research had far reaching policy implications. For example, as far as communication development and the Third World was concerned, implicit in these models of research (but rarely explicitly stated) was the idea that development in the Third World should be measured in terms of the adoption and assimilation of western technology and culture.

The main emphasis of the work was on increasing efficiency within the accepted and unquestioned value framework. In general, prior to Montreal, the research and projects sponsored by UNESCO (deficient in theories, models, concepts and methods) tended to legitimate and reinforce the existing system and the established order, and in the Third World it tended to strengthen economic and cultural dependence rather than promote independence.

Prior to Montreal, the research and projects sponsored by UNESCO tended to legitimate and reinforce the existing system and the established order.

It would appear that it is this research tradition and its advocates which are approved, and the break from which is clearly deplored, by Rosemary Righter, her sponsors and associates.

James Carey, one of the few American scholars experienced in both mass communication research and journalism education, who adopts a moderate critical position, makes some interesting points about the development of mass communication research in the USA in the post-war years and about some of the factors that impinged on this development. Referring to the change in "emphasis" first from the "powerful influence model" to the "limited effects model" and then back via "uses and gratifications" to a re-defined influence model, he writes:

"The history of mass communication research is more than the history of 'findings', the history of the autonomous processes of theoretical and empirical development. This history of mass communication research must include, as a parallel, a history of the changing world of mass communications: of the purposes to which these institutions are put, the audiences that gather to them, the social structures which they more or less shape. In terms of this latter history, it can be argued that the basic reason behind the shift in the argument about effects from a powerful to a limited to a more powerful model is that the social world was being transformed over this period, transformed by a series of cycles moving around a linear trend. That is, the basic model for studying communication effects is that of business cycles: the inflation and deflation of effects around a linear historical movement. Powerful effects of communication were sensed in the thirties because the depression and the political currents surrounding the entrance to war created a fertile bed for the production of certain kinds of effects. Similarly. the normalcy of the 50's and 60's led to a limited effects model. In the late 60's a period of war, political

The history of mass communication research must include a history of the changing world of mass communication.

discord and inflation again conspired to expose the social structure in fundamental ways and to make it permeable by the media of communication. These cyclical movements occurred around a fundamental social process, however; the progressively deeper penetration of the media of communications into the social structure and its constituent institutions. One need only look at the role of popular culture and the media in the schools for example.

The shift from a powerful effects model to a limited effects model paralleled a shift in the outlook of social scientists from a prophetic to a priestly class.

The history of communication effects, however, intersects at every point with the history of communication researchers: their interests and implicit ideological position. When I say the 'interests' of researchers I mean that often maligned word in a dual sense: the problems which interest researchers and the self-interest, particularly the status interests of researchers.

I elsewhere argued that the shift from a powerful effects model to a limited effects model paralleled a shift in the outlook of social scientists from a prophetic to a priestly class: from a group of outsiders hurling critical barbs at established society to a group of insiders. Researchers were joined to the establishment and research underwent what Kenneth Burke called a 'bureaucratization of the imaginative'. This incorporation in turn paralleled a depoliticization of the social structure, a declaration of the end of ideology and a convergence of status interests between university researchers and other powerful elements within society, In turn the repoliticization of the social structure in the late 60's was marked by the decided tension between these groups, a slight but significant radicalization of faculties, a re-attentiveness to propaganda and manipulation, and the growing necessity within universities under the force of students (and the drying up of federal funds) of adopting critical and prophetic stances. But researchers retained certain status interests however realigned: look, for example, at the differing tones and conclusions of the commission reports on violence and on pornography in the USA.''

The problem of communication effects is a diachronic not a synchronic one.

Carey goes on to argue that his main point is a simple one, namely that the problem of communication effects is a diachronic not a synchronic one. The failure to grasp this implies that the essential nature of the communication process is not understood. It means that research will still be carried out within the frameworks of inadequate behaviouristic and functional models; that cause and effect questions will still be asked and, above all from our point of view, that questions will *not be asked* that do not meet the requirements of these simple models.

It is worth noting that Carey makes these comments in criticism of the proposals for future research made by Elihu Katz following his BBC sponsored enquiry. As I have argued elsewhere, the Katz proposals may be seen as yet another example of the media establishment using paid servants, (who in general subscribe to the old ways and appear suspicious of the critical approach) to counter the challenge from critical research without rejecting research altogether. It performs a form of alibi function.

Katz and Righter have something in common. Should the BBC back the Katz research proposals *and finance them,* then it would certainly lead to a shift in direction and emphasis in mass communication research in Britain — a shift away from the critical and back towards the administrative. From all accounts Righter would welcome this type of development. In both cases — and there are other examples from other countries — there would be less of a challenge to the establishment, the status quo, or to the accepted ways of doing things. There are many examples in recent developments in mass communication research of this backlash or counter-attack.

But, as Carey states, "scholarship like many of the arts flourishes when it stands in determined opposition to the established order. If you are in opposition you have to work very much harder to get a hearing at all." It is worth remembering in this connection that, unlike most other institutions, the media control what is presented about them. It could be that the extra effort makes the critical difference. But "more importantly," writes Carey, "to attract and hold major scholars the field of communication must formulate puzzles and dilemmas that are intellectually challenging and provocative."

As I see the position, it was only after Montreal that the questions raised by UNESCO about mass communication became relevant, challenging and provocative at both intellectual and political levels, and quite clearly this is what the trouble is all about. Those who run international media operations and those who serve them are not interested in challenge, stimulation and povocation at any level. In fact, it is just the opposite. They want the programme to go on without disturbance or change.

The Katz proposals may be seen as yet another example of the media establishment using paid servants to counter the challenge from critical research without rejecting research altogether.

It was only after Montreal that the questions raised by UNESCO about mass communication became relevant, challenging and provocative and this is what the trouble is all about.

Not surprisingly,
these people also
appear quite
incapable of viewing
the research
developments of the
last decade as
genuine intellectual
developments with a
sound social
scientific base.

Not surprisingly, these people also appear quite incapable of viewing the research developments of the last decade as genuine intellectual developments with a sound social scientific base. Admittedly, such developments can be used and abused by those whose prime interests is neither social science nor human welfare. This has happened and it is still happening, but this exploitation and abuse should not prevent us from recognizing the validity and usefulness of the developments. If, as a result of research, conclusions are reached and points made about the nature of media operations or communication processes, they do not become invalid simply because they are also accepted and made use of by those who might have other equally unsatisfactory objectives in mind. With regard to the points made by Righter in this connection, it is worth noting that whether a communications industry is free or "controlled" is not determined by a particular ideology but by the prevailing power structure. Government controlled media exists in countries with widely different ideologies.

But to return to the "history". After Montreal some changes did occur. Gradually (although only in certain areas) UNESCO research became more critical, and eventually this led to the production of research reports, which, for the first time, spelled out in detail the true nature of the flow of international information, media materials, etc; described the influence on this flow, of historical, economic and political factors; and pointed to the inevitable outcomes of the operation of the free-flow doctrine in a world where national and regional media resources and capabilities were so unbalanced.

It was this detailed and well substantiated exposure of the implications of free-flow, coming from several different sources, UNESCO-supported and elsewhere, that provoked the attack on UNESCO's research policy and those associated with it from those who until that time had shown little interest in research.

UNESCO has not only
supported more
systematic, social
scientific research
in mass communication
than it did before
Montreal but that
research has also
been more diverse, more
critical and more
challenging.

Although there have been inconsistencies and quite recently some signs of ambivalence and confusion, over the last decade, UNESCO has not only supported more systematic, social scientific research in mass communication than it did before Montreal (and this is to its credit) but that research has also been more diverse (breaking the monopoly of conventional western behaviouristic/functional models), more critical and more challenging. These research policies demonstrate a recognition of the realities of the inter-

national situation, and of the true potential of research as
well as an acceptance that research cannot be carried out in
a vacuum and that it inevitably has cultural, political and
economic implications.

Again, this is also what the trouble is about. UNESCO, and
this type of research, is being criticized now, despite its
increased pluralism and diversity, primarily because some of
the research is critically oriented, and that because of this it
is likely to challenge the status quo and the vested interests
of the international media establishment and reject the conventional wisdom of the service research which supports
this establishment. It must be repeated and emphasized that
until relatively recently there had been no systematic or
sustained challenge from research to any established media
structures or communication policies. Its function was to
support.

*Until recently, there
had been no
systematic or
sustained challenge
from research to any
established media
structures or
communication
policies.*

Many people previously unconcerned, or perhaps not aware
of the problem, now feel with regard to "free flow", "new
information order", etc., that the Third World has a good
case. But who, before the results from this new research
were made available, was able to support this case with hard
evidence, and who was able to challenge the myths about
the universal benefits of freedom (freedom to select from a
strictly limited agenda) which appear to be readily accepted
by the news agencies, their clients and supporters? What
part did the now vociferous advocates of "free flow" play
in facilitating free and informed discussion on this question? What research or enquiries on this score did they ever
sponsor? They only became interested, they only sponsored
research, when challenged — when their interests were
threatened, and of course it was intended that such research
would produce results that would help them in their
defence.

*We must remember that
it is only recently
that anyone questioned
the prevailing
system at all.*

On the other side, so to speak, it is now argued, even by
some of those sympathetic to the Third World, that "the
virtues and benefits of the present system are in danger of
being ignored in the current debate". This may be so, but
we must remember that it is only recently that anyone
questioned the prevailing system at all. Balance has only
just been introduced into the debate. The virtues and benefits of the existing system were taken for granted, although
not always specified or substantiated. What some of us see
today as obvious inadequacies have been wrapped in a cloak
of silence for years. Clearly the lifting of the cloak is
regretted by many of those who speak and write in terms of

"freedom". It is not without significance that those who lifted the cloak with their research are now attacked by those who so obviously benefited from the silence.

It is now suggested that UNESCO research should be shifted away from such questions as "the right to communicate" to "more concrete problems". But what are these "concrete problems"?

This is no doubt why in some quarters it is now suggested that UNESCO research should be shifted away from such questions as "the right to communicate" to "more concrete problems". But what are these "concrete problems"? The same as, or similar to, the safe, "value-free", micro-questions of the old-time positivists who served the system so well, whether they realized it or not? All this represents a definite and not very well disguised attempt to put the cloak back to the days when the function of research was to serve the system as it was, and not to question, challenge or attempt to improve it. This then is the political arena in which mass communication research operates. It is not that research has suddenly become politicised; it is more a question of the emergence of a balance, as *latently politicised* research is challenged by more *overtly politicised* developments.

I shall deal now, albeit briefly, with some more specific aspects of communication research in an attempt to further illustrate some of the differences between the new and the old approaches. I have already mentioned some of the essential features of both approaches. Extending these and applying them to the Third World and the question of media and development, it needs to be stressed that the emphasis by the conventional researcher in this field, within the un-questioned framework of the Protestant ethic, on such psychological or individualistic concepts as empathy, psychic mobility, development consciousness, imitation, attitude change, etc., reflected an inadequate understanding of both the concept of development and society and the nature of the communication process.

We now know that to restrict our understanding of media influence to that which can be assessed by way of attitude change, imitation or identification, presents a very misleading picture of the part played by the media in society.

As indicated earlier, we now know that to restrict our understanding of media influence to that which can be assessed by way of attitude change, imitation or identification, presents a very misleading picture of the part played by the media in society. There is no need here to dwell at length on the question of influence or effects, but over the past few years we have moved to a position where we now think of media influence in terms of association, amplification, legitimation, agenda setting, and so on. We also take into account units other than the individual as we attempt to assess the influence of the media on other institutions, in defining social reality, and on culture and society more

This challenging situation calls for more ability, more imagination, insight, discipline, dedication, effort — not less.

generally. Of course, these phenomena are not so easily susceptible to what passes for scientific measurement as are attitude change and imitation, and in one way this is what caused a problem. The issues deemed worthy of investigation have tended to be those which could be measured by the *approved* available techniques. It is encouraging to see the newer approaches to mass communication research favouring a more flexible, imaginative, insightful, adventurous, less hidebound approach to the study of media influence than we have had in the past. It is important to remember, however, that to support this change is not to offer support for some of the sloppy, unsystematic, impressionistic, soft options that have appeared in recent years. This challenging situation calls for more ability, more imagination, more insight, more discipline, more dedication, more effort — not less.

We may also find evidence of another hangover from the past when we examine the general questions on communication and information. There are many examples across a wide range of communication issues (development, health education, family planning, agricultural innovation and adoption, social action, social policy, etc.) where one still has the impression that those responsible for information campaigns and educational programmes work on the assumption that their main — perhaps even their sole — task is to provide information and the rest will follow.

There are many examples across a wide range of communication issues where one has the impression that those responsible for information campaigns and educational programmes work on the assumption that their main — perhaps even sole — task is to provide information and the rest will follow.

Yet research shows this is not the case. The adoption of a sociological perspective where the information process and the relevant individuals and groups are studied in the appropriate historical and social contexts illustrates the importance of many other non-media factors. People may possess the necessary information on any given issue, but may not possess the social skills to translate the information into the appropriate social action. Others may possess the information too, but they might also have conflicting information or opposing attitudes or experiences in the past which act as obstacles and get in the way of the translation. The effective conversion and utilization of information may also depend on other institutional arrangements and support factors in the social structure generally. All these intervening factors are extremely important· in any analysis of communication/information problems. An analysis may indicate, for example, that in any given campaign it would be more fruitful to concentrate on the transfer, the obstacles, the intervening factors, the conversion and utilization of information, etc., than on its provision. Generally, we

*Information is a
necessary but never a
sufficient cause of
social action,
although there are
some instances where
it may be used as a
substitute for action.*

may say that information is a necessary but never a sufficient cause of social action, although there are even some
instances where it may be used as a substitute for action.

I referred earlier to research priorities, and I also suggested
that as far as research problems were concerned, despite the
differences stemming mainly from dependency relationships, both developing countries and the so-called developed countries had many things in common. Twelve years
ago I listed my own research priorities — the sort of questions I felt we ought to be asking, nationally and internationally, about the role of the media and the nature of
the communication process. In general the list still holds
good, although more progress has been made in some areas
than in others. It should, of course, be noted that the questions, as listed, are not mutually exclusive.

The questions I asked were as follows:

1. In what way, to what extent, and over what time period will the new developments in media technology
   render existing communication technology obsolete?

2. Does the 'communications revolution' represent an
   entirely new factor in the socialization process and, if
   so, how?

3. Does the new technology demand an entirely new
   institutional and organizational structure, or can existing structures be suitably adapted?

4. How should one decide between

   (a) private interests and public control?
   (b) public accountability and freedom of speech?

*Is it not inevitable
that the "free flow
of information" will
work to the advantage
of those who possess
the information and
the means to
disseminate it?*

5. Many decisions in media policy are made in the name
   of 'the public good' and 'the national interest'. But
   what do these terms really mean, and who decides
   what is good?

6. Granted existing structures of newsgathering, selection,
   and presentation, is it not inevitable that the 'free flow
   of information' will work to the advantage of those
   who possess the information and the means to disseminate it?

7. Is it not time that the media were demystified, and
   that we began to question the restrictions and the

possible tyranny of professionalism? Must we always have the few talking about the many to the many?

8. Will the multiplicity of channels made possible by the new technology lead to cultural diversity and better opportunities for minority interests? In any case, who will control the software, the input, or the programmes?

9. Is public monopoly the only real guarantee of diversity?

10. Granted existing systems of ownership and control and the prevalence of western news values, are the media ever likely to provide the amount and quality of information necessary for people to act intelligently in a participatory democracy?

11. Is there not a grave risk that we shall become paralysed by an overload of information? How much can we tolerate? How much can we understand?

12. Internationally, will the 'communications revolution' lead to an increase or a decrease in the gap between the haves and the have-nots?

13. As far as the developing countries are concerned, is not the main, perhaps even the sole, concern — how to use the media in the interests of national identity and development? Never mind objectivity, impartiality, or balance. How can one harness the new technology to national as distinct from sectional objectives?

14. How can we guard against the possible homogenizing influence of the new technology as traditional cultures may become swamped by the commercial off-loading of cheap alien material?

15. What do we know about the processes of media influence?

At this stage, with the benefit of many years' work in the field, I would now want to develop the point about cultural homogeneity and pose some additional questions about the media and national culture. I would also wish to give more attention to the very important question of participation. But for the moment let the list suffice to give a more concrete illustration of the sorts of questions that critical researchers are, or should be, asking.

Is public monopoly the only real guarantee of diversity?

As far as the developing countries are concerned, is not the main, perhaps even the sole, concern how to use the media in the interests of national identity and development?

Perhaps the level where the various bands of critical research appear to have the most in common is at the level of research operation and practice.

It is necessary now for me to deal, at slightly greater length, with the points mentioned earlier about the usefulness or validity of classifying such diverse groups and individuals under a general "critical" heading. In fact, it has been said that the rejection of positivism and the conventional research referred to earlier, together with a vague, ill-defined concern with social problems and policy, is about all this motley collection of critical researchers have in common.

Perhaps the level where the various bands of critical research appear to have most in common is at the level of research operation and practice. It is beyond dispute that the aforementioned rejections of positivism, behaviouristic psychology with its simple causal hypotheses, and the extremes of functionalism, together with a preference for models of the communication process which, if nothing else, include sociological concepts, have led to research programmes and projects which were not much in evidence a decade or so ago.

Of course, there is much more to be done; other questions to be asked, a need for more evidence or recognition of underlying assumptions and for more precise and clear articulations of theoretical principles. But only the blind, the ignorant, or the profoundly prejudiced could fail to recognize that the questions that are being asked now represent a fundamentally different approach to mass communication research than the approaches which prevailed in the not so distant past, and which still persist in places today. Admittedly, the questions, the research approaches, and the social and policy concerns, do not represent a single, clearly articulated 'theoretical" position. But, for me, with a clear preference for a plurality of models, this is all to the good, and a situation to be welcomed and encouraged. There are, however, those from widely different standpoints, who think the label is misleading, concealing more than it reveals, perhaps even concealing quite dangerous and disruptive tendencies not appropriate to any scientific endeavour.

But only the blind, the ignorant, or the profoundly prejudiced could fail to recognize that the questions being asked now represent a fundamentally different approach to mass communication research.

To recapitulate briefly, the last twenty years or so have seen changes in mass communication research reflecting changes in social science generally. One of the outcomes, more apparent in Europe and Britain than in the USA, has been the development of a critical, sociological approach which has challenged not only the supremacy of earlier, mainly positivistic research approaches, but also the service and administrative functions of these approaches and the claims and presumptions of the media systems which they serve. In more recent years similar challenges, perhaps representing an interesting fusion between regional initiatives in the Third World, particularly in Latin America, and the aforementioned critical approach have also developed.

There are those who now see a crisis in sociology which is bound to be reflected in some way or other in mass communication research.

So far, so good. But there are those who now see a crisis in sociology which is bound to be reflected in some way or other in mass communication research. A prominent British sociologist, John Rex, has argued that we have gone astray. He welcomed the dethroning of the old approaches, but is not very happy with the new claimants and usurpers. Instead of the considered and thoughtful development of plural paradigms which enjoy complementary relationships (and which he and I would favour) he fears that a situation has developed not of complementarity but of conflict between "warring" schools. As he sees it, this situation is not marked by speculative and reflective approaches or by careful examination, respect for evidence, consideration of alternatives, or the caution and tolerance that one might expect from social science, but by dogma, doctrinaire statements, selective use of evidence, unsubstantiated assertions and, at times, an arrogance and hostile intolerance. He likens the situation to the religious wars of the past. The positions, firmly held by the new high priests, brook no contradictions, and evidence must not be allowed to get in the way of faith. Like others who claim to be social scientists, he is more than a little worried about a situation where, if one hundred hypotheses derived from a theory or set of beliefs were invalidated in research, the theory might still remain inviolate. This has certainly little in common with the "rational, moderate and democratic approach advocated by many of those who would consider themselves to be critical researchers.

If one hundred hypotheses derived from a theory or set of beliefs were invalidated in research, the theory might still remain inviolate.

An outsider might be forgiven for assuming (many of them have so assumed) that whatever the specific nature of the various perspectives within the critical field, all or most of them would enthusiastically welcome the overall change in research direction which has been outlined. But that this is not necessarily so, even amongst those who would call themselves sociologists, is clear from recent divisions and disagreements within the critical school, some of which reflect the disputes and the "religious wars" that are currently being waged within the wider field of sociology. This may seem strange to the outsider, although it should not surprise anyone familiar with the field. Moreover, it needs to be emphasized here that this is not just another illustration of the interminable, incestuous, wranglings and ramblings of sociologists — so boring and irrelevant to the rest of the world. It may well exhibit many unfortunate characteristics, but it is at the heart of the relationship between research and ideology and is central to an understanding of the recent history, the current state, and no doubt the future development of mass communication research.

It has been argued that institutionalized sociology would not necessarily be the source of inspiration for critical enquiry.

It has been argued that institutionalized sociology (it has, of course, been institutionalized in different ways in different places) would not necessarily be the source of inspiration for critical enquiry. According to Golding and Murdock, this inspiration is more likely to be found in a commitment to the basic questions that they would regard as providing sociology with its original impetus.

To them, and others holding similar views, what matters is that society is defined by the system of class relationships which prevail and thus the prime focus for study should be "the mass media . . . and the class system". The second focus should be on the way in which the media constitute one of the means by which that system is legitimated, and the third focus should be on the sources of social dissent and political struggle. The task of "research" is to show how the prevailing distributions of poverty and power and the dominant principles of control shape the structure of symbolic arrangements, how they enter into experience as interpretative procedures, and the conditions of their repetition and change. In order to accomplish this successfully it is suggested that research must be grounded more solidly and consistently than hitherto in general social theory, apparently in one specific social theory.

It is suggested that research must be grounded more solidly and consistently than hitherto in general social theory.

Some of the researchers and students of the media who adopt this or some similar stance are genuinely committed to research which attempts to demonstrate the validity of the abovementioned relationships. But there are others who are more concerned with assertion than with validation, or with the provision of concrete evidence from the systematic observations of social reality which might enable social theory to be put to the test. Some of them pay lip service to data collection and analysis, but others are dismissive of such laborious and irrelevant procedures (which also happen to be difficult to master and have the unfortunate tendency of proving one wrong) and readily accept that their main task — the main function of research — is to attempt to make reality appear to conform to ideology.

There is an increasing number of ideologists who present their work as social science, perhaps seeing no incompatibility between the two or not regarding it as a problem at all.

It is ideology that we are now talking about and in mass communication research, as elsewhere, there are an increasing number of ideologists who present their work as social science, perhaps seeing no incompatibility between the two, or not regarding it as a problem at all. I presume it all depends on what one means by ideology and what one means by social science.

But some researchers and social scientists do see it as a problem, and wonder if they fail to find their source of inspiration and their basic theoretical underpinnings in "institutionalized sociology in academia", then where do they find them? It has been suggested that the answer is in sociology *as it should be* rather than as it is. But to some, this answer fails to distinguish between sociology and ideology, and this has led them to conclude that the primary objective of the research that is carried out under the heading of this type of sociological investigation is not "the objective recording of reality", "the systematic description of the present", but the prescriptions for a preferred future.

This is not the place for a full discussion on the nature of ideology and its relationship to social science, but in view of the general theme of this paper and the issues covered in it, there are some questions that cannot be ignored.

Ideology which, according to Maurice Cranston, rests on what it believes to be knowledge and *pretends* to wear the "crown of reason", has had a chequered history, being defined, interpreted and regarded in a variety of ways. Even Marx himself used the word in more than one sense, moving from a perjorative to a more favourable interpretation over the years.

Lewis Feuer explains that ideology contains elements of more than one logical category.

Lewis S. Feuer, in what some regard as the most important sociological study of ideology to have yet appeared, explains that ideology contains elements of more than one logical category. He says the most important are perhaps the following: (a) it claims to provide a more or less scientific or systematic account of human experience, (b) it sets forth a programme of individual and collective action, (c) it seeks not merely to persuade the mind but also to recruit the commitment of its adherents, (d) while it conceives the realisation of its programme as a fight in which all must participate, and thus seeks mass participation, it also calls into being an "officer-type" elite to lead the struggle and a "bookish type" elite to interpret the theory.

*Ideology, according
to Raymond Aron, is
incompatible with
social science for by
its very nature it
already knows the
answers to the
questions which
research exists
to explore.*

According to Feuer, Cranston and those of like mind,
ideological thought, by its very nature, is an exercise subject to very strict limitations for any proposition that calls
into question the doctrine of the ideology itself is excluded.
No matter what happens as the result of research or social
scientific enquiry, the ideologist will not renounce his
ideology. Cranston writes that to subscribe to an ideology is
to enrol for a package tour, where every decision and all
arrangements are made, and where no one has to think for
himself on any matter of importance. From this standpoint
ideology, "the opium of intellectuals" according to Raymond Aron, is incompatible with social science (as many
would define it) for by its very nature it already knows the
answers to the questions which research exists to explore.
Let the ideologist make his statements by all means, but
why waste money, time, resources, energy, etc. on a
phoney research exercise when whatever is discovered will
not result in any change — is a point of view with regard to
mass communication research which stems from this
particular interpretation of ideology.

It has been suggested that we should work for and accept
plural or conflicting ideologies, but this idea is not supported by Cranston, who believes that ideology, whatever its
source or colour, is by its very nature incompatible with the
free enquiry, respect for evidence, open discussion and exchange that should be the hallmarks of social science.

*Why waste money,
time resources,
energy, etc. on a
phoney research
exercise when
whatever is
discovered will not
result in any change.*

The authors of papers such as this one, just like the mass
media and mass communication researchers, are clearly not
uninfluenced by their background and experience. So far
this paper has been written from the standpoint, albeit a
critical one, of a social scientist who has been brought up
and works in a western, industrialized society. Several years
ago Walery Pisarek, in preparing an international bibliography for a monograph published by the International
Association for Mass Communication Research, said that he
would be well satisfied "even if the sole effect of introducing certain publications . . . would be to give some of its
users grounds for suspicion that the frontiers of the science
of mass communication are wider than those normally
delineated by the English language literature" Since that
time Pisarek and others, through IAMCR, have made further attempts to redress the imbalance but there is still a
long way to go and, in any case, as we have seen, without
denying the validity of Pisarek's concern, it is much more
than a question of language. Pisarek obviously recognises
this, for he reminded us, at a conference some years ago,

that researchers from East and West had difficulty in finding a level for mutual understanding, not only because their
national languages differed, but because they classified
reality in different ways.

*Researchers from East
and West had
difficulty in finding
a level for mutual
understanding, not
only because their
national languages
differed, but
because they
classified reality in
different ways.*

The same conference provided us with some good examples
of what Pisarek probably had in mind. On the one hand we
can read the following from the conference papers:

> "It follows in both socialist and capitalist societies that
> the mass media have to fulfil diametrically opposed
> missions — deformation of the masses is vital to impe-
> rialism but formation of all human capabilities is a pre-
> condition for socialism. Television interprets and re-
> directs (the needs of children) in such a way as to make
> them conform to standardized capitalist patterns of
> work, decision making and leisure behaviour."

> "Practice shows phenomena appearing in journalism of
> both capitalist and socialist countries, which are for-
> mally and structurally of the same kind — such as the
> recent increase in local reporting, the growing number
> of specialized journals and magazines — increasing
> differentiation in radio and television programmes."
> (It might appear then that there is common ground
> here, and a good base for comparative study and ex-
> changes, but the author goes on to argue that in capita-
> list countries the process of differentiation just referred
> to) ". . . entails, as intended, real separation, limita-
> tions, isolation and one-sidedness of people who are
> becoming increasingly incapable of understanding
> social contexts, whereas in socialist countries the pro-
> cess of differentiation helps to develop the ability of
> exercising active democracy by striving for maximum
> comprehensibility and forcefulness of messages."

*In both socialist
and capitalist
societies the mass
media have to fulfil
diametrically opposed
missions.*

> "The author demonstrates that in both socialist and
> capitalist societies the mass media have to fulfil diame-
> trically opposed missions (deformation of the masses of
> the people is vital to imperialism; but formation of all
> human capabilities is a precondition for socialism). This
> is illustrated especially by the objectives and methods
> of portraying man in the two social orders, as well as
> by references to advertising and influences on people's
> leisure time behaviour. It is demonstrated that the
> collaboration of the masses with their media is a per-
> manent principle under socialism while under imperia-
> lism the inclusion of the audience merely serves, in the

On the whole assertion tends to prevail over evidence and demonstration.

the first place, to obtain 'feedback' information on the effectiveness of the media and, in the second place, to better carry out the manipulation intended. Criticism is permitted only if it does not endanger the system."

We can read many other similar statements which appear to manifest a clearly committed position or standpoint both with regard to the role of media in society and the part that should be played by mass communication research. Moreover, on the whole assertion tends to prevail over evidence and demonstration.

On the other hand, other papers at the same conference reflect an approach, or perhaps I should say a series of individual approaches, characterized by such statements as the following.

Research shows that:

"teachers make no use of the considerable time spent by their students with the new media."

"The family is evidently a potential mediator of the impact of television."

"Television is an indispensable instrument for conveying information on extra family reality."

"Television is playing a major role in the socialization process of children that differs from that of the school and the family."

Teachers make no use of the considerable time spent by their students with the new media.

Incidentally, it should be emphasized that in selecting these statements from both sides, so to speak, no criticism is intended. They are selected simply to illustrate what are obviously clear differences in approach and in views about the nature of research.

One way of looking at this with regard to the concept of socialization is to see the latter approach as the "so what" approach. Research is carried out, information provided about the role of the media and other institutions in the socialization process, and there the work of the debate ends as far as the researcher is concerned. We are left to make use of this information as we think appropriate. The research does not address itself to an evaluation of the content of the media, still less to an analysis of the structure and organization of the media, in any purposive or critical way.

In contrast to this the other approach to socialization — the one which I illustrated first — at times implicitly, at other times very explicitly, approaches socialization in the sense of How can or should the media be used? How can our research illuminate the process of socialization in such a way that clearly stated, predetermined social objectives may be achieved? How can we demonstrate that our interpretation, our system, our approach, are essentially different from, and superior to, other systems etc?

Most researchers, whatever their school of thought, have a great deal in common.

It could be argued, of course, that I am both stating the obvious and deliberately maximising the differences — that the statements are not typical or representative — that there may be striking differences in the approaches, but that there are also equally striking similarities where common ground can be occupied and meaningful exchanges can take place. There is a point here, and I am sure that those supporting such a line of argument could also turn to the conference papers and other exchanges and illustrate, without much difficulty, the scope and nature of this common ground.

They would no doubt show that in actually teasing out the role of the media in society, in studying the relationship to other media institutions, reactions to the media, the effects of the media, the nature of the communications process, comprehensibility, and so on — most researchers, whatever their school of thought, have a great deal in common.

An example of this agreement might be that they would probably be able to show from many of the contributions that at long last researchers seem to have dropped studying the media in isolation and now accept, albeit belatedly, that the media can only be adequately studied in relation to other institutions within the appropriate wider historical, political and national contexts. The need for theoretical developments (of some form or other) would also receive wide acceptance.

The media can only be adequately studied in relation to other institutions within the appropriate wider historical, political and national contexts.

International exchanges at conferences, seminars, etc. — learned, stimulating and insightful though they undoubtedly are — in one way tend to reinforce the observation by Pisarek, for scholars from different parts of the world approach themes and problems from their different perspectives. But this position can be, and often is, oversimplified. We have seen that there are differences within the west and we shall see that the "eastern bloc" is not as

There are similarities between some of the western critical approaches and some of the approaches favoured in Eastern and Central Europe, but not necessarily at all levels.

homogeneous as some would have us believe. Moreover, there are similarities between some of the western critical approaches and some of the approaches favoured in Eastern and Central Europe, but not necessarily at all levels (e.g. targets of criticism). It has been suggested that these similarities may be a reflection of the fact that the main theoretical lines have, in their own ways, developed in opposition to Western social science (although not in isolation from it), and "as criticisms of the present state of Western theory". It is worth noting that the most widely known challenges to Western social science are those developed in the West, but, as far as I am aware, from my limited knowledge of Eastern literature, a parallel state of affairs does not exist in the East. Of course, the circumstances are quite different, and the differences are reflected in the nature, aims, purposes and scope of social science and research.

In passing, it is important to note that the International Association for Mass Communication Research has an important task to perform in this connection. The Association is not so unrealistic as to think that continuing exchanges would remove all differences. In any case, this need not be desirable for research approaches, perspectives, etc. are bound to reflect the system from which they stem and within which they operate, and the differences may therefore be necessary and healthy. Nevertheless, the International Association would not be accepting its responsibilities if it did not attempt to provide an opportunity for exchanges — a forum, a place where the different perspectives and their implications can be presented, examined and compared.

The Association is not so unrealistic as to think that continuing exchanges would remove all differences.

At the 1976 conference, the Association did provide an opportunity for Dr Lothar Bisky from the DDR to present his particular evaluation of the "state of the art" of mass communication research. Dr Bisky emphasized from the outset that as mass communication systems vary between the capitalist and socialist states, then the theoretical and methodological perspectives of mass communication researchers must also vary. He stated quite unequivocally that he approached his task from an historical-materialistic point of view. Although recognising the difficulties of his position, he preferred a positive, future-oriented exposition to an indulgence in critical post-mortems.

He maintained that internationally mass communication research was like a universal reservoir into which arbitrary points of view, and in fact anything which had any relevance to the mass media, flowed frequently but haphazardly. In drawing attention to the expansion of research he went on to argue that the main problems were qualitative rather than quantitative. He was certainly not convinced that the increase in the research effort in recent years had led to an increase in our understanding of the mass media or of the communication process.

In drawing attention to the expansion of research Bisky went on to argue that the main problems were qualitative rather than quantitative.

What we needed to do, according to Bisky, was to empty the reservoir and begin again by establishing more clearly the relationships between the various disciplines employed by mass communication researchers (sociology, psychology, aesthetics, etc.), and also to define more precisely the special character of mass communication research, its subject matter, and its theoretical and methodological bases.

Bisky maintained that the reason why research had not established this clarity of definition and purpose and had become, in his terms, a 'reservoir' was because it tended to avoid "basic research" (for example, attempting to be precise about what one understands by the term "communication'), and that this had led to false theoretical premises, associated conceptual confusions and methodological mistakes. He illustrated the consequences of this, stressing throughout that the necessary connections between theory and empiricism had been ignored and that we were now paying the price for this neglect.

Bisky would like to see the focus of mass communication research shift to investigations of the "method of mass media transmitted *communication processes* (communication includes the production *and* reception of information)". He recognised, however, that this could only be done within the context of a broader concept of the relationship of man and society.

The reason why research had not established this clarity of definition and purpose and had become a "reservoir" was because it tended to avoid "basic research".

The concept he favoured was that of mass communication as a component of social communication, which itself was part and parcel of an historically defined system of social production and reproduction. To Bisky, social communication is "an essential part of the cooperation of man, whereby its contents and form arise from the historic, concretely defined manner of social production and reproduction, and therefore can only be explained in this manner". A theoretical explanation of mass communication is possible only on the basis of the social character of mass communication, and within the framework of a social theory.

It would appear to follow from this, then, that within a bourgeois society the media system will be bourgeois, with bourgeois ideas, and the dominant classes will dominate the system to spread their own bourgeois ideology. Presumably it would also be argued that a free mass communication system can only function in a classless society.

Presumably it would also be argued that a free mass communication system can only function in a classless society.

When applied to the recipients of mass media products, i.e. the audience, the Marxist analysis favoured by Bisky would focus on their total social action and relationships, and not just on their reactions to media output.

Summarizing and looking to the future, Bisky stated that he was trying to develop the varying ramifications of theory and empiricism in mass communication research, and that he hoped that the quality of such an effort would decide the scientific quality of mass communication research in the future.

Briefly, he would like mass communication research in the future to:

1. concentrate on the subject proper and not act as a universal reservoir;

2. clarify its theoretical basis; and

3. develop an effective interchange between theoretical and empirical research to produce true scientific development.

What really matters is the critical quality of theory — not just theory as such or theory for the sake of theory.

It has been argued, however, from the same general position, that what really matters is the *critical quality* of theory — not just theory as such or theory for the sake of theory. Not everyone would agree with Bisky when he says that empiricism in mass communication research has been built up largely atheoretically. It could be argued that empiricism itself was a theory based on scientific ontological assumptions. It might also be argued that empirical research ought not to be explained theoretically, as Bisky suggests, for research should not *explain* reality anyway. Putting the results of empirical research afterwards in a theoretical framework (albeit critically) tends to ignore the necessity of designing the whole research process from the perspective of critical social theory from the very beginning. This means that, rather than upholding a separation between empirical and theoretical research, mass communication research could be more fruitfully guided by the dialectical relationship of theory and praxis.

Another criticism also from a Marxist position is that Bisky has not given enough attention to the "recently emerged concepts of situation and communication situation". It is claimed that these new approaches are opposed both to "the deterministic, mechanical approaches of cybernetics and systems theory, and also to the subjective interpretations of situational interactionalism and existentialism".

These new approaches are opposed both to "the deterministic, mechanical approaches of cybernetics and systems theory, and also to the subjective interpretations of situational interactionalism and existentialism".

Apparently the "situation" approach, characteristic of much of the mass communication research in Hungary, tries to grasp the notion of communication situations by establishing socio-historical categories at several levels. It is claimed that setting out from broader historical situations and working down to the situational micro elements of an act of communication, this approach is capable of systematically depicting communication as a socially determined process.

Tamas Szecsko has written that

"The relatively fast development of communication research in Hungary from the middle of the 1960s is incomprehensible without realizing two basic trends characteristic of Hungary's domestic policy and public life in the 1960s and 1970s: the comprehensive economic reform called "new economic mechanism" and the further development of the country's political and public institutions in the direction of "socialist democratism". Both trends concern basic social relations and, as opposed to the overcentralized political, governmental and economic system of the 1950s, afford a more extensive field of decision, action, and responsibility for different social and economic units. At the same time, because of the increased social relevance of such actions, both trends involve more social planning, particularly planning of the more complex and long-range varieties.

Besides material information, the particular content of social consciousness is getting more attention.

Under such conditions, the leading political bodies' and social organizations' demands for information have rapidly increased. Furthermore, there has been a structured change within these demands. Besides material information, the particular content of social consciousness is getting more attention. The leadership of the Party and the government have increasingly been encouraging the research of public opinion and mass communication. Consequently, the findings of such research are integrated more and more often into information, cultural and communication policies on a national level.

The development of communication research has been influenced by advances in Marxist social theory and the integration of the results of empirical methods with social theory.

The development of communication research has been influenced by advances in Marxist social theory and the integration of the results of empirical methods with social theory. Linguistics also bears on the trends of communication research, and Hungarian linguistics may well be proud of its traditions, especially in historical linguistics. Recently, it has started integrating structuralism, generative grammar, and other linguistic approaches and probing adjacent fields such as sociolinguistics and psycholinguistics. Since 1960 scholars in the theory of literature have also been adopting methods of communication research such as the quantitative content and semiotic approaches to art analysis. From the middle of the 1960s there have been contributions from the concepts and logic of cybernetics, information theory, mathematical theory of games, and general theory.''

Szecsko goes on to outline the issues constituting the key reference points of Hungarian mass communication policies as follows:

— *Mass orientation and stratum orientation*: to find a dynamic balance between the two in programming, partly with a view to the differentiating demands of the audiences, partly with respect to the expanding technical possibilities of production.

— *Centralization and decentralization*: to work out — parallel with the development of the system of political institutions — a territorial structure of the mass communication system which is decentralized enough to promote

Since 1960 scholars in the theory of literature have also been adopting methods of communication research.

and give voice to the democratism of public life on a regional and local level and is at the same time centralized enough to have the whole society's interests asserted.

— *Connections between communication media and institution-systems*: to go beyond technical aspects of multimedia development and try to integrate the institution-systems of political communication, public education, and culture in a way that enables the optimal allocation of intellectual resources and energies for development of the interest in attaining the most important social objectives.

— *Communication policy and social policy*: to create material conditions, partly by means of social policy, partly by economic policy, under which differences between different social strata are gradually eliminated as regards their effective use of mass media potentialities.

— *Fields of tolerance*: contrary to the communication policies that emphasize data of the "head-counting" type of audience research and thus preserve the existing demands and taste levels, to make a more conscious use of those so-called "fields of tolerance" in which cultural content is received favourably by the public but without being a commercial mass-production.

— *Creation of demands*: to create, beyond existing demands and necessities new, more conscious, and humanized intellectual demands of a higher level within the public.

— *Relaxation, "re-engagement"*: to solve the basic dilemma of mass entertainment so that relaxation should not mean an escape from reality. The "light programmes" should not block the reception of cultural values, and the intellectual loosening should not suggest that culture could be obtained without efforts.

— *Creation of community*: the communication systems should be consciously applied to support the strengthening of real communities formed by common activities instead of quasi-communities produced by the sheer communication experience.

— *Stability and conflict*: to reflect events and phenomena of the world in mass communication in a way that presents the steady trends of the development of mankind and society and at the same time shows the conflicts and contradictions of the development as well.

— *Continuity and discontinuity*: to try to make people conscious of historically new traits, values, and norms of the socialist society and at the same time to guarantee that they appreciate, integrate, and pass on the age-old cultural heritage of mankind and of the nation.

— *Value-orientation*: to devise mechanisms within the system of communication so that both the direct messages and the indirect ones (in the metatext) may globally reflect the system of norms and the hierarchy of values of the new society.

— *News-value*: to reappraise the informative functions of the communication system, reinterpreting the "news-value" concept of journalism, which, in its traditional sense, meant no more than unexpectedness, interest, and rapidity. Now it should be based on the "image-improvement" function of the given information — namely by helping people to recognize the substantial aspects of objective reality.

— Need of information: starting from the objective need of information of groups and strata of society, to guarantee that the communication system regularly supplies for all strata and groups more information about substantial issues, which demand publicity, rather than merely the "subsistence-level" of information, and to ensure that the system teaches the public how to find their own information, how to select consciously, and how to interpret.

— The unexpectedness and the planned: to establish an institution of social communication, which in its basic aspects can be planned with scientific accuracy (and thus can be integrated in the system of social planning) but which is flexible enough in its actual operation to adapt itself to the rhythm of unforeseeable events and rapid differentiation of social demands.

Szecsko also stresses the historical perspective, the educative or social-strategic role and the importance of the policy orientation of Hungarian mass communication research.

Hungarian mass communication research is well known internationally and produces many publications, quite a number of them in the English language. At one level of analysis (admittedly a relatively superficial one) an overview of the titles of recently published articles by Hungarian mass communication researchers might lead one to conclude that they were not all that different from those produced by their counterparts in the USA, and there are in fact significant similarities which go beyond mere titles. However, in making such comparisons one should not forget that Szecsko also stresses the historical perspective, the educative or social-strategic role and the importance of the policy orientation of Hungarian mass communication research. He also refers to the compelling need to keep close ties with social practice and the role of research in changing phenomena as well as in describing them.

On the whole he regards the above outline as a series of unresolved issues.

"The rapidly transforming communication system of a socialist society is trying to create its own structure, institutions, and mechanisms amid these points of reference. And while these principles are assuming the shapes of communication policies, all those participat-

It is not uncommon in the West for different institutions in the same society to be pursuing diametrically opposed social goals.

ing in the job — politicians, communicators, or researchers — are not only trying to find solutions but have to face new dilemmas and devise new strategies for finding the proper balance between the teleology of social values and the historical and social necessities."

Perhaps this reference to institutional integration and collaboration points to one of the most important differences between East and West. It is not uncommon in the West for different institutions in the same society to be pursuing diametrically opposed social goals.

It was suggested earlier that in the world of mass communication research there was a reasonably wide agreement on the need to develop appropriate theories. In fact, mass communication research, for much of its history, has been obsessed with the quest for theory. However, judging from recent international conferences, there is no clear agreement as to the most appropriate level of theorizing. Two suggestions have recently been made:

1. a call for a "grand theory", an approach which is usually related to the desire to link mass communication research with the main issues of society.

2. mass communication researchers should pursue theorizing of the middle range, since the time is not yet ripe for the formulation of a "grand theory".

It is relatively easy to point to the pitfalls of arid empiricism, but the issue remains as to the best ways in which fruitful links should or could be forged between empirical research and the development of theory.

Even allowing for the difficulties raised in this comment, it seems to be fairly generally acknowledged that we must pay due attention to the relationship between theory and empirical research (and the results of empirical research). It is, of course, relatively easy to point to the pitfalls of arid empiricism, but the issue remains as to the best ways in which fruitful links should or could be forged between empirical research and the development of theory. Most of us accept that the importance of empirical research lies not in the data themselves. But we also recognise that in the interpretations made of the data, if we do embrace some form of grand theory, we must not fall into the trap of remaining at a level of theorizing which would not or could not provide the possibility of generating hypotheses designed to test critically such theoretical issues.

The weaknesses and inadequacies of research, which are not consciously tied to an articulated theory, have been well illustrated and they reflect what Carey has referred to as "the absence of any informing relation between communications and social theory".

Perhaps it might also be stated again that this does not mean that the conventional work has no theoretical implications. It represents a standpoint, a value position, even if this is not made explicit. In fact, one of the problems is that because the position is never articulated it can never be adequately criticised. Without an underlying theory of society any research programme will fragment into bits and pieces that can never possibly tell us anything about the relationship of media to society, and this is one of the reasons why the conventional approach is likely to be welcomed by the media establishment.

Carey suggests that there can be a theory of communication (and research) which has developed from a history of society, or one that is explicitly a theory of society.

A theory of society is necessary — on this, perhaps, many of us can agree. But what theory? Carey suggests that there can be a theory of communication (and research) which has developed from a history of society, or a theory of communication that is explicitly a theory of society. We need not pursue this question here, but we may quote Carey again and emphasize "that powerful and fundamental work in this field, as in the other social sciences, will only proceed under the reflexive guidance and criticism of such theory".

There is a task for us here, then, and the clearer articulation and exposition of our theories would make it easier for us all to understand what we were all about. Another way of bridging gaps, finding common denominators, coming together and possibly carrying out research exercises, might be to focus more on the individual and his communication needs. We have already noted the Hungarian interest here.

Structural, organizational and institutional changes should not be regarded as ends in themselves, but as means towards the achievement of the goals of individual development.

We might ask if structural changes, although absolutely essential nationally and internationally, can never be sufficient in themselves. Structural, organizational and institutional changes should not be regarded as ends in themselves, but as means towards the achievement of the goals of individual development. We must have independent criteria relating to the human person that go beyond mere structure. Structural changes must be evaluated in terms of their contribution to the fulfilment of human communication needs which we must be prepared to identify and spell out. This is not an either/or situation, but we must pay attention to types of individual *as well as* to types of society. We are in danger of forgetting this, and seem to assume that a given type of society and set of institutional arrangements will inevitably be in the best interests of all individuals in that society. We should know, both from history and from the contemporary situation, that there is no guaranteed or automatic relationship between any given structure on the one hand and individual freedom and human development on the other. We must avoid the self-fulfilling prophecy.

Genuine, critical research is a continuing process — it must be applied without fear or favour to the new as well as to the old.

Here is another vitally important area, calling for systematic comparative research. This is a real challenge for communication researchers, for they must continue to expose the imbalance and inequities of the existing order, seeking at the same time a more just order which itself must be evaluated in terms of the type of independent criteria just mentioned. Genuine, critical research is a continuing process — it must be applied without fear or favour to the new as well as to the old. We must be careful not to jump out of the frying pan into the fire and replace the old, imbalanced system with one which rests more on slogans, tautologies, wishful thinking and self-fulfilling prophecies than on substantiated achievements judged according to generally acceptable and consistently applied criteria.

It is possible that a suitable area for exploration and co-operative research in this connection might focus on participation. Participation is a key concept in the general debate at both national and international levels, but it is not always precisely defined, uniformly interpreted or consistently applied. There is plenty of lip service to the notion, but this is often little more than a thinly disguised cover-up for the arrogance and intolerance of the media professionals and political technocrats who are likely to be impatient of experimentation and resistant to radical change. Efficiency is their watch-word, and in their terms participation is not likely to be efficient or professional. A form of professional tyranny is never far from the surface.

Participation is a key concept in the general debate at both national and international levels, but it is not always precisely defined, uniformly interpreted or consistently applied.

Should we not all be working towards situations where people will have the opportunity, and be encouraged, to participate at all levels in their own development? Should we not strive for conditions where people would be free to develop themselves as individuals, to increase their understanding and awareness by means of discussion, decision making, involvement and so on?

Unfortunately, the media systems in most parts of the world are not geared to this form of participation. The technology that might facilitate greater participation is available, but there are signs that this availability is being countered by an increasing reluctance on the part of the communication establishment to share their powers in any meaningful way. So-called experiments in participation often serve little more than an alibi function. Moreover, it is not always appreciated that access and participation do not necessarily work in the same direction, but often need to be balanced one against the other.

Is it being too naive to think that we might possibly carry out international comparative studies covering all types of socio-economic systems, using agreed operational definitions of participation? We could then see what was meant by participation, and how it was practised in the different systems.

We rightly call for more balance in the international flow of information; let us apply the same principles to the development of our research activities and the dissemination of our results.

In very general terms I think this is the way ahead, and it points to possible days of collaboration and cooperation. Of course there are tremendous difficulties to be overcome, but even so I am basically optimistic. I would like to think we could look forward to change, to a new economic order, to a new information order, and to a situation where every researcher in any country will always be willing to examine alternatives and where he will always have the opportunity to do this. One of our main tasks should be to encourage the pursuit of these objectives in a rational, moderate and balanced way. We rightly call for more balance in the international flow of information; let us apply the same principles to the development of our research activities and the dissemination of our results.

PART II

INTERNATIONAL COMMUNICATION

The long-awaited report of the UNESCO International Commission for the Study of Communication Problems, chaired by Nobel and Lenin prizewinner Sean MacBride of the Republic of Ireland, appeared in 1981 under the title *Many Voices, One World*. The work of the commission and its report have had repercussions around the world, and it is inconceivable that this *Yearbook* not take account of the report.

Included in this section are excerpts from the report itself, nine comments by communication scholars from as many countries, and the Declaration of Talloires, a statement issued by Western journalists meeting in Talloires, France, in May 1981, after the release of the MacBride Commission Report. These commentaries all give various points of view on the report and on the assumptions the authors see underlying it.

Two additional articles in this section are devoted to the corollary concept of media imperialism, but as the reader will discover, they approach it from very different viewpoints.

Communication policies and different ways of regarding international communication have received much attention in recent years. A document that has provided and will provide material for many and lengthy discussions about the fields in various groups is the so-called MacBride Report. Sean MacBride of Ireland has been the president of the UNESCO International Commission for the Study of Communication Problems since it started its work in December 1977. In late 1980 the commission issued its report, Many Voices, One World. In his preface to the report, MacBride gives a background to the work of the commission: the aims, development, and problems. He describes the report as generally "a consensus of how the Commission sees the present communication order and foresees a new one." From the report itself we have selected "Conclusions and Recommendations" and "Issues Requiring Further Study," from Part 5: Communication Tomorrow. This part of the report is commented upon in the subsequent sections.

6

MANY VOICES, ONE WORLD

UNESCO International Commission for the Study of Communication Problems

PREFACE

The International Commission for the Study of Communication Problems began its work in December 1977. My feelings then, at the outset of our long journey in the world of communications, were a mixture of excitement and trepidation: excitement at the opportunity to preside a sixteen member group from all corners of the globe in the exploration of a subject so basic to peace and human development; trepidation because of the vast range of topics and the crucial nature of the problems to be studied.

Nor did the background to the establishment of the Commission permit any optimistic temerity in anticipating the difficulties of the task ahead or of reaching agreed conclusion.

In the 1970s, international debates on communications issues had stridently reached points of confrontation in many areas. Third world protests against the dominant flow of news from the industrialized countries were often construed as attacks on the free flow of information. Defenders of journalistic freedom were labelled intruders on national sovereignty. Varying concepts of news values and the rôle, rights and responsibilities of journalists were widely contended, as was the potential contribution of the mass media to the solution of major world problems.

Given this divisive atmosphere which surrounded the start of the Commission's work, my concern from the beginning was how to achieve a balanced, non-partisan, objective analysis of today's communication scene and how to meet the challenge of reaching the broadest possible consensus in our views on the major issues before us.

Another primary concern was the breadth of our mandate: "to study the totality of communication problems in modern societies". Among all the documentation and literature in the field which this Commission perused during the course of its work, none attempted such an all-encompassing review. Ours does not purport to be anything near a definitive work, but we have tried to transcend the conventional issues and to come close to the terms of our mandate.

Hence, ours is not simply a report on the collection and dissemination of news or on the mass media, although the major problems in these areas were starting-points for our discussion. We have been immediately involved in a wider historical, political and sociological perspective. Likewise, concentration on information had to be broadened to include all aspects of communication, considered in an overall socio-economic, cultural and political context. Moreover, as communication is so central to all social, economic and political activity at community, national and international levels, I would paraphrase H. G. Wells and say human history becomes more and more a race between communication and catastrophe. Full use of communication in all its varied strands is vital to assure that humanity has more than a history . . . that our children are ensured a future.

The Commission's sixteen members — largely representative of the world's ideological, political, economic and geographical spectrum — reached what I consider a surprising measure of agreement on major issues, upon which opinions heretofore had seemed irreconcilable. It was not simply a matter of reaching conclusions; more important, perhaps, was the identification and analysis of the problems and the possible solutions. In the inevitable continuing debates on facets of the developing new world information and communication order we hope that these may be of assistance.

For me, and I venture to think that this also applies to all my colleagues on the Commission, the most rewarding experience was the mutual sense of respect and friendship which we developed for each other in the course of our work. I hope that the constructive effort which dominated our work will persist when our report comes to be examined by Governments and others.

When the final draft of the report came before us for approval I felt impelled by a desire to rewrite it from beginning to end. I am sure that all my colleagues and Members of the Secretariat felt the same impulse. The style of writing varied, parts were prolix. Apart from the fact that we did not have the time necessary to undertake such a task, we felt that, despite the stylistic imperfection the report conveyed our views clearly. The reader must bear in mind the many linguistic, cultural and philosophical strands that were woven into this vast mosaic on communication.

Despite the large area of consensus reached on most major issues, it is obvious that many questions remain open; in addition, many subjects require further analysis. Many difficulties lie ahead, particularly in organizing and implementing concrete measures to help to construct the new order, which call for continuing review. There are many varying views as to the meaning of the "New Order" and as to what it should encompass, just as there are diverse opinions on ways and means of achieving it. But, in spite of these divergences, there was nobody in the Commission not convinced that structural changes in the field of communication are necessary and that the existing order is unacceptable to all.

There is obviously no magic solution to efface by a single stroke the existing complicated and inter-connected web of communication problems. There will be many stages, strategies and facets in the patient step-by-step establishment of the new structures, methods and attitudes which are required. Thus, the "New World Information and Communication Order" may be more accurately defined as a process than any given set of conditions and practices. The particulars of the process will continually alter, yet its goals will be constant — more justice, more equity, more reciprocity in information exchange, less dependence in communication flows, less downwards diffusion of messages, more self-reliance and cultural identity, more benefits for all mankind.

The Commission's analysis and its consensus on major guidelines for the development of a New World Information and Communication Order were themselves the result of a lengthy process. We owe much to Ambassador Mustapha Masmoudi and to Dr. Bogdan Osolnik, not only for their persistent advocacy of the "New Order" but for their constructive elucidation of its major aspects. But besides rich discussions between the Members of the Commission, during eight sessions from December 1977 to November 1979, our basic approach was constantly to reach outwards, to the extent practically feasible, to examine broad subjects directly with professionals and specialists involved, representing national, regional and international participation.

We started by organizing a large international gathering on issues such as contents of information, accuracy and balance in facts and images presented, infrastructures for news supply, rights and responsibilities of journalists and organizations engaged in news gathering and distribution, as well as technical and economic aspects of their operations. For that purpose an International Seminar on the Infrastructures of News Collection and Dissemination held in April 1978 in Stockholm, with the generous assistance of the Swedish government, attended by some 100 representatives of news agencies, broadcasting organizations, major newspapers, research institutes and international non-governmental organizations of regional or world-wide scope.

Apart from meetings held at Unesco Headquarters in Paris, the Commission held four sessions in countries as various as Sweden, Yugoslavia, India and Mexico. This permitted a closer insight into disparate cultural and social issues involved. It also permitted contacts with professionals and researchers sharing different views on basic aspects of communication in divergent societies. Round tables were organized on topics which were of particular importance for the Commission; with Yugoslav media and government representatives, we discussed the interaction between society and communication media; we had another debate on cooperation among developing countries on the same occasion. Our Indian hosts organized a wide ranging discussion on the relationship between communication and development; we also discussed with them the impact of future technological advances. With a large group of Latin American writers, professors and media personnel we focused on the correlation between culture and communication.

These direct consultations on central themes provided us with invaluable insights into the interlocking nature of fundamental issues in communications; particularly, they confirmed that these issues are structurally linked to wider socio-economic and cultural patterns. Thus, finally — and inevitably — communication problems assume a highly political character which is the basic reason why they are at the centre of the stage today in national and international arenas.

Further background material for our deliberations was provided by some one hundred descriptive and opinion papers prepared on specific aspects of communication by specialists from around the world. This represented particularly valuable substantive material for purposes of comparative analysis and for stimulating rethinking on communication issues.

Our professional contacts were further enriched by the opportunities afforded myself and other Members of the Commission and the Secretariat to attend more than a score of conferences, meetings, seminars and discussion groups organized by international organizations, international professional associations, the Non-Aligned countries, regional and national institutions concerned with various aspects of information and communication.

In addition, during the course of the Commission's work, dozens of international, regional and national institutions — research and documentation centres, schools of journalism, universities, professional associations and similar bodies — collaborated actively by the generous supply of research findings, topical documentation and substantive commentary.

Finally, we had the benefit of hundreds of individual, institutional and governmental comments on our Interim Report, which was submitted in 1978 to the Twentieth Session of Unesco's General Conference.

Thus, while our report represents the Commission's collective vision of the communication scene it has been based on a virtually worldwide survey of opinions, both individual and institutional, and a mountain of documentation from myriad sources. This wealth of information covered the widest possible spectrum of ideological, political, socio-economic and cultural colourings. Each member of the Commission considered it from his or her own viewpoint, then it was collectively reviewed in our deliberations.

The resulting distillation makes up our Report. Generally it is a consensus of how the Commission sees the present communication order and foresees a new one. Where there were differences those are reflected by way of comment or dissent. But given its broad base, plus its formulation by a representative international group which the Commission was, our Report — its presentations, findings and proposals — will, I trust, reach a wide like-minded audience. With this belief, my initial trepidations have been dissipated. I am confident that, with good will governing future dialogues, a new order benefiting all humanity can be constructed.

A. CONCLUSIONS AND RECOMMENDATIONS

The survey contained in this Report has recorded a dramatic expansion of communication resources and possibilities. It is an expansion that promises great opportunities, but also raises anxieties and uncertainties. Everything will depend on the use made of the new resources — that is, on crucial decisions, and on the question of who will make the decisions. Communication can be an instrument of power, a revolutionary weapon, a commercial product, or a means of education; it can serve the ends of either liberation or of oppression, of either the growth of the individual personality or of drilling human beings into uniformity. Each society must choose the best way to approach the task facing all of us and to find the means to overcome the material, social and political constraints that impede progress.

We have already considered many suggestions for further development. Without repeating them it might be useful to begin our recommendations by summarizing previous main conclusions:

1. Our review of communication the world over reveals a variety of solutions adopted in different countries — in accordance with diverse traditions, patterns of social, economic and cultural life, needs and possibilities. This diversity is valuable and should be respected; there is no place for the universal application of preconceived models. Yet it should be possible to establish, in broad outline, common aims and common values in the sphere of communication, based on common interests in a world of interdependence. The whole human race is threatened by the arms race and by the persistence of unacceptable global inequalities, both of which generate tensions and which jeopardize its future and even its survival. The contemporary situation demands a better, more just and more democratic social order, and the realization of fundamental human rights. These goals can be achieved only through understanding and tolerance, gained in large part by free, open and balanced communications.

2. The review has also shown that the utmost importance should be given to eliminating imbalances and disparities in communication and its structures, and particularly in information flows. Developing countries need to reduce their dependence, and claim a new, more just and more equitable order in the field of communication. This issue has been fully debated in various settings; the time has now come to move from principles to substantive reforms and concrete action.

3. Our conclusions are founded on the firm conviction that communication is a basic individual right, as well as a collective one required by all communities and nations. Freedom of information — and, more specifically the right to seek, receive and impart information — is a fundamental human right; indeed, a prerequisite for many others. The inherent nature of communication means that its fullest possible exercise and potential depend on the surrounding political, social and economic conditions, the most vital of these being democracy within countries and equal, democratic relations between them. It is in this context that the democratization of communication at national and international levels, as well as the larger role of communication in democratizing society, acquires utmost importance.

4. For these purposes, it is essential to develop comprehensive national communication policies linked to overall social, cultural and economic development objectives. Such policies should evolve from broad consultations with all sectors concerned and adequate mechanisms for wide participation of organized social groups in their definition and implementation. National governments as much as the international community should recognize the urgency of according communications higher priority in planning and funding. Every country should develop its communication patterns in accordance with its own conditions, needs and traditions, thus strengthening its integrity, independence and self-reliance.

5. The basic considerations which are developed at length in the body of our Report are intended to provide a framework for the development of a new information and communication order. We see its implementation as an on-going process of change in the nature of relations between and within nations in the field of communications. Imbalances in national information and communication systems are as disturbing and unacceptable as social, economic, cultural and technological, both national and international disparities. Indeed, rectification of the latter is inconceivable in any true or lasting sense without elimination of the former. Crucial decisions concerning communication development need to be taken urgently, at both national and international levels. These decisions are not merely the concern of professionals, researchers or scholars, nor can they be the sole prerogative of those holding political or economic power. The decision-making process has to involve social participation at all levels. This calls for new attitudes for overcoming stereotyped thinking and to promote more understanding of diversity and plurality, with full respect for the dignity and equality of peoples living in different conditions and acting in different ways.

Thus our call for reflection and action is addressed broadly to governments and international organizations, to policy-makers and planners, to the media and professional organizations, to researchers, communication practitioners, to organized social groups and the public at large.

I. Strengthening Independence and Self-reliance

Communication Policies

All individuals and people collectively have an inalienable right to a better life which, howsoever conceived, must ensure a social minimum, nationally and globally. This calls for the strengthening of capacities and the elimination of gross inequalities; such defects may threaten social harmony and even international peace. There must be a measured movement from disadvantage and dependance to self-reliance and the creation of more equal opportunities. Since communication is interwoven with every aspect of life, it is clearly of the utmost importance that the existing "communication gap" be rapidly narrowed and eventually eliminated.

We recommend:

1. Communication be no longer regarded merely as an incidental service and its development left to chance. Recognition of its potential warrants the formulation by all nations, and particularly developing countries, of comprehensive communication policies linked to overall social, cultural, economic and political goals. Such policies should be based on inter-ministerial and inter-disciplinary consultations with broad

public participation. The object must be to utilize the unique capacities of each form of communication, from interpersonal and traditional to the most modern, to make men and societies aware of their rights, harmonize unity in diversity, and foster the growth of individuals and communities within the wider frame of national development in an interdependent world.

2. As language embodies the cultural experience of people, all languages should be adequately developed to serve the complex and diverse requirements of modern communication. Developing nations and multilingual societies need to evolve language policies that promote all national languages even while selecting some, where necessary, for more widespread use in communication, higher education and administration. There is also need in certain situations for the adaptation, simplification, and standardization of scripts and development of keyboards, preparation of dictionaries and modernized systems of language learning, transcription of literature in widely-spoken national languages. The provision of simultaneous interpretation and automated translation facilities now under experimentation for cross-cultural communication to bridge linguistic divides should also be envisaged.

3. A primary policy objective should be to make elementary education available to all and to wipe out illiteracy, supplementing formal schooling systems with non-formal education and enrichment within appropriate structures of continuing and distance learning (through radio, television and correspondence).

4. Within the framework of national development policies, each country will have to work out its own set of priorities, bearing in mind that it will not be possible to move in all directions at the same time. But, as far as resources allow, communication policies should aim at stimulating and encouraging all means of communication.

Strengthening Capacities

Communication policies should offer a guide to the determination of information and media priorities and to the selection of appropriate technologies. This is required to plan the installation and development of adequate infrastructures to provide self-reliant communications capacity.

We recommend:

5. Developing countries take specific measures to establish or develop essential elements of their communication systems: print media, broadcasting and telecommunications along with the related training and production facilities.

6. Strong national news agencies are vital for improving each country's national and international reporting. Where viable, regional networks should be set up to increase news flows and serve all the major language groups in the area. Nationally, the agencies should buttress the growth of both urban and rural newspapers to serve as the core of a country's news collection and distribution system.

7. National book production should be encouraged and accompanied by the establishment of a distribution network for books, newspapers and periodicals. The stimulation of works by national authors in various languages should be promoted.

8. The development of comprehensive national radio networks, capable of reaching

remote areas should take priority over the development of television, which, however, should be encouraged where appropriate. Special attention should be given to areas where illiteracy is prevalent.

9. National capacity for producing broadcast materials is necessary to obviate dependence on external sources over and beyond desirable programme exchange. This capacity should include national or regional broadcasting, film and documentary production centres with a basic distribution network.

10. Adequate educational and training facilities are required to supply personnel for the media and production organizations, as well as managers, technicians and maintenance personnel. In this regard, co-operation between neighbouring countries and within regions should be encouraged.

Basic Needs

All nations have to make choices in investment priorities. In choosing between possible alternatives and often conflicting interests, developing countries, in particular, must give priority to satisfying their people's essential needs. Communication is not only a system of public information, but also an integral part of education and development.

We recommend:

11. The communication component in all development projects should receive adequate financing. So-called "development support communications" are essential for mobilizing initiatives and providing information required for action in all fields of development — agriculture, health and family planning, education, religion, industry and so on.

12. Essential communication needs to be met include the extension of basic postal services and telecommunication networks through small rural electronic exchanges.

13. The development of a community press in rural areas and small towns would not only provide print support for economic and social extension activities. This would also facilitate the production of functional literature for neo-literates as well.

14. Utilization of local radio, low-cost small format television and video systems and other appropriate technologies would facilitate production of programmes relevant to community development efforts, stimulate participation and provide opportunity for diversified cultural expression.

15. The educational and informational use of communication should be given equal priority with entertainment. At the same time, education systems should prepare young people for communication activities. Introduction of pupils at primary and secondary levels to the forms and uses of the means of communication (how to read newspapers, evaluate radio and television programmes, use elementary audio-visual techniques and apparatus) should permit the young to understand reality better and enrich their knowledge of current affairs and problems.

16. Organization of community listening and viewing groups could in certain circumstances widen both entertainment and educational opportunities. Education and information activities should be supported by different facilities ranging from

mobile book, tape and film libraries to programmed instruction through "schools of the air".

17. Such activities should be aggregated wherever possible in order to create vibrant local communication resource centres for entertainment, education, information dissemination and cultural exchange. They should be supported by decentralized media production centres; educational and extension services should be location-specific if they are to be credible and accepted.

18. It is not sufficient to urge that communication be given a high priority in national development; possible sources of investment finance must be identified. Among these could be differential communication pricing policies that would place larger burdens on more prosperous urban and elite groups; the taxing of commercial advertising may also be envisaged for this purpose.

Particular Challenges

We have focused on national efforts which must be made to lead to greater independence and self-reliance. But there are three major challenges to this goal that require concerted international action. Simply put, these are paper, tariff structures and the electro-magnetic spectrum.

We recommend:

19. A major international research and development effort to increase the supply of paper. The worldwide shortage of paper, including newsprint, and its escalating cost impose crushing burdens upon struggling newspapers, periodicals and the publication industry, above all in the developing countries. Certain ecological constraints have also emerged. Unesco, in collaboration with FAO, should take urgent measures to identify and encourage production of paper and newsprint either by recycling paper or from new sources of feedstock in addition to the wood pulp presently produced largely by certain northern countries. Kenaf, bagasse, tropical woods and grasses could possibly provide alternative sources. Initial experiments are encouraging and need to be supported and multiplied.

20. Tariffs for news transmission, telecommunications rates and air mail charges for the dissemination of news, transport of newspapers, periodicals, books and audiovisual materials are one of the main obstacles to a free and balanced flow of information. This situation must be corrected, especially in the case of developing countries, through a variety of national and international initiatives. Governments should in particular examine the policies and practices of their post and telegraph authorities. Profits or revenues should not be the primary aim of such agencies. They are instruments for policy-making and planned development in the field of information and culture. Their tariffs should be in line with larger national goals. International action is also necessary to alter telecommunication tariffs that militate heavily against small and peripheral users. Current international consultations on this question may be brought to early fruition, possibly at the October 1980 session of the 154-nation International Telegraph and Telephone Consultative Committee, which should have before it specific proposals made by a Unesco-sponsored working group on "Low Telecommunication Rates" (November 1979). Unesco might, in cooperation with ITU, also sponsor an overall study on international telecommunication services by means of satellite transmission in collaboration with

Intelsat, Intersputnik and user country representatives to make proposals for international and regional coordination of geostationary satellite development. The study should also include investigation of the possibility and practicalities of discounts for transmission of news and preferential rates for certain types of transmission to and from developing countries. Finally, developing countries should investigate the possibility of negotiating preferential tariffs on a bilateral or regional basis.

21. The electro-magnetic spectrum and geostationary orbit, both finite natural resources, should be more equitably shared as the common property of mankind. For that purpose, we welcome the decisions taken by the World Administrative Radio Conference (WARC), Geneva, September–November 1979, to convene a series of special conferences over the next few years on certain specific topics related to the utilization of these resources.

II. Social Consequences and New Tasks

Integrating Communication into Development

Development strategies should incorporate communication policies as an integral part in the diagnosis of needs and in the design and implementation of selected priorities. In this respect communication should be considered a major development resource, a vehicle to ensure real political participation in decision-making, a central information base for defining policy options, and an instrument for creating awareness of national priorities.

We recommend:

22. Promotion of dialogue for development as a central component of both communication and development policies. Implementation of national policies should be carried out through three complementary communication patterns: first, from decision-makers towards different social sectors to transmit information about what they regard as necessary changes in development actions, alternative strategies and the varying consequences of the different alternatives; second, among and between diverse social sectors in a horizontal information network to express and exchange views on their different demands, aspirations, objective needs and subjective motivations; third, between decision-makers and all social groups through permanent participatory mechanisms for two-way information flows to elaborate development goals and priorities and make decisions on utilization of resources. Each one of these patterns requires the design of specific information programmes, using different communication means.

23. In promoting communication policies, special attention should be given to the use of non-technical language and comprehensible symbols, images and forms to ensure popular understanding of development issues and goals. Similarly, development information supplied to the media should be adapted to prevailing news values and practices, which in turn should be encouraged to be more receptive to development needs and problems.

Facing the Technological Challenge

The technological explosion in communication has both great potential and great danger. The outcome depends on crucial decisions and on where and by whom they are taken. Thus, it is a priority to organize the decision-making process in a participatory manner on the basis of a full awareness of the social impact of different alternatives.

We recommend:

24. Devising policy instruments at the national level in order to evaluate the positive and negative social implications of the introduction of powerful new communication technologies. The preparation of technological impact surveys can be a useful tool to assess the consequences for life styles, relevance for under-privileged sectors of society, cultural influence, effects on employment patterns, and similar factors. This is particularly important when making choices with respect to the development of communication infrastructures.

25. Setting up national mechanisms to promote participation and discussion of social priorities in the acquisition or extension of new communication technologies. Decisions with respect to the orientation given to research and development should come under closer public scrutiny.

26. In developing countries the promotion of autonomous research and development should be linked to specific projects and programmes at the national, regional and inter-regional levels, which are often geared to the satisfaction of basic needs. More funds are necessary to stimulate and support adaptive technological research. This might also help these countries to avoid problems of obsolescence and problems arising from the non-availability of particular types of equipment, related spare parts and components from the advanced industrial nations.

27. The concentration of communications technology in a relatively few developed countries and transnational corporations has led to virtual monopoly situations in this field. To counteract these tendencies national and international measures are required, among them reform of exisiting patent laws and conventions, appropriate legislation and international agreements.

Strengthening Cultural Identity

Promoting conditions for the preservation of the cultural identity of every society is necessary to enable it to enjoy a harmonious and creative inter-relationship with other cultures. It is equally necessary to modify situations in many developed and developing countries which suffer from cultural dominance.

We recommend:

28. Establishment of national cultural policies, which should foster cultural identity and creativity, and involve the media in these tasks. Such policies should also contain guidelines for safeguarding national cultural development while promoting knowledge of other cultures. It is in relation to others that each culture enhances its own identity.[1]

29. Communication and cultural policies should ensure that creative artists and

---

(1) Comment by **Mr. S. MacBride:** "I wish to add that owing to the cultural importance of spiritual and religious values and also in order to restore moral values, policy guidelines should take into account religious beliefs and traditions."

various grass-roots groups can make their voices heard through the media. The innovative uses of film, television or radio by people of different cultures should be studied. Such experiments constitute a basis for continuing cultural dialogue, which could be furthered by agreements between countries and through international support.

30. Introduction of guidelines with respect to advertising content and the values and attitudes it fosters, in accordance with national standards and practices. Such guidelines should be consistent with national development policies and efforts to preserve cultural identity. Particular attention should be given to the impact on children and adolescents. In this connection, various mechanisms such as complaint boards or consumer review committees might be established to afford the public the possibility of reacting against advertising which they feel inappropriate.

Reducing the Commercialization of Communication

The social effects of the commercialization of the mass media are a major concern in policy formulation and decision-making by private and public bodies.

We recommend:

31. In expanding communication systems, preference should be given to non-commercial forms of mass communication. Promotion of such types of communication should be integrated with the traditions, culture, development objectives and socio-political system of each country. As in the field of education, public funds might be made available for this purpose.

32. While acknowledging the need of the media for revenues, ways and means should be considered to reduce the negative effects that the influence of market and commercial considerations have in the organization and content of national and international communication flows.[1]

33. That consideration be given to changing existing funding patterns of commercial mass media. In this connection, reviews could be made of the way in which the relative role of advertising volume and costs pricing policies, voluntary contributions, subsidies, taxes, financial incentives and supports could be modified to enhance the social function of mass media and improve their service to the community.

Access to Technical Information

The flow of technical information within nations and across national boundaries is a major resource for development. Access to such information, which countries need for technical decision-making at all levels, is as crucial as access to news sources. This type of information is generally not easily available and is most often concentrated in large techno-structures. Developed countries are not providing adequate information of this type to developing countries.

(1) Comment by **Mr. E. Abel:** "At no time has the commission seen evidence adduced in support of the notion that market and commercial considerations necessarily exert a negative effect upon communication flows. On the contrary, the commission has praised elsewhere in this report courageous investigative journalism of the sort that can be sustained only by independent media whose survival depends upon their acceptance in the marketplace, rather than the favors of political leaders. The commission also is aware that market mechanisms play an increasingly important role today even in so-called planned economies."

We recommend:

34. Developing countries should pay particular attention to: (a) the correlation between education, scientific and communication policies, because their practical application frequently overlaps; (b) the creation in each country of one or several centres for the collection and utilization of technical information and data, both from within the country and from abroad; (c) to secure the basic equipment necessary for essential data processing activities; (d) the development of skills and facilities for computer processing and analysis of data obtained from remote sensing.

35. Developed countries should foster exchanges of technical information on the principle that all countries have equal rights to full access to available information. It is increasingly necessary, in order to reduce inequalities in this field, to promote cooperative arrangements for collection, retrieval, processing and diffusion of technological information through various networks, regardless of geographical or institutional frontiers. UNISIST, which provides basic guidelines for voluntary cooperation among and between information systems and services, should further develop its activities.

36. Developing countries should adopt national informatics policies as a matter of priority. These should primarily relate to the establishment of decision-making centres (inter-departmental and inter-disciplinary) which would inter alia (a) assess technological alternatives; (b) centralize purchases; (c) encourage local production of software; (d) promote regional and sub-regional cooperation (in various fields, including education, health and consumer services).

37. At the international level, consideration should be given to action with respect to: (a) a systematic identification of existing organized data processing infrastructures in various specialized fields; (b) agreement on measures for effective multi-country participation in the programmes, planning and administration of existing or developing data infrastructures; (c) analysis of commercial and technical measures likely to improve the use of informatics by developing countries; (d) agreement on international priorities for research and development that is of interest to all countries in the field of informatics.

38. Transnational corporations should supply to the authorities of the countries in which they operate, upon request and on a regular basis as specified by local laws and regulations, all information required for legislative and administrative purposes relevant to their activities and specifically needed to assess the performance of such entities. They should also provide the public, trade unions and other interested sectors of the countries in which they operate with information needed to understand the global structure, activities and policies of the transnational corporation and their significance for the country concerned.

III. Professional Integrity and Standards

Responsibility of Journalists

For the journalist, freedom and responsibility are indivisible. Freedom without responsibility invites distortion and other abuses. But in the absence of freedom there can be no exercise of responsibility. The concept of freedom with responsibility necessarily includes a concern for professional ethics, demanding an equitable approach to events, situations or processes with due attention to their diverse aspects. This is not always the case today.

We recommend:

39. The importance of the journalist's mission in the contemporary world demands steps to enhance his standing in society. In many countries even today, journalists are not regarded as members of an acknowledged profession and they are treated accordingly. To overcome this situation, journalism needs to raise its standards and quality for recognition everywhere as a genuine profession.

40. To be treated as professionals, journalists require broad educational preparation and specific professional training. Programmes of instruction need to be developed not only for entry-level recruits, but also for experienced personnel who from time to time would benefit from special seminars and conferences designed to refresh and enrich their qualifications. Basically, programmes of instruction and training should be conducted on national and regional levels.

41. Such values as truthfulness, accuracy and respect for human rights are not universally applied at present. Higher professional standards and responsibility cannot be imposed by decree, nor do they depend solely on the goodwill of individual journalists, who are employed by institutions which can improve or handicap their professional performance. The self-respect of journalists, their integrity and inner drive to turn out work of high quality are of paramount importance. It is this level of professional dedication, making for responsibility, that should be fostered by news media and journalists' organizations. In this framework, a distinction may have to be drawn between media institutions, owners and managers on the one hand, and journalists on the other.

42. As in other professions, journalists and media organizations serve the public directly and the public, in turn, is entitled to hold them accountable for their actions. Among the mechanisms devised up to now in various countries for assuring accountability, the Commission sees merit in press or media councils, the institution of the press ombudsman and peer group criticism of the sort practised by journalism reviews in several countries. In addition, communities served by particular media can accomplish significant reforms through citizen action. Specific forms of community involvement in decision-making will vary, of course, from country to country. Public broadcasting stations, for example, can be governed by representative boards drawn from the community. Voluntary measures of this sort can do much to influence media performance. Nevertheless, it appears necessary to develop further effective ways by which the right to assess mass media performance can be exercised by the public.

43. Codes of professional ethics exist in all parts of the world, adopted voluntarily in many countries by professional groups. The adoption of codes of ethics at national and, in some cases, at the regional level is desirable, provided that such codes are prepared and adopted by the profession itself — without governmental interference.

Towards Improved International Reporting

The full and factual presentation of news about one country to others is a continuing problem. The reasons for this are manifold: principal among them are correspondents' working conditions, their skills and attitudes, varying conceptions of news and information values and government viewpoints. Remedies for the situation will require long-term, evolutionary action towards improving the exchange of news around the world.

We recommend:

44. All countries should take steps to assure admittance of foreign correspondents and facilitate their collection and transmission of news. Special obligations in this regard, undertaken by the signatories to the Final Act of the Helsinki conference, should be honoured and, indeed, liberally applied. Free access to news sources by journalists is an indispensable requirement for accurate, faithful and balanced reporting. This necessarily involves access to unofficial, as well as official sources of information, that is, access to the entire spectrum of opinion within any country.[1]

45. Conventional standards of news selection and reporting, and many accepted news values, need to be reassessed if readers and listeners around the world are to receive a more faithful and comprehensive account of events, movements and trends in both developing and developed countries. The inescapable need to interpret unfamiliar situations in terms that will be understood by a distant audience should not blind reporters or editors to the hazards of narrow ethnocentric thinking. The first step towards overcoming this bias is to acknowledge that it colours the thinking of virtually all human beings, journalists included, for the most part without deliberate intent. The act of selecting certain news items for publication, while rejecting others, produces in the minds of the audience a picture of the world that may well be incomplete or distorted. Higher professional standards are needed for journalists to be able to illuminate the diverse cultures and beliefs of the modern world, without their presuming to judge the ultimate validity of any foreign nation's experience and traditions.

46. To this end, reporters being assigned to foreign posts should have the benefit of language training and acquaintance with the history, institutions, politics, economics and cultural environment of the country or region in which they will be serving.

47. The press and broadcasters in the industrialized world should allot more space and time to reporting events in and background material about foreign countries in general and news from the developing world in particular. Also, the media in developed countries — especially the "gatekeepers", editors and producers of print and broadcasting media who select the news items to be published or broadcast — should become more familiar with the cultures and conditions in developing countries. Although the present imbalance in news flows calls for strengthening capacities in developing countries, the media of the industrialized countries have their contribution to make towards the correction of these inequalities

48. To offset the negative effects of inaccurate or malicious reporting of international news, the right of reply and correction should be further considered. While these

(1) Comment by **Mr. S. Losev:** This paragraph doesn't correspond to the Helsinki Final Act (see section 2 — information, point (c)), contradicts the interests of developing nations, and therefore is completely unacceptable and I object against it being included. I suggest to replace this recommendation by the following text: "All countries should take appropriate measures to improve the conditions for foreign correspondants to carry out their professional activities in the host countries in accordance with the provisions of the Helsinki Final Act and with due respect to the national sovereignty and the national identity of the host country".

concepts are recognized in many countries, their nature and scope vary so widely that it would be neither expedient nor realistic to propose the adoption of any international regulations for their purpose. False or distorted news accounts can be harmful, but the voluntary publication of corrections or replies is preferable to international normative action. Since the manner in which the right of reply and correction as applied in different countries varies significantly, it is further suggested that: (a) the exercise of the international right of reply and correction be considered for application on a voluntary basis in each country according to its journalistic practices and national legal framework; (b) the United Nations, in consultation with all concerned bodies, explore the conditions under which this right could be perfected at the international level, taking into account the cumbersome operation of the 1952 Convention on the International Right of Correction; (c) media institutions with an international reach define on a voluntary basis internal standards for the exercise of this right and make them publicly available.

49. Intelligence services of many nations have at one time or other recruited journalists to commit espionage under cover of their professional duties. This practice must be condemned. It undermines the integrity of the profession and, in some circumstances, can expose other journalists to unjustified suspicion or physical threat. The Commission urges journalists and their employers to be on guard against possible attempts of this kind. We also urge governments to refrain from using journalists for purposes of espionage.

Protection of Journalists

Daily reports from around the world attest to dangers that journalists are subject to in the exercise of their profession: harassment, threats, imprisonment, physical violence, assassination. Continual vigilance is required to focus the world's attention on such assaults to human rights.

We recommend:

50. The professional independence and integrity of all those involved in the collection and dissemination of news, information and views to the public should be safeguarded. However, the Commission does not propose special privileges to protect journalists in the performance of their duties, although journalism is often a dangerous profession. Far from constituting a special category, journalists are citizens of their respective countries, entitled to the same range of human rights as other citizens. One exception is provided in the Additional Protocol to the Geneva Conventions of 12 August 1949, which applies only to journalists on perilous missions, such as in areas of armed conflict. To propose additional measures would invite the dangers entailed in a licensing system since it would require some body to stipulate who should be entitled to claim such protection. Journalists will be fully protected only when everyone's human rights are guaranteed.[1]

---

(1) Comment by **Mr. S MacBride:** "I consider this paragraph quite inadequate to deal with what is a serious position. Because of the importance of the role of journalists and others who provide or control the flow of news to the media, I urge that they should be granted a special status and protection. I also urge that provisions should be made to enable a journalist to appeal against a refusal of reasonable facilities. My views on these issues are embodied in a paper entitled *The Protection of Journalists* (CIC Document No. 90) which I submitted to the Commission; I refer in particular to paragraphs 1–17 and 35–53 of this paper."

51. That Unesco should convene a series of round tables at which journalists, media executives, researchers and jurists can periodically review problems related to the protection of journalists and propose additional appropriate measures to this end.[2]

IV. Democratization of Communication

Human Rights

Freedom of speech, of the press, of information and of assembly are vital for the realization of human rights. Extension of these communication freedoms to a broader individual and collective right to communicate is an evolving principle in the democratization process. Among the human rights to be emphasized are those of equality for women and between races. Defence of all human rights is one of the media's most vital tasks.

We recommend:

52. All those working in the mass media should contribute to the fulfilment of human rights, both individual and collective, in the spirit of the Unesco Declaration on the mass media and the Helsinki Final Act, and the International Bill of Human Rights. The contribution of the media in this regard is not only to foster these principles, but also to expose all infringements, wherever they occur, and to support those whose rights have been neglected or violated. Professional associations and public opinion should support journalists subject to pressure or who suffer adverse consequences from their dedication to the defence of human rights.

53. The media should contribute to promoting the just cause of peoples struggling for freedom and independence and their right to live in peace and equality without foreign interference. This is especially important for all oppressed peoples who, while struggling against colonialism, religious and racial discrimination, are deprived of opportunity to make their voices heard within their own countries.

54. Communication needs in a democratic society should be met by the extension of specific rights such as the right to be informed, the right to inform, the right to privacy, the right to participate in public communication — all elements of a new concept, the right to communicate. In developing what might be called a new era of social rights, we suggest all the implications of the right to communicate be further explored.

Removal of Obstacles

Communication, with its immense possibilities for influencing the minds and behaviour of people, can be a powerful means of promoting democratization of society and of widening public participation in the decision-making process. This depends on the structures and practices of the media and their management and to what extent they facilitate broader access and open the communication process to a free interchange of ideas, information and experience among equals, without dominance or discrimination.

(1) Comment by **Mr. S. MacBride:** "I urge that such a Round Table be convened annually for a period of five years; I refer to paragraphs 50–57 of my paper on *The Protection of Journalists* (CIC Document No. 90)."

We recommend:

55. All countries adopt measures to enlarge sources of information needed by citizens in their everyday life. A careful review of existing laws and regulations should be undertaken with the aim of reducing limitations, secrecy provisions and other constraints in information practices.

56. Censorship or arbitrary control of information should be abolished.[1] In areas where reasonable restrictions may be considered necessary, these should be provided for by law, subject to judicial review and in line with the principles enshrined in the United Nations Charter, the Universal Declaration of Human Rights and the International Covenants relating to human rights, and in other instruments adopted by the community of nations.[2]

57. Special attention should be devoted to obstacles and restrictions which derive from the concentration of media ownership, public or private, from commercial influences on the press and broadcasting, or from private or governmental advertising. The problem of financial conditions under which the media operate should be critically reviewed, and measures elaborated to strengthen editorial independence.

58. Effective legal measures should be designed to: (a) limit the process of concentration and monopolization; (b) circumscribe the action of transnationals by requiring them to comply with specific criteria and conditions defined by national legislation and development policies; (c) reverse trends to reduce the number of decision-makers at a time when the media's public is growing larger and the impact of communication is increasing; (d) reduce the influence of advertising upon editorial policy and broadcast programming; (e) seek and improve models which would ensure greater independence and autonomy of the media concerning their management and editorial policy, whether these media are under private, public or government ownership.[3]

Diversity and Choice

Diversity and choice in the content of communication are a pre-condition for democratic participation. Every individual and particular groups should be able to

---

(1) Comment by **Mr. S. Losev:** "This whole problem of censorship or arbitrary control of information is within the national legislation of each country and is to be solved within the national, legal framework taking in due consideration the national interests of each country."

(2) Comment by **Mr. S. MacBride:** "I also wish to draw attention to the provisions of Article 10 of the European Convention for the Protection of Human Rights which I consider as wholly inadequate. I urge that Articles 13 and 14 of the Inter-American Convention on Human Rights (1979) are much more comprehensive and effective than the equivalent provisions of the European Convention. The matter is discussed in paragraphs 26–29 of my paper on *The Protection of Journalists* (CIC Document No. 90)."

(3) Comment by **Mr. E. Abel:** "Regarding (a) and (c), anti-monopoly legislation, whether more or less effective, is relevant only in countries where a degree of competition can be said to exist. It is a travesty to speak of measures against concentration and monopolization in countries where the media are themselves established as state monopolies, or operate as an arm of the only authorized political party. (b) Transnational corporations are expected to comply with the laws of the countries in which they do business. (d) Where it can be shown to exist, the influence of advertisers upon editorial content or broadcast programming would warrant careful study. But a sweeping demand that such influence be reduced, without pausing to examine or attempting to measure that influence in particular circumstances, is a symptom of ideological prejudice."

form judgments on the basis of a full range of information and a variety of messages and opinions and have the opportunity to share these ideas with others. The development of decentralized and diversified media should provide larger opportunities for a real direct involvement of the people in communication processes.

We recommend:

59. The building of infrastructures and the adoption of particular technologies should be carefully matched to the need for more abundant information to a broader public from a plurality of sources.

60. Attention should be paid to the communication needs of women. They should be assured adequate access to communication means and that images of them and of their activities are not distorted by the media or in advertising.

61. The concerns of children and youth, national, ethnic, religious, linguistic minorities. people living in remote areas and the aged and handicapped also deserve particular consideration. They constitute large and sensitive segments of society and have special communication needs.

Integration and Participation

To be able to communicate in contemporary society, man must dispose of appropriate communication tools. New technologies offer him many devices for individualized information and entertainment, but often fail to provide appropriate tools for communication within his community or social or cultural group. Hence, alternative means of communication are often required.

We recommend:

62. Much more attention be devoted to use of the media in living and working environments. Instead of isolating men and women, the media should help integrate them into the community.

63. Readers, listeners and viewers have generally been treated as passive receivers of information. Those in charge of the media should encourage their audiences to play a more active role in communication by allocating more newspaper space, or broadcasting time, for the views of individual members of the public or organized social groups.

64. The creation of appropriate communication facilities at all levels, leading towards new forms of public involvement in the management of the media and new modalities for their funding.

65. Communication policy-makers should give far greater importance to devising ways whereby the management of the media could be democratized — while respecting national customs and characteristics — by associating the following categories: (a) journalists and professional communicators: (b) creative artists; (c) technicians; (d) media owners and managers; (e) representatives of the public. Such democratization of the media needs the full support and understanding of all those working in them, and this process should lead to their having a more active role in editorial policy and management.

V. Fostering International Cooperation

Partners for Development

Inequalities in communication facilities, which exist everywhere, are due to economic discrepancies or to political and economic design, still others to cultural imposition or neglect. But whatever the source or reason for them, gross inequalities should no longer be countenanced. The very notion of a new world information and communication order presupposes fostering international cooperation, which includes two main areas: international assistance and contributions towards international understanding. The international dimensions of communication are today of such importance that it has become crucial to develop cooperation on a world-wide scale. It is for the international community to take the appropriate steps to replace dependence, dominance and inequality by more fruitful nd more open relations of inter-dependence and complementarity, based on mutual interest and the equal dignity of nations and peoples. Such cooperation requires a major international commitment to redress the present situation. This clear commitment is a need not only for developing countries but also for the international community as a whole. The tensions and disruptions that will come from lack of action are far greater than the problems posed by necessary changes.

We recommend:

66. The progressive implementation of national and international measures that will foster the setting up of a new world information and communication order. The proposals contained in this report can serve as a contribution to develop the varied actions necessary to move in that direction.

67. International cooperation for the development of communications be given equal priority with and within other sectors (e.g. health, agriculture, industry, science, education, etc.) as information is a basic resource for individual and collective advancement and for all-round development. This may be achieved by utilizing funds provided through bilateral governmental agreements and from international and regional organizations, which should plan a considerable increase in their allocations for communication, infrastructures, equipment and programme development. Care should be taken that assistance is compatible with developing countries' priorities. Consideration should also be given to provision of assistance on a programme rather than on a strict project basis.

68. The close relationship between the establishment of a new international economic order and the new world information and communication order should be carefully considered by the technical bodies dealing with these issues. Concrete plans of action linking both processes should be implemented within the United Nations system. The United Nations, in approving the international development strategy should consider the communications sector as an integral element of it and not merely as an instrument of public information.

Strengthening Collective Self-reliance

Developing countries have a primary responsibility for undertaking necessary changes to overcome their dependence in the field of communications. The actions needed begin at the national level, but must be complemented by forceful and decisive agreements at the bilateral, sub-regional, regional, and inter-regional levels.

Collective self-reliance is the cornerstone of a new world information and communication order.

We recommend:

69. The communication dimension should be incorporated into existing programmes and agreements for economic cooperation between developing countries.

70. Joint activities in the field of communication, which are under way between developing countries should be developed further in the light of the overall analysis and recommendations of this Report. In particular, attention should be given to cooperation among national news agencies, to the further development of the News Agencies Pool and broadcasting organizations of the non-aligned countries, as well as to the general exchange on a regular basis of radio, TV programmes and films.

71. With respect to cooperation in the field of technical information, the establishment of regional and sub-regional data banks and information processing centres and specialized documentation centres should be given a high priority. They should be conceived and organized, both in terms of software and management, according to the particular needs of cooperating countries. Choices of technology and selection of foreign enterprises should be made so as not to increase dependence in this field.

72. Mechanisms for sharing information of a non-strategic nature could be established particularly in economic matters. Arrangements of this nature could be of value in areas such as multilateral trade negotiations, dealings with transnational corporations and banks, economic forecasting, and medium- and long-term planning and other similar fields.

73. Particular efforts should be undertaken to ensure that news about other developing countries within or outside their region receive more attention and space in the media. Special projects could be developed to ensure a steady flow of attractive and interesting material inspired by news values which meet developing countries' information needs.

74. Measures to promote links and agreements between professional organizations and communication researchers of different countries should be fostered. It is necessary to develop networks of institutions and people working in the field of communication in order to share and exchange experiences and implement joint projects of common interest with concrete operational contents.

International Mechanisms

Cooperation for the development of communications is a global concern and therefore of importance to international organizations, where all Member states can fully debate the issues involved and decide upon multi-national action. Governments should therefore attentively review the structures and programmes of international agencies in the communications field and point to changes required to meet evolving needs.

We recommend:

75. The Member States of Unesco should increase their support to the Organization's programme in this area. Consideration should be given to organizing a distinct

communication sector, not simply in order to underline its importance, but to emphasize that its activities are inter-related with the other major components of Unesco's work — education, science and culture.[1] In its communications activities, Unesco should concentrate on priority areas. Among these are assistance to national policy formulation and planning, technical development, organizing professional meetings and exchanges, promotion and coordination of research, and elaboration of international norms.

76. Better coordination of the various communication activities within Unesco and those throughout the United Nations System. A thorough inventory and assessment of all communications development and related programmes of the various agencies should be undertaken as a basis for designing appropriate mechanisms to carry out the necessary consultation, cooperation and coordination.

77. It would be desirable for the United Nations family to be equipped with a more effective information system, including a broadcast capability of its own and possibly access to a satellite system. That would enable the United Nations to follow more closely world affairs and transmit its message more effectively to all the peoples of the earth. Although such a proposal would require heavy investment and raise some complex issues, a feasibility study should be undertaken so that a carefully designed project could be prepared for deliberation and decision.[2][3]

78. Consideration might be given to establishing within the framework of Unesco an International Centre for the Study and Planning of Information and Communication. Its main tasks would be to: (a) promote the development of national communication systems in developing countries and the balance and reciprocity in international information flows; (b) mobilize resources required for that purpose and manage the funds put at its disposal; and (c) assure coordination among parties interested in communication development and involved in various cooperation programmes and evaluate results of bilateral and multilateral activities in this field; (d) organize round tables, seminars, and conferences for the training of communication planners, researchers and journalists, particularly those specializing in international problems; and (e) keep under review communications technology transfers between developed and developing countries so that they are carried out in the most suitable conditions. The Centre may be guided by a tripartite coordinating council composed of representatives of developing and developed countries and of interested international organizations. We suggest Unesco should undertake further study of this proposal

---

(1) Comment by **Mr. M. Lubis:** "I strongly believe that the present set-up in Unesco (Sector of Culture and Communication) is adequate to deal with the problems of Communication."

(2) Comment by **Mr. M. Lubis:** "I am of the opinion that the present communication potential of the UN system has not been effectively and efficiently used and managed. And I cannot foresee for a long time to come that the UN system will be able to speak with one voice on the really relevant issues of the world, disarmament, peace, freedom, human rights. However, I support the suggestion about a feasibility study, contained in the same paragraph."

(3) Comment by **Mr. S. MacBride:** "I would point out that the phenomenal growth of international broadcasting highlights the absence of a UN International Broadcasting System. Some thirty countries broadcast a total of *12,000 hours* per week in one hundred different languages. I urge that the UN should establish a broadcasting system of its own that would broadcast 24 hours round the clock in not less than 30 different languages. See my paper on *The Protection of Journalists* (CIC Document No. 90, paragraph 46) and the paper on *International Broadcasting* (CIC Document No. 60)."

for consideration at the 1980 session of the General Conference.[1]

Towards International Understanding

The strengthening of peace, international security and cooperation and the lessening of international tensions are the common concern of all nations. The mass media can make a substantial contribution towards achieving these goals. The special session of the United Nations General Assembly on disarmament called for increased efforts by the mass media to mobilize public opinion in favour of disarmament and of ending the arms race. This Declaration together with the Unesco Declaration on fundamental principles concerning the contribution of the mass media to strengthening peace and international understanding, to the promotion of human rights and to countering racialism, apartheid and incitement to war should be the foundation of new communication policies to foster international understanding. A new world information and communication order requires and must become the instrument for peaceful cooperation between nations.

We recommend:

79. National communication policies should be consistent with adopted international communication principles and should seek to create a climate of mutual understanding and peaceful coexistence among nations. Countries should also encourage their broadcast and other means of international communication to make the fullest contribution towards peace and international cooperation and to refrain from advocating national, racial or religious hatred, and incitement to discrimination, hostility, violence or war.

80. Due attention should be paid to the problems of peace and disarmament, human rights, development and the creation of a new communication order. Mass media both printed and audiovisual, should be encouraged to publicise significant documents of the United Nations, of Unesco, of the world peace movements, and of various other international and national organizations devoted to peace and disarmament. The curricula of schools of journalism should include study of these international problems and the views expressed on them within the United Nations.

---

(1) Comment by **Ms. B. Zimmerman**: "Although I agree that a coordinating body in the field of communication development could serve a useful purpose, I cannot support this precise recommendation. All members of the Commission did not have the opportunity to discuss thoroughly the advantages and disadvantages of various objectives and structures for such a coordinating body. As a Unesco Intergovernmental Conference is to be held in 1980 to cover that topic, I feel the Commission should welcome the careful study that the Unesco Conference is in a position to give the matter, rather than offering any recommendation at this time."

Comment by **Mr. E. Abel:** "This proposal is premature, unnecessary and unwise. The design of an appropriate mechanism for promoting and coordinating communications development demands more time and resources than this Commission possesses. Essentially the same proposal here advanced was one of two submitted to a Unesco experts meeting in November; neither one was endorsed. The question is on the agenda for an intergovernmental meeting at Unesco in April. The UN General Assembly has now taken a strong interest in the matter and has requested the Secretary-General to intervene. As it stands, this proposal can only deter the necessary cooperation of both the competent UN bodies and the developed nations whose cooperation is indispensable to further progress."

Comment by **Mr. S. MacBride:** "I suggest that if any steps are taken in this direction prior consultation and accord should be reached with journalists' organizations and other NGOs involved in the mass media."

81. All forms of co-operation among the media, the professionals and their associations, which contribute to the better knowledge of other nations and cultures, should be encouraged and promoted.

82. Reporting on international events or developments in individual countries in situations of crisis and tension requires extreme care and responsibility. In such situations the media often constitute one of the few, if not the sole, link between combatants or hostile groups. This clearly casts on them a special role which they should seek to dischàrge with objectivity and sensitivity.

☐ ☐ ☐

The recommendations and suggestions contained in our Report do not presume to cover all topics and issues calling for reflection and action. Nevertheless, they indicate the importance and scale of the tasks which face every country in the field of information and communication, as well as their international dimensions which pose a formidable challenge to the community of nations.

Our study indicates clearly the direction in which the world must move to attain a new information and communication order — essentially a series of new relationships arising from the advances promised by new communication technologies which should enable all peoples to benefit. The awareness already created on certain issues, such as global imbalances in information flows, suggests that a process of change has resulted and is under way. The power and promise of ever-new communication technologies and systems are, however, such as to demand deliberate measures to ensure that existing communication disparities do not widen. The objective should be to ensure that men and women are enabled to lead richer and more satisfying lives.

B. ISSUES REQUIRING FURTHER STUDY

We have suggested some actions which may help lead towards a new world information and communication order. Some of them are for immediate undertaking; others will take more time to prepare and implement. The important thing is to start moving towards a change in the present situation.

However, there are other issues that require examination, but the International Commission lacked time or sufficient data or expertise to deal with them. The proposals listed below have not been approved by the Commission; several were not, in fact, even discussed. Members felt free, nevertheless, to submit individual or group proposals which, in their judgment, called for study in the future. While these suggestions have not been endorsed by the Commission, they may still indicate some preliminary ideas about issues to be pursued, if and when they arouse interest.

I. Increased Interdependence

1. Studies are necessary to define more precisely the inter-dependence of interests of rich and poor countries, as well as of countries belonging to different socio-political systems. Research undertaken to date has not adequately explored this community of interests; more substantial findings are desirable as background for eventual future measures leading to wider cooperation. Similar studies are necessary to prepare more diversified cooperative efforts among developing countries themselves.

2. For the same purpose, indicators should be worked out to facilitate comparison of the results obtained through various media in different countries.

3. As international cooperation depends on mutual understanding, language barriers are a continuing problem. There is a certain imbalance in the use of international languages and studies might be undertaken with a view to improving the situation.

II. Improved Coordination

4. A new information and communication order cannot be developed on the basis of sporadic projects and initiatives, and without a solid research base. Feasibility studies are needed to ensure better coordination of activities in many fields, particularly at an initial stage, involving (a) news collection and supply; (b) data banks; (c) broadcast programme banks for exchange purposes; (d) exchange of data gathered by remote sensing.

III. International Standards and Instruments

5. The texts of international instruments (of the League of Nations, the United Nations and UN Agencies, intergovernmental organizations, etc.) as well as draft texts which have long run up against political barriers should be reviewed in order to promote further international legislation in this area, since only by extending its scope will it be possible to overcome certain difficulties and to regulate certain aspects of

the new world communication order.

6. Studies should be undertaken to identify, if possible, principles generally recognised by the profession of journalism and which take into account the public interest. This could also encompass further consideration, by journalists' organizations themselves, of the concept of an international code of ethics. Some fundamental elements for this code might be found in the Unesco Declaration on the mass media, as well as in provisions common to the majority of existing national and regional codes.

7. Studies should be undertaken on the social, economic and cultural effects of advertising to identify problems, and to suggest solutions, at the national and international levels, possibly including study of the practicability of an international advertising code, which could have as its basis the preservation of cultural identity and protection of moral values.

IV. Collection and Dissemination of News

8. The scope of the round tables, mentioned in Recommendation 51 above, could be enlarged, after appropriate studies, to include other major problems related to the collection and dissemination of international news, particularly professional, ethical and juridical aspects.

V. Protection of Journalists

9. Further studies should be made for the safeguarding of journalists in the exercise of their profession. The possibility might be explored for setting up some mechanism whereby when a journalist is either refused or deprived of his identity card he would have a right of appeal to a professional body, ideally with adequate judicial authority to rectify the position. Such studies should also look into the possibility of the creation of an international body to which a further appeal could be made in the final resort.

VI. Greater Attention to Neglected Areas

10. The concentration of the media in the developed regions, and the control of or access to them enjoyed by the affluent categories of the population, should be corrected by giving particular attention to the needs of the less developed countries and those of rural areas. Studies should be undertaken to evaluate these needs, to determine priorities and to measure the likely rate of return of future investments. Consideration might be given for example to (a) the feasibility of generalizing sound and television broadcasting and expanding telephone networks in rural areas; (b) the efficacy of possible government measures to expand distribution of receiving sets (e.g. through special facilities, tax exemptions, low-interest loans, subsidies, etc.) and (c) technological possibilities and innovations (e.g. the production of high-power generators for areas without electricity, etc.).

VII. More Extensive Financial Resources

11. The scarcity of available resources for communication development, both at national and international levels, highlights the need for further studies in three

different areas: (a) identification of country priorities for national and international financing; (b) evaluation of the cost-effectiveness of existing investments; (c) the search for new financial resources.

12. As far as new resources are concerned, several possibilities might be explored: (a) marshalling of resources deriving from surplus profits on raw materials; (b) establishment of an international duty[1] on the use of the electromagnetic spectrum and geostationary orbit space for the benefit of developing countries; (c) levying of an international duty[2] on the profits of transnational corporations producing transmission facilities and equipment for the benefit of developing countries and for the partial financing of the cost of using international communication facilities (cable, telecommunications networks, satellites, etc.).

□   □   □

Responding to its wide mandate, the Commission has sought to identify major problems and trends and has recommended certain lines of action. Apart from recommendations coming from the Commission as a whole, some of its members made additional suggestions, considering that the interest for new issues will continue to grow.

It is important to realise that the new order we seek is not only a goal but a stage in a journey. It is a continuing quest for ever more free, more equal, more just relations within all societies and among all nations and peoples. This Report represents what we believe we have learned. And this, above all, is what we wish to communicate.

---

(1) Comment by **Mr. S. Losev:** "The idea of an international tax for whatever good reasons or causes does not seem just or justifiable to me."

(2) Comment by **Mr. S. MacBride** and **Ms. B. Zimmerman:** "The examples cited, particularly those proposing international duties, seem to have been insufficiently considered in terms of their validity or practicability in the international sphere, and indicate the need for further careful study in this area."

"Many Voices, One World," the report of the UNESCO International Commission for the Study of Communication Problems, chaired by Sean MacBride, has caused a great number of reactions. Cees Hamelink of the Institute of Social Studies, The Hague, Netherlands, has edited a book with comments on the report. From that book we have chosen nine chapters that mirror different reactions. In the first of these pieces, Alfred E. Opubor of the University of Lagos, Nigeria, argues that although the report is useful to those who have little prior knowledge of the problems, it has little to contribute to those who look for new theories and data about the field. The report is in general atheoretical and it reifies communication as capable of "doing," intervening and motivating social action in itself, Opubor argues.

7

GROPING TOWARD ELUSIVE CONCEPTS

Alfred E. Opubor

The Report reminds one of the folktale about the Three Blindmen and the Elephant. Each blind man having touched the elephant at a different part of its anatomy, promptly declared his view of what an elephant was. Consequently, although they disagreed about its essence, the blind men achieved consensus about the fact of the elephant's existence. There is however a slight twist in the McBride story; all the blindmen here declare that they have resolved their conflicting views of the essential elephant, having "reached a surprising agreement on major issues, upon which opinion heretofore had seem irreconcilable" (p. XVIII). But one gets the impression that as in the traditional folktale, so it is in the modern exploration; the nature of the elephant has eluded the explorers! We are no nearer an understanding of "the totality of communication problems in modern Societies", in spite of the far-ranging and assiduous deliberations of this multinational and high-powered Commission.

The basic difficulty of the Report seems to be its atheoretic approach. There is no clarity about the nature of communication and how it may be productively studied. The "Schemes or models for the study of communication", as well as the "definition" of communication contained in Appendix 2 indicate the ambivalence of the Commission's approach to matters of theory. While it is clear that the Commission gives priority to communication through the mass media and allied technology, the relationship of these modalities of communication to the phenomenon of human communication as a social and psychological process is left unexplored. This situation leads to the view that each form of communication is *sui generis*, a unique phenomenon with no radical or fundamental linkages to other forms.

From Alfred E. Opubor, "Groping Toward Elusive Concepts," pp. 4-7 in Cees J. Hamelink (ed.) *Communication in the Eighties: A Reader on the MacBride Report.* Rome: IDOC International, 1981. Reprinted by permission of IDOC.

Perhaps because of this atheoretic approach, the Report at many points slips into the "pathetic fallacy", in which Communication is reified, and endowed with capacities for "doing", for intervening and for motivating social action on its own. Communication is thus conferred with the status of an actor in the drama of human history, as a result of the confusion, in the Report, between the technology, its use and effects, and the social process involving technology.

Examples of the reification of communication are especially numerous in Part I of the Report which attempts an overview of the conceptual territory. We will select three of these examples as illustrations.

1) "Communication's ability to activate, socialize, homogenize and even adapt people to their own culture has always been over-estimated, while at the same time the standardizing and distorting consequences of audio-visual media have been under-valued." (p. 16).

2) "Despite the considerable influence of communication, it would be wrong to attribute to it more virtues, more faults, or greater powers than it truly possesses", (p. 17).

3) "Communication turns its eyes more naturally to modernisation and to fitting young people to take their place in a world that is being remade. Its mission is to bring to light social possibilities which have not yet been explored or applied", (p. 29).

Part I of the Report attempts to be analytical; yet it is also implicitly prescriptive. But the bases of prescriptions are unclear. Do they represent deductions from the analysis, or a value-system pre-determined by the terms of reference of the Commission?

Because it presumes to cover "the spectrum of communication in contemporary society... (which)... almost defies description because of its immense variety and range of its components". The Report contains a wide variety of ideas, many of which have been treated cursorily, and whose relevance to the total picture is unspecified or undeveloped. Does this reflect the priority accorded to these problems by the Commission, or is it the result of the quite variable amount and depth of supporting documentation for the different issues under consideration by the Commission?

Part II, Chapter 3, which is concerned with "Integration: Changing pattern", devotes a scanty three paragraphs to the "Combination of Traditional and Modern". While recognizing the importance of "traditional communication" in the Third World, the Report offers no new insights about their contribution to the study of communication in society. In a pluralistic world the potential value of different models of communication to our understanding of the process and values which can influence the organisation of human relationships, need to be seriously explored. We argue that the so-called "traditional media", like any socio-technological system of communication embody perspectives which deserve more serious attention and analysis than provided by the Report. And especially since they represent a potential area of contribution by Third World Societies to human knowledge and possibly even to the solution of communication problems, it is unfortunate that the Report has treated them in such casual terms. At the recent

Intergovernmental Conference on Communication Policies in Africa, a recommendation advocating a scientific approach to the study of traditional systems of communication was adopted.

Its implications could be far-reaching for future work directed towards understanding questions of the ethics of communication and the issue of freedom of expression especially from the point of view of non-Western thought.

The discussion of "free flow" is a succint and lucid review of the history and development of this problematic concept. The Report makes a contribution to our understanding especially by linking "free flow" to the concept of "freedom of information" both at the individual and institutional levels, and involving consideration of the influence of economic as well as the usual political forces in the restriction of freedom of information. It is this level of analysis that begins to expose the kinds of practical solutions which must emerge for the correction of the "flaws in communication flow" which constitute a major problem of the communication situation in the world today, and which tend to become obscured by partial discussions of the pros and cons of "free flow". A recognition of the similarity between flaws in international communication flows and intra-national flows provides a basis for the harmonisation of policies at the national level with strategies for achieving a more equitable international communication flow. This is important because of the tendency in some societies to dissociate internal realities from the more polemical approach to external environment.

However, the links between the communication policies of a single nation and the mechanisms for stipulating and implementing communication policies at regional or supra-national levels are still unclear. While there are a few pragmatic actions, especially in the Third World, to pool resources for news dissemination, or to exchange news and cultural material, the underlying assumptions for such action are far from being clarified, and their total scope has yet to be subjected to the kind of systematic thinking and planning which has been advocated as an approach to communication policies.

The Report rightly draws attention to the disparity in infrastructural development, in institutionalization, in training facilities, research abilities and technological know-how between the developing and developed regions of the world. However the impression is created that major problems would be solved, if, somehow, the developing countries could attain the same levels of endowment as the developed countries. There is the suggestion that the training needs of the developing countries are peculiar to them, that the development of professionalism is a "given" which can be assured through training. Yet the international debate seems to have emphasised the need for re-examination of the nature of "professional" values for communicators in a pluralistic and increasingly interdependent world. It has been suggested, for example, that the training of Western journalists might involve more emphasis on interpersonal and intercultural skills, to enable them to function more effectively in their processing of news from a wide variety of cultural backgrounds.

It has even been suggested that multi-cultural training programmes might be set up in Third World countries to assist in the international socialization of communicators from the developed world, through a process of values-sharing.

The Reports' "Recommendations and Conclusions" contain a baffling array of courageous and innovative insights, as well as impractical and banal suggestions, coupled with unclear prescriptions of dubious validity. The sheer spread of the territory covered and the volume of the concerns exposed for study, reflection and action, ensures that this Report will be regarded by its primary audience-governments, policy-makers and international agencies, as a document with "a little morsel for everyone". And that is no small achievement. The Report will for many in that audience provide the first contact with ideas related to communication policies and their international implications. However, for the scholar, seeking either new theoretic insights or new data, or even new analyses of familiar data and problems, the Report is indeed a slim harvest.

Professor Kaarle Nordenstreng of the University of Tampere, Finland, is critical of the MacBride Report on several grounds. The approach is generally ahistorical, Nordenstreng claims. It looks at the history of communication in isolation, in a paradigm where communication is seen as related to but not organically linked to other social phenomena. The report further does not contain any coherent picture of the "one world" it sets out to describe. Also, the conception of man lacks the aspect of human consciousness, an ahumanistic view that is typical of a functional-positivistic approach.

8

THE PARADIGM OF A TOTALITY

Kaarle Nordenstreng

It may not be unreasonable to expect that a book of some 300 pages, entitled "Many voices, one world. Communication and society, today and tomorrow", would provide the reader with a fairly comprehensive picture of three objects: world, society and communication. Even more so since the book is the outcome of a mandate "to study the totality of communication problems in modern societies" (see Preface by Sean MacBride, p. XVII).

Therefore, it is appropriate to ask what kind of "one world" emerges from the Report, what kind of a concept of society is there, and what is the nature and place of communication in this "totality"? What is the explicit and implicit conceptualization — paradigm — of such central objects as suggested by the Report?

Looking firstly at the world as portrayed by the Report, one is delighted to see Chapter 1 entitled "The historical dimension". History is indeed an indispensable key to any thorough analysis of social problems (and the Commission was created as a response to a need precisley for "more thorough analysis of all communication and information problems" as indicated in Appendix 3, p. 295). Following the title however, one finds little that might be called "history of the world"; rather it is an outline of the history of human communication faculties and media.

To be precise, we may read that "the world has advanced", (p. 3), that there were "societies with distinct economic, moral and cultural traditions", there was "the era of imperialism", there are "the now independent nations of Africa and Asia", also called "States" (p. 4). Furthermore, we may read about "Chinese emperors", "Hindu Temples", and "the teachings of Buddha, of Christ and Mohammed" (p. 5), about "such civilizations as the Chinese, the Indian, the Egyptian, or the Greco-Roman" (p. 6), and even about

From Kaarle Nordenstreng, "The Paradigm of a Totality," pp. 8-16 in Cees J. Hamelink (ed.) *Communication in the Eighties: A Reader on the MacBride Report.* Rome: IDOC International, 1981. Reprinted by permission of IDOC.

the "struggle for democratic rights and national liberation", about "socialist movements in the capitalist world" (p. 8), and finally that "the socialist politico-economic system was established in the 20th century", and that more recently there have been "broader political and economic changes, both within many countries and on a world scale" (p. 10).

The problems with all these historical facts — certainly correct as such — is that they have been made as passing remarks alongside a much more elaborate story of how various forms and means of communications have developed throughout history. Thus the world itself, its development and nature at different stages in history — including the nation-states and international relations — is left outside the scope of the study. Or to put it more politely, the world history is taken for granted such as it is normally described in textbooks and encyclopedias. Is it necessary however, in such a context to go into "history beyond communications"?

It is indeed necessary to go beyond the particular phenomena of communications, if one wants to do more than just describe the surface of historical development, that is, if one wants to study the relations between communications and society. Unless we embrace what might be called "real world history", we are left with the history of communications *in isolation* from fundamental social and global developments. Such a picture of communication history is not only incomplete: it amounts to a crucial choice of methodology carrying with it a particular concept of communication, a paradigm where communication is understood as a phenomenon *related* to a number of other social phenomena but not *organically linked with* them. A distinct communication history — however accurate and useful it may be in its details — can never provide us with an understanding of that kind of "totality" which the Report was supposed to discover. Indeed, such a "historical dimension" provides us with pseudo-history since the approach is strictly speaking *ahistorical*.

This fundamental criticism cannot be met by pointing to such paragraphs as for example the one where the Report declares it "worth taking a closer look at the historical circumstances in which this concept of press freedom emerged" (p. 8). Again one is delighted to face such a promising formulation, and again one is disappointed to find little that goes beyond passing remarks only regarding social, political and economic history. It can hardly be considered a closer look at the historical circumstances if only abstract references are made to "authoritarian rulers" or "authority, which claimed the right to control, by prior censorship or otherwise, the chief medium for the spreading of ideas..." (p. 8). The French revolution is just mentioned in this connection without even hinting to the fact — recognized by historians of all orientations — that it was a turning point not only in terms of demands for abstract freedom but also and above all in terms of the total life situation of social classes. Such a ahistorical approach leads to the logical consequence that central concepts like freedom and authority remain abstract words — or sometimes worse, turn into ideological vehicles which are used as political slogans rather than scientifically based solid concepts (*). (This metholodogical position by no

means suggests that the development and functioning of communications is mechanistically determined by i. a. economic etc.,
factors; there is always space for relative autonomy).

An example: The development of news agencies is correctly
connected to "the opening up of further trade and commerce, and
to making the world a much smaller place. At the same time,
since this was the heyday of colonialism, they promoted the
interests of the colonial powers, helped to sustain the existing
political and economic order and to expand the commercial and
political interests of the metropolitan powers". (p. 9). Yet the
concepts of colonialism, metropolitan powers, interests, trade and
commerce are left in the text completely open, without any
concrete historical substance. In such a situation the text might
appear quite radical — or as it is viewed under the influence of
western ideology: "political" — but in reality it is radical only in
a superficial way. Radical words do not necessarily embody radical
ideas, true radicalism equals depthness and a clarity of thought
broader than distinct slogans. Accordingly, "the existing political
and economic order" may here invite some frightening connotations
in the minds of those who are not particularly fond of articulating
the world in terms of old and new "orders". A closer look however,
will convince the reader that little more than hollow words are
involved. The defenders of the "existing order" need not worry too
much since they are not the target of radical analysis but of radical
rhetorics only.

Here one cannot but observe that such bourgeois versions of
press history as the well-known (but now largely outdated) "Four
theories of the press" by U.S. professors Siebert, Peterson and
Schramm contains more of a "real world history" than the Report
does. Considering also the recent revival of research on the history
of mass communications (especially in Great Britain), we must
conclude that the Report is clearly more ahistorical in its writing
of history than is the existing tradition of mass communications
research.

The chapters to follow the "historical dimension" provide the
reader with much more material on the basis of which "the world"
of the Report can be constructed. But the dilemma of the first
chapter is present throughout the Report: the picture of the
contemporary world is little more coherent, socio-economico-
politically concrete and conceptually clear than the description of
the world in historical perspective. This is only logical since it is
precisely through a historical analysis that a picture of the
contemporary world can be meaningfully constituted.

This becomes especially clear in Chapter 3 of Part I where
"The international dimension" is singled out for discussion. Symptomatically, it follows "The contemporary dimension" of Chapter 2
suggesting that international consideration of communication is
something distinct from both the historical and the contemporary
perspective. In defining "The issue", this international chapter makes
a serious attempt to go beyond the obvious communications
phenomena and to characterize the global situation by bringing
communications into the total picture as an organic component

(p. 34-35). Indeed, here the contours of the world of the Report get somewhat more specific than in the chapter on history: dependency, domination and related inequalities appear as main characteristics — both in general politico-economic relations and in the particular relations of communication. Yet the nature of these dependencies remains quite abstract and historically- conceptually vague. The crucial question "Why"? has hardly been asked, let alone answered.

It is typical that in such a situation prominence is given to the coverage of the international debate which has taken place on various political and professional fora during the 1970s. Evidently a short overview of this debate is only welcome (although it is by no means original given the existing abundant literature on the topic), but it becomes problematic when attention to this politically flavoured polemics seems to largely substitute a proper analysis of the objective state of affairs. Thus also the context for the setting up of the Commission itself appears as a political debate rather than as a certain stage in the global relation of socio-economico-political forces. This debate and its heated political nature is certainly a fact, but nevertheless there is a need to go beyond the obvious and to ultimately embrace the fundamental, historically determined forces operating on the world scale.

The Commission might have benefitted from an intellectual in-depth exercise of clarifying to itself why it was established in the first place. If pushed far and deep enough, such an exercise would have led the Commission to provide a more comprehensive picture of the real world — both past and present — instead of an abstract notion of "one world" around which a number of more or less disconnected communications phenomena and debates about them occur.

The world of the Report is further illuminated by several chapters in Part II and III, but the methodological approach continues to be the same as in the beginning: communication with all its means, trends (including transnationalization), disparities, etc., is kept in the focus of attention to the extent that the reader is even tempted to forget that a world exists. Yet, after arriving at Chapter 4 of Part III one cannot help recalling that the Report does contain a concept of the world, however abstract and distant from the actual communications phenomena it did appear to be. This chapter, entitled "Images of the world", has some twenty pages of text devoted to one of the four main lines of inquiry which the Commission was supposed to pursue according to its mandate, namely "to define the role which communication might play in making public opinion aware of the major problems besetting the world, in sensitizing it to these problems and helping gradually to solve them by concerted action at the national and international levels".

The chapter begins with listing "crucial problems facing mankind today" such as the protection of the environment, the rational use of natural resources, employment, inflation, the defence of human rights, the struggle against the legacy of colonialism, the safeguarding of peace and disarmament (p. 175).

Seven problem areas are then singled out for further discussion: (1) war and disarmament, (2) hunger and poverty, (3) "North-South split", (4), East-West interface, (5), violation of human rights, (6) equal rights for women, and (7) "interdependence and co-operation". It is made clear that the Report has no ambitions "to seek solutions to the major issues over-shadowing the final decades of this century. More modestly, we aim to show that communication means and systems are not always making contributions they may be expected to do and to highlight the contributions which communication in general, and the media in particular, can and should make in encouraging critical awareness of these problems..." (p. 175).

This all looks at first sight once more very appropriate and indeed promising —— if not radical in the sense of deep and comprehensive. The chapter adds little to our understanding of the nature and reasons of the crucial problems. It is true that many important aspects of the problems are described and many well-intentioned value positions are taken, in line with the established thinking of the international community as this has been expressed for example in several resolutions and declarations of the United Nations, yet such central documents as the Declaration on the Establishment of the New International Economic Order would have deserved a more prominent place in the text than just a footnote (see p. 181).

As was the case in examining world history, we may say that such a listing of main characteristics of the problems will hardly help "in encouraging critical awareness" of them — neither the awareness of the Report nor that of public opinion. In fact, the Report suggests a deceptive way of looking at global problems which should serve as a warning example rather than as a model for the mass media and other promoters of public opinion: an ahistorical, nominalistic and overtly political way to go about it — however convenient it may be in terms of eliminating theoretical and political controversies — does not usually lead us to facing objective reality but on the contrary easily obscures reality by preventing us from seeing the deep interrelationships and the totality of social phenomena.

Clear example of this dilemma are provided by the chapter in its dealing with the "North-South" and "East-West" problems. Well-known determinants for both cases are mentioned, such as "world wide imbalance", "legacy of colonial past", and a minority that "possesses the majority share of resources and income", for the "North-South split", and "cold war", "détente", "peace, co-operation and international undestanding", for the "East-West interface" (pp. 183-184). All this is most welcome but insufficient. After all, the Report is not supposed to be a political resolution — as was the case with the famous Mass Media Declaration — but a thorough analytical study of the problems involved. Therefore in this connection there is little excuse for leaving the argumentation and conceptualization at the level of political documents and debates (or even below them as indicated by the treatment of the new international economic order). The fundamental problems of "North-South" and "East-West" remain equally hazy and impressionistic as they usually are in everyday reasoning, and, moreover, not even an attempt is made to bring these two "axes'" together under an overall global analysis. Thus the Report helps to maintain a reasoning where the world has been artificially compartmentalized according to international-political cross currents which again easily serves as an ideological distortion of the true nature of reality.

Once more we must add that a simple recognition of these problems is welcome and that such an eclectic way of characterizing them is the natural first stage of a comprehensive understanding of their nature and origin, or to put it in terms of the Report, of a "critical awareness of these problems". The point is that the problems are too crucial to be left just to some descriptive remarks, and what is more, such a methodological approach leaves the communication problems related to these global problems hanging in a political air without scientifically based solid conceptual links with the totality of social, economic and political realities. This is so even if the summarising passages of the two sub-chapters under discussion do contain quite good formulations, such as "to go beyond the need for assistance; the elimination of unjust and oppressive structures, the revision of the present division of labour, the building of a new international economic order", (p. 183), or "improved international communication in Europe will not mean the dissolution of all ideological, political, social and cultural differences between various European countries" (p. 185). These are excellent statements at the level of a political discussion but they have little to offer at the level of a scientific analysis since the preceding text contains only sketchy material to substantiate those statements in terms of in-depth analysis.

But the crucial issues of the world as outlined in the Report do not only suffer from insufficient depthness and comprehensiveness. Another serious problem with the way the Report sees the world is created by the display of priorities. Typical of the eclectic approach is that issues of quite different magnitude and nature are listed as if they were comparable in terms of theoretical understanding and political priority (compare for example, in the list of seven problem areas above "North-South" with the demand for equal rights for women). This again is a logical consequence of the lack of coherent analysis of the issues and their interrelationships: one is led to relativism and ultimately to a political choice of more or less arbitrarily understood distinct problems.

At first glance it looks as if the big issues raised to the focus of global attention would not be very much different from what is nowadays customarily discussed on fora such as United Nations and Unesco. However, a careful look at the totality advocated by the Report leads us to conclude that the priorities of the Report do after all depart in some crucial aspects from those of the international community (the latter defined by decisions of UN, Unesco and such significant bodies as the non-aligned movement). Let us take the question of peace and international understanding as an example.

Matters of peace and war are treated in the first four parts of the Report, firstly as one of several aspects along "the international dimension" and subsequently as one of the seven "crucial problems" covered in the chapter discussed above. None of these passages deals to any satisfactory degree with the nature of a nation state, the relations between nation-states, or ultimately the global system of international relations. Thus also the field of international law is practically forgotten, including the fundamental principles which are supposed to guide relations between states as universally recognised by the international community. Such an omission is not only peculiar for the sponsor of the Report — after all, Unesco is a United Nations organisation, that is to say, it is an instrument of the international community, — but more profoundly it has led to the undermining of the prime importance of peace and security in the Report.

It should not be forgotten that matters of peace and war occupy the very core of international relations and that, furthermore, the purpose of Unesco, according to Article I of its Constitution, is to "contribute to peace and security...", the well-known phrase on the "free flow of ideas by word and image" being clearly subordinated to this overall objective. Yet the Report displays this question as a matter of secondary or even tertiary importance. This state of affairs is easily detectable already in the synopsis of the Report, especially in Part V (Conclusions and recommendations). The latter, in its summary of "previous main conclusions" (pp. 253-254) makes only passing reference to the arms race as a factor threatening the human race. In any case not one of the five points of the summary focuses on international relations and the role of information in this field — with the exception of a strong stand for freedom of information as a fundamental human right. The same kind of emphasis on the human rights aspect of information, at the expense of equally or even more fundamental aspects of obligations vis-à-vis the nature of information as determined by international law, can be found in Part I where it poses the issue of "The international dimension" (p. 35).

The unreasonably low priority to matters of peace and war in Part V is further indicated by the structure of the five areas of recommendations which follow the brief summary. The first area "Strengthening in independence and self-reliance" makes only in passing a reference to "even international peace" (p. 254); it is mainly concerned with national communication policies, with international relations brought into this picture only indirectly through administrative aspects of telecommunication. The second area is concerned with "Social consequences and new tasks" with politically quite radical positions on cultural identity and commercialization of communication, including the control of transnational corporations. Although international relations are involved here, they are projected at the particular level of transnational corporations, which however crucial they may be in view of communication policies, should be legally speaking seen as subordinated to the overall principles of international relations. The third area on "Professional integrity and standards" devotes one third of its attention to "improved international reporting" which comes already very close to what is being discussed here, but again the politically quite advanced recommendations lose much of their power since they are not backed by proper references to international law and by duly theoretical conceptualization in the previuos parts of the Report. The fourth area invites for "democratization of communication", another laudable and in this exceptional case even innovative recommendation, but without notable emphasis on international relations (although the demand for democratization is also relevant to them). The final area is devoted to "Fostering international co-operation", and here we shall find what was missing elsewhere: "The strengthening of peace, international security and co-operation and the lessening of international tensions are the common concern of all nations. The mass media can make a substantial contribution towards achieving these goals". (p. 271). It is not difficult to see that here we have in a nutshell the essence of the 1978 Mass Media Declaration (which, as is reminded by Appendix 3, p. 295, was a central reason for the establishment of the Commission).

Politically speaking it can be argued that it is all there: international relations including matters of peace and war have been covered in the Report. However, it is evident that the totality of the Report, or looking momentarily just at Part V, does not underline the central location of this question, since the passage on international relations occupies the status of just one topic out of four — all formally equal by emphasis — within the context of five broad areas covered. This is no doubt a lower position than it should deserve in view of Unesco's Constitution and also taking into account major resolutions of the Unesco General Conference, not to mention the positions of the UN General Assembly.

Such a judgement is only strengthened by the two short paragraphs which conclude the chapter of proper conclusions and recommendations (p. 272). Here it is stated that the recommendations and suggestions "indicate the importance and scale of the tasks which face every country in the field of information and communication, as well as their international relations..." Furthermore, at the end of that part of the Report which was "really and definitively discussed" by the Commission, to use the words by Mr. Sergei Losev (who in his supplementary comment reveals that Parts I - IV have not been thoroughly discussed by the Commission, let alone written by it), we are faced with the following sentence: "Our study indicates clearly the direction in which the world must move to attain a new information and communication order — essentially a series of new relationships arising from the advances promised by *new communication technologies* which should enable all peoples to benefit" (p. 272, emphasis added).

Does this not indicate that not only the outcome but even the determined line of the Report serves to undermine the Mass Media Declaration, on the one hand, and to elevate matters of technology to the degree of mystification, on the other?

To return to the problem of "one world", it is by now clear that the Report does not contain any coherent picture of the world — neither of the world of today or of tomorrow, or for that matter the world of yesterday. That is why a demand or a programme towards a "new order", whatever attributes are attached to it, remains also a fairly empty slogan with more political connotations that theoretical insight. The fact that "interdependence" is one of the few salient attributes attached to this abstract notion of the world throughout the Report only confirms the political nature of the "one world" — to be specific, its Western ("trilateral") political bias.

But this does not mean that no world exists in the Report; it is implicit and hidden — probably not even realized by those who wrote the Report. It is a hidden paradigm with fundamental philosophical and methodological implications. Indeed, it is part of an overall paradigm which we will find if we begin to search also for the concepts of society and communication in this Report. As is the case with the world, the Report offers no adequate definition or even proper elements for description of these two central concepts — not even to the degree offered by today's social sciences (including bourgeois sociology).

'   But again, the scattered elements involved do constitute an implicit picture of society and of communication, as well as of the nature of a human being. This paradigm, if carefully analyzed, turns out to be not far from the mainstream of bourgeois liberalism (ahistorical and abstract notion of society, value pluralism, etc).

The concept of communication implied by the Report falls logically into this overall picture. It follows the model where communication is understood as exchange with many connections to other social phenomena but without really organic links with them. Moreover the paradigm practically eliminates human consciousness as a factor in the communications process. Such an ahumanistic view is typical of the functional-positivistic approach — the mother of those models of communication which dominate in the West and which have served as a source of inspiration also for the Report (as indicated in Appendix 2). In fact, man without subjective consciousness is a logical component in the overall paradigm where nature and society are so "pluralistically" composed that there is no room left for objective reality.

The report is an excellent illustration of the dilemma of eclecticism: you try to be comprehensive but you lose the totality which you are supposed to discover. In this respect the Report could well be called "Mission impossible".

The title of the following section alludes to what the author, Tamàs Szecskö, regards as the main merit of the MacBride Report. To Lasswell's classical paradigm have been added the questions of who owns and who dominates the market. The report will have an eye-opening impact on the broader public, Szecskö says, but he is at the same time critical on a number of points. For example, he maintains that the report has very little to say about the social history of communications and it covers inadequately the experiences of developing and socialist countries. Tamàs Szecskö is at the Research Center of Hungarian Radio and TV, Budapest, Hungary.

9

BROADENING LASSWELL'S PARADIGM

Tamàs Szecskö

For all those who had thought that the Report could play a similar role in revolutionizing the "Ancien regime" of the international information order as the Great Encyclopedia did in paving the way towards the French Revolution, browsing through the 312 pages volume might be a disappointment. Although encyclopedic in its approach, the Report is by far not a revolutionary manifesto. The reasons are manyfold. Here only two of them are given. We find ourselves already in the process of making the new international information order — its fore-runners were not the very distinguished members of the McBride Commission, but those politicians, communicators and researchers, who, one decade ago, began criticizing, both in theory and practice, both politically and morally, those inequalities and disparities of the global information flows and structures that the world has inherited from the colonial period of modern history. Moreover, Diderot, d'Alambert and the other encyclopedists basically shared the same world view, while the Commission's members cannot be accused of this. Rather the opposite: the metabolism of this body was regulated by the fact that its members had expressedly different political, ideological backgrounds, possessed varied expertises in the communications field and represented — without a formal type of legally binding representativeness — different regions of the world. And last, but not least, the old French authors did not work in a commission, with the necessity of finding — or trying to find — a consensus at every cornerstone of their argumentation. Our modern encyclopedists, by their very mandate, had this obligation which, moreover, was burdened with strong exogeneous stresses and strains and a permanent attack on behalf of the international press and news monopolies, as one of the Commission's members hinted to in his

From Tamàs Szecskö, "Broadening Lasswell's Paradigm," pp. 17-22 in Cees J. Hamelink (ed.) *Communication in the Eighties: A Reader on the MacBride Report.* Rome: IDOC International, 1981. Reprinted by permission of IDOC.

presentation of the Report at the recent Conference of the IAMCR, in Caracas.

Given these circumstances the character of the outcome of the Commission's work could only be uneven, and sometimes eclectic. Paraphrasing the title of the Report's commercialized version, "Many Voices, One World" — the Report echoed on different registers. Meeting everybody's demand, however, is almost identical with denying everybody's needs. So, there are certainly readers who will find the text too much descriptive, while for others it may have a prescriptive, normative character. For some its value-loadedness will be embarassing, others will spot and criticize the inconsistencies in its value-system, or just that kind of approach which seems to them of a value-free nature. Some politicians and practitioners in the communications field will probably speak out against its quasi-scientific terminology and the lengthy, sometimes redundant argumentation, even expressing acid remarks regarding its abstract nature, while, on the other hand, researchers and scholars may attack it because of its theoretical deficiencies and exaggerated practice-orientedness. In view of all these different perceptions the Report has to be seen as a *political* document prepared by a *small group* of experts for a *large international* audience. This is the overall perception guiding my forthcoming remarks which will rather than pursuing the scholarly qualities of the Report, meditate on its intrinsic values, its analytical depth and its possible social uses.

It is not merely by chance that encyclopedic analogies occur to the reader's mind when leafing through the volume. The Report is really an encyclopedia-like inventory of the problems of — let me borrow its subtitle — "communication and society: today and tomorrow". It enlists the most vital issues of the national and international communication scenes, and, going beyond their enumeration, tries to detect their socio-historical origin. In this sense, it is much more than a static and skeleton-like inventory: it is a kind of documentary, unveiling those currents and undercurrents, those information flows, institutions and structures, those forces and interests of global communications in the 70's, which hinder the progress towards a more just, equal, democratic international order of speaking to each other, listening to each other, understanding — or even sharing —— each other's social, cultural and moral values. Consequently, I am convinced, it will have an eye-opening impact even on the broader public, making it aware of this vitally important segment of contradictory realities in today's world.

Stating the assets and liabilities of the world communications system, the Report generally — if not always particularly — follows that line of thinking and argumentation which, during the last decade, has been taken up at several fora: at the last four General Conference of Unesco, at the regional inter-governmental conferences on communication policies, at numerous international seminars and workshops organized under the auspices of Unesco, and in such important documents as the Helsinki Final Act or the Declaration on the Mass Media. Nevertheless, it would be a mistake to consider the Report as a kind of well-documented summary of the disparate resolutions and recommendations which were born in the UN family during the last years. On some points the Report goes further than hitherto any international document in this field, elsewhere it proves shorter, milder or more hesitant than some earlier international intellectual ventures. Yet — and this is what I find of utmost importance — the Report is the first international document that provides a really global view on the world's communication problems and that, because of this type of approach, is capable of convincingly showing the urgent necessity of giving the communications issues a high priority, both on the national and the international level. It does not only state that — as the often-quoted saying goes — "today's world is like a drum: you beat it anywhere and it trembles everywhere", but also tries to show the possible and necessary interrelations between the different kinds of "drum-beats" and the rhythm of the development processes. World public opinion (it is worth noting that a separate subchapter deals with its growing importance!) could and should be made aware of these interrelations, and the Report does its best in this direction.

The traditional approach to mass communications phenomena — dominant for a long time and having rear-guards even now — usually cuts the communications processes into two parts, both logically and methodologically. On one side, there was the consumer — readers, listener, viewer — and the consumption of communication contents itself. All this could be studied by the social sciences, could be "nose-counted", multi-variate analyzed, and anything else you may wish. The other side, that of the production of the communication contents has mainly been the realm of technology, of engineers and technicians, where social scientists normally did not wander, with perhaps the exception of some organizational sociologists and one or two psychologists addicted to "gate-keeper" studies. This artificial and, in its impact conservative, polarisation of mass communications processes was no longer dominant in the 70's and was replaced by a much more revealing model which regards mass communications as a complex production process of communication contents (signs, images, consciousness), which certainly has its distribution aspects as well. With this change of viewpoint two hitherto neglected although by any means not negligible aspects, came suddenly into the forefront of scholarly interest: that of economic and political power. It is to the merit of the Report that, if not in the directly theorizing parts, but in the logical sequence of its argumentation, it has chosen this approach, and consequently added to Lasswell's basic five "W"-s (*) other rather pertinent questions: such as "Who owns"?, "who dominates the market?", and "who screens the information?". The fruitfulness of this approach is easily perceivable in those parts of the text which deal with concentration and monopolies, with the process of transnationalization, with the national and international commercial companies. Even in some of the more abstract and theoretical discussions, like e.g. the refreshingly new brief subchapter on "news-values", one can feel the fertilizing effect of this approach.

(*) Who says what in which channel to whom with what effect.

Setting the priorities in a global context and deploying the argumentation of the logics of message-production: these are the first two very positive aspects of the Report, while the third, not less important one is the concept of democratization which is an underlying value in the whole body of the Report. The Latin American members of the Commission, Gabriel Garcia Marquez and Juan Somavia, in their first comments on the Report (Appendix 1) stress this fact and to cite their words: "The relevance given to the issue of democratization is of the highest significance. More democratic communication structures are a national and international need of peoples everywhere. Promoting access, participation, decentralization, open management, and the diffusion of the power, concentrated in the hands of commercial or bureaucratic interests, is a world-wide necessity. This is particularly crucial in Third World countries dominated by repressive minority regimes" (p. 281).

The Hungarian delegate to the Unesco General Conference in 1978, after the debate and acceptance of the Declaration on the Mass Media, in explanation of his vote, called attention to the fact, that the newly accepted document expressedly marked the end of the classical liberalist ideology in the domain of international information. If this is true and I think it is — then the Report seems to be a first endeavour to build, on the ruins of the manipulative information liberalism, a new theoretical and operational framework for a more just international information order. Even if one takes into consideration all its contradictions, shortcomings and mistakes. There are indeed quite a few of them.

To begin with, there is the lack of consistency in the theoretical foundations of the Report. If the editor of the volume was trying to demonstrate — or to excuse for — the deficiencies in the theoretical base by inserting the two first parts of Appendix 2 ("Definitions", Some Schemes or Models for the Study of Communication"), this task has been accomplished perfectly. Looking at these parts, one cannot pardon the consequent and laborious mixing up of the concepts of information, communication and mass communication. Practically minded readers of the Report might object and wonder what this slightly theoretical lapse has to do with the macro-level processes and structures of a new international information order? I touch here only one aspect of the problem: when communication, information and mass communication are taken apart, the exact — or even the guessed — meaning of the "right to communication" fades away. Stricter theoretical definitions taken into consideration, the "right to communicate" seems to be a pleonasmus or a non sense, just like the "right to breathe", or the "right to sleep". The "right to inform and be informed" may come under the traditional umbrella of the human and civil rights, while the eventual "right to mass-communicate" (which probably covers the access and the participation aspects) is a brand-new problem for any kind of constitutional and legal regulations.

Technology's role is not less controversial either in the Report. On the one hand, the text duly states the primacy of socio-historical relations and social needs over the technology, but, on the other hand, it leaves open quite a few back-doors for the technological

determinism to creep in. Moreover, the whole Chapter 1 seems
to be restricted to the technological dimension, although its title
is "The Historical Dimension". A participant in the IAMCR conference in Caracas rightly remarked, that nowadays an average
secondary school textbook has much more to say on the social
context of the history of communications than this ominous
chapter has.

Another shortcoming of the Report is that, while analyzing
communications in general, it concentrates almost exclusively on
the transfer and exchange of news, that is on mediated information,
in a stricter sense. As for the cultural aspect, the limitations of
the Report's basic standpoint are clearly expressed in the statement,
that "communication is a part of culture as much as an influence
upon it" (p. 161). But what about the communication — or even
mass communication — of culture itself? Handling the cultural
aspects of communication so economically, the whole problem of
"cultural imperialism" becomes diluted in some vague remarks and
defensive statements, even though there are subchapters which, at
least in their titles, seem to deal with it. Antonio Pasquali, deputy
assistant director-general of Unesco has rightly remarked in his
address at the conference of the IAMCR that "it is worthwhile to
note the slow movement of scientific interest towards a new more
comprehensive notion, that of 'cultural industry' of which communication systems constitute the substantial part. This new category
of socio-economic thought, to this day not well defined in operational terms and without norn.lized taxonomy, at the end will
favor a more global approach to the problem through an analysis
of production modes and the forms of action that imply a more
rigorous and substantial scientific description of the phenomenon".
I think, this problem-area should have also been reflected in the
Report.

If slightly near-sighted in the matters of culture, the Report
proves to be rather hesitant and timid in relation to national
communication policies. Certainly, it stresses the importance of the
elaboration and implementation of such policies, but less convincingly than many earlier Unesco documents, including the
biennial action plans and the recommendations of intergovernmental conferences on the subject. Besides this hesitative attitude —
or rather hand in hand with it — the paragraphs dealing with
communication policies seem to hide just that liberalist attitude
that it could not only avoid, but — as I have shown earlier —
very creatively surpassed at other places. In this frame of thinking
the most important task of policies seems to be a kind of technical
allocation of resources, while the regulative motions of the society
are usually tagged as "State intervention", as if there were no other
forms of common action or national policy implementation than
State intervention, and as if there were no other forms of the
State's actions (promotion, development, etc.), than intervention.
The strong screening effect of the liberalist terminology can be
felt most markedly in the fact, that the concepts of "plan and
planning" have entirely vanished from the text, like four-letter
words in the Victorian novels. (The absurdity of this situation is
clearly demonstrated in the index of the Report, where the reader

finds the item "Political and Economic Planning", but when going back to the indicated page, realizes that it is only the title of a source quoted there.)

The disappearance of the concept of planning does not only show a detour from Unesco's philosophy and practice of the last decade, in which, on many instances, communication policies and planning were treated in conjunction with each other, but clearly indicates another deficiency of the McBride Report: that of inadequate covering of the experiences of the developing nations and socialist societies. Although the Commission put the main emphasis in its work on the developing world and was supposed to deal with the socialist countries as well, the empirical material and the examples used in the text come overwhelmingly from Western developed societies. But, after all, one should not wonder, because among the 100 titles enlisted in the List of Documents prepared for the Commission (Appendix 3) one cannot find but 10 documents authored by people coming from socialist countries, and even the combined number of authors coming from developing and socialist countries is remarkably less than of the authors from the Western countries. I know, of course, that regional affiliation is not always a decisive factor in scientific or ideological attitudes. Nevertheless, these structural disproportions are too large to be considered merely a trick of chance.

I shall not discuss here the research aspects of the Report. There will be times and places to do that, because, after all, this is only the beginning of the debate which — and this is not a paradox — could be effective and fruitful only if it does not concentrate solely on the Report itself, but rather on those problem-areas which are successfully outlined in the text. The world of communications and the communications of the world need this debate and need even more badly forthcoming actions. The road to a new international information order will probably be long and tiresome. The Report gives us some instruments of orientation to begin this long journey. But it does not provide us with a strategy. I suspect, that for the time being, only the transnational corporations have complete strategies of the long-term development of the world communications system. Here I am less optimistic that the McBride Commission.

Oswaldo Capriles does not believe that the MacBride Report will contribute to a better understanding of international communication. The reason for this is that NIIO (the New International Information Order) is not properly defined and discussed, in spite of its being a key concept. This is to the disadvantage of the developing countries. The author is at the Central University of Venezuela, Caracas, Venezuela.

10

SOME REMARKS ON THE NEW INTERNATIONAL INFORMATION ORDER

Oswaldo Capriles

The "new order" is present already in the subtile of the Report and the reader is thus led to believe that the new international information order (NIIO) occupies a key position. It is striking, however, to discover upon reading the whole report that it contains nowhere a proper definition of the NIIO.

In general terms, the NIIO formulations and documents produced up to 1979, before the submission of the Report to Unesco, have suffered from a strong degree of confusion between theory and practice, analytical diagnosis of reality and concrete models for social change, and between objectives to be met and strategies to be applied.

One can think here of such documents as the Report of the Tunis Symposium of non-aligned countries (March 1976), the Report of the ILET Seminar in Mexico City (May 1976), the reports from the non-aligned meetings in New Delhi and Colombo in Summer 1976 or the papers by Masmoudi and Osolnik produced for the McBride Commission (in 1978).

Confusion has been present particularly in the presuppositions of these papers rather than in their concrete proposals. Very often reference was made to the NIIO as an already existing reality. In their reaction most of the Western media translated this reference in its most simplistic terms in order to reinforce fears against alleged totalitarian aims inherent in a type of secret conspiracy stemming from radical Third World groups.

It is unfortunate that the Report has little to add to this state of affairs concerning the NIIO. It hardly helps us to go beyond the existing confusion. Thus the same critical remarks apply to the

From Oswaldo Capriles, "Some Remarks on the New International Information Order," pp. 30-32 in Cees J. Hamelink (ed.) *Communication in the Eighties: A Reader on the MacBride Report.* Rome: IDOC International, 1981. Reprinted by permission of IDOC.

Report as can be made with respect to the majority of available documents on the NIIO.

Under the term NIIO one generally encounters:

1) A non-homogeneous *set of criticisms* directed against the currently dominant condition of international communications. This critical diagnosis, even where it appears as relatively organically related, tends to become confused due to its connection with critical claims of a different nature or with utopian statements.

2) A *set of proposals*, similarly non-homogeneous and insufficiently based upon critical analytical research. Most of the proposals tend to be utopian statements and reinforce conformist attitudes vis-à-vis current global domination.

3) A *strategy* which attempts to locate the criticisms and the proposals in the concrete time and space of the international political reality. Again the lack of homogeneity constitutes a major problem. Strategies devised thus far have been incapable of relating the theoretical statements on the issue with the concrete political experience. Therefore they appear as sporadic and unrelated actions.

A recurring problem with the NIIO debate is the adoption of imprecise terminology, usually on loan from economic statements about unequal international exchange relations. This has led to the lack of a precisely defined subject, clear objectives and methodological principles.

Compared with earlier descriptions one finds a broad though useful definition of the NIIO in a resolution of the Fourth meeting of the Intergovernmental Coordinating Council for Information of the non-aligned countries (Bagdad, June 5-7-1980). This document, summarising a number of earlier positions of the non-aligned movement, Unesco, and the UN, states that:
the NIIO is based on,

"(a) the fundamental principles of international law, notably self-determination of peoples, sovereign equality of states and non-interference in international affairs of other states,

(b) the right of every nation to develop its own independent information system and to protect its national sovereignty and cultural identity, in particular by regulating the activities of the transnational corporations,

(c) the right of people and individuals to acquire an objective picture of reality by means of accurate and comprehensive information as well as to express themselves freely through various media of culture and communication,

(d) the right of every nation to use its means of information to make known worldwide its interest, its aspirations and its political, moral and cultural values,

(e) the right of every nation to participate, on the governmental and non-governmental level, in the international exchange of information under favourable conditions in a sense of equality, justice and mutual advantage,

(f) the responsibility of various actors in the process of information for its truthfulness and objectivity, as well as for the particular social objectives to which the information activities are dedicated".

This resolution demonstrates that there exist fairly advanced formulations in the field of international law and politics that represent the original and genuine aspirations of the Third World and that are based on principles already adopted by the international community.

The Report did not develop its discussion of the NIIO on the basis of such formulations and hence falls behind the thinking of the key actors in this field: the non-aligned countries. This is clearly reflected in the subtitle of the Report which reads: "Towards a new, more just and more efficient world information and communication order". In fact, this typical compromise formula indicates that though the point of depature for the Report may have been a challenging of the "old order" dominated by the western transnational corporations, throughout the writing of the Report an accomodation was achieved that is strikingly western in its bias. The core question of the NIIO — and the related question of the national communication policies — has been dealt with in such obscure and fragmented manner that the Report does not contribute to our better understanding.

Nabil H. Dajani of the American University of Beirut, Lebanon, finds the MacBride Report reflecting materialistic values too much, at the expense of moralistic ones. The author warns that the technological promises are neither neutral nor value free and proposes that the Third World countries should develop the traditional effective media instead of looking for new technology. Too much discussion is devoted to balanced flows between nations instead of between the rich and the poor, the rulers and the ruled and between the minorities and the majority, he says.

11

PERSPECTIVE FROM THE MIDDLE EAST

Nabil H. Dajani

"It is obvious that many questions remain open... many subjects require further analysis. Many difficulties lie ahead, particularly, in organising and implementing concrete measures to help to construct the new order..." One finds these words in Sean McBride's introduction to the Report. Viewing this Report as a student of communications in a small Third World country in the Middle East I could not agree more with this introduction.

The Report provides a most welcome discussion of the historical, political, and sociological perspectives of communication. However, it is clear that in drawing their recommendations its members, divided by numerous ideological and political differences, had to make many compromises that led to the production of a document that does not excite anybody, except, perhaps, its publishers.

As an Easterner who considers moral and spiritual values supreme, I find the Report reflecting many of the materialistic values which I do not endorse. The overemphasis of modern technology and the de-emphasis of the moral obligations of nations and governments is one of my objections to the Report. I find the discussion of the issues of "social participation", of a "just and democratic social order", and of other such morally oriented issues too westernized in its emphasis. Even the elimination of a social inequality is resolved in the report by recommending more technology. This, to my Middle Eastern mind, is recommending neo-dependence on the West in either of its materialistic versions, capitalism and communism.

Technological assistance by advanced societies may lead to the commitment to their type of technology which will eventually lead to the economic control by these advanced societies, as well as the control of the messages transferred through this technology. Thus,

From Nabil H. Dajani, "Perspective from the Middle East," pp. 33-36 in Cees J. Hamelink (ed.) *Communication in the Eighties: A Reader on the MacBride Report.* IDOC International, 1981, Reprinted by permission of IDOC.

through the domination of U.S. messages on Lebanese television, a character like J.R. Ewing of the U.S. T.V. program "Dallas" may represent in my Lebanese society the values of success, power and ability while that of Ayatullah Khomeini may represent fanaticism and ridicule. And "human rights" may become more of an issue when such rights concern few Jewish dissidents in Russia than when they concern hundreds of innocent civilian Lebanese killed by Israeli bombs in South Lebanon. Indeed, as two of the Commission members (Marquez and Somavia) rightly point out, the "technological promise" which this report glorifies is neither neutral nor value free and "decisions in this field have enormous political and social implications. Each society has to develop the necessary instruments to make an evaluation of alternative choices and their impact." (p. 281)

I should, however, hasten to state that I do not oppose technology but rather the emphasis on technology itself. I believe that Third World countries and especially countries of the Middle East, should develop the technology which is based on, or the extension of, their effective traditional media. This will allow for minimum possible foreign control and maximum utilization of both local funds and professional potentials.

Another point I wish to emphasize here is that the Report after a stimulating discussion section, comes up with recommendations paying only little service to the moral problems involving the new world information and communication order. The recommendations, although contributing positively to the present state of affairs of communication, represent a victory for the two Northern blocks in the sense that both of them managed to maintain what I consider "illegal gains." After Nairobi and Paris, and after the discussion section of the report one would expect better and firmer recommendations.

This victory, however, does not seem to be satisfactory to representatives of both blocks. The Report includes many interventions in the form of footnotes, which are clearly motivated by political maneuvers, to preserve value systems and realities favorable to them. Abel's intervention supporting advertising (p. 266) and Losev's intervention indirectly supporting arbitrary control of information (p. 266) are two such examples.

And while the report clearly makes its position that the world is not a global village, that the integrity of different cultures should be preserved, and that diversity is valuable and should be respected, yet the recommendations do not always support this position. In the sections on "professional integrity and standards" as well as on "democratization of communication" one senses attempts at stressing universal standards over those dealing with the protection and needs of individual societies. The call on all countries for the assurance of admittance of foreign correspondents and for facilitating their collection and trasmission of news, while at the same time admitting that "intelligence services of many nations have at one time or another recruited journalists to commit espionage under cover of their professional duties" (p. 264), is hardly compatible with the right of each society to safeguard its own security and safety.

In addition to this contradiction the Report, in its discussion and recommendations sections, emphasizes a professional information approach rather than a communication one. Professional journalistic issues are dealt with in more detail and attention than those pertaining to communications issues. Regrettably the Report provides only a short section on communications research and the recommendations include only one short neutral paragraph on this most important subject which should be at the heart of all efforts to bring about a new world information and communication order.

And the new world information and communication order is left undefined by the Report. This order has been the subject of endless ideological and political negotations at Unesco, the UN and at numerous conferences. The Report comes out for the new order, for how can anyone accept the present order? How can anyone openly support corruption and exploitation? McBride asserts that "there was nobody in the Commission not convinced that structural changes, in the field of communication are necessary and that the existing order is unacceptable to all" (p. XVIII). Yet despite this assertion the recommendations do not provide more than generalities about this new order. Interestingly the Report introduces talks of "structural" changes, that is material changes, and no reference is made to moral changes. I contend that no matter how good the structure is, it is doomed if the morals are bad. In the final analysis the driver is more important than the car and the one who uses the technology determines its output. I also contend that the disease in the present order was moral before it became structural.

But I concede that while structural changes may be possible, moral changes are next to impossible at this juncture of time when the world is dominated by materialistic forces. The moral thrust into the new world order should come, if it is at all to come, from countries of the Third World that uphold their spiritualism and stand firm to their moral values. These Third World countries should oppose universalistic values and refuse to lose or dilute their moral superiority over the west for the sake of acquiring the junk of Western technology.

To be practical, therefore, we should go ahead with the structural changes that may lead to a new world information and communication order but we should not compromise in these structural changes. The structural changes needed should not be determined by the dominant powers. The need is for changes that will allow the moral thrust for which the world order is in bad need. These changes, I believe, will be resisted by the present materialistic powers dominating the world.

The present debate on the role of communication in society, to which the McBride Commission, among other bodies, was an active forum, provides an opportunity to push forward for structural demands that are as free of political or ideological motives as possible. And here the Third World countries are faced with the challenge of being honest to the values they are publicly supporting. They should not allow for double standards, one standard on the international scene and another at home. The call for an equal and balanced flow of information and communication between nations should also include a call for an equal and balanced flow of information within nations.

The Report argues for a balanced flow between nations but not for a balanced flow between the rich and the poor, the ruler and the ruled, the minorities and the majority, etc... And when such a balanced flow is mentioned (in the section on democratization of communication) the Report does not spell it out as forcefully as it does on the subject of the flow on the international scene. The Report also argues that two-way communications is among the basic needs in relation to development policies but not in every matter of government and social living. Of course development here has a materialistic economic connotation and not a moral one.

If the supporters of the call for a new world information and communication order succeed in producing an international declaration on the new world order, at the heart of this declaration should be the need for a new information and communication order for the individual within the modern state.

Finally I should confess that I have focused my remarks on the negative aspects of the Report. Its positive aspects are numerous. Its best contribution is that it exposes the old world order and provides hope for a new order. It sheds light on the road that, hopefully, will lead us to a better world where morals have a prominent place.

Eapen K. Eapen's reaction to the MacBride Report is pessimistic: "The Report, with minor faltering, tackles the four W's—what, when, where, and who—but not the 'how.' The diagnoses are not carried to the logical treatment." He finds that the experiences of India do not support the technologically positive approach of the report. The expressed demand for research is also problematic for the Third World countries: how to do research without researchers? The author is at the University of Trivandum, India.

12

PERSPECTIVE FROM ASIA

Eapen K. Eapen

For one who quickly runs through the 312-page document what immediately strikes is the gap between the first four chapters and the fifth, viz. of conclusions and recommendations. The earlier portions are often inspiring compared to the rather utopian final section. Probably the descriptive parts were less controversial and more amenable to clear thinking and easier writing than the concluding pages which had to carry the element of consensus.

The conclusions do not easily flow from the preceding sections. Apparently, a meeting of the minds on the historical development of communication and the status of media, modern and traditional, was easier to achieve than agreeing on their social role and relevance. Societies differ and, therefore, expecting unanimity of views from their representatives is unrealistic. However, even where overt agreements on descriptive material have been arrived at, conflicting interpretations are possible.

Communications literature of the 1960s related to its role in development, tended to list what media *could* do. The Report's conclusions are in the direction of what communications *should* do, Some of these are saying the obvious. For example, "A primary available objective should be to make elementary education available to all and to wipe out illiteracy, supplementing formal schooling systems with non-formal education and enrichment within appropriate structures of continuing and long distance learning (through radio, television and correspondence)." (p. 255). Non-controversial and desirable goals like these are incorporated into other well-written documents such as the Indian Constitution, 30 years old. Aspirations do not get easily translated into action. Those who successfully come out of the Indian school tunnel are largely the young ones of upper classes (be they urban or rural) and mostly

From Eapen K. Eapen, "Perspective from Asia," pp. 37-39 in Cees J. Hamelink (ed.) *Communication in the Eighties: A Reader on the MacBride Report*. Rome: IDOC International, 1981. Reprinted by permission of IDOC.

boys. Year after year statistics have shown that some six out of ten who enter the school at the elementary level leave within three or four years for extremely complicated, though valid, reasons. These dropouts join the legions of illiterates. Considering the vastness of India, there are regional variations to this pattern but given the rural social structures this is generally true.

The platitude of the UN development decades is another example where the paper plans have not delivered the goods of development.

Radio and television as educational aids, for leapfrogging decades and for their audiovisual propensities, are unquestioningly accepted. But the Indian experiences belie such optimism. One cannot go into all the reasons for failure here but it needs to be mentioned that film as a medium has been in India for over eight decades and radio for over five. The former is part of the private industry, the latter public. According to the Report, of some 3,000 films produced globally each year, about a fifth are in India. They come in all principal Indian languages. Of the 16 languages which the Report mentions as spoken by more than 50 million people each, five are from the Indian sub-continent: Bengali, Hindi, Tamil, Teluga and Urdu. The Report tells, also, that there are 1650 languages and dialects in use in India representing a rich linguistic culture. Impressive as this information and statistics are, single language situations of England, France or Japan offer no models for "enrichment within appropriate structures of continuing and long distance learning."

Television, unlike other modern media, has been late in coming to India. It arrived as an experiment in the national capital (Delhi) in 1959, courtesy West German Government transmitter, primarily for educational purposes: education during day within school walls, and outside during evening for rural adults. The Satellite Instructional Television Experiment of 1975-76, courtesy NASA, was again an educational adventure in school as well as non-formal. Those who are aware of these electronic media evaluations know that the software exercises did not turn out the way national committees had foreseen and international expertise had forecast.

There is little TV in the India of 1980 — less than a million sets for some 650 milion people. Most of these sets are in the metropolitan cities of Bombay, Calcutta, Delhi and Madras. As for radio, of the estimated 30 million sets, over 90% are in urban India — in a nation where eight out of ten inhabitants live in villages. This picture gives the availability of radio and TV, of whose use the Report is hopeful about for purposes of education. Equating availability with effective use is a dangerous presumption.

On the one hand it is argued that technology is neutral, on the other that it embodies values. Without taking issues on this dichotomy of positions, it remains to be stressed that acculturation of technology in a given society is necessary before it can be made to serve pre-determined national purposes such as education.

While the McBride Commission was an omnibus type, representing various regional and ideological segmentations of the international family, it has to be pointed out that hardly any of them was a communications scholar. So when it generalises about effective mass media use for solving illnesses of the mosaic this good earth of ours is, one does not want to question the intentions individually or collectively of the persons who composed it.

The chapter on "Research Contributions" begins: "There is a continuously felt need for more analytical thinking about, and above all more comprehensive and critical inquiry into, communications phenomena and their relation to the way societies function. Greater interest is now attached to research covering the role, purpose and forms of communication and all the problems which it raises in the overall development of contemporary society." (p. 223). This is non-controversial whether one belongs to the empirical research tradition or the emerging critical research orientation. The dilemma, however, with much of the Third World would remain: How can we have socially relevant, policy generating research without local researchers?

There are few areas of research which have received as much attention in the less developed countries as the one based on information dissemination-adoption models. As the Report rightly points out these have been carried out by specialists who either came from abroad or who had been trained abroad, carrying ideological and cultural approaches alien to the situations studied. The dependency on imported theories and research tools is mentioned and the lack of in-country training facilities hinted at. This thread of reasoning is carried on to the next chapter on "The Professional Communicators" (p. 227).

One is not quite sure as to the nature of the audience perceived for *Many Voices, One World*. Though the two brief chapters referred to above do highlight the paucity of trained professionals and researchers in the Third World, considering the crucial nature of human resources required for communication systems, the arguments could have been pushed further and more forcefully dealt with in the concluding sector.

"Appropriate structures of continuing and distance learning" need not remain the mirage during the decades ahead, if personnel shortcomings are plugged. How to go about it is not the strong point of what the Report concedes, "this is not an academic question, but a practical necessity."

The Report, with minor faltering, tackles the four "Ws" — what, when, where and who but not the "How." The diagnoses are not carried on to the logical treatment. As a "review of all the problems of communication in contemporary society", the document does not add significantly to the knowledge of the scholar and offers little of realistic solutions for the non-scholars' dilemmas.

Jorg Becker of Frankfurt, Federal Republic of Germany, is of the opinion that the MacBride Report will fill an important research gap in the FRG, because it deals with problems seldom dealt with in that country's research. Still, there are flaws in the report. Becker finds that although the authors realize that media technology and media content cannot be analyzed detached from one another, they do not proceed to discuss it within a dialectic perspective. Also, sometimes the media are treated as having a technological life of their own, without reference to specific economic, political, and social conditions.

13

THE SCIENTIFIC AND POLITICAL SIGNIFICANCE IN THE FEDERAL REPUBLIC OF GERMANY

Jorg Becker

1. Epistemological Criticism

Harald Vocke, the political editor of the *Frankfurter Allgemeine Zeitung*, the most important daily in the Federal Republic of Germany within the conservative spectrum, attacked the Report in the May 5, 1980 issue with the following commentary: "There is a growing interest among the majority of Unesco member states for the concept propagated by the Irishman MacBride in favour of a planned world order for the information system". On July 4, 1980, the conservative *Neue Züricher Zeitung*, which also carries considerable journalistic weight in the FRG, followed with the following remarks: "The attempt being made by the MacBride Commission to seek solutions by means of compromise between differing media philosophies is doomed to failure if Marxist communications theoreticians have the say on the one side". These strongly anti-communist commentaries were already predominant in the West German press on the occasion of the passing of the so-called Mass Media Declaration of Unesco in November 1978, upon publication of the Interim Report from the MacBride Commission and in relation to other similar media-political events. They constitute something of a basso continuo, always played, irrespective of the actual composition of the individual musical work.

To qualify the Report as "Marxist" is neither true in the political sense, nor on a scientific level. On political level this is evident if one examines the footnotes in which Sergei Losev from the USSR presented his dissenting votes to the overall report — most certainly a highly specific and narrow perspective within Marxist thought. In the scientific sense, a Marxist-oriented report

From Jorg Becker, "The Scientific and Political Significance in the Federal Republic of Germany," pp. 40-45 in Cees J. Hamelink (ed.) *Communication in the Eighties: A Reader on the MacBride Report*. Rome: IDOC International, 1981. Reprinted by permission of IDOC.

would be bound to present mainly materialistic argumentation. But this is just what the Report does not do. To a large extent it reflects idealistic positions within internationally oriented communications science in the west in the post-war period (1). Although it is true that the Report argues on a level of control supremacy sociological thought, it is nonetheless inconsistent in its epistemological substantiation, rooted in outdated model systems from the social sciences and has "remained true" to the idealistic bias of many a Unesco document.

This can be clarified by the following three points:

1. There is agreement in many European and non-European philosophies to the effect that technic and substance aspects of social processes cannot be analysed detached one from another. This principle is also of validity for problems of media policy. The technical form in the construction of the Viewdata (Prestel) medium, for example, does not permit the textual reproduction of lengthier statements of facts, thus preventing the possibility as far as coverage is concerned for a storage and transmission of a argumentative statements. In other words: the decision of the Third World to take over a specific media technology automatically involves the effect exercised by this on the content presented in this medium.

The Report, however, refers only in the introduction to the recommendations in Part V to the varying political possibilities for utilization. It states here: "Communication can be an instrument of power, a revolutionary weapon, a commercial product, or a means of education; it can serve the ends of either liberation or of oppression, of either the individual personality or of drilling human beings into uniformity" (p. 253) (This attitude to technology is also characteristic of the view taken by many a group calling itself progressive or Marxist).

Anyone who believes that once in possession of new media technology it will be possible to pour into the present form the content which appears suitable, overlooks the fact that the new media technology is in itself the expression of a new social change which has yet to be defined in terms of its concrete content.

The British journalist Rosemary Righter, who is closely associated with the International Press Institute, reproached the Report at the annual conference of this Institute in Florence in May 1980 with the words: "Unesco shows no signs of wishing to separate the medium from the message" (2), and in so doing demands something which is absolutely impossible in theoretical terms. The Report has succeeded in overcoming this naively idealistic position; it in fact recognizes clearly and unmistakably

---

(1) Heikki Hell, Kaarle Nordenstreng and Waris. Paper presented at the IAMCR conference, August 1980, Caracas.

(2) Paper presented at the IPI General Assembly, May 1980.

that the content and form of the media are fused with each other, but reduces this fusion to the question of use only, instead of discussing the dialectic unity of media form and content. This position of neutral optimism in the face of technology sometimes leads to uncritical recommendations and glorifications in technological questions in the Report; nonetheless, it is not quite as uncritical in its approach to the problems of technology transfers as in the recently presented report from the Brandt Commission "North-South: A programme for Survival".

2. This lack of dialectic perspective leads often enough in the Report to an uncritical relationship towards the problems of media growth. By virtue of the fact that the widely varying communications needs of people in different countries and cultures around the world are not referred back clearly enough to their respective specific economic, political and social conditions, the Report reveals in many places a concept of the media which has to a certain extent acquired a life of its own in technological terms.

3. The framework of explanation for the North-South conflict appears in many instances in the Report as that of the contrast between developing and industrial countries, but rarely as the contrast between metropolitan capital and countries and social strata kept in a state of peripheral dependence. In so doing, the Report relapses again and again into the modernist ideology which is at the same time considered as overcome. Both an analysis of the conflict of interests between the industrial countries, the socialist countries and those of the Third World, between the impoverished peasant population and the western-oriented elite in the Third World is missing in general, as well as that of the transnational media corporations. In view of the enormous amount of research material concerning the penetration of the Third World by the transnational corporations, this part of the Report is in particular to be described as decidedly unsatisfactory from a scientific point of view. A more detailed, more copious, differentiating and more logical examination could and should have been made in particular of the (historically growing) activity of transnational media corporations. On this point the Report falls far behind the level of scientific discussion already reached.

2. Relevance in Terms of Research

Despite the general theoretical shortcomings, the Report fills a tremendously important research gap in the FRG, one to the fact that the questions handled here concerning the change of the international information order have scarcely been dealt with or not at all in private or university research. A glance at reading lists from the West German universities over the past five years would serve to demonstrate that the topics presented in the Report have virtually been ignored as far as their thematic examination is concerned.

Concentrated presentations of the topic by individual specialist journals consist mainly of translations from papers already published abroad, a collection of essays is conspicuous only because of the inconsistent compilation of different conference papers (Informationsfreiheit, eds Hans Bohrmann, Josef Hackforth and Hendrik Schmidt, Munich, 1979), the only empirical examination of the position of the FRG in the media North-South conflict is revealed as nothing more than an unbalanced summary of statistics and business reports lacking any indication of a theoretical approach (Klaus Winckler: *Medienförderung privater und öffentlicher Institutionen der Bundesrepublik Deutschland für Drittländer*, Munich, 1979), and the first recently presented international legal papers on *The Problem of Transnational Information Flow and of the "Domaine Réservé* (Jochen A. Frowein and Bruno Simma: *Das Problem des grenzüberschreitenden Informationsflusses und das "domaine réservé"*, Heidelberg, 1979), only serve to demonstrate yet again the traditional style of argumentation on this subject in the Federal Republic (which is similarly true of papers on international law coming from the Federal Republic concerning the International Maritime Law Conference or the Problems of a New International Economic Order). Only the work of Richard Dill and Dietrich Berwanger remains to be mentioned: (Richard Dill: "Information als Ware Was ist die Neue Welt Informationsordnung?" in *Uerberblick*, 1/1979, pp. 47-49; id, "Die Mediendeklaration der Unesco," in *ARD, Jahrbuch*, 1979, pp. 17-21; Dietrich Bergwanger: "Die Neus Internationale Informationsordnung and die Unesco Mediendeklaration" in *Rundfunk und Fernsehen*, 1/1980, pp. 7-20) but nonetheless, as knowledgeable as their work is, as little they are able to open up new horizons. Not least of all this should be traced back to the fact that both occupy top positions the West German broadcasting system, that is to say, precisely in those institutions whose legitimacy is being questioned in principle by the Report: the former as International Affairs' Coordinator for the West German broadcasting institutes, the latter as the Director of the Berlin Radio Station (SFB) training school for Third World journalists. All West German papers have the following characteristics in common: an affirmative attitude towards the media policy expressed in the activities directed by the Federal Republic towards the Third World (Deutsche Welle, Trans Tel, the media project policy of the political foundations, training of journalists from the Third World in the Federal Republic, the business activities abroad of the media and electronic corporations AEG/Telefunken, Siemens, Bertelsmann, etc.), the lack of valid empirical material, the failure to debate media interrelationships, the inability to implement a structural analysis of peripheral capitalism, the modernist ideology and the lack of both historical and also futurist perspectives.

The Report does however support the papers published hitherto in the Federal Republic by the dependency theoreticians and critics of modernism in the sector of international communications research, such as Hartmut Deckelmann, Georg Michael Luyken and the author (3).

3. Political Relevance

In view of the level of political awareness as to the importance of the information and communications industry in international politics, a level which is so underdeveloped in the FRG in particular, the Report should be compulsory reading for all those interested in these questions: development and media politicians, ministry officials in Bonn, sociology, political science and journalism students, Third World groups and journalists. Compulsory reading in particular for the reason that this volume contains such a wealth of empirical and statistical material that it will be impossible in the future to claim carelessly and with impunity that the structural disadvantage of the Third World in the global information system has not yet been proven.

This report should above all become compulsory reading for the ministerial bureaucracy in Bonn: the Report sets itself agreeably apart from the 9 volume report brought out in 1976 under the coordinating direction of the Federal Post Ministry by the *Kommission für den Ausbau des Technischen Kommunikationssystems* (Commission for the Expansion of the Technical Communications System) for the FRG, since the Report grasps that communications questions are of political and not merely technological nature; the Report sets itself agreeably apart from the uncoordinated media political guidelines from the Foreign Office, the Ministry of the Interior, the Research and Development Aid Ministry, the Report also agreeably fills the research gap in the Federal Government's media research policy, which has meant that in the allocation of several hundred research projects in the past decade, at the most a small (and cheap) handful of projects on Third World media questions were involved.

Finally, the Report fills the gap in the report presented by the North-South Commission under the direction of Willy Brandt: incomprehensibly and irresponsibly, the Brandt Report contains not a single passage on the international information system. Winfried Böll, a committed and competent critic of the development aid policy of the Federal Government, could also thus justifiably characterize the Brandt Commission report as too « economic », since culture and religion also fail to appear here, the problems of identity in the Third World are also only dealt with in passing. (4)

Since the three Unesco Commissions in the FRG, Switzerland and Austria are at present working on preparations for a translation of the Report into German, it will be able to fulfil a very important role within the political situation of the media in the FRG. The Re

---

(3) Jörg Becker, i.a. *Free flow of information? Informationen zur Neuen Internationalen Informationsordnung*, Frankfurt, 1979; Hartmut Deckelmann: *Fernsehen in Afrika, Kultureller Imperialismus oder Erziehung für die Massen?* Berlin, 1978; George-Michael Luyken: "25 Jahre Communication and Development Forschung in den USA", in *Rundfunk und Fernsehen*, 1/1980, pp. 110-122).

port will be able to advance its arguments against the highly ve-
hement activities of the conservative forces on the sphere of international media policy, since, interestingly enough, this overall
topic has been dealt with far more carefully and as far
more important by conservative forces in the Federal Republic than
by the Social Democrats. Within the Social Democratic Party the
Report can and must serve to support the socialist wing which has
turned its close attention in the past two years to questions of the
democratization and decommercialization of the media within the
FRG (i.e. cable TV, media growth, viewdata), but has scarcely realized the international dimensions.

The Report, with its two central demands for democratization
and decommercialization thus fulfils an eminently important
function within the FRG, in that it defines the global framework which
in fact applies to the media the political debate at present being
conducted with intensity in internal terms.

The measures the MacBride Report proposes be taken against the impact of the large transnational communication industry are insufficient and can only lead to "cosmetic surgery," argues Cees J. Hamelink of the Institute of Social Studies, The Hague, Netherlands. The economic structure of this information industry, its interlocking overall structure, and its part in national economies are overlooked by the commission. Through the information industry, the access to vital economic information will be confined. Hamelink argues that the key concepts of the report are in favor of the Western communication industry and very much to the disadvantage of the Third World nations.

14

ONE WORLD

Marketplace for Transnational Corporations

Cees J. Hamelink

Part V of the Report entitled "Communication Tomorrow" points to some problems in the field of international communications. Paragraph 27 states:

> "The concentration of communications technology in a relatively few developed countries and transnational corporations has led to virtual monopoly situations in this field" (p. 259).

and in paragraph 57:

> "Special attention should be devoted to obstacles and restrictions which derive from the concentration of media ownership, public or private, from commercial influences on the press and broadcasting or from private or governmental advertising" (p. 266).

In order to counteract such monopoly situations, obstacles and restrictions the Commission proposes a number of measures.

Among them the most important are mentioned in paragraph 27:

> "... reform of existing patent laws and conventions, appropriate legislation and international agreements" (p. 259),

in paragraph 38:

> "Transnational corporations should supply to the authorities of the countries in which they operate, upon request and on a regular basis as specified by local laws and regulations, all information required for legislative and administrative purposes relevant to their activities and specifically needed to assess the performance of such entities. They should also provide the public, trade unions and other interested sectors of the countries in which they operate with information needed to understand the global structure, activities and policies of the transnational corporation and their significance for the country concerned" (p. 261)

From Cees J. Hamelink, "One World: Marketplace for Transnational Corporations," pp. 46-52 in Cees J. Hamelink (ed.) *Communication in the Eighties: A Reader on the MacBride Report.* Rome: IDOC International, 1981. Reprinted by permission of IDOC.

and in paragraph 58:

> "Effective legal measures should be designed to:
> (a) limit the process of concentration and monopolisation; (b)
> circumscribe the action of transnationals by requiring them to
> comply with specific criteria and conditions defined by national
> legislation and development policies; (c) reverse trends to reduce
> the number of decision-makers at a time when the media's
> public is growing larger and the impact of communication is
> increasing; (d) reduce the influence of advertising upon editorial
> policy and broadcast programming; (e) seek and improve models
> which would ensure greater independence and autonomy of the
> media concerning their management and editorial policy, and
> whether these media are under private, public or government
> ownership" (p. 266).

The proposed measures — mainly legal in nature — seem to
me totally inadequate in confronting the vast politico-economic power exercised by those transnational corporations that play a key
role in international communications. This inadequacy is due to
the fact that the report has not sufficiently critically and substantially analysed the role of transnational corporations in the field of
international communications. In this contribution I intend to indicate where the report's analysis (mainly in Part II, chapter 4 on
Concentration) has important shortcomings that consequently lead
to the proposal of measures that can only be "cosmetic surgery".

Communication Industry

The report rightly describes the industrialisation, oligopolisa-
tion and transnationalisation of communication in a process leading towards the formation of an influential "communication industry". An industry which "deserves particular scrutiny" and calls
for more "attention from policy makers, planners and media practitioners". In the report's scrutiny two crucial elements are insufficiently dealt with.

a. *The economic dimension.* It is exactly the economic scope
of those transnational corporations that constitute the communication industry that gives them their powerful role in international relations. Their impact is not primarily due to the much debated
contents but to economic parameters omitted in the Report:

— the commercial activities of the 80 transnational corporations that among them account for 3/4 of world production and
distribution of communication goods and services have reached such
a scope as to make the communication industry the fourth largest
industry in the world after energy, automotive and chemical industries;

— in 1980 the goods and services produced and distributed by
this industry contribute some 20% to total world trade;

— the investments in Research & Development by the corporations in this branch exceed similar investments in any other
branch; R&D for communication technology is some 30% of the
global R&D budget;

— there is fast growing interest for investing in this industry
from corporations that are involved in totally different fields, but
countries". Many of them, in fact, are on their way of becoming
information economies (see table).

that occupy vital locations in the totality of transnational industry, such as B.P., General Motors, Volkswagen, BASF and Exxon;
— the capital intensity of the communication industry leads to a strong interlocking with the world's largest institutional investors: the group of leading transnational banks.
b. *The complex*. The report mentions in passing the relations with other branches of industrial activity. This, however, is a key characteristic of the communication industry. Its power is derived from its economic scope and its interlocks. The communication industry is a strongly interlocked web of corporations. In spite of all the publicly professed competitive spirit the most important corporations of the industry have very strong direct and indirect interlocks among them (see Cees J. Hamelink, International finance and the information industry, forthcoming publication from ILET and ISS). Additionally these corporations have strong interlocks with other industries, the banks and the military.

Information Economy

The role of the communications-industry complex is only increasing with the shift in many developed countries from the industrial economy to the information economy. In this process the communication industry gets an ever more central place in national economies. Actually, already since the 50's the classical core industries: textile, steel, automotive and rubber, lose their significance and are replaced by such new industries as electronics, space, biochemistry and exploitation of the seas. In these industries the processing of information is a key factor. Corporations that are important in the communication industry also play an essential role in these industries, such as General Electric (in biochemistry) and Lockheed (in sea-exploitation).

In most industrial production processes the importance of information has drastically increased. In the manufacturing of complex machinery the factor information has taken over from manual skill and labour force.

It has been estimated that costs of industrial production are nowadays approximately 70% costs for the processing of information (i.a. in market exploitation, advertising, R&D, intracompany communications).

A large corporation with sales of $1 bilion will spend some 14 million dollar on telecommunication alone (W.N. Barnes, vice-president of Collins Communications Switching Division-Rockwell International, in Fortune, January 28, 1980). In corporate management it is estimated that daily activities are for 80% made up by some 150-300 information acts.

In the shift towards the information economy the role of the so-called services sector of the economy is essential. Many of its activities (in banking, administration, telecommunications, etc.) are in fact related to the processing of information. This sector contributes in the US, Canada, Japan, and several Westeuropean countries more to the Gross National Product than the combined agricultural and industrial sectors. This is also the case in a group of countries that is usually referred to as "the newly industrialising

Contribution Services Sector to the Economy (1976)

COUNTRY	Distribution GNP in % AGRICULTURE	INDUSTRY	SERVICES
Korea	27	34	39
Mexico	10	35	55
Brazil	8	39	52
Hong Kong	2	34	64
Greece	18	31	51
Singapore	2	35	63
Spain	9	39	52

(Sources: World Development Indicators, World Bank).

Computer-Industry

In the development towards the information economy the communication industry plays a significant role. This is particularly true for the nucleus of the communications-industrial complex: the computer industry. Computer technology and especially its micro-components will decisively shape the structure of the information economy. This technology is strongly concentrated in the hands of those few corporations that — in the core of the communications-industrial complex — have oligopolised access to essential hardware-software interlocks. Whatever is being written about the social transformation to be brought about by the "chips": the micro-electronic revolution and its social impact will be steered by the managers of the communication industry.

Financial Information

In the information economy the key problems are not posed by the mass media, the journalists or the international newsflows. Crucial problems will be caused by the privileged access to specialised information. Now already in North-South negotiations the unequal property of specialised technical, scientific and financial information is more important and complicated as politico-economic issue than questions relating to media flows.

The Report refers to this but does not elaborate the most important aspect. This is the fact that the interlocking of the communication industry with the transnational banks leads to an oligopolised access to such a vital resource as financial information. Financial information flows across the globe in the form of computer data through the banking networks and in the form of economic news through transnational newsagencies and newspapers. Financial data — an important segment of overall transborder data flows — is controlled by the large transnational banks that own and/or operate transnational computer-communication systems. Also through more traditional means they have privileged access to vital financial information.

Financial data base services controlled by Chase Econometrics, Reuters and the AP-Dow Jones combination supply most of the world's demand for financial information. Financial information to the business community at large is mainly accounted for by the 7 leading financial newspapers: The Financial Times (U.K.), the Wall Street Journal (USA), the Australian Financial Review, the Gazeta Mercantil (Brazil), the Handelsblatt (FRG), Il Sole-24 Ore (Italy) and the Nihon Keizai Shimbun (Japan).

Financial information flows follow the general pattern of international communications. There is a two-way traffic among the countries of the North and between those countries and the countries of the South. The nature of the traffic differs with its direction. From the South flow primarily "raw" materials (data in unprocessed form) and the reversed flow contains primarily ready-made information packages. In the North the USA transmits to Western Europe and Japan information goods and services and receives to a lesser degree similar goods and services. Western Europe sends large volumes of data for processing to the USA. Between the USA, Western Europe and Japan processed data are exchanged with a majority participation from the USA.

Access to the whole range of financial information is the privileged property of few private enterprises in the North. It needs only little imagination to see the disadvantages this implies for the countries of the South.

Here the convergence of economic and informational structures becomes most transparent. At this crossroad the strongest interests are invested, the problems are most acute and — at the same time — rapid technological developments make chances for their solution increasingly slim.

The New International Order

The Report supports — with qualifications — the Third World's case for a new international information order. It misses, however, an essential point by not seriously analysing the role of the transnational corporations in the movement towards a new international order.

The 1978 Unesco General Conference is a turning point in the international debate in so far as at this meeting the opposition against a new information order is transformed into its unanimous acceptance. Kaarle Nordenstreng sees this acceptance as part of a strategic design geared towards achieving "a stage of mutual accommodation in a spirit of compromise" (in "Struggle around the new international information order", a paper that was partly published in the Journal of Communication, Spring, 1979).

The likelihood of such a design is strengthened by the fact that at the meeting the key concept of the debate was reformulated. The original concept coined by the non-aligned movement (the "new international information order") was replaced by a "new, more just and more effective world information and communication order". It is unlikely that this is coincidental since the formula "new international information order" (in its combination with the new economic order) stood for a challenge to Western politico-economic interests: the global and fundamental reallocation of the infra-structures of international information flows and a qualitative change in the contents of these flows.

As US Ambassador John E. Reinhardt indicated at the Unesco conference in his intrepretation the new order would imply "a more effective programme of action" including "American assistance, both public and private, to suitably identified centers of professional education and training in broadcasting and journalism in the developing world" as well as "a major effort to apply the benefits of advanced communications technology — specifically communications satellites — to economic and social needs in the rural areas of developing nations".

In line with Reinhardt's statement is one of the resolutions adopted at the conference in which the Director-General is requested "to intensify the encouragement of communications development and to hold consultations to lead to the provision of developing countries of technological and other means for promoting a free flow and a wider and better balanced exchange of information of all kinds".

The "new order" in its reformulation seems to be acceptable because it reduces the problems of international information mainly to the transfer of professional know-how, technology and financial resources.

Since 1978 the "new order" has been accepted by Western governments and rather than maintaining the former critical attitude, there is an active desire "to shape the future course of the new world order as co-architects" (John E. Reinhardt in "Towards an acceptable concept of the new world information order", an address given at the US-Japan symposium, Boston, October, 1979).

The question is of course "whose new order" is now so unanimously embraced and about to be implemented. As some US corporations have quickly understood, the emphasis on transfer of resources can be exploited as a welcome legitimation for Western market expansion. It can be hardly coincidental that immediately after the Unesco meeting several large communications corporations advertised their goods and services to the Third World. Such as electronics manufacturer G.T.E.: "One of the Third World's first needs is good communications. G.T.E. is in a unique position to help bring modern communications to these nations". As the advertisement aptly says "it is another demonstration of how we try to be in the right place at the right time for all our markets".

The "new world information and communication order" could very well be the world order of the transnational corporations (the "corporate village" with international political blessing). A similar development seems possible as Karl Sauvant observes with regard to the new economic order "with its reliance on transnational enterprises (it) is not likely to be a framework for a new and more equitable world economic order, but rather designed to stabilise the present order and thus contain a further deterioration of the position of the developing countries" (in his chapter on "The role of transnational enterprise in the establishment of the new international economic order: a critical review", in Strategies for the NIEO, edited by Ervin Laszlo and Jorge A. Lozoya, Pergamon, 1979).

The expansion of international information flows will primarily benefit the networks of large transnational industrial and financial corporations. As Herbert Schiller notes "Increased linkages, broadened flows of information and data, and above all, installation of new communication technology, are expected to serve nicely the world business system's requirements. That they can be considered as constituting a new international information order is so much additional icing on the cake of the transnationals" (in "Whose new international economic and information order?" a paper for the conference on Alternative Development Strategies and the Future of Asia, New Delhi, October, 1979).

The new international information order seems to follow the same route as the new international economic order. The basic framework is created by the transnational corporations. As former IBM chairman Jacques Mainsonrouge observed recently "They (transnational corporations) have become agents of change and progress for they are building what, for all intents and purposes, must be considered a new world economic system". The Report although rightly pointing to the crucial role of transnational corporations in the field of international communications, did not sufficiently recognise that the new international information order is indeed likely to be the order of the transnational corporations. The "one world" the Report ambitiously refers to in its title may very well be the global marketplace for transnational corporations.

In his contribution to the comments on the MacBride Commission Report, Professor Herbert I. Schiller of the University of California, San Diego, concentrates on the technology issue. The commission has realized that communication technology is not neutral and that it is not capable of solving social problems. The report offers evidence that technology raises a number of problems: For example, it is commanded by a few corporate groups, it tends to extend material dependency, and it may damage cultural autonomy. But when it comes to offering solutions to these problems, the report becomes unclear, failing to deal with those systematic patterns that can be observed. Also, the report does not acknowledge the real role played by the transnational system in the movement toward "informatization" of international communication, Schiller says.

15

ELECTRONIC UTOPIAS
AND STRUCTURAL REALITIES

Herbert I. Schiller

Many Voices, One World, the Report of the International Commission for the Study of Communication Problems, devotes some space to the implications and possible consequences of the new communications technology. The discussion however, is not centered in any one section and as a result, the comments on technology appear intermittently throughout the Report. Actually, this is indicative of the study in general — a subject is considered but the analysis often is neither systematic nor thorough.

Still, it would be mistaken to conclude from this criticism that the Report's discussion of technology lacks utility. To the contrary, some very pertinent and, given the prevailing views on this matter, refreshingly unorthodox comments on technology — its creation, development, installation and utilization in the current world economic order — are made.

In fact, it is not too much to say that the Report, in a somewhat scattered and unfocused way, comes fairly close to identifying and criticizing the vital part new communications technology plays in maintaining and extending the present order of global control and authority.

The Report challenges, although regretably well along in its discussion, the central thesis held by the enthusiasts of Western technology — the idea that technology is neutral. Flatly, it states, technology "is seldom neutral". And the use of technology "even less so". (p. 214). Moreover, it notes that frequently the fields that are selected for research — and consequently the ones that may produce new technological concepts and operating machinery — are determined by powerful interest groups. And, as might be expected, the utilization of the research results are highly concentrated in the hands of these same interests. Technological development therefore, "demands careful scrutiny". (p. 214).

As a general course of action therefore, the Report recommends that the decision-making process, which affects technology all along the line, from the inception of an idea to its application in hardware,

From Herbert I. Schiller, "Electronic Utopias and Structural Realities," pp. 53-57 in Cees J. Hamelink (ed.) *Communication in the Eighties: A Reader on the MacBride Report*. Rome: IDOC International, 1981. Reprinted by permission of IDOC.

and its installation and operation, be opened up to as large a number of participants and involved groups as possible. It calls this "socializing" the decision-making process. (p. 215).

All this leads the Report to the consistent, but still startling conclusion that, in some circumstances, the introduction of new technology should be delayed, if not indefinitely postponed. "However inviting", the Report states, "introduction of some new technologies should be seriously considered, and perhaps delayed, in certain developmental situations. It must also be remembered that introduction of new technologies is often easier than subsequent provision of software required for their optimum utilization. This requires the attention of each national community and all its elements — governmental and non-governmental, public and private". (p. 95).

The delay in introducing new technology is more than justified, the Report believes, because rapid and heedless installation could mean the transfer or application of instrumentation that may be irrelevant, inappropriate or actually harmful. The Report is quite explicit here:

> "Although it is difficult to generalize about harmful effects, since they differ so considerably, the charges most frequently levelled are that such transfers (I) have consisted primarily in simple exportation of western technology, which reflects the economic and social conditions and practices of one part of the world only; (II) have generally tended to be capital rather than labour-intensive; (III) have created dependence upon foreign capital, foreign supply sources and foreign tastes and expectations; (IV) have been effected mostly by transnational corporations, which have maintained control over the technology; (V) have benefitted elite sectors (news-papers, television, telephone) more than the masses; (VI) have contributed little to economic self-reliance and co-operation among developing countries; (VII) have fostered the rural exodus and increased migration". (p. 217).

Not only is technology lacking in neutrality. It is also nowhere near as capable as some claim it to be, as a social problem-solver. The Report notes this and cautions against regarding new technology "as an all-purpose tool capable of superseding social action and eclipsing effort to make structural transformations in the developed and developing countries. The future largely depends upon an awareness of the choices open, upon the balance of social forces and upon the conscious effort to promote optimum conditions for communication systems within and between nations". (p. 33).

Additionally, the Report recognizes that the technological advances that are so highly regarded today may, in a decade or more, be found to "have produced unforeseen effects, uncertainties and imponderables". It is essential, therefore, the Report declares, that the technology be put at the service of democratization and popular benefit, and "not to be used to reinforce vested interests of established powers". (pp. 79-80).

Easier said than done! It is precisely to prevent awareness of the choices that may exist, and the necessity to make structural changes *before* embarking on technological journeys, that the transnational system urges the early adoption and installation of the new technology. It is no exaggeration to state that adoption now of the new instrumentation means almost certain shutting out of the democratic forces that the Report calls upon to be determining agents in the decision-making process. The existing balance of economic and technological power make this inevitable.

On data bases, the Report's views are also perceptive. While acknowledging their potential for making available a huge amount of information, data bases' present limitations are grasped accurately:

> "... their utility is limited due to the often narrow criteria for the selection of data being put into data banks or other systems for news storage. The usefulness of these modern and powerful devices for data processing depends not only on whom they serve, but also on the plurality and diversity of data collected and stored". (p. 70).

Additionally, the Report declares that to utilize these data bases fully, requires preparatory work and the understanding that the bases now are being organized only in a few countries — again, conferring on these nations, de facto control of what the French call the "collective memory" of society.

> "...all these informatic networks with their quantities of information and data are bringing about a new mode of communication. It does not seem premature to start preparatory work in all countries for new opportunities such as these, even if they have to be on a limited scale for quite some time. However, since the distribution and development of many of these recent technological advances are mainly concentrated in a few areas around the world, the equitable distribution of their potential benefits is a major subject of international concern. There can be no doubt that these data exchanges cross political frontiers. This, however, is not a wholly new phenomenon; previous services were already highly concentrated and confined to certain points in the world. International study — not limited to industrialised countries alone — of the flow of data across frontiers, leading to proposals for action, would help in bringing about a recognition of its importance and its implications, and thus facilitate a more equitable development" (n. 71).

In sum, the Report offers ample evidence that the new communications technology raises more problems than it solves:

1. It is concentrated and at the command of only a few, powerful corporate groups, located in two or three advanced industrial nations.

2. It is systematically-structured. The data bases, for example, include the biases, outlooks, interests of the system and interest groups that put them together. The information obtained will, as a matter of course, promote these outlooks.

3. The technology promises to extend material dependency — equipment, replacement parts, servicing and new models will continue to be administered by a few supplying nations and companies.

4. The training programs and institutional forms required by the new technology suggest further erosion of national cultural autonomy.

What then are we to make of these rather harsh assessments of the most advanced Western communications technology? Unfortunately, not too much! One unresolved ambiguity of the Report itself on technology, and two related weaknesses in the criticisms offered by the Report, seriously reduce the overall impact of its technology discussion. First the ambiguity that threads through the Report. It moves uncertainly and erratically between warning about and at the same time, promoting the new technology, sometimes in the very same paragraph. Consider for example this schizoid passage toward the end of the Report.

> "Two observations may be added to these conclusions. First, international co-operation should not be limited to the conventional domain of the press, radio and television but should be extended to such new activities as the creation of new infrastructures, the strengthening of existing means, the establishment of new agencies, data banks, the development of informatics, satellite links, etc. Secondly, attention should be given to the potential distortions resulting from the massive introduction of new technologies into systems that remain fragile". (p. 222).

In the same few sentences are included encouragement for establishing all kinds of new communications technologies and, simultaneously, a warning that these processes may seriously distort already weak national systems. How can this contradiction be accounted for? It is a consequence, it would seem, of two other related weaknesses in the Report.

These is, first, a lack of specificity that diminishes greatly the strong general comments which have been quoted earlier in this chapter. The names and national locations of the actors in the information scenario are hard to find. Closely related, and apparent throughout the study, — not only in the technology sections — is an inability to demonstrate that international communication developments today are not merely an ad hoc aggregation of random actions — some good, some bad, some uncertain. Admittedly, not everything that is now occurring is an outcome of deliberate planning or special long-range intention. However, a *systematic pattern* can be observed. Also, it is connected to some very tangible infrastructural and economic institutions. It is this pattern which is missing in the Report.

An earlier, but still ongoing communication development, is illustrative. Commercialization of West European broadcasting is a case in point. Beginning with the acceptance of commercialization in the United Kingdom in 1954, the procession of commercialization throughout Europe can be viewed as a series of entirely discrete developments — first the British, then the French, then the Italians, now the Germans, etc. And, it would be correct to see in each national setting, a specificity of local, regional or national factors that make each country's situation unique.

Yet, when all the individual national examples are examined, with due respect given to the individual differences with which the process unfolded in each country, a pattern emerges — and an explanation for the design is also ascertainable. This phenomenon, the commercialization of the media, can be attributed to the pressure of the world business system, the transnational system in particular, to re-organize media systems for its own needs and objectives — in a word, consumerism. To be sure, how the transnational system imposes itself in any one national locale is a highly specific matter, requiring detailed examination.

Broadcasting is an important area of communications. It provides a preview of what is now beginning to happen in the sphere of electronic communications — what some call telematics or informatisation or computer communications. The appearance of advanced communications technology — computers, satellites, cable TV, portable recording equipment and video discs — is following a pattern not unlike that which characterized the spread of commercial broadcasting. In this instance, also, it would be incorrect to claim that a master plan exists to computerize Western Europe or North America or the developing nations.

What is occurring in this field, is the outcome of a complex intermixture of economic influence and competitive pressure, technological development, and changing domination-dependency relationships. The interactions are taking place at local, national and international levels. In the process, the main actors are the major business corporations, some of which produce the new equipment and aggressively search out new markets. Others sell new information services. Still others, possibly the most important grouping, adopt the new equipment and services because they promise to maintain or open up a competitive edge over industrial rivals.

Additionally, there are the governmental and military bureaucracies that find the new instrumentation indispensable in fulfilling their functions of administration, co-ordination and protection of the system overall.

These are the forces that are propelling the technology and advancing its installation, globally. The Report nowhere acknowledges the specificity of *the transnational system as the engine* behind the accelerating movement toward informatisation in the international communications arena at this time. As a consequence, the market-military economy and its needs, and the transnational system as the embodiment of this grouping, when mentioned at all, are always marginal and never accorded their significance as determining agents in the process underway.

We are left therefore, in *Many Voices, One World*, with several cutting phrases, some acute insights and quite a bit of cautionary comment about the lurking dangers of the new communications technology. These cannot do more than thinly cover a great gap in the Report — the absence of any comprehensive analysis of, as well as a regrettable unwillingness to confront, a powerful transnational business system which is, as we write this, using every means and technique to do what the Report warns against.

The publication of the MacBride Commission Report also prompted a response from First World journalists. Meeting in May 1981 in Talloires, France, journalists and other media representatives were sharply critical of sections of the report and their import. The group issued the following declaration upholding its view of press freedom.

16

DECLARATION OF TALLOIRES

Voices of Freedom Conference

We, members of the journalistic profession from many parts of the world—editors, publishers, broadcasters, reporters, photographers—linked by our mutual dedication to a free press;

Meeting in Talloires, France, from May 15 to May 17, 1981, to consider means of improving the free flow of information worldwide, and to demonstrate our resolve to resist any encroachment on this free flow;

Determined to uphold the objectives of the Universal Declaration of Human Rights, which in its Article 19 states, "Everyone has the right to freedom of opinion and expression; this right includes freedom to hold opinions without interference and to seek, receive and impart information and ideas through any media and regardless of frontiers";

Mindful of the commitment of the Constitution of the United Nations Educational, Scientific and Cultural Organization to "promote the free flow of ideas by word and image";

Conscious also that we share a common faith, as stated in the Charter of the United Nations, "in the dignity and worth of the human person, in the equal rights of men and women, and of nations large and small";

Recalling moreover that the signatories of the Final Act of the Conference on Security and Cooperation in Europe concluded in 1975 in Helsinki, Finland, pledged themselves to foster "the freer flow and wider dissemination of information of all kinds, to encourage cooperation in the field of information and exchange of information with other countries, and to improve the conditions under which journalists from one participating state exercise their profession in another participating state," and expressed their intention in particular to support "the improvement of the circulation of, access to, and exchange of information";

Declare that:

1. We affirm our commitment to these principles and call upon all international bodies and nations to adhere faithfully to them.

From Voices of Freedom Conference, "Declaration of Talloires," May 1981.

2. We believe that the free flow of information and ideas is essential for mutual understanding and world peace. We consider restraints on the movement of news and information to be contrary to the interests of international understanding, in violation of the Universal Declaration of Human Rights, the Constitution of UNESCO, and the Final Act of the Conference on Security and Cooperation in Europe; and inconsistent with the Charter of the United Nations.

3. We support the universal human right to be fully informed, which right requires the free circulation of news and opinion. We vigorously oppose any interference with this fundamental right.

4. We insist that free access, by the people and the press, to all sources of information, both official and unofficial, must be assured and reinforced. Denying freedom of the press denies also the freedom of the individual.

5. We are aware that governments, in developed and developing countries alike, frequently constrain or otherwise discourage the reporting of information they consider detrimental or embarrassing, and that governments usually invoke the national interest to justify these constraints. We believe, however, that the people's interests, and therefore the interests of the nation, are better served by free and open reporting. From robust public debate grows better understanding of the issues facing a nation and its peoples; and out of understanding, greater chances for solutions.

6. We believe that in any society the public interest is best served by a variety of independent news media. It is often suggested that some countries cannot support a multiplicity of print journals, radio and television stations because there is said to be a lack of an adequate economic base. Where a variety of independent news media is not available for any reason, existing information channels should reflect differing points of view.

7. We adhere to the principle that editorial decisions must be free of all advertising influence. At the same time, we acknowledge the importance of advertising as a consumer service, and in providing financial support for a strong and self-reliant press. Without financial independence, the press cannot be independent.

8. We recognize that new technologies have greatly facilitated the international flow of information and that the news media in many countries have not sufficiently benefitted from this progress. We support all efforts by international organizations and other public and private bodies to correct this imbalance and to make the new technology available to promote the worldwide advancement of the press and broadcast media and the journalistic profession.

9. We believe the debate on news and information in modern society that has taken place in UNESCO and other international bodies should now be put to constructive purposes. We reaffirm our views on several specific questions that have arisen in the course of this debate, being convinced that:

• Censorship and other forms of arbitrary control of information and opinion should be eliminated; the people's right to news and information must not be abridged.

• Access by journalists to diverse sources of news and opinion, official or unofficial, should be without restriction. Such access is inseparable from access of the people to information.

• There can be no international code of journalistic ethics; the plurality of views makes this impossible. Codes of journalistic ethics, if adopted within a country, should be formulated by the press itself, and should be voluntary in their application. They cannot be formulated, imposed or monitored by governments without becoming an instrument of official control of the press and therefore a denial of press freedom.

• Members of the press should enjoy the full protection of national and international law. We seek no special protection nor any special status and oppose any proposals that would control journalists in the name of protecting them.

• Journalists should be free to form organizations to protect their professional interests. However, there should be no restriction on any person's freedom to practice journalism.

• Licensing of journalists by national or international bodies should not be sanctioned, nor should any special requirements be demanded of journalists in lieu of licensing them. Such measures submit journalists to controls and pressures inconsistent with a free press.

• The press's responsibility is the pursuit of truth. To legislate or otherwise mandate responsibilities for the press is to destroy its independence. The ultimate guarantor of journalistic responsibility is the free exchange of ideas.

• All journalistic freedoms should apply equally to the print and broadcast media. Since the broadcast media are the primary purveyors of news and information in many countries, there is particular need for nations to keep their broadcast channels open to the free transmission of news and opinion.

10. We pledge cooperation in all genuine efforts to expand the free flow of information worldwide. We believe the time has come within UNESCO and other intergovernmental bodies to abandon attempts at regulating news content and formulating rules for the press. Effort should be directed instead to finding practical solutions to the problems before us, such as improving technological training, increasing professional interchanges and equipment transfers, reducing communications tariffs, producing cheaper newsprint and eliminating other barriers to the development of news media capabilities.

Our interests as members of the press, whether from the developed or the developing countries, are essentially the same; ours is a joint dedication to the freest, most accurate and impartial information that is within our professional capability to produce and distribute. We reject the view of press theoreticians and those national or international officials who claim that while the people in some countries are ready for a free press, those in other countries are insufficiently developed to enjoy that freedom.

We are deeply concerned by a growing tendency in many countries and in international bodies to put government interests above those of the individual, particularly in regard to information. We believe that the state exists for the individual and has a duty to uphold individual rights. We believe that the ultimate definition of a free press lies not in the actions of governments or international bodies, but rather in the professionalism, vigor and courage of individual journalists.

Press freedom is a basic human right. We pledge ourselves to concerted action to uphold this right.

Different approaches to concepts such as dependency, cultural imperialism, media imperialism, media diffusion, and technological determinism are here discussed by Chin-Chuan Lee. In the conclusion to this discussion, Lee maintains that there is no "independent, well-articulated, and convincing body of theory about cultural imperialism." When it comes to solving communication policy problems, neo-Marxists advocate revolution, non-Marxists evolution. The former cannot be limited to the media area alone but includes redefinition of man in society and culture. Evolution can take place within the media realm. Lee is doubtful whether the neo-Marxist alternative of media policy will bring integrity and freedom but finds, on the other hand, that conservative non-Marxist analysts are far too positive in defending the established interests of the strong nations. Third World countries must accept neither an unrestrained free flow nor a repressive and authoritarian media control, but choose a synthesis, being both fair and positive to national goals of development. Chin-Chuan Lee will be joining the School of Journalism and Mass Communication at the University of Minnesota.

17

ECONOMIC DEPENDENCY AND CULTURAL IMPERIALISM

Theoretical Perspectives

Chin-Chuan Lee

The clash of doctrines is not a disaster, it is an opportunity.

—Alfred North Whitehead,
Science and the Modern World.

The purpose of this chapter is to (1) evaluate economic dependency as an explanation of underdevelopment; (2) compare the structures of logical statements made about economic dependency and cultural imperialism; (3) show the different loci of explanation, by neo-Marxists and non-Marxists, about the international communication imbalance; (4) extend an alternate theoretical model of the spread of American multinational corporations to the examination of media flow; (5) suggest the possibility of "socialist media imperialism"; (6) discuss the applicability of technological determinism to media flow; and (7) suggest the close correspondence between media flow patterns and the stratification of international power structure. This chapter will set the foundation for the next chapter, which will attempt to clarify the concept of "media imperialism."

ECONOMIC DEPENDENCY: ARGUMENTS

Lenin (1952) argues that imperialism is a necessary result of advanced monopoly capitalism with its concentration on production and capital; international cartels or monopolies would have to be organized to strengthen and sustain the advantageous position for the outlets of their capital.[1] This by-now familiar theoretical exposition has not only revived the vitality of the original theory-ideology of

Karl Marx (Mills, 1962; Lichtheim, 1974) but also provoked the current version of economic dependency perspective. Many neo-Marxists have borrowed heavily from Lenin's formulation to account for historical and contemporary underdevelopment. Andre Gunder Frank (1972) and Immanuel Wallerstein (1974) have successfully popularized the terms "dependency" relations between the "metropolitan" or "center" (economically advanced capitalist exploiting countries) and the rest of the world, known as "periphery" or "satellite" (the economic, and political by implication, exploitee).

What is "dependency?" It is defined by Frank (1972: 9) as "no more than a euphemism that cloaks subjection, oppression, alienation, and imperialist, capitalist racism, all of which are internal as well as external."[2] In other words, dependency is an embodiment of the neo-colonial international relation between the strong and the weak, the rich and the poor, and the exploiting and the exploited. Despite its lack of clarity and specificity, the concept has produced a voluminous literature in economic (and secondarily, political) development. We shall review some of the major arguments implied by the dependency analyses, only insofar as they will help to understand the ensuing examination of "cultural imperialism."

There are four major arguments of economic dependence. First, dependence causes underdevelopment.[3] The prosperity of the West has been taken from the Third World. Frank (1969: 3–17) declared that the underdevelopment of Latin American countries was not original or traditional but, rather, resulted from the centuries-long participation in world capitalist development. The development of the national and other subordinate metropolises, argues Frank, is limited by their satellite status; the satellites experience their greatest economic development if and when their ties to the metropolises are weakest. Or, the underdevelopment of Latin America is *caused* by the economic (and political, by implication) exploitation of the capitalist "centers" in conjunction with willing local bourgeoise "conspirators." Wallerstein (1974a, 1974b) claims that rapid industrial growth in the West could not have occurred without the conditioning of a "periphery" from which an economic surplus is extracted and necessary raw materials secured.

The second argument is that the West has strived to perpetuate this dependency of the Third World. The West has become richer and richer at the expense of the poor Third World by ensuring the latter's continued economic dependency.

Third, dependence is considered the central feature of the current international economic system, both when it takes the form of colonialism and also when it expresses itself in neo-colonialism in all its forms (Bauer and Yamey, 1977).[4] More specifically, the West has dictated the economic prospects of the Third World by all sorts of schemes: investments in directions guided by American economic and political interests, trade barriers to Third World exports, foreign aid, calculated overpricing of exports by the subsidiaries of multinational corporations, and so forth.[5]

Fourth, following the previously mentioned allegations, a policy prescription to correct this dependency malaise is offered: a severance of ties to the external capitalist powers. Frank (1972) was not hesitant to single out Castro's Cuba as the "nondependent" route for other Latin American nations to follow. This desire to "go socialist" is most succinctly put by the title of a book by Frank (1969): *Latin America: Underdevelopment or Revolution*. The alternative is a categorically either-or proposition as if there were no bargaining ground for the Third World. Contrary to Marx, who expected revolution only after the phase of advanced capitalism had been reached, neo-Marxists have maintained that revolution *can, will,* and *ought to* occur in the Third World. Higgins (1977) thinks this confuses argument, prediction, and sermon. This policy position as advocated by neo-Marxists has aroused more heated controversy than the other three arguments.

ECONOMIC DEPENDENCY: A CRITIQUE

Most literature on economic dependency depends on *economic reductionism* and *class conflict* reductionism. Radical theorists have claimed that the dependency of the Third World on the capitalist powers is a transformation of economic and class structure, which tends to reflect the expression of the dominant class within and without nations.

The advantage of a radical perspective lies in its ability to account for the *intra*national and *inter*national power structures and the close (although imperfect) interdependence between them. Its historical world-system analysis lends to a more parsimonious interpretation of statemaking (Tilly, 1975), international conflict, and social change (Skocpol, 1977). In repudiating the traditional disdain of American quantitative economists for dependency analyses, Higgins (1977) notes that development is unlikely to take place in many Third World countries where there is an entrenched elite resolutely opposed to all economic and social measures that might bring change. Additionally, he thinks the real world is dominated by conflict (not harmony) of interests, tendency toward disequilibrium (rather than equilibrium), and recurring breaks in the continuity of development (rather than nondisruptive change).

On the other hand, a Marxist-Leninist theory of imperialism, along with its contemporary version in dependency literature, has serious defects in many respects. Criticism directed toward a radical perspective can be summed up in four categories: (1) the doubt cast on the usefulness of "dependency" as a scientific concept; (2) its overemphasis on economic determinism; (3) its emphasis on the world-system analysis to the neglect of many national states and the internal dynamics of national states; and (4) the questionable policy prescription of the so-called "socialist alternative." All of these criticisms bear important implications for the theory of cultural imperialism too.

First, the usefulness of "dependency" as a theoretical concept is still much in doubt, although it is increasingly being used as a comprehensive, if not sweeping, explanation of the state of underdevelopment. For example, Lall (1975), a critic generally sympathetic to the dependency perspective, notes that most of its arguments are aimed at the intrinsic cost of the *capitalist system* in general rather than *dependency* as such.[6] He writes: "Many of its conclusions about the effect of dependence on development may apply to particular cases but cannot be generalized, and as an analytical tool 'dependence' is not conducive to a useful analysis of underdevelopment." According to Lall, this is because of its failure to (1) lay down certain characteristics of dependent economies which are not found in nondependent ones, and (2) show these characteristics to affect adversely the course and pattern of development of the dependent countries.

For the dependency analysts, cases such as Canada, Australia, New Zealand, and Switzerland always constitute anomalies that are not easily incorporated into their overarching model. These deviant cases tend to be treated as "accidental" and explained in an ad hoc fashion. For example, Wallerstein's categories (1976) of "core," "semi-periphery," and "periphery" countries in a world market appear to be of dubious utility, because this classification, like the concept of "dependency," fails to meet the two criteria Lall outlines. It is particularly disturbing that Wallerstein uses "semi-periphery" as a residual, mixed-bag category incorporating cases ranging from Canada and Australia, to Spain and Chile, to Zaire.

Second, dependency analysts' reliance on economic determinism—and reductionism—has uneven plausibility. Berger (1976: 228) thinks that in some areas of the World interpretations based on it have considerable plausibility, at least on the surface; this is notably the case in Latin America. In other areas, according to him, "only the most tortuous argumentation can squeeze the empirically available facts into the strait jacket of the theory." The American *military* venture into Vietnam in the 1960s clearly involved less prominent *economic* motives, for example. That the United States and the Soviet Union have been guided by the geopolitical calculus of balance of power in their formulation of China policy demonstrates the inadequacy of economic reductionism. This similar concern leads Tilly (1975) to conclude that analysts have not formed a distinct, well-articulated, and convincing theory of *political* dependence. Nor is the economic dependence perspective capable of accounting for the military activities, fiscal policies, and cultural autonomy in the process of state-making and current development. Marxist-Leninists' reluctance and failure to attribute separate importance to political *and* cultural spheres appears to be a serious flaw.

Third, the uncritical use of a "dependency" focus has the risk of becoming political rhetoric, as Portes (1976) cautions. Dependency perspectives tend to be insensitive to the substantial variance of dependency itself, both in *kind* and *degree*. More seriously, the dependency analysts, especially those politically left-leaning, attempt to conform various interpretations to the Marxist deductive theoretical system without much empirical or logical substantiation. Their over-emphasis on the world system as an analytical context tends to over-look the importance of national variations and their potential possibil-ity to muster internal forces to counteract foreign influences. Tilly (1975), Skocpol (1977) and Moore (1966), among others, have de-monstrated the importance of *within-nation class coalitions*. Eisen-stadt (1977) has also argued the importance of relations between responses to modernization of different societies and patterns of their respective historical traditions.[7]

Fourth, radical perspectives have argued for a withdrawal from the world capitalist system as the sole remedy to dependency. The prob-lem is that "going socialist" itself does not necessarily guarantee in any way a national independence, and that Cuba has not found its way toward escaping from the heavy economic, political, and military dependency on the Soviet Union provides a graphic illustration. This Berger (1976: 88) calls "a simple exchange of one dependency for another." If the *economic* dependency dynamics as formulated by radical analysts have validity, it appears that many *political* depen-dency dynamics may also exist among the socialist countries. Radical analysts seem reluctant to recognize the latter dependency and fail to provide satisfying explanations. The deliberate efforts by Vietnam, after the conquest of the south, to cultivate American aid and by Castro to seek a lifting of the American trade embargo, offer very intriguing cases for analysis.

T. B. Bottomore (1976: 67–68), a scholar specializing in the inter-pretation of Marxist class conflict theory, also has reservations about such a "socialist alternative." He argues that there is a lack of infor-mation to determine what the policies of the communist industrial countries are or how these policies are carried out because of their limited participation in the international development agencies and in multinational aid programs. Strategic aims and military aid, he con-tends, also play an important part in the relations between the com-munist nations and developing nations. The denunciation of the So-viet Union as "socialist imperialist" by the Chinese Communists (Lichtheim, 1974) eminently fits this general argument. More impor-tantly, Bottomore maintains, judgment on whether the development policies of the communist countries constitutes a real socialist alternative to the expansion of capitalism must "depend on how one assesses the socialist potential of societies in which public ownership of the principal means of production and a degree of socialist planning is associated with an authoritarian, and often repressive, political system."

Higgins (1977) further criticizes the radical perspective for lack of policy prescriptions. What comes after the revolution? The requirements remain the same as before, argues Higgins, in terms of technological change, education and training, capital accumulation, improved resource allocation, and the like. Dependency perspectives offer very little about what to do for a national development planner.

CULTURAL IMPERIALISM: NEO-MARXIST PERSPECTIVES

We have examined the arguments of capitalist imperialism and economic dependency at considerable length in the hope of illuminating the topic of "cultural imperialism." So far most of the literature on "cultural imperialism" appears to be drawing heavily on the theoretical analogues of economic dependence; there has *not* developed a distinct and coherent theory of cultural imperialism. Much of the discussions in the previous two sections seem to fit cultural imperialism well, as do their critiques.

Nordenstreng and Varis (1973) argue that "bourgeois journalism," or mass communication in capitalist societies, serves three major functions: (1) to conceal class antagonism inside society and to compensate for the symptoms of alienation; (2) to illegitimize the concrete social alternatives to the existing order of society; and (3) to make profit as a branch of commercial industry. Mass media, in short, are important tools for profit-making and consciousness control to maintain the existing socioeconomic status quo.

Transposing the intrasocietal class conflict to the international communication system, they further maintain that the national oligarchies of developing countries are allied with international corporate capitalism but opposed to the poor mass publics. They explicitly conclude that the international streams of communication are "a manifestation of the ruling interests of the societies from which they originate and not a unanimous output of the nations involved." The extremely asymmetrical flow of communication materials, therefore, is thought of not only as a commercial exchange, but as a Third World being mind-managed or dictated by the insidious communication ideologies of external capitalist powers. Another way of looking at it is that the West, especially the U.S., has sought to drag Third World countries into the market-oriented capitalist world economies by offering, to use an analogy, sugar-coated exogenous cultures in seemingly harmless communication media products. It is the internal contradiction of the capitalist system, including its industrial, advertising, military, and cultural structures, that forces the external expansion of market and control in communication. Other writers (Schiller, 1976; Szeckso, in Gerbner, 1977; Nedzyski, in Gerbner et al., 1973) have echoed the same point of view.

These kinds of arguments about cultural imperialism appear to resemble closely the logical structure of economic dependency. First, like economic dependency the cultural imperialism analysis pushes class conflict to international development; it is assumed that there are levels of dominance among stratified groups or nations: the "exploiting" ("centers") and the "exploited" ("peripheries"). They are in constant conflict, but the latter is waging a losing battle. Second, the stratification of class systems seems to be based primarily upon the means of economic production and ownership, and only secondarily (by implication) upon the control of political power or what Dahrendorf (1959) has strongly argued as "authority relations."

Salinas and Paldan (1979) present a more sophisticated argument of cultural imperialism in the process of what they call "dependent development." Multinational conglomerates of monopoly capitalism open possibilities for industrialization of some peripheral areas, so it is a simultaneous process of dependence and capitalist development. This, according to the argument, co-opts the expanded local bourgeoisie and middle class into the sphere of metropolitan cultural influences, while intensifying the marginalization of lower classes. As a result, the local culture industry, in seeking larger profits in the market economy, is especially responsive to the conditioning of the metropolis—and thus drives toward cultural homogenization. Contrary to what Nordenstreng and Varis (1973) would claim, they optimistically argue for the prospect of ultimate "cultural liberation" because the existence of domination is full of structural contradictions which serve as a vivid lesson for "pedagogy of the oppressed." In the process the oppressed will acquire experience and organizational skills in culture, the will to overcome ideological polarization, the possibility to express the lived reality of the dominated, and the sensitivity to alternative products and models.

In transferring the logical structure of economic dependency to communication-cultural areas, there emerge two variants. One variant views the cultural-communication imperialism as part of the larger monolithic imperialism syndrome. Media products (such as television programming) are drawn to parallel other marketable commodity exchanges.[8] Another variant sees it, however, as more or less independent of socioeconomic or political dependency structures. If the former exposition is more credible, efforts ought to be made to articulate, elaborate, and apply the general economic dependency perspective to the analysis of imbalanced communication flow and cultural ramifications. If the latter exposition is more credible, a body of theory about cultural-communication imperialism is urgently called for (more discussion will follow shortly).

Military-Industrial Complex

Schiller (1969), in his *Mass Communication and American Empire*, traces the structure of the U.S. military-industrial complex and its logic and drive in expanding the "free" enterprise system throughout the world. His analysis focuses on multinational enterprises, although also scratching the surface of other extremely important factors existing in the "exploited" nations. Communication imperialism is, to him, a conscious and organized effort taken by the U.S. military-communication conglomerates to maintain a commercial, political, and military superiority.

This military-industrial complex in the communication field, according to Schiller (1969), takes two forms. Directly, the U.S. Department of Defense, not the Federal Communications Commission, is in charge of the allocation of frequencies and the making of national telecommunications policy. Indirectly, major electronic companies, like RCA-NBC, are holders of major defense contracts. American media dominance stems from U.S. foreign and defense policies and in turn are important instruments of such policies. In short, mass media are the extension of the American empire, coming to global ascendancy during the postwar period when the majority of the noncommunist countries were eager for freedom and were so weak as to accept American influence.

The omnipresence of the U.S.-made television programs throughout the nonsocialist countries (and increasingly some socialist countries) is but one manifestation of the cultural imperialism. To Schiller the powerful U.S. communication industry forces a global commercialization of the international broadcasting system and it has put other countries totally on the defensive so far as the cultural integrity of their mass communication system is concerned.

Deviating from his more dispassionate and better researched earlier work (1969), Schiller (1976) relied on updated favorable quotes in an attempt to codify a theory of cultural imperialism. In it he denounces almost all forms of Western communication styles and systems (including tourism, media technology, professional value, and educational training) as totally unacceptable to the Third World countries. It is fair to note that Schiller has tended to exaggerate the dysfunctional consequences of Western communication systems and products, without due regard for their functional consequences. He goes so far as to call for a policy of self-reliance and a policy of national, socialist planning, yet leaves both policies unarticulated. Schiller vehemently attacks the principle of "free flow of information" as benefiting only the strong parties in the deal, but fails to suggest effective means through which to achieve self-reliance.

While national planning is essential for all countries involved in introducing media technologies which might alter or affect the existing system, the conclusion does not necessarily follow that socialism is the only viable alternative. Mass media are part of social life; formulation of a national communication policy goes to the heart of the problems concerning man and society, individualism and collectivism (Yu, 1977). A sound communication policy critically depends on the question of how willing a country is to pay what price for what policy. There may be no such thing as *the* best way, as Schiller seems to suggest. The Third World countries display a great variety of differences in history, culture, social structure, and the problems facing them. As there are many ways to capitalist development, there are many ways to socialism and socialist communication policies. The socialist alternatives, as advocated by Schiller (1976) and other radical writers (such as Smythe and Nordenstreng), are yet to be shown as capable of being free from authoritarian and even repressive control by regimes in power.[9]

Class Coalitions

Derivative of the economic dependency thesis, the interests of elites in the Third World correspond to those of international capitalism and thus form an alliance to create and perpetuate the cultural dependence of the Third World. The oversimplification of elite class versus mass class within and between nations often obscures useful discussion. Just who constitutes the elite ruling class? Even when there is a consensus it seems less useful to study the *class* itself rather than to study *class coalitions*. The elite class in the media realm should not be limited to those who have superior positions in the economic means of production and ownership. There are many types of elites: government elites, commercial elites, intellectual elites, religious elites, and so forth, whose concerns and interests may coincide at times but may diverge at other times. They all participate in the politics of media.[10]

The coming of television was not universally accepted in the majority of nations. Religious hierarchies in Israel, Chile, Saudi Arabia, Italy, Mexico, Denmark, Sweden, and other countries have allied with other social groups to oppose the inauguration of television for fear of its adverse effects on moral standards and religious codes. For example, ex-King Faisal of Saudi Arabia authorized television in 1964 as part of modernization efforts only after he arrived at an understanding on television morality (such as prohibiting the showing of females for the initial six months) with local religious leaders (Boyd, 1970–1971). Former Prime Minister Golda Meir of Israel, concerned with the likely effect of television in creating a "conspicuous consumption" pattern, found allies in orthodox religious elites (Katz, 1971; Green, 1972). These examples serve to illustrate that different elite classes may coalesce around quite different concerns.

Joining forces to oppose television were other media elites whose direct interests were in jeopardy. The film industries in the United States, England, Spain, France, Mexico, and Taiwan have at one time or another opposed television; some opposition still exists. Newspaper and magazine owners may coalesce with television to establish joint ownership or affiliations (such as in the Philippines, Australia, and several Latin American countries), but they may vehemently oppose each other (such as in India, Greece, and Scandinavian countries).

Different elites may also present contradictory demands. The intellectual elites in India rejected television as an unnecessary luxury. This conflicted with pressures from the economically well-off urban elites for private commercial television offering programs and advertising to their tastes. Moreover, these demands and pressures conflicted with the government's goals to plan for national development, on the one hand, and to use broadcasting as foreign propaganda tools, on the other.

Government elites, in power or in opposition, would also coalesce with different social groups for different media solutions. Even intellectual elites have very different opinions and coalitions in the controversy of television politics.[11]

We have, in short, tried to suggest that examination of different class coalitions is more fruitful than that of class conflict. The simple statement about linkage between international capitalism and domestic elites, even if it is partially true, is a gross oversimplification. Amid the outcries against American media imperialism in Canada, the concerns of government elites for indigenous economic control have merged with those of nationalist intellectual elites for cultural expression. This merger, however, stands in opposition to the concerns of commercial elites (such as private broadcasters, cable television operators, and advertisers) whose profits depend directly upon, and correspond with, the international media capitalism of the United States. In contrast, the government elites and media commercial elites coalesce to diminish foreign dependence of television products in Taiwan partly because local programming finds greater market acceptability, despite many intellectuals' demands for "sleeker" foreign programs.[12]

CULTURAL IMPERIALISM AND MEDIA IMPERIALISM

That neo-Marxists prefer to deal with "cultural imperialism"—or even "imperialism" per se—instead of "media imperialism" must be understood in terms of their theoretical and ideological orientations. They adopt a more holistic view of the role of the media, focusing on "the relationship between ownership and control of the media and the power structure in society, the ideological signification of meaning in media messages and its effects in reproducing the class system" (Curran et al., 1977: 10). They are primarily concerned with the totality of dependence and dominance relationships by which stronger and weaker nations, and classes within nations, relate to each other. Because of the economic reductionism and class conflict reductionism that guide their inquiries, neo-Marxists are also generally antagonistic to the tripartite analysis of economics, politics, and culture (Murdock and Golding, 1977).

"Media imperialism" is too constricting for neo-Marxists because they regard it as part of "cultural imperialism." In a self-evident truism as typified by Schiller (in Nordenstreng and Schiller, 1979: 30), transnational media of capitalist countries provide "in their imagery and messagery the beliefs and perspectives that create and reinforce their audiences' attachment to the way things are in the (capitalistic) system overall." He regards it "pointless" to measure the impact of any individual medium or message. He does not think the consequences of the transnational media's heavy outputs are measurable. He (1976) defines "cultural imperialism" vaguely as "the sum of process by which a society is brought into the modern world system and how its dominating stratum is attracted, pressured, forced into shaping social institutions to correspond to, or even to promote, the values and structures of the dominant center of the system." A definition like this is less receptive to rigorous empirical test of the between-media differences, nor does Schiller appear to think the test desirable or necessary.

Murdock and Golding (1977) took fellow Marxist writers to task for insisting on the top-heavy centrality of cultural analysis without first focusing on the economic base that shapes cultural production. Murdock and Golding appear to take a more orthodox Marxian position in which economic infrastructure and class conflict are chief determinants of cultural forms.

Conversely, non-Marxists seem to prefer to deal with "media imperialism" rather than the all-encompassing "cultural imperialism" or "imperialism." Generally they are willing to accord the mass media institutions with "a considerable degree of autonomy within a pluralist model of industrial society" (Curran et al., 1977: 10). Boyd-Barrett (1977) affirms the value of "media imperialism" as a distinct analytical tool because it refers to a more specific range of phenomenon that lends itself more easily to a rigorous examination. Conceivably others may also argue that "media imperialism" should not be confused with "cultural imperialism" and "imperialism" because all three correlate in varying degrees of strength in different cases. The media are important components of culture, but analysis that fails to differentiate the media, educational institutions, family, and so on may obfuscate more than it illuminates. The linkage between economics, politics, and culture cannot be taken for granted but must be demonstrated. This perspective is exemplified by Boyd-Barrett's (1977) definition of "media imperialism": "the process whereby the ownership, structure, distribution or content of the media in any one country are singly or together subject to substantial pressure from the media interests of any other country or countries without proportionate reciprocation of influence by the country so affected." Works by Tunstall (1977) and Katz and Wedell (1977) are mainly informed by this line of thought. For the most part this book will use "media imperialism" in place of "cultural imperialism" except where the cultural implications of media are explicit.

MEDIA IMPERIALISM: NON-MARXIST PERSPECTIVES

While non-Marxists may assign varying degrees of weight to the *external* exploitative entrepreneurship of the American media conglomerates, their general willingness to emphasize the complex *internal* causes existing in individual recipient nations is at variance with the crude version of the neo-Marxist view of media imperialism.

Specifically, these analysts (1) pay considerable attention to the economies of scale of American media; (2) recognize the importance of national variations, the variance in media dependence itself, and the complex internal dynamics variables other than—or in addition to—the world-system analysis; (3) maintain that each individual country is capable, within limits, of mustering internal forces to counteract external foreign media influences in the process of change; and (4) argue that the international communication flow may result in both good and bad (not just bad) cultural influences on the participating countries. We shall deal with these points one by one.

Economies of Scale

The imbalanced communication flow is to non-Marxists in large part a function of supply and forced pseudo-demand; thus, the political overtones of "cultural imperialism" and conspiracy may be lessened.

The marketplace activity should be looked at from both the seller's side and from the buyer's side. From the seller's side, the large and powerful countries (especially the United States) are equipped with an elaborate and efficient media infrastructure that puts them in an advantageous position in programming, production, and distribution. They have a large amount of talent, money, equipment, and experience. These resources, put together, enable them to maintain an undisputed lead and initiative which leads further to global media predominance. Further, television programming is a cultural product closely following the economies-of-scale principle; additional film copies can be made at a small fraction of the original cost (Owen et al., 1974). The U.S. communication conglomerates in Hollywood can thus afford to sell their products at a price much less expensive than that which local production might otherwise have cost. Foreign sales are a bonus for them.

From the buyer's side, Katz (1973) attributes the homogeneity of television programming to (1) voracious demands of the medium for materials to fill up airtime, and (2) the Western production and management models which most countries take as their guides. He sees the situation as one of inflated demand and supply, with the emphasis on the demand side of the equation. Specifically, Katz observes that as television was developed by the American radio companies it also inherited many of radio's norms uncritically, which were further exportable to other countries.[13] These norms are: (1) nonstop broad-casting, which small countries do not have the talent to sustain; (2) a quest for the largest audience, which renders television to market and rating competition and thus leads it to content homogeneity; and (3) up-to-the-minute news, which discourages the production of news based on thorough research and interpretation. These norms, especially nonstop broadcasting, gives television a "runaway charac-ter" that favors foreign imports. Katz and Wedell (1977) find strong evidence for this hypothesis in their eleven-nation case study. Tun-stall (1977) also argues that the fierce competition between multi-channel commercial television in Latin America and the ex-British white commonwealth colonies was partially responsible for the pres-sure that brought in inexpensive U.S. telefilms. Perhaps this helps to explain why such economically wealthy and developed countries as Canada and Australia are, contrary to the expectation of "media dependency" theory, avid consumers of U.S. telefilms.

Internal Dynamics

Non-Marxists are also willing to assign more weight to internal dynamics than neo-Marxists, who insist on exploring the subject at a world-system level without concern for variances in political and social systems *within and between* recipient countries.

Katz and Wedell (1977) and Tunstall (1977) can be categorized as making efforts to trace the social causes of this television content homogeneity. Tunstall's case-historical analysis tracks down the in-tricate roots of media infrastructure, its ownership pattern, social and political arrangements, as well as foreign involvement to account for the outcome of media dependency relationships. This locus of ex-planation has obviously met with Schiller's disapproval. He says Tunstall "sometimes gets lost in *excessive* detail chronicling individ-ual national media experience" [emphasis added].[14] Katz and Wedell, on the other hand, try to give an account of the role of American media dominance from a Third World vantage point. They evaluate the performance of broadcasting in light of its promises as originally mapped out by the Third World nations. Both studies have shown large variations in the kind and degree of media dependency, as influenced by the interaction of internal variables (media infrastructure, sociopolitical systems, cultural traditions, economic structure), and external variables (imposed influences by the "metropolitan" nations). This media dependency variance, like other internal dynamics of individual societies, tends to be ignored or glossed over by radical writers.[15]

Autonomous Internal Forces

Non-Marxist writers have been more willing to recognize the possibility of autonomous internal forces and their potential role in the process of change.

This position is closely linked with the previously mentioned analyses of the economies of scale (supply-demand market functions) and the importance of internal dynamics variables on media dependency. The diffusion of innovations (including that of television programming) is a random process (or an S-shaped logistic cumulative curve) unless structural constraints are externally imposed upon it (Rogers and Shoemaker, 1970; Chaffee, 1975). The implication is that market forces, without interference, would normally work to the advantage of the communication-developed or media-rich countries.

But allowances must be made for the possibility that the Third World nations, consumers in the international media marketplace arrangement, may take necessary actions against further foreign exploitation. For example, the government can impose a ceiling on the proportion of the foreign-imported programs or reduce daily airtime to curtail foreign dependence. This has occurred in such countries as Canada, Thailand, Malaysia, Taiwan, Australia, and most of Europe. Purchasers in the developing countries also have some autonomy in looking for bargains among different offers, for the interest among the competitive exporters is not necessarily in accord or unchanging. The Third World countries (such as India and Colombia) may also convert commercial television into political, social, or educational uses, thus cutting off the necessity for large amounts of foreign entertainment films. All these actions may seem highly infeasible, if not impossible, for the radical proponents of the "cultural imperialism" perspective.

Katz and Wedell (1977), whose allegiance is Anglo-American

although they also show sympathy for the Third World countries, are not committed to the proposition that "the media are capable of sowing the seeds of cultural homogeneity and thus, ultimately, of dependence on the West and its trinkets." They claim that the question of what can be done about the homogeneity of programs, whether the media can be harnessed to authentic cultural expression, is still open. They further reject the attempt to seal frontiers against all news and influence from abroad as futile and dangerous.

There are obviously no fixed rules to strike a balance between the weights of internal autonomy and those of external dependence, for it must be responsive to a complex array of historical and contemporary conditions. Carey (1977) is rather skeptical about the strength of internal autonomy as it relates to the dilemma of Ireland. Ireland represents an extreme case where a small nation cannot afford to have television and also cannot afford not to. It established television to signal the status of national identity, and yet finds itself powerless in the face of the omnipresent television onslaught from neighboring Britain. The overwhelming presence of British television resulted in a failed attempt by a cabinet member in the government of Ireland to introduce the BBC signal as Ireland's second national channel.

Extreme cases notwithstanding, there are many variations in the dynamic process of accommodating the media to local constraints and national needs. Katz and Wedell (1977) observe that many Third World nations have come to a "sense of purpose" for television in their countries around the early 1970s, and this realization has been expressed in their media policies. This is obviously a strong manifestation of an enduring internal autonomy, although one may disagree with specific policies taken by each government.

Cultural Benefits

Contrary to a radical perspective, non-Marxists have contended that international communication flow may also bring about both positive and negative effects on indigenous cultural growth. This position is deeply anchored in the anthropological theory of cultural diffusion and a business-organization "product life cycle" model of multinational enterprise expansion (see the following two sections for elaboration). Cultural diffusion means, to use an analogy, absorbing the new lifeblood of alien cultures into a native organism to strengthen and rejuvenate the tissue and fabric of existing cultural heritage. The "product life cycle" model maintains that interaction with foreign media would make local learning of advanced technology possible so that the recipient nations are better equipped to harness media to indigenous cultural development. This business model, which has been applied to media flows in Read (1976) and Pool (1977), may contain some rather grave romantic fallacies—the most salient of all the failure to account for the possibilities of furthering foreign dependence.

Although, in these views, the foreign inflow of media products are allegedly beneficial to the recipient nations, there should be serious concern that if such flows are allowed to take place with no hindrance, they are bound to consolidate the interests of the stronger parties; the weaker states may suffer from negative consequences economically and culturally before positive benefits are in sight. Many realistic non-Marxists do not dispute this but claim that remedies are available short of a radical route of closed-door cultural isolation. These remedies include, to name just a few, initiating regional cooperation among nations, regrounding media professionals in native cultures, diversifying the source of foreign media product supply, and utilizing group efforts at the local community level to assist the media function of education and information.

"PRODUCT LIFE CYCLE" AND MEDIA FLOW

Non-Marxists have in the past decade developed a "product life cycle" theory, as an alternative to popular exposition of capitalist imperialism, to explain the rhythm of corporate expansion. Foreign expansion is considered a law of life for the oligopolistic firm which must constantly innovate to maintain or increase its huge market share and high profit. The chief "engine" of such expansion is a quest for a global profit maximization, rather than a political or economic "conspiracy".[16] Many efforts have been made to apply this "product life cycle" to industrial organizations; some have tried a limited application of this approach to explain the multinational media corporations.

"Product life cycle" grew out of industrial organization theory and came to academic prominence through works by the Multinational Enterprise Project at the Harvard Business School.[17] The major body of theory has been spelled out by Raymond Vernon (1966, 1971).

Vernon (1971) defines a multinational corporation as a cluster of corporations of different nationalities that are joined together by a parent company through bonds of common ownership, that respond to a common strategy, and that draw on a common pool of financial and human resources. It is characterized by: (1) a large structure, (2) an oligopolistic nature, and (3) control by a parent company usually located in the United States. He further specified four stages which a multinational corporation must go through:

First, innovation of products in the United States: Vernon maintains that the U.S.-controlled enterprises generate new products and processes in response to the high per capita income and the relative availability of production factors, including large internal market demand as well as swift and effective communication.

Second, growth through foreign export and spread of products: Once the new industrial products are introduced, the monopoly is likely to be upset as competition arises from the rapid spread of knowledge in research and development. This perceived domestic threat prompts large corporations to capitalize on the relatively affluent markets of other industrialized nations, thus entering a second phase of the cycle marked by an exponential growth in profit through active export activities.

Third, slowdown or maturation of foreign expansion: Foreign companies in the importing (industrialized) nations rush to existence on the basis of transferred technology and pose a challenge to American companies. The American corporations may establish overseas subsidiaries and cost-reducing manufacturing facilities to maintain market advantage and oligopolistic equilibrium.

Fourth, decline of multinational corporations and rise of foreign industries: Finally, the American enterprises can no longer protect their oligopolistic advantage. Their large size and elaborate organizational structure become relative diseconomies with increasingly strong competition. While the American parent companies lose the cost advantages, their overseas subsidiaries operate in an environment that may not accord to them a special competitive edge. Thus, they may slough off some products, invest in cost-saving developing nations, launch aggressive advertising campaigns to create a demand for their products, or make product changes. The industrialized nations, and eventually some developing nations, may develop their industries so as to be capable of exporting their products to the United States, thus completing a product life cycle.

Following Vernon's lead, Barnet and Muller (1974: 128–133) have examined the life cycle of television receiver manufacturing in terms of four stages: (1) childhood (1948 to the mid-1950s), (2) adolescence (mid-1950s), (3) adulthood (early 1960s), and (4) aging (after the mid-1960s). Similar attempts have been made by Read (1976) and Douglass (1963) to explain world development of the motion picture industry.[18] It appears that other media businesses (such as radio and advertising) are equally susceptible to a product life cycle analysis, although such applications have not been seriously attempted. Attempts by Read (1976), however, to extend this model to the expansion of American newspapers, news magazines, and international news agencies seem strained.

Product life cycle is essentially an evolutionary performance cycle. Once a threshold is exceeded, the process enters the next phase of the cycle and never stays the same. When we evaluate the life cycle of television programs flow, we find the goodness of fit less satisfying (Chapter 3), especially with regard to the *cultural* significance of the multinational media enterprise expansion. As we will argue in Chapter 3, the product life cycle is an oversimplified business-organization model, failing to openly specify social, political, and ideological considerations.[19] It has been primarily applied to industrial and manufacturing products. Little has been done to apply the model to cultural products; where it has been tried (Chapter 3), the model appears to be of uneven applicability.

The four stages of the product life cycle (innovation-expansion-maturation-decline) seem to have some heuristic value, but the dynamic demarcating characteristics associated with each stage are by no means clear. It is therefore a descriptive model at best and lacking in explanatory power. We shall return to examine this model in Chapter 3.

MEDIA DIFFUSION VERSUS MEDIA IMPERIALISM

There have been some efforts made to draw on the implications of "product life cycle" for cultural significance, in spite of the ambiguities of the model. These implications seem to coincide with the concern of anthropologists for cultural diffusion. Together they offer explanations for the global media flow and diagnoses for the Third World radically different from those given by the media imperialism theme. Some of the points have been alluded to in the previous exposition; we now return to take further look at this issue.

Cultural anthropologists have long argued that diffusion always had a catalytic function in sociocultural development. The independent replication of innovations has been exceedingly rare, particularly when compared to the enormous effects of diffusion (Heine-Geldern, 1967). Pool (1977) and Read (1976) have basically relied on "product life cycle" to argue for the same point.

The two frameworks (media diffusion versus media imperialism) for analyzing international media flow can be contrasted by considering their answers to three basic questions (Table 2.1):

(1) What is the "engine" of multinational media enterprise expansion?
(2) What are the consequences for media dependence by the Third World on the "metropolitan" cultures?
(3) What are the diagnoses for the media policy of the Third World?

Engine of Expansion

As we have discussed previously, proponents of "media imperialism," as represented by Schiller (1976), point to the U.S. military-industrial complex as the major "engine" of its global media supremacy. To them the efforts were consciously orchestrated.[20] But more importantly, they see "media imperialism" as a manifestation of the internal contradictions of advanced capitalism.

In contrast, analysts of "media diffusion" (at least in its product life cycle form) see foreign expansion of American multinational enterprises as geared toward a purely economic goal of profit maximization on a global scale, nothing more or nothing less (see Read, 1976). It is an institutional necessity. In the case of media products, the

TABLE 2.1 Competing Explanations to the Imbalance of Global Media Flow

Locus of Explanation	Media Diffusion	Media Imperialism
Engine of multinational media expansion	The pure market strength of the United States to seek profit maximization	The military-industrial complex as an outgrowth of internal contradiction of advanced capitalism
Consequences for media dependence	Initial dependence, followed by a relative growth of domestic capabilities	Perpetuation of further, even permanent, dependence
Diagnosis for media policy	Maintenance of an open interaction with cosmopolitan cultures	Withdrawal from the global capitalist system and its dominant cultures

American corporations began exportation of television programs on a random and casual basis, and often at the request of the Third World countries.[21] It was not until later that the perceived threat to the U.S. market supremacy by domestic competition motivated the leading American media conglomerates to seek foreign markets. Their activities were not necessarily collaborative with the U.S. government. But it is fair to say that Read (1976) has exaggerated the purely commercial function of the laissez-faire marketplace to the exclusion of more politico-economic mechanisms.

Dependence

As we have discussed previously, proponents of "media imperialism" claim that the present dependence by the Third World on the dominant cultures will lead to further, and even permanent, dependence. That means a long-term exploitation by the capitalist powers and a continued underdevelopment of the Third World.

No, say media diffusionists. They believe every society can grow because of its ability to borrow elements from other cultures and to incorporate them into its own. In many instances it is not the actual cultural trait that is adopted by the borrowing culture but merely the principle on which it is based (Heine-Geldern, 1967). The process of adoption is always selective and adaptive. Imported elements acquire meaning and features that integrate them with the new environment and make them quite different from what they were in their place of origin (Pool, 1977). Therefore, they seem to maintain that the present dependence is only temporary and not at all dysfunctional. In their opinion, the Third World can learn, adapt, and borrow the technology *and* culture from the advanced nations in developing an indigenous cultural or media expression. Pool (1977) says:

> There is an enormous amount of adoption of cultural elements from abroad, the items adopted are modified to adapt to the adopting culture, and in this process there is a *cycle of initial dependence on interaction with the source culture, but it is followed by a patriation of the new activity and a relative growth of domestic interactions* [emphasis added].

The present uneven flow, for them, will be self-correcting.

Media diffusionists have such confidence in the positive functions of open interaction that they appear to be relatively unconcerned with the unanticipated latent dysfunctions that might result. They point with pride to the development of production "subcenters" (such as Mexico and Egypt) as one of the major achievements of media diffusion.

It is questionable, however, whether these "subcenters" ever change their fundamental dependency relationship with the metropolitan centers, or whether the bulk of their media products are necessarily conducive to the national development needs.[22] After all, technology is much easier to learn and be modified than is culture. To this, diffusionists may contend that although heavy imitation of media products by the Third World exists at present, they will be adapted and incorporated into indigenous cultures in the future. Why? Because in many parts of the world television is still in the process of development or on its way to completing the product life cycle, and it is too early to write off the model.

The unreserved optimism of media diffusionists may turn out to be a romantic fallacy. If they think the Third World countries have to learn the technology to produce products that are suitable to indigenous cultures, then the model seems to actually refer to the *technology* diffusion rather than *culture* diffusion. If they think, on the other hand, that given a longer period of time—to invest today for the benefit of tomorrow, so to speak—the Third World countries will achieve both technological and cultural ends, this process is less than clear and convincing evidence does not seem to be forthcoming.

The tension between the two schools of thought will continue. Some tensions center around ideological characters, but others arise from incomplete data. Meanwhile, it seems necessary that questions continue to be raised in the hope that the arguments will be codified, specified, and amenable to better research.

Diagnoses for Media Policy

Following directly from the previous reasoning, the critics of the media imperialism theme seem to insist on diagnosing the present symptom of imbalanced global communication flow by withdrawing from the global capitalist system and its dominant cultures (Schiller, 1976; Smythe, 1973). Many of the problems are still unresolved with such suggestions, especially with respect to the repressive nature of the media control.

Media diffusionists, in contrast, insist on an open interaction with metropolitan (or what they may prefer to call as "cosmopolitan") cultures. For them, cultural protectionism is self-defeating in three senses. First, one country loses the opportunity to learn, borrow, and adapt from other cultures if it unwisely closes its doors. Pool (1977) emphasizes that domestic producers, as soon as they learn to produce the kind of attractive things that had come from abroad, have a distinct advantage in the competition for an audience.[23] Second, they seem to suggest that cultures, like other commercial commodities, must submit themselves to an "open market" competition; any cultures that can exist only with cultural protectionism policies are not worthy of protection. They tend to pay the price of primitiveness and mediocrity for their self-sufficiency. Third, Pool (1974b) argues: "American commerce seeks to reflect world cultural tastes; the product in turn feeds back into the system and reinforces that which was already found popular." In addition, what the American public wants is "not so very different from what other publics want." Pool claims that cultural protection is a result of the painful process of "men's *emotional* resistance to the change in values, habits and style of life as they came to know early in life" [emphasis added].

Media diffusionists neither find the status quo in the international flow of information inherently wrong or undesirable, nor suggest ways of redressing this imbalance. A strong case can be made, however, for the policy of media self-sufficiency insofar as possible, *and* have it be useful to national development goals, even at some price of primitiveness and mediocrity. After all, the definitions of "primitiveness" and "mediocrity" are often rather arbitrary Western definitions based on the level of technological sophistication instead of cultural values and developmental functions seen from the Third World's vantage point.

Whether American media products truly reflect world cultural tastes is, to say the very least, debatable—there is ample evidence to demonstrate that they reflect American middle-class aspirations and fantasies (e.g., Wilensky, 1964) which are often at variance with cultural values of other countries (Tunstall, 1977; Katz and Wedell, 1977). It is difficult to take seriously the argument that such popularly marketed products of American commerce as *Kojak* or *I Love Lucy* represent the convergence of world cultural tastes and that Third World markets ought to embrace them wholeheartedly even at the sacrifice of the slice of airtime that could have been allocated to, say, farming demonstrations or health knowledge. With perfect sincerity, Pool (1974b) claims: "In general, culture does not need protection. Culture is what people are already attached to. If the culture is satisfactory, if it is not itself already in the process of decomposition, if local media are doing the job of providing products that fit the culture, the audience will not look abroad." A slightly far-fetched analogy may go like this: "If the Ching Dynasty of Imperial China was satisfactory, if it was not itself in the process of decomposition, if local merchants were doing the job of providing products that fit public needs, people would not have had to look to the British—for opium."

At issue is whether Third World countries have legitimate reasons to protect cultures from what they consider undesirable foreign influences. It is fair to say that while radical writers (Nordenstreng and Varis, 1973; Schiller, 1976) have a tendency to deny the *desirable* consequences of media/culture diffusion, liberal writers (Pool, 1977, 1974b) have a reverse tendency to ignore the *undesirable* consequences of entrenched American media/culture foreign domination. In short, media/culture diffusion can and ought to be selective; Third World nations are entitled to minimizing what they deem as undesirable elements of foreign culture and media products lest the desirable elements of the indigenous culture be threatened. The indigenous culture may need protection not just because it is unsatisfying or decaying, but because it is devoid of a strong metropolitan economy for support. Cultural exchange is two-way; it is not so cut and dried as an either-or proposition. The argument for a wholesale cultural import—in the free and unrestrained world market—may put the economically weak nations at an unwarranted disadvantage.

In sum, what does this lengthy discussion leave for the Third World? We believe that it is incumbent upon individual Third World nations to formulate clear policies to control their own media destiny. They must not fall into the trap of accepting either unrestrained "free flow" or repressive and authoritarian media control. What they need, it seems to us, is the freedom to choose any appropriate synthesis of media models and alternatives as long as it is fair *and* beneficial to their national development goals.

SOCIALIST MEDIA IMPERIALISM

The theory of imperialism—along with its manifestations in media and culture—has its origin in Lenin (1952), who aimed at explaining the consequences of the internal contradictions of advanced monopoly capitalism. The power and ideological splits between Communist China and the Soviet Union have cast doubt on the popular image of a monolithic communist bloc. Communist internationalism, as predicted by Lenin, has been empirically refuted by the outgrowth of nationalist socialisms in the Third World, especially by that of Maoism (Lichtheim, 1974). It is intriguing that the Chinese Communists have denounced the Soviet Union as a major social imperialist and Cuba and Vietnam as minor social imperialists. These denunciations undoubtedly motivated by ideology and power struggle, nonetheless suggest that (1) the definition of "imperialism" stands in urgent need of reexamination; (2) contrary to what Marxist-Leninists would have postulated, imperialism may not be limited to international capitalism but also exists in socialism; and (3) different mechanisms and manifestations may exist between capitalist imperialism and socialist imperialism. In fact different Marxian scholars (Bottomore, 1974; Mills, 1962) and non-Marxist scholars (Aron, 1965; Lichtheim, 1974) have expressed grave apprehension about the trend of the Soviet territorial and military-political, if not necessarily economic, expansion. The encroachment upon Eastern Europe by the Soviet tanks certainly paints no rosier—if anything, bloodier—image than the horde of greedy American businessmen scurrying for money abroad.

In relating social imperialism to the field of media, the Chinese Communists have blasted Soviet hegemony for outdating Mark Twain's old characterization of the international news monopoly by the Associated Press. (To paraphrase, Twain said that only the sun in the sky and the AP on the earth could brighten every corner of the globe.) Radio Moscow's forty high-power transmitters used exclusively for international propaganda broadcasting, according to this charge, have made the technologically advanced BBC look quite ashamed. Soviet spies and agents, in the name of journalism, have been accused of infiltrating Third World nations. Worse yet, the Soviet airwaves have "tended to turn international problems from black to white and to confuse right and wrong—their technique for manufacturing rumors is unsurpassed in this world."[24]

The Chinese Communists' denunciation of Soviet foreign expansion in propaganda and mass media paradoxically casts themselves in the same category—in foreign propaganda broadcasting, at least. This denunciation cannot be dismissed lightly, not because of its journalistic sensationalism or our intention to side with either, but because of its inherent challenge to the established theory of "media imperialism." Conceivably some may dispute the empirical accuracy of China's accusations. Others may rightly note that the ascendance of Soviet socialism as a major world force has a rather short history compared with Western liberal democracies or capitalism, and therefore has failed to develop a communication media infrastructure so sophisticated as to equal the ability in media domination (in terms of product sales and so on). But none of these arguments either dispels the Soviet intention and its potential for media hegemony or undercuts the power of China's implied challenge to the theory of "media imperialism."

Needless to say, our understanding of socialist imperialism—in the media and in other fields—is greatly hampered by the secretive nature and the strict control of information flow within and without totalitarian countries, especially when these materials hinge upon military and political operations. For instance, the kind of basic official documents Guback (1969) or Schiller (1969) relied on for their expositions of capitalist media imperialism cannot be ascertained in the Soviet Union with the same degree of ease and richness.

The challenge to the existing "media imperialism" theory helps to illuminate a number of points. First, contrary to what Schiller (1976) argues, media technology is not necessarily an *inherent* manifestation and embodiment of capitalism; both advanced capitalist and advanced socialist countries may in fact employ the same technological means for their specific objectives. (We shall pursue this point further in the next section.) Second, we ought to look for different causal mechanisms that account for commonalities and differences, in terms of process and outcome, between capitalist and socialist media imperialisms. So far capitalist media imperialism, as noted, has been attacked by the left as an inevitable consequence of advanced capitalism (Schiller, 1973), and defended by the right as the outcome of the unequaled market strength of the United States in the freely flowing world economic structure (Read, 1976). While many Marxists and non-Marxists disavow the "conspiracy" implied in the capitalist expansion, the Chinese Communists' attack on socialist media imperialism contains an unmistakably sharp overtone of Soviet conspiracy. Third, socialist media imperialism does not appear to offer a viable alternative to capitalist media imperialism; its implications for the Third World are serious and important. These questions, thus stated, constitute candidates for further inquiry but this book shall not deal with them for the most part.

TECHNOLOGICAL DETERMINISM AND MEDIA FLOW

Both neo-Marxists and non-Marxists have invoked—but never quite wholeheartedly—technological determinism to explain the global homogenization of television culture.

The crudest version of technological determinism is offered by

Head and Gordon (1976). They claim that broadcasting has the *intrin-sic* characteristic of *continuance*—it is not there all at once as a physical entity like a newspaper, book, or film, but arrives continu-ously, minute by minute. Audiences exposed to this continuous flow of communication, they contend, have the intrinsic characteristic of limited attention span for "difficult" material and thus favor less demanding program materials: entertainment. This explanation, based primarily on a hedonist perspective as proposed by William Stephenson's play theory (1967), is hardly a satisfying explanation of the media flow or homogenous television program structure. Evi-dence shows that radio's program schedule is much more varied and indigenous than television in most countries although both media have to comply with what Head and Gordon term the "continuous" technical requirement.[25]

Schiller (1976, 1973), arguing from the radical perspective, rejects the "neutrality" of technology as a myth. He believes that the prod-ucts, introduction, and uses of technology "are in fact political and ideological acts which either support or threaten world monopoly capitalism," meaning the United States and its upper-class allies in various capitalist nations. This is a position consistent with his gen-eral thesis that media technology is an embodiment of capitalist ideol-ogy and interests. It is instructive to note that Maoists in China subscribed to the same view whereas the post-Mao pragmatists do not (see Epilogue).

Tunstall (1977) seems to have shown a somewhat contradictory, or at least ambivalent, attitude toward technological determinism. In his more despairing and pessimistic moments he says:

> In my view a non-American way out of the media box is difficult to discover because it is an American, or Anglo-American, built box, and this, with the possible exception of the Chinese, no nations seem willing to do [1977: 63].

The title of his book, *The Media Are American,* succinctly illustrates this fear. In other words, all media are essentially American; the American media superiority is inherently inevitable and not just a result of its faster and more prolific media development. Elsewhere, however, he has taken pains to explain that this does not have to be the case. Specifically, Tunstall (1977: 266–269) tries to refute two theses: (1) that new technology determines the media patterns which subsequently follow in the importing nation; and (2) that an American pattern of media follows more or less automatically from industrialization.

Technology *alone* determines neither how people encounter and respond to the mass media (DeFleur and Ball-Rokeach, 1975: 199–217) nor how the American media have come to dominate the world. McLuhanist explanations of media flow are likely to be devoid of (1) the social *intention* of those who developed the media technology, (2) the international power stratification, and (3) the media tradition and social system of the recipient nations.

Television is being used chiefly as an entertainment medium not because of its inherent technical character as Head and Gordon suggest, but because of social, political, and cultural milieus. In short, it has deep-rooted Anglo-American cultural origins. There is no reason to believe that the technological know-how could have prevented an utterly different medium from being devised, but the cultural inputs dictated otherwise. Williams (1975: 25) states:

> Unlike all previous communications technologies, radio and television were systems primarily devised for transmission and reception as abstract processes, with little or no definition of preceding content. When the question of content was raised, it was resolved, in the main, parasitically. . . . It is not only that the supply of broadcasting facilities preceded the demand; it is that the means of communication preceded their content.

The American television system, like other media, is characterized by a system of centralized cultural packaging, local distribution, and privatized reception. This is the dominant mode of media structure adopted by the majority of nations in the world.

It has been argued that television content requires "certain" standard practices in mass production and consequently has to exhibit a "certain" kind of program. It rewards an ability to draw the largest share of audience rather than aesthetic excellence. If that were to be true, the implication could be quite discouraging for cultural protectionists because technological and cultural origin of the medium will not guarantee successful cultural expression by individual countries even if they decide to do away with the imported programs. However, such interpretation is unsatisfying on at least two counts. First, it unduly discounts the potential chances for internal national media policy in stemming foreign dependence. The fact that television sets in China, as Tunstall himself implies in the previous quote, are displayed in public places for ideological indoctrination (see Epilogue), undercuts the explanatory power of the technological-cultural determinism. Japan's NHK channel and the BBC, despite pressure to meet capitalist competition to some extent, provide evidence to invalidate the assertion that advanced technologies are inherent products of modern capitalism and hence cannot be expected to take up a cultural mission.[26] Second, we are at a loss to separate that part of the outcome which is attributable to technological constraints versus that which is due to cultural values or social uses.

INTERNATIONAL POWER STRATIFICATION AND MEDIA FLOW

Neo-Marxists resort to economic reductionism and class conflict to explain the inequity of global media flow, whereas non-Marxists tend to ignore or avoid both variables. In this section we suggest that the pattern of world communications flow may have a close (but not perfect) correspondence with the stratification of the international *power* structure, which has more to do with the relative ranking of politico-economic strength of individual countries than with the conventional Marxist dichotomies of economic capitalism and socialism. Quantitatively speaking, the correlation between communications flow and the stratification of the international power structure is fairly strong but never approaches unity. There are always exceptions to this general pattern. To sum up, this is meant to be a modest probabilistic statement rather than a sweeping, overarching deterministic claim.

In the international capitalist system, countries that are politically and economically strong (the United Kingdom, France, West Germany, Japan) tend to be the most media-independent.[27] They are all major exporters of media products to the Third World and significant importers of American media products; this further illustrates the pecking order of international power resources. Among them, Tunstall (1977) persuasively argues that the British media have played the role, not of a progressively defeated competitor, but of a prosperous junior partner to the dominant American media enterprises. With the strategic help of British media, the American media penetrate and reach into other countries in Europe and elsewhere. Of the twenty or so great corporations which dominate world media exports, some five are British; British media exports to the rest of the world are still approximately one-third, by cash value, of U.S. exports.

What is more, many rapidly thriving regional media leaders appear to be also the most dominant political powers in specific regions: Mexico and Argentina in Latin America; Egypt in the Arab world; Sweden among the Nordic countries. The second-tier capitalist countries which are too close to the world-dominant capitalist centers to strive for political and economic autonomy seem to have the greatest difficulty in asserting media independence. This is especially the case with Canada (see Chapter 4), Australia (Haskell, 1977), and Ireland (Carey, 1977; Howell, 1979) and Nordic nations. It is generally ignored that an inequitable communication flow exists between the First World and the Second World or among the highly industrialized nations; such inequity is *not* limited to the politically and economically advanced nations and the Third World only.

More important, the inequity of communication flow exists among the international socialist system. The Soviet media model has been imported by the Eastern European nations and the Soviet—although not U.S.—media products appear to dominate in those countries too (Paulu, 1974). This is an illustration that socialist countries also display a stratified political and economic power structure and with it a stratified media structure. This stratified media hierarchy may be less distinct and manifest in the international socialist system than in the capitalist system, but it nevertheless exists. In Eastern Europe the dominant political and social objectives have high priorities in all media; there is virtually no political or commercial competition to the media either. Advertising plays a small part in the revenue makeup, except in Yugoslavia where the Western influences seem to be stronger (Yugoslavia belongs to Eurovision rather than to Intervision).

Eurovision and Intervision are television programming consortiums made up of the Western European and Eastern European broadcasting organization respectively. Both have engaged in news exchange since 1965, but there is a great disparity in such exchange. While Intervision members take about 65% of all Eurovision offers, less than 10% of Intervision's offerings are acceptable to Eurovision (Sherman and Ruby, 1974: Kressley, 1978). This divergence in part reflects the imbalance of power resources between Western and Eastern Europe and is in part due to the difference in news philosophy. The Western television news is mainly devoted to straight descriptive news and the sensation of disaster, which is amenable to reinterpretation by the socialist countries. In contrast, Intervision newscasts generally favor heavier doses of commentary and consciously set "good news," with 90% of political news dealing with visiting heads of state or other important public figures in foreign countries. Therefore, while the socialist countries adopt a high percentage of Eurovision's offerings, the Western countries only choose from Intervision those items that suit their established preference patterns (such as sports and descriptive political coverage) but hardly anything from the realm of culture, science, and economic affairs. Kressley (1978) suggests that Intervision's participation pattern in Eurovision closely resembles that of less affluent Eurovision affiliates in the West. He also observes a gradual movement of socialist broadcasting, especially in Eastern Europe, from a consciously managed didactic style toward greater responsiveness to popular tastes, and he predicts that this will increase further imbalance of communication media flow in the future.

CONCLUDING REMARKS

In this chapter we have examined the arguments of economic dependency made by neo-Marxist scholars and have offered a critique. We have compared the logical structure of economic dependency with that of media-cultural-communication imperialism; there is a great similarity between them. No independent, well-articulated, and convincing body of theory about cultural imperialism has been developed. Non-Marxists have very different ideas about how to explain the present state of unequal world communication flow.

In sum, radical writers are good at diagnosis but poor at therapy. They have performed a very important sensitizing function in exposing the potential and actual pitfalls of liberal expectancy as symbolized by such principles as "free (unrestrained) flow of information." However they have tended to undermine their case by overstatement. Their suggestions for policy solutions tend to be unrealistic and always stop short of enough specification and elaboration to be empirically testable. They thus resemble the aura and illusion of political rhetoric and dogma.

The crucial difference between neo-Marxists and non-Marxists is the difference between revolution and evolution. Revolution cannot be limited to the media realm alone; it is a redefinition of the relationship between man and society, media and politics. Evolution, however, can take place in the media realm without overhauling and restructuring politics, society, economics, and culture.

Both perspectives appear to have valid points as well as share a "mirror trap" of romantic fallacy. This radical challenge to the status quo has made all parties rethink the present global communication flow. The burden of proof still remains with the neo-Marxists that the socialist alternative is able to achieve cultural integrity *and* freedom. The more conservative elements of non-Marxist analysts, in contrast, appear to defend the established interests of the strong nations under an illusion of a bright and rosy future. That time and market will not automatically take care of the present inequity in media production and distribution if no actions are to be taken resolutely by the nations involved does not deter them at all.

After examining the media imperialism controversy between neo-Marxist and non-Marxist scholars, we have suggested the theoretical possibility of "socialist media imperialism," and have tried to refute the appropriateness of invoking technological determinism to explain media flow. Finally we suggest that the present media flow may closely correspond to the stratification of international power arrangements rather than the conventional perspective of international class conflict.

The concept of "media imperialism" is generally vague and stands in need of a more precise definition. We will attempt to redefine it at different levels of generality in the next chapter.

NOTES

1. Economists Schumpeter (1951) and Boulding (1972), along with sociologist Berger (1976), among others, all offer counterarguments to Lenin's theory.

2. It is important to note that when Frank and other radical writers (e.g., Nordenstreng and Varis, 1973, Schiller, 1976) speak of *internal* processes, they often refer to the class conflict *within* nations. See Note 7 for a contrasting non-Marxist definition.

3. It is often unclear whether "underdevelopment" is meant as an absolute or as relative to the "developed" countries. Rhetorically, the term "underdevelopment" can sometimes be seen as pejorative, in view of the accusations made in recent years by environment-conscious pressure groups that the U.S. is "overdeveloped."

4. Colonialism is a historical reference to distant territories politically governed by an imperial center after the conquest of the native population. Neo-colonialism is a contemporary reference to strong external economic, political, and cultural dependency on the dominant powers; this can take place even long after the national independence of the weaker nations. Colonialism and imperialism are often used interchangeably, as are neo-colonialism, neo-imperialism, and dependency.

5. See Bottomore (1976: 55–71) for foreign aid and dependency, Barnet and Muller (1974) for monopoly pricing, Frank (1972: 92–137) for investment and dependency, Bauer and Yamey (1977) and Nove (1974) for dissenting views on economic dependency.

6. Weisskopf (1976) offered a useful extension of Lall's critique in empirical terms.

7. Elsewhere Eisenstadt (1976) listed variables of internal dynamics for consideration: level of resources available, the pattern of impingement of modern sectors on the respective societies (dualism), the structure of the change situation in which they are caught (historical processes), the different traditions of the premodern socioeconomic structures, perception of choice by different elites and groups in given historical situations, center-periphery relations, and types of coalescence.

8. See, for example, Smythe's statements in Nordenstreng and Varis (1974: 50).

9. Smythe (1973) held out high promise for a media policy of isolated self-reliance during the Cultural Revolution of the People's Republic of China. His account should be reexamined in the context of the present post-Mao leadership, which has accused the "Gang of Four" (said to have masterminded the Cultural Revolution) of manipulating the media to serve their ill-intentioned political ambitions. Whether the present regime is committed to a different media policy or is simply condemning foes for its own political ends will have to be seen (see Epilogue).

10. We benefited from the "resource management" perspective which Gamson (1975) used to analyze social protest. Much of the following descriptive data draws on Dizard (1966).

11. See Orlik (1970) and Harrison and Eckman (in Gerbner, 1977) for examples in the case of South Africa.

12. See Chapter 4 (Canada) and Chapter 5 (Taiwan) for a detailed examination.

13. According to Katz (1973: 382), "The administrative and creative structures, the technical infrastructure, even the governmental superstructure (the FCC, etc.) all acted as agents for the transfer of a conception of broadcasting, its content and its norms, from radio to television." Williams (1975) has also examined how American commercial broadcasting institutions could determine or affect cultural forms of television technology, which also means the exclusion of alternative uses.

14. See Schiller's book review in *Journal of Communication* 27: 226–228, 1977.

15. In fairness, it should be noted that Nordenstreng and Varis (1974), in summarizing the collective opinion of a UNESCO-sponsored media flow symposium, have suggested an examination of four internal variables more acceptable to a non-Marxist's locus of explanation. These variables include history of the media, economic resources and demographic characteristics (size of audience), tariffs on exported programs and the expenses involved in program purchasing, and national conditions such as overall economic structures within and between nations.

16. The use of the word "conspiracy" has elicited intense emotional response. While many popular writers have often interpreted the neo-Marxist stand as a "conspiracy" on the part of the United States, some sophisticated neo-Marxists have generally shunned such characterizations. To these Marxists, there may not necessarily be a plot; what happens is the natural working of the economic system that is apart from the intent of any group of conspirators. They also attribute imperialism to the alliance of local bourgeoise in the exploited nations and international capitalism.

17. Since its founding in 1965, the project has produced two score journal articles, a dozen theses, a 500-page book of tables, and five volumes of which Vernon's book (1971) was the first in the series. See the preface in Vernon (1971). Unfortunately, few bear direct relevance to multinational media organizations.

18. Read (1976) acknowledged the intellectual assistance of Raymond Vernon, Ithiel de Sola Pool, and Samuel Huntington, among others. Douglass (1963) completed his doctoral thesis at MIT where this school of thought is influential.

19. Vernon's (1971) aim was admittedly modest. But when the model is extended to analyze the media flow, the failure to specify noneconomic variables is serious. Evans (1979) has attempted to incorporate these social and political variables into the product life cycle model to examine the relationship between dependence and underdevelopment in Brazil.

20. As a most extreme case, see U.S. Senate (1975. 15–29) and Schiller (1976: 98–109) concerning the U.S. Central Intelligence Agency in relation to media efforts to oust the Marxist Allende government in Chile. See also Tunstall (1977: 222 231).

21. See Katz and Shinar (1975) for such an example in Thailand. See also Read (1976) and Dizard (1966).

22. Incidentally but not insignificantly, the development of regional media production centers has been interpreted as a positive result of the free flow of information and cultural diffusion (Pool, 1977) on the one hand, and on the other as a proof of media imperialism since these countries happen to be significant importers of Anglo-American products. Indeed, different ideological lenses do provide different views.

23. Browne (1968), Katz and Wedell (1977), Katz and Gurevitch (1976), Hsu et al. (1975), and Tsui (in G. Chu et al., 1977: 46) have provided some empirical support for this point. Canada, on the other hand, has not fared so well on this score.

24. *Hsin Wen Chan Hsien* [News Front] 1: 71–72, 1979.

25. Jamison and McAnany (1978) examine the role of radio in national development. Suine and Kline (1975) and Hirsch (1971) argue that radio in the United States, faced with television's competition, has sought specialized formats and audiences to be economically viable.

26. Having so said, one may take note of the criticisms, usually by radical writers, directed toward the BBC for "holding the middle ground." See, for example, Curran et al. (1977) and McQuail (1972).

27. This is a case in point where different media may lead to somewhat different conclusions. In the case of the film industry, Guback (1969) shows that the United Kingdom and West Germany have little autonomous local production.

References

ADELMAN, I. and C.T. MORRIS (1973) Economic Growth and Social Equality in the Developing Countries. Stanford, CA: Stanford University Press.

ADHIKARYA, R. (1977) Broadcasting in Penisular Malaysia. Boston: Routledge & Kegan Paul.

ADLER, R. and D. CATER [eds.] (1976) Television as a Cultural Form. New York: Praeger.

ALISKY, M. (1976) "Government-press relations in Peru," Journalism Quarterly 53: 661–665.

ALKER, H.R., Jr. (1966) "Causal inference and political analysis," in J. Bernd (ed.) Mathematical Applications in Political Science. Dallas, TX: Southern Methodist University Press.

ALMOND, G. and S. VERBA (1963) The Civic Culture. Princeton, NJ: Princeton University Press.

APPLETON, S. (1976–1977) "Survey research in Taiwan." Public Opinion Quarterly 40: 468–481.

ARON, R. (1965) Main Currents in Sociological Thought. Two volumes. Harmondsworth: Penguin.

BABE, R.E. (1975) Cable Television and Telecommunications in Canada: An Economic Analysis. East Lansing: Michigan State University International Business and Economic Studies.

BARNET, R. and R. MULLER (1974) Global Reach: The Power of the Multinational Corporations. New York: Simon & Schuster.

BARNETT, A.D. (1977) "Round one in China's succession: the shift towards pragmatism," Current Scene, 15, 1.

———(1967) "A note on communication and development in Communist China," in D. Lerner and W. Schramm (eds.) Communication and Change in the Developing Countries. Honolulu: University of Hawaii/East-West Center Press.

BARNOUW, E. (1975) Tube of Plenty: The Evolution of American Television. New York: Oxford University Press.

BAUER, P.T. (1972) Dissent on Development. Cambridge, MA: Harvard University Press.

———and B.S. YAMEY (1977), "Against the new economic order," Commentary 63, 4: 25–31.

BEKE, A.J. (1970) Broadcasting and the Freedom of Choice. S.J.D. dissertation, University of Michigan.

BELTRAN, L.R. (1976a) "Social structure and rural development communication in Latin America: the 'radiophonic schools' of Colombia," in G.C. Chu and S.A. Rahim (eds.) Communication for Group Transformation in Development (Monograph No. 2). Honolulu: East-West Communication Institute.

———(1976b) "Alien premise, objects, and methods in Latin America." Communication Research 3: 107–134.

_____ and E. Fox de Cardona (1977) "Latin America and the United States: flaws in the free flow of information," in J. Richstad (ed.) New Perspectives in International Communication. Honolulu: East-West Communication Institute.

BENDIX, R. (1970) Embattled Reason, Essays on Social Knowledge. New York: Oxford University Press.

_____ (1967) "Tradition and modernity reconsidered." Comparative Studies in Society and History 9: 292–346.

BERGER, P. (1976) Pyramids of Sacrifice: Political Ethics and Social Change. New York: Anchor.

BLACK, E. R. (1968) "Canadian public policy and the mass media," Canadian Journal of Economics 2: 368–379.

BLOCKER, J. (1976) "The bad news from UNESCO." Columbia Journalism Review (March/April): 57–59.

BLUMLER, J. G. and M. GUREVITCH (1975) "Towards a comparative framework for political communication research," in S. H. Chaffee (ed.) Political Communication. Beverly Hills, CA: Sage.

BOGART, L. (1958) The Age of Television. New York: Ungar.

BORDENAVE, J. D. (1976) "Communication of agricultural innovations in Latin America: the need for new models." Communication Research 3: 135–154.

BOTTOMORE, T. B. (1974) Sociology as Social Criticism. New York: Scott, Foresman.

BOULDING, K. E. (ed.) (1972) Economic Imperialism. Ann Arbor: University of Michigan Press.

BOYD-BARRETT, O. (1977) "Media imperialism: towards an international framework for the analysis of media systems," in J. Curran et al. (eds.) Mass Communication and Society. London: Edward Arnold.

BOYD, D. A. (1970–1971) "Saudi Arabian television." Journal of Broadcasting 15: 73–78.

BRZEZINSKI, Z. (1956) "The politics of underdevelopment." World Politics 9: 55–75.

BROWN, L. (1971) Television: The Business Behind the Box. New York: Harcourt Brace Jovanovich.

BROWNE, D. (1975) "Television and national stabilization: the Lebanese experience." Journalism Quarterly, 52: 692–698.

_____ (1971) "The BBC and the pirates: a phase in the life of a prolonged monopoly." Journalism Quarterly, 48: 85–99.

_____ (1968) "The American image as presented abroad by U.S. television." Journalism Quarterly, 45: 307–316.

BUNCE, R. (1976) Television in the Corporate Interest. New York: Praeger.

BURES, O. [ed.] (1975) Developing World and Mass Media. Prague: International Organization of Journalists.

de CAMARGO, N. and V. B. NOYA PINTO (1975) Communication Policies in Brazil. Paris: UNESCO Press.

Canada, Consultative Committee on the Implications of Telecommunications for Canadian Sovereignty (1979) Telecommunications and Canada. Ottawa: Minister of Supply and Services Canada.

Canada, Department of Communications [DOC] (1975) The Impact of Cable Television on the

Canadian Broadcasting System. Ottawa: Social Policy and Programs Branch.

Candad, Special Senate Committee [SSC] (1970a) The Uncertain Mirror. Ottawa: Information Canada.

——— (1970b) Words, Music and Dollars. Ottawa: Information Canada.

——— (1970c) Good, Bad, or Simply Inevitable? Ottawa: Information Canada.

Canadian Radio-Television and Telecommunications Commission [CRTC] (1979a) Canadian Broadcasting Corporation's Television and Radio Network Licences. Ottawa: Minister of Supply and Services Canada.

——— (1979b) Special Report on Broadcasting in Canada 1968–1978. Ottawa: Minister of Supply and Services Canada.

——— (1979c) A Review of Certain Cable Television Programming Issues. Ottawa: Minister of Supply and Services Canada.

CARDONA, E. (1977) "American television in Latin America," in G. Gerbner (ed.) Mass Media Policies in Changing Cultures. New York: John Wiley.

——— (1975) "Multinational television." Journal of Communication 25: 122–127.

CANTOR, M. G. (1971) The Hollywood TV Producer. New York: Basic Books.

CAREY, J. W. (1977) "The politics of popular culture: a case study." Presented to the Association for Education in Journalism, Madison, August 22.

——— (1975) "Communication and culture." Communication Research 2: 173–191.

CHAFFEE, S. H. (1975) "The diffusion of political information," in S. H. Chaffee (ed.) Political Communication. Beverly Hills, CA: Sage.

CHAO, T. (1969) Drama Reform in Mainland China, 1942–67 (in Chinese). Hong Kong: Chinese University Press.

CHENG, C. M. [ed.] (1976) Selected Readings in Journalism (in Chinese). Taipei: College of Chinese Culture Press.

CHINN, D. L. (1977) "Distributional equality and economic growth: the case of Taiwan." Economic Development and Cultural Change 26: 65–79.

CHODAK, S. (1973) Societal Development. New York: Oxford University Press.

CHU, G. C. (1977) Radical Change Through Communication in Mao's China. Honolulu: University of Hawaii Press.

——— and F. L. K. HSU [eds.] (1979) Moving a Mountain: Cultural Change in China. Honolulu: University of Hawaii/East-West Center Press.

CHU, G. C. et al. [eds.] (1977) Research on Mass Communication in Taiwan and Hong Kong. Honolulu: East-West Communication Institute.

CHU, J. (1975) "The PRC journalists as a cadre." Current Scene 13, 1: 1–14.

——— and W. FANG (1972) "The training of journalists in Communist China." Journalism Quarterly 49: 489–497.

CHU, L. L. (1978) "Flow of international news on China's television." Asian Messenger 3, 2: 38–42.

——— (1977a) Planning Birth Campaigns in China 1949–1976 (Case Study No. 5). Honolulu: East-West Communication Institute.

——— (1977b) "Television in Mainland China." Ming Pao (in Chinese) April 26–27.

COLEMAN, J. S. (1971) "Conflicting theories of social change." American Behavioral Scientist 15: 633–650.

COMPTON, N. (1964) "Television and Canadian culture." Commentary 38, 5: 75–79.

CONTRERAS, E. J. LARSON, J. K. MAYO, and P. SPAIN (1976) Cross Cultural Broadcasting. Reports and papers on mass communication (No. 77). Paris: UNESCO Press.

CREAN, S. (1976) Who's Afraid of Canadian Culture? Don Mills, Ont.: General.

CURRAN, J., M. GUREVITCH, and J. WOOLLACOOTT [eds.] (1977) Mass Communication and Society. London: Edward Arnold.

CUTRIGHT, P. (1963) "National political development: measurement and analysis," American Sociological Review 28: 253–264.

DAHRENDORF, R. (1959) Class and Class Conflict in Industrial Society. Palo Alto, CA: Stanford University Press.

DAVISON, W. P. and F. T. C. YU [eds.] (1974) Mass Communication Research. New York: Praeger.

DeFLEUR, M. L. and S. BALL-ROKEACH (1975) Theories of Mass Communication, 3rd ed. New York: McKay.

DERVIN, B. and B. S. GREENBERG (1972) "The communication environment of the urban poor," in F. G. Kline and P. Tichenor (eds.) Current Perspectives in Mass Communication Research. Beverly Hills, CA: Sage.

DIZARD, W. P. (1966) Television: A World View. Syracuse, NY: Syracuse University Press.

DONOHUE, G. A., P. J. TICHENOR, and C. N. OLIEN (1975) "Mass media and the knowledge gap: a hypothesis reconsidered." Communication Research 2: 3–21.

DOUGLASS, G. K. (1963) Product Life Cycle and International Trade in Motion Pictures. Ph.D. dissertation, MIT.

EISENSTADT, S. N. (1977) "Dynamics of civilizations and development: the case of European society." Economic Development and Cultural Change, vol. 25 supplement, pp. 123–144.

_____ (1976) "The changing vision of modernization and development," in W. Schramm and D. Lerner (eds.) Communication and Change: The Last Ten Years—and the Next. Honolulu: University of Hawaii/East-West Center Press.

ELLIOT, P. and P. GOLDING (1974) "Mass communication and social change: the imagery of development and the development of imagery," in E. De Kadt and G. Williams (eds.) Sociology and Development. London: Tavistock.

EMERY, W. B. (1969) National and International Systems of Broadcasting. East Lansing: Michigan State University Press.

ETTEMA, J. S. and F. G. KLINE (1977) "Deficits, differences, and ceilings: contingent conditions for understanding the knowledge gap." Communication Research 4: 179–202.

EVANS, P. B. (1979) Dependent Development. Princeton, NJ: Princeton University Press.

FAIRBANK, J. K. (1976) "Our one-China problem." Atlantic Monthly 328 (September): 4–12.

FISCHER, H. D. and J. C. MERRILL [eds.] (1976) International and Intercultural Communication. New York: Hastings. (Second edition)

_____ [eds.] (1970) International and Intercultural Communication. New York: Hastings. (First edition)

FRANK, A. G. (1972) Lumpenbourgeoisie: Lumpendevelopment: Dependence, Class, and Politics in Latin America. New York: Monthly Review.

_____ (1969) Latin America: Underdevelopment or Revolution. New York: Monthly Review.

FREY, F. W. (1973) "Communication and development," in I. de Sola Pool and W. Schramm (eds.) Handbook of Communication. Chicago: Rand McNally.

FURTADO, C. (1973) "The post-1964 Brazilian 'model' of development." Studies in Comparative International Development 8: 115–127.

_____ (1970) Obstacles to Development in Latin America. Garden City, NY: Anchor.

_____ (1964) Development and Underdevelopment. Berkeley: University of California Press.

GALLOWAY, J. J. (1977) "The analysis and significance of communication effects gap." Communication Research 4: 363–386.

GALLOWAY, J. F. (1972) The Politics and Technology of Satellite Communications. Lexington, MA: D. C. Heath.

GAMSON, W. (1975) The Strategy of Social Protest. Homewood, IL: Irwin.

GANS, H. J. (1974a) Popular Culture and High Culture. New York: Basic Books.

――――(1974b) More Equality. New York: Vintage.

――――(1962) The Urban Villagers. New York: Macmillan.

GEERTZ, C. (1973) The Interpretation of Culture. New York: Basic Books.

GERBNER, G. [ed.] (1977) Mass Media Policies in Changing Cultures. New York: John Wiley.

――――L. P. GROSS, and W. H. MELODY (eds.) (1973), Communication Technology and Social Policy. New York: John Wiley.

GOFFMAN, E. (1961) The Asylum. New York: Anchor.

GOLDING, P. (1974) "Media role in national development: a critique of a theoretical orthodoxy," Journal of Communication 24: 39–53.

GOLDTHORPE, J. E. (1975) The Sociology of the Third World. New York: Cambridge University Press.

GOULET, D. (1977) The Uncertain Promise: Value Conflicts in Technology Transfer. New York: IDOC/North America.

GRANT, G. P. (1970) Lament for a Nation. Toronto: McClelland & Stewart.

GREEN, T. (1972) The Universal Eye: The World of TV. New York: Stein & Day.

GREW, R. (1977) "Modernization and its discontents." American Behavioral Scientist 21: 289–312.

GRIFFITH, W. E. (1973) "Communist esoteric communications: explication de texte," in I. de sola Pool and W. Schramm (eds.) Handbook of Communication. Chicago: Rand-McNally.

GROSSBERG, L. (1977) "Cultural interpretation and mass communication," Communication Research 4: 339–360.

GRUNIG, J. (1971) "Communication and the economic decision-making process of Colombian peasants." Economic Development and Cultural Change 18: 580–597.

GUBACK, T. (1974a) "Film as international business." Journal of Communication 24: 90–101.

――――(1974b) "Cultural identity and film in the European Economic Community." Cinema Journal 14: 2–12.

――――(1969) The International Film Industry: Western Europe and America Since 1945. Bloomington: Indiana University Press.

――――and D. J. DOMBKOWSKI (1976) "Television and Hollywood: economic relations in the 1970s." Journal of Broadcasting 20: 511–527.

GUITE, J.-M. (1974) CATV and the Wired-City in Canada. Ottawa: Department of Communications. (mimeo)

GUSFIELD, J. (1967) "Tradition and modernity: misplaced polarities in the study of social change." American Journal of Sociology 72: 351–362.

HACHTEN, W. A. (1971) Muffled Drums: The News Media in Africa. Ames: Iowa State University Press.

HALLMAN, E. S. (1977) Broadcasting in Canada. Boston: Routledge & Kegan Paul.

HALLORAN, J. D. and P. CROLL (1972) "Television programs in Great Britain: content and control," in G. A. Comstock and E. A. Rubinstein (eds.) Television and Social Behavior. Vol. 1: Media Content and Control. Washington, DC: Government Printing Office.

HARDIN, H. (1974) A Nation Unaware: The Canadian Economic Culture. Vancouver: Douglas.

HASKELL, D. (1977) "Accountability in Australian television." Gazette 23: 89–104.

HEAD, S. [ed.] (1974) Broadcasting in Africa. Philadelphia: Temple University Press.
_____ (1972) Broadcasting in America. Boston: Houghton Mifflin.
_____ and T. F. GORDON (1976) "The structure of world broadcast programming: some tentative hypotheses." Gazette 22: 106–114.
HEINE-GELDERN, R. (1967) "Cultural diffusion," in International Encyclopedia of the Social Sciences. New York: Macmillan.
HESTER, A. L. (1973) "International information flow." Gazette 19, 4.
HIGGINS, B. (1977) "Economic development and cultural change: seamless web or patchwork quilt?" Economic Development and Cultural Change. Vol. 25 supplement, pp. 99–122.
HIRSCH, P. M. (1971) "Sociological approaches to the pop music phenomenon." American Behavioral Scientist 14: 371–388.
HOGGART, R. (1967) "Television and its place in mass culture," in International Encyclopedia of the Social Sciences. New York: Macmillan.
HORNIK, R. (1977) "Mass media use and the 'revolution of rising frustrations': a reconsideration of the theory." Communication Research 4: 387–414.
HOUN, F. W. (1961) To Change A Nation. New York: Macmillan.
HOWELL, N. J., Jr. (1979) "Ireland's second television channel: seeking national culture and viewer choice." Journalism Quarterly 56: 77–86.
HSU, C.-S. (1977) "Communication revolution and the Republic of China." Chung Ho Monthly (in Chinese) (November): 63–64.
_____ (1972) "Electronic media in the Republic of China." (unpublished).
_____ S. J. YANG, and J.-C. PANG (1975) Communication Behavior of Residents in Taiwan. Taipei: National Chengchi University Graduate School of Journalism (Monograph, in Chinese).
_____ S. J. YANG and J. C. PANG (1976) The Process of Mass Communication and Audience Processes in Taiwan. Taipei: National Chengchi University Graduate School of Journalism (Monograph, in Chinese, 2 vol.).
HSU, K.-Y. (1975) The Chinese Literary Scene: A Writer's Visit to People's Republic. New York: Vintage.
HU, S.-H. (1977) "An analysis of current broadcasting in Communist China." Pao Hsueh (in Chinese) 5, 8: 121–130.
HUAI-YU (1977) "Broadcasting in Communist China." Studies on Chinese Communism (in Chinese) 11, 3: 73–78.
HUANG, M. (1976) Intellectual Ferment For Political Reforms in Taiwan, 1971–1973 (Michigan papers in Chinese studies No. 28). Ann Arbor: University of Michigan Center for Chinese Studies.
HULL, W. H. N. (1962) "The public control of broadcasting: the Canadian and Australian experiences." Canadian Journal of Economics and Political Science 28: 114–126.
HULTEN, O. (1973) "The INTELSAT system: some notes on television utilization of satellite technology." Gazette 19: 29–37.
HUNTINGTON, S. P. (1968) Political Order in Changing Societies. New Haven: CT: Yale University Press.
INKELES, A. and D. SMITH (1974) Becoming Modern. Cambridge, MA: Harvard University Press.
Iran Communication and Development Institute (1977) "Modernization revisted—an interview with Daniel Lerner." Communications and Development Review, 1, 2–3: 4–6.
JACOBS, B. J. (1973) "Taiwan 1972: political season." Asian Survey 13, 1.
JAMISON, D. T. and E. G. McANANY (1978) Radio for Education and Development. Beverly Hills, CA: Sage.

JOHANSEN, P. W. (1973) "The CRTC and Canadian content regulation." Journal of Broad-casting 17: 465–474.

JOWETT, G. (1976) Film: The Democratic Art. Boston: Little, Brown.

KATZ, E. (1977) Social Research on Broadcasting: Proposals for Further Development. London: BBC.

———— (1973) "Television as a horseless carriage," in G. Gerbner et al. (eds.) Communication Technology and Social Policy. New York: John Wiley.

———— (1971) "Television comes to the people of the book," in I. L. Horowitz (ed.) The Use and Misuse of Social Science. New Brunswick, NJ: Transaction Books.

———— and D. FOULKES (1962) "On the use of the mass media as 'escape': clarification of a concept." Public Opinion Quarterly 26: 377–388.

———— and D. SHINAR (1975) The Role of Broadcasting in National Development: Thailand Case Study. Jerusalem: Hebrew University Communications Institute. (mimeo).

———— and M. GUREVITCH (1976) The Secularization of Leisure: Culture and Communication in Israel. Cambridge, MA: Harvard University Press.

———— and G. WEDELL (1977) Broadcasting in the Third World: Promise and Performance. Cambridge, MA: Harvard University Press.

KATZMAN, N. (1974) "The impact of communication technology: promises and prospects." Journal of Communication 24: 47–58.

KELMAN, H. C. (1961) "Processes of opinion change." Public Opinion Quarterly 25: 57–78.

KINCAID, D. L., H.-J. PARK, K.-K. CHUNG, and C.-C. LEE (1975) Mothers' Clubs and Family Planning in Rural Korea: The Case of Oryu Li. (Case Study, No. 2). Honolulu: East-West Communication Institute.

KING, A. Y. C. (1978) From Tradition to Modernity (in Chinese). Taipei: Chung Kuo Shih Pao Press.

———— (1977) "A voluntarist model of organization: the Maoist version and its critique." British Journal of Sociology 28, 3: 363–374.

KLINE, F. G. (1976) "Policy options for protection of the Canadian Broadcasting System." Ottawa: Department of Communications, Social Policy and Programs Branch. (mimeo)

———— K. KENT, and D. DAVIS (1971) "Problems in causal analysis of aggregate data with applications to political instability," in J. V. Gillespie and B. A. Nesvold (eds.) Macro-Quantitative Analysis. Beverly Hills, CA: Sage.

KRASNOW, E. G. and L. D. LONGLEY (1978) The Politics of Broadcast Regulation. New York: St. Martin's.

KRESSLEY, K. (1978) "East-West communication in Europe: the television nexus." Communication Research 5: 71–86.

LALL, S. (1975) "Is 'dependence' a useful concept in analyzing underdevelopment?" World Development 3: 799–810.

LAZARSFELD, P. F. and R. K. MERTON (1949) "Mass communication, popular taste, and organized social action," in L. Bryson (ed.) The Communication of Ideas. New York: Institute for Religious and Social Studies.

LeDUC, D. R. (1976) "Cable TV control in Canada: a comparative policy study." Journal of Broadcasting 20: 435–450.

LEE, J. A. R. (1976) Towards Realistic Communication Policies. Reports and papers on mass communication (No. 76). Paris: UNESCO Press.

LEE, T. C. (1976) "Comments on the broadcasting and television law." Radio and Television (in Chinese) 29: 29–31.

———— (1975) Media Policies in Taiwan (in Chinese). Taipei: Association of Journalists.

_____(1973) Comparative Television System: Direction of the Development of Chinese Television (in Chinese). Taipei: National Chengchi University.

_____(1970) "The fundamental spirit of the proposed broadcasting act." Pao Hsueh (in Chinese) 4, 4: 14–27.

LENIN, N. (1952) "Imperialism: a special stage of capitalism," in Selected Works. Moscow: Foreign Languages Publishing House.

LENT, J. A. (1978) Broadcasting in Asia and the Pacific. Philadelphia: Temple University Press.

_____(1976) "Commonwealth Caribbean mass media." The Democratic Journalist (October): 8–11.

_____(1975) "Government policies reshape Malaysia's diverse media." Journalism Quarterly 52: 663–669, 734.

_____(1972) Philippine Mass Communications. Manila: Philippine Press Institute.

_____(1970) "Philippine media and Nation-building: an overview." Gazette 16: 2–12.

LERNER, D. (1967a) "Communication and the prospects of innovative development," in D. Lerner and W. Schramm (eds.) Communication and Change in the Developing Countries. Honolulu: University of Hawaii/East-West Center Press.

_____(1967b) "International cooperation and communication in national development," in D. Lerner and W. Schramm (eds.) Communication and Change in the Developing Countries. Honolulu: University of Hawaii/East-West Center Press.

_____(1963) "Toward a Communication theory of Modernization," in Lucian W. Pye (ed.) Communications and Political Development. Princeton, NJ: Princeton University Press

_____(1958) The Passing of Traditional Society. New York: Macmillan.

_____and W. SCHRAMM [eds.] (1967) Communication and Change in the Developing Countries. Honolulu: University of Hawaii/East-West Center Press.

_____and L. NELSON [eds.] (1977) Communication Research—A Half-Century Appraisal. Honolulu: University of Hawaii/East-West Center Press.

LEYS, S. (1978) Chinese Shadows. Harmondsworth: Penguin.

LICHTHEIM, G. (1974) Imperialism. Harmondsworth: Penguin.

LIPSET, S. M. (1965) "Revolution and counter-revolution —the United States and Canada," in T. R. Ford (ed.) The Revolution Theme in Contemporary America. Lexington: University of Kentucky Press.

LITVAK, I. and C. MAULE (1974) Cultural Sovereignty: The Time and Reader's Digest Case in Canada, New York: Praeger.

LIU, A. P. L. (1971) Communication and National Integration in Communist China. Berkeley: University of California Press.

Maclean Hunter Research Bureau (1977) A Report on Advertising Revenues in Canada. Toronto: Author.

MAO TSE-TUNG (1977) Selected Works. Vol. 5. Peking: Foreign Language Press.

_____(1969) Selected Works. Vol. 4. Peking: Foreign Language Press.

_____(1965) Selected Works. Vol. 1–3. Peking: Foreign Language Press.

McBEATH, G. (1978) "Taiwan in 1977: holding the reins." Asian Survey 18: 17–28.

McCORMACK, T. (1969) "Folk culture and the mass media." European Journal of Sociology 10: 220–237.

McCRONE, D. J. and C. F. CNUDDE (1967) "Towards a communications theory of democratic political development: a causal model." American Political Science Review 61: 72–79.

McQUAIL, D. (ed.) (1972) Sociology of Mass Communication. Harmondsworth: Penguin.

MARCUSE, H. (1969) "Repressive Tolerance" in R. Wolff et al., A Critique of Pure Tolerance. Boston: Beacon.

MELODY, W. (1973) Children's Television: The Economics of Exploitation. New Haven, CT: Yale University Press.

MENDAL, D. (1970) The Politics of Formosan Nationalism. Berkeley: University of California Press.

MILLER, R. E. (1973) "The CRTC: guardian of the Canadian identity." Journal of Broadcasting, 17: 189–200.

MILLS, C. W. (1962) The Marxists. New York: Dell.

MOORE, B. Jr. (1966) Social Origins of Dictatorship and Democracy. Boston: Beacon.

MORTON, W. L. (1965) The Canadian Identity. Madison: University of Wisconsin Press.

MOU, S. Y. (1971) "The process of formulating the broadcasting and television law." Radio and Television (in Chinese) 29: 14–21.

MURDOCK, G. and P. GOLDING (1977) "Capitalism, communication and class relations," in J. Curran et al. (eds.) Mass Communication and Society. London: Arnold.

MURRAY, J. and M. C. GERACE (1972) "Canadian attitudes toward the U.S. presence." Public Opinion Quarterly 36: 388–397.

MURRAY, J. A. and L. LeDUC (1976–1977) "Public opinion and foreign policy options in Canada." Public Opinion Quarterly 40: 488–496.

NAM, S. and I. OH (1973) "Press freedom: function of subsystem autonomy, antithesis of development." Journalism Quarterly 50: 744–750.

NATHAN, A. J. (1979) "Mass mobilization and political participation in China." Unpublished paper, East-West Communication Institute.

NIELSEN, R. P. (1976) "International marketing public policy: U.S. penetration of the Canadian television program market." Columbia Journal of World Business 11: 130–139.

———— and A. B. NIELSEN (1976) "Canadian TV content regulation and U.S. cultural 'overflow.'" Journal of Broadcasting 20: 461–466.

NISBET, R. A. (1969) Social Change and History. New York: Oxford University Press.

NORDENSTRENG, K. and T. VARIS (1974) Television Traffic—A One-Way Street? Reports and papers on mass communication (No. 70). Paris: UNESCO Press.

———— (1973) "The nonhomogeneity of national state and the international flow of communication," in G. Gerbner et al. (eds.) Communication Technology and Social Policy. New York: John Wiley.

NORDENSTRENG, K. and H. I. SCHILLER [eds.] (1979) National Sovereignity and International Communication. Norwood, NJ: Ablex.

NOVE, A. (1974) "On reading Andre Gunder Frank." Journal of Developing Studies 10: 445–455.

OKSENBERG, M. [ed.] (1973) China's Developmental Experience. New York: Praeger.

ORLIK, P. B. (1970) "South Africa: how long without TV?" Journal of Broadcasting 14: 245–258.

OWEN, B. M., J. H. BEEBE, and W. G. MANNING, Jr. (1974) Television Economics, Lexington, MA: D. C. Heath.

OWENS, E. and R. SHAW (1974) Development Reconsidered: Bridging the Gap Between Government and the People. Lexington, MA: Heath.

PACKENHAM, R. (1973) Liberal America and the Third World. Princeton, NJ: Princeton University Press.

PAULU, B. (1978) "United Kingdom: quality with control." Journal of Communication 28, 3: 52–58.

———— (1974) Radio and Television Broadcasting in Eastern Europe. Minneapolis: University of Minnesota Press.

PEERS, F. W. (1975) "Canadian media regulation," in G. J. Robinson and D. F. Theall (eds.) Studies in Canadian Communications. Montreal: McGill University Printing Service.

_____(1969) The Politics of Canadian Broadcasting, 1920–1951. Toronto: University of Toronto Press.

POOL, I. de SOLA (1977) "The changing flow of television." Journal of Communication 27: 139–149.

_____(1974a) "The rise of communications policy research." Journal of Communication 24: 31–42.

_____(1974b) "Direct broadcasting satellites and the integrity of national culture," in Control of the Direct Broadcast Satellite: Values in Conflict. Palo Alto: Aspen Institute, Program on Communication and Society.

_____(1973) "Communication in totalitarian societies," in I. de Sola Pool and W. Schramm (eds.) Handbook of Communication. Chicago: Rand-McNally.

_____and W. Schramm [eds.] (1973), Handbook of Communication. Chicago: Rand McNally.

PORTES, A. (1976) "On the sociology of national development: theories and issues." American Journal of Sociology 82: 55–85.

_____(1974) "Modernity and development: a critique." Studies in Comparative International Development 9: 247–279.

_____(1973) "The factorial structure of modernity: empirical replications." American Journal of Sociology 79: 15–44.

PYE, L. W. (1978) "Communication and Chinese political culture." Asian Survey 18, 3: 221–246.

_____[ed.] (1963) Communication and Political Development. Princeton, NJ. Princeton University Press.

RAO, Y. V. L. (1963) Communication and Development: A Study of Two Indian Villages. Minneapolis: University of Minnesota Press.

RAHIM, S. A. (1976) Communication and Rural Development in Bangladesh. (Case Study No. 3). Honolulu: East-West Communication Institute.

READ, W. (1976) America's Mass Media Merchants. Baltimore: Johns Hopkins University Press.

RICHSTAD, J. [ed.] (1977) New Perspectives in International Communication. Honolulu: East-West Communication Institute.

ROBINSON, G. J. and D. F. THEALL [eds.] (1975) Studies in Canadian Communications. Montreal: McGill University Printing Service.

ROGERS, E. M. (1976) "Communication and development: the passing of the dominant paradigm." Communication Research 3: 213–240.

_____(1974) Communication Strategies for Family Planning. New York: Macmillan.

_____(1973) "Communication for development in China and India: the case of health and family planning at the village level." Unpublished paper, East-West Communication Institute.

ROGERS, E. M. with L. SVENNING (1969) Modernization Among Peasants: The Impact of Communication. New York: Holt, Rinehart & Winston.

ROGERS, E. M. and F. SHOEMAKER (1971) Communication of Innovations. New York: Macmillan.

ROLING, N. G., J. ASCROFT, and F. WA CHEGE (1976) "The diffusion of innovations and the issue of equity in rural development," Communication Research 3: 155–170.

ROMANOW, W. I. (1976) "A developing Canadian identity: a consequence of defensive regulatory posture for broadcasting." Gazette 22: 26–37.

ROSENBERG, B. and D. M. WHITE [eds.] (1971) Mass Culture Revisited. New York: Nostrand Reinhold.

———— [eds.] (1957) Mass Culture. New York: Macmillan.

SALINAS, R. and L. PALDAN (1979) "Culture in the process of dependent development: theoretical perspectives," in K. Nordenstreng and H. I. Schiller (eds.) National Sovereignty and International Communication. Norwood, NJ: Ablex.

SCHILLER, H. I. (1977) "The imposition of communications domination: genesis of the free flow of information principles," Democratic Journalist (April): 7–13.

———— (1976) Communication and Cultural Domination. White Plains, NY: International Arts and Sciences Press.

———— (1973) The Mind Managers. Boston: Beacon.

———— (1969) Mass Communication and American Empire. New York: Kelly.

———— (1967) "National development requires some social distance." Antioch Review 27: 63–75.

SCHRAM, S. [ed.] (1974) Mao Tse-tung Unrehearsed. Harmondsworth: Penguin.

SCHRAMM, W. (1977) Big Media, Little Media. Beverly Hills, CA: Sage.

———— (1964) Mass Media and National Development. Palo Alto, CA: Stanford University Press.

———— and D. LERNER [eds.] (1976) Communication and Change: The Last Ten Years—And the Next. Honolulu: University of Hawaii/East-West Center Press.

SCHUMPETER, J. (1951) The Theory of Economic Development. Cambridge, MA: Harvard University Press.

SCHWARTZ, M. (1967) Public Opinion and Canadian Identity. Berkeley: University of California Press.

SHAPLEN, R. (1977) "Letter from Taiwan." New Yorker (June 3): 72–95.

SHERMAN, C. E. and J. RUBY (1974) "The Eurovision news exchange." Journalism Quarterly 51: 478–485.

SHERMAN, C. E. and D. BROWNE [eds.] (1976) Issues in International Broadcasting. Washington, DC: Broadcast Education Association.

SHILS, E. A. (1967) "The intellectuals," in International Encyclopedia of the Social Sciences. New York: Macmillan.

SHINGI, P. M. and B. MODY (1976) "The communication effects gap: a field experiment on television and agricultural ignorance in India." Communication Research 3: 171–190.

SIGNITZER, B. (1976) Regulation of Direct Broadcasting from Satellites: The U.N. Involvement. New York: Praeger.

SINGER, B. [ed.] (1975) Communication in Canadian Society. Toronto: Copp Clark.

———— (1973) "Mass media and the transformation of minority identity," British Journal of Sociology 24: 140–150.

SKOCPOL, T. (1977) "Wallerstein's world capitalist system: a theoretical and historical critique." American Journal of Sociology 82: 1075–1090.

SMYTHE, D. (1973) "Mass communications and cultural revolution: the experience of China," in G. Gerbner et al. (eds.) Communication Technology and Social Policy. New York: John Wiley.

SNOW, M. S. (1976) International Commercial Satellite Communications: Economic and Political Issues of the First Decade of INTELSAT. New York: Praeger.

SOMMERLAD, E. L. (1975) National Communication Systems: Some Policy Issues and Options. Reports and papers on mass communication (No. 74). Paris: UNESCO.

SPAIN, P. L., D. T. JAMISON, and E. G. McANANY [eds.] (1977) Radio for Education and Development: Case Studies (Staff working paper 266; 2 vol.). Washington, DC: World Bank.

SPARKES, V. M. (1976) "Community cablecasting in the U.S. and Canada." Journal of Broadcasting 20: 451–460.

Starch, INRA, Hooper and International Advertising Association (1976) World Advertising Expenditures. New York: Author.

STEPHENSON, J. B. (1968) "Is everyone going modern? A critique and a suggestion for measuring modernism." American Journal of Sociology 74: 265–275.

STEPHENSON, W. (1967) A Play Theory of Mass Communication. Chicago: University of Chicago Press.

STINCHCOMBE, A. L. (1968) Constructing Social Theories. New York: Harcourt Brace Jovanovich.

SUINE, K. and F. G. KLINE (1975) "Communication, Mass Political Behavior, and Mass Society," in S. H. Chaffee (ed.) Political Communication. Beverly Hills, CA: Sage.

SUSSMAN, L. R. (1978) "Mass news media and the Third World challenge," in Sage Papers in Communications (480046). Beverly Hills, CA: Sage.

Taiwan, Television Academy of Arts and Sciences of the Republic of China (1978) Television Yearbook of the Republic of China, 1967–1977. Taipei: Author.

_____ (1976) Television Yearbook of the Republic of China, 1961–1975. Taipei: Author.

Taiwan, Executive Yuan (1977a) Taiwan Statistical Data Book. Taipei: Economic Planning Council.

Taiwan, Executive Yuan (1977b) The Republic of China Yearbook. Taipei: Government Information Office.

Taiwan, Executive Yuan (1977c) The rules regulating enterprises supplying broadcasting and television programs; the rules regulating responsible personnel and staff members of the broadcasting and television enterprises. Taipei: Government Information Office.

TEHRANIAN, M., F. HAKIMZADEH, and M. L. VIDALE [eds.] (1977) Communication Policy for National Development. A comparative Perspective. Boston: Routledge & Kegan Paul.

TICHENOR, P., G. A. DONOHUE, and C. N. OLIEN (1970) "Mass media flow and differential growth in knowledge." Public Opinion Quarterly 34: 159–170.

TILLY, C. (1975) "Western state-making and theories of political transformation," in C. Tilly (ed.) The Formation of National States in Western Europe. Princeton, NJ: Princeton University Press.

TING, W. [ed.] (1973) A Compilation of Press Articles on Peking's News Policy During the Cultural Revolution (in Chinese). Hong Kong: Chinese University Press.

TIPPS, D. C. (1973) "Modernization theory and the comparative study of societies: a critical perspective." Comparative Studies in Society and History 15: 199–226.

TOOGOOD, A. (1971) "The Canadian broadcasting system: search for a definition." Journalism Quarterly 48: 331–336.

TSOU, T. (1977) "Mao Tse-tung thought, the last struggle for succession, and the post-Mao era." China Quarterly 71: 498–527.

TUNSTALL, J. (1977) The Media Are American: Anglo-American Media In the World. New York: Columbia University Press.

U.S. House of Representatives (1974) United States-Canadian Broadcasting Relations. Hearing Before the Subcommittee on Inter-American Affairs of the Committee on Foreign Affairs, April 25. Washington, DC: Government Printing Office.

U.S. Senate, Select Committee Study (1975) Covert Action in Chile 1963–1973. Staff Report of the Select Committee to Study Governmental Operations with Respect to Intelligence Activities. Washington DC: Government Printing Office.

VERNON, R. (1971) Sovereignty At Bay. New York: Basic Books.

———— (1966) "International investment and international trade in the product life cycle." Quarterly Journal of Economics 80: 190–207.

WALLERSTEIN, I. (1976) "Semi-peripheral countries and the contemporary world crisis." Theory and Society 3: 461–484.

———— (1974a) The Modern World System. New York: Academic.

———— (1974b) "The rise and future demise of the world capitalist system." Comparative Studies in Society and History 16: 387–415.

WANG, C. H. (1977) Television, Television (in Chinese). Taipei: Yuan-Cheng.

WANG, H. C. (1976) "A critique on the spirit of the broadcasting and television law." Radio and Television (in Chinese) 29: 25–28.

WEAR, D. D., Jr. (1977) "French television and radio loosen ties with government—adding some new concern." Television/Radio Age (April 11): A25–35.

WEDELL, E. G. (1968) Broadcasting and Public Policy. London: Joseph.

WEIR, E. A. (1965) The Struggle for National Broadcasting in Canada. Toronto: McCllelland & Stewart.

WEISS, E. F. (1974) "Tearing the fabric of Canada: the broadcast media and Canadian identity." Presented to the Mass Communications and Society Division of the Association for Education in Journalism, San Diego.

WEISSKOPF, T.(1976) "Dependence as an explanation of underdevelopment." Presented to the Sixth National Meeting of Latin American Studies Association, Atlanta, March 25–28.

WELLS, A. F. (1972) Picture-Tube Imperialism? The Impact of U.S. Television on Latin America. Maryknoll, NY: Orbis.

WHITING, G. C. and J. D. STANFIELD (1972) "Mass media use and opportunity structure in rural Brazil." Public Opinion Quarterly 36: 56–68.

WHYTE, M. K. (1974) Small Groups and Political Rituals in China. Berkeley: University of California Press.

———— (1973) "Bureaucracy and modernization in China: the Maoist Critique." American Journal of Sociology 38.

WILENSKY, H. L. (1964) "Mass society and mass culture: interdependence or independence?" American Sociological Review 29: 173–193.

WILLIAMS, R. (1976) Keyword: A Vocabulary of Culture and Society. New York: Oxford University Press.

———— (1975) Television: Technology and Cultural Form. New York: Schocken.

WOLF, E. R. (1969) Peasant Wars of the Twentieth Century. New York: Harper & Row.

WU, E. K. (1976) "News editing and reporting at Chiehfung Jihpao," Asian Messenger 1, 2: 18–19.

YEN, P. C. (1977a) "Television may rise to be No. 1 advertising medium." Radio and Television (in Chinese) 31: 26–31.

———— (1977b) "Advertising surpassed U.S.$100 million last year." Chung Yang Jih Pao (in Chinese) February 23.

———— (1976) "The growth of broadcasting advertising in 1975–1976." Radio and Television (in Chinese) 29: 35–40.

———— (1974) A Study of Advertising Volume in Taiwan (in Chinese). Taipei: Hua-Hsin.

YU, F. T. C. (1979) "China's mass communication in historical perspective," in G. C. Chu and F. L. K. Hsu (eds.) Moving a Mountain: Cultural Change in China. Honolulu: University of Hawaii/East-West Center Press.

———— (1977) "Communication policy and planning for development: some notes on research." in D. Lerner and L. Nelson (eds.) Communication Research—A Half-Century Appraisal. Honolulu: University of Hawaii/East-West Center Press.

_____ (1967) "Campaigns, communications and development in Communist China," in D. Lerner and W. Schramm (eds.) Communication and Change in the Developing Countries. Honolulu: University of Hawaii/East-West Center Press.

_____ (1964) Mass Persuasion in Communist China. New York: Praeger.

Without a proper theory, research about media imperialism lacks a fruitful future. Without a theory, "media imperialism" may end up as a pseudo-concept. Fred Fejes, an assistant professor of communication at Wayne State University, is thus concerned about the development of the study of media imperialism. One way of studying this aspect of international communication is to tie it to a dependency approach, which offers a broad context for the study of the relations between, for example, developing and developed countries. But social researchers in the field seem to be ignorant about the work of communication researchers, and communication researchers seldom relate to other forms of developmental studies. Media imperialism studies should pay more attention to the historical dimension, to culture and to forms of communication other than mass media, Fejes argues. But his most urgent demand seems to be that of a theory, and not a narrow one but a broad "conceptual framework, a set of concepts, hypothesized linkages and above all an optic that attempts to locate and clarify a wide range of problems."

18

MEDIA IMPERIALISM

An Assessment

Fred Fejes

Within the last ten years, the view of what is important in global communications and of the rôle modern communications play in the development of Third World countries has undergone a drastic change. While during the 1960s communication researchers focused on ways in which modern media could assist in the social development of the nations of Africa, Latin America and Asia, this last decade has witnessed the emergence of an approach to the study of communications and development which has an entirely different perspective and evaluation of the rôle of modern communications. Although there is by no means complete agreement, the term 'media imperialism' is frequently used to describe the concerns of this new approach. While there have been several attempts to give this term some conceptual precision (Boyd-Barret, 1977; Lee, 1980; Tunstall, 1977), on the whole it still remains vague as an analytical concept. For the purposes of this discussion, media imperialism shall be used in a broad and general manner to describe the processes by which modern communication media have operated to create, maintain and expand systems of domination and dependence on a world scale.

As has been noted by others (Nordenstreng and Schiller, 1979; Cruise O'Brien, 1979), the media imperialism approach evolved in an attempt to deal with those questions and areas of concern which earlier communication models and thinking generally ignored. In contrast to earlier models which focused on the national level and on social psychological factors in order to determine the ways in which modern communications media could help accelerate the process of development and modernization, the media imperialism approach is based on 'an emphasis on global structure, whereby it is precisely the international socio-political system that decisively determines the course of development within the sphere of each nation' (Nordenstreng and Schiller, 1979: 7) Whereas earlier models viewed modern communications media as a 'tool' for development, the media imperialism approach viewed the media, situated as they were in a transnational context, as an obstacle to meaningful and well balanced socio-economic progress. Seen in a larger context, the growth of the media imperialism approach is one reflection of the general critical assessment and rejection by many Third World countries of Western models of modernization of which the earlier communication models were a part, a development which has produced calls for a 'New International Information Order' as an essential component of a 'New International Economic Order'.

The major thrust and greatest accomplishment of the work undertaken within the media imperialism approach so far has been an empirical description of the manner in which communications media operate on a global level. As reflected, for example, in works by Schiller (1971), Mattelart (1979), Varis (1973) and many others, the research in this area on the whole tends to focus on the operatior of transnational agents, either transnational corporations or transnational media industries, and their rôle in the structuring and flow of media products at an international level. Such works attempt to describe in detail the manner in which such transnational agents dominate the international structure and flow of communications. Yet while at the empirical level there has been much progress dealing with the concerns of media imperialism, such progress has not been matched at the theoretical level (Mosco and Herman, 1979; Subveri, 1979). Although there have been individual attempts to formulate and analyse media imperialism as a 'theory' (Boyd-Barret, 1977; Lee, 1980), on the whole the development of media imperialism as a theoretical approach, in contrast to empirical descriptions of concrete examples of media imperialism, has not formed an important element of the agenda of work in this area.

This, of course, should not imply that the empirical progress achieved thus far is of any less value. In contrast to the common complaint that radical and critical researchers and scholars overemphasize the development of a theoretical exactness to the point of irrelevance, the work done on media imperialism, because of its empirical nature, has been eminently clear, accessible and relevant, characteristics which account for the dissemination of its ideas over a wide audience. Nonetheless, it must be recognized that the lack of an explicit and well formulated theoretical basis involves dangers. Without any type of accepted theoretical framework, one is unable to formulate a research agenda, distinguishing those questions and issues that are important and need to be pursued from those less important or that have been over-studied, thus moving the field in general from mere replication of previous work to the breaking of new grounds. Without theory delineating the bounds of explanation, there is the danger of media imperialism becoming a pseudo-concept, something which can be used to explain everything in general about the media in developing countries and hence nothing in particular. Most importantly, without theory, there is lacking the critical standpoint and set of standards and concepts by which one can judge and evaluate the research efforts which deal with the issues raised by this approach. A good example of this last point is William Read's study *America's Mass Media Merchants* (1976). As an empirical work the subject of this study—the expansion of American media overseas—falls within the concerns of the media imperialism approach. But the study's overall purpose and conclusion—to demonstrate that 'through the market place system by which America's mass media merchants communicate with foreign consumers, both parties enjoy different, but useful benefits' (Read, 1976: 181)—is diametrically opposed to the central thrust of the previous work done in this area. Read's study aptly demonstrates how, lacking an explicit theoretical foundation, the critical outlook that motivated the early progress of this approach can be diluted and its concerns coopted.

To say, however, that media imperialism researchers lack a developed theory does not mean that they do not work within the context of some underlying theoretical concepts and notions. In one sense the research on media imperialism can be situated within the broad tradition of a Marxist critique of capitalism in that in the global growth of western communications media researchers see a reflection of the general imperialist expansion of Western capitalist societies. Yet it is mistaken to label this approach Marxist in any detailed and precise sense of the word. While the motivation and sources behind the work on media imperialism are varied, such work perhaps can be better understood both as a research approach and as a theoretical endeavor by putting it in the larger context of the work and thinking done on the questions and problems of Third World development in general over the past decade. Earlier models of the rôle of communications in the developmental process of course were formulated in the context of more general models of development that defined the entire process as one of 'modernization'. Within the last ten years, however, such general models have been challenged by a different view of the development process. The new view has been generally termed the dependency model. The impact and success of the dependency model in reshaping thinking and work on Third World development has been so fundamental that some commentators see in the emergence of this new model and its replacement of earlier notions of development an example of a Kuhnian social scientific revolution (Valenzuela and Valenzuela, 1979). As the emergence and growth of the media imperialism approach can thus be seen as one aspect of the larger change in development thinking that has occurred with the appearance of the dependency model, some of the basic theoretical notions that underlie the media imperialism approach can be best articulated and understood by presenting a brief overview of the major points of the dependency model.

While the history of the dependency model and a detailed exposition of its argument has been presented elsewhere (see Chilcote and Edelstein, 1974; Portes, 1976, Cardoso, 1977; Valenzuela and Valenzuela, 1979), it is important to note that the dependency model is radically different with regards both to its assumptions and its analysis of the problems of development than prior theories of modernization. While the modernization theories focused on the internal processes of development and of the rôle of social values, the dependency theory proceeds from an analysis of the relationships between developed and under-developed countries and examines the developmental problems of the Third World in terms of these relationships. Its major conclusion is that the Third World countries occupy a subordinate position in the international economic and political systems which are seen as being structured primarily according to the needs of the developed countries. Developed countries maintain their dominant position and continue their own process of development at the expense of the developmental needs of the Third World countries. The penetration of Third World countries by multinational corporations, the political objectives and foreign aid policies of developed countries, the subordinate position of Third World countries in the international market and credit system, all are seen as aspects of the dependency phenomenon. Just as important, dependency relationships are seen as reproducing themselves in the structure of internal relationships. Underdeveloped countries are seen as being polarized between the urban sector, whose interests are often allied with the developed countries, and the rural sector which exists in an exploitative relationship to the urban sector. As a result of this overall structure of dependency, Third World countries are seen as having little chance of achieving self-sustained internal growth or modernization in the Western sense as presumed by the previous developmental models. Indeed as Third World countries remain within this system over time they encounter increasingly serious internal difficulties and a deterioration of their position in international trade and finance.

While earlier theories of modernization can be viewed as by-products of classical

Western social theory which stressed the evolutionary nature of the social developmental process and rôle of ideas and values, the dependency model, in contrast, can be seen as a counterpart of earlier theories of imperialism, particularly the Marxist-Leninist concept of imperialism, reformulated from the point of view of the underdeveloped countries (Portes, 1976). The implications of dependency models are likewise radically different. Effective national development comes to be interpreted as the 'liberation from dependency', a concept which could mean anything from the formation of Third World raw material cartels to revolutions of national liberation. The generally optimistic picture which was presented by previous theories of modernization and which assumed a basic mutuality of interest between developed and Third World countries has been confronted by an alternative theory of development that presents a pessimistic view of development and is based on a conflictual model of the world system.

Aside from noting briefly the major elements of the dependency approach, it is important to stress some additional aspects of the dependency model which are of direct relevance to an understanding and assessment of the work done under the media imperialism approach. First, rather than being a set of propositions that are universally valid, the dependency approach is based on an analysis of the particular historical context of dependent societies. The relationships of dependency can only be understood in the context of concrete historical situations. This then requires that an analysis be based on an examination of the specific historical forces and factors involved in a nation's incorporation into and situation within a system of extra-national relationships. Thus, in an attempt to understand the notion of dependency, one must be wary of talking about dependent societies or the relationships of dependency in general without specifying the concrete historical situation in which societies and relationships exist (Villamil, 1979).

A second important aspect of the dependency analysis is its emphasis on the rôle of extra-national forces and factors that create and support the maintainence of underdevelopment in the Third World. Particular importance is laid on the rôle that transnational corporations play in Third World countries (Sunkel and Fuenzalida, 1979). Yet, while in the present stage of the capitalist world economy, the transnational corporations are the dominant institution, the dependent condition of a particular nation cannot be regarded only in terms of the domination by transnational interests and other external forces and factors. The condition of dependency involves the dynamic relationship between internal factors such as a nation's class structure and history and external factors such as transnational corporations, international financial institutions and so on. Dependency analysis is essentially a dialectical analysis which stresses the complex manner in which internal and external factors operate over time. Underdevelopment and dependency are not simply the result of 'external constraints' on peripheral societies, nor can dependency be operationalized solely with reference to external factors (Valenzuela and Valenzuela, 1979). Fernando Cardoso, one of the major figures of the dependency school, has noted that in the dissemination of the dependency model, particularly in the United States, the attention to external variables—'the intervention of the CIA in foreign policy, the invisible and Machiavellian hand of the multinationals, etc.'—while justified and necessary, has come to assume priority over an understanding of the specific and historically situated internal factors that operate in the maintenance of the dependent status of peripheral societies (Cardoso, 1977: 14). This misplaced emphasis lends itself well to grand theories of conspiracy, but does little to develop an understanding of the complexities of Third World societies and their relations to the developed world.

A third aspect of the dependency approach is its theoretical status and methodology. The dependency approach does not pretend to be a precisely articulated model comprised of formal and testable propositions (Villamil, 1979). Rather it is more correctly, as noted by Richard Fagen (1977: 7), a 'way of framing' the problems of underdevelopment. Given the wide range of complex problems and relationships which the approach attempts to explore, isolating and narrowly defining a set of variables and relationships does violence to the dialectical interrelationships among the elements of dependency. It is a bias on behalf of such formalistic models which, while conforming well to North American ideas of social science, has resulted in the overemphasis on the external factors of dependency and the neglect of the factors operating at the national level and the dynamic movement that exists within the entire complex whole.

As is hopefully obvious, it is within the broad context of the dependency approach that most of the substantive concerns of communication scholars and researchers investigating media imperialism can be located. If one were to view the intellectual history of development thinking in the 1970s, one would conclude that the formulation of the media imperialism approach was, objectively speaking, developed as a corollary to the dependency model. Nonetheless, in spite of the great affinities that exist, there seems to be very little active interaction between social scientists doing work within the dependency approach and communication researchers doing work on media imperialism. Those working in sociology, economics and political science generally tend to be ignorant of the work of communication researchers in this area or even tend to dismiss communications as an unimportant element in the overall structures of dependency. Aside from an occasional perfunctory citation or quote from the works of someone like A. G. Frank, a dependency theorist whose work, written in English, is generally more accessible but should not be taken as the definitive statement of the dependency model (Valenzuela and Valenzuela, 1979), communication researchers likewise rarely explicitly acknowledge what is happening elsewhere in developmental studies. Of course there are exceptions. Social scientists such as Osvaldo Sunkel and Edmundo F. Fuenzalida, associated with the Institute of Development Studies at the University of Sussex, show a keen appreciation and knowledge of the issues of culture and communication and attempt to relate such issues to the larger concerns of dependency (Sunkel and Fuenzalida, 1975, 1979). The work of Ritu Cruise O'Brien, also associated with the Institute of Development Studies, provides an excellent example of how an awareness of the larger dimensions of dependency can inform a study of media imperialism (Cruise O'Brien, 1979). Salinas and Paldán (1979) have applied a dependency analysis to a discussion of culture in a dependent society. Lee (1980), basing himself primarily on the works of A. G. Frank, has used the dependency theory to discuss the theoretical and methodological aspects of the work on media imperialism.

Yet such work has made, as yet, little impact. It is unfortunately the case that many communication scholars, researchers and students address the topic of media imperialism with little or no acquaintance with the dependency approach and, failing to see the broad context in which media imperialism falls, make numerous mistakes and misinterpretations that could easily have been avoided. If progress is to be made in the study of media imperialism, it is necessary that those working in this area integrate their efforts into the larger framework of dependency analysis in order to draw upon its concepts, formulations and insights to inform their own work. Drawing from the above discussion of the dependency model, the following brief comments and assessments are offered about the present state of work on media imperialism to demonstrate how the dependency approach can both strengthen the work on media imperialism and point to new issues and areas which need to be explored.

As noted earlier, a major focus of the media imperialism approach has been on the rôle of transnational corporations or media interests in shaping communications between developed and Third World countries. While such a focus is, of course, a necessary corrective to earlier models of communication and development and does perform the very necessary task of establishing the over-whelming dominant rôle of transnational interests in world communications, such a focus nonetheless leads to an imbalanced perspective that views media imperialism as primarily the consequence of factors external to a dependent society. This tends to ignore, as noted above, the forces and factors operating on a national and local level that assist and react against the perpetuation of media imperialism and, more importantly, it tends to obscure the complex relationships and dynamics that exist among the external and internal factors and forces. Thus it is important that, under the rubric of the media imperialism approach, studies of transnational communicators and media be complemented with studies focusing on communications media and interests at the national level. Such studies would attempt to place the development and function of the various communications media in the context of the class and power dynamics that operate within a nation and in the context of that nation's status as a dependent society. For example, what groups control the media and to what ends are the communications and information media put; what rôle does a nation's media play in maintaining or changing the structure of power in society. Such questions need to be explored and then linked to an analysis of how that nation and its media is tied into the international system of domination and dependence. The need for such studies is all the more important given the movement among some Third World nations towards the intervention of the state through the formulation of national communication policies. To many observers at the international level, such a movement represents a progressive move to overcome the consequences of media imperialism. But can such a general assessment be valid if practically next to nothing is known about the factors and forces that operate at the national level?

Closely linked to the need for an analysis of internal factors and the dynamics between such factors and external forces and interest is the need for an analysis of media imperialism as an historical phenomenon, that is, how it exists in particular historical situations and periods. The media imperialism approach, tied as it is to the pressing concerns over current problems, does not have much to offer about the rôle of communications media in relations of domination and dependence prior to World War II. Yet it is important to place the study of media imperialism in a larger historical perspective, not only to give the approach more breadth and power, but also to reveal the extremely complex interrelationships that have existed over time between the development and expansion of communications media and the forces and factors associated with the relations of dominance and dependence. Only with knowledge of media imperialism as a concrete historical phenomenon operating in the larger context of domination, can one hope to assess and formulate effective and meaningful contemporary strategies to overcome it.

A third concern that the media imperialism approach must address if it is to progress is the issue of culture. While a great deal of the concern over media imperialism is motivated by a fear of the cultural consequences of the transnational media—of the threat that such media poses to the integrity and the development of viable national cultures in Third World societies—it is the one area where, aside from anecdotal accounts, little progress has been achieved in understanding specifically the cultural impact of transnational media on Third World societies. All too often the institutional aspects of transnational media receive the major attention while the cultural impact, which one assumes to occur, goes unaddressed in any detailed manner. Generally a perception of the cultural consequences of the content of various media products is based on a view of the mass media as primarily manipulative agents capable of having direct, unmediated effects on the audience's behavior and world view. No one, of course, can deny that the study of the cultural dimension of the media is one of the most difficult areas of communication studies. There is very little consensus as to the basic formulation of the questions to be asked, much less agreement on methods and criteria. In recent years there have been attempts to address the question of culture within the context of a dependency perspective, both in terms of the impact of media products and in terms of the broader impact that dependency has on the overall structure of human relationships within a dependent society (see, for example Dagnino, 1973; Sunkel and Fuenzalida, 1975; Schiller, 1976; Matterlart, 1978; Burton and Franco, 1978; Salinas and Paldán, 1979). As yet, however, no compelling formulation has emerged to guide future work. Nonetheless the issue of culture must be addressed. One avenue of research that shows hope of progress particularly to communication researchers is the work by literary scholars and some communication researchers which attempts to explicate the symbolic universe that is contained in the content of the mass media in dependent societies and relate this to the overall system of dependency (Dorfman and Mattelart, 1975; Kunzle, 1978, Flora and Flora, 1978). Generally such studies demonstrate how the relations of dominance–dependence are reproduced within the content of the popular media. Such works are useful to communication researchers in that they establish a baseline for the content of the media which enables researchers to say something about the products of the transnational media in dependent societies. The next step—going from a discussion of the content of the popular media to a study of its actual impact on the lives and human relationships of Third World populations—is, of course, an extremely difficult step that represents a major challenge.

Another necessary direction of advance is broadening the study of media imperialism from a primary focus on the mass media to an analysis of other communications and information media and associated questions and areas of concerns. In spite of the popular conception held by many communication researchers who address the topic, media imperialism is not simply the flow of particular products of the mass media such as television programs or news stories between the developed countries and Third World nations. Such a narrow view ignores or obscures many important dimensions of the process and misinterprets the basic concern. Fortunately, as shown by the works of Cruise O'Brien (1979) and Golding (1977) on the transference of communication technology and professional models, and of Schiller (1979) on transnational data flow, progress has already been made in defining and analysing media imperialism with the scope and breadth that the phenomenon requires. Such efforts must be continued and expanded.

Finally attention must be paid to the development of the media imperialism approach as a theoretical endeavor. As noted earlier, the lack of theoretical development that would match the empirical progress already achieved in this area endangers the underlying critical outlook and concern behind this work. Yet one should be very cautious in the construction of theoretical formulations. The basic question which the media imperialism approach should seek to explore both on a theoretical and empirical level is: how does modern communication—its media, its practices and its products—relate to the larger structures and dynamics of dependency. The theoretical formulation and the development of a specific methodology should match the breadth of this basic concern. An attempt to define either dependency and media imperialism as a precisely articulated model consisting of strictly defined variables and relationships totally distorts the basic notions behind these two areas of work. Attempting to reduce the notions of dependency and media imperialism to a set of narrow empirical propositions replaces the dynamism and organicism essential to these ideas with a set of formal, mechanistic relationships.

One must recognize that empirical social science as it has developed today is not equipped and does not have the tools to study the phenomenon of dependency or media imperialism in the manner in which these notions were originally conceived. Unfortunately the response by some in the social science community to this problem has been to redefine dependency and media imperialism in order to make them amenable to the available empirical techniques. Thus for some social scientists dependency is seen as a set of correlations between data and trade patterns between developed and Third World countries and levels of GNP. For some communication researchers, media imperialism is largely a question of how many episodes of *Kojak* are shown on Bolivian television. While such information is no doubt useful, and while not denying that there are numerous discreet aspects of both dependency and media imperialism that can be profitably examined in this manner, what is being studied through primary reliance on such narrow measures is not the phenomenon of dependency or media imperialism. In the attempt to move the study of media imperialism from detailed description to a concern with wider theoretical issues, it is necessary to eschew a narrow conception of what theory is and what it is supposed to do. It is far better to utilize the broad notion of the purpose and use of theory best described in Fagen's words, seeing a 'theory' of media imperialism as 'a conceptual framework, a set of concepts, hypothesized linkages, and above all an optic that attempts to locate and clarify a wide range of problems' (Fagen, 1977: 7). Hopefully in this manner, both the critical import of the notion of media imperialism and the complexity of the phenonemon which such a notion attempts to describe will be maintained and appreciated.

Bibliography

BOYD-BARRET, O. (1977). Media imperialism: towards an international framework for the analysis of media systems, in Curran, J., Gurevitch, M. and Woolacott, J. (eds) *Mass Communication and Society*, London, Arnold
BURTON, J. and FRANCO, J. (1978). Culture and imperialism, *Latin American Perspectives* vol. V, no. 2
CARDOSO, F. H. (1977). The consumption of dependency theory in the United States, *Latin American Research Review* vol. XII, no. 3

CHILCOTE, R. H. and EDELSTEIN, J. C. (1974). Introduction: alternative perspectives of development and underdevelopment in Latin America, in Chilcote, R. H. and Edlestein, J. C. (eds) *Latin America: The Struggle with Dependency and Beyond*, Cambridge, Mass., Schenkman

CRUISE O'BRIEN, R. (1979). Mass communications: social mechanisms of incorporation and dependence, in Villamil, J. J. (ed.) *Transnational Capitalism and National Development*, Atlantic Highlands, Humanities Press

DAGNINO, E. (1973). Cultural and ideological dependence: building a theoretical framework, in Bonilla, F. and Girling, R. (ed.) *Structures of Dependency*, East Palo Alto, Nairobi Bookstore

DORFMAN, A. and MATTELART, A. (1975). *How to read Donald Duck: Imperialist Ideology in a Disney Comic*, New York, International General

FAGEN, R. R. (1977). Studying latin American politics: some implications of the *Dependencia* approach, *Latin American Research Review* vol. XII, no. 2

FLORA, C. B. and FLORA, J. L. (1978). The fotonovela as a tool for class and cultural domination, *Latin American Perspectives*, vol. V, no. 2

GOLDING, P. (1977). Media professionalism in the Third World, in Curran, J., Gurevitch, M. and Woolacott, J. (eds) *Mass Communication and Society*, London, Arnold

KUNZLE, D. (1978). Chile's *La Firme* versus ITT, *Latin American Perspectives*, vol. V, no. 2

LEE, C. (1980). *'Media Imperialism' Reconsidered: The Homogenizing of Television Culture*, Beverly Hills, Sage

MATTELART, A. (1978). The nature of communications practice in a dependent society, *Latin American Perspectives* vol. V, no. 2

MATTELART, A. (1979). *Multinational Corporations and the Control of Culture*, Atlantic Highlands, Humanities Press

MOSCO, V. and HERMAN, A. (1979). Radical social theory and the communications revolution, paper presented to the Fourth Annual Conference on the Current State of Marxist Theory, University of Louisville, Louisville, Kentucky

NORDENSTRENG, K. and SCHILLER, H. I. (1979). Communication and national development: changing perspectives—introduction, in Nordenstreng, K. and Schiller, H. I. (eds) *National Sovereignty and International Communication*, Norwood, Ablex

PORTES, A. (1976). On the sociology of national development: theories and issues, *American Journal of Sociology*, vol. 82, no. 1

READ, W. (1976). *America's Mass Media Merchants*, Baltimore, Johns Hopkins University Press

SALINAS, R. and PALDAN, L. (1979). Culture in the process of dependent development: theoretical perspectives, in Nordenstreng, K. and Schiller, H. I. (eds) *National Sovereignty and International Communication*, Norwood, Ablex

SAUVANT, K. (1976). The potential of multinational enterprises as vehicles for the transmission of business culture, in Sauvant, K. and Lavipour, F. (eds) *Controlling Multinational Enterprises: Problems, Strategies, Counter-Strategies*, Boulder, Westview Press

SCHILLER, H. I. (1971). *Mass Communication and American Empire*, Boston, Beacon

SCHILLER, H. I. (1976). *Communication and Cultural Domination*, New York, International Arts and Sciences Press

SCHILLER, H. I. (1978). Computer systems: power for whom and for what? *Journal of Communication* vol. 28, no. 4

SUBVERI-VELEZ, F. A. (1979). The mass media as the dependent variable, xerox, Mass Communication Research Center, University of Wisconsin, Madison

SUNKEL, O. and FUENZALIDA, E. (1975). The effects of transnational corporations on culture, Institute of Development Studies at the University of Sussex

SUNKEL, O. and FUENZALIDA, E. F. (1979). Transnationalization and its national consequences, in Villamil, J. J. (ed.) *Transnational Capitalism and National Development*, Atlantic Highlands, Humanities Press

TUNSTALL, J. (1977). *The Media Are American*, New York, Columbia University Press

VALENZUELA, J. S. and VALENZUELA, A. (1979). Modernization and dependence: alternative perspectives in the study of Latin American underdevelopment, in Villamil, J. J. (ed.) *Transnational Capitalism and National Development*, Atlantic Highlands, Humanities Press

VARIS, T. (1973). *International Inventory of Television Programme Structure and the Flow of Programmes Between Nations*, University of Tampere, Finland

VILLAMIL, J. J. (1979). Introduction, in Villamil, J. J. (ed.) *Transnational Capitalism and National Development*, Atlantic Highlands, Humanities Press

PART III

ON TELEVISION

Television research is burgeoning, moving along new theoretical avenues with increased methodological diversity. Five articles on television research in this section represent the changing conceptual and methodological interests of scholars of television. Critical scholars such as Kellner are examining the institutional structures of monopolistic capitalist enterprises, such as network television, and relating such structures to the production of culture. Kellner's piece, however, is not a restatement of leftist dogma; rather, he challenges conventional Marxist critiques of the television industry for ignoring the inherent contradictions among the various roles network television plays in American society. His methodology is certainly critical and his analysis is unusual and informative.

Several of the authors examine television audiences. These studies, however, differ greatly from the large body of social-learning-theory research on television effects. The authors represented here do not direct their attention solely to behavioral effects of television—a much researched topic. Rather, these studies examine such wide-ranging audience interactions as the subjective motivations of television-audience viewers (several schools of thought assume audiences of television are passive; here, empirical evidence for such assumptions is provided) and the information-processing activities of child television viewers. Through highly controlled laboratory observations, Anderson and his colleagues examine the relationship between the children's abilities to comprehend the content of television programming and their attention to that content. In these studies, Anderson et al. challenge current notions of the major role of production features of programming as the major determinant of young children's attention.

Two studies also present arguments for the need for qualitative and observational research on television audiences. Lull's presentation of the usefulness of ethnographies of television viewing is both instructive and heuristic. Similarly, Messaris and Sarett present an argument for reevaluating the role of parent child interaction about television as a determinant of children's learning outcomes. They, too, recommend more qualitative approaches to such research.

This article reports on two experimental studies testing the hypothesis that preschoolers' attention to television is determined by the comprehensibility of the program being viewed. The findings reported here dispute the popular notion that young children's attention to TV is primarily determined by the fast pace and other visual and auditory production features of the programming. Daniel R. Anderson is associate professor in the Department of Psychology, University of Massachusetts. Elizabeth Pugzles Lorch, Diane Erickson Field, and Jeanne Sanders are doctoral students in the Department of Psychology at the University of Massachusetts.

19

THE EFFECTS OF
TV PROGRAM COMPREHENSIBILITY ON
PRESCHOOL CHILDREN'S VISUAL
ATTENTION TO TELEVISION

Daniel R. Anderson, Elizabeth Pugzles Lorch,
Diane Erickson Field, and Jeanne Sanders

It is popularly believed that young children's TV viewing is an essentially passive cognitive experience (e.g., Lesser 1977; Mander 1978; Winn 1977) An implicit assumption is that the young child's attention is captured by dynamic formal attributes of the medium (e.g., Bandura 1977; Huston-Stein & Wright, Note 1) leaving the viewer ". . . little more than a vessel of reception" (Mander 1978, p. 204). This conception of TV viewing has influenced educational TV program production. In the development of "Sesame Street" (Lesser 1974), for example, emphasis was placed on the use of formal attributes to attract the child's visual attention, the underlying notion being that attention is a necessary prerequisite to understanding and retention. Insofar as these ends have been accomplished, "Sesame Street" has also been criticized for leaving ". . . little time for the response and reflection . . ." necessary for retention, presumably because the children keep ". . . their eyes glued to the set . . ." (Singer & Singer 1979; also see Lesser 1977). Thus, in both the conception and critique of

"Sesame Street," the underlying assumption of the nature of TV viewing is that TV captures and holds attention by means of salient formal attributes leading to passive reception of content.

Recently Lorch, Anderson, and Levin (1979) reported a study which they interpreted as strongly casting doubt on this prevailing assumption. They showed "Sesame Street" to two groups of 5-year-olds: one group viewed without toys, and another group viewed with toys available. Visual attention to the TV in the no-toys group was double that of the toys group (87% vs. 44%). Following the viewing session, the children were tested for comprehension of the program. There was no significant difference in comprehension between the two groups, but there was a significant correlation between comprehension and attention within groups such that "those portions of the program which were most poorly understood received relatively low attention, whereas those portions which were better comprehended received relatively high attention." Lorch et al.

This research was supported by a grant from the National Science Foundation, by funds from Children's Television Workshop through a contract with the U.S. Office of Education, and by a Research Scientist Development Award to D. R. Anderson from the National Institute of Mental Health. We appreciate the assistance of Cynthia Moss and Rex Bradford. Requests for reprints should be addressed to Daniel R. Anderson, Department of Psychology, University of Massachusetts, Amherst, Massachusetts 01003.

From Daniel R. Anderson, Elizabeth Pugzles Lorch, Diane Erickson Field, and Jeanne Sanders, "The Effects of TV Program Comprehensibility on Preschool Children's Visual Attention to Television," *Child Development* 52 (March 1981), pp. 151-157. Reprinted by permission of the Society for Research in Child Development and the authors.

(1979) interpreted these results as indicating that variations in visual attention to the TV are caused in part by variations in the comprehensibility of the TV program. They suggested that young children's attention to television is not passive and involuntary, but instead reflects the development, with TV-viewing experience, of sophisticated strategies for optimally distributing visual attention to the most informative parts of the TV program. Formal attributes were interpreted as being effective insofar as they provide information to the child about the comprehensibility of the program (Alwitt, Anderson, Lorch, & Levin 1980; Lorch et al. 1979; Anderson & Lorch, Note 2). This point of view is, therefore, essentially the opposite of that implicit in the popular conception of TV viewing.

The Lorch et al. (1979) arguments are based in part on within-program positive correlations between visual attention and comprehension. It is possible that there is a natural correlation between attractive production techniques and comprehensibility such that the relation between attention and comprehension is an indirect product of professional TV production. Bryant, Hezel, and Zillman (1978), in fact, recently performed a content analysis of "Sesame Street" in which they noted that "apparently the producers of *Sesame Street* reserved . . . electronic embellishments of the basic messages for times when critical material was present" (p. 53).

The present studies are aimed at testing the hypothesis that variations in TV program comprehensibility cause variations in visual attention to television in young children. In the first study an a priori index of program comprehensibility—immediacy of dialogue—was related to visual attention. The second study experimentally reduced TV program comprehensibility while holding the nonsemantic formal attribute structure of the program constant. If young children's visual attention to television is caused in part by program comprehensibility, then attention should be enhanced in the presence of immediate concrete dialogue in the first study, and it should be reduced to program segments rendered less comprehensible in the second study.

Study 1

Television dialogue that has its referent immediately and concretely present should, in general, be more comprehensible to a preschooler than dialogue that has its referent dis-

placed in time and space (e.g., Brown 1976; de Villiers & de Villiers 1978). If program comprehensibility is a determinant of visual attention in preschoolers, then dialogue that is concrete and immediate should receive greater attention than other dialogue. In study 1, dialogue from 15 "Sesame Street" programs was rated for "immediacy" (i.e., the referent of the dialogue was concretely present visually and/or auditorily; see Rice [Note 3]). Preschoolers' visual attention to the programs was compared in the presence of dialogue with immediate referents, nonimmediate referents, and in the absence of dialogue.

Method

Subjects.—Subjects were 149 3-year-olds (average age = 3.5 years, SD = 0.3 years, 75 girls) and 150 5-year-olds (average age = 5.5 years, SD = 0.3 years, 75 girls). The children were predominantly white and from a wide range of socioeconomic backgrounds.

Design.—With one exception, 20 children (equal numbers of 3- and 5-year-olds, and equal numbers of boys and girls within each age) viewed one of 15 different "Sesame Street" programs. The children viewed either singly or in groups of two or three, always with one parent present. At each age for each program three children viewed singly, four viewed in two groups of two, and three viewed as one group of three (a procedural error eliminated one 3-year-old from one group of three). The influence of peer presence on TV viewing behavior is the subject of a separate report (Anderson, Lorch, Smith, Bradford, & Levin, in press). Presently the concern is with the children's visual attention in the presence and absence of immediate dialogue.

Procedure.—The children were individually brought to the University of Massachusetts Child Study Center by a parent. After the parents and children were greeted and the study explained, the children were brought to a pleasantly furnished 7 (2.1-m) × 12-foot (3.6-m) viewing room. The program appeared in black and white on a 17-inch (42.5-cm) TV monitor in one corner of the room. Distractor slides were rear-projected on a one-way mirror such that a 17-inch color slide image appeared at a 45° angle about 3 feet (1 m) away from the TV screen. The slides appeared every 8 sec, with each slide change signaled by a distinct "beep" from a box located just below the slide image. The slides, which consisted of a large variety of scenes from Disneyland, animals, posters for movies, artworks, and the like, never repeated themselves throughout the viewing session.

Observation procedure.—The children were observed viewing the program through a one-way mirror, with one observer present for each child in the viewing room. When, in an observer's judgment, the child looked at the TV, the observer depressed a button until the child looked away. The button was connected to an electronic device which automatically recorded the time of onset and offset of each button push. Visual attention is straightforwardly measured in this manner and produces highly reliable data (about 98% agreement, $\phi = .95$ or greater; Alwitt et al. [1980]; Anderson & Levin [1976]).

Dialogue rating.—Observers practiced rating the presence of dialogue and immediacy of dialogue on a "Sesame Street" program different from the ones watched by the subjects. Rating was accomplished by pressing a button connected to a small computer. When, in the observer's judgment, dialogue was present on the sound track (singing was not included as dialogue), she pressed the button, releasing it when dialogue was judged to be absent. Immediacy of dialogue was defined as the referent of the dialogue being visually or auditorily present. Examples of immediacy include narration about a puppet whose arms were too short to reach a nectarine (puppet shown trying to reach the nectarine) or discussion of a background noise (an airplane motor). An example of nonimmediate dialogue is a conversation about a shopping trip which occurred earlier in the day. After two observers reviewed and rated the practice tape, they rated each of the 15 "Sesame Street" programs. Although an observer might repeat a rating if she was not satisfied with her judgments (especially for immediacy), the observers did not discuss their ratings with each other. Interobserver agreement on the 15 tapes combined was 87.7% ($\phi = .733$) for presence of dialogue and 84.0% ($\phi = .493$) for immediacy of dialogue. The ratings for each tape were combined by a

logical "and" operation such that dialogue or immediacy was considered present at a given point in time only if both observers rated it present. By removing instances of immediacy from all instances of dialogue, the attribute "nonimmediate" dialogue was created. By removing instances of dialogue from the total program, absence of dialogue was determined. Thirty percent of the program time contained absence of dialogue, 14% contained immediate dialogue, and 56% contained nonimmediate dialogue.

Results and Discussion

The percentage of visual attention was calculated in the presence of immediate dialogue, nonimmediate dialogue, and the absence of dialogue using the technique developed by Anderson and Levin ([1976]; described in detail in Levin & Anderson [1976]). The data were subjected to an age × dialogue type (immediate, nonimmediate, no dialogue) analysis of variance. The data for the missing 3-year-old was replaced with mean scores for that viewing group, with appropriate adjustments in degrees of freedom (Myers 1972). Although scores of individual subjects were analyzed, error terms were recomputed in order to take into account variability due to particular viewing groups (Myers, DiCecco, & Lorch, in press).[1] As seen in table 1, 5-year-olds visual-

TABLE 1

MEAN PERCENTAGE VISUAL ATTENTION AS A
FUNCTION OF DIALOGUE
TYPE AND AGE

	DIALOGUE TYPE			
AGE	Immediate	Nonimmediate	Absent	Average
3 ($N = 149$)	65.3	58.1	63.0	62.2
	(18.7)	(17.9)	(17.0)	
5 ($N = 150$)	79.4	71.1	74.6	75.1
	(11.9)	(13.9)	(12.7)	
Average	72.1	64.6	68.9	...

NOTE.—Values in parentheses are standard deviations.

[1] Subjects and individual viewing groups were considered random-effects variables. Because the expected mean squares for treatment effects contain components representing each random-effects variable, error terms based on subject variability alone would yield a positively biased F test. Frequently, the recommended procedure (Clark 1973; Myers 1972, pp. 308–309) would be computation of quasi-F ratios, with appropriate error terms derived as linear combinations of mean squares providing the necessary components. In this case, however, error terms with appropriate expected mean squares could be found in an analysis of data from the groups of two (with variables age, tape, groups within age by tape, and language). The groups within age × tape term (30 degrees of freedom) was used to test the age effect, and the language × groups within age × tape term (60 degrees of freedom) was used to test the effect of language and the interaction of age and language.

ly attended to the TV more than 3-year-olds, $F(1,30) = 25.71$, $p < .001$. There was a significant dialogue type main effect, $F(2,60) = 107.17$, $p < .001$, but the age × dialogue type interaction was not significant, $F(2,60) = 2.90$, $p > .05$. The dialogue type main effect was due to greater attention in the presence of immediate dialogue than nonimmediate dialogue or absence of dialogue. Absence of dialogue received greater attention than nonimmediate dialogue (Bonferroni F tests; overall type I error rate does not exceed .01).

The assumption underlying study 1 is that immediate TV dialogue is, in general, more concrete and thus more understandable to young children than is nonimmediate dialogue. Although no detailed linguistic analyses of the dialogue were performed, it was our impression that nonimmediate dialogue often employed more complex linguistic structures and used a more abstract vocabulary than immediate dialogue. The finding that preschoolers' visual attention was greater in the presence of immediate dialogue supports the contention of Lorch et al. (1979) that TV program comprehensibility is a major determinant of young children's attention to television. The results also replicate those of Krull and Husson (1979), who reported similar findings after the present study was already in progress.

Study 2

Although the results of study 1 are consistent with the notion that TV program comprehensibility determines preschoolers' attention, it is also possible that immediate dialogue maintains visual attention not because it is more understandable but because it usually refers to objects or events that are visually present and thus invite visual inspection. A more convincing demonstration requires experimental manipulation of TV program comprehensibility while holding the formal attribute structure (the "look" and the "sound" of the program) constant. Study 2 approached this demonstration in three ways. One technique used was to rearrange scenes so that the sequence of actions was logically inconsistent and difficult to comprehend (as suggested from Collins, Wellman, Keniston, & Westby [1978]). A second technique involved professionally dubbed foreign language dialogue using voices with qualities similar to the original. The third technique employed the original dialogue dubbed in backward, utterance for utterance, so that the original voice qualities and intonations were retained, but were semantically unintelligible.

Method

Subjects.—Subjects were 96 children, age 2, 3.5, or 5 years (± 1 month). They were predominantly white and from a wide range of socioeconomic backgrounds.

Design.—Forty-eight children (16 at each age and equal numbers of boys and girls within each age) viewed one of two specially prepared 1-hour "Sesame Street" shows. Each videotaped show consisted of 33 different segments ("bits"). The shows were identical except that bits which were normal on tape *A* were selectively distorted on tape *B* so as to be less comprehensible, and vice versa. Three techniques were used to distort bits: random editing, foreign language dubbing, and backward speech dubbing. Tape *A* consisted of 17 normal bits (31.1 min), 8 randomly edited bits (12.2 min), 5 foreign language bits (10.2 min), and 3 backward speech bits (6.4 min). Tape *B* consisted of 16 normal bits (28.8 min), 9 randomly edited bits (17.3 min), 5 foreign language bits (7.0 min), and 3 backward speech bits (6.8 min).

Editing procedures.—The 17 randomly edited bits were structurally rearranged so that scenes within the bits were reordered. Professional electronic video-editing equipment was used. Only preexisting edit points were used as edit points for the rearrangement; typically only one to three video frames are lost in such professional quality video editing. An average of nine scenes averaging 12.0 sec in length were rearranged per bit.

The six bits with backward speech were constructed by physically splicing an audiotape so that each utterance occurred in reverse at its original location in the bit after being dubbed back onto the videotape. Lip synch was thus roughly retained and voice quality and intonation were unchanged.

The 10 foreign language (Greek) bits were provided by Children's Television Workshop's International Division. These bits were visually identical to the English version bits and were professionally dubbed with an attempt made to match voice quality with that in the English language version.

Procedure.—The setting and procedure were the same as in the first study except that the children viewed the color videotape individually with a parent present. A variety of toys was available and the children were free to play, watch TV, or interact with the parent. There was no slide distractor.

Results and Discussion

The design of the experiment allows both within and between-subjects comparisons of the level of attention in normal and distorted segments. Analyses were done separately for each distortion type: random editing, foreign language, and backward speech. Two between-subjects analyses of variance and one within-subjects analysis of variance on percentage of visual attention were performed for each distortion type. In the age × sex × bit type between-subjects analyses, subjects who viewed normal bits on one tape served as controls for subjects who viewed those same bits distorted on the other tape. Subjects who served as controls in one analysis served as experimental subjects in the other. In the age × sex × bit type within-subjects analysis of variance, a subject's attention to normal bits was compared with the same subject's attention to each type of distorted bit. Because there was substantially less within- than between-subjects variance, more significant effects were obtained when the comparisons were within subjects. A significant increase in visual attention with age was found in all analyses (with the exception of one between-subjects analysis of backward dialogue), and there were no main effects of sex or interactions with sex.

Random editing.—Other than main effects of age, the two between-subjects analyses revealed no significant effects. In the within-subjects analysis, there was a significant bit type main effect, $F(1,90) = 13.47$, $p < .001$, such that attention was greater to the normal than to the distorted segments (as shown in table 2). The more sensitive within-subjects analysis thus revealed a slight decrease in visual attention to the randomly edited bits.

Foreign dialogue.—Normal bits received higher attention than distorted bits, as indicated by significant effects of bit type in the between-subjects analyses, $F(1,84) = 13.63$ and 13.64, $p < .001$, and in the within-subjects analysis, $F(1,90) = 74.17$, $p < .001$. The within-subjects analysis also revealed a significant age × bit type interaction, $F(2,90) = 4.56$, $p < .05$, due to a somewhat smaller reduction in attention by foreign language bits in younger children. Post hoc analyses revealed, nevertheless, that the reduction was significant at each age.

Backward dialogue.—The results for bits with backward dialogue were nearly identical to the results for bits with foreign dialogue. The between-subjects analyses revealed significant bit type main effects, $F(1,84) = 17.53$ and 7.39, $p < .01$, but no significant interactions. The within-subjects analysis indicated a significant bit type main effect, $F(1,90) = 122.31$, $p < .001$, and an age × bit type interaction, $F(2,90) = 10.07$, $p < .001$. As with foreign dialogue, the interaction was due to a smaller difference from normal in the younger children. Again, post hoc analyses indicated that the difference between normal and backward dialogue bits was significant at each age level.

Adult ratings of bit comprehensibility.—After the attention data were collected, 20 adult observers (college students, 10 for each tape) were asked to rate each bit on a scale of 1–5 as to how well they felt they understood each bit and how easy it was to understand each bit. Since the ratings on the two questions were highly correlated, they were combined to provide an adult estimate of bit comprehensibility. The experimental distortions of comprehensibility were successful: whereas normal bits received an average rating of 4.7 (a 5 indicated perfect comprehensibility), random editing, foreign dialogue, and backward

TABLE 2

PERCENTAGE VISUAL ATTENTION AS A FUNCTION OF AGE AND BIT TYPE
(Within-Subjects Analysis)

	BIT TYPE				
AGE	Normal	Random Editing	Foreign Dialogue	Backward Dialogue	Average
2 ($N = 32$)	32.4	28.9	24.5	24.3	28.3
	(18.5)	(16.2)	(20.4)	(18.1)	
3.5 ($N = 32$)	45.1	38.0	28.8	26.0	35.5
	(19.5)	(16.9)	(20.3)	(18.4)	
5 ($N = 32$)	63.2	62.0	42.8	37.9	50.6
	(19.9)	(21.2)	(21.9)	(27.4)	
Average	46.9	43.0	32.0	29.4	...

NOTE.—Values in parentheses are standard deviations.

dialogue bits received average ratings of 3.8, 2.8, and 2.4, respectively (each significantly different from normal, t [19] = 8.72, $p < .001$). Although the randomly edited bits were rated as less comprehensible than normal bits, they were rated as more comprehensible than the foreign and backward dialogue bits, t (19) = 6.39, $p < .001$. Notice that even the language distortions left the bits moderately understandable according to the adult ratings. This residual comprehensibility was probably due to the undistorted concrete visual actions of the "Sesame Street" characters. When correlations of average adult comprehensibility ratings for each bit and the children's attention to each bit were calculated, the correlations were significant at each age level, r (64) = .285, .507, and .426, $p < .05$, for the 2-, 3.5-, and 5-year-olds, respectively. Since these correlations could primarily reflect the difference between the normal and distorted bits, the correlations were calculated excluding the normal bits. The resulting correlations, r (31) = .299, .441, and .412 for the 2-, 3.5-, and 5-year-olds, respectively, were still significant for the two older groups. Thus, differences in adult ratings of comprehensibility of the distorted bits were appropriately reflected in differences in the children's visual attention to those bits. The minimal depression of the children's visual attention to the randomly edited bits reflected the adults' ratings of those bits as actually being more comprehensible than the bits which had dialogue distorted. The attention paid to those bits, in turn, may have been as much due to the residual comprehensibility of the visual actions as to the attention-maintaining power of the formal features inherent in those bits.

General Discussion

The present results, combined with the findings of Krull and Husson (1979) and Lorch et al. (1979), strongly support the hypothesis that a major determinant of young children's visual attention to a television program is the degree to which they are able to comprehend it.

An intriguing aspect of the present studies was the importance of understandable dialogue in maintaining young children's attention to television. This finding stands opposed to reports by Friedlander and his associates (Bohannon & Friedlander 1973; Friedlander & Cohen de Lara 1973) that, when given the choice between garbled and semantically sensible audiotracks, preschoolers showed nonsig-

nificant preferences. Since the choice required operation of a switch according to a Sidman avoidance type of schedule of reinforcement to avoid the garbled audio, it is possible that for young children the complexities and novelty of the task itself decreased their semantic processing of the TV program audio.

Although understandable dialogue appears to be an important factor in maintaining young children's attention, a meaningful sequence of scenes appears to be less important. In the present study, randomly rearranging scenes within "Sesame Street" bits led to little change in visual attention. One reason for the relative lack of effect may be that the children perceived the randomly edited bits as more comprehensible than bits in which dialogue was distorted (as adults did), probably because each short scene (averaging 12.0 seconds in length) was individually understandable. Additionally, young children may comprehend TV primarily at the level of such short scenes. Collins (1979), for example, has suggested that young children have considerable difficulty integrating information across scenes in television programs. Foreign and backward dialogue, on the other hand, may produce much larger decrements in attention because within-scene comprehensibility is reduced.

We suggest that the present results have implications for the development of a theory of children's television viewing. There is currently no such theory, with the exception of preliminary speculations by social learning theorists (Bandura 1977; Bandura & Walters 1963) who adopt a sequential model which represents attentional processes as necessary precursors to the comprehension, encoding, and retention of modeled events. Although comprehensible modeled events are seen by social learning theorists as necessary for subsequent matching performance by the child (Bandura 1977; Brown 1976), attention is seen as primarily determined by the intrinsic reward value of the stimulus as well as past reinforcement for attention. Television, presumably because of the distinctive formal features which characterize the medium, is seen as ". . . so effective in capturing attention that viewers learn much of what they see without requiring any special incentive to do so" (Bandura 1977, p. 25). Our perspective is instead that the young viewer learns that these formal features of television can be predictive of learnable informative content (Alwitt et al. 1980; Lorch et al. 1979; Anderson & Lorch, Note 2). The young child ordinarily uses these features to effectively divide attention between TV viewing and other activities such as toy play. The present results indicate that when the content is not understandable the child's attention is substantially reduced, despite the presence of these formal features. There is as yet no evidence that the television medium has any unique control over the young child's attention separate from its content.

Reference Notes

1. Huston-Stein, A., & Wright, J. C. Modeling the medium: effects of formal properties of children's television programs. Paper presented at the Society for Research in Child Development biennial meeting, New Orleans, 1977.
2. Anderson, D. R., & Lorch, E. P. A theory of the active nature of young children's television viewing. Presented at the Society for Research in Child Development biennial meeting, San Francisco, 1979.
3. Rice, M. Television as a medium of verbal communication. Presented at American Psychological Association annual meeting, New York City, September 1979.

References

Alwitt, L. F.; Anderson, D. R.; Lorch, E. P.; & Levin, S. R. Preschool children's visual attention to attributes of television. *Human Communication Research*, 1980, **7**, 52–67.

Anderson, D. R., & Levin, S. R. Young children's attention to "Sesame Street." *Child Development*, 1976, **47**, 806–811.

Anderson, D. R.; Lorch, E. P.; Smith, R.; Bradford, R.; & Levin, S. R. The effects of peer presence on preschool children's television viewing behavior. *Developmental Psychology*, in press.

Bandura, A. *Social learning theory*. Englewood Cliffs, N.J.: Prentice-Hall, 1977.

Bandura, A., & Walters, R. H. *Social learning and personality development*. New York: Holt, Rinehart & Winston, 1963.

Bohannon, J. N., & Friedlander, B. Z. The effect of intonation on syntax recognition in elementary school children. *Child Development*, 1973, **44**, 675–677.

Brown, I., Jr. Role of referent concreteness in the acquisition of passive sentence comprehension through abstract modeling. *Journal of Experimental Child Psychology*, 1976, **22**, 185–199.

Bryant, J.; Hezel, R.; & Zillman, D. Humor in children's educational television. *Communication Education*, 1978, **28**, 49–59.

Clark, H. H. The language-as-fixed-effect fallacy: a critique of language statistics in psychological research. *Journal of Verbal Learning and Verbal Behavior*, 1973, **12**, 335–359.

Collins, W. A. Children's comprehension of television content. In E. Wartella (Ed.), *Children communicating: media and the development of thought, speech, understanding*. Beverly Hills, Calif.: Sage, 1979.

Collins, W. A.; Wellman, H.; Keniston, A. H.; & Westby, S. O. Age-related aspects of comprehension and inference from a televised dramatic narrative. *Child Development*, 1978, **49**, 389–399.

Friedlander, B. Z., & Cohen de Lara, H. Receptive language anomaly and language/reading dysfunction in "normal" primary grade school children. *Psychology in the Schools*, 1973, **10**, 12–18.

Krull, R., & Husson, W. Children's attention: the case of TV viewing. In E. Wartella (Ed.), *Children communicating: media and development of thought, speech, understanding*. Beverly Hills, Calif.: Sage, 1979.

Lesser, G. S. *Children and television*. New York: Random House, 1974.

Lesser, H. *Television and the preschool child*. New York: Academic Press, 1977.

Levin, S., & Anderson, D. R. The development of attention. *Journal of Communication*, 1976, **26**, 126–135.

Lorch, E. P.; Anderson, D. R.; & Levin, S. R. The relationship between visual attention and children's comprehension of television. *Child Development*, 1979, **50**, 722–727.

Mander, J. *Four arguments for the elimination of television*. New York: Morrow, 1978.

Myers, J. L. *Fundamentals of experimental design*. Boston: Allyn & Bacon, 1972.

Myers, J. L.; DiCecco, J. V.; & Lorch, R. F. The statistical analysis of the effects of social grouping on individual performance. *Journal of Personality and Social Psychology*, in press.

Singer, J. L., & Singer, D. G. Come back Mister Rogers, come back. *Psychology Today*, 1979, **12**, 56–60.

de Villiers, J. G., & de Villiers, P. A. *Language acquisition*. Cambridge, Mass.: Harvard University Press, 1978.

Winn, M. *The plug-in drug*. New York: Viking, 1977.

This is a theoretical examination of the relationship between parent-child interaction about television and children's learning from television. The authors argue that parent-child interaction has consequences for children's interpretations of television, their development of cognitive categories regarding the real world, their acquisition of behaviors from TV, and their development of social relationships. Paul Messaris is assistant professor of communications at the Annenberg School of Communications, University of Pennsylvania. Carla Sarett was a doctoral candidate at the Annenberg School of Communications, University of Pennsylvania, when this article was written. She is now assistant professor of communications at Queens College, the City University of New York.

20

ON THE CONSEQUENCES OF TELEVISION-RELATED PARENT-CHILD INTERACTION

Paul Messaris and Carla Sarett

Studies of mass-media exposure as a potential learning context for children sometimes conceptualize the learning process in question as occurring independently of, or in competition with, the learning processes inherent in intrafamily relationships (e.g., Chaffee, Ward, & Tipton, 1970, pp. 657-658; Hollander, 1971). However, as Chaffee (1972, p. 108) has pointed out, this kind of separation between medium and family is not always feasible or permissible for the researcher. A child's behavior with regard to a certain medium may be conditioned by the structure of its family, while the medium may—in a loose sense, reciprocally—provide the pretexts for certain orders of interaction between parents and children. In short, situations with these characteristics present the investigator with the problem of a single learning context, in which the roles of medium and family members must be accounted for at the same time.

An apparently increasing number of investigators have been applying this kind of inclusive perspective, in varying degrees of explicitness, to research on television. The immediate focus of much of this research has been on the ways in which children's viewing patterns and preferences are affected by parents, either through direct control (e.g., Barcus, 1969; Hess & Goldman, 1962; Himmelweit, Oppenheim, & Vince, 1958, p. 378; Mohr, 1979) or by virtue of other features of the relationship between parent and child (e.g., Chaffee & McLeod, 1972; Chaffee, McLeod, & Atkin, 1971; Forsey, 1963; Maccoby, 1954; Riley & Riley, 1951). Implicitly, at least, much of this work has also had a broader concern with the consequences of television-related parental influence for behavior outside the immediate television-viewing situation (McLeod & Brown, 1976, p. 203). Among the studies that have focused directly on parental influence on these other consequences, a particularly prominent position is occupied by research on the role of parents in modifying the effects of advertising (Robertson, 1979, for a review). This paper is an attempt to outline certain consequences of one particular class of potential learning contexts in which both family and television play a part, namely, parent-child interac-

Paul Messaris (Ph.D., University of Pennsylvania, 1975) is assistant professor of communications at the Annenberg School of Communications, University of Pennsylvania, Philadelphia, Pennsylvania 19104. *Carla Sarett* (M.A., Annenberg School of Communications, University of Pennsylvania, 1978) is a doctoral candidate at the Annenberg School of Communications, University of Pennsylvania, Philadelphia, Pennsylvania 19104.

From Paul Messaris and Carla Sarett, "On the Consequences of Television-Related Parent-Child Interaction," *Human Communication Research* 7, 3 (Spring 1981), pp. 226-244. Reprinted by permission of the publisher and authors.

tions focused explicitly on television. In other words, the concern of this paper is with parent-child interactions in which the content of television programming appears as explicit subject matter, e.g., as the topic of a verbal exchange, as the premise for a game, and so forth. The discussion of the consequences of this kind of behavior will be theoretical, although descriptive statements about the interactional sequences involved will be based primarily on empirical findings.

The extent to which television is a subject of interaction in the family has received some documentation in previous studies. To begin with, several investigators have gathered data on the frequency with which children watch television in the company of their parents. Although more recent studies (e.g., Halloran, Brown, & Chaney, 1970, pp. 108-109; Lyle & Hoffman, 1972, p. 166) tend to give lower figures for this kind of behavior than earlier work did (e.g., Friedson, 1953, p. 232; Himmelweit, Oppenheim, & Vince, 1958, p. 377; Schramm, Lyle, & Parker, 1961, p. 268), even the more recent data suggest that joint viewing by parents and children is a modal pattern of high frequency (Bower, 1973, p. 149). Furthermore, whereas some earlier writers in this area (e.g., Maccoby, 1951; Steiner, 1963, pp. 101-103) tended to argue that such joint-viewing situations were characterized by relatively little interaction among family members, more recent findings (e.g., Barcus, 1969; Lyle & Hoffman, 1972, p. 152) do not support this notion. In general, then, the viewing situation itself appears to be an important context of parent-child interaction involving television. However, subject matter drawn from television can also enter family interaction on a variety of other occasions, such as games between parents and children (cf. Williams, Smart, & Epstein 1979), parental comments on children's play, children's descriptions of programs they have watched alone, as well as after-the-fact discussion of programs viewed together (cf. LoSciuto, 1972, p. 57; Lyle & Hoffman, 1972, pp. 170-171). It need hardly be added that these patterns vary depending on the child's age and any number of other variables.

The aim of this paper is to develop a theoretical framework for the examination of certain conse-

quences, for a child's subsequent behavior, of the kinds of interactions adumbrated above. The consequences to be examined here may be grouped into four general categories. The first category comprises changes in the way in which a child interprets televised material. Within this general category, two more specific kinds of changes will be discussed: those involving the child's development of interpretational competence regarding the narrative conventions of commercial television and those contributing to the child's acquisition of a set of beliefs regarding the validity and generalizability of various types of televised material. The second general category of consequences discussed below includes changes in a child's repertory of cognitive categories regarding the real world. The specific focus of the discussion of this category will be on the child's acquisition of a system of verbal labels for "translating" the visual content of television programming into a socially validated system for the representation of reality. The third category of consequences covered here includes changes in a child's patterns of overt behavior, that is, a child's overt action upon, or interaction with, features of his/her environment other than television itself. Included in this discussion will be an examination of the formation of opinion, considered here purely as overt verbal behavior. Finally, under a fourth general category of consequences, this paper will focus on changes in one specific aspect of a child's overt behavior, namely, his/her social relationships. It should be emphasized that the list of specific processes and consequences to be discussed under the four headings outlined above is not intended to be exhaustive. Notably absent from this list is any discussion of parental influence on children's television-viewing patterns; and several other issues, such as parental definitions of incidental vocabulary items encountered by a child in a television program, will be mentioned only in passing. It should also be pointed out that, although the four categories of consequences will be discussed separately from one another, they are not unrelated, since various second-order effects may be conceived of as linking one area with another. Thus, changes in a child's system for the cognitive classification of environmental objects and events (the second category of consequences discussed here) presumably have certain implications for his/her patterns of overt behavior toward them (the third and fourth categories) (cf. Bronfenbrenner, 1979, pp. 27-28), whereas the first category (changes in a child's way of interpreting televised material) may be thought of as involving a "reflexive" change, that is, a change in part of the learning context itself, with repercussions for all the other categories of consequences (cf. Bateson, 1972).

The discussion that follows makes frequent use of illustrations taken from the findings of a project in which the authors are currently engaged. The goal of this project is to compile an inventory and to map the features of television-related parent-child interactions in several social contexts. Although the project is aimed at eventual direct observation of selected situations of family interaction, in its present phase it is based on interviews with parents, and it is from some of these interviews that excerpts will be drawn here. Further details on this project are contained in the concluding section of this paper. The findings themselves will be presented in full elsewhere.

THE DEVELOPMENT OF INTERPRETATIONAL SKILLS

Parent-child interactions centered on television may affect in at least two important ways a child's skills in interpreting television programming: first, by developing the child's proficiency regarding the representational conventions of commercial television and, second, by contributing to the child's perception of the validity and the generalizability of specific types of programming (cf.Leifer, Gordon, & Graves, 1974, pp. 239-241).

Television is frequently regarded as a medium whose representational substance, that is, the flow of televised images and sounds, is so isomorphic with the objects it represents, that is, the appearances and sounds of the material world, that little or no learning is required in order to be able to match the two. In the case of individual images, there is considerable evidence that this is indeed the case. For example, in a somewhat extreme study of this issue, a child raised with no exposure whatsoever to

pictures was able to identify immediately the subject (an animal) of the first television image he encountered (Hochberg & Brooks, 1962). When it comes to the relationship between images, however, the situation appears to be different. In particular, the isomorphy between reality and its televised presentation cannot be said to hold in the case of many of the narrative devices, such as flashbacks, parallel editing, and the like, by which the sections of the typical fictional program are joined together. Devices of this sort can therefore properly be considered to be arbitrary conventions, in the sense that one should expect them to vary cross-culturally (cf. Bellman & Jules-Rosette, 1977) and, more important, to require learning on the part of the audience members in a particular culture. Several studies provide evidence of this kind of learning, although the medium of reference in each case is film, rather than television. For example, in an experiment based on three filmed versions of a single story, age-related differences in comprehension were found to increase with increasing presence of certain editing devices in the films (Mialaret & Melies, 1954). In a study by Zazzo (1952), similar results were found for variations in editing style within a single film. Indirect evidence on this point is also provided by Carey (1974), in a study of devices indicating space-time transitions.

Aside from the possibility that a child may have to learn the meaning of particular narrative devices, however, it may also be true that the very act of treating the separate sections of a narrative as parts of a whole, rather than as successive unrelated events, requires specific learning, i.e., is not a tendency transferable automatically to television from one's experience with raw reality. This point has been argued in theory by Worth & Gross (1974); and the argument is supported by a series of studies, summarized in Messaris & Gross (1977), in which young children's misinterpretations of a visual narrative appear to have been occasioned by a failure to take into account the implications of one scene for the meaning of another. Studies by Collins and his associates (cf. Collins, 1975, 1979) also support the notion that the ability to deal with a visual narrative as a set of interrelated parts, subordinate to a whole, is an acquired skill; and an impressive example of differences in degrees of acquisition of this skill is provided by Noble (1975, p. 91).

In general, then, the development of the ability to interpret a television program as a coherent narrative is one potential area on which a child's interactions with parents—or, in fact, any more experienced viewer—can have an effect. It is our assumption that the actual process involved here takes place primarily during, or immediately following, joint-viewing situations and consists not only of explicit teaching but also—and, perhaps, more frequently—of indirect learning, contingent upon a parent's indication of the correct interpretation of a particular point, although not necessarily of the principle on which the interpretation is based. More specifically, in our interviews with parents, it was reported repeatedly that joint-viewing situations were punctuated continuously by two kinds of questions from their children: why had a particular event occurred (or not occurred) and what was going to happen next. Since the answers to these kinds of questions frequently involve the establishment of appropriate connections between segments of a program, these answers can, if accumulated over a sufficient number of cases, supply a child with the material necessary to infer, consciously or not, the principle behind the connection. It should, however, be emphasized that the principle itself need not be cited explicitly by the parent, who may, in any case, not be able to give an explicit rule for a particular interpretation. One example of this kind of situation in our data involved an episode of "The Incredible Hulk" in which a young woman whom the Hulk saves from drowning remembers, in flashback, the death by drowning of her sister. The interviewee's child, apparently failing to understand the correct sequence of events, wanted to know why the Hulk had allowed the second sister to drown after having saved the first one. While this child's mother did not, by her own account, give her daughter a general rule for recognizing and interpreting flashbacks, it seems reasonable to argue that, by supplying the correct interpretation of this particular flashback, she was making possible the eventual inductive recognition of the rule on the child's part. An intriguing extension of this argu-

ment is developed by Appell (1963, p. 312), who suggests that, even before a child can talk, it can begin to learn appropriate patterns of response to television by adjusting its own behavior to the nonverbal responses of older viewers.

A second way in which parent-child interactions may affect the development of a child's interpretational skills has to do with the child's perception of the validity and generalizability of the situations depicted on television programs. A common belief regarding this issue is that younger children either cannot distinguish television's portrayal of the world from the real thing or that, at any rate, they are uncritical in their acceptance as "the truth" of whatever they see on television. For example, the father of two preschoolers told our interviewer that "they'll accept anything they see as gospel, unless you tell them it's not for real." It should be added that the prevalent belief that this kind of situation is typical of most children is usually supported by the claim that the situation arises from the extreme naturalism with which commercial television is thought to portray everyday life. On the other hand, however, there were also several accounts in our data of children who reportedly do question the veridicality of televised representations. According to one mother, her children (aged 4, 8, and 11) are continually asking her, "Is this a true story?" or, "Did this really happen?" This mother also described her children as "very critical" of television in general and then explained: "But they just do what their father does. They're doing that by example." The existence of cases of this sort suggests, then, that the origin of children's perceptions of the truth value of television programming is best considered problematical and that parent-child interactions may well contribute, in certain cases, to the formation of these perceptions. Indeed, the argument concerning television's naturalism is by no means impregnable, since, for one thing, the flagrant antinaturalism of "superhero" stunts is frequently cited by parents as a stimulus for their children's developing understanding of television's fictitiousness.

The most obvious way in which a parent may affect a child's tendency to accept certain kinds of televised portrayals as true or false and representative or unrepresentative would seem to be that of direct statement, as in the following account of a mother's comments to her 7-year-old son on the series "Roots": "I didn't see all of that, but parts I did see, I remember saying, I don't believe any of this, I'm sure that this is all played up." (Interviewer: "What kind of thing?") "Well, like the way they were treated, the attitude and the personality of the slaves at the time." In this case, of course, it is a particular series which is being indicted, whereas the husband in the previous example seems to be more generally critical. In any event, what matters in the long run, presumably, is the cumulative pattern of parental comments on particular *types* of programming or on television in general. Patterns of this sort may account for the results of a study by Gross & Morgan (in press), who found a negative association between, on the one hand, the degree of parental intervention, through rule imposition, advice, and the like, in their children's television viewing and, on the other hand, the children's adherence to "versions" of reality presented on television. It must not be assumed, however, that explicit commentary or intervention are the only ways in which parent-child interaction can impinge on a child's assessment of the credibility of televised material. For example, the work of McLeod and his associates indicates that there is a relationship between adolescents' beliefs in the verisimilitude of television violence and certain aspects of intrafamily communication patterns *in general*: these beliefs were highest for adolescents from families with a joint—and seemingly self-contradictory—emphasis both on subordination to established authority and on the adolescent's development of his/her own position on an issue (McLeod, Atkin, & Chaffee, 1972b, p. 296). This datum becomes particularly important in the light of other findings by McLeod and his associates of relationships between family positions on these two dimensions—"socio-orientation" and "concept orientation"—and various other aspects of adolescents' responses to the mass media (McLeod & O'Keefe, 1972; McLeod & Brown, 1976), since these findings, taken together, make it possible to incorporate the issue of children's perceptions of television's truth value within a more general theory

of the relationship between family communication patterns and children's responses to television. A study conducted by Lull (in press-b) within the terms of this theory has yielded several findings of potential importance to the issue at hand: most notably, a positive relationship between socio-orientation and the use of television for the illustration of experience and for "intellectual validation"; and a positive relationship between concept-orientation and the use of television for the selective regulation, by parents, of children's experiences. It seems reasonable to make the tentative assumption that a family's use of television in any one of these ways also has implications for a child's developing sense of the validity and generalizability of programs, although Lull's analysis is not concerned explicitly with this aspect of the matter.

It should also be mentioned that validity and generalizability can, of course, be matters of degree and not merely of kind. For example, as is often assumed, the credibility of a medium may be a relative matter, and it may therefore be pertinent to ask how children learn to discriminate among television, the press, and so forth as possible sources of information. A potential instance of direct parental influence on this process may be present in the following case of a mother who uses the newspaper to validate a TV-news report of suicide that her child had questioned: "This guy committed suicide. So, you know: Did this guy really jump off? And the next day in the paper, somebody jumped off the Tacony Bridge, and I said, see, here it is, this kind of thing really happens." As suggested earlier, of course, parental influence in these matters may also occur less directly.

THE ARTICULATION OF COGNITIVE CATEGORIES

There are several ways in which television viewing may lead, through parental intervention, to an augmentation or refinement of a child's stock of information about reality. Parents are frequently called upon to provide contextual information (e.g., historical or technical/scientific facts) necessary to the understanding of a television program, to explain the meaning of words a child has not encountered before, or, most importantly, to integrate disturbing material into an acceptable philosophy of existence, as can happen when a parent must deal with a child's reaction to an irrefutable portrayal of suffering. In this discussion, we shall concentrate on two aspects of this cognitive development, both having to do with the elaboration and refinement of the child's system of cognitive categories: first, what may be termed the "translation" of the concrete information provided by television into the abstract categories of social intercourse; and, second, the imposition on reality of "new" categories derived from television through a process to be explained below.

It is an inherent property of "photographic" media such as television that their representations of reality are concrete, in the sense that these representations correspond always to a particular object or event (cf. Gombrich, 1972). By contrast, the linguistic representation of reality is largely a matter of abstract categories (e.g., the words *object*, *event*) and only secondarily, as with proper nouns, involves concrete reference. As de Saussure (1959) and Whorf (1956) have pointed out, this means that the use of language involves, of necessity, the imposition, on the real world, of a system of categories given in the language itself and, ultimately, ascribable to the needs of the societies in which this language is in use (cf. Berlin & Kay, 1969; Gould, 1979). Furthermore, it is a commonplace observation that, to the extent that the category system of language furnishes the terms in which the members of a society interact with each other and, indirectly, act upon the material environment, this system can be said to constitute the reality of a given society (cf. Berger & Luckmann, 1966). Practical illustrations of some of the senses in which this argument may be valid are provided by a variety of studies demonstrating the consequences of verbal labels for several types of behavior (e.g., Kanouse, 1972; Kraut, 1973; Gurwitz & Topol, 1978). It follows from this argument that the requirements of social intercourse necessitate the continuous "translation," by the viewer, of some of the information provided by a medium such as television into the terms of an abstract system. To a great extent, this translation

process is an "automatic" by-product of any use of language in reference to televised material, and in such cases the issue may be said to be trivial. However, in situations in which the existence of variant categories is a matter of current social consequence, rather than an obsolete survival, the issue obviously becomes important. An example of such a situation will also illustrate how the interaction between parent and child may enter into this process of "translation."

In several instances in our data, parents reported having been asked by a child why a particular television character had committed an evil act. A frequent response to this kind of question appears to be the classification of the characters in the program into several categories and the explanation of the evil act by assignment of the perpetrator to the category of "bad guy." For example, one mother says that she told a daughter who was upset over an incident in "Lassie," "there are some people who are good in this world, and some people who are bad"; and a father reportedly explained to his daughter, in reference to a western, that "the good guy is the one with the white hat and the bad guy is the one with the black hat, so you can always tell the difference." On the other hand, the following account was given by the mother of three grade-school children: "Sometimes you would have to explain why the bad guy was really good, something like that. 'Cause they wouldn't understand why the bad guy was doing all these terrible things, but they didn't understand the *background* behind why he had ended up being such a rotten character, and why he always somehow got it in the end but you felt sorry for him, and maybe the children didn't really understand, why you did feel sorry for him. So, there are a lot of times when I'll say, well, I felt sorry for him because he had so many rough breaks, or whatever, and it really wasn't his fault that he ended up the way he did." In this case, the mother's category system for the distribution of good and evil in society is more complex than the simple dichotomies of the previous examples and may, perhaps, be identified with a "liberal" position on these matters. Which of these alternative systems a child ends up operating with would seem to be a matter of some consequence, and the same can therefore be said of the potential role of the parent as "category-pro-vider" in this kind of situation.

A second type of process, involving television, through which the interaction of parent and child may shape a child's system of cognitive categories, is best introduced by example. Many parents in our interviews report having compared a television character to a real-life person in the presence of their children. The television character cited most frequently in this respect is Archie Bunker. For example: "My son was watching Archie Bunker the other day and he said, mommy, do you know that Archie Bunker looks a lot like grandpa, and I said, yeah, and I guess he *thinks* a lot like grandpa too." "I call her daddy Archie Bunker when he's being particularly redneck in my opinion, and she will kid him to that effect, ay, you're Archie Bunker! Well, he plays—and it's obviously a play: don't you call me Archie Bunker! Oh yes, you are, you are! No, I'm not, no, I'm not!—kind of thing."

The most obvious intended effect of such comparisons, on the part of the parent, is probably that of giving an inoffensive frame to criticism. (For a description of the use of comic strip characters in this way, see Bogart, 1955.) However, it may also be the case that an important additional effect—probably unintended—of this kind of situation is the creation of a new classificatory category for the child. It seems reasonable to suggest that such a category is already within the awareness of the parent in this kind of situation. In the second example cited above, for instance, the mother gives direct evidence of having such a category ("particularly redneck"); but, independently of such evidence, it might be expected that the conceptual type of the "house reactionary as buffoon" would exist, prior to its televised fictionalization, in the awareness of the kind of adult who would be likely to use such a conceptual type in a critical vein. On the other hand, it also seems quite likely that the child in this kind of situation has not yet developed such a conceptual type or cognitive category. In such a case, the situation itself, i.e., the comparison between a fictional character and a real-life person, may be the stimulus for the creation of such a category.

What may happen, in other words, is that the indication, by a parent, of the existence of a set of traits common to the two or more people compared may direct the child to abstract this set of traits into a "new" type. In such cases, then, the parent's contribution to this category formation is indirect, and the category, or set of categories, is not actually given in abstract terms. On the other hand, the applicability of this category, or set of categories, to reality is given in the very process of formation. In both of these respects, therefore, this kind of process differs from the process of "translation" described earlier. Both types of process, however, may be assumed to have the following important consequence: Once a child has acquired a particular category system, future encounters with the relevant concrete content of television programming (e.g., a particular episode of "All in the Family") may now presumably lead directly, that is, without parental intervention, to the elaboration of the content of the corresponding abstract categories.

PARENTAL INFLUENCE ON OVERT BEHAVIORAL RESPONSES TO TELEVISION

It may be assumed that the cognitive developments discussed above are of ultimate consequence for a child's overt behavior as well. In this section, however, the focus will be on some of the processes by which television-related parental interaction with children may affect their behavior directly. A number of the parents we have interviewed described instances in which the content of a television program gave them the opportunity to inject a moral precept into discussions with their children (cf. Barcus, 1969), as in the following instances: "One of the episodes (of "The Brady Bunch") there was a broken vase, one of the mother's favorite vases, and they had glued it together, and I said, well, I'm sorry, I would be very disappointed if you didn't come and tell me that you broke this favorite vase, 'cause if I find out you were trying to cover up you're in a lot more trouble than if you'd come and told me the truth." "I'll say certain things like, oh, wasn't that girl nice, how she just shared things so willingly. I'll make comments like that sometimes in a program to point out that sharing's a very important part of life." There is a variety of evidence on the effectiveness of this kind of advice. A series of studies of children's imitation of filmed aggression found that degree of imitation was controllable by the use of appropriate rewards (Bandura, 1965), that verbal approval or disapproval of the filmed behavior by an adult was an effective positive or negative reinforcer (Hicks, 1968), and that the physical presence of the adult during the period of potential imitation was necessary for this effect among younger children (5-year-olds) but not among older ones (10-year-olds) (Grusec, 1973). (In fact, it has been argued that imitation cannot occur at all without prior or concomitant environmental reinforcement—whether by parents or otherwise—of the class of behavior involved, e.g., Skinner, 1953, pp. 119-122; Gewirtz, 1969, pp. 159-160.) In an experiment in which mothers, rather than adult experimenters, administered the reinforcement, successful countering of the message of a commercial was found under certain conditions, namely, with a relatively less attractive commercial and, more importantly, when the mothers reasoned with their children, rather than giving authority-based advice (Prasad, Rao, & Sheikh, 1978).

In all the instances cited above, the parent's or experimenter's advice or other comments preceded the behavior that they were intended to affect. This kind of situation may be contrasted with cases in which, once a child has actually performed a certain type of behavior that may be linked to television, the parent administers positive or negative reinforcement after the fact. For example, one of our interviewees reportedly uses the young son from the television series "Eight Is Enough" as a point of comparison when she is trying to stop her 7-year-old son's crying ("see what happened to Nicholas, and *he* didn't cry, so why are you crying?"), while another points to a television character as a warning in attempting to control her daughter's eating habits ("see, if you keep eating, you're going to be fat like that when you're older"). Also of potential relevance here are findings reported by Linne, which can be interpreted as indicating that children's long-term aggressive responses to a violent television series were tempered in those cases in which the children's immediate reactions to the programs could be monitored by their parents and other family

members (Brown & Linne, 1976). In the examples from our data, of course, the link with television was introduced into the situation by the parents themselves, whereas in the situation studied by Linne the link preceded parental intervention. The common element that distinguishes both types of situation from those cited earlier, however, is that the coincidence between reinforcement and behavior is here more direct. From this it may tentatively be inferred that the potency of reinforcement is here greater.

Aside from the findings mentioned above, there are several instances of research that has suggested a connection between children's behavioral responses to television and various features of the family environment, although in these cases it is less clear that parent-child interaction focused directly on television is involved. Thus, it has been shown that the relationship between children's or adolescents' aggression levels or aggressive tendencies and amounts of viewing television violence may vary with degree of parental emphasis on nonaggression (McLeod, Atkin, & Chaffee, 1972a, p. 238; 1972b, p. 312), with the extent to which family attitudes towards aggression are clear to the child (Dominick & Greenberg, 1972, p. 323), or with the degree to which parental disciplinary practices are oriented toward internalization vs. external control of behavior (Korzenny, Greenberg, & Atkin, 1979). Also of relevance here may be the findings of several studies that have indicated that children's responses (variously measured) to advertising may be related to the frequency of family discussions about the consumption of goods and services (Ward & Wackman, 1971), to the degree of parental approval of a product (Atkin, 1978, p. 79), or to differences in family environment associated with parental education (Rossiter & Robertson, 1974; Roberston & Rossiter, 1977). It must be repeated, however, that in most of these instances the extent to which parental influence is exercised through interactions specifically focused on the subject of television is unclear.

There is evidence from a variety of sources, then, that parents may affect their children's overt behavioral responses to television—through advice before the fact, through approval/disapproval or other reward/punishment once a type of behavior has been initiated, or through the control of aspects of a child's environment less specifically oriented toward a particular type of behavior. It must not be assumed, however, that action (e.g., aggression, consumer behavior) is the only kind of overt behavior that may be influenced by parental advice or approving/disapproving comments occasioned by, or linked to, television. Rather, it may well be the case that an important additional consequence of such advice, and so forth, is the conditioning of a child's verbal behavior. An interesting example of this possibility is the case of a mother from a wealthy suburban community who reportedly warned her 7-year-old son at length to avoid the kinds of criminal entanglements that were shown, on television, to have landed a 10-year-old heroin addict in jail. Although a child's involvement with drugs cannot be precluded, regardless of social background, it is probably true that, for this particular child, the circumstances that might lead to general criminal entanglements are not likely to materialize. In this sense, then, his mother's advice on that aspect of the matter may never have any direct bearing on his actions. This does not mean, however, that the consequences of advice of this sort are unimportant.

While the child in this example is only remotely likely to face a jail term for the kind of "non white-collar" criminal activity his mother was warning him about, his future as an adult will almost certainly occur in a society in which such activity is a public issue, requiring the expression of opinion. There is in fact a whole range of experiences that any particular child can never expect to encounter directly but on which he/she will be expected, as a member of society, to make a verbal contribution towards the attainment of community consensus. It is, then, to the shaping of verbal behavior of this sort that much of the parental commentary discussed above may be said to contribute. Indeed, several parents reported that they used joint-viewing situations to elicit and to regulate the opinions of their children on salient moral issues—or that their children themselves used such situations to have their opinions monitored. For example: "Sometimes I

might ask *him* to explain it to me to see whether he understands something, you know, the difference between a good character and a bad character, something like that, and, why is one good and one bad." "The kids will come with it, they'll say, that's the kind of thing you shouldn't do, right? Or, that's not very nice. They'll say, he's not very nice is he, he shouldn't do that. And I'll say, yes, you're right, he's not very nice, he's hurting someone." It can be argued, incidentally, that such occasions, on which children actively voice an opinion, which is then either accepted or modified, are the most likely to result in the stabilization of these opinions (cf. Hovland, Janis, & Kelley, 1968, pp. 215-240). The use of cases from television as pertinent referents for the clarification of values has also been reported by Lull (1980), while Anderson et al. (1979) give an example of a parent who avoids watching certain programs with his children because of the likelihood of questions on difficult moral issues.

The notion that situations that call forth comments on matters of public concern are institutionalized means for the regulation of public opinion is an old one (cf. Durkheim, 1900; Malinowski, 1926). The role of the mass media in such situations has been described by Lazarsfeld & Merton (1964), in their discussion of what Wright (1959) has labeled the "ethicizing function" of mass communication. Their argument was that public exposure of wrongdoing through the mass media generates discussions in the course of which private moral standards are adjusted against societal norms. An implicit part of this argument, too, was the notion that the end result of these discussions is an actual adjustment of individual action as a consequence of internalization of public standards of morality. The position advanced here differs somewhat from that of Lazarsfeld and Merton on this latter point. Since any connection between verbal opinions and action is problematic (cf. Mischel, 1968; Wicker, 1969) and since the process that Lazarsfeld and Merton describe is, in the first instance, primarily one of equilibration between verbal pronouncements, it may be wise to see the primary function of this process as the regulation of public opinion considered purely as overt verbal behavior. With this view, conformity to public opinion in one's actions need be seen only as a matter of response to the social pressure generated by concerted public declaration on a certain issue, and the assumption of internalization need not be made.

THE DEVELOPMENT OF SOCIAL RELATIONSHIPS

The final area to be considered here is the development of the child as a participant in social relationships. In this area, the discussion will focus on three ways in which the interaction between parents and children, in combination with various uses of television content, may contribute to the developmental process. The first two of these involve parental intervention in the processes attendant upon a child's identification with a particular television character. The third entails the assumption by parents and children of complementary roles in situations modeled after television portrayals.

The term "identification" can be used in several ways. Here it will be used relatively loosely to refer to a child's perception of, or assumption of, a commonality of personality traits between himself/herself and a particular television character. In the first of these two situations, in which the commonality is perceived to exist, rather than assumed in the absence of its existence, identification may lead a child to use his/her televised counterpart as a guide for future social behavior. More important, from the present perspective, a parent may intervene in such a situation, by placing selective emphasis on particular aspects of the commonality and their implications. In two separate cases in our data, for example, parents reported that one of their children identified with the TV-cartoon character, Charlie Brown, with respect to his constant victimization by other characters. ("A lot of kids can relate to Charlie Brown, because I think these are things that have always happened to them, just like poor little Charlie.") Both of these parents said that they responded to this situation by pointing out the importance of perseverance in the case of the "real" Charlie Brown ("in the end they all become his friends . . . . The school year isn't over yet, the *day* isn't over

yet"). Assuming that statements of this kind do, in certain circumstances, affect the nature of a child's continuing relations with his/her peers or any other persons, this sort of parent-child interaction would appear to be a relatively simple instance of the type of process under examination here.

More complicated is the case of a child's identification with a television character who is in fact perceived to be different from the child, in the sense that this character's personality and social situation are clearly other than those of the child in question—for example, the obedient child of wealthy parents identifying with the TV version of a penniless juvenile delinquent. It is generally argued (e.g., Kennedy, 1978) that the value, from the point of view of the child's development, of cases such as these is that they increase the child's understanding of the types he/she is identifying with. However, a more precise formulation of this issue was given by G.H. Mead (1925, p. 276), in a discussion of the role of fiction in the development of the self. To his well-known position that the social self (or person) is a relational entity encompassing appropriate patterns of response to specific other members of society as well as to a "generalized other," Mead added in this instance the observation that identification with fictional characters is one way in which these patterns of response may be formed. The specific processes implicit in Mead's formulation are internal to the organism. However, in the situations we are concerned with here, these processes can take partly external form in the interaction between parent and child.

An example of what we have in mind occurs in the following description of a mother's response to her 7-year-old daughter's imitation of "the Fonz." "I guess that particular character annoyed me, the Fonz. I'm not terribly pro-TV anyway, as you may have noticed at this point, but I think they showed what is essentially a hood and a creep and gave him many positive characteristics that the type he represented wouldn't have, and I didn't like that, so I would tend to put him down when she was imitating him, or when he happened to be on TV. 'Oh, he's so neat!' 'Oh, Jenny, he's such a creep!'" Identification in this case takes the overt form of imitation. By putting herself in this position, the child elicits from her mother the kind of (negative) response that is the appropriate form of her relationship to the type of person she is imitating. This much of the process is therefore external, and it is only the necessary final step, that is, internalization by the child of a "relational tendency" modeled after that of her mother, which is not. It must be assumed further, of course, that identifiable real-life counterparts of "the Fonz" are a salient component of the child's social environment. Incidentally, in reference to the process described here and to the previous case, it might be mentioned that H.S. Sullivan (1953, pp. 223-225) considered imitation in the presence of parents to be an indispensable component of adequate socialization.

The third and final type of process to be discussed in this section may also be said to involve identification, although of a very different order. In this type of process, two or more members of a family will adopt a set of television-derived roles during the course of a game or other type of play. This sort of thing occurs quite typically among children, of course (cf. Himmelweit, Oppenheim, & Vince, 1958, p. 381; Desmond, 1978, pp. 205-206), and some of its functions in such circumstances appear to be relatively clear. In the course of systematic observation of children's play in a day-care center, for instance, we have noted such patterns as: male "superheroes" saving female "damsels in distress" from assorted perils; male "vampires" attacking female "victims" in aggressive/erotic fashion; aggressive older "monsters" (e.g., the "Incredible Hulk") terrorizing more retiring, younger, "helpless masses," and so forth. It is easy to see such play as "rehearsal" with obvious stimuli and also, perhaps, fairly obvious consequences. Play involving parents with their children, however, is another matter.

There are two particularly vivid examples of play of this latter variety in our data. One case is that of a father who takes the role of the "joker" and other villains in games with his two sons, "Batman" and "Robin." The other is that of a mother who on at least one occasion allowed her son to tie her up and come to her rescue as a "superhero." The com-

plexity of the relationships that such situations temporarily give rise to should be evident. The children of the first example, for instance, must be able to balance the game's intensification of certain dimensions of the father-son relationship against its reversal of certain others of these dimensions. Furthermore, they may also have to contend with the possibility that the reversals actually correspond to latent elements. In the second case, the difference in sex between parent and child makes the situation even more complex. It would be rash to hazard an interpretation of the consequences of these specific interactions without much more study of the particulars in each case. As a general principle, however, it may be suggested that perhaps one of the most important consequences of such interactions as a class is the training they provide in the skills of performance in delicate social positions (cf. Bateson, 1956).

SUMMARY

The contents of the preceding four sections have yielded several assumptions about potential consequences of television-related parent-child interaction, which the following summary will attempt to present in compact form.

(1) Assumptions concerning the learning of interpretational skills: (a) By furnishing the necessary information for adequate interpretations of problematic program elements, parents may be contributing to their children's mastery of television's narrative conventions and of the implicit principle that the parts of a program should be treated as components of a superordinate whole. (b) Explicit parental commentary on the truth value of television programming may be one basis on which children's perceptions of the validity and generalizability of television programming are formed. However, parental influence in this regard can apparently be less explicit, too.

(2) Assumptions concerning the articulation of cognitive categories: A child's classification system for environmental objects and events may be affected by the addition or elaboration of categories derived from: (a) the parental "translation" of tele-

vised images into verbal concepts or (b) the classificatory principles implicit in parental comparisons between television characters and real-life people.

(3) Assumptions concerning overt behavioral consequences: (a) Children's overt behavior in response to television may be affected by: (i) parental advice in connection with a televised situation capable of being linked to some response by the child; (ii) parental approval/disapproval or other reward/ punishment following the initiation of behavior that may be linked to television. (Less explicit means of parental influence are, however, also a possibility.) (b) Aside from potential consequences for children's future actions, parental advice occasioned by television may also be an important element in the formation of their children's patterns of overt verbal behavior.

(4) Assumptions concerning the development of social relationships: Parental responses to children's identification with television characters may affect children's developing social relationships by: (a) providing guidance concerning social characteristics that a child perceives himself/herself as sharing with the television character; or (b) providing a model for the child's own pattern of response to the social type exemplified by the television character in question. Furthermore, (c) social "skill," in general, rather than any particular type of relationship, may be affected by parental participation in children's identificatory play.

IMPLICATIONS FOR RESEARCH

The final subtype of consequence referred to immediately above would, of course, be a very poor candidate for empirical testing and has been included in this discussion primarily as an indication of the complexity of the subject and as a hint at how much has been left unsaid. On the other hand, this exception aside, the preceding discussion has been oriented towards types of processes and attendant consequences that appear to the authors to be more readily subject to empirical investigation. In this section, methodological issues involved in such an investigation will be discussed. The discussion will deal separately with two orders of evidence required for the verification of the propositions developed thus far: (a) evidence that the sequences of parent-child interaction do occur as described or, where the description is incomplete, evidence on the missing segments; and (b) evidence confirming, failing to confirm, or modifying the posited consequences of these interactions.

The descriptions of television-related parent-child interactions given above have been based primarily on the series of interviews with parents from which illustrations have been excerpted throughout this paper. These are open-ended interviews, soliciting information on 26 prespecified types of television-related parent-child interaction and on whatever additional types a parent can supply. In connection with each of the items covered by the interview, the respondent is first asked to indicate whether a certain kind of situation occurs in his/her family (e.g., children's questions about things they haven't understood, discussions of the accuracy of televised portrayals, comparisons between real-life people and television characters, and so on). Positive responses are followed by a request for specific examples, and various probes are used to obtain descriptions of the behavior of all participants in a cited occurrence, as well as of its time and place.

This kind of interview is probably the most convenient way of getting information on television-related parent-child interaction. However, data from such interviews are very likely to contain at least two types of bias. First, because of the controversial nature of the subject (viz., the role of television in people's lives), respondents may assume a defensive posture and skew their answers accordingly. In the data drawn upon for this paper, for example, parents occasionally appeared to be exaggerating the importance of educational television in their children's lives, under-reporting the amount of television-based interaction, and so forth. Second, regardless of the intentions of the respondent, inaccuracies in reporting are bound to result from the respondent's lack of specific training as an observer of the complex behavior under investigation (cf. Birdwhistell, 1970, pp. 190-191; Messaris, 1977). These inaccuracies are likely to involve imperfect recall, unconscious assimilation of the reconstructed information to social stereotypes of parent-child interaction (cf. Bartlett, 1932), and selective inattention to aspects of the interaction—in particular, modalities of behavior other than the lexical—that are not ordinarily included in everyday accounts of one's past social encounters.

Because of the potential for these types of bias, it seems necessary for research in this area to use other sources of data in addition to interviews with parents, despite their privileged access to the events being investigated. Above a certain age, children are one obvious source of supplementary data. However, as Greenberg, Ericson, and Vlahos (1972) and Rossiter and Robertson (1975) have noted, children's accounts of television-related family interaction may also be biased, partly in the same ways as parental accounts, but partly also in an opposite direction, that of minimizing the extent and impact of parental control in these matters. In view of these potential limitations of self-report data, the needs of the investigator in this general area may, depending on the problem, require going beyond interviews to observation.

Because of the technical difficulties and the expense entailed in installing video (cf. Bechtel, Achelpohl, & Akers, 1972) or even less complicated (cf. Allen, 1965) recording devices in people's homes, observation must involve the actual presence of an observer in the houses of informants. Furthermore, because the observer's presence may, before it ceases to be a novelty, generate unacceptable adjustments in the behavior observed, this kind of observation cannot be limited to the briefer period of contact typically employed in interviews. Thus, Murray (1972), Anderson et al. (1979), Reid (1979), and Lull (1980) have all conducted repeated visits with informant families, while Lull (in press-a) has also employed observers who actually "lived in" with families for several days. Some accomodation to the presence of the observer obviously must persist, regardless of the length of the period of observation. There is some evidence, however, that television-related behavior is less vulnerable to this kind of accommodation than other aspects of family life (Lull, in press-a).

The time requirements of observational work have obvious consequences for limits in sample size. It is, therefore, appropriate to think of it as the stage in which hypotheses can be formed and elaborated, rather than as the actual arena in which they will be tested (cf. Anderson, 1979). In an area like the one under consideration here, any explicit hypothesis intended for immediate empirical testing cannot easily avoid having to account for several variables simultaneously (age of the child, SES, several dimensions of parent-child interaction, etc.). Thus, large sample sizes are also unavoidable, and observational data must eventually yield to other measures. However, as Lull (1979) demonstrates with a particularly vivid example, observational data may be an indispensable adjunct to the elaboration of hypotheses in the preliminary stages of research in the area discussed here, and the emphasis placed on such data in the preceding paragraphs has been predicated on that assumption. With reference to the processes of parent-child interaction described above, direct observation would make possible: (a) greater detail and specificity in the formulation of these processes; (b) the specification of situational variables related to these processes; and (c) estimates of frequencies of occurrence of each process. In combination with interviews, then, direct observation should furnish the first order of data required for the validation of statements about these processes, namely, data necessary for the verification or completion of descriptions of the interactional sequences involved.

The Measurement of Consequences

The measurement of the posited consequences of the processes discussed above involves methodological problems which go beyond those discussed thus far. These problems differ, to a certain extent, depending on which of the several categories of consequence covered in this paper is involved.

Interpretational competence. Children's abilities to interpret visual narratives are typically measured in one of three ways: (a) through verbal "reconstruction" of the narrative (e.g., Murphy, 1973;

Zazzo & Zazzo, 1951); (b) through questions about the content of specific incidents, about the connections between incidents, and so forth (e.g., Desmond, 1978); (c) through picture-sequencing tasks, in which children are asked to order still pictures extracted from a videotape, film, and the like (e.g., Leifer et al., 1971). In a methodological study in which children's performance on the first of these tasks was compared with their performance on the third, Zazzo (1952) found that "visual" reconstruction was consistently more easy than "verbal" reconstruction. Although this particular finding was confounded by the fact that the amount of initial information available to the children in the two situations was very different, it nevertheless suggests the possibility that the visual task taps the measured skill (comprehension) more directly and is, therefore, the more valid measure. It may be useful, therefore, to inject here a word of caution on the appropriateness of such a conclusion. For one thing, it is not at all certain that the process of attending to even a purely visual narrative is, under ordinary circumstances, devoid of some form of "inner verbalization" (cf. Bandura, 1969; Bandura, Grusec, & Menlove, 1966). Perhaps more important, it should be pointed out that the task of verbal reconstruction does have an equivalent in most children's everyday experience, whereas that of visual reconstruction does not. Specifically, investigators who have studied children as viewers in their homes have repeatedly encountered, especially among young children, spontaneous verbal "reportage" concerning the unfolding televised events (cf. Murray, 1972; Winick & Winick, 1979). Indeed, in one study on children's responses to film (Siersted & Lund Hansen, 1951), such "spontaneous" remarks, coupled with photographs, were used as the main source of evidence on children's interpretations. In short, it is not clear that the visual measures are the most appropriate, despite the possibility that verbal reconstructions, especially when they occur after the fact, may contain elaborations not necessarily corresponding to the nature of the original experience (cf. Williams, 1969). In any event, if the investigator is interested in the child's perception of characters' motives, causal links in the plot, and so on (e.g., Collins, 1979), some use of verbal mea-

sures, especially of the second kind listed above, seems inevitable.

Perceptions of validity and generalizability of program content. The degree to which children perceive various categories of television programming as accurate portrayals of reality has been investigated through explicit questions in several studies. For example, respondents have been asked to indicate degree of agreement with statements such as: "The programs I see on TV tell about life the way it really is" (Greenberg & Dominick, 1969, p. 338); "The people I see in adventure stories are just like the people I meet in real life" (McLeod, Atkin, & Chaffee, 1972a, p. 208). While direct questioning may be the best method to use with older children or adolescents, as in the two cases cited above, its use with younger children is problematic: As long as one does not believe that young children treat television as real "by default," a child's possible inability to verbalize a distinction between reality and television, that is, to deal with the *concept* of a potential difference between the two realms, cannot be taken as conclusive evidence that he/she implicitly treats the content of television programming as a valid contribution to his/her developing stock of knowledge about the real world. It would seem desirable, instead, to use some indirect method of validation in such cases. For example, degree of belief in certain stereotypes associated with television can be taken as one indirect measure of the truth value implicitly or explicitly assigned to the medium (cf. Gross & Morgan, in press)—but only so long as other sources of confirmation or development of these stereotypes can be ruled out.

Cognitive categories. Although certain features of a child's system of cognitive classification may be explicit, it cannot be assumed beforehand that this kind of material is accessible to direct questions. Measurement of the number, type, and salience of classificatory dimensions that a child—or its parents—imposes on various aspects of reality must therefore be a matter of inference from less direct data. Perhaps the simplest kinds of test of this type are the various sorting tasks developed initially by anthropological linguists (e.g., Carroll & Casagrande, 1958) for the measurement of covert categories. In a study by Quarfoth, for example, children were asked to sort pictures of television characters into piles, "to put the ones together that belong together" (Quarfoth, 1979, p. 212). This kind of task permitted the investigator to infer the presence of a cartoon-puppet-"human" character distinction, and so forth. Somewhat more demanding on the subject, perhaps, are various scaling techniques in which degree of similarity between pairs of objects must be judged and the underlying structure of classificatory dimensions is obtained on the basis of a large set of judgments (e.g., Reeves & Greenberg, 1977; Reeves & Lometti, 1979; Alexander, 1980). The disadvantage of measures involving sorting or scaling is that they require the subject to perform a relatively unusual task. The use of these techniques presupposes, therefore, an assumption that the cognitive patterns being measured are relatively constant across types of situations that elicit them. In an attempt to avoid having to make this assumption, Peevers & Secord (1973) have introduced what they consider a less "artificial" measurement instrument, namely, subjects' "free" or "naturalistic" descriptions, which are then analyzed for classificatory principles by the investigators. A written version of this kind of measure has been used by Alexander & Wartella (1979) to assess the relationship between children's perceptions of television characters and their perceptions of real people. However, as Alexander (1980) points out, the cognitive processes involved in discriminating among objects and sorting them into categories may differ from those involved in describing individual objects. Therefore, the assumption that tasks involving "free" description will give the investigator access to a subject's system of classification should be treated with caution.

Overt behavior. With regard to validity, direct observation is obviously the most desirable method of measurement of overt behavioral patterns. However, while in-home observation, even when a family is not directly engaged in television viewing, may not be too problematic to negotiate, the observation of older children in other contexts and, in particular, in unsupervised peer-group situations is likely to be hampered by serious initial barriers of trust (cf. Fine & Glassner, 1979). At the very least, the problem becomes one of excessive time requirements. Hence the obvious need, especially in large-sample work, for reliance on self- and other-report. These considerations apply also to the measurement of opinion, viewed, as it is here, purely as overt verbal behavior. In other words, opinions in this sense should either be observed directly or be reported on in connection with specified classes of eliciting situations. The latter alternative differs from that of typical opinion polling, in which the possibilities of cross-situational variation are usually unaccounted for, since only one situation—namely, that of the interview itself—is examined. As an alternative or in addition to reports of actual behavior, investigators sometimes ask respondents to describe their behavior in a hypothetical situation (e.g., Dominick & Greenberg, 1972). Answers to questions of this sort may not be good indicators of a child's past behavior, but, as indicators of likely future behavior, they may be extremely useful, for reasons to be discussed below, with reference to the measurement of social relationships.

Social relationships. If the interest of the investigator is in the observation of changing patterns in a child's current social relationships, the methodological considerations noted above apply here, too. However, if one's interest is in the contribution that present learning may make to unobservable future behavior, the situation is much more complicated. Since the types of future behavior that one is interested in (e.g., parenthood, relationships with employers, etc.) may have no direct counterpart in the present behavior of the child, the question becomes: Is there any realm of a child's overt behavior in which one can observe that "portion" of its future roles that it has already learned (and may, of course, subsequently unlearn)? The answer may, of course, be no, but there is some evidence to support the notion that certain kinds of play may fit this requirement. While games with conventional rules have been seen as providing training for expected future roles, and associations between game style and social structure have been demonstrated empirically (e.g., Caillois, 1979; Eifermann, 1971; Roberts, Sutton-Smith, & Kendon, 1963), an argument can be made that "fantasy play"—play involving make-believe and lacking conventional rules—is the arena in which a child rehearses what he/she has already learned (cf. Piaget, 1962; Vygotsky, 1979). On the basis of this argument, contexts involving some element of "make-believe" (i.e., questions about hypothetical situations, semiprojective tests, observations of natural play, etc.) can be used deliberately to elicit clues to future behavior; and, in at least one case (Erikson, 1955; 1972), long-term follow-up studies have been claimed to support the methodological presupposition of this kind of measurement.

Other Research Considerations

In concluding, it should be noted that any work in this general area that attempts to go beyond the exploratory stage must deal explicitly with at least two variables not discussed here, namely, children's age and family's social class. The precise manner in which age is accounted for will vary, of course, depending on whether the researcher is working within a general theoretical framework that posits uniform developmental stages; but, so long as he/she makes some assumption of structural discontinuity in the developmental path (cf. Overton & Reese, 1973), age, as the best initial index of a child's position on this path, must be controlled for: As Ward, Wackman, & Wartella (1977, pp. 105-106) have argued, it is obviously possible that unvarying family environments may differ in their developmental implications at different ages.

Considerations of social-class differences, on the other hand, are a necessary part of any research that would seek to link the kinds of intrafamily processes discussed here to the operation of the broader social system. A prominent possibility for such a link is provided by the work of McLeod and his associates, mentioned earlier, on family communication patterns (McLeod & Brown, 1976). On the one hand, the family types that they describe appear to be associated with characteristic patterns of television-related interaction among family members (e.g., Lull, in press-b). On the other hand, the

dimensions along which these types are distinguished may also be related to class differences: While McLeod has repeatedly cautioned against the assumption of a simple relationship here (McLeod & Chaffee, 1972, 84, pp.86-87; McLeod & O'Keefe, 1972, pp. 129-131), the partly parallel work of Bernstein (1971) and his associates—especially Douglas's (1973) admittedly tentative discussion of social mobility—suggests that the search for connections, even if very complex ones, between "micro-interaction" patterns and social-structural variables may not be fruitless.

REFERENCES

ALEXANDER, A. Children's perceptions of television characters: Validity in the multidimensional scaling approach. Presented to the International Communication Association, Acapulco, 1980.
ALEXANDER, A., & WARTELLA, E. Children's impressions of television characters and real people. Paper presented to the International Communication Association, Philadelphia, 1979.
ALLEN, C.L. Photographing the TV audience. Journal of Advertising Research, 1965, 5(1), 2-8.
ANDERSON, J.A. Ethnology and hypothetico-deductive research. Paper presented to the International Communication Association, Philadelphia, 1979.
ANDERSON, J.A., TRAUDT, P.J., ACKER, S.R., MEYER, T.P., & DONOHUE, T.R. An ethnological approach to a study of televiewing in family settings. Paper presented to the Western Speech Communication Association, Los Angeles, 1979.
APPELL, C.T. Television viewing and the preschool child. Marriage and Family Living, 1963, 25, 311-318.
ATKIN, C.K. Effects of drug commercials on young viewers. Journal of Communication, 1978, 28(4), 71-79.
BANDURA, A. Influence of models' reinforcement contingencies on the acquisition of imitative responses. Journal of Personality and Social Psychology, 1965, 1, 589-595.
BANDURA, A. Social-learning theory of identificatory processes. In D.A. Goslin (Ed.), Handbook of socialization theory and research. Chicago: Rand McNally, 1969.
BANDURA, A., GRUSEC, J.E., & MENLOVE, F.L. Observational learning as a function of symbolization and incentive set. Child Development, 1966, 37, 499-506.
BARCUS, F.E. Parental influence on children's television viewing. Television Quarterly, 1969, 8, 63-73.
BARTLETT, F.C. Remembering. Cambridge, England: Cambridge University Press, 1932.
BATESON, G. The message "This is play." In B. Schaffner (Ed.), Group processes. New York: Josiah Macy, Jr. Foundation, 1956.
BATESON, G. The logical categories of learning and communication. In G. Bateson, Steps to an ecology of mind. New York: Ballantine Books, Inc., 1972, 279-308.
BECHTEL, R.B., ACHELPOHL, C., & AKERS, R. Correlates

between observed behavior and questionnaire responses on television viewing. In E.A. Rubinstei, G.A. Comstock, & J.P. Murray (Eds.), *Television and social behavior*, Vol. 4, *Television in day-to-day life: Patterns of use*. Washington, D.C.: U.S. Government Printing Office, 1972.

BELLMAN, B.L., & JULES-ROSETTE, B. *A paradigm for looking: Cross-cultural research with visual media*. Norwood, N.J.: Ablex Publishing Corporation, 1977.

BERGER, P.L., & LUCKMANN, T. *The social construction of reality*. Garden City, N.Y.: Doubleday Anchor, 1966.

BERLIN, B., & KAY, P. *Basic color terms: Their universality and evolution*. Berkeley: University of California Press, 1969.

BERNSTEIN, B. *Class, codes and control*. New York: Schocken Books, 1971.

BIRDWHISTELL, R.L. *Kinesics and context*. Philadelphia: University of Pennsylvania Press, 1970.

BOGART, L. Adults talk about newspaper comics. *American Journal of Sociology*, 1955, 61, 26-30.

BOWER, R.T. *Television and the public*. New York: Holt, Rinehart & Winston, 1973.

BRONFENBRENNER, U. *The ecology of human development: Experiments by nature and design*. Cambridge: Harvard University Press, 1979.

BROWN, J.R., & LINNE, O. The family as a mediator of television's effects. In R. Brown (Ed.), *Children and television*. Beverly Hills: Sage, 1976.

CAILLOIS, R. *Man, play, and games*. New York: Schocken, 1979.

CAREY, J. Temporal and spatial transitions in American fiction films. *Studies in the Anthropology of Visual Communication*, 1974, 1, 45-50.

CARROLL, J.B., & CASAGRANDE, J.B. The function of language classifications in behavior. In E.E. Maccoby, T.M. Newcomb, & E.L. Hartley (Eds.), *Readings in social psychology* (3rd ed). New York: Holt, Rinehart & Winston, 1958.

CHAFFEE, S.H. The interpersonal context of mass communication. In F.G. Kline & P.J. Tichenor (Eds.), *Current perspectives in mass communication research*. Beverly Hills: Sage, 1972, 95-120.

CHAFFEE, S.H., & McLEOD, J.M. Adolescent television use in the family context. In G.A. Comstock & E.A. Rubinstein (Eds.), *Television and social behavior* (Vol. 3), *Television and adolescent aggressiveness*. Washington, D.C.: U.S. Government Printing Office, 1972.

CHAFFEE, S.H., McLEOD, J.M., & ATKIN, C.K. Parental influences on adolescent media use. In F.G. Kline & P. Clarke (Eds.), *Mass communications and youth: Some current perspectives*. Beverly Hills: Sage Publications, 1971.

CHAFFEE, S.H., WARD, L.S., & TIPTON, L.P. Mass communication and political socialization. *Journalism Quarterly*, 1970, 47, 647-659, 666.

COLLINS, W.A. The developing child as viewer. *Journal of Communication*, 1975, 25(4), 33-44.

COLLINS, W.A. Children's comprehension of television content. In E. Wartella (Ed.), *Children communicating*. Beverly Hills: Sage, 1979.

DESMOND, R.J. Cognitive development and television comprehension. *Communication Research*, 1978, 5, 202-220.

DOMINICK, J.R., & GREENBERG, B.S. Attitudes toward violence: The interaction of television exposure, family at-

titudes, and social class. In G.A. Comstock & E.A. Rubinstein (Eds.), *Television and social behavior* (Vol. 3), *Television and adolescent aggressiveness*. Washington, D.C.: U.S. Government Printing Office, 1972.

DOUGLAS, M. *Natural symbols*. New York: Vintage, 1973.

DURKHEIM, E. Deux lois de l'evolution penale. *L' Annee Sociologique*, 1900, 4, 65-95.

EIFERMANN, R.R. *Determinants of children's game styles*. Jerusalem: The Israel Academy of Sciences and Humanities, 1971.

ERIKSON, E.H. Sex differences in the play configurations of American pre-adolescents. In M. Mead & M. Wolfenstein (Eds.), *Childhood in contemporary cultures*. Chicago: The University of Chicago Press, 1955.

ERIKSON, E.H. Play and actuality. In M.W. Piers (Ed.), *Play and development*. New York: Norton, 1972.

FINE, G.A., & GLASSNER, B. Participant observation with children: Promise and problems. *Urban Life*, 1979, 8, 153-174.

FORSEY, S.D. The influence of family structures upon the patterns and effects of television viewing. In L. Arons & M.A. May (Eds.), *Television and human behavior: Tomorrow's research in mass communication*. New York: Appleton-Century-Crofts, 1963, 64-80.

FRIEDSON, E. The relation of the social situation of contact to the media in mass communication. *Public Opinion Quarterly*, 1953, 17, 230-238.

GEWIRTZ, J.L. Mechanisms of social learning: Some roles of stimulation and behavior in early human development. In D.A. Goslin (Ed.), *Handbook of socialization theory and research*. Chicago: Rand McNally, 1969.

GOMBRICH, E.H. The visual image. *Scientific American*, 1972, 227, 82-96.

GOULD, S.J. A quahog is a quahog. *Natural History*, 1979, 88(7), 18-26.

GREENBERG, B.S., & DOMINICK, J.R. Racial and social class differences in teen-agers' use of television. *Journal of Broadcasting*, 1969, 13, 331-344.

GREENBERG, B.S., ERICSON, P.M., & VLAHOS, M. Children's television behaviors as perceived by mother and child. In E.A. Rubinstein, G.A. Comstock, & J.P. Murray (Eds.), *Television and social behavior* (Vol. 4), *Television in day-to-day life: Patterns of use*. Washington, D.C.: U.S. Government Printing Office, 1972, 395-407.

GROSS, L., & MORGAN, M. Television and enculturation. In J.R. Dominick & J. Fletcher (Eds.), *Research in broadcasting—Readings*. Broadcast Education Association, in press.

GRUSEC, J.E. Effects of co-observer evaluations on imitation: A developmental study. *Developmental Psychology*, 1973, 8(1), 141.

GURWITZ, S.B., & TOPOL, B. Determinants of confirming and discomfirming responses to negative social labels. *Journal of Experimental Social Psychology*, 1978, 14, 31-42.

HALLORAN, J.D., BROWN, R.L., & CHANEY, D.C. *Television and delinquency*. Leicester: Leicester University Press, 1970.

HESS, R.H., & GOLDMAN, H. Parents' views of the effect of television on their children. *Child Development*, 1962, 33, 411-426.

HICKS, D.J. Effects of co-observer's sanctions and adult presence on imitative aggression. *Child Development*, 1968, 39, 303-309.

HIMMELWEIT, H.T., OPPENHEIM, A., & VINCE, P. *Television and the child*. London: Oxford University Press, 1958.

HOCHBERG, J., & BROOKS, V. Pictorial perception as an unlearned ability. *American Journal of Psychology*, 1962, 75, 624-628.

HOLLANDER, N. Adolescents and the war: The sources of socialization. *Journalism Quarterly*, 1971, 58, 472-479.

HOVLAND, C.I., JANIS, I.L., & KELLEY, H.H. *Communication and persuasion: Psychological studies of opinion change*. New Haven: Yale University Press, 1968.

KANOUSE, D.E. Language, labeling, and attribution. In E.E. Jones, D.E. Kanouse, H.H. Kelley, R.E. Nisbett, S. Valins, & B. Weiner (Eds.), *Attribution: Perceiving the causes of behavior*. Morristown, N.J.: General Learning Press, 1972.

KENNEDY, J.M. Identification and different arts media. In S.S. Madeja (Ed.),*The arts, cognition, and basic skills*. St. Louis: Cemrel, Inc., 1978, 214-227.

KORZENNY, F., GREENBERG, B.S., & ATKIN, C.K. Styles of parental disciplinary practices as a mediator of children's learning from antisocial television portrayals. In D. Nimmo (Ed.), *Communication yearbook 3*. New Brunswick, Transaction Books, 1979.

KRAUT, R.E. Effects of social labeling on giving to charity. *Journal of Experimental Social Psychology*, 1973, 9, 551-562.

LAZARSFELD, P.F., & MERTON, R.K. Communication, popular taste and organized social action. In L. Bryson (Ed.), *The communication of ideas*. New York: Cooper Square Publishers, 1964.

LEIFER, A.D., COLLINS, W.A., GROSS, B., TAYLOR, P., ANDREWS, L., & BLACKMER, E. Developmental aspects of variables relevant to observational learning. *Child Development*, 1971, 42, 1509-1516.

LEIFER, A.D., GORDON, N.J., & GRAVES, S.B. Children's television: More than mere entertainment. *Harvard Educational Review*, 1974, 44, 213-245.

LoSCIUTO, L.A. A national inventory of television viewing behavior. In E.A. Rubinstein, G.A. Comstock, & J.P. Murray (Eds.), *Television and social behavior* (Vol. 4), *Television in day-to-day life: Patterns of use*. Washington, D.C.: U.S. Government Printing Office, 1972.

LULL, J. Ethnographies of mass communication. Paper presented to the International Communication Association, Philadelphia, 1979.

LULL, J. The social uses of television. *Human Communication Research*, 1980, 6, 197-209.

LULL, J. Doing ethnographic research on broadcast media audiences. In J.R. Dominick & J. Fletcher (Eds.), *Research in broadcasting—Readings*. Broadcast Education Association, in press-a.

LULL, J. Family communication patterns and the social uses of television. *Communication Research*, in press-b.

LYLE, J., & HOFFMAN, H.R. Children's use of television and other media. In E.A. Rubinstein, G.A. Comstock, & J.P. Murray (Eds.), *Television and social behavior* (Vol. 4), *Television in day-to-day life: Patterns of use*. Washington, D.C.: U.S. Government Printing Office, 1972.

MACCOBY, E.E. Television: Its impact on school children. *Public Opinion Quarterly*, 1951, 15, 421-444.

MACCOBY, E.E. Why do children watch television? *Public Opinion Quarterly*, 1954, 18, 239-244.

MALINOWSKI, B. *Crime and custom in savage society*. London: Routledge and Kegan Paul, 1926.

McLEOD, J.M., ATKIN, C.K., & CHAFFEE, S.H. Adolescents, parents, and television use: Adolescent self-report from Maryland and Wisconsin samples. In G.A. Comstock & E.A. Rubinstein (Eds.), *Television and social behavior* (Vol. 3), *Television and adolescent aggressiveness*. Washington, D.C.: U.S. Government Printing Office, 1972a.

McLEOD, J.M., ATKIN, C.K., & CHAFFEE, S.H. Adolescents, parents, and television use: Self-report and other-report measures from the Wisconsin sample. in G.A. Comstock & E.A. Rubinstein (Eds.), *Television and social behavior* (Vol. 3), *Television and adolescent aggressiveness*. Washington, D.C.: U.S. Government Printing Office, 1972b.

McLEOD, J., & BROWN, J.D. The family environment and adolescent television use. In R. Brown (Ed.), *Children and television*. Beverly Hills: Sage, 1976.

McLEOD, J.M., & CHAFFEE, S.H. The construction of social reality. In J. Tedeschi (Ed.), *The social influence process*. Chicago: Aldine-Atherton, 1972.

McLEOD, J.M., & O'KEEFE, G.J., JR. The socialization perspective and communication behavior. In F.G. Kline & P.J. Tichenor (Eds.), *Current perspectives in mass communication research*. Beverly Hills: Sage, 1972.

MEAD, G.H. The genesis of the self and social control. *The International Journal of Ethics*, 1925, 35, 251-277.

MESSARIS, P. Biases of self-reported "functions" and "gratifications" of mass-media use. *Et Cetera*, 34, 316-329.

MESSARIS, P., & GROSS, L. Interpretations of a photographic narrative by viewers in four age groups. *Studies in the Anthropology of Visual Communication*, 1977, 4, 99-111.

MIALARET, G., & MELIES, M.G. Experiences sur la comprehension du langage cinematographique par l'enfant. *Revue Internationale de Filmologie*, 1954, 5, 221-228.

MISCHEL, W. *Personality and assessment*. New York: John Wiley & Sons, 1968.

MOHR, P.J. Parental guidance of children's viewing of evening television programs. *Journal of Broadcasting*, 1979, 23, 213-228.

MURPHY, J.P. Investigation of the nature and development of interpretive competence. Paper presented to the International Communciation Association, Montreal, 1973.

MURRAY, J.P. Television in inner-city homes: Viewing behavior of young boys. In E.A. Rubinstein, G.A. Comstock, & J.P. Murray (Eds.), *Television and social behavior* (Vol. 4), *Television in day-to-day life: Patterns of use*. Washington, D.C.: U.S. Government Printing Office, 1972, 345-394.

NOBLE, G. *Children in front of the small screen*. Beverly Hills: Sage, 1975.

OVERTON, W.F., & REESE, H.W. Models of development: Methodological implications. In J.R. Nesselroade & H.W. Reese (Eds.), *Life-span developmental psychology: Methodological issues*. New York: Academic Press, 1973.

PEEVERS, B.H., & SECORD, P.F. Developmental changes in attribution of descriptive concepts to persons. *Journal of Personality and Social Psychology*, 1973, 27, 120-128.

PIAGET, J. *Play, dreams, and imitation in childhood*. New York: Norton, 1962.

PRASAD, V.K., RAO, T.R., & SHEIKH, A.A. Mother vs. commercial. *Journal of Communication*, 1978, 28(1), 91-96.

QUARFOTH, J.M. Children's understanding of the nature of television characters. *Journal of Communication*, 1979, 29(3), 210-218.

REEVES, B., & GREENBERG, B.S. Children's perceptions of television characters. *Human Communication Research*, 1977, 3, 113-127.

REEVES, B., & LOMETTI, G.E. The dimensional structure of children's perceptions of television characters: A replication. *Human Communication Research*, 1979, 5, 247-256.

REID, L.N. Viewing rules as mediating factors of children's responses to commercials. *Journal of Broadcasting*, 1979, 23, 15-26.

RILEY, M.W., & RILEY, J.W., JR. A sociological approach to communications research. *Public Opinion Quarterly*, 1951, 15, 445-460.

ROBERTS, J.M., SUTTON-SMITH, B., & KENDON, A. Strategy in games and folk tales. *Journal of Social Psychology*, 1963, 61, 185-199.

ROBERTSON, T.S. Parental mediation of television advertising effects. *Journal of Communication*, 1979, 29(1), 12-25.

ROBERTSON, T.S., & ROSSITER, J.R. Children's responsiveness to commercials. *Journal of Communication*, 1977, 27(1), 101-106.

ROSSITER, J.R., & ROBERTSON, T.S. Testing the defenses. *Journal of Communication*, 1974, 24(4), 137-144.

ROSSITER, J.R., & ROBERTSON, T.S. Children's television viewing: An examination of parent-child consensus. *Sociometry*, 1975, 38, 308-326.

de SAUSSURE, F. *Course in general linguistics*. New York: McGraw-Hill, 1959.

SCHRAMM, W., LYLE, J., & PARKER, E.B. *Television in the lives of our children*. Stanford: Stanford University Press, 1961.

SIERSTED, E., & LUND HANSEN, H. Reactions de petits enfants au cinema. *Revue Internationale de Filmologie*, 1951, 2, 241-245.

SKINNER, B.F. *Science and human behavior*. New York: The Free Press, 1953.

STEINER, G.A. *The people look at television: A study of audience attitudes*. New York: Alfred A. Knopf, 1963.

SULLIVAN, H.S. *The interpersonal theory of psychiatry*. New York: Norton, 1953.

VYGOTSKY, L.S. *Mind in society: The development of higher psychological processes*. Cambridge, Harvard University Press, 1979.

WARD, S., & WACKMAN, D. Family and media influences on adolescent consumer learning. In F.G. Kline & P. Clarke (Eds.), *Mass communications and youth: Some current perspectives*. Beverly Hills: Sage, 1971, 113-125.

WARD, S., WACKMAN, D.B., & WARTELLA, E. *How children learn to buy*. Beverly Hills: Sage, 1977.

WHORF, B.L. Science and linguistics. In J.B. Carroll (Ed.), *Language, thought, and reality*. Cambridge: The M.I.T. Press, 1956.

WICKER, A.W. Attitudes versus actions: The relationship of verbal and overt behavioral responses to attitude objects. *Journal of Social Issues*, 1969, 25(4), 41-78.

WILLIAMS, F. Social class differences in how children talk about television. *Journal of Broadcasting*, 1969, 13, 345-357.

WILLIAMS, F., SMART, M.E., & EPSTEIN, R.H. Use of commercial television in parent and child interaction. *Journal of Broadcasting*, 1979, 23, 229-235.

WINICK, M.P., & WINICK, C. *The television experience: What children see*. Beverly Hills: Sage, 1979.

WORTH, S., & GROSS, L. Symbolic strategies. *Journal of Communication*, 1974, 24, 27-39.

WRIGHT, C.R. *Mass communication: A sociological perspective*. New York: Random House, 1959.

ZAZZO, B. Analyse de difficultes d'une sequence cinematographique par la conduite du recit chez l'enfant. *Revue Internationale de Filmologie*, 1952, 3, 25-36.

ZAZZO, B., & ZAZZO, R. Une experience sur la comprehension du film. *Revue Internationale de Filmologie*, 1951, 2, 159-170.

By using an innovative technique for sampling measurement periods with the aid of an electronic paging device, this study examines adults' self-reported mood states at random times over the course of a week. When the experience of television viewing is compared to other activities, adults report less cognitive involvement with television than other activities. Mihaly Csikszentmihalyi is professor in the Departments of Behavioral Science and Education and chairman of the Committee on Human Development of the University of Chicago. Robert Kubey is a doctoral student in the Committee on Human Development of the University of Chicago, and a lecturer in psychology at the University of Wisconsin.

21

TELEVISION AND THE REST OF LIFE

A Systematic Comparison of Subjective Experience

Mihaly Csikszentmihalyi and Robert Kubey

TELEVISION'S IMPACT on American life, according to Robinson's (1969, 1972) studies of time budgets, has been responsible for a greater rearrangement of life activities than the automobile. Not only has the time devoted to television cut into time previously committed to other mass media, but it has absorbed significant portions of time formerly spent in social and other leisure activities (Goldsen 1977); Comstock, 1980). The present research offers a behavioral and experiential account of TV viewing and addresses the following questions: In what combination of activities is television watching typically embedded? How does the subjective experience of watching television differ from other typical activities? How is TV watching related to one's experience of family life?

Previous research on how people feel while watching television has been conducted either in artificial laboratory conditions or retrospectively, with respondents relying on their memories (Bower,

1973; Steiner, 1963). Few researchers have examined how adults feel while watching TV in their homes or how the subjective experience of viewing contrasts with the variety of other activities which people engage in on a daily basis. For example:

(1) With little supporting empirical evidence, most writers on the subject have assumed that television watching is a passive, uninvolving, and generally boring experience. A minority of observers have suggested that television programs subject the viewer to harmful levels of stress or that they increase existing tensions within the family (Caprio, 1976; Rosenblatt and Cunningham, 1976).

(2) Television is often compared to print media (Krugman, 1977; McLuhan, 1978). Yet very little is known of the differences in people's experience while reading or watching TV. To better understand how TV viewing differs from reading we compared the two activities on a number of experiential variables.

(3) Similarly, although little research has been conducted, various observers have feared that the quality of family interaction has been drastically altered by the presence of TV sets in the home. One of the very few empirical studies addressing this concern dates back to Maccoby (1951), who concluded that "the television atmosphere in most households is one of quiet absorption on the part of family members who are present. The nature of the family social life during a program could be described as "parallel" rather than interactive, and the set does seem quite clearly to dominate family life when it is on." One recent study, by Rosenblatt and Cunningham (1976), has suggested that TV watching may function as a family coping mechanism and a means for avoiding tense interaction, especially in crowded homes where conflict avoidance through spatial separation is impossible. Television, according to these authors, may help to keep some families together by keeping them apart. Our method offers new and unique data on the question of how television watching effects familial experience.

To approach these questions, we have utilized a body of data collected via the recently developed Experience Sampling Method (ESM), which fulfills the requirement of tapping mood states in a relatively unobtrusive manner while people are actually involved in their normal life activities (Csikszentmihalyi et al., 1977).

Method

PROCEDURE

The data were obtained from a sample of 104 adult workers, each of whom filled out self-report forms at random times during a period of one week. The scheduling of self-reports was controlled by one-way radio communication. Each respondent (R) carried a pocket-sized electronic paging device which was activated by radio signals emitted from a transmitting tower with a 50-mile effective radius. The signals caused the pagers to make a series of audible "beeps" which served as the stimulus for Rs to complete the self-report form. On average, each R was signaled 56 times in a week during the waking hours only. The average number of self-reports completed by each R was 45. The difference between signals sent and reports completed was due to occasional signal failure (3 to 4 per week), and to R's forgetfulness, or to unsuitable circumstances, or because Rs were out of range of the transmitter. Nearly 4,800 records were thus collected. Most of the analyses to follow focus on those 91 Rs who reported watching television at least once during the week.

THE SAMPLE

The sample consisted of full-time male and female employees from five large companies in the Chicago area who volunteered for the study without compensation. Sixty-three percent of the respondents were female, 30 percent single and never married, 80 percent white, and 43 percent over 35 years of age with an age range of 18–63 years. The average annual earned income was about $14,000 and few respondents earned a great deal less or more than this figure. Ninety percent of Rs had completed high school, 44 percent worked on assembly line jobs, 29 percent were clerical workers or secretaries, and 27 percent were supervisors, buyers, and engineers.

This sample of full-time working adults is not a representative cross-section of TV viewers. Unemployed and retired persons (Kubey, 1980), and students and housewives, not represented in the sample, may well use and experience television somewhat differently. Though all respondents are working men and women, their reports are still applicable to the research questions posed, and the findings should characterize general trends in viewing. Still, we recognize the need for replication with more representative samples.

In this study, no data were collected as to which programs were being watched when Rs were signaled. We have chosen to emphasize "exposure" and "social context" variables rather than "content," in line with the "uses and gratifications" school (Katz et al., 1973), which has observed that these are the more neglected and basic aspects of media use appropriate for study (see also Hirsch, 1980). Furthermore, we believe that at the outset it is useful to examine television viewing behavior as a total experience without consideration to content, just as one might examine eating behavior without concern for the types of food consumed.

Each R was provided with a bound booklet of self-report forms to complete in response to each signal: (1) Activities which Rs reported were later coded into 20 categories (e.g., working at work, driving, reading, watching TV). (2) They rated their mood and physical states on 7-point scales at the moment signaled; a factor analysis divided these items into two clusters: "affect" (consisting of such variables as cheerful-irritable, relaxed-tense, sociable-lonely), and "potency" (alert-drowsy, strong-weak, active-passive). (3) The quality of R's "cognitive" interaction with the environment (whether the subject felt challenged by the activity, whether he or she was concentrating, and how high the person perceived his or her skills for each activity to be).[1]

Results

AMOUNT OF VIEWING

The estimates of time allocation to various activities obtained in this study are consistent with those reported by Robinson and Converse (1967), who used diary-based time sampling.[2] Over comparable activities the two methods produced a Spearman rank-order correlation of .92 (Csikszentmihalyi and Graef, 1980). Robinson and Converse's respondents watched approximately 20 percent more television but this discrepancy may have been because our subjects were not being signaled past 10:00 P.M. when a large percentage of adult TV viewing typically takes place, and because of their working status, which meant they did 85 percent of their television viewing after 5:00 P.M.

---

[1] For a discussion of the reliability and validity of the ESM see Csikszentmihalyi and Graef (1980) and Larson et al. (1981). As an example, the average correlation coefficient for individual affect and potency means between the first and second halves of the week was .72, and for the cognitive variables it was .61 (N=104). In a follow-up study of 28 adolescents, the average correlation between individual means after a two-year interval was .47 for affect and potency, and .61 for the cognitive variables.

[2] Respondents reported television watching as a main activity 7.2 percent of the time (344 responses) and as a secondary activity 2.8 percent of the time (136 responses). These figures are almost identical to those reported in studies conducted by Szalai (1972) and Robinson (1977). In total, they add up to an estimated average of 1.5 hours of television watching per person during the 14 hours of each day when beepers were activated. No other leisure activity involved as much time.

SECONDARY ACTIVITIES ACCOMPANYING TELEVISION WATCHING

The design of the self-report form allowed us to ask respondents if they were engaged in a secondary activity in addition to the one which they described as primary. Roughly 10 percent of all primary mealtime activity, for example, was accompanied by television viewing, and for nearly 25 percent of the time that TV was described as a secondary activity, meals were marked as primary.[3] Television watching was also a frequent accompaniment to the main activities of talking (14 percent) and reading (12.5 percent).

Secondary activities were reported as accompanying primary television watching 67.4 percent of the time. Thus, television occupied Rs' undivided attention during only 32.6 percent of viewing occasions. For our sample, television watching almost always occurred after work and in a context of physical relaxation and orally pleasurable activities.

TV viewing was contrasted with a wide variety of other typical activities. For this discussion the comparison will be limited to four major activities plus a "total" which includes all activity reports after subtracting those given while watching TV. The four activities are as follows: working at work (all work activity while on the job, excluding such activities as socializing, coffee breaks, and lunch); public leisure (activities such as eating out, parties, sports and games, club meetings, and cultural events); idling (waiting, sitting and not doing anything, staring out a window, daydreaming); and meals.

Table 1 presents a rank ordering of averaged individual self-report means. Activities whose means were significantly different from TV watching are noted.

COGNITIVE STATES

Television watching in our sample was experienced as the least challenging activity and the one involving the least amount of skill. With the exception of "idling activities," the differences between TV watching and the other activities were quite significant. For example, the mean levels for "concentration," "challenges," and "skills" are

---

[3] Respondents indicated that eating and smoking occurred during 17 percent of primary viewing. This incidence of "oral consumption" activity while watching television was extremely high compared to its less frequent occurrence in conjunction with other pursuits. Adding talking (18 percent) as another oral pursuit raises the "oral" percentage accompanying TV to over 35 percent. This predominance of talking and eating behavior with television was also observed by Bechtel et al. (1972) and by Allen (1965), who used videotape and film to record viewing behavior in the home.

significantly lower for watching television than the average levels for all other activities combined.[4]

MOOD STATES

Most notable among the findings in Table 1 is that TV watching is experienced as the most relaxing of all activities; this is consistent

Table 1. Rank Ordering of Individual Self-Report Means in Five Selected Activities and for Total Responses Minus TV Watching

Response Variables	Activities					
	TV Watching $(N=91)$[a,b]	Total Activity[c] $(N=91)$	Working at Work $(N=91)$	Public Leisure $(N=71)$	Idling $(N=79)$	Meals $(N=82)$
Cognition						
Concentration						
(Rank)	4	2[d]	1*	3	6*	5
(Mean)	4.94	5.29	6.03	5.23	3.83	4.75
Challenges	6	2*	1*	3*	5	4
	2.49	3.77	4.84	3.72	2.58	2.65
Skills	6	2*	1*	3[d]	5	4*
	3.74	5.36	6.38	4.90	3.91	4.63
Affect						
Cheerful-irritable	3	4	5	1*	6*	2
	4.89	4.85	4.73	5.50	4.44	5.04
Relaxed-tense	1	5*	6*	2	4*	3
	5.36	4.83	4.54	5.28	4.86	5.20
Sociable-lonely	5	3	4	1[d]	6[d]	2[d]
	4.74	4.86	4.82	5.62	4.47	5.14
Potency						
Alert-drowsy	5	3*	2*	1*	6*	4*
	4.76	5.29	5.57	5.76	4.07	5.27
Strong-weak	5	4*	2*	1*	6[d]	3*
	4.48	4.79	4.95	5.09	4.24	4.94
Active-passive	5	3*	1*	2*	6	4*
	4.06	4.79	5.08	5.02	3.97	4.60

NOTE: Higher means refer to more positive states.

[a] Number of subjects range from 71 to 91. Only those subjects who reported doing each activity were included in each analysis.

[b] Total number of signals for each activity are as follows: TV = 344, Total Activity = 4,447, Working at Work = 1,280, Public Leisure = 116, Idling = 411, and Meals = 331.

[c] Total activity refers to all activities minus television viewing.

[d] Activities whose means are significantly different from TV watching means on a t-test (two-tails) by a factor of $p < .05$.

* $p < .005$.

[4] People also reported that there was virtually nothing at stake while watching TV. Yet television watching was found to be one of the activities which respondents, when signaled, most frequently checked "wanting to do" as opposed to "having to do." Only when reading or participating in sports and games did people report wanting to do it more often. Our subjects reported "wanting" to watch television with nearly 90 percent of "TV" signals—this in sharp contrast to their "wanting" to work only 15 percent of the time. Thus, television viewing can be thought of as among the most freely chosen activities in which our Rs became involved.

with survey research by Bower (1973) and Steiner (1963), which has also indicated that the public perceives "relaxation" to be among the most characteristic functions of television watching. The degree to which people felt "relaxed" rather than "tense" in our research suggests that viewing is usually not the stress-producing experience that some have claimed it to be.

Potency states accompanying TV watching were all relatively low. People tended to report feeling "drowsy," "weak," and "passive" when viewing. Thus, the typical viewing experience is characterized by low feelings of potency, moderate cheerfulness, and high relaxation.

To understand the dynamics of the relaxed TV viewing state in greater depth we chose to focus on relaxation in two other major types of activities: working at work and public leisure. Table 2 shows correlations between level of reported relaxation and the nine cognitive, affective, and potency variables. This provides a view of how people experience relaxation in different contexts. When viewing television, relaxation is significantly related to feelings of cheerfulness and sociability. Relaxation at work is also strongly related to these same feelings.

Most striking, however, is that in public leisure activities relaxation was even more intimately tied to cheerfulness and sociability, while at the same time Rs also reported being quite alert, strong, and active, and having high concentration, challenges, and skill. Thus, it is clear that relaxation in other forms of leisure is compatible with heightened cognitive and potency states, while relaxation during television watching is neutral in respect to such states.

Table 2. Correlates of Relaxation in Three Different Activities

	Activities		
Response Variables	TV Watching[a]	Working at Work	Public Leisure
Cognition			
Concentration	−.06	−.02	.65**
Challenges	−.03	−.16	.49**
Skills	.07	.13	.57**
Affect			
Cheerful-irritable	.76**	.76**	.90**
Relaxed-tense	1.00**	1.00**	1.00**
Sociable-lonely	.60**	.67**	.87**
Potency			
Alert-drowsy	.27*	.34**	.86**
Strong-weak	.23*	.40**	.89**
Active-passive	.22*	.28*	.82**

NOTE: All correlation coefficients are Pearson Product Moment Correlations.
[a] Number of respondents and signals are identical to those in Table 1.
   * $p < .05$.
  ** $p < .001$

Television Viewing in Different Contexts

TELEVISION VERSUS READING

Affective states reported while watching TV and while reading are nearly identical. Individual self-report means for the two activities are presented in Table 3. People report being as cheerful, relaxed, and sociable when reading as when they are viewing television. But reading, in comparison to television, is experienced as having greater cognitive requirements (more concentration, more challenges, more skills) and involving higher feelings of potency (greater alertness, strength, and less passivity). So, again, in relative terms, television is characterized by reduced mental investment and a drop in feelings of potency.

TELEVISION AND FAMILY LIFE

Of particular interest to social critics of television are its possible effects on family life. Table 4 examines the TV viewing experience as a function of whether the familial experience was altered by television watching.

Television watching was a significantly more challenging, cheerful, and sociable experience with the family than alone. These findings follow the trend of all "alone" experiences, which tend to be more generally negative than "family" experiences, regardless of the activity engaged in. In other words, as a function of being alone or with

Table 3. Comparison of Subjective States while Watching Television and While Reading

	Activities		
Response Variables	TV Watching (N=344)		Reading (N=182)
Cognition			
Concentration	4.82	**	5.72
Challenges	2.39	*	2.90
Skills	3.51	**	4.97
Affect			
Cheerful-irritable	4.80		4.89
Relaxed-tense	5.29		5.33
Sociable-lonely	4.68		4.65
Potency			
Alert-drowsy	4.68	**	5.12
Strong-weak	4.36	*	4.58
Active-passive	3.90	**	4.23

NOTE: Comparisons between means were made by t-tests (two-tailed). Higher means refer to more positive states.

  * $p < .05$.
  ** $p < .01$.

Table 4. Comparison of Subjective States While Watching Television with the Family, Compared to Family Interaction Without Television, and Television Watching Alone

Response Variables	Activity and Context		
	TV Watching with Family (N = 201)	Being with the Family Without TV (N = 923)	Watching TV Alone (N = 105)
Cognition			
Concentration	4.79	4.99	5.07
Challenges	2.59	3.55**	1.89*
Skills	3.42	4.90**	3.37
Affect			
Cheerful-irritable	4.91	5.00	4.56*
Relaxed-tense	5.35	5.00**	5.11
Sociable-lonely	4.93	5.11	4.08**
Potency			
Alert-drowsy	4.66	5.18**	4.68
Strong-weak	4.33	4.71**	4.37
Active-passive	3.88	4.79**	3.97

NOTE: Comparisons between means were made by t-test (two-tailed). Higher means refer to more positive states.
* $p < .05$

the family, the television watching experience is modified in much the same manner as most other activities. One exception is the increased challenges accompanying family viewing, which does not normally differentiate aloneness. Thus, the most striking finding in this comparison is that TV watching is a considerably more challenging experience when done with the family. Respondents' experiences with their families, however, were clearly affected by the presence of television. When television was being viewed with members of the family, in contrast to being with the family without TV, subjects reported feeling significantly less challenged, less skilled, more relaxed, less alert, less strong, and less active. The strongest negative changes, then, occurred in the cognitive and potency variables.

To understand such phenomena more fully, we also looked at how the experience of being with one's family was affected by reading newspapers, magazines, or books. As with television, people felt significantly more relaxed ($p < .004$), passive ($p < .004$), and less challenged ($p < .035$) while reading in the presence of family members than when interacting with them. However, there was no drop in perceived skills or in the other two potency variables as was the case with television.

Discussion

Television viewing was consistently and closely tied to relaxation, to weaker cognitive investments, and to lower feelings of potency when compared to other activities. The study suggests that this experience is modified to some extent by the context in which people view, but that the general trends associated with TV viewing remain largely intact regardless of context. Affective states appear to change least as a function of TV viewing and potency states are the most vulnerable to change. At the same time, however, our findings may apply only to the viewing experience of adult workers, but not to children or retired persons, for whom television might provide a more active involvement.

It is important to point out that we cannot conclude from this research whether television *itself* causes all the variations we have observed. In other words, is it the case that when people feel passive or weak they choose television as an activity which accommodates their mood or is it that TV actually causes people to feel more passive and weak? Pearlin (1959), for one, has compared TV viewing to the coping function of alcohol, suggesting that some people use television to withdraw periodically from troubles or stress. Television's influence on moods is surely mediated by a person's affective and cognitive state prior to viewing. The in-depth examination of such affective and behavioral sequences and the relationship of needs to gratifications are intended for future studies.

Goldsen (1977) has observed, as has McLuhan ("the medium is the message"), that most television content is received by viewers in much the same way. There are exceptions, such as live reports of assassinations, moon landings, Watergate hearings, or sporting events. Such events *do* command undivided attention and we respond almost as if we were there. After a few replays, however, these live events become part of the sameness of the vast television landscape.

What is the future of television's role in human experience? New developments, such as video games, television with computer interface, and home video equipment all involve the common behavioral component of participation. If television viewing is at present a passive enterprise, the future promises to allow the viewer greater opportunities to interact with and exert control over the TV set and its content. Nonetheless, the results of this study suggest that television, in its present form, may frequently be chosen for the very reason that it *is* unchallenging, relaxing, and relatively uninvolving. To be sure, then, much of television watching in the future will still fulfill these same needs for escape and relaxation. Much of its content will go unchanged because there will be continued demand for such experiences. Modern technological innovations, therefore, will only present new and different viewing opportunities in addition to the existing standard forms of television experience.

References

Allen, C.
  1965 "Photographing the TV audience." Journal of Advertising Research 5:2–8.
Bechtel, R., C. Achelpohl, and R. Akers
  1972 "Correlates between observed behavior and questionnaire response on television viewing." In E. Rubinstein, G. Comstock, and J. Murray (eds.), Television and Social Behavior, Vol. 4, Television in Day-to-Day Life: Patterns of Use. Washington, D.C.: Government Printing Office.
Bower, R.
  1973 Television and the Public. New York: Holt, Rinehart, and Winston.
Caprio, F.
  1976 Personal communication to the authors.
Comstock, George
  1980 TV in America. Beverly Hills, Calif.: Sage.
Csikszentmihalyi, M., and R. Graef
  1980 "The experience of freedom in daily life." American Journal of Community Psychology 8:401–14.
Csikszentmihalyi, M., R. Larson, and S. Prescott
  1977 "The ecology of adolescent activities and experience." Journal of Youth and Adolescence 6:281–94.
Goldsen, R.
  1977 "Changing channels: how TV shapes American minds." Human Behavior 2:63–67.
Gorney, R., D. Loye, and G. Steele
  1977 "Impact of dramatized television entertainment on adult males." American Journal of Psychiatry 134:170–74
Hirsch, P.
  1980 "A research agenda for approaching the study of television." Paper commissioned for the Aspen Institute Conference on Proposals for a Center for the Study of Television.
Katz, E., J. Blumler, and M. Gurevitch
  1973 "Uses and gratifications research." Public Opinion Quarterly 37:509–23.
Krugman, H.
  1977 "Memory without recall, exposure without perception." Journal of Advertising Research 17:7–12.
Kubey, R.
  1980 "Television and aging: past, present, and future." Gerontologist 20:16–35.
Larson, R., M. Csikszentmihalyi, and R. Graef
  1980 "Mood variability and the psycho-social adjustment of adolescence." Journal of Youth and Adolescents 9:469–90.
Maccoby, E.
  1951 "Television: its impact on school children." Public Opinion Quarterly 15:421–44.
McLuhan, M.
  1978 "The brain and the media: the 'western' hemisphere." Journal of Communication 28:54–60.

Pearlin, L.
  1959 "Social and personal stress and escape television viewing." Public
        Opinion Quarterly 23:256–59.
Robinson, J.
  1969 "Television and leisure time: yesterday, today and (maybe) tomor-
        row." Public Opinion Quarterly 33:210–22.
  1972 "Television's impact on everyday life: some cross-national evi-
        dence." In E. Rubinstein, G. Comstock, and J. Murrya (eds), Televi-
        sion and Social Behavior, Vol. 4, Television in Day-to-Day Life:
        Patterns of Use. Washington, D.C.: Government Printing Office.
  1977 How Americans Use Time: A Social-Psychological Analysis of
        Everyday Behavior. New York: Praeger.
Robinson, J., and P. Converse
  1967 Basic Tables of Time-Budget Date for the United States. Ann Arbor,
        Mich.: Survey Research Center.
Rosenblatt, P., and M. Cunningham
  1976 "Television watching and family tensions." Journal of Marriage and
        the Family 31:11.
Steiner, G.
  1963 The People Look at Television. New York: Knopf.
Szalai, A. (ed.)
  1972 The Use of Time: Daily Activities of Urban and Suburban Popula-
        tions in Twelve Countries. The Hague: Mouton and Co.

In this article, James Lull argues for ethnographic studies of television audiences. He presents a typology of the social uses of television based on findings from systematic participant observation of families viewing television at home. This article received the Speech Communication Association's Golden Anniversary Monograph Award for 1980. James Lull is assistant professor of speech at the University of California, Santa Barbara.

22

THE SOCIAL USES OF TELEVISION

James Lull

Elihu Katz, director of the Hebrew University's Communication Institute, recently told the British Broadcasting Corporation that he would give "a large prize to anybody who succeeded in developing a method for the sampling of everyday conversation to supplement the probing of survey research" on mass communication (Katz, 1977). He described the potential advantages of these data in the analysis of the media's role in setting conversational agendas, television's place in the development of interpersonal interaction patterns within families, the socialization effects of media, and the consequences of media programming on the use of language, patterns of speech, and thought.

The purpose of this essay is to elaborate theoretically and practically on Katz's recommendation for increased sensitivity by mass communication researchers to the nature of the social uses which audience members make of television. This will be accomplished by first suggesting that audience members create specific and sometimes elaborate practical actions involving the mass media in order to gratify particular needs in the social context of family television viewing. Second, a research method (ethnography) will be presented which allows for investigation of these media-related behaviors. Finally, evidence will be presented from ethnographic research in conjunction with pertinent findings from the uses and gratifications literature in support of a typology of the social uses of television.

MASS MEDIA AS SOCIAL RESOURCES

Social actors can be thought to actively employ the tools of communication in order to purposively

James Lull (Ph.D., University of Wisconsin-Madison, 1976) is assistant professor of speech at the University of California, Santa Barbara, California 93106. This study accepted for publication July 12, 1979.

From James Lull, "The Social Uses of Television," *Human Communication Research* 6, 3 (Spring 1980), pp. 197-209. Reprinted by permission of the publisher and author.

construct their social realities. Symbolic interactionism (Blumer, 1969), language-action (Frentz & Farrell, 1976), and communicative constructivism (Delia, 1977) are, to varying degrees, contemporary derivatives of the social constructivist position. The uses and gratifications paradigm in mass communication is another manifestation of the constructivist view. Adherents to this perspective posit that individuals selectively use mass media in order to satisfy their human needs. In Katz' words, "this is the research tradition which asks not what the media do to people, but what people do with the media" (Katz, 1977). According to the modern conception, "uses" of media are observable evidences of the audience's control over the receptive instruments of mass communication.

Less obvious social uses of television, many of which are embedded in the taken-for-granted communicative substance which surrounds the viewing experience, generally have not been examined. However, the recent tradition of ethnomethodology, wherein the assumptive world of social interaction is itself treated as a phenomenon (Garfinkel, 1967; Zimmerman & Pollner, 1970; Mehan & Wood, 1975; Zimmerman, 1978), provides a perspective to disclose additional insights into the nature of human communication, including interpersonal uses of the mass media.[1] Common social instances of media consumption can be viewed as delicate and situated accomplishments created by the persons involved.

In the study of human communication, specimens of language, occasions for talk, and the structural properties of interaction patterns can all be identified among available resources for the accomplishment of such interpersonal objectives as the creation of communicative displays which attest to the social competency of an interlocutor or to the correct fulfillment of role incumbencies (Hymes, 1964; Philipsen, 1975). These resources are so central to daily living that verbal strategies are even known to be utilized together with a host of other communicative provisions in order for a social member to display gender effectively (Garfinkel & Stoller, 1967).

Mass media can also be viewed as important and uniquely employed social resources in interpersonal communication systems. They are handy expedients which can be exploited by individuals, coalitions, and family units to serve their personal needs, create practical relationships, and engage the social world. Television and other mass media, rarely mentioned as vital forces in the construction or maintenance of interpersonal relations, can now be seen to play central roles in the methods which families and other social units employ to interact normatively. The interpersonal uses one makes of the mass media constitute the construction of a particular subset of actions which find many practical applications in the home environment. One approach to documenting these behaviors is participant-observational research, which leads to ethnographies of mass communication.

THE ETHNOGRAPHIC METHOD IN THE STUDY OF MEDIA AUDIENCE BEHAVIOR

In mass communication research, the most fundamental aspects of human interaction—those distinct and detailed events which social actors create *in their own terms and on their own grounds* in order to make the substance of their ordinary routines meaningful—are seldom taken into account by researchers. The rough edges, special cases, and subtle peculiarities of the social world are sometimes ignored in order to facilitate cleanliness, parsimony, and predictive strength in mathematically induced designs and theories.

Participant observational strategies offer alternatives to the methods which are commonly employed. The use of participant observation for documentation of intensive naturalistic case studies in mass communication allows for theory building which binds together conceptual communicative elements, messages linkages, and exchanges by social actors as holistic units-in-interaction (Blumer, 1969). The family, television's primary audience, is a natural unit for this kind of analysis. Through ethnographic inquiry, the researcher can study actual communication contexts and ways in which media experiences enter the lives of family members.

A naturalistic research method which gains access to audience members' conversations alone, however, has not proven to be sufficient. This investigatory approach has been attempted with only moderate success by researchers from the Kansas City Mental Health Foundation (Bechtel, Achelpohl, & Akers, 1972). Television cameras were placed on top of the television sets of a small sample of families (20) in order to document viewing behavior. Microphones were placed around the rooms to record conversations and personal reactions to the shows. With this equipment, the researchers were able to observe behavior which accompanies television viewing (e.g., singing, ironing, sorting clothes, talking, mimicking the television, dancing, doing exercises, posing, dressing, fighting, eating). They also investigated the degree of agreement between the actual and estimated amounts of television viewing done by their subjects. A considerable discrepancy between the two measures was found, with significant overreporting of viewing time made by nearly half the family members.

By examining one distinct aspect of family life (the viewing experience), the researchers concluded that "Television viewing does not occur in a vacuum; it is always to some degree background to a complex behavior pattern in the home.... No doubt an aim of future research is determining the relationship among viewing time, viewing styles, and the larger framework of a family's life style" (Bechtel et al., 1972, p. 299).

Bechtel and his associates concluded that even the most accurate record of movements and conversations in front of the set failed to provide much insight into the nature of interpersonal networks which characterize family communication systems. Further, the sampling of conversation alone did little to advance knowledge of the uses, gratifications, or meanings that media hold for their audiences. Patterns or styles of viewing were not regarded in relation to the substance of subjects' everyday interpersonal communications, their personality characteristics, family roles, or the structural properties of the families. Also, as one might suspect, viewing habits were reported by many subjects in this study to have been substantially altered by the presence of a vidicon camera pointing at them from a position on top of their television sets.

The more elaborate method of ethnography, which is organized around (1) participant observation, (2) the use of informants, and (3) in-depth interviewing, can be used by the social researcher as an integrated means for understanding the everyday world of social groups, their patterns of interpersonal communication, and their uses of the mass media. The intent of the ethnography of mass communication is to allow the researcher to grasp as completely as possible with minimal disturbance the "native's perspective" on relevant communicative and sociocultural matters indigenous to him (Bruyn, 1966; Glaser & Strauss, 1967). The method, when applied to the study of television's primary audience, requires that the researcher enter the natural domain of his subjects—the family home. The willingness and abilities of the researcher are strongly tested by the prospect of this intrusion into such a small and private social unit.

The presence of the investigator in the habitat of his subjects, the usual objection to participant observation research, need not severely disrupt the natural behavior of the family unit (Lull, 1976, 1978). Recently, some research was conducted on the ways in which families select television programs for group viewing in their homes (Lull, 1978). In order to collect these data, families were asked to gather in their homes when all members could be present. Family members were given six independent sets of fabricated program selections to choose from. Conversations were audiotape-recorded as families decided what televison shows to "watch." The nature of their overall discussion patterns, comparative willingness to express preferences, the degree of selection consensus, and perceptions of interpersonal influence in the family were later reported.

When he placed himself in the homes of families on these occasions, a variety of unexpected observations took place. The researcher became convinced that a more encompassing form of systematic, in-home participant observation could provide even more valuable insights into families' uses of the media. His arrival at subjects' residences during the study described above sometimes interrupted normal television viewing. In several cases, the negotiation of *real* choices for television viewing resumed before he had departed the home at the conclusion of the research exercise. The researcher was encouraged that, in this early study, where he had entered the homes of 20 families personally unknown to him, apparently normal televison-viewing behavior took place with the researcher still present. Subsequent research, where observers spent from three to seven days with families, has demonstrated that, in the vast majority of cases (more than 80 percent), families indicated at the conclusion of the observational period that no major behavioral alterations had taken place due to the presence of the investigator.

When documenting the social uses of television by the ethnographic method, the researcher uses observations and interview data as a means for internal behavioral validation. Since multiple ob-server-coder strategies are impractical in most ethnographic research, the investigator combines detailed observations of the social unit with postob-servational in-depth interviewing of his subjects. Further checks on the observed behaviors are made with the use of informants—in this case, other family members.

Three or four essential forms of raw data exist at the conclusion of the data-gathering process. Writ-ten materials include the observational notes made by the observer during the time spent in family homes. The observer also has produced a written summary at the end of each day of observation. Audiotape recordings have been made by inter-viewing each family member at the conclusion of the observational period. Written transcripts are made from the tape recordings.

A simple but useful technique has been to type-write onto paper or cards all the observational notes (including interview information) which will be used for compiling the ethnographic report. Then, after a careful review of the data for themes to be explored in the analysis, observations and interview comments are placed together by cutting the type-written pages into units or placing the cards in the desired sequence. In this way the researcher can arrange and rearrange the "bits" of data until the proper internal consistency is found within each topic. These data help the ethnographer of mass communication demonstrate the internal validity of

areas which are to be developed theoretically.

While participant observational strategies can be designed to test specific hypotheses posited in ad-vance of the period of observation, this is typically done after an initial process of discovery has been undertaken utilizing the same essential method (Ci-courel, 1974, p. 203).

The ethnography of mass communication is meant to be a sustained, microscopic, inductive examination of the natural interactional communi-cations which connect human beings to the mass media and to each other. From data generated by ethnographic inquiries with this purpose, and by means of a review of the contributions made by other researchers to the uses and gratifications liter-ature, a beginning typology of the social uses of television has been constructed and is presented in the next major section of this paper. Evidence pre-sented in support of the typology derives from a review of the major findings in the uses and gratifi-cations literature and from ethnographic data col-lected at the University of Wisconsin and the Uni-versity of California.

More than 200 families, representing blue-collar, white-collar, and farm types, were studied during the past three years at these locations. They were contacted through social agencies such as girls' clubs, boys' clubs, community nursery schools, university resources, and religious groups. In the variety of studies, families have been randomly selected from mailing lists, telephone lists, or members present at general meetings attended by the researcher. The acceptance rate for families contacted was about 30 percent. This figure is less when "normal" families only (two parents present) are used (Bechtel et al., 1972). Observational periods ranged from two to seven days per family.[2] Observers studied these groups from mid-afternoon until bedtime. Intensive independent interviewing of each family member followed the last day of observation in each case. Following the writing of the reports, family members were asked to read and confirm the validity of the observations.

Families at first were given only a general intro-duction to the purpose of the research. They were told that the observers were students in communi-cation who were interested in "family life." It was not possible to reveal the researchers' particular interests since that knowledge probably would have influenced families' media activities during the observational period. Debriefing followed the collection of all data.

Observers' procedures for data gathering were standardized as much as possible from family to family. Each observer maintained a preprinted log on which the ongoing behavior of families was documented throughout the day. Since they were known to the families only as students, the observers took most of their notes in the guise of "homework" chores conducted while they sat in the living rooms or television-viewing areas of the homes. In this way, observers were able to take many notes on the premises and record the details of interpersonal interaction and media use as they occurred. A reconstruction of daily behavior was made by each observer after returning home following the observation periods each night.

Observers took part in the routines of the families for the duration of the observation period. They ate with the families, performed household chores with them, played with the children, and took part in group entertainment, particularly television watching. Families were told from the beginning that in no case should they change their routines in order to accommodate the observer.

Observers looked for regularity in communicative acts reflected in the interpersonal roles and relationships associated with the use of mass media. Particular interactional behaviors such as dominance strategies and talk patterns were noted. Interpersonal behaviors involving mass media, such as the dynamics of the television program selection process and the viewing experience, were other primary areas for observation.

A full accounting of the data collected in studies such as this is not well suited for journal reports because of the lengthy analyses which typify ethnographic research. Family communication is so vivid, detailed, and theoretically intriguing under naturalistic conditions that the alert ethnographer becomes seemingly inundated by pertinent observations. Henry, in his accounts of five mentally disturbed families (Henry, 1965), used about 100 pages of text to discuss each family. Lewis discus-

sed the behavior of five Mexican families in 300 pages (Lewis, 1959) and required nearly 700 pages to present a single Puerto Rican extended family (Lewis, 1965). Other classic ethnographies of neighborhoods, gangs, and cultures have also been reported in book-length form (Gans, 1962; Liebow, 1967; Whyte, 1943; Anderson, 1923). Ethnographic data presented in support of the following typology is, necessarily, a distillation of the findings.

THE SOCIAL USES TYPOLOGY

A previous attempt to organize audience uses of the mass media into a descriptive typology has been made by McQuail, Blumler, and Brown (1972). Their category system is arranged into four components: (1) diversion—the use of television and other media for escaping routines and problems, emotional release; (2) personal relationships—social utility, companionship; (3) personal identity—personal reference, reality exploration, value reinforcement; (4) surveillance.

In the following paragraphs, an accounting for the primary social uses, opposed to the personal uses implicit in much of the McQuail et al. schema, is presented. It is somewhat arbitrary to distinguish between the personal and interpersonal uses of television, however the inventory and explication of the uses of television described here focus directly on their communicative value as social resources.

Social uses of television in the home are of two primary types: structural and relational (Figure 1). The focus of this section will be on the latter category, but a brief discussion of the former is helpful in clarifying the different uses of the medium. Examples which illustrate components of the typology are by no means thought to be exhaustive of the individual categories. The evidence presented here is meant to provide an introductory agenda of behaviors which can be classified according to the factors which are described.

Structural Uses of Television

Television is employed as an *environmental resource* in order to create a flow of constant back-

FIGURE 1
Social Uses of Television

Structural

Environmental (background noise; companionship; entertainment)

Regulative (punctuation of time and activity; talk patterns)

Relational

Communication Facilitation (experience illustration; common ground; conversational entrance; anxiety reduction; agenda for talk; value clarification)

Affiliation/Avoidance (physical, verbal contact/ neglect; family solidarity; family relaxant; conflict reduction; relationship maintenance)

Social Learning (decision-making; behavior modeling; problem solving; value transmission; legitimization; information dissemination; substitute schooling)

Competence/Dominance (role enactment; role reinforcement; substitute role portrayal; intellectual validation; authority exercise; gatekeeping; argument facilitation)

ground noise which moves to the foreground when individuals or groups desire. It is a companion for accomplishing household chores and routines. It contributes to the overall social environment by rendering a constant and predictable assortment of sounds and pictures which instantly creates an apparently busy atmosphere. The activated television set guarantees its users a nonstop backdrop of verbal communication against which they can construct their interpersonal exchanges. Of course, it always serves its timeless environmental function as a source of entertainment for the family.

Second, television has the structural characteristic of being a *behavioral regulator*. Television punctuates time and family activity such as mealtime, bedtime, choretime, homework periods, and a host of related activities and duties. Patterns of talk are affected by viewing routines. External family communication is similarly regulated by television. Taking part in community projects, recreational activities, or outside entertainment are directly influenced by the scheduling of television programs.

Television viewing takes place in social units other than families. Viewing in various settings can be free and selective, as it is in college dormitories,

or it can be parceled out as a reward granted by the proper authorities. Children in nursery schools are allowed to watch television after they pick up their toys. Girls in a California reform school can view only when their rooms pass inspection and when they complete their evening chores. Television in a retirement home is an attractive alternative to sitting alone in a private room. Under all these conditions, television viewing contributes to the structuring of the day. There is a time for viewing. That time is often related to other responsibilities and activities in which the individual is involved.

Relational Uses of Television

The ways in which audience members use television to create practical social arrangements can be organized into a behavioral typology of four major divisions. While the exclusivity of the categories is not absolute, an argument for the internal validity of the components of the schema described below will be made. Further, the order of presentation of the four relational functions (communication facilitation, affiliation/avoidance, social learning, competence/dominance) is made sequentially in order to demonstrate the relative complexity of the constructs.

Communication Facilitation

Television's characters, stories, and themes are employed by viewers as abundant illustrators which facilitate conversations. Children, for example, use television programs and characters as primary known-in-common referents in order to clarify issues they discuss. Television examples are used by children to explain to each other, and to their parents and teachers, those real-world experiences, emotions, and beliefs which are difficult to make interpersonally transparent in attempts at verbal communication.

A child often uses television in order to enter an adult conversation. When a child is ignored during conversations held by adults, he or she can gain entry to the discussion by using a television example which illustrates a point being made by one of the adult interactants. If participants in the conversation are familiar with the television example, the child has introduced a common referent in order to gain access to the conversation from which he or she was otherwise left out.

The viewing experience itself can be facilitative. Conversational discomfort is sometimes reduced when the television is turned on and in view of the interactants. The uneasiness of prolonged eye contact is lessened since the television set ably attracts attention during lulls in conversation. Also, the program being watched creates an immediate agenda for talk where there may otherwise be none.

The medium is used as a convenient resource for entertaining outside guests in the home. To turn on the set when guests arrive is to introduce instant common ground. Strangers in the home may then indulge in "television talk"—verbal responses to television programs which allow audience members to discuss topics of common experience which probably have little personal importance. Television viewing under these circumstances provides an opportunity for abundant talk with little substance—an exercise in conversational form for the interlocutors. In this way, viewers become better acquainted but invest minimal personal risk. Television also helps some family members clarify interpersonally their attitudes and values, especially in recent years since the medium has presented more controversial programming.

Affiliation/Avoidance

A fundamental social use of television is its potential as a resource for the construction of desired opportunities for interpersonal contact or avoidance. One uses and gratifications researcher believes that this is the primary social use of the medium (Nordenstreng, 1970). The proxemic nature of audience positioning in front of the television set is often used to advantage by young children who desire to engage physically or verbally their admired older siblings. Some adults orchestrate rare moments of physical contact in front of the television screen, an intimacy which need not be accompanied by conversation. An entertainment medium, however defined, is useful for this purpose. In one family which was observed, the husband and wife

touched each other only twice during the seven-day period. The first time the man playfully grabbed his wife and seated her on his lap while his daughter, acting as a kind of medium, told a humorous story about something that had happened at school that day. The other occasion for physical contact during the week took place one night while the couple watched television. The man was a hard-working laborer who nearly always fell asleep when he watched television at night. He dozed as he sat in a recliner rocking chair with his shoes off. He snored loudly with his mouth open. His wife, who had been sitting on the floor in the same room, pushed herself along the floor until she was close to his chair. She leaned back until her head rested against his bare feet and smiled as she created this rare moment of "intimacy."

Television viewing is a convenient family behavior which is accomplished *together*. The medium is used to provide opportunities for family members or friends to communally experience entertainment or informational programming. A feeling of family solidarity is sometimes achieved through television-induced laughter, sorrow, anger, or intellectual stimulation (Katz & Foulkes, 1962). Confirmation of the family as a unit of interdependent personalities is made by the attempts of viewers to predict consensually the outcomes of television shows while they watch or by the creation of on-going discussions of the details or implications of the televised stories. Audience members also use television as a family relevant whereby group viewing promotes family harmony by reducing interpersonal discord, at least during the viewing period.

Television can lessen the demand for the manufacture of talk and the exchange of thought by providing a sustaining focus for attention which can be employed as a kind of social distractor, rendering less intense the communicative formalities which might otherwise be expected. Since television is used by the viewer as a focus for attention, creating "parallel" rather than interactive viewing patterns, it also becomes a resource for escape—not just from the personal problems or responsibilities of the individual viewer, but from the social environment (Walters & Stone, 1975). Anthropologist Edmund

Carpenter (1972) reported that a U.S. Army official in Germany recently blamed the high divorce rate among his troops on the lack of an English-language television station in the area where they live. The officer said, "That means a soldier and his wife have got to talk to each other in the evenings and they suddenly discover that they really don't like each other" (Carpenter, 1972, p. 10). A blue-collar family which was observed said it was grateful for television since it occupies so much of the grandparents' time in the evening, thereby keeping them away from their home which is located just three doors away. This young couple preferred not to be bothered by their parents. Television limits unwanted visits.

Television functions as a social resource in a unique way which helps married couples maintain satisfactory relationships. Unlike print media which transmit bits of information, television can provoke a vicarious, evanescent fantasy world which serves for some the psychological purpose of a desirable, if temporary, occupation of an alternative reality.

Psychological transformations triggered by program viewing become resources put to use by the inventive social actor. An example is revealed in the case of a farm woman who 15 years ago resigned her premed scholarship to a major midwestern university, married her high-school boyfriend, and attended vocational school in order to become a medical secretary. Her first child was born one year following her marriage, causing her to quit her job at the medical office.

The *only* television shows watched by this woman during the research period were programs which featured settings and themes directly related to the medical profession ("Marcus Welby, M.D.," "Medical Center," "Medical Story"). When these programs were aired, she engaged in a continual and intense commentary about the nature of the story, particularly as it related to medical considerations. She remarked about the appropriateness of operating-room procedures. She evaluated the work of subordinates and always referred to the doctors by their formal titles. She praised medical work well done and found fault with mistakes made by the staff. The Caesarean section of quintuplets during one melodrama fasci-

nated her as she remarked instructively about the importance of quickly trimming "all five cords."

During an interview probe following a week-long observation period conducted by the researcher, the woman said:

> I've always been interested in anything medical, in anything to do with the medical field. So, that's what I like . . . I usually find that their (medical) information is pretty accurate for their diagnosis of disease and so forth . . . so, I enjoy it because I worked around a lot of that and it just kinda' keeps me in the business, I guess.

Her husband appeared to recognize the desirability of using television as a fantasy stimulant for his wife. Although his wife knew full well what times her favorites were televised, he reminded her of these and encouraged her to watch. He even changed the television channel from "Monday Night Football" in order to insure that she watched a medical program which was presented by a competing network at the same time. His encouragement of her participation in the dream world which their marriage and child raising denied her may have helped him dismiss whatever guilt he harbored for having been, in part, responsible for curtailing her vocational opportunities.

Social Learning

Television is widely regarded as a resource for learning (Lyle, 1972). Of special interest here are the social uses made of the many opportunities for learning from television. Much information for daily living is available from the electronic media. Obvious examples are the consumer and political spot messages which provide an agenda for decision making, actions which have important implications for the society, the family unit, and the individual (Schiller, 1973; Mander, 1977). But more subtle learning experiences have been noted as well. Early studies of the soap operas demonstrated that these melodramas provide practical suggestions for social interaction which are widely imitated by audience members (Lazarsfeld & Stanton, 1949; Herzog, 1944). These imitations may be useful in the solving of family problems which bear resemblance to difficulties resolved in television dramas. At the very least, television provides an abundance of role models which audience members find socially useful.

Parents encourage their children to watch television game shows, public television, or network specials as substitute school experiences. Themes and values implicit in television programs are used by the parents to educate their children about the topics being presented in accord with their own view of the world. In this way, the value system of the parent is transmitted to the child and attitudes already in place are reinforced (Katzman, 1972).

Scholarly research on how individuals learn from the mass media, then pass the information along in predictable interpersonal diffusion patterns, dates back more than 30 years (Lazarsfeld, Berelson, & Gaudet, 1948; Merton, 1949; Berelson, Lazarsfeld, & McPhee, 1954; Katz & Lazarsfeld, 1962). The two-step flow and the multistep flow theories implied that opinion leaders, who are heavy media consumers in their areas of expertise, learn much about their specialities from television and other media. These informational experts then transmit their knowledge to a network of human acquaintances.

In accomplishing the information-dissemination task, opinion leaders use information from the media to not only educate their friends, acquaintances, or coworkers, but also to assert themselves as valued members of society. The opinion leader uses television and other media to help create and then fulfill an interpersonal role which may have the effect of demonstrating competence.

Competence/Dominance

There are a variety of ways in which television provides unique opportunities for the demonstration of competence by means of family role fulfillment. The regulation of childrens' television viewing by a parent is one means for accomplishing this objective. For those adults who desire to supervise closely or restrict the flow of unwanted external information into the home, the methodical and authoritative regulating of television viewing is useful

as an occasion for the undertaking of a gatekeeping function. In doing so, the parent, often the mother, makes observable to the children and spouse a correct role-determined and rule-governed action which confirms the individual as a "good parent" or "good mother." Successful enactment of the television regulatory function directs media experiences of the children into forms which are consistent with the parents' moral perspective. Simultaneously, the parent asserts an expected jurisdictional act which confirms proper performance of a particular family role.

The symbolic portrayal of roles by television characters may confirm similar roles which are undertaken by audience members. When behavior by an actor or actress on television resembles the way in which the viewer behaves under similar circumstances, the experience may be useful to the viewer as a means for demonstrating role competence to the other audience members. Similarly, a family member may use television in order to learn acceptable role behavior, then imitate this behavior in a way which results in acceptance of the role enactment by other family members.

The role of a missing parent can be played by a television character. It is convenient in some single-parent families for the adult who is present to encourage the watching of particular television programs where a favored image of the missing parent is regularly presented. Implicitly, the role of the lone parent can be preserved or clarified as the substitute parent's complementary actions are portrayed on the screen.

Some viewers capitalize on the one-way nature of television by verbally assaulting the characters, newscasters, or commercials. One man who was observed constantly disagreed out loud with the evening news reports on television. He clarified the reports and chided the announcer for not knowing the "real facts." Vocal criticisms of programs or commercial announcements also serve as ways for viewers to reassure one another that, despite the fact that they are now watching, they know how *bad* television is, a self-promoting evaluation.

In another case, a housewife who majored in French in college repeatedly corrected the poor pronunciation of French words uttered by an American actor who attempted to masquerade as a Frenchman. Gans, in a study of poor Italian families in Boston, found that his subjects received attention from other viewers when they noticed that activities on the screen were technically unfeasible or when they pointed out "anachronisms or mistakes [that] appear in the plot" (Gans, 1962, p. 194).

A television viewer may or may not use the medium to demonstrate competence for purposes of dominating other family members. But, cases in which this occurs are numerous in ethnographic research. For instance, family members often use television as a validator of contested information, thereby demonstrating intellectual competence. In one family, for example, the capture and arrest of William and Emily Harris of the Symbionese Liberation Army was a topic of conversation at the dinner table on the evening the couple was apprehended in San Francisco. There were conflicting reports among family members as to whether or not Patty Hearst had also been captured. The highly authoritarian father had heard an early report on radio that only the Harrises had been arrested. He had not learned the later news that Hearst had been taken into the custody of police as well. His wife and daughter both told him that they had heard on the car radio that Hearst had been arrested too. He arrogantly denied the validity of their reports and said that the family could find out the "true situation" by watching the news on television. The husband later was embarrassed to discover on the news that Hearst had indeed been apprehended, a turn of events which falsified his version of the incident. "See," his wife said emphatically when the news was revealed. "We were right! I told you that Patty Hearst had been caught and you wouldn't believe me." The medium had confirmed her and disconfirmed him on the issue. A few minutes later television provided an opportunity for him to recapture his dominant position. During a commercial message, he voiced an opinion about some attribute of the product which was being promoted. His wife disagreed. Seconds later the television announcer on the commercial gave information which supported the husband. He quickly and defiantly turned to his wife and said, "I don't talk much. But when I do you should listen."

Men, women, boys, and girls use television to communicate to each other attitudes toward the appropriateness of male and female behavior with respect to sex roles. Teenaged boys were observed shouting criticism at the female detectives on the program "Charlie's Angels" with their sisters in the room. The program provided an opportunity for the boys to vocalize their negative feelings about the qualifications of the television actresses for doing "men's work." Similarly, adolescent girls competed to correctly identify wardrobe fashions of various historical periods during a program which featured this topic. The girls tried to identify the periods before the announcer on the program did so. Correct identification gave status to the girl who guessed right, validating her as a relative expert on women's fashions and placing her in an esteemed position in the eyes of her peers.

Interpersonal dominance strategies involve television in other ways. Television viewing in many homes is authoritatively granted or taken away as a reward or punishment. Adults and children argue to decide who will watch what programs, thereby creating an opportunity for the airing of personal differences. For family members who are angered by each other, television viewing (the program decision-making process or the viewing experience) provides incessant opportunities for argument, provoking possible dominance struggles among family members.

More subtle uses of the medium are made by some viewers to influence other audience members. In one case, a married couple watched a television program in which the lead actor passionately embraced a young woman. The husband at home asked his wife during this scene if the two on the screen were married. She answered, "Do they look married to you?" They both laughed quietly without taking their eyes off the screen. By coorienting and commenting on the television program, these family members spoke to each other indirectly, but made their positions about relational matters clearly known.

CONCLUSIONS

Although the natural television audience, the

family, has been identified in social theorizing as a "unit of interacting personalities" since the work of Burgess (1926), the study of various family processes as they occur at home has seldom been tried. Further, researchers who study family behavior today have recognized that "communication is increasingly emphasized as both the keystone of family interaction and the key to understanding family dynamics" (Anderson & Carter, 1974, p. 111). Hopefully, this paper has helped demonstrate that the methods which individuals construct, using television and other media, constitute important subsets of unique and useful communicative behaviors which are central to family life.

The typology of social uses of television presented here is different from previous ones in that the categories were derived by examining accumulated instances of observed audience behavior, detailed reports from audience members whose confidence had been won due to prolonged contact with field researchers, discussions by these same family members about the television uses employed by their peers, and by the relevant findings produced by other researchers using traditional data-gathering techniques. The contribution made to this work by the ethnographic method complements the data rendered by quantitative techniques and perhaps discloses some insights not otherwise obtainable. Knowledge of audience behavior in the family home can perhaps be maximized with a multimethod approach to this general area of inquiry, wherein data retrieved by traditional methods is considered in conjunction with ethnographic data.

While the typology of social uses presented here implies no particular ordering of the constructs other than by their apparent relative complexity, they can be considered ordinal and interdependent. As has been discussed, the social-learning process on some occasions necessarily precedes the demonstration of role competence. Similarly, demonstration of role competence may take the more elaborate form of an interpersonal dominance strategy. Interpersonal affiliation may also be regarded as a precursive behavior with competence demonstration or domination as intended consequences of the move toward another family member. Communication facilitation seems intuitively fundamental to the three other categories.

It may be very helpful to construct indices based on the four major divisions of the relational uses of television to develop "viewer types" or "family types." In doing so, it may be possible to determine if a person or a particular family uses television essentially for the facilitation of effective family communication; for the potential to construct the desired degree of interpersonal affiliation; for learning about how to behave in the social world; or for demonstrating competence or dominating others in the viewer group. Distinguishing these family types would generate an index of audience behavior as an independent variable. From this, researchers could design studies which would employ "social uses types" as predictors of media exposure, interpersonal communication satisfaction, family harmony, or other relevant dependent measures of theoretical value. Audience behavior may then contribute more significantly to the growing interest in styles and strategies of family communication. The relational uses which families make of television certainly represent a range of communicative behaviors which reveal much about the nature of the group. A precise understanding of the particular uses made of television by families may even hold implications for family therapy.

Typologies are inherently descriptive and heuristic devices. The classification of social uses which has been presented here requires further elaboration and validation. Methodologically, an argument has been made for more ethnographies of mass communication, using triangulated data-collection techniques: naturalistic observation, self-reports, and other-reports. In this way, novel and complex social uses of television and other media can be documented. Another approach would be to operationalize the constructs proposed in the previous discussion in the form of fixed-alternative statements for survey research. By generating quantitative scores and applying statistical tests, it may be possible to establish or modify the components of the typology into scientifically intercorrelated factors. Of course, this method assumes that audience members are sufficiently self-aware to recognize or gauge some rather subtle uses of the media which have been discovered ethnographically, an assumption which may not be comfortably met.

NOTES

1. Ethnomethodology is, in a general sense, a manner for conducting social research since it is a way of thinking about social structure and process. But, the term is intended to direct researchers to observation and interpretation of the social "methods" of their subjects as the substance for analysis, particularly routine behaviors which are often overlooked. The "method" in "ethnomethodology" refers to the ways in which people construct their social realities, not to a research strategy.

2. For family research, a one-week-long observation period per family is most efficient. Henry (1965, pp. xv-xxiii) makes a convincing argument for this length of observation. Certainly some additional data would be gathered in a longer stay, but the researcher must utilize the time wisely in order to maximize sample size while simultaneously retrieving the most valuable data.

REFERENCES

ANDERSON, N. *The hobo*. Chicago: University of Chicago Press, 1923.
ANDERSON, R.E., & CARTER, I.E. *Human behavior in the social environment*. Chicago: Aldine, 1974.
BECHTEL, R., ACHELPOHL, C., & AKERS, R. Correlates between observed behavior and questionnaire responses on television viewing. In E.A. Rubinstein, G.A. Comstock, and J.P. Murray (Eds.), *Television and social behavior, 4*: Television in day-to-day life: Patterns of use. Washington, D.C.: Government Printing Office, 1972, 274-344.
BERELSON, B. LAZARSFELD, P., & McPHEE, W.N. *Voting: A study of opinion formation in a presidential campaign*. Chicago: University of Chicago Press, 1954.
BLUMER, H. *Symbolic interactionism*. Englewood Cliffs, N.J.: Prentice-Hall, 1969.
BRUYN, S. *The human perspective in sociology: The methodology of participant observation*. Englewood Cliffs, N.J.: Prentice-Hall, 1966.
BURGESS, E.W. The family as a unit of interacting personalities. *The Family*, 1926, 1, 3-9.
CARPENTER, E. *Oh! What a blow that phantom gave me*. New York: Holt, Rinehart and Winston, 1972.
CICOUREL, A.V. *Theory and method in a study of Argentine fertility*. New York: Wiley, 1974.
DELIA, J.G. Constructivism and the study of human communication. *Quarterly Journal of Speech*, 1976, 1, 66-83.
FRENTZ, T.S., & FARRELL, T.B. Language-action: A paradigm for communication. *Quarterly Journal of Speech*, 1976, 4, 333-349.
GANS, H.J. *The urban villagers*. New York: Free Press, 1962.
GARFINKEL, H. *Studies in ethnomethodology*. Englewood Cliffs, N.J.: Prentice-Hall, 1967.

GARFINKEL, H., & STOLLER, R.J. Passing and the managed achievement of sex status in an 'intersexed' person-part 1. In H. Garfinkel, *Studies in ethnomethodology*. Englewood Cliffs, N.J.: Prentice-Hall, 1967.
GLASER, B.G., & STRAUSS, A.L. *The discovery of grounded theory: Strategies for qualitative research*. Chicago: Aldine, 1967.
HENRY, J. *Pathways to madness*. New York: Vintage Books, 1965.
HERZOG, H. What do we really know about daytime serial listeners? In P. Lazarsfeld and F.N. Stanton (Eds.), *Radio research: 1942-43*. New York: Duell, Sloan, and Pearce, 1944.
HYMES, D. Toward ethnographies of communication. *American Anthropologist*, 1964, 6, part 2.
KATZ, E. The two step flow of communication: An up-to-date report on an hypothesis. *Public Opinion Quarterly*, 1957, 1, 61-78.
KATZ, E., & LAZARSFELD, P. *Personal influence: The part played by people in the flow of mass communications*. Glencoe, Ill.: Free Press, 1962.
KATZ, E., & FOULKES, D. On the use of mass media as 'escape.' *Public Opinion Quarterly*, 1962, 4, 377-388.
KATZ, E., BLUMLER, J.G., & GUREVITCH, M. Uses of mass communication by the individual. In W.P. Davison and F.T.C. Yu (Eds.), *Mass communication research*. New York: Praeger, 1974.
KATZ, E. Looking for trouble: Social research on broadcasting. Lecture given to the British Broadcasting Corporation, London, 1977.
KATZMAN, N. Television soap operas: What's been going on anyway? *Public Opinion Quarterly*, 1972, 2, 200-212.
LAZARSFELD, P., BERELSON, B., & GAUDET, H. *The people's choice*. New York: Columbia University Press, 1948.
LAZARSFELD, P., & STANTON, F.N. (Eds.). *Communications research: 1948-1949*. New York: Harper, 1949.
LEWIS, O. *Five families*. New York: Basic Books, 1959.
LEWIS, O. *La Vida*. New York: Random House, 1965.
LIEBOW, E. *Tally's corner*. Little, Bown & Company, 1967.
LULL, J. *Mass media and family communication: An ethnography of audience behavior*. Doctoral dissertation, University of Wisconsin-Madison, 1976.
LULL, J. Choosing television programs by family vote. *Communication Quarterly*, 1978, 26, 53-57.
LYLE, J. Learning from television. In E.A. Rubinstein, G.A. Comstock, and J.P. Murray (Eds.), *Television and social behavior, 4*: Television in day-to-day life: Patterns of use. Washington, D.C.: Government Printing Office, 1972, 19-21.
McQUAIL, D., BLUMLER, J.G., & BROWN, J.R. The television audience: A revised perspective. In D. McQuail (Ed.), *Sociology of mass communication*. Harmondsworth, England: Penguin Books, 1972, 135-165.
MANDER, J. *Four arguments for the elimination of television*. New York: Morrow, 1977.
MEHAN, H., & WOOD, H. *The reality of ethnomethodology*. New York: Wiley, 1975.
MERTON, R.K. Patterns of influence. In P. Lazarsfeld and F.Stanton (Eds.), *Communications research: 1948-1949*. New York: Harper, 1949.
NORDENSTRENG, K. Comments on 'gratification research' in broadcasting. *Public Opinion Quarterly*, 1970, 2, 130-132.

PHILIPSEN, G.F. Speaking like a man in teamsterville: Culture patterns of role enactment in an urban neighborhood. *Quarterly Journal of Speech*, 1975, 1, 13-22.

SCHILLER, H.I. *The mind managers*. Boston: Beacon Press, 1973.

WALTER, J.K., & STONE, V.A. Television and family communication. *Journal of Broadcasting*, 1975, 4, 409-414.

WHYTE, W.F. *Street corner society*. University of Chicago Press, 1943.

ZIMMERMAN, D.H., & POLLNER, M. The everyday world as a phenomenon. In J.D. Douglas (Ed.), *Understanding everyday life*. Chicago: Aldine, 1970.

ZIMMERMAN, D.H. Ethnomethodology. *The American Sociologist*, 1978, 1, 6-15.

This article presents a critical/institutional analysis of network television as a monopolistic business enterprise and as a cultural apparatus. In his theoretical development of the notion of "network," Kellner argues that there are frequent tensions and conflicts among the various roles networks perform. Furthermore, he strongly chastises previous critiques of the industry for ignoring these inherent contradictions; theorizing in the area must address these issues, he says. Douglas Kellner is in the Department of Philosophy, University of Texas at Austin.

23

NETWORK TELEVISION AND AMERICAN SOCIETY

Introduction to a Critical Theory of Television

Douglas Kellner

Network television, one of the most powerful social forces in America, is assuming increasingly important and complex social functions in contemporary societies. Television networks determine the structure and content of news and information, as well as the dominant forms, values, and ideologies in television entertainment. Network televsion serves as an instrument of social control, promoting capitalist commodities and consumerist values, social conformity, law and order, authority figures, and the family. Its advertising is one of the major managers of consumer demand; its ideas, images, information, entertainment are ubiquitous forces of socialization. Moreover, network television is an extremely profitable business institution, connected with great corporations and banks, and is itself a rapidly growing economic conglomerate which controls many other businesses. Network television is also a political force contributing to the ritualization of politics; reinforcing spectator politics, it is itself an autonomous political power. Not only does the network system constitute the form of American television, but it fashions images and ideas for many other countries in the world. American network television is thus one of the most far-reaching communication apparatuses and information and entertainment transmitters that has ever existed. Despite this, there has been relatively little theoretical analysis of the American broadcasting system, and there exists no adequate critical-institutional theory of television. In view of the heated debates over the effects of American television, it is surprising that television has not received the sort of theoretical scrutiny directed toward other major institutions, such as the state, the educational system, the corporation, or the family. Of all major contemporary institutions, network television is the most neglected and mystified. In the following pages, I shall propose aspects of a critical theory of television while challenging dominant paradigms and conventional wisdom. I begin by situating television within the fundamental socioeconomic processes of advanced capitalism and then analyze

From Douglas Kellner, "Network Television and American Society: Introduction to a Critical Theory of Television," *Theory and Society* 10 (1981), pp. 31-62. Reprinted by permission of Elsevier Scientific Publishing Company and the author.

its social functions within American society today, focusing on its contradictory imperatives and social effects, as well as the contradictions between
business, the state, and network television.

Television and Advanced Capitalism

Histories of broadcasting reveal that the electronic communication media
first caught the attention of business, the military, and politicians during
World War I.[1] In a sense, the development of broadcasting was bound up with
the development of imperialism. For example, corporations such as United
Fruit became interested in broadcasting to coordinate their foreign investments, and the military was interested in electronic communications to aid
in the planning and execution of warfare.[2] The miliary usefulness of radio
became apparent when it was perceived that although telegraph wires could
be destroyed, radio signals were not as vulnerable. Broadcasting played an
important role in World War I, while World War II held up the introduction of
television because the military needed the technical resources and labor-power
for the war effort.[3] After World War II, television entertainment and advertising became an important force in constituting the consumer society as the
dominant social form.[4] Television subsequently helped mobilize public opinion against communism during the Cold War.[5] Since then military and
imperial ventures have aided in the development of electronic communications and have helped produce satellite television, the NASA space program,
and the "electronic battlefield". As Herbert Schiller and others have argued,
American television has been instrumental in selling American values, commodities, and ways of life to other countries, and is thus a major force of
cultural hegemony.[6]

American television is rooted in the fundamental economic processes of
corporate capitalism. The development of the telecommunications system
followed the railroad, oil, steel, and automobile industries in concentrating
the means of communication in the hands of giant corporations. Thus American
Telephone and Telegraph (AT&T) monopolized the telephone industry;
Western Union monopolized the telegraph industry; RCA, Westinghouse, and
General Electric controlled the industries producing radio and electric appli-
ances. Network television was in turn established in the radio broadcasting
industry and grew out of the monopolistic aspirations of RCA corporate executives.[7] With the invention of television, the struggle for hegemony of the
telecommunications industry reached fever pitch in the 1930s. In their remarkable book, *Television: A Struggle for Power* (1938), Frank Waldrop and
Joseph Borkin recount how AT&T and RCA battled for supremacy in the
communications industry.[8] AT&T wanted to use telephone lines to broad-

cast television into homes, whereas RCA wanted to use wireless, over-the-air broadcasting to maintain control of radio and to secure control of television.[9] During this period, RCA considered developing facsimile electronic reproduction which would deliver newspaper and other print material into the home, as well as two-way televisual phone communication via broadcast waves, which would have given them almost total control of the communications industry.[10] In the 1930s and 1940s, these two giants compromised, establishing the basis for the present system of American television.[11] AT&T retained control of telephone lines and RCA dropped development of over-the-air two-way televisual phone communication. The introduction of facsimile reproduction was postponed and publishing interests retained control of print material. For these concessions, RCA was allowed to remain foremost in broadcasting. As a counter-tendency, however, to increasing monopolization of the American economy, there were government efforts to regulate and in some cases to break up monopoly. Government uproar over monopoly of the broadcast industry forced RCA to divest itself of one of its two networks (which became ABC).[12] In the heyday of radio in the 1940s, then, the three networks which would dominate television were the oligopolistic kingpins of broadcasting. Henceforth, members of the broadcast industry would dominate the government broadcasting regulatory agency (The Federal Communications Commission), and would advance industry private interests rather than enforce the "public interest, convenience, and necessity". Here too the broadcast industry falls within the central dynamics of advanced capitalism where government regulatory agencies advance the interests of the industries supposedly under regulation.[13]

Network television is also an important part of the social processes in advanced capitalism that produced a consumer society. As leisure time increased in the earlier part of the century as a result of a shortened working day, people spent more time engaged with popular culture. Advertising became increasingly central in producing the consumer demand necessary to reproduce a consumer society, and broadcasting began to play a crucial role in selling commodities.[14] Popular culture and broadcasting also began playing a fundamental role in providing advertisements for the new consumer and commodity society. In this way, broadcasting played a crucial role in engineering consent for advanced capitalism, and advanced capitalism could now assign a less important role to force in maintaining social control.[15] But this role has been a strange and contradictory one from the 1950s until the present. The television networks are part of an advancing economic sector and have become increasingly profitable and powerful in the past decades.[16] They are now an important socioeconomic force, owning and controlling many other industries and businesses.[17] They have benefited from technological-electronic marvels which have produced satellite television, cable television, and new television home technologies. Today network television occupies a central place within advanced capitalism whose fate as a social system is ever more closely bound together with the broadcasting industry. What, then, is the nature, structure, and function of network television?

Towards a Theory of Network

Network television is a complex system of production and distribution. As a technical phenomenon, "Network" is a web of cables, satellites, and microwave relay stations radiating from centers in New York to affiliates all over the United States.[18] As a system of syndication it pays studios to produce programs and then pays affiliates to broadcast them. In turn, affiliates agree to play a certain amount of Network programming. Advertisers then pay the networks a fee depending on how many viewers are watching at a particular time according to Nielsen and Arbitron ratings.[19] Network thus comprises the "television overlords" while the affiliates are their sometimes docile, sometimes restive, vassals. Conceived as a totality, Network is a system of enormous centralized corporations, local broadcasting outlets, advertisers who sell their products, production studios that supply the programs, and ratings research companies who provide the numbers that shape advertising rates and incomes. Network is the structure which holds the commercial system of broadcasting together. It is the conglomerate of institutions, practices, rules, and personnel which comprise the commercial broadcasting system.

This theory of network television presupposes a distinction between *Network* as a system of commercial broadcasting and *a specific network* like CBS or ABC. According to Gaye Tuchman, "A network is a corporation that seeks stations as affiliates. It leases airtime from its affiliated stations and sells portions of that leased time to commercial advertisers. Networks also own and operate stations."[20] Simply conceptualizing Network as a corporation seeking affiliates fails to grasp that the network system of commercial broadcasting encompasses network corporations and their affiliates, production studios, a star-publicity system, advertising agencies, sponsors, ratings agencies, trade magazines, journals, and popular magazines such as *TV Guide.* Thus, "Network" refers to the totality of the broadcast system and its intricate workings. The theory of Network assumes that despite competition and differences between the specific networks (ABC, CBS, and NBC), each is similar in its operations, its goals, and its interchangeable personnel and programs. An analogy would be to the concept "Hollywood" which has come to refer to the system of American film as a distinguishable mode of production and product. American television too has developed a unique system of production; consequently, "Network" refers to the type of broadcasting and programming developed in America.

Network then is a commercial system of television production and distribution, governed by the profit motive and so-called market competition,
relatively free of government regulation.[21] A product of American capitalism,
its structure and programming are deeply embedded in the capitalist mode of
production and the American power structure. Unlike broadcasting systems
in other major countries, where government finances, regulates, and sometimes controls television, no other alternative but a "free market" system of
broadcasting has ever been seriously considered in America.[22] From the beginning, Network was the child of private enterprise and only in America is television so free from accountability to the public and government. Most radical
theories of television have highlighted its dual functions of producing both
profit and hegemonic ideology, seeing television as a business machine and an
ideology machine within a monolithic capitalist society. Theodor Adorno and
Max Horkheimer, for instance — whose essay "The Culture Industry" provided
the model for many radical theories of television, the media, and popular
culture — posit capitalism as "an iron system" which "is uniform as a whole
and in every part."[23] Foreshadowing Marcuse's one-dimensional society thesis,
they argue that the "culture industry" serves to "make the individual all the
more subservient to his adversary — the absolute power of capitalism."[24] The
goals of the culture industry are profit and social control; it follows a "necessity inherent in the system not to leave the customer alone, not for a moment
to allow him any suspicion that resistance is possible."[25] Its job is to "defend
society" and it provides something for everyone "so that none may escape."[26]
"The stronger the position of the culture industry becomes, the more sum
marily it can deal with the consumer's needs, producing them, controlling
them, disciplining them, and even withdrawing amusement."[27] Thus the culture industry is a powerful "instrument of social control."[28]

Most theories which conceptualize television's dual functions as producer of
profit and ideology have utilized a "critical theory" model of capitalism and
the media, conceptualizing television as the "cultural arm of the industrial
order" (Gerbner), an instrument that "maintains hegemony and legitimates
the status quo" (Tuchman), and as an "ideological state apparatus" (Althusser
and his followers).[29] This is also the dominant model in the work of the
Network Project which partially carried out an ambitious attempt to provide
an institutional analysis of network television.[30] Their panel discussions, radio
broadcasts, and publications from 1971—75 provide valuable material, but no
systematic analysis was ever developed. Although their theoretical presuppositions were never adequately spelled out, they too saw Network as a monolithic
instrument of corporate domination, engaged solely in the pursuit of profit
and the goal of maintaining capitalist hegemony, and thus serving as an instrument of corporate manipulation. Consequently, they failed to discern any

emancipatory potential in public television, cable and satellite television, the public access movement, or any other aspect of American television.[31]

Commerce versus Communication

All such theories fail to describe the contradictory imperatives built into the American broadcasting system. The network system is grounded in a fundamental contradiction between the airwaves as a public domain, supposedly owned by the public and to be used in the "public interest, convenience, and necessity," and the private ownership of network television.[32] This contradiction is expressed in the conflict between private enterprise and government regulation and between the profit motive and public interest, as well as in the contradictions between the myth of "objective news" and the actual control and censorship of information. This results in contradictions between the mandates calling for the free flow of information necessary for democracy and the constraints on information and entertainment congenial to the profit imperatives of privately owned corporations. The history of American broadcasting has been governed by the drive for profit maximization, and Network has battled government regulation and stifled attempts at expanding channels of communication, thus repeatedly sacrificing entertainment and information for commercial interests.[33] In the early 1930s, pressure from newspaper publishers severely limited the amount of news on radio and there were no detailed or adequate radio news broadcasts until World War II.[34] The defeat of the Wagner-Hatfield Bill in 1935, offered as an amendment to the Federal Communications Act of 1934, eliminated an attempt to allot "to educational, religious, agricultural, labor, cooperative, and similar non-profit-making associations one-fourth of all the radio broadcasting facilities within their jurisdiction."[35] Government and industry frequently suppressed technologies of communication in the interests of their exploitation by hegemonic corporations, such as postponing FM radio, leading to the suicide of its inventor, Edwin Armstrong,[36] the de facto choice in the 1940s of VHF over UHF television systems, thus effectively reducing the possible number of television stations,[37] and hampering the development of cable and pay television.[38] Again and again, the major broadcasting powers suppressed technologies that would have expanded the media of communication and produced a more diverse and innovative broadcast system. Consequently, there were attempts by the broadcast industry, supported by their allies in government, to make broadcasting a wholly private business enterprise with little regard for the public interest.

In 1946, the head of the National Association of Broadcasters, Justin Miller, declared the idea that the people owned the airwaves – central to the 1934

Federal Communications Act — was "hooey and nonsense."[39] Although occasionally members of the FCC, isolated government spokespersons, congressional members, or other federal agencies attempted to regulate the broadcasting industries, on the whole they have operated as private industries.[40] Operating in the "public interest" was generally interpreted as providing a minimum of public affairs programming and there were few instances of stations being denied renewal of their licenses because of poor programming.[41] The commercial nature of the system was highlighted by advertising agencies and sponsors actually producing many radio programs — a practice common during the first years of television.[42] Contradictions between commerce and communication, private enterprise and the public interest intensified in the 1950s, and with the turmoil over the quiz show scandals and mounting criticism of television, the networks took over responsibility for programming from advertisers.[43] By the late 1950s, there was a widespread uproar over the low quality of American television, dominated by quiz shows, westerns, violent action-adventure shows, and insipid situation comedies. At the time, FCC Commissioner Newton Minow made his famous "vast wasteland" speech and pushed for the development of public television.[44] With the emergence of public television in the early 1960s, a potentially new form of American television appeared, but for the most part PBS reproduced the network system — without advertising and enormous pressure for ratings — hence it is sometimes called the "fourth network."[45]

This previous discussion might make it appear that network television is simply a typical capitalist business institution driven solely by the interests of profit-maximization. Unlike other monopolistic businesses, however, it has the unique role of maintaining the free flow of information necessary for a healthy democracy and of transmitting ideologies necessary for stabilizing capitalism. Hence, the "public interest" proviso requires that Network maintain a free flow of information as well as a cash flow to satisfy its owners and stockholders. Here again business has predominated over communication, forcing William Paley both to regret the day that CBS issued corporate stock and to tell Bill Moyers the CBS simply could not afford to produce quality documentary or discussion shows regularly because "the minute is worth too much now."[46] Most critics of network television have argued that the drive for maximum ratings and profit is responsible for the "lowest common denominator" programming and the sacrifice of television's higher potential as a vehicle of communication and entertainment. Corporate restraints and censorship have produced a contradiction between the First Amendment right to free speech and the democratic concept of a public sphere contrasted to actual restrictions on public debate, alternative views, and critical discourse. In the 1934 Federal Communications Act, earnest attempts were made by Congress to have the broadcast system conform to the classical principles of democracy and to direct broadcasting to produce a public sphere of free discussion and debate. Although the airwaves were deemed part of the public domain, subject to government regulation, broadcasting was to remain free of political control and censorship.[47]

Curiously, there was nothing in the Federal Communications Act discussing the sale of broadcasting time for commercial purposes. In fact, even such a person concerned with business as Herbert Hoover conceived of broadcasting as a non-commercial medium when he was Secretary of Commerce: "Radio is not to be considered merely as a business carried on for private gain, for private advertisement, or for the entertainment of the curious. It is to be considered as a public concern, impressed with a public trust, and to be considered primarily from the standpoint of the public interest."[48] In 1922, Hoover stated that radio was one of the few instances where the public was unanimously in favor of an extension of federal government powers, and both Hoover and Coolidge were in favor of a public utility attitude toward broadcasting.[49] When commerce had obviously dominated the form and content of the broadcast media by the 1940s, the FCC commissioned a study, *Public Service Responsibility of Broadcast Licensees* (the so-called "Blue Book"), which reaffirmed the public, democratic, and non-commercial principles which were to govern the broadcast media.[50] Moreover, a variety of court and FCC decisions have reaffirmed democratic principles of communication for the broadcast media. These principles and decisions specify what is meant by broadcasting serving the "public interest" and include: (1) a 1944 Supreme Court decision that the people have a First Amendment right to receive information from the widest possible, diverse, and antagonistic sources; (2) a 1949 FCC decision which asserts that the people have the right to be informed and hear competing sides of an issue; and (3) a court decision which affirms a right to reply to one-sided or distorted discourse (the "fairness doctrine" in the 1967 Red Lion Case).[51] Consequently, there is a contradiction between First Amendment freedoms of speech, as interpreted by Congress, the FCC, and the courts, and communicative practices that limit the spectrum of opinion and constrain communication.[52]

Capitalism Versus Democracy

We have here an example of the contradiction between capitalism and democracy historically typical of the American experience.[53] A democratic social order would engage in popular debate of the central issues in a society, would give all sides of an issue an opportunity to make a case, and would then decide the issue after sufficient debate through democratic participation. In an advanced industrial technological order, access to the means of public communication is necessary to ensure that adequate presentation of various points of view and debate can take place. However, in a capitalist society in which the means of communication are concentrated in powerful corporations, access is denied or limited to minority, oppositional, or alternative views. Studies have shown that the opinion spectrum presented is severely limited and many groups and individuals are denied access to broadcast media.[54] Restriction of access to the media and limitations on public debate contradict the need for an informed public that can participate in democratic politics. That the mass media have sacrificed public communication for commerce plainly exhibits that their private ownership contradicts their avowed purpose of serving the "public interest, convenience, and necessity."

There are then contradictions between the nature and purpose of commercial television and a democratic social order. Paul Klein claims that people choose "the least objectionable program" and that network television maximizes its audience by offering non-controversial programs to keep from offending people.[55] Other network observers claim that this leads to "lowest common denominator" programming which, in seeking a mass audience, avoids culture or controversy that challenges or provokes the audience. In this view, television is perceived as a commercial medium which seeks to attract, entertain, and pacify its audience, while selling commercial goods and ideology. Consequently, those who call television a "democratic" or "populist" art fail both to understand the nature of democracy, and to see how television has been replacing democratic participation by providing political spectacles and by reducing elections to a manipulation of political images.[56] Furthermore, there are contradictions between democracy and advertising which are the lifeblood that sustains the network operation.[57] Advertising seeks to show that whatever problems people have can be resolved by something they can purchase. It contains images that celebrate the society as it is and do not stir people to political action or social participation. It suggests that happiness and value are located in the private sphere, encouraging a privatized, consumer existence. Democracy, however, thrives on controversy and requires participation in social processes, presupposing that people are motivated enough to want to get involved in public life. Democracy requires a lively public sphere where there is discussion, debate, and participation in collective, public decision making.

By attracting the audience with the lure of "free entertainment," television produces immense profits and gains enormous sociocultural power over its audience. Eventually, however, the audience pays for its "free entertainment". The advertiser pays the television network for the time-spot purchased according to how many people are supposedly watching at a given time, and its advertising expenses are in turn passed to the consumer. Thus even in the privacy of one's home, one is being exploited by corporate capital. Not only is leisure "colonized" (Aronowitz), but it is a form of unwaged labor in which networks derive profits from the aggregate size of audience-viewing, while advertisers not only increase aggregate consumer demand, but also force the audience to pay higher prices for its commodities as the cost of viewing "free" TV.[58]

John Brenkman argues that the isolation which the consumption of mass media experience in the home imposes on audiences breaks down other forms of association and substitutes vicarious consumption of media images for active, participatory, associative culture.[59] The separation of the consumers of mass culture from each other at once produces an alienation from active cultural production and collective social experience, as well as a replacement of the public sphere (Habermas) by cultural consumption.[60] In this way, "leisure" time activity reproduces types of alienation, fragmentation, and domination found in the labor process.[61] These analyses demystify any view of television as "harmless entertainment" and show the important social functions television has within advanced capitalism. Most such theories, however, assume that popular culture and the mass media simply and unproblematically reproduce the social relations of advanced capitalism. In this view, the mass media have only conservative social functions and network television is assigned a central and especially pernicious role in this process.[62] Such analyses fail to see, however, certain contradictions and tensions within this process and consequently do not indicate how the mass media might conceivably be utilized to promote social change which might subvert the hegemony of monopoly capitalism. This issue will occupy the next several sections, which propose new paradigms to conceptualize the role of network television in contemporary society.

Profitability, Legitimation, and the Production of News and Entertainment

In contrast to vulgar leftism, I will argue that there are frequent tensions and conflicts among Network's drive toward profit-maximization, its production of hegemonic ideology to engineer social consent, and its production of news and entertainment according to professional codes. To maximize profit, network television must produce programs that appeal to the audience and must hire people who can produce appealing programs. Therefore, the short-range economic interests of a network may lead them to broadcast news which puts in question aspects of the socioeconomic order, thus jeopardizing their long-range economic interests.[63] For example, in order to gain maximum ratings and profits, the networks must deal with the crucial problems, scandals, and crises in society which attract the interests of the audience. Their own corporate interests may lead them to sacrifice what might be perceived as their interest in legitimating the whole system. Likewise, if the audience is attracted to entertainment programs dealing with current social problems and issues, the networks may well play these more controversial shows, even if they are critical of established society. Consequently, the imperatives to maximize profits and yet defend the established power structure, of which Network is a significant part, is conducive to conflicts and tensions within Network and between Network and other institutions in American society.

Furthermore, tensions may arise between the "cultural apparatus" of producers, directors, writers, and actors and the "consciousness industry" in New York with its corporate executives, managers, and censors.[64] Here manifold conflicts between business and culture emerge. Producers in the cultural apparatus are often interested in producing original, realistic, or controversial works. Interviews with television cultural workers show that many people working within television do not want to produce bland, conformist programming and constantly struggle against network censorship in order to produce more provocative programming.[65] The network executives and managers, however, are primarily concerned with profits and ratings, desiring programs that will not offend its massive audience, corporate sponsors, special interest groups, or government regulators by creating controversy. Yet Network also depends on "creative talent" who may not share traditional values or capitalist ideology, and who may be quite critical of some aspects of American society. Corporate managers must therefore make some concessions to the cultural apparatus which may occasionally produce critical-realist, satirical, or non-conformist works that subvert hegemonic ideology and criticize established society.[66] For instance, in the 1970s, topical and controversial shows such as *All in the Family, Mary Hartman*, and other Norman Lear comedies, broke previous television taboos and opened new space for social critique and satire. Then mini-series like *Roots, Washington: Behind Closed Doors, Wheels*, and *Holocaust* opened new space for historical drama dealing with oppression, political corruption, class conflict, and offered a more realistic picture of the central problems of American life and modern history.[67] These shows are often anti-business and deal sympathetically with oppressed poor, black, and working people. Beyond making concessions to the cultural apparatus, network must also hold an audience. It cannot simply reproduce the old stale ideology and formulas and must produce new programs that may well subvert traditional ideology. Hence, as the race for ratings and profits intensifies, and as new communications technologies are introduced, Network may be forced to expand the limits of censorship and broadcast programs that may sacrifice previous ideologies and idealizations of American life.

Conflicts emerge, too, between producing a news product which affirms and legitimates the existing society and professional news codes that call for objectivity, neutrality, and adversary or investigative reporting. Although many studies show how network news organizations, codes, and personnel policies restrict adversary views and criticism,[68] there are also times when professional codes and organizational imperatives lead to news production that may contradict the interests of the network managers and the power structure to which they and their corporations belong. Fred Friendly, Daniel Schorr, and others have written of the struggles waged with network executives over criticisms of Joe McCarthy, various corporations, the Vietnam War, the CIA, etc.[69] Although top management often exerts heavy-handed control over news production, many news personnel see themselves as journalists with professional codes and responsibilities.[70] These codes may lead network news personnel to broadcast news which criticizes existing practices, policies, and even institutions within the society. Moreover, in an era of "investigative journalism," the adversary functions of the press may intensify conflicts within the broadcast media as well as between Network and other dominant institutions.

Thus whereas television news and entertainment have tended to legitimize the existing society, its profit-imperative no less than its professional code render networks unreliable defenders of the existing order. As television's economic and cultural power increases, it becomes relatively freer of control by the state and dominant corporations. Whereas advertisers once produced programs and exerted control over content, today the networks can resist advertisers' censorship because many other sponsors are willing to buy any commercial time-spots refused.[71] Likewise, the state, at least in the United States, has never controlled effectively the media, as conflicts between the Johnson and Nixon Administrations with television have shown.[72] Network's race for profits may thus induce them to sacrifice conventional ideology and traditional values if the audience prefers adversary reporting or more novel, satirical, or critical entertainment. Moreover, professional codes and the special interests of the television production community have also helped drive television in this direction. The result is increasingly contradictory television images and social effects which current radical and conservative theories of television have failed to conceptualize.

Network's Contradictory Images and Social Effects

Network is subject to a variety of social pressures, including those from women, blacks, and other minorities, as well as political, educational, labor, and religious groups. Hence, Network was forced to make concessions to the civil rights movement, the women's movement, the gay movement, the sexual revolution, and portrayed other changes which took place in the 1960s. Therefore, in the late 1960s and 1970s, images of women, blacks, gays, and other minorities were progressive in contrast to the racism and sexism that prevailed, and still prevails, in large parts of the country. There are also pressures by conservative and liberal groups to curtail portrayals of sex and violence and to defend traditional values such as the family and religion. Caught between conservative and progressive segments of American society, Network's programs are full of contradictions and tensions.

In general, there is a lag between social experience and the world of television entertainment belatedly portraying social change after the turmoil has abated. Television thus often puts its benediction (or damnation) on changes after the fact. Hence television is often out of sync with social experience, and there may be dissonance between the Today of its news and the Yesterday of its entertainment programs. After the tumultuous civil rights struggles in the early sixties, for example, blacks finally began to be accepted in the television world from the mid to late sixties. After the agitation of the woman's liberation movement and manifold sexual rebellions in the 1960s, independent working women, unmarried couples, broken families, singles living together, and homosexuals were increasingly portrayed on television. Such changes should not be exaggerated, however, for representatives of women and minority groups continue to complain that television has not actually broken with sexist and racist stereotypes and has not actually produced realistic and complex portraits of women or minorities.[73] Moreover, when television portrays social change or oppositional movements, it often blunts the radical edge of new social forces, values, or changes and tries to absorb, coopt, and defuse any challenges to the existing power structure.[74] Nonetheless, because America consists of various regions, groups, and individuals with different values, ideologies, and culture,[75] television records changes that have taken place in certain regions and groups to other groups. In this way, programs about pre-marital sex, drugs, or the breakdown of the family, as well as political-economic scandal and corruption, may be unsettling to traditionalist groups. While television may adjust some groups to social changes which they have not yet experienced, it can also challenge others with new ideas and experiences which they may resist. Although it is often suggested that American television is a cultural homogenizer imposing its mainstream culture on the entire country,[76] these homogenizing effects can be overstated. Indeed, contradictions between the television world and individual experience, or between TV encoding and audience decoding, may render television a vehicle of culture homogeneity and social control less powerful than many claim. Despite television's attempt in the 1950s and early 1960s to idealize and celebrate American life, a decade of social conflict did take place in the 1960s. Likewise, in the mid-1970s and early 1980s, despite television's preference for a mild version of women's liberation or liberalism, a traditionalist, conservative revolt is taking place that is often critical of television. Recently both conservatives and radicals have been attacking television with equal vehemence and often in similar terms, suggesting that many people are not pacified or being homogenized by the tube.

Network's drive to increase profit, often at the expense of traditional ideology, is behind the complaints of conservative critics about the disintegrating effects of television on traditional values. Daniel Bell argues that television and the mass media are instrumental in promoting a new consumer ethic and hedonistic lifestyle that contradicts the older capitalist-protestant production ethic with its emphasis on hard work, saving, delayed gratification, the family, religion, and other traditional values.[77] Neoconservatives such as Aaron Wildavsky, Daniel Moynihan, Robert Nisbet, and Samuel Huntington all argue that television has eroded respect for authority by exposing political scandals, business corruption and failures, while fostering cynicism, distrust, and disrespect for the system. They complain that the media have gone too far in their adversary function and have eroded the President's power (Wildavsky and Moynihan), thus "seriously and dangerously" weakening the state's ability to govern."[78] Moynihan and Bell maintain that television has promoted an "adversary culture," while Huntington holds that it has promoted a "democratic distemper".[79] Many conservatives have been critical of the "new class" within the cultural apparatus whose biases, they claim, are liberal, "collectivist," and anti-"free enterprise," thus promoting an "adversary culture".[80] Edith Efron, for example, has often attacked television's "left-wing" bias, arguing that television has been a mouthpiece for "ecological stop-growth types," "nuclear Luddites and plutonophobes," and "Third World and socialist tyrannies"; on the other hand, she claims that television has been hostile to "U.S. business, U.S. labor, the U.S. military and U.S. technology".[81] In short, she claims that the television networks are promoting the agenda of the New Left![82] Ben Stein, in *The View From Sunset Boulevard*, has attacked television entertainment as anti-business, anti-military, and anti-traditional American values.[83] He contends that the Hollywood TV production community, which actually does the programming and writing, is an "extremely energetic and militant class" which uses its cultural power to attack competing social elites and to propagate its ultra-liberal views.

The views of conservatives such as Efron and Stein coincide with the Nixon-Agnew administration's critiques of television's "liberal bias".[84] Some of the conservative critique is exaggerated — the Efron article cited above is ludicrous — and critics of television's "subversive" effects fail to see its ideological service on behalf of the established order. The conflict between radicals who conceptualize television as a hegemonic tool of the established society and stress its integrating-stabilizing effects, and conservatives who decry its disintegrating-destabilizing effects, exhibits the opposing poles of the contradictory and ambiguous social effects of American television. Television *does* have different effects on different audiences and can even have contradictory effects on a given individual. Some individuals may be frightened and made passive by television violence, as Gerbner and his associates argue, whereas others may be led to carry out aggressive or violent acts.[85] Because audiences select the shows they are attracted to, television probably reinforces pre-existing dispositions, although that it is so pervasive and ubiquitous indicates it is increasingly shaping basic attitudes, beliefs, values, and behavior.

It is therefore mistaken to define television as a monolithic tool of a unified ruling class. Instead, television reflects divisions and conflicts within the ruling class and the entire society about the direction of public policy. The struggles surrounding Vietnam and Watergate demonstrate that the media are not simply expressing a unified ruling class ideology. Indeed, the intra-capitalist rivalries and power struggles visible on American television suggests that there is really no one, unified "ruling class" with a unitary strategy, goals, and (what Enzensberger calls) a "politics of control". As Enzensberger argues, "The degree to which the power struggles within the ruling class are extroverted by Western television is without precedent in history, and all currrent theories of manipulation only serve to obscure this fact."[86] Against the neoconservatives, Enzensberger is also probably correct that the overall effects of television are to stabilize the social order and contain opposition: "Like Congress, only much more so, it can therefore be seen as a sort of homeostatic machine expressing, and at the same time containing, the contradictions which arise within the ruling class. The in-fights of this minority are acted out symbolically on the screen, as a kind of strategic simulations game which tends to prevent open clashes from occurring in reality. On balance, television thus works as a servo-mechanism increasing the overall stability of a given social system. Obviously, such a setup is much more sophisticated than a simple switch, and far more effective as a means of controlling complex and fluid situations."[87]

This analysis of network television's contradictory images and social effects helps explain, I believe, the inadequacies of the dominant and conflicting theories of television today. Those theories focusing solely on television's hegemonic-legitimating images and homogenizing social effects are one-sided and limited, as are those theories primarily seeing "subversive" effects. Both sorts of theories fail to see the contradictions within television messages and

its contradictory social effects; both exaggerate the power of television an
assume a passive spectator and manipulation theory. A critical theory o
television must attend to contradictory images, messages, and social effects
while also rejecting monolithic theories of advanced capitalism.

Network, the State, and Business

The relationship between Network and the state has been fraught with contradictions and ambiguities. Most FCC commissioners have been Network
allies, although a few have challenged, threatened, and at times controlled
aspects of Network practice.[88] Although Network has often expressed state
ideology on other occasions, Network has challenged and subverted state
ideology and practice. The broadcast media commonly publicize and mobilize
support for government programs. FDR's New Deal, Kennedy's New Frontier,
Johnson's Great Society program, various state Vietnam policies, Nixon's
Watergate defense, and Carter's Middle East diplomacy and responses to the
Iran and Afghanistan events all used the media to explain state policy, programs, and positions to the American people. In the initial stages of new
policy and programs, Network tends to be a sympathetic amplifier and to
present, explain, and interpret government policies and programs in a generally
favorable light. However, as soon as criticisms and failures of government
policies develop, Network reflects opposition and raises doubts about government action. If the failures become too obvious, television sharpens focus on
the policies' deficiencies and in this way subverts state practice. Television
thus often contributes to political stalemate or instability in ways which
might injure state practice, hindering both its steering and legitimation functions.

Many critical theories of the media have failed to note the contradictions and
tension between network television and the state. Claus Mueller, for example,
assumes in *The Politics of Communication* that the media are simply a mouthpiece for state propaganda, as do Althusser and the structural marxists.[89]
Such theories fail to see the contradictions in the state apparatus, the lack of
a unifying hegemonic state ideology and practice, and the contradictions in
the media's alternating criticism and promotion of the state. Part of the
problem derives from a crude model which posits the state as the tool of the
dominant economic interests and the media as the mouthpiece of the state
and ruling class. Such theories fail to perceive the relative autonomy of both
state and media from the dominant economic class and both fail to observe
the manifest conflicts between the state, Network, and business in contemporary society.[90] In the most dramatic instances, conflicts between the state
and Network take the form of media exposure of the worst failures of govern-

ment. For example, television presentations of Vietnam, Watergate, and the crimes of the CIA, FBI and other government agencies seriously delegitimated state practice.[91] While early television coverage of the Vietnam war defended government policy, after the Tet offensive television coverage raised serious doubts about the war policy.[92] Soon after, Johnson announced that he would not seek re-election and more attention was given to the anti-war movement. With Nixon's war policy, Network tended to present uncritically Nixon's view that American involvement was scaling down, but at the same time exposed various scandals such as the Calley affair at My Lai, troop insubordination and the shooting of officers, the murder of white American students at Kent State, and corruption in the South Vietnamese government. Although Network defined Vietnam as a pragmatic failure, never really analyzing why we were there in the first place, the coverage of the fall of Saigon — capped by incredible pictures of helicopter flight from the American embassy — made it clear that Vietnam was not merely the defeat but the rout of state policy. In a three hour documentary soon after the fall of Saigon, CBS tried to present itself as the enlightened critic of the war whose coverage and exposure of the failures of state policy helped us out of a morass into which we should have never fallen. Aside from the obvious self-promotion of the heroic role of the CBS coverage of Vietnam, the program exhibited an actual contradiction between the state and Network, as well as television's attempt to gain some of the prestige and cultural power lost by the state.

That television news often focusses on conflict also led it to popularize the ideas and practice of the New Left in the 1960s.[93] Although the Network text often criticized the "violence" and "anarchy" of student demonstrators, the powerful images of struggle made New Left activism attractive to many young people and perhaps even to viewers conditioned to enjoy action-adventure programs. However, as Todd Gitlin points out, television's focus on sensational action disposed the New Left into a dangerous adventurism, and never really explained the New Left criticisms of the existing society or visions of a new society.[94]

Although network coverage of Watergate at first accepted the Nixon Administration's explanation of the Watergate affair as a "third-rate burglary," as the scandal escalated, television played a crucial role in the downfall of the Administration. The network executives knew that Nixon's vindictive nature (as exposed in his "enemies list") and his hatred of the media would lead him to retaliate if he maintained the Presidency. They nonetheless decided to televise the Watergate Hearings and involved a fascinated nation in one of the great political passion plays of recent times. Network processed the Watergate affair as the drama of a Bad Man against the Good System — a typical formula that fit in well with the Gothic vision of popular culture. So much corruption was exposed, however, and public opinion was so firmly mobilized against Nixon that he had to resign, and it is doubtful that the drama of his resignation washed away the stench of political corruption in the American political system Watergate coverage so relentlessly exposed. In the Post-Watergate and Post-Vietnam era, Network has gained much power and legitimacy as a result of state failures and it continues to expose the failings of state practice and political corruption. The Bert Lance affair and "Abscam," "Brilab," and other political scandals reveal once again the power of the media and network television's adversary functions.

Network also stands in an ambiguous and contradictory role to business today. Although Network has been the dedicated salesman of corporate products and the most effective promulgator of capitalist ideology, today tensions are evolving between Network and business. Network news, documentaries, and special events programs have been calling attention to business malpractice, environmental pollution, greed, and disdain for the public. Network is so profitable and powerful that advertisers flock to it in an increasingly lopsided seller's market; thus, Network has less and less to fear from business pressure and threats.[95] Because there is a widespread hostility toward big business and corporate ripoffs, shows such as *60 Minutes* win big ratings in their exposés of corruption and practical advice on how to avoid being cheated by business malpractice. Although *60 Minutes* provides morality plays that expose individual corruption, rather than critical analyses of the system as a whole, and although it reduces the issue to individual cases of corruption, it also creates suspicion and mistrust of business. More important, the evening news presents business failures and scandals in a way that prompt a more radical questioning of the functionality of the capitalist system. The evening news often portrays accounts of products such as the Pinto automobile, whose rearend gas tank was said to explode upon impact, or Firestone radial tires which frequently burst, causing serious injury. Network news regularly broadcasts government studies of dangerous food additives, pesticides, herbicides, and false advertising. It reveals, often graphically, pollution and environmental destruction by profit-pursuing industries. Many presentations on the "energy crisis" showed the failures of the energy system, and especially after Three Mile Island, the dangers of and resistance to nuclear energy. Furthermore, the trials and tribulations of the economy are daily broadcast in tales of stagflation, rising interest rates, exorbitant mortgage rates, wildly fluctuating gold prices, and a jittery stock market — all of which show an economy saturated with failures, irrationality, and crises. Network news thus broadcasts messages which suggest that the American dream is over and that perpetual crisis is on the agenda of the day.

Business has recently been increasingly vocal in its criticisms of network television, claiming that it is biased against business.[96] James L. Ferguson, Chairman of General Foods, accused the media of an "underlying hostility toward the business community and all its works," while another top industrialist claimed that "the press is biased in favor of the public interest groups."[97] Oil corporations have been intensely critical of how television news presents oil company profits and policies, and have been buying ads in top newspapers attacking the networks, when they were not allowed to buy network time to present their own point of view.[98] Walter Wriston, the Chairman of Citibank, argues that the media are hypercritical of all American institutions and are eroding public confidence: "the accent today is not on the evidence of progress in a multitude of fields; the heaviest emphasis is upon failure. The media, supported by some academic 'liberals', would have us believe that things are not just going badly, they are growing progressively worse. The dominant theme is the new American way of failure. No one wins; we always lose. Jack Armstrong and Tom Swift are dead."[99] More documentation of conflicts between business and the media surface in A. Kent MacDougall's series of articles in *The Los Angeles Times* during February, 1980. Mac-Dougall's first article, "Flaws in Press Coverage Plus Business Sensitivity Stirs Bitter Debate," began: "Businessmen who rank journalists with bureaucrats and environmentalists as their most irksome tormentors are starting to strike back at newspaper and television news coverage they consider biased against them."[100] MacDougall then documented a series of criticisms and lawsuits by major corporations against the networks and some newspapers. In a later article MacDougall focused on TV coverage of business, where he wrote: "Mobil's low opinion of TV news is shared by other oil producers and by big business in general. While regarding most newspapers and news magazines as neutral-to-sympathetic, the oil industry looks on television as often unfriendly, inaccurate and superficial — and at least partly responsible for turning public opinion against it. Large corporations especially resent TV for biting the hand that feeds it. Television has no income other than what it gets from corporate advertisers, who poured more than $10 billion into TV last year. As Leonard S. Matthews, president of the American Association of Advertising Agencies, warned recently, 'To expect private companies to go on supporting a medium that is attacking them is like taking up a collection among the Christians for money to buy more lions.'"[101]

Even Network's attempt to sell commodities and consumer ideologies may prove to be dysfunctional for the capitalist system. Advertising intensifies needs for new products, luxury items, success, and happiness. Programs such as *The Love Boat, Fantasy Island,* or *Three's Company* intensify desires for romance and erotic gratification. The many idealized family dramas and situation comedies promote hopes for a happy family life. Programs such as

Laverne and Shirley and *Starsky and Hutch* reinforce needs for friendship and close relationships. *Mary Tyler Moore* and programs that glamorize professional jobs help create aspirations for exciting work. Game shows intensify desires for a lucky break and winning prizes. Soap operas help reinforce desires for a life with drama and intense experience. Cop and action-adventure shows reinforce desires for the triumph of Good and elimination of Evil. Cumulatively, these programs and advertising help create rising expectations and hopes for a better life. If frustrated by actual social conditions, network television may unintentionally spur deep dissatisfaction with the present society and the demands for a better one. Jack Schierenbeck argues that television is dysfunctional for current capitalist stabilization strategies since it continues to provide images of abundance, hedonism, and good times as business wants to impose a regime of scarcity.[102] In 1974 the editors of *Business Week* wrote: "It will be a hard pill for many Americans to swallow the idea of doing with less so that big business can have more. . . *nothing. . . compares in difficulty with the selling job that must now be done to make people accept the new reality.*"[103] While significant sectors of big business want to halt the growing state sector, dismantle or contain the social welfare complex, enforce a lower standard of living, discipline labor, and impose a reign of scarcity, TV advertising and entertainment continue to promote individual fulfillment, economic progress, and consumerism. Whereas members of the Trilateral Commission and others want to curtail democracy and political struggle,[104] TV news shows growing labor unrest, as once quiescent municipal workers, schoolteachers, firemen, and police strike to gain higher wages and better working conditions. TV news continues to sell a version of corporate liberalism when significant sectors of business want to dismantle the welfare state and return to an unregulated, "free market" economy and TV shows the benefits of government regulation when industry wants to do away with it. TV news broadcasts anti-nuclear struggles and exposes the dangers, excessive costs, and irrationality of nuclear energy, as the energy corporations try to promote and sell nuclear energy to the public.

For those who care to see, television news reflects, not the harmonious integration, but the growing disintegration of the world capitalist system. It shows the chaos of the international capitalist economy and monetary system, and the triumph of the National Liberation Movements. One nightly gains images of the breakup of imperialism, as TV dramatically portrays revolts and struggles against dictatorships and repression supported by the CIA and American military and financial aid. It reveals post-World War II American foreign policy to be a failed attempt to stabilize capitalism and to impose a Pax Americana on Europe and the Third World. In this sense, the news shows a world in turmoil and revolution, albeit through the lenses of media which reduce political struggle to bloodshed and violence, thus failing to explain what they exhibit. This is not to say that network television is an instrument of revolution that will overthrow capitalism. Rather, television is an ambiguous mirror. It reflects the system's worst failures, intra-ruling class contradictions, and such serious threats as economic and energy crises, national liberation movements, terrorism, and explosively unstable parts of the world. But, as some argue, the format of television news often blunts its potentially radical messages,[105] serving as a headline service that presents fragments of social events abstracted from their socio-historical context. Network news leans toward the sensational, dramatic, and pictorial. It omits detailed analysis or interpretation that would situate the news in the context of the vicissitudes of advanced capitalism. It usually simplifies its presentation and ignores material that is not suited to packaged news formats. Interspersing news with commercials, which dramatize the tribulations of the body, blunts responses to the significance of the events portrayed. The news might possibly promote cynicism, confusion, and despair, but who knows? Individuals process television events in different ways and the nightly dramas of the evening news may also generate sparks of critical consciousness. Surely, the contradictory messages of network television preclude any simplistic view that television news and information is single-mindedly functional or dysfunctional for the capitalist system as a whole.

Thus although network television never broadcasts adequate analyses or critiques of advanced capitalism, or never proposes any radical alternatives to its problems, it may contribute to what Habermas calls the "legitimation crisis" by expanding awareness of the system's failings.[106] Television is caught in the contradictions of American capitalism and reproduces these in its programming.[107] There is no one monolithic ideology or ideological strategy discernable today, and television reflects and reinforces this ideological confusion. Although American television is saturated with values and ideology, they often contradict each other, and sometimes undermine more traditional values. Although the immediate effects may promote cynicism and apathy, the cumulative effects may create a reservoir of discontent that could be mobilized in struggles for social transformation. Thus the contradictions between the state, business, and network television may end up creating the space for social change that it has so far helped to contain.

The End of Network Hegemony?

The contradiction between a commercial system of broadcasting dominated by three networks and the potential of the emerging new technologies of cable and satellite TV have led many to predict the end of Network hegemony.[108] The expansion of the television channel spectrum and development of alternative television would finally end Network domination of American television, making possible a pluralistic system of diverse broadcasting aimed at a variety of audiences. Cable-satellite TV might break through the limitations of the series form and produce a taste for unique and diverse programming. Home video-recorders, video-discs, and television games would give viewers more control over their television environment. Network television would thus become only one supplier among many, competing with hundreds of other television producers and distributers, including local groups producing their own videotapes for public access. This vision of video pluralism is promising, but there remains the danger that Network will continue to control the vast majority of programming, to capture and control the new technology, or to impose its system on competitors.[109] Nonetheless, there is exciting potential in the new broadcast technology that might decisively undermine Network's domination of the American broadcast system and cause some important changes in American television and society.

For example, two-way interactive cable systems make it possible to envisage "television democracy" as a real possibility.[110] Local, state, and national issues could be debated on network, public, and local cable TV, viewers could have the opportunity to respond immediately; representative views could be expressed, and after sufficient discussion and debate, the electorate could vote on the issue, using buttons on the television apparatus which would feed the information through the cable system to a central computer.[111] Such systems are already in operation,[112] and their widespread introduction could make possible a new sort of democratic participation. Thus, although so far television has usurped some of the functions of representative democracy and has increased spectator politics, it is possible that the technology of the emerging communications systems might make possible a resurgence of democracy. Public access television also makes it possible for various groups and individuals to communicate their ideas and images to the vast TV audience. The current situation is, however, precarious. FCC rules mandating that every cable system with more than 3,500 subscribers must provide a public access channel were struck down in the Supreme Court in 1979, ruling that the FCC exceeded its authority.[113] The decision did, however, leave open the right for communities who franchise cable system to demand public access, or for Congress to pass laws requiring cable systems to provide public access channels and facilities. This uncertain situation means that some of the crucial political debates and struggles of the coming years will revolve around communications policies. Public access television holds the promise of a more democratic television system and its suppression or elimination could prevent a more progressive type of television and public communication from developing.[114]

There are also contradictions and tensions within the network broadcasting system itself which provide the space for a different kind of television. If Public Television produced more appealing, popular television, attracting large audiences, it might pressure the network system to improve their programs. Although Public Television has so far had negligible effects on network programming or practice, it nonetheless contains the promise of a different television system. Its lack of commercials serves as a reminder that American television is one of the few systems in the world not funded by the government, that is generally unresponsive to a wide variety of groups and interests, and that is not free from commercial interruption. An audience that spent a large amount of viewing time watching television devoid of commercial interruption might well come to find commercial television intolerable. Although up until the present, Public Television has prevailed as "high brow" entertainment and has not produced programs with large ratings, it remains a specter haunting the irrationality and crass commercialism of the network system. There are also internal conflicts within the network system between network producers, their affiliates, and independent television stations. Although so far the relationship between the centralized network corporations in New York and their affiliates throughout the country has been cozy, with the affiliates a grateful part of the network system, there is increasing disagreement here as profits multiply and the networks and affiliates compete for the surplus. For example, there is a contradiction between nation ally originated programs and local tastes and values. Affiliates have refused to carry certain programs, thus sealing their doom in the ratings race; they are increasingly contesting network programming and operations, leading the networks to tell the affiliates not "to bite the hand that feeds you."[115] Realizing the importance of local autonomy, the FCC ruled that local affiliates be granted an extra half-hour of prime time to develop local programming. Although the profit-driven and unimaginative local affiliates for the most part merely replayed stale network reruns or syndicated game shows, the FCC move indicated that there is a real distinction between national networks and local affiliates by calling for independent affiliate production.[116]

Because independent stations play reruns of network programs and old movies, there has been little tension here, but increased independent production bypassing Network mediation could result in some changes in television programming and practice. Production and distribution of *Mary Hartman, Mary Hartman* and other Normal Lear productions not developed by Network, and productions of mini-series and television movies especially for independents and maverick affiliates show possible ways to circumvent network hegemony and to offer competition to Network domination of programming.[117] Such possibilities are enhanced by new cable-satellite television technology, and the growing popularity of cable and pay TV. Home Box Office, for example, is offering recent movies, uncut and uncensored, over cable systems and by satellite from New York to millions to homes. There are also syndicated religious programs and a Christian Broadcasting Network, as well as sports events, special programming and pornography — all of which show possibilities of breaking network hegemony. "Affiliate Power" and autonomy, the increase of independent, non-affiliated stations, and cable-satellite TV may, however, be a mixed blessing. Local affiliates seem to be both more conservative and more profit-hungry than even the networks.[118] Cable television might become saturated with Hollywood ideological-extravaganzas, pornography, old-time religion, sports or mind-numbing rock music. But on the other hand, the development of cable and non-network television might make possible the opening of new channels of communication and produce a more democratic, diverse, and pluralistic broadcast system.

As more and more people purchase television games, home video recorders, prerecorded video cassettes and discs, and subscribe to cable systems offering a wealth of programming, Network television faces a loss of audience and profit if it does not broadcast programs offering more exciting, interesting, varied, and novel entertainment. The drive for profits and ratings would then lead television to ease censorship and to offer programs which are not simply reproductions of capitalist ideology and conventional formulas, thus diminishing television's function as an instrument of social control. New technology alone, of course, will not break Network domination of American television, or produce better television, hence the need for a media politics to try to bring about more diverse, pluralistic programming, public access to the media, and an end to censorship, by government or business, of controversial programming.

It is impossible to offer a clear prognosis for American television, partly because a shroud of secrecy covers the operations of Network, and partly because of uncertainty surrounding legislation for a new Federal Communications Act which might crucially influence the development of American broadcasting.[119] All the drafts of the new communications bill so far proposed contain provisions that would eliminate the "public interest" proviso and such stepping stones to media access as the "fairness doctrine" and public access cable channels. Since the proposed bills contain no guarantee of public access, a new communications act might lead to increased monopolization of the broadcast media. A communications act, however, aiding the expansion of cable and satellite television and guaranteeing public access might open up new channels of communication and make possible a new plurality of media voices, offering diverse channels of communication to video producers and political activists, as well as alternative views and visions for television consumers. Both public interest groups and broadcast industry people have opposed various aspects of the proposed communications bills. There will be years of intense debate and struggles which will probably lead to many tradeoffs and compromises. Up until now, Network has completely dominated American television. Although there are many contradictions and internal and external conflicts in the system, Network has been able to manage them. It is by no means inevitable, however, that it will continue to do so in the future; possibly, new broadcast technologies, public access struggles, and other social, political, or cultural changes may end total network domination of the broadcast system. The current contests over access, and the public debates over the proposed communications acts, will thus probably play a crucial role in the future of American broadcasting. The stakes are enormous. Whereas continued domination of the broadcast media by the networks could contribute to a withering away of democracy and increased powerlessness, a greatly democratized and expanded broadcast system, allowing significant segments of society, groups, and individuals access to broadcasting, could provide political enlightenment and participation in political debate and public affairs. Consequently, struggles over communications policy and practice could structure the political agenda for the rest of the century and determine whether monopoly capitalism or democracy will be the dominant force in American life. As Alvin Gouldner puts it:

> It is through the mass media and through them alone that there is today any possibility at all of a truly mass public enlightenment that might go beyond what universities may elicit, i.e., beyond small elites and educated elitism. It is through the media that the system may be made to "dance to its own melody," or to expose itself. From *l'affaire Dreyfus* to the Watergate scandal, the powerful role of the media in monitoring the management of public affairs has been notable, even if sporadic. For those who can see, it is profoundly at variance with any simple-minded stereotype of media simply as an agency reproducing the existent system of domination. The path from critical theory to the long march through the institutions must go over the bridge of the mass media, and undertake the struggle for and critique of these media for what they are: a complex system of property interests, technologies, professionalizing skills, strivings for domination and for autonomy, all swarming with the most profound inner contradictions.[120]

NOTES

1. On the history of broadcasting, see the books by Gleason L. Archer, *Big Business and Radio* (New York, 1939; reprinted by Arno Press, 1972) and *History of Radio to 1926* (New York, 1938; reprinted by Arno Press, 1972); Frank C. Waldrop and Joseph Borkin, *Television: A Struggle for Power* (New York, 1938; reprinted by Arno Press, 1972); Erik Barnouw, *A History of Broadcasting in the United States*, 3 vols. (Oxford University Press, 1966–1970) and the one volume condensation which focuses on television, *Tube of Plenty* (Oxford, 1977); and Christopher Sterling and John Kitross, *Stay Tuned* (Wadsworth, 1978).
2. Barnouw, *A Tower in Babel* (Oxford University Press, 1968), 20, 29, 42, 72–3, 88–9, and 161.
3. *Ibid.*, 34ff, and Barnouw, *The Golden Web* (Oxford University Press, 1968), 133ff.
4. Stuart Ewen, in *Captains of Consciousness* (McGraw-Hill, 1976), writes of the

origins of consumerism and indicates how consumerism failed to penetrate American life and culture during the 1930s because of the Depression and then World War II. Consequently, during the postwar period, when television was first introduced on a grand scale, consumer society became a primary reality.

5. Barnouw, *Tube of Plenty*, 112, 213, and 366. On the anti-communist film genre, see Russell E. Shain, "Hollywood's Cold War," *Journal of Popular Film* (Fall 1974) and on television and the Cold War, see J. Fred MacDonald, "The Cold War as Entertainment in 'Fifties Television," *Journal of Popular Film and Television* (1978).

6. See Herbert Schiller, *Mass Communications and American Empire* (Beacon Press, 1971) and *Communication and Cultural Domination* (IASP, 1976). See also Jeremy Turnstall, *The Media are American* (Columbia University Press, 1977); *Communication and Class Struggle, Vol. 1, Capitalism, Imperialism,* ed. Armand Mattelart and Seth Siegelaub (International General, 1979); and Armand Mattelart, *Multinationals and Systems of Communication* (Humanities Press, 1979).

7. See Waldrop and Borkin, and Carl Dreher, *Sarnoff: An American Success* (Quadrangle/New York Times Press, 1977).

8. Waldrop and Borkin. 9. *Ibid.*

10. *Ibid.* On "facsimile," see John V. L. Hogan, "Facsimile and its Future Uses," in *The Annals of the American Academy of Political and Social Sciences* (January 1941).

11. See Barnouw, *The Golden Web* and *Tube of Plenty.*

12. In 1941, the FCC forced RCA to sell one of its two networks in order to break its overwhelming dominance of American broadcasting; thus, in 1943 RCA sold its "blue" network, which became ABC. See Barnouw, *The Golden Web,* 168ff.

13. On Federal Regulatory agencies and capitalism, see Grant McConnell, *Private Power and American Democracy* (Knopf, 1966); Theodore J. Lowi, *The End of Liberalism* (Norton, 1964). On the Federal Communications Commission, see the studies by Erwin G. Krasnow and Lawrence D. Longley, *The Politics of Broadcast Regulation* (St. Martin, 1973); Richard Bunce, *Television in the Corporate Interest* (Praeger Publishers, 1976); Barry Cole and Mal Oettinger, *Reluctant Regulators* (Addison-Wesley, 1978); Vincent Mosco, *Broadcasting in the United States* (Ablex, 1979); and the inside criticism of the FCC by former commissioner Nicholas Johnson, *How to Talk Back to Your Television* (Little, Brown and Company, 1970).

14. Ewen. For a penetrating early study of how advertising shaped television, see Lawrence Laurent, "Commercial Television: What Are Its Educational Possibilities and Limits?," in *Television's Impact on American Culture,* ed. William Y. Elliot (Michigan State University Press, 1956), 125–174.

15. On the distinction between force and consent as modes of social control, see Antonio Gramsci, *Prison Notebooks* (International Publishers, 1971) and Douglas Kellner, "Ideology, Marxism, and Advanced Capitalism," *Socialist Review* (Nov.– Dec. 1978). For a study of the use of the mass media to induce consent to advanced capitalism, see Paul F. Lazarsfeld and Robert K. Merton, "Mass Communication, Popular Taste, and Organized Social Action," in *Mass Communications,* ed. Wilbur Schramm (University of Illinois Press, 1960), 492ff.

16. For recent figures on television profits, see *Broadcasting,* July 30, 1979, 28ff. and December 3, 1979, 63ff.

17. On network ownership, conglomerates, and interlocking directorates, see the Network Project, *Directory of the Networks,* Notebook Number Two (February 1973) and *Control of Information,* Notebook Number Three (March 1973); James Monaco, "Who Owns the Media?," in *Media Culture* (Delta, 1978), 286; and *Who Owns the Media?,* ed. Benjamin M. Compaine (Harmony Books, 1979).

18. The concept of "Network" developed here is indebted to discussions with Bill Gibson and to his unpublished paper on the history of network broadcasting.

19. On the business of television, see Les Brown, *Television: The Business Behind the Box* (Harcourt Brace Jovanovich, 1971); *Inside the TV Business,* coordinated by Sonny Fox and edited by Steve Morganstern (Sterling Publishing Company, 1979); and A. Frank Reel, *The Networks: How They Stole the Show* (Scribner's, 1980).

20. Gaye Tuchman, "Introduction," *The TV Establishment* (Prentice-Hall, 1974), 7.

21. Anthony Smith writes: "America finds itself in a different position from all other societies where the institutional machinery of the mass media has been the direct product of social decision-making. Even in societies with a very highly developed preoccupation with media freedom (e.g., Sweden) it has been unquestionably assumed that governments are responsible for guaranteeing an institutional structure though not the informational content. Only in the United States has structure as well as content been left to a combination of free market forces working within

a loose system of spectrum regulation. The literature which television developed in its greatest decade of expansion treated the institutions as somehow inexorable; at most they could be subjected to further regulatory procedures, never to fundamental and fresh political choice." " 'Just a Pleasant Way to Spend an Evening' – The Softening Embrace of American Television," *Daedalus* (Winter 1978), 197. There are no adequate comparative studies of international television. On this topic, see Wilson P. Dizard, *Television: A World View* (Syracuse University Press, 1966); Walter Emergy, *National and International Systems of Broadcasting* (Michigan State University Press, 1969); and Timothy Green, *The Universal Eye* (Stein and Day, 1972).

22. See Sidney Head, *Broadcasting in America* (Houghton Mifflin, 1972): "American broadcasting developed relatively unhampered within the permissive framework of the competitive free-enterprise system. The style of American broadcasting has been characterized by all the pragmatism, aggressiveness, materialism improvisation, expansionism, and free-swinging competitiveness of American marketing" (11). It is, however, an ideological distortion to conceptualize network television in terms of a competitive "free enterprise" system, for, up to the present, Network has been an oligopoly run by three major networks – ABC, CBS, and NBC – who dominate television production and distribution.

23. T. W. Adorno and Max Horkheimer, "The Culture Industry," in *Dialectic of Enlightenment* (Seabury Press, 1972). In a forthcoming paper, I shall trace out the impact of the Adorno-Horkheimer theory on concepts of popular culture and the mass media held by Dwight Macdonald, Herbert Marcuse, George Gerbner, Herbert Schiller, and Gaye Tuchman.

24. *Ibid.* 25. *Ibid.*, 141. 26. *Ibid.*, 123. 27. *Ibid.*, 144. 28. *Ibid.*, 149.

29. Among Gerbner's many articles, see "Television: The New State Religion," *et cetera* (June 1977) and George Gerbner and Larry Gross, "Living with Television: The Violence Profile," *Journal of Communications* (Spring 1976), 177, Tuchman, "Introduction," 5; and Louis Althusser, "Ideology and Ideological State Apparatuses," in *Lenin and Philosophy* (Monthly Review Press, 1971). A similar model is in Herbert Schiller's influential book *The Mind Managers* (Beacon Press, 1974).

30. See the Network Project *Notebooks* 1–10 (New York: 1972–5) and the transcripts of their radio broadcasts collected in *Performance* (July–August 1972).

31. *Ibid.* For criticisms of the Network Project on these points, see Kellner, "TV, Ideology, and Emancipatory Popular Culture," *Socialist Review* (May–June 1979).

32. For a similar view of American society and network television as systems beset with contradictions, see Alvin W. Gouldner, *The Dialectic of Ideology and Technology* (Seabury Press, 1976). By "contradictions" I mean oppositions between structures, institutions, social functions, and goals that produce tensions and conflicts which provide the potential for change and development. I am not using contradictions in the strict marxian sense of irreconcilable opposites which do not allow of any possible reconciliation without structural transformation. Indeed, American broadcasting has proven itself capable of containing its contradictions within an ever more powerful and profitable broadcast system. The contradictions are there, however, and manifest themselves daily in a manifold of tensions and conflicts, internally and externally. Thus the contradictions of network television discussed in the following pages may well be containable within the present network system and system of American capitalism, but they may also help produce changes in the broadcast system and in turn promote social change. These contradictions are therefore important for they provide the space for cultural political intervention in the media. Moreover, they contain the possibilities for a different system of broadcasting; on this topic see the last section of this paper. For an illuminating discussion of the concept of contradiction, see Alvin W. Gouldner, *The Two Marxisms* (Seabury Press, 1980), especially 12 and 168.

33. See the sources cited in notes 1 and 13.

34. See Barnouw, *Golden Web*, 18 and Mitchell Charney, *News by Radio* (Macmillan, 1948). Pressure from newspaper publishers in 1933 led the radio networks to disband their newly founded news organizations and to set up a Press-Radio Bureau which would supply broadcasters with news from AP, UP, and INS news services. No item would exceed 30 seconds and the bulletins would only provide material for two five minute news broadcasts a day. Rising interest in the events in Europe led the networks to break this agreement in the 1930s.

35. Barnouw, *Golden Web*, 24.

36. Barnouw, and Mosco. 37. *Ibid.* 38. *Ibid.*

39. Barnouw, *Golden Web*, 221–2.

40. The heroes of Barnouw's epic history of American Broadcasting are FCC Com-

missioners such as Fly, Durr, and Minow who stood up to the network titans and seriously tried to regulate broadcasting in the public interest, attacking monopoly, banal programming, and overly restrictive network control of the communications spectrum. These Commissioners were frequently targets of vicious attacks by Congress, whose members were dependent on Network for political advertising and publicity; consequently, on the whole Congress has a woefully pathetic record in communications legislation. For an interesting discussion of these issues by Fly, Durr, and others, see *Broadcasting and Government Regulation in a Free Society* (Center for the Study of Democratic Institutions, 1959).

41. See Barnouw, *Golden Web* and the studies of the FCC cited in note 20.
42. Barnouw, *The Sponsor* (Oxford University Press, 1978).
43. *Ibid.*
44. For the text of Minow's speech, see Newton Minow, *Equal Time* (Atheneum, 1964).
45. The Network Project, *The Fourth Network* (1972) and Brown, 314ff.
46. William Paley, cited in David Halberstram, *The Powers That Be,* 734.
47. The text of the Communications Act of 1934 is in *Documents of American Broadcasting,* ed. Frank J. Kahn (Appleton-Century-Crofts, 1968); see, especially, sections 307a and d, 315, and 322.
48. Herbert Hoover, cited in *Broadcasting and Government Regulation,* 10.
49. *Ibid.*
50. The Federal Communications Commission, *Public Service Responsibility of Broadcasting Licensees,* March 7, 1946. Text in *Documents of American Broadcasting,* 125ff.
51. For discussions of these issues, see Jerome A. Barron, *Freedom of the Press for Whom?* (Indiana University Press, 1973) and Fred Friendly, *The Good Guys, The Bad Guys and the First Amendment* (Vintage, 1977).
52. These contradictions provide the space for media politics and the legal ground for public access struggles which will be discussed in the concluding section. See also my article, "TV, Ideology, and Emancipatory Popular Culture."
53. This discussion is indebted to conversations with Jack Schierenbeck. On the dual tradition of capitalism and democracy, see Alan Wolfe, *The Limits of Legitimacy* (Free Press, 1977). On conflicts between democracy, FCC policy, and commercial broadcasting, see Bunce and Mosco.
54. See Robert Cirino, *Don't Blame the People* (Random House, 1971); *Power to Persuade* (Bantam, 1974); and *We're Being More Than Entertained* (Lighthouse Press, 1977).
55. Paul Klein, "Feedback 5: Entertainment," *Performance* (July–August 1972).
56. For example, former CBS President Robert Wood tried to present TV as a "democratic" art by claiming, "I think that probably one of the most democratic institutions in this country is the television industry, because, unlike candidates, who run every two years or four years or six years, our candidates . . . that is, our programs, are being voted upon 365 days and nights, every single year." Cited in *Prime Time TV: The Decision Makers,* broadcast by ABC, Monday, September 2, 1974; network transcript, II–10. Fred Silverman likes to describe TV as a "populist art"; see, for example, "The Crapshoot for Half a Billion," *Life Magazine,* Sept. 10, 1971, 58.
57. Jacques Ellul, *Propaganda* (Vintage Books, 1973).
58. Developing this line of argument, Dallas Smythe, in "Communications: The Blindspot of Western Marxism," *Canadian Journal of Political and Social Theory* (1977), describes the labor activity engaged in while watching television. He argues that the mass media produce the audience as a commodity by attracting viewers to television programs and then managing consumer demand and engaging in "ideological teaching". (Smythe directs his criticism at Baran and Sweezy's *Monopoly Capital* which he believes fails to adequately conceptualize the role of advertising and the media within captialist societies. He is also polemicizing against Enzensberger and others who claim that "the mind industry is monstrous and difficult to understand because it does not, strictly speaking, produce anything." Cited in Smythe, "Critique of *The Consciousness Industry,*" *Journal of Communications* (1977), 199. Smythe argues that the "mind industry" produces "the audience as commodity" as it manages consumer demand and produces social consent to capitalism through advertising and ideology. Smythe claims to fill a blindspot in marxist theory concerning advertising and the communications media. His article sparked a lively debate. See Graham Murdock, "Blindspots about Western Marxism: A Reply to Dallas Smythe," *Candian Journal of Political and Social Theory* (1978); a rejoinder by Smythe in the same issue; and Bill Livant, "The Audience Commodity," *Ibid.* (Winter 1979). My discussion in the following

pages suggests "blindspots" in Smythe's theory: failure to see the contradictions in network television.) Smythe feels that by at once mobilizing people to attend to advertising and ideological messages, while keeping them separate in their homes, television serves both commercial and social control functions. Thus, for Smythe, the broadcast media produce "audiences with predictable specifications who will pay attention in predictable numbers and at particular times to particular means of communication" (4). News and entertainment attracts the audience and advertisements produce demands which are "satisfied by purchases of consumer goods" (3).

59. John Brenkman, "Mass Media: From Collective Experience to the Culture of Privatization," *Social Text* (Winter 1979).

60. See Jürgen Habermas, *Strukturwandel der Offentlichkeit* (Luchterhand, 1962) and "The Public Sphere," *New German Critique* (Fall 1974).

61. On the nature and function of "leisure" under capitalism, see Smythe, and T. W. Adorno, "Freizeit," in *Stichworte* (Suhrkamp, 1970).

62. See Smythe, and Barnouw, *Tube of Plenty*, 468–70. This is the position taken by Adorno, Gerbner, The Network Project, Tuchman, and many others.

63. There is a parallel here to the contradictions which James O'Conner finds in the capitalist state between its accumulation and legitimation functions; see *The Fiscal Crisis of the State* (St. Martin Press, 1973). Both Network and the state are concerned with accumulating wealth (i.e., capital), with aiding in the total accumulation of social wealth, and with legitimating the system as a whole, although, of course, in different ways. In both institutions, these functions often are in conflict with each other and attest to contradictions at the center of contemporary capitalist societies.

64. On the contradictions between the "cultural apparatus" (a term introduced by by C. Wright Mills) and the "consciousness industry" (Hans Magnus Enzensberger), see Gouldner, *The Dialectic of Ideology*.

65. For a vivid sense of Network censorship and repression of dissidents see the writing on television and discussion of his experiences as a scriptwriter by Harlan Ellison, *The Glass Teat* (Pyramid Books, 1975). Censorship is also discussed by television writers in "View From the Typewriter," *TV Guide*, Aug. 3, 1974, 2–8; in the 1977 PBS Documentary, "You Should See What You're Missing"; and in David Rintel's testimony before the Senate Subcommittee on Constitutional Rights, Febr. 8, 1972. The liberal views of many television cultural workers are documented in Stein.

66. Kellner, "TV."

67. *Ibid.*

68. See Edward Jay Epstein, *News From Nowhere* (Vintage, 1974); The Glasgow University Media Group, *Bad News* (Routledge and Kegan Paul, 1976); Peter Dahlgren, *Network TV News and the Corporate State* (Ph. D. Dissertation: The City University of New York, 1977); Gaye Tuchman, *Making News* (Free Press, 1978); Herbert Gans, *Deciding What's News* (Pantheon, 1979); and Todd Gitlin, *The Whole World is Watching: Mass Media in the Making and the Unmaking of the New Left* (University of California Press, 1980).

69. Fred Friendly, *Due to Circumstances Beyond Our Control* (Random House, 1967); Alexander Kendrick, *Prime Time* (Avon, 1969); and Daniel Schorr, *Clearing the Air* (Houghton Mifflin, 1977).

70. Todd Gitlin, "News as Ideology and Contested Area," *Socialist Review* (Nov.– Dec. 1979), 27ff.

71. See *Broadcasting*, Aug. 14, 1978, 38, for a discussion of Network's record $1.4 billion profits in 1977, and its increased power over advertisers, who are competing more fiercely than ever for network airtime, which is usually sold out before the season begins.

72. For valuable information on television and politics, see the series *Survey of Broadcast Journalism*, ed. Marvin Barrett (Grosset & Dunlap).

73. See *Window Dressing on the Set: Women and Minorities in Television*, A Report of the United States Commission on Civil Rights, August 1977. On images of women in the mass media, see the articles in *Hearth and Home*, ed. Gaye Tuchman, Arlene Kaplan Daniels, and James Bennet (Oxford University Press, 1978) and on images of blacks, see Norman L. Friedman, "Responses of Blacks and Other Minorities to Television Shows of the 1970's About Their Groups," *Journal of Popular Film and Television* (1978).

74. Gitlin.

75. On the concept of non-synchronicity, see Ernst Bloch, "Nonsynchronism and Dialectics," *New German Critique* (Spring 1977).

76. On the concept of "mid-cult" and the allegedly homogenizing effects of popu-

lar culture, see Dwight Macdonald, *Against the American Grain* (Vintage, 1962); see also Daniel J. Boorstin, *The Americans. The Democratic Experience* (Vintage, 1974), 390, and Paul Hirsh, "The Role of Television and Popular Culture in Contemporary Society," in *Television: The Critical View,* ed. Horace Newcomb (Oxford University Press, 1979).

77. Daniel Bell, *The Cultural Contradictions of Capitalism* (Basic Books, 1976).
78. Daniel Patrick Moynihan, *Coping: On the Practice of Government* (Vintage Books, 1973), 315.
79. Bell; Samuel Huntington, "The Democratic Distemper," in *The Crisis of Democracy,* ed. Michael Crozier, Samuel Huntington, and Joji Watanuki (New York University Press, 1975); for several years, Edith Efron, Patrick Buchanon, Kevin Phillips, and others argued in the *TV Guide* "Newswatch" column that TV was subversive of traditional values and was affected by a "liberal bias". See the Efron article cited below for an extreme example.
80. Kevin Phillips, *Mediacracy* (Doubleday, 1975). For insights into the thrust of the neoconservative critique of television, I am indebted to Stuart Hersh.
81. Edith Efron, "New Lineup of Charges Against Media," *TV Guide,* Oct. 8, 1977, A–5–6.
82. *Ibid.,* A–6.
83. Ben Stein, *The View from Sunset Boulevard* (Basic Books, 1979).
84. For discussion of the Nixon Administration attack on the news media, see *Survey of Broadcast Journalism, 1969– 70.* Ben Stein is the son of Nixon's director of communications Herbert Stein and has himself worked in the Nixon Administration.
85. See Gerbner and Gross, "Living with Television," and Bradley S. Greenberg and Thomas F. Gordon, "Social Class and Racial Differences in Children's Perception of Violence," in *Television and Social Behavior,* Vol. V (National Institute of Mental Health, 1972).
86. Hans Magnus Enzensberger, "Television and the Politics of Liberation," in Douglas Davis and Allison Simmons, *The New Television: A Public/Private Art* (MIT Press, 1977), 249.
87. Enzensberger, 250.
88. FCC Commissioners James Fly and Clifford Durr often tried to regulate broadcasting in the public interest in the 1930s and the 1940s, and in the 1960s Newton Minow and Nicholas Johnson tried to reform broadcasting from within the FCC regulatory structure.
89. Claus Mueller, *The Politics of Communication* (Oxford University Press, 1973), and Louis Althusser, "Ideology and Ideological State Apparatuses." Althusser describes the ideological apparatus in advanced capitalism as a "state ideological apparatus," assuming that the state controls the means of ideological production. Nicos Poulantzas takes a similar position on the state and media in a discussion with Ralph Miliband, republished in *Ideology in Social Science* (Vintage Books, 1973).
90. A similar error is found in the many studies that perceive television as a powerful instrument of the state, and especially the President. See, for example, Bernard Rubin, *Political Television* (Wadsworth Publishing Company, 1967) and Newton N. Minow, John Bartlow Martin, and Lee M. Mitchell, *Presidential Television* (Basic Books, 1973).
91. John Stockwell has told me that fear of exposure after Watergate revelations has frightened CIA officials and helped make it possible for him to write his book exposing CIA operations in Angola without fear of violent reprisals (discussions in Austin, Texas in October 1978; broadcast on "Alternative Views News Magazine," November 14, 1978). See Stockwell's book, *In Search of Enemies* (Norton, 1978).
92. My discussion of network coverage of Vietnam is indebted to conversations with Bill Gibson and to his Ph.D. dissertation, *Vietnam, Network News, and the Ruptures of the Sixties.*
93. Gitlin, "Sixteen Notes on Television and the Movement," in George White and Charles Newgram, *Literature and Revolution* (Holt, Rinehart and Winston, 1972).
94. *Ibid.*
95. See *Broadcasting,* Aug. 14, 1978, 38ff.
96. See the discussions in *Media and Business,* ed. Howard Simons and Joseph A. Califano, Jr. (Random House, 1979) and the sources cited in Gitlin, "News as Ideology and Contested Area," 54, n. 57.
97. Simons and Califano, xii–iii.
98. *Ibid.* Mobil's attack on CBS News' presentation of their profit increases was

published, among other places, in *Broadcasting*, Nov. 12, 1979, 76–7; earlier, Mobil published an attack on ABC's "20/20" for their coverage of the issue of gas deregulation in *The Wall Street Journal*, Thursday, Aug. 31, 1978, 7. Mobil, Kaiser, and other major corporations have been irritated that the networks refuse to sell them time for "public service" advertising (i.e., corporate propaganda) and have thus been placing ads in print attacking network coverage of various issues and presenting their point of view: see *Broadcasting*, June 25, 1979, 72. If the networks sold time to the corporations to promote their positions, public interest groups could demand time to rebut the corporations under the Fairness Doctrine, and the networks fear "clutter" of airtime with political messages. On the desirability of pressuring the networks to present "public service" spot advertising, see Phil Jacklin, "Access to the Attention System," *Access*, May 17, 1976, 9–10.

99. Simons and Califano, xiii.
100. A. Kent MacDougall, *Los Angeles Times*, February 3, 1980.
101. MacDougall, *Los Angeles Times*, February 5, 1980.
102. Jack Schierenbeck, in an unpublished study of television and capitalism, has been arguing this position in discussions with the Austin Television Group.
103. Editors, *Business Week*, October, 1974.
104. See Crozier, et al., *The Crisis of Democracy*.
105. See the sources cited in note 68.
106. Jürgen Habermas, *Legitimation Crisis* (Beacon Press, 1975). It has been argued that the very existence of television serves as an effective instrument of social control, and that its fragmentation of ideology is functional in keeping diverse groups of individuals passively captured in their homes, partaking of artificial, vicarious experience which keeps them from actively participating in the social world. See Jerry Mander, *Four Arguments for the Elimination of Television* (William Morrow, 1978).
107. Kellner, "TV."
108. See Richard Reeves, "The Dangers of Television in the Silverman Era," *Esquire*, April 25, 1978, 56, and "Television Enters the 80's," *Media Digest* (Winter 1980), 1.
109. This is the conclusion of the Network Project in their extremely pessimistic studies of cable and satellite TV. See their *Notebooks*, No. 1, 5, 7, and 8. The Network Project analysis sees only new vehicles for capitalist hegemony and manipulation in the emerging technology. As early as 1974 they wrote a premature obituary on any emancipatory possibilities in cable TV (*Notebook 8*); dismissed public access in 1975 (*Notebook 11*) and made "the case against satellites" (*Notebook 1*) without any consideration of possible beneficial developments, such as the possibility of breaking network hegemony and opening new channels of communication. They failed to take account of the struggles for public access and drew their pessimistic conclusions on cable television mainly from a short-term investigation of New York City Cable TV. A careful study is needed of the emerging new technologies and legal and social struggles for their use and development.
110. On interactive cable, see the articles in *Journal of Communications* (Spring 1978), 142ff.
111. This possibility was anticipated by Robert Paul Wolff, *In Defense of Anarchism* (Harper and Row, 1968).
112. See the articles on the "QUBE" system in Columbus, Ohio, by James Monaco, *American Film*, May 1977 and November 1978, and David Lachenbruch, *TV Guide*, Dec. 24, 1977.
113. See *Broadcasting*, April 9, 1979, 59–60 and Joshua N. Koenig, "Access in Jeopardy," *NFLCP Newsletter*, (April–May 1978) and "Court Strikes Down FCC Access Rules," *Community Television Review* (Spring 1979).
114. See Kellner, "TV."
115. On conflicts between network corporations in New York and their affiliates, see Steve Knoll, "Showdown at Clearance Gap," *TV Guide*, April 10, 1976, and "Affiliate Power," April 17, 1976. When Bob Wood resigned as President from CBS, he cited pressures from restive and demanding affiliates as one of his chief headaches and reasons for resigning. See Les Brown, "CBS President Ducks Pressure," *New York Times News Service*, 1976.
116. Brown, *Television*, 351ff. On the abortive "family hour," see Geoffrey Cowan, *See No Evil* (Simon and Schuster, 1979).
117. See Jon Carroll, "What Hath Mary Hartman Wrought? TV Syndicators Threaten Networks," *Village Voice*, March 22, 1976 and Bill Davidson, "Signs of Rebellion," *TV Guide*, May 20, 1978.
118. Affiliates often refuse to play controversial network programming and have rarely produced innovative, quality programming. See Brown.

119. On debates over the proposed communications acts, *Broadcasting* and *Access*
      provided the best coverage from June 1978 until the present. The issue was
      barely even mentioned on network television.
120. Gouldner, *Dialectic of Ideology*, 160.

Acknowledgments

This study has evolved out of work with a group in Austin, Texas which has
been meeting regularly for over five years studying and discussing American
television, as well as producing a one-hour weekly news magazine for cable
television. I am indebted to members of this group for comments and criticisms on earlier drafts of this study: Bill Gibson, John Gibson, Jim Greene,
Stuart Hersh, Frank Morrow, Harry O'Hara, and Jack Schierenbeck. Helpful
comments and criticisms were also offered by, among others, Joe Heuman,
Alvin Gouldner, C. A. Kellner, and Joel Rogers.

PART IV

LEISURE AND MEDIA USE:
TIME AND MONEY

How and why people use media, and what media they use, is certainly a central focus in media studies. The five articles in this section are linked in that they approach these questions macroscopically: People, or aggregates, are not so much viewed as using media per se, but as locating patterns of use within their lives.

For several of the authors in this section, formulating answers to these questions requires coming to grips with the definition of leisure; the approaches are varied, but the authors turn their attention to the resources people have available to frame those portions of their lives over which they are customarily assumed to exercise control. These resources are time and money. They are scarce, and for individuals, their employment represents a zero-sum game; that which is allocated to some use is not available for another.

Moreover, the use of time and money for cultural and leisure pursuits implies the availability of choices in use. Choices of two types are foremost: Will resources be devoted to use of media or to something else, and if the choice is for use of media, what sort of media will be chosen?

Approaching these questions illuminates several things. Such research may be clearly administrative, as one seeks to understand how leisure choices are made so as to prepare a strategy for capturing a market or audience. It also may be critical, as one attempts to understand how meaning is made from choices and uses, and how such meanings are constrained by the structures that made the cultural materials available; or they may cross such lines and consider both. We are fortunate in this section to have examples of each of these approaches.

This article notes that understanding culture, leisure, and time use is dependent upon the ways available for its measurement. Richard Peterson reviews data indexing these and calls for more and better statistics organized within a comprehensive framework. Peterson is professor of sociology at Vanderbilt University; work on this article was begun when he was visiting research specialist at the National Endowment for the Arts in Washington, D.C., 1979-1980.

24

MEASURING CULTURE, LEISURE, AND TIME USE

Richard A. Peterson

Richard A. Peterson is a professor of sociology at Vanderbilt University. An industrial sociologist by training with a Ph.D. from the University of Illinois, much of his research since leaving the University of Wisconsin for Vanderbilt has been on the structure of the commercial music industry and related aspects of the production of culture. He spent 1979–80 as a visiting research specialist with the National Endowment for the Arts in Washington, D.C., where he gave advice on the establishment of a set of statistics and on the conceptualization of indicators of culture. This has led to his current interest in identifying the patterns of cultural choice to be found in contemporary American life-styles.

The perspective for this paper was developed while the author was on research leave from Vanderbilt University as a visiting research specialist with the Research Division of the National Endowment for the Arts in Washington, D.C.

From Richard A. Peterson, "Measuring Culture, Leisure, and Time Use," *The Annals of the American Academy of Political and Social Science* 453 (January 1981), pp. 169-179. Reprinted by permission of the publisher.

A RECENT compendium of measures of culture, leisure, and time use[1] asserts that, unlike many other areas of social concern for which historical data are both well established and quite abundant, indicators of culture, leisure, and time use are relatively new and fairly scarce. To be sure, there is no coherent and widely accepted set of measures, but the reason is not so much a scarcity of information—a wide range of data of varying quality is available. Rather, the prime problem is a lack of agreement on how best to define such key terms as culture, art, leisure, recreation, and free time. Philip Ennis made this point in a 1968 essay devoted to the definition and measurement of leisure. "Of all the great categories of life," he suggested, "leisure is surely one of the most untidy."[2]

A good deal of information has accumulated since he made that observation, and the quality of leisure has become of more widespread concern, but the definition of the field is not conspicuously more tidy than it was in 1968. Necessarily then, any review of recent trends needs to define the field of study.

This chapter begins by reviewing some currently available information, then suggests the elements of a scheme for organizing information on culture, leisure, and time use. Along the way, data that are available, or soon will be, are noted.

FREE TIME

The prime question is how Americans use their free time—the time not devoted to paid work, household and family maintenance, personal care, or sleep.[3] Such time is "free" at least in the sense that it is free of these other obligations. But free time costs something because the time is not spent in gainful employment.[4] At the same time, the ways it is spent may benefit the individual or society.

The average urban adult in 1975 had 38.5 free hours per week. This is a bit more than a half hour more free time available per day than in 1965.[5] An increase in free time was enjoyed by all sex, race, age, occupational, and marital groups, but only persons 18 to 25 showed a marked jump in the amount of leisure time available. Of course, the increase in free time is not always voluntary. In some instances it is due to unemployment or forced retirement. The available data suggest, however, that in the aggregate, the amount of time devoted to work, sleep, and personal care has changed very little, while the time devoted to family care has declined about three quarters of an

1. U.S. Bureau of the Census, *Social Indicators III* [Washington, DC: U.S. Government Printing Office (USGPO), 1980] (hereafter cited as *Social Indicators III*). The state of the art of culture indicators represented in this compendium is taken as the point of departure for the discussion that follows.

2. Philip H. Ennis, "The Definition and Measurement of Leisure," in *Indicators of Social Change*, eds. Eleanor B. Sheldon and Wilbert Moore (New York: Russell Sage Foundation, 1968), p. 525.

3. Free time is sometimes referred to by the more normative term "leisure." *See*, for example, Ennis, p. 528; and Joffre Dumazedier, *Sociology of Leisure* (New York: Elsevier, 1974), pp. 67–91.

4. On this point, *see* Gary S. Becker, "A Theory of the Allocation of Time," *J. Economics*, 75: 493–517 (Sept. 1965); Staffan Linder, *The Harried Leisure Class* (New York: Columbia University Press, 1970); and Barry Gruenberg, "How Free is Free Time?: An Analysis of some Determinants of Leisure Time-Use Patterns" (Ph.D. diss., Ann Arbor: University of Michigan, 1974).

5. *Social Indicators III*, Table 11/13. The most comprehensive analysis of time use patterns is provided by John P. Robinson, *How Americans Use Time: A Social-Psychological Analysis of Everyday Behavior* (New York: Praeger, 1977).

hour per day.[6] This reflects less time devoted to meal preparation and the reduced likelihood of there being dependent children or elderly persons in the home.

In line with having more free time, people reported feeling less rushed in 1976 than in 1965.[7] In another survey, over half of those reporting expressed a great deal of satisfaction with "nonwork activities, hobbies and the like," but there was no patterned change in the level of satisfaction with leisure time activities measured in annual surveys between 1973 and 1978.[8]

Spending free time

Authors differ on how best to classify the various uses of free time, but the following seven categories reflect the way data sets are organized and administrative agency boundaries are drawn. The seven are: passive leisure (such as most television viewing); active recreation (camping, bowling, and the like); amateur art and craft activity (Sunday painting, quilting, or stamp collecting); arts participation (as a consumer of any professional arts activity, such as museum, concert, or play attendance); folk life (any ethnic communal activity); informal social life (parties, conversation, and the like); and organized social participation (volun-

tary civic, fraternal, political, and religious activity).[9]

Little is known about folk life. This is unfortunate because there are research and policy concerns about "Americanization of ethnics," "massification," and "the preservation of cultural diversity" which make it important to chart the vitality or atrophy of folk–culture participation. In practice, however, it has proved difficult, using standard survey techniques, to separate authentic folk activities that are rooted in ongoing, communal groups from the broader range of craft activities or from the family, religious, and local civic activities in which they are often embedded.[10]

TELEVISION VIEWING

Folk life is underrepresented in the available data, but television receives a great deal of coverage. In 1975, passive leisure consumed 19 hours, or 49 percent of all free time per week, of which 15.2 hours, or 40 percent of all free time, was de-

6. Ibid., Tables 11/13, 11/14.

7. Ibid., Table 11/2.

8. Ibid., Table 11/1. This finding, that the levels of stated satisfaction do not correlate with changes in objective conditions, fits the general observation that between 1957 and 1978, roughly the same proportion of persons reported being "very happy" in the face of wide swings in unemployment, inflation, and military turmoil around the world. See on this point, Richard Curtin, "Facing Adversity with a Smile," Public Opinion, 3:17–19 (April 1980).

9. There is nothing final or fixed about these categories. Their sources include: Ennis; Dumazedier, pp. 77–84; Alvin Toffler, "The Art of Measuring the Arts," The Annals of the American Academy of Political and Social Science, 373:145–155 (1967); Jiri Zuzanek, Leisure and Social Change (Waterloo, Canada: University of Waterloo Press, 1967); Jiri Zuzanek, "Evaluation of the Instruments Used in Leisure Studies—Canada 1972, 1975, 1976, and 1978: Suggestions for Further Research" (Report prepared for Statistics Canada, 1979); UNESCO, "Preliminary Study on the Scope and Coverage of a Framework for Cultural Statistics" (Paris: CES/AC.4/8); and Bryan L. Kinsley, "Defining Cultural Activities" (Paper presented at the Second Canadian Congress on Leisure Research, Toronto, Canada, 1978).

10. These observations were sharpened through conversations with Allan Lomax, Bess Lomax Hawes, Eudora H. Moore, and John Schafer; the last three are associated with the National Endowment for the Arts.

voted to television viewing by urban adults. This represents a marked increase in television viewing, because a comparable sample in 1965 devoted 10.4 hours per week, or 30 percent of all free time, to television.[11] This increase averages about 40 minutes more viewing per day. Thus in effect, all of the half-hour gain in leisure noted earlier, and more, was absorbed by additional television viewing, and none was available to go to any of the other six categories of free time use. Seven polls conducted by the Roper Organization between 1964 and 1974 show a comparable rise in the hours of television viewing.[12]

Has the increase continued since 1975? The evidence is mixed. Figures for each season from 1974–75 through 1978–79, provided by the Nielson television program rating service, show that adult viewing time has increased slowly but steadily.[13] In contrast to this, however, figures from the National Opinion Research Center's General Social Survey show that between 1975 and 1978, the number of persons reporting viewing no television and the number reporting one hour of television per day both went up slightly, while the number reporting four or more hours dropped 5.4 percent.[14] The third available data series does not clarify the situation. Polls conducted by the Roper Organization in 1974, 1976, and 1978, show no appreciable change in the hours of reported television viewing.[15] The Institute for Social Research of the University of Michigan is conducting a time–budget survey in 1981–82, so a more comprehensive answer to the questions about the dynamics of television viewing time should become available in the foreseeable future.

If the trends in television viewing in recent years are not clear, the data on satisfaction with the medium are unambiguous. In 1960, 28 percent listed television as the favorite leisure activity. In 1966 and 1974, the level was up to 46 percent—three times higher than the next most favored activity, reading. But by 1977, just 30.7 listed television as the favorite leisure activity.[16] In effect, though people may be viewing television more, they are apparently enjoying it less.

Television has become an important source of news for many people. Between 1959 and 1978, the proportion reporting getting most of their news from television rose from one half to two thirds of all respondents. This finding has been widely remarked by those who lament the atrophy of newspaper reading. It is less often reported that these same data show that the gain for television has been less at the expense of newspapers, which dropped 8 percent, than at the expense of radio, which dropped 14 percent.[17]

Heavy television viewers tend to be nonworking women, blacks, the elderly, the poor, and children. But there is some evidence that the viewing rates of men and teens are approaching these other groups.[18]

11. *Social Indicators III*, Table 11/15.
12. Ibid., Table 11/17.
13. Ibid., Table 11/16.
14. Ibid., Table 11/18.
15. Ibid., Table 11/17.

16. Ibid., Table 11/9.
17. These are Roper polls. *See Social Indicators III*, Table 11/3.
18. Ibid., Table 11/16, supplemented by Michael Hughes and Richard A. Peterson, "Television Watching and Socio-Political Attitudes: An Empirical Study of Sexism, Racism, Conservatism, Alienation, Quality of Life Indicators, and Attitudes about Violence" (Unpublished paper, Nashville, TN:

Incidence and frequency

Television absorbs the greatest amount of free time and has received the greatest amount of research attention. The other sorts of free time use, such as arts participation and active recreation, command so much less time relative to passive leisure, work, and sleep that they are not reliably measured using the time–budget method that asks how every minute of the day is spent.

But other sorts of time measures, appropriate for learning about activities that garner less time, are available. They measure whether (incidence) or how often (frequency) people have spent time engaged in activities of interest during some longer reference period, such as a month or a year. Several tables illustrate the measurement of incidence or frequency, but the information is too fragmentary to warrant comment here.[19]

A good deal of information about the incidence and frequency of a wide range of free time activities will become available in the near future. The National Outdoor Recreation Survey will have been replicated and the results of the 1981–82 Leisure Activity Survey (LAS) conducted for the National Endowment for the Arts by the U.S. Bureau of the Census will be available. The LAS is being administered to a sample of 24,000 respondents. It includes questions asking about the incidence and frequency of many different sorts of arts participation and craft activities. Passive leisure, active recreation, folk life, and social participation variables are also covered, although in less detail.

Results of the LAS will help to clarify the findings of a secondary analysis conducted by DiMaggio, Useem, and Brown of the characteristics of attenders found in 270 studies of museum and performing arts institutions.[20] Their findings suggest that the participants in these cultural activities are disproportionately well educated, well-to-do professionals. They found no evidence that the audience for major high arts events has become any more diverse from 1960 through 1976. Since the studies on which the tables are based vary widely in their quality, it is not possible to draw any firm conclusions at this time.

When the LAS findings are available, however, it will be possible to more reliably characterize the audience for the various art forms and other leisure activities as well. In addition, key questions from the LAS will be repeated on the Institute for Social Research 1981 time–budget survey, so it will be possible to link the incidence and frequency data from the LAS with the duration data in the time–budget survey.

Vanderbilt University, 1080); George Comstock, Steven Chaffee, Nathan Matzman, Maxwell McCombs, and Donald Roberts, *Television and Human Behavior* (New York: Columbia University Press, 1978), pp. 173–310. Comstock et al. is the best available review of research on television and its effects. An excellent recent study which seeks to identify the various patterns of cultural choice in the selection of television viewing is provided by Ronald E. Frank and Marshall G. Greenberg, *The Public's Use of Television* (Beverly Hills, CA: Sage, 1980).

19. *See Social Indicators III*, Tables 11/10 and 11/11. The first reports the incidence of selected outdoor activities, and the second reports the frequency of participation in selected recreational activities during the period of a year.

20. Paul DiMaggio, Michael Useem, and Paula Brown, "Audience Studies of the Performing Arts and Museums: A Critical Review," Research Division Report #9 (Washington, DC: National Endowment for the Arts, 1978).

MEASURES ALTERNATIVE TO TIME

The incidence, frequency, and duration of time spent are not the only possible measures of leisure participation. There are subjective and monetary measures as well.[21] Monetary measures are those which index the money rather than the time spent at leisure. Monetary measures will be discussed after first looking at subjective measures.

Subjective measures

Subjective measures are those that gauge the desire for, preferences among, or satisfaction with leisure activities.[22] Such subjective measures are attractive to policymakers because they point to unmet needs, rather than chronicling past participation or money spent. Whether they ask about the time or money allocations or ask about feeling states, they can be prospective. As such, they are considered helpful in predicting future demand. A major limitation of most subjective measures is that to approve of more leisure and cultural services does not "cost" respondents anything.[23] Subjective measures can therefore be poor predictors of actual behavior. In the words of the old adage, "If wishes were horses, beggars would ride."

The free-floating nature of subjective measures has brought their collection into question,[24] and the few established U.S. government statistical series which now regularly collect subjective measures are under review.[25]

In addition, few subjective measures of leisure have been initiated with an eye to establishing a time series. Rather, they have been generated to fill the immediate policy needs of administrators or the short-term needs of scientific researchers for numerous variables measured at one point rather than time–series measures collected at regular intervals over time. It is not clear that better subjective measures of leisure will become available in the near future.

Monetary measures

There is a large class of measures that uses money as the unit of enumeration. Money, like time, is a scarce resource. Thus the allocation of money to leisure activities can serve as an indicator of changing

21. The distinctions between, and the relative strengths of, time, money, and subjective measures of leisure time consumption are detailed by Richard A. Peterson, "Arts Audience Statistics and Culture Indicators: A Review of Complementary Approaches" (Washington, DC: Research Division, National Endowment for the Arts, July 1980), chs. 4–7 (hereafter cited as "Arts Audience Statistics").

22. Tables dealing with general satisfaction are 11/1 and 11/2, while those dealing with the subjective satisfaction with television are Tables 11/8 and 11/9 Social Indicators III.

23. Peterson, in "Arts Audience Statistics," reviews means of anchoring subjective measures in prior behavior and experience, pp. 7.2–7.8.

24. Comptroller General, Better Guidance and Controls Are Needed to Improve Federal Surveys of Attitudes and Opinions (Washington, DC: General Accounting Office GGD-78-24, 1978); Allen R. Wilcox, "Dissatisfaction with Satisfaction: Subjective Social Indicators and the Quality of Life" (Presentation at the 74th annual American Sociological Association meetings, Boston, 1979); and Donald W. Katzner, Choice and the Quality of Life (Beverly Hills, CA: Sage, 1979).

25. See A Framework for Planning, U.S. Federal Statistics for the 1980s (Washington, DC: Office of Federal Statistical Policy and Standards, USGPO, 1978); and Developments in the United States Federal Statistical System, 1977–1979 (Washington, DC: Office of Federal Statistical Policy and Standards, USGPO, 1979).

patterns of activity.[26] Suffice it to note that while personal consumption expenditures have been stable at about 64 percent of the gross national product over these 19 years, the expenditures for leisure and cultural activities as a percent of personal consumption expenditures has grown from 5.5 percent to 6.8 percent, with virtually all of the growth coming in the decade of the 1960s.

Some information is available for a variety of leisure time activities. Several of these, including "motion picture theaters" and "clubs and fraternal organizations," are homogeneous enough to be readily interpretable, but several are composed of elements which, from a consumer point of view, are quite heterogeneous. "Nondurable toys and sports supplies" provides a case in point. The allocation of money to these together has gone down slightly over the period, but this probably masks a dramatic shift in which expenditures for toys have declined while expenditures for sports supplies have risen as the baby-boom cohort reached adolescence and early adulthood.

The annual figures come from a number of different sources of varying reliability, so more detailed classification would not be justified. Every five years, however, the figures come from the Census of Business. A number of organizations have assisted in making the census categories more meaningful. For example, the National Endowment for the Arts has helped to clarify the categories of arts performance organizations listed in the 1977 census, and further

improvements are planned for the 1982 census. Thus it will be possible to represent leisure expenditures in much finer detail in future social indicator reports.

Finally, the Continuing Consumer Expenditure Survey under the sponsorship of the U.S. Bureau of Labor Statistics should be mentioned as another source of monetary measures of leisure consumption. Beginning in October 1979, the survey has canvased 16,000 households, or as they are called in this study, consumer units, each quarter of the year. Interviewers return three times so that a full year's data is collected from each household. The survey instrument is detailed enough so that it will become a rich source of information on changes in the major categories of leisure expenditures.[27]

Two Alternative Perspectives

To this point, the focus has been on the uses of free time, and more briefly, subjective measures and expenditures for leisure activities. But there are other sorts of measures that rightfully have their own place.

Process measures

Numerous productive activities must take place before consumption is possible in most areas of leisure and culture.[28] Before books are read,

---

26. Peterson, in "Arts Audience Statistics," ch. 6, describes and evaluates numerous alternative measures which might be used in the development of money measures of arts and cultural indicators.

27. For a discussion of the Continuing Consumer Expenditure Survey, see the Consumer Price Index: Concepts and Content over the Years (Washington, DC: Bureau of Labor Statistics, Report 517, 1978). For a discussion of how the survey may fit into the development of culture indicators, see Peterson, "Arts Audience Statistics," pp. 6.7–6.10.

28. For a discussion of the production of culture, see Richard A. Peterson, "Revitalizing the Culture Concept," Annual Review of Sociology, 5: 152–58 (1979).

for example, they must be conceived, written, edited, published, printed, distributed, critiqued, and archived in a library. A set of comprehensive cultural statistics would include measures of all these stages which together with the time and money measures of consumption comprise what can conveniently be called the "process perspective" for organizing the divers measures relevant to culture and leisure.

The Cultural Statistics Division of the Canadian census bureau, Statistics Canada, has developed a scheme to organize its data collection and analysis that exemplifies the process perspective. The relevant statistics are sought to measure creation, production, presentation, distribution, conservation, and consumption in each of 12 visual, audio, and written media.[29] An even more comprehensive "framework for cultural statistics" is under development through the United Nations Educational, Scientific, and Cultural Organization (UNESCO).[30] In addition to the arts and cultural activities included in the Canadian design, the UNESCO framework includes measures of "cultural heritage," "sports and games," "nature and environment," and "sociocultural activities."

United States' statistics are not currently organized in terms which fit either the Canadian or UNESCO process perspectives, but a good deal of the relevant data is currently available or could be assembled from existing time series.[31] Bringing the materials together in one place would go a long way toward fulfilling the promise implied by the term "culture."

Product measures

All the measures discussed to this point show one or another aspect of human activity, including creation, production, distribution, and consumption, related to culture and leisure. An alternative approach is to focus on the products of these activities.

Divers product measures are possible.[32] In common, they focus on the products that are created, disseminated, or consumed. Such measures make it possible to trace the quality of cultural products, leisure, and time use. Cultural anthropologists have regularly used artifacts as a means of understanding characteristics of a society,[33] and the approach has been applied by numerous research scholars to aspects of contemporary industrial nations.[34]

The call for product indicators of culture has an analog in the arena of science indicators. The system of science indicators developed by the National Science Board details the processes by which new knowledge

29. Culture Statistics Program (Ottawa, Canada: Joint Agreement between Statistics Canada and the Secretary of State, 1976).

30. "Preliminary Study on the Scope and Coverage of a Framework for Cultural Statistics" (Paris: UNESCO CES/AC.4/8). For commentaries on the framework for cultural statistics, see Louis Bohner, "Indicators of Cultural Development within the European Context" (Paris: UNESCO ST-79/Conf. 602/Col. 2, 1979); and Serge Fanchette, "Cultural Indicators: Theory and Practice" (Paris: UNESCO ST-79/Conf. 602/III, 1979).

31. For a discussion and critique of both the Canadian and UNESCO schemes, see Peterson, "Arts Audience Statistics," pp. 3.2–3.17.

32. For a review of product statistics and indicators of the arts, see Peterson, "Arts Audience Statistics," ch. 8.

33. Mary Douglas and Baron Isherwood, The World of Goods (New York: Basic Books, 1979).

34. Pierre Bourdieu, La Distinction: Critique Social de Jugement (Paris: Les Editions de Minuit, 1979).

is made.[35] The set of indicators has not, however, included measures of scientific achievement per se. To fill this void, there is a call for what Zuckerman and Miller call "knowledge indicators."[36]

No government agency now regularly publishes product statistics. What is more, there is no generally agreed on scheme within which to organize the divers indices that do exist. One possible organizing principle is to view products as the tangible part of a communication process measured at three points: creation, dissemination, and appreciation, or inculcation.[37]

For creation, the question is, How many new works of various types or genres have been offered for consumption within a given period of time—ordinarily a year? The U.S. Copyright Office is a useful source of such information for new written and musical works. In some fields, industry service organizations, trade associations, and technical magazines regularly list new works.

For dissemination the question is, What sorts of works, whether new or not, are widely disseminated during a given period of time? Here again, trade associations, magazines, and commercial pollsters often collect statistics on the relative popularity of particular works. In addition,

scholars have compiled great amounts of information on the particular art or media forms in which they are interested. For example, Mueller has compiled the complete performed repertoire of the 27 major symphony orchestras from the date of their founding through the 1969–70 season.[38] With these data, it is possible to chart the availability of different types of classical music in America year by year.

Besides tracing the popularity of whole works, it is possible to trace changes in the content of works which are newly created or are popular. A team headed by George Gerbner at the University of Pennsylvania and another team coordinated by Karl Rosengren in Sweden are engaged in ongoing content analyses. The Gerbner group has focused on violence and sexism in commercial television,[39] whereas the Rosengren group has focused on five aspects of the Swedish symbol system: literature, advertising, religion, domestic political debate, and international confrontation.[40]

For appreciation, the question is, How well do Americans understand aspects of culture and is this level of understanding or appreciation

35. The most recently published science indicators report is Science Indicators, 1978 (Washington, DC: National Science Board, USGPO, 1979). For a discussion of the various alternative ways of conceptualizing science indicators, see Manfred Kochen, "Models of Scientific Output," in Toward a Metric of Science, ed. Y. Elkana (New York: John Wiley & Sons, 1978) pp. 97–138.

36. Harriet Zuckerman and Roberta B. Miller, "Indicators of Science: Notes and Queries," Scientometrics (in press).

37. This model of product indicators is developed and illustrated in Peterson, "Arts Audience Statistics," pp. 8.1–8.13.

38. Kate Mueller, Twenty-Seven Major American Symphony Orchestras (Bloomington, IN: University of Indiana Press, 1973).

39. The rationale for Gerbner's research program can be found in George Gerbner, "Cultural Indicators," The Annals of the American Academy of Political and Social Science, 388: 69–80; and George Gerbner, "Cultural Indicators: The Third Voice," in Communications, Technology and Social Policy, eds. George Gerbner, Larry P. Gross, and William H. Melody (New York: John Wiley & Sons, 1973), pp. 9–28.

40. Karl Eric Rosengren, "Cultural Indicators: The Swedish Symbol System, 1945–1975" (Lund: University of Lund, 1976); and Karl Eric Rosengren, "Cultural Indicators: Sweden, 1945–1975" (Presentation to the International Conference on Communication, Acapulco, Mexico, 18–23 May 1980).

changing over time? Psychologists have made numerous studies of aesthetic appreciation, but for the most part their interest has been in comparing various subpopulations with each other rather than in showing changes over time.[41] The national polling organizations have collected information on the levels of political knowledge of the U.S. population, but there are no comparable available measures of cultural appreciation of the adult population.

There is more information available on the school-age population. The National Assessment of Educational Progress twice during the decade of the 1970s has asked large samples of children and youth comprehensive batteries of questions about literature, the visual arts, and music.[42] The assessments have probed the knowledge of classical works, aesthetic appreciation, and the rudiments of creative ability. Details of the comparisons between the early and the late 1970s data will become available during the next several years.

41. A comprehensive review of the formative stages of this research strategy is provided by Irving L. Child, "Esthetics," in *Handbook of Social Psychology*, eds. Gardner Lindsey and Elliot Aaronson (Reading, MA: Addison-Wesley, 1964), pp. 853–916.

42. The scope and research strategies of the National Assessment of Educational Progress can be found in "What the National Assessment Is" (Washington, DC: National Assessment of Educational Progress, USGPO, 1975); and "Act Technical Report; Summary Volume. Arts Report Number 06-A-21" (Denver, CO: Educational Commission of the States, 1977).

CONCLUSION

The arena of culture, leisure, and time use is nearly as untidy as Ennis found it in 1968. Consequently, this chapter has focused less on reporting data in order to focus more on exploring means of structuring the area and pointing to possible data sources. This has been done with a view to making possible a more conceptually coherent and empirically founded chapter for subsequent social indicator reports and to suggesting ways the field can develop.

Several recommendations can be drawn. The first is to include more monetary and subjective measures to complement the time measures of culture and leisure consumption. The second recommendation is to include selected measures of creation, production, distribution, and preservation to put the consumption measures into the more inclusive perspective of the process model. The third recommendation is to include a selection of product measures—what has been created, what has been widely disseminated, and what is appreciated—to complement the process measures of leisure and culture activity. Finally, the scope of the available measures as well as the amount of current research activity and policy interest is such that the time is ripe to establish a regularly updated compendium of culture statistics comparable to the biannual report of science indicators compiled by the National Science Board.

Table 8/1
Personal Consumption Expenditures for Leisure and Cultural Activities, Selected Years: 1960–1978

ITEM	1960	1965	1970	1975	1978
Gross National Product (GNP) (in billions of constant 1978 dollars)	1,114.7	1,422.8	1,650.6	1,853.1	2,107.6
Personal consumption expenditures (in billions of constant 1978 dollars)	715.7	889.5	1,039.7	1,188.4	1,340.1
Personal consumption expenditures as a percent of GNP	64.2	62.5	63.0	64.1	63.6
Personal consumption expenditures for leisure and cultural activities (in millions of constant 1978 dollars)	39,333	53,569	68,884	80,641	91,244
Expenditures for leisure and cultural activities as a percent of all personal consumption expenditures	5.5	6.0	6.6	6.8	6.8
Total expenditures for leisure and cultural activities (in percent)	100.0	100.0	100.0	100.0	100.0
Nondurable toys and sport supplies	13.9	13.8	13.4	12.9	12.8
Wheel goods, durable toys, sports equipment, boats, pleasure aircraft	11.1	11.1	13.4	14.4	15.9
Commercial participant amusements* ..	6.7	6.5	5.7	5.3	5.0
Spectator sports	2.0	2.6	2.6	2.2	2.0
Books and maps	6.4	6.4	5.7	5.4	5.9
Magazines, newspapers, sheet music ...	12.1	10.3	9.5	11.3	10.9
Legitimate theaters and opera and entertainments of nonprofit institutions†	1.9	1.5	1.4	1.2	1.4
Clubs and fraternal organizations‡	4.1	3.3	2.9	2.3	2.0
Radio and television receivers, records, and musical instruments	16.8	19.5	21.7	22.3	21.4
Radio and television repair	4.3	3.6	2.6	2.1	1.9
Motion picture theaters	5.4	4.1	3.7	3.8	4.7
Flowers, seeds, and potted plants	3.9	4.9	5.2	5.1	5.5
Parimutuel net receipts	3.0	3.1	2.8	2.5	2.2
Other§	8.4	9.2	9.4	9.0	8.3

Sources: U.S. Bureau of Economic Analysis, *The National Income and Product Accounts of the United States*, 1929–1974, and *Survey of Current Business*, July 1976 and 1979.

Note: These data represent the market value of purchases of goods and services by individual and nonprofit institutions. Detail may not add to total shown because of rounding.

* Consists of billiard parlors, bowling alleys, dancing, riding, shooting, skating, and swimming places, amusement devices and parks, golf courses, sightseeing buses and guides, and private flying operations.

† Except athletic.

‡ Consists of dues and fees, excluding insurance premiums.

§ Consists of net receipts of lotteries and expenditures for purchase of pets and pet care services, cable TV, film processing, photographic studios, sporting and recreational camps, and recreation services, not elsewhere classified.

This analysis of consumer expenditures on mass media from 1968 to 1977 finds that constant-dollar spending for U.S. periodicals rose somewhat in the decade. Looking across all spending on media, however, Maxwell McCombs and Chaim Eyal note that a "principle of relative constancy" McCombs earlier advanced appears to have held firm with these more recent data. McCombs is John Ben Snow Professor in the School of Public Communication, Syracuse University; Eyal is on the faculty of social sciences in the Communication Institute of Hebrew University, Jerusalem.

25

SPENDING ON MASS MEDIA

Maxwell E. McCombs and Chaim H. Eyal

*Analysis of economic expenditures on media
for 1968-1977 indicates that public support
for printed materials is relatively stable.*

One way of looking at the value a society places on reading is to examine the actual financial expenditures which people make for reading materials. Such a research strategy heeds the familiar admonition to augment attitudinal measures with behavioral ones.

We first monitored trends in spending for individual media for 1929 through 1968 (1). For those years spending on mass media products was largely limited to a fixed proportion of the total economy. This study will trace the patterns for consumer spending during the last decade to determine whether this pattern remained stable or whether there have been changes in personal income and leisure time over recent decades which have changed the marketplace for the mass media.

Data used are aggregate national statistics for annual consumer expenditures for 1968-1977 provided by the U.S. Department of Commerce (3). While there is a certain Philistinism in the use of economic statistics to trace the public's appreciation of printed materials and other mass communication, nevertheless, these statistics have the great advantage of availability and comparability across media and time.

The total number of dollars spent annually by Americans for all mass communication has more than doubled since the beginning of the last decade. In 1977, the last year for which final figures are available, consumers spent more than $38 billion on mass communications (see Table 1). This compares with expenditures of just under $17 billion in 1968. However, this also was a decade of major population growth and significant inflation, so comparisons were adjusted

Maxwell E. McCombs is John Ben Snow Professor in the School of Public Communication, Syracuse University, where Chaim H. Eyal is a post-doctoral research associate. This article continues the reporting of trends in consumer spending on mass media since the study of trends for 1920–1968 (1). The authors acknowledge the assistance provided by Robert J. Coen at McCann-Erickson.

Table 1: Consumer expenditures on mass communications, 1968–1977 (in billions of dollars)

	News-papers, maga-zines, sheet music	Books, maps	Total printed media	Radio, TV receivers, records, musical instruments	Radio and TV repairs	Total radio and TV	Motion picture admis-sions	Other admis-sions	Total admis-sions	Total audio and audio-visual media	Total all media
1968	3.41	2.67	**6.08**	7.85	1.23	**9.08**	1.05	.63	**1.68**	**10.76**	16.84
1969	3.85	3.13	**6.98**	8.27	1.27	**9.54**	1.10	.68	**1.78**	**11.32**	18.30
1970	4.23	3.45	**7.68**	9.44	1.31	**10.75**	1.16	.73	**1.89**	**12.64**	20.32
1971	4.56	3.72	**8.28**	9.78	1.39	**11.17**	1.17	.74	**1.91**	**13.08**	21.36
1972	4.68	2.53	**7.21**	10.96	1.22	**12.18**	1.64	.63	**2.27**	**14.45**	21.66
1973	5.84	2.77	**8.61**	12.29	1.33	**13.62**	1.96	.67	**2.63**	**16.25**	24.87
1974	7.04	3.03	**10.07**	13.27	1.24	**14.51**	2.49	.73	**3.22**	**17.73**	27.81
1975	7.55	3.60	**11.15**	14.84	1.36	**16.20**	2.54	.80	**3.34**	**19.54**	30.69
1976	8.14	3.70	**11.84**	16.47	1.50	**17.97**	2.99	.93	**3.92**	**21.89**	33.73
1977	9.04	4.34	**13.38**	18.00	1.74	**19.74**	4.07	1.08	**5.15**	**24.90**	38.28

Note: Subtotals appear in bold.

in a second set of trend measures. All the trend measures are correlation coefficients (or partial correlation coefficients) summarizing the comparison between the appropriate economic statistics from Table 1 and the time series 1968-1977. A perfectly monotonic increase across the ten years would yield a trend measure of +1; a perfectly monotonic decrease, −1. Within this range of values, the sign indicates the direction of the trend and the value, its strength. Trend measures are reported for all media in Table 2, both with and without controls for personal income.

Table 2: Trends in consumer spending on mass media, 1968-1977 (with controls for increases in population growth, inflation and personal income)

	Trend	Trend with controls
Total spending		
Actual $[a]	+.975	−.586
Actual $ per household[b]	+.968	.578
Constant $ per household[c]	−.423	−.324
By media (actual $)[a]		
Newspapers, magazines, sheet music	+.981	−.103
Books and maps	+.580	−.295
All print media	+.954	−.286
Radio/TV receivers, records, musical instruments	+.987	−.131
Radio/TV repairs	+.705	−.528
All radio/TV	+.985	.366
Movie admissions	+.945	−.742
All audio and audio/visual media	+.978	−.785
By media (actual $ per household)[b]		
Newspapers, magazines, sheet music	+.977	−.078
Books and maps	+.187	−.321
All print media	+.925	−.301
Radio/TV receivers, records, musical instruments	+.987	−.050
Radio/TV repairs	+.120	−.591
All radio/TV	+.983	−.350
Movie admissions	+.942	−.710
All audio and audio/visual media	+.975	−.768
By media (constant $ per household)[c]		
Newspapers, magazines, sheet music	+.736	+.832
Books and maps	−.817	−.876
All print media	−.520	−.530
Radio/TV receivers, records, musical instruments	+.182	+.715
Radio/TV repairs	−.957	−.963
All radio/TV	−.514	−.501
Movie admissions	+.889	+.894
All audio and audio/visual media	+.088	+.472

[a] The control variable is total personal income
[b] The control variable is average personal income per household
[c] The control variable is average personal income per household in constant $

Thus, the near monotonic increase in total spending on mass communication is reflected in the trend measure of +.975 but is best restated in terms of constant dollars spent per household for mass communication. With this restatement, there actually was a modest decline (−.423) in consumer expenditures on all mass communication during the decade.

Consumer spending on print from 1968 to 1977 parallels the general trend for all mass communication. From about $6 billion in 1968, consumer spending on all print media more than doubled by 1977, when it exceeded $13 billion. In terms of actual dollars spent, the ten-year trend for print media (+.954) is nearly monotonic, much like the trend for all mass communication.

But spending on periodicals and books, the two chief components of print media, show disparate trends. While spending on newspapers and magazines nearly tripled, spending on books and maps did not even double. This disparity among print media is clearly visible in the trend figures for actual dollar expenditures of +.981 for newspapers and magazines, compared to +.580 for books and maps.

Again, it is necessary to control for population growth and inflation, factors which increase the total number of dollars in the marketplace. When these controls are added, the disparities in consumer spending on periodicals and books are accented. Even accounting for inflation and population growth, spending on periodicals still shows a healthy increase across the decade, a strong +.736. But the trend in spending on books is its mirror image, −.817.

Part of this dramatic decline in spending on books results, undoubtedly, from the declining enrollments of our schools and colleges. As our society moves farther and farther past the crest of the baby boom, there is a slackened demand for school textbooks, everything from kindergarten primers to college textbooks. This substantially smaller market for books also is coupled with heightened pressure recently for reduced government spending and an actual drop in federal education spending (2, p. 10). It is easy to visualize the impact of all this on large, institutional orders for school books, which are a major portion of book publishers' revenues.

Further insight into the recent declining trend for spending on books is found in the statistics on how total consumer spending on print is divided between periodicals and books (see Table 1). During the past decade the picture is one of shifting ratios, with books receiving a smaller and smaller share. In 1968 nearly 45 percent of the spending on print media was for books. But this steadily declined and by 1977 books received only about one-third of the money spent on print. This declining share of spending on books is consistent with the trends shown for books and periodicals in Table 2.

But this picture of decline is a misleading one when viewed in the isolation of a single decade. If the division of money between periodicals and books is examined for the entire period from 1929 to 1977 (see 1), it is obvious that, historically, periodicals have claimed about two-thirds of the money spent on print compared to one-third for books. However, books began to receive a larger share of this spending during the late 1950s and continued to do so until 1971. In other words, the historical share of dollars spent on print that was received by periodicals declined from the mid-1950s until 1971. These were, of course, the very years in which the major mass circulation periodicals failed. *Collier's* disappeared in 1956 to be followed in time by *Coronet, American, Look, Saturday Evening Post,* and finally, in 1972, *Life.* But by that time periodicals' share of the market sharply rebounded, and books' share of the market steadily declined until it reached its historic plateau of one-third of the spending on print media. In short, the long-range picture of the distribution of spending between periodicals and books is a highly stable one. Our view of the short-range changes during 1968-1977 caught a major, but apparently short-lived, deviation in this long-running trend.

> *A brief comparison of the trends for spending*
> *on print with the trends for spending on*
> *audio-visual media also provides*
> *a useful context for studying print.*

The trend for spending on all audio-visual media over the past ten years in terms of constant dollars per household is one of stability, as reflected in the trend figure, + .088. This average reflects a melange of ups and downs. Interestingly, the only figure which exceeds the upward trend for periodicals is the trend for movie admissions. This reflects the strong recovery of the movies during the past ten years from the disastrous decade following World War II when the advent of television devastated the movie industry.

These trends on spending for various mass media need to be considered in a larger context summarized by the Principle of Relative Constancy. This principle asserts that the pattern of economic support for mass communication is approximately constant relative to the general economy. It holds that mass communication products have become staples of consumption in our society much like food, clothing, and shelter. As staples, they receive a fixed, constant share of the economic pie, a relatively fixed proportion of all expenditures. The analysis (1) of consumer spending on mass communication from 1929 through 1968 found good evidence for this economic constraint. Have the social and communication changes of the past decade altered this constraint?

To determine this we examined the trend from 1968 to 1977 in consumer spending on all mass communication as a percentage of four measures of the general economy. These measures range from the broadest possible measure of the general economy, the Gross National Product (GNP), to more specific consumer income and spending measures.

For all three trends where the base of the percentage is some measure of consumer spending or income, the evidence from 1968-1977 is uniform and supportive of the Principle of Relative Constancy. Whether taken as a percentage of total income expenditures (−.238), of average personal income per household

(−.365), or of total recreation expenditures (−.369), spending on mass communication is highly consistent across the decade, resulting in trend measures very close to zero. To the extent that the patterns diverge from this benchmark of absolute constancy across time, there is a modest decline in the proportion of funds devoted to mass communication. The sole exception is the trend measure based on GNP for which a trend of +.801 was measured. GNP is a broad measure of total economic activity that is subject to shifts and fluctuations well beyond the influence of consumers.

> *Collectively, these trends in spending*
> *on mass communication document a*
> *continuing public appreciation of reading.*

Even with a proliferation of audio-visual communication services and devices during the past decade, the historical patterns of spending on print and other mass media remain much the same. Of course, the sheer size of mass communication has grown. The actual number of dollars spent by consumers on mass communication more than doubled from 1968 to 1977. But when this upward trend in spending (+.975) is restated in constant dollars spent per household, the trend actually is modestly downward (−.423).

The trend for print is parallel. But for the short-range trends it is necessary to consider periodicals and books separately. Stated in terms of constant dollars per household, their trends are almost exact opposites: +.736 for periodicals and −.817 for books. This disparity results from some short-term shifts in the historical division of consumer spending between periodicals and books. But by 1977 the historical ratio of 2:1 (periodicals over books) in consumer spending on print had reappeared.

Despite these short-term perturbations in the division of spending on periodicals and books, the long-range trend in public support for print media has continued undisturbed. During the last ten years the share of total consumer spending on mass communication devoted to print continued at its historical level, slightly more than one-third of all expenditures.

The larger economic context of mass communication expenditures, summarized in the Principle of Relative Constancy, also remained stable between 1968 and 1977. This stability, both in the overall pattern of mass communication expenditures and in spending on print media, allays many misgivings about the impact of technology on our society. Society's use of mass communication, in terms of manifest behaviors as well as the underlying motivations and gratifications, seems remarkably resilient in the face of rapid technological change.

REFERENCES

1. McCombs, Maxwell. "Mass Media in the Marketplace." *Journalism Monographs* 24, 1972.
2. Sterling, Christopher H. and Timothy R. Haight. *The Mass Media: Aspen Institute Guide to Communication Industry Trends.* New York: Praeger, 1978.
3. U.S. Department of Commerce. *Survey of Current Business*, Vols. 53–58, No. 7 in each year.

It is more than television—specifically, it is the pursuit of differing circulation, advertising, and prestige-political goals—that has increasingly polarized the British press along social class lines, Jeremy Tunstall argues. Moreover, he notes, either a Marxist or a functionalist interpretation of the British transition would be appropriate. Tunstall is professor of sociology at the City University, London.

26

THE BRITISH PRESS
IN THE AGE OF TELEVISION

Jeremy Tunstall

THIS article seeks to provide an overview of some major trends in the British press during 'the age of television'. While the press industry remains in a broadly healthy financial state, television has played an important part in other major changes in the press. Social class polarisation within the press audience has increased, as have other related forms of polarisation such as the national/provincial and the popular/prestige divides.

Television has indirectly played its part in major changes in the pattern of British press ownership. Broadly since 1945 there has been a change from a predominantly *family* pattern of ownership to a *conglomerate* pattern. This article concludes by noting that the empirical facts can be seen as illustrating both Marxist and functional accounts of mass media in market economies.

The impact of television on the press

Firstly, in terms of advertising revenue, the press still does rather well. Ever since commercial television became firmly established around 1960, television has taken between 22% and 26% of total media advertising expenditure in Britain. The total press share has always since 1960 remained around 70%. However there has been a major change within the press—with *national newspapers* getting a smaller, and *provincial* newspapers a larger, slice. While national press display advertising has been hit by TV, provincial press classified advertising has expanded.[1]

Secondly, in terms of audience time, the press has remained broadly static. Television has cut into radio time, and also greatly increased total

From Jeremy Tunstall, "The British Press in the Age of Television," pp. 19-36 in Harry Christian (ed.) *The Sociology of Journalism and the Press,* Sociological Review Monograph 29, University of Keele, October 1980. Reprinted by permission of the Editorial Board of the SOCIOLOGICAL REVIEW.

audience media time. The British public now divides its media time roughly as follows: One quarter to ITV, a half to BBC television and to radio, and one quarter to newspapers and magazines.

Thirdly, there is now a different social class pattern as between the media. Although the ITV audience is more working class, both BBC1 TV and television overall in Britain have an audience relatively undifferentiated by social class (Table 1). But the *national* press has become much the most social class polarised of the major British mass media (Table 2). Television influences have played a large part in destroying the middle-brow, middle-market, sector of the British national press.

TABLE 1

Average amounts of viewing and listening per head, per week, mid February 1975

		BBC's Three Socio-Economic Groups		
		A	B	C
Television	BBC1	6.58hrs	7.43hrs	6.47hrs
	BBC2	2.15	1.47	1.26
	ITV	4.47	7.08	11.49
	Total TV	14.00	16.38	20.02
Radio	BBC Radio 1	1.45	3.20	4.09
	2	2.18	2.58	2.58
	3	1.03	0.28	0.07
	4	4.15	2.55	1.20
Total Radio (BBC 1—4 & Luxembourg)		9.27	9.47	8.40
Total TV and Radio		23.27	26.25	28.42

Source: Annual Review of BBC Audience Research Findings.

TABLE 2

Newspapers and Social Class 1974-5

Percentage within each of six social class categories reading the newspaper

	Total	Upper Middle A	Middle B	Lower Middle C1	Skilled Working C2	Working D	Subsistence E
Daily Mirror	32	7	13	26	40	41	22
Sun	29	5	11	23	38	39	17
Daily Express	21	24	23	25	20	17	17
Daily Mail	12	15	16	17	11	9	9
Daily Telegraph	9	42	28	14	4	2	3
The Guardian	3	17	9	5	1	1	—
The Times	3	20	9	4	1	1	—
Financial Times	2	14	7	3	1	1	—
Total	111	144	116	116	115	111	68

Source: JICNARS

   This social class polarisation is linked to other forms of polarisation. The divide in the British press between popular tabloids and prestige broadsheets now greatly exaggerate real differences in education and reader interest, because the two types of newspaper have two different forms of revenue. The prestige nationals are dependent on advertising revenue, which exaggerates their 'up market' inclinations (because premium rates can be charged for delivering 'AB' readers to advertisers). The popular tabloids, in contrast, are almost wholly dependent on sales revenues and these papers are locked into a sales war to the death which exaggerates their 'down market' inclinations.

   Another form of polarisation which takes an unusually sharp form in Britain is that between the *national* and *provincial* press. Provincial papers typically have an all-class audience, depend on advertising revenue, and do not confer prestige on their owners. Britain (apart from Scotland) is unusual in no longer having any examples of provincial papers which sell, not just in a single urban centre or county, but over an entire major region The *Daily Star*, a popular daily newspaper published in Manchester since 1978, has achieved a sizeable national readership.

1930-1956: The Golden Period

   In retrospect the years 1930 to 1956 can nostalgically be seen as the golden period, when records of all kinds were achieved. In Western Europe at large the Second World War obviously produced enormous dislocation for the press; but in Britain despite newsprint rationing—or more accurately because of it the 1940s were a comfortable period of low competition and high profits. Then in 1955 both newsprint rationing finally ended and commercial TV arrived. After 1956 the British press was off the plateau and sliding. As Table 3 shows, the level of daily

TABLE 3

Daily Press—Total Circulations

	National Morning	London Evening	Provincial Morning and Evening	Total Daily
1920	5,430	1,940	7,300	14,670
1930	8,650	2,030	7,270	17,950
1938	10,400	1,850	7,000	19,250
1948	15,500	3,500	9,970	28,970
1956	16,780	2,810	10,320	29,910
1960	15,880	2,220	10,400	28,500
1966	15,591	1,886	8,780	26,257
1971	14,176	1,461	8,653	23,290
1976	14,006	992	8,141	23,129

Sources: N. Kaldor and R. Silverman, *A Statistical Analysis of Advertising Expenditure and of the Revenue of the Press;* Advertising Association, *Advertising Expenditure 1960;* RCP 1977.

circulation by 1976 had fallen back by some six million on 1956, but was still above 1938 levels; on a per population basis, however, 1976 daily sales were almost identical to those of 1938.

Indeed, on a per population basis daily circulations in 1976 were only slightly above 1930 levels.[2] Nevertheless since 1930 several important internal adjustments have occurred. Whereas in the 1930s daily newspaper reading was still heavily skewed towards the middle class (Table 4), it is now much more evenly spread (Table 2).

TABLE 4

Penetration of National Daily Newspapers by Income Groups, 1935

	Income Groups				
	1	2	3	4	5
	£1,000+	£500-1,000	£250-500	£125-250	Under£125
	%	%	%	%	%
The Times	54.1	20.7	2.6	0.1	0.02
Daily Telegraph/Morning Post	48.1	35.6	14.0	2.0	0.4
Daily Mail	31.6	35.0	31.7	12.3	4.5
Daily Mirror	26.0	19.1	12.8	5.2	2.0
Daily Sketch	11.5	8.4	7.5	4.6	2.1
Daily Express	12.3	16.8	26.4	20.0	7.8
News Chronicle	4.0	5.6	10.2	13.4	7.6
Daily Herald	1.2	1.2	6.2	21.4	20.9
All national newspapers per Income group	188.8	142.4	111.4	79.0	45.3
Families in income group as percentage of total populations	0.9	3.4	14.3	57.5	24.0

Source: Political and Economic Planning (1938) *Report on the British Press*, p. 77 (Based on national sample survey conducted by Incorporated Society of British Advertisers).

The geographical spread of national newspaper penetration has not greatly altered as Table 5 indicates. Nor has the sex composition of newspaper readership much altered—in 1935 as in 1976 men were slightly more likely than women to read newspapers. It was the 'Northcliffe revolution' of around 1900 which successfully reached women as well as men readers and—by printing in Manchester—achieved a *nationally* spread sale.

Nor has the loss of titles been very great compared with some other countries. For example the number of provincial evenings in Britain between 1890 and 1970 was always around eighty. But within this relatively stable overall number there has been much change; in particular in 1921 twenty-four provincial towns had evening newspaper competition, whereas none have now. There was also a very considerable drop in the number of provincial *mornings* from fifty-two in 1900 to only eighteen in 1970.

TABLE 5

Penetration of National Newspapers in selected regions, 1935-1975

Percentage* within region reading each newspaper

	South East	(West) Midlands	North West	NE and North	Scotland
Daily Express 1935	20.7	15.0	14.8	10.1	20.2
Daily Express 1975	19	16	24	17	29
Daily Mail 1935	16.9	12.7	13.4	12.9	8.9
Daily Mail 1975	15	13	13	9	4

* For 1935 the data relate to families, for 1975 to all adults.
Sources: PEP (1938) *Report on the British Press*, JICNARS Jan.—Dec. 1975.

In 1900 both the national and provincial press were still organised on the basis of competition between political parties and factions. In London both the morning and evening press was organised on political party lines; today the London press is mainly a morning press organised on social class lines. Whereas in 1900 the larger provincial cities each had four or five partisan dailies under several ownerships, by 1970 the provincial daily press had been re-organised around the principle of monopoly; larger provincial cities typically had a lucrative evening and a weak morning daily under a single ownership. Small provincial centres had merely a monopoly evening. The evenings had also followed the spread of population into the suburbs.

As if to emphasise the national/provincial polarity even more, by the 1970s local weekly newspapers were the ultimate in non-partisanship and often the ultimate in profitable local monopoly.

Party Involvement

No detailed study exists of the political involvement of the whole British press during the twentieth century. But several broad generalisations can be made. Firstly while partisanship has not disappeared, the partisanship in the press which remains tends to 'fit' with the social class composition of the audience. Publications—like provincial evenings or weeklies—which appeal today across social class and educational differences tend to be a-political. This focuses most interest on the middle of the national spectrum (Table 6).

TABLE 6

National Daily Newspaper Circulations 1930-79 (in thousands)

	1930	1937	1947	1961	1971	1979
The Times	186	191	269	257	340	—
The Guardian	—	—	—	240	332	379
Financial Times	—	—	—	132	170	206
Daily Telegraph	175	559	1,016	1,248	1,446	1,477
Morning Post	120	—	—	—	—	—
Daily Express	1,693	2,204	3,856	4,321	3,413	2,406
Daily Herald/The Sun	1,119	2,033	2,134	1,407	2,293	3,793
Daily Mail	1,845	1,580	2,077	2,649	1,798	1,944
News Chronicle	1,452	1,324	1,623	—	—	—
Daily Sketch (Graphic)	926	684	772	991	—	—
Daily Mirror	1,072	1,328	3,702	4,578	4,384	3,623
TOTAL	8,568	9,903	15,449	15,823	14,176	13,828

Source: RCP, 1947, RCP, 1977.
1979, (Jan.—June) *The Times* was not appearing. *Daily Star* not included.

Secondly, in this middle area the last two overtly partisan newspapers, the Liberal *News Chronicle* and Labour *Daily Herald* have disappeared. One lesson drawn from their deaths by the press at large is that partisanship should be flexible rather than permanent.

Thirdly, the political coverage in newspapers has altered. Political speeches—one of the old partisan staples of the late nineteenth century—now get much less coverage.

Nevertheless it would not be correct to think of press partisanship as in rapid and steady decline throughout the twentieth century. For one thing, as Alan Lee tells us[3] over a third of provincial dailies were independent or neutral in 1900. And in the 1970s plenty of partisanship still remained.

Moreover during the period when the Labour Party was taking over from the Liberals there appears to have been an increase in partisanship, with the Labour Party receiving hostile partisan coverage of increased ferocity. Indeed the relatively *small* increase in total daily circulation between 1920 and 1938 (Table 3) is probably partly accounted for by the unpopularity of a predominantly Conservative press with many of the potential new readers. This was also *par excellence* the era of the eccentric press Lords—especially Beaverbrook and Rothermere.

As so often in the press, political partisanship and business went hand in hand. The transformation in the inter-war period of the provincial press—the growth of chains and local monopolies—involved both the building of Conservative bastions for political ends and of commercial bastions for monopoly profit.

Nevertheless between 1900 and 1970 the British press gave up many of its party concerns in favour of entertainment and/or information. While some partisanship remained, the common 1900 idea disappeared of the paper owned by a political figure or with the main purpose of supporting a party. Partisanship became more tactical and diffuse; the 'political' goal slowly evolved into a 'prestige' goal. Not that prestige is unconnected with power; but it is a different conception of how to use and pursue power through a newspaper.

The mid Century Plateau

One version of conventional wisdom presents the British press in mid century as the world's most competitive. But there is more image than substance to such a view. Newspapers were still a sheltered industry—until 1955 there was no competition for advertising from either television or radio. For a large slab of the period 1939 to 1955 newsprint rationing was operated in such a way as largely to freeze the circulation status quo. Even in the 1930s there was only one period of moderately fierce national press competition—and this was confined to the very early 1930s.

The famous canvassing sales war of the early 1930s involved new readers being bought with subsidised copies of Dickens, saucepans, and other impedimenta. This is usually portrayed as extravagant and wasteful competition. Such a view is mistaken. The *Daily Herald* in particular was trying to acquire new readers—it was encouraging working class people to start taking a daily paper. As Table 4 shows, by 1935 the *Daily Herald* had met with some, but only sóme, success in this endeavour—about one-fifth of working class families took the *Daily Herald*. But in 1935 the *Daily Mirror* was an up market newspaper read as a second daily by wealthy families; like the *Daily Sketch*, it was not a tabloid in the more recent popular working class sense. But even the *Daily Herald* did not constitute severe head on competition for the other dailies; true, it raised its sale from a few hundred thousand in 1929 to a million in 1930 and to two million by 1937—but Table 4 suggests that this was done largely by attracting readers completely new to newspaper buying. The ferocity of these sales wars (before the days of TV promotion) can be exaggerated—they ran only for a few months at a time in 1930, 1931 and finally from March to June 1933.

These sales wars may be better understood as one of several occasional bursts of competition which disturbed the rather uncompetitive—indeed semi-cartel—arrangements of the inter-war British press.

Apart from the *Daily Herald*—which suddenly began to take competition so seriously in 1929—the only other national daily to adopt firmly competitive ways was Lord Beaverbrook's *Daily Express*. In 1930, however, the *Daily Mail* still had the largest sale; moreover the Harmsworth family, in addition to the *Daily Mail*, still also owned the *Daily Mirror*. These three dailies—*Mail, Mirror* and *Express*—had 52% of national daily circulation; and the owners of these three dailies, the Harmsworth family and Beaverbrook, were business partners. Until 1934 the Harmsworths and Beaverbrook jointly owned on a 49:51% basis, the London *Evening Standard*. The only other big daily sales belonged to the *News Chronicle* (it was a merger in 1930 of the *Daily News* and *Daily Chronicle*); under Cadbury management and with Liberal policies its competitive position continued to slip.

Nor was the inter-war *provincial* newspaper scene exceptionally competitive. True, there was a war between the Berry and Harmsworth/Rothermere provincial chains—but this was largely confined to only two cities, Bristol and Newcastle, and was resolved by each group retreating from one city.[4]

Why did the newspaper groups so dislike competition? One important reason was perhaps the very success of the Harmsworth group in the first decade of the century—which had shown how devastating competition could be. After 1918 the Rothermere/Harmonsworth competitive thrust weakened, while its political concerns strengthened; other groups went the same way.

When the war came in 1939 circulations were pegged. Newsprint was very severely rationed and in 1945 paper consumption was down to only a quarter of 1939 levels; with dollar problems, this rationing continued. In 1947 the national dailies were still only a quarter or a third of their pre-war size (Table 7). But in several other respects, newsprint rationing was the answer to a newspaper owner's prayers. While pages were cut back, the sale price stayed the same and there was a surplus of advertising; selling a one-third size paper at the full price was extremely profitable. For a short period after the war sales were allowed to expand— and the *Daily Mirror's* sale boomed—but in 1947 the dollar crisis brought back severe restrictions.

Fleet Street managers liked some aspects of newsprint rationing and were reluctant to see it go. Beaverbrook in 1946 indicated his awareness

TABLE 7

Size of Six national Newspapers (1937, 1947, 1975)

	1937	1947		1975	
	Mean number of pages	Mean number of pages	Mean printed area per issue (sq. in.)	Mean number of pages	Mean printed area per issue (sq. in.)
The Times	25.7	9.6	3,600	26.2	8,810
Daily Telegraph	25.0	6.2	2,200	28.5	9,853
Daily Express	20.0	4.6	1,560	17.3	5,270
Daily Mail	19.3	4.6	1,390	33.7*	4,975
Daily Mirror	22.5	9.2	1,320	27.9	3,952
Daily Worker/ Morning Star	8	6.1	1,170	6.0	1,442

* The Daily Mail changed to tabloid size in 1971.

Source: Denis McQuail, *Analysis of Newspaper Content* p. 15, HMSO for Royal Commission on the Press 1977.

of troubles to come; he claimed that the government had given the press four new freedoms—freedom from competition, advertising revenue, newsprint and freedom from enterprise.[5] *The Times* became increasingly restless with the harsh restriction on pages. In 1955 as the ending of these controls approached, only *The Times* was enthusiastic. The others actually wanted the government to dismantle the controls more slowly.[6]

Some of the ills to which Fleet Street was already prone in 1939, after 15 years in the deepfreeze, emerged in 1956 in impressively virulent strength. And 1956 was no ordinary year. This was the year in which commercial television turned the corner. Fleet Street was never to be the same again.

After Television: the Press in Decline?

There is one explanation of the effect of television which sees it as an unmitigated disaster for the press. But the rival case is that the press has not been damaged at all; James Curran argued that the apparent circulation falls in the national press were misleading because the high sales figures had been of very thin paper-rationed newspapers. Television had hit, not newspapers, but other media more functionally similar to TV—such as consumer magazines, posters and cinema. On meaningful criteria—such as total page area of newspaper sold, or proportion of consumer expenditure—Curran argued, British national newspapers had not declined at all.[7]

There was some merit in Curran's arguments—certainly well into the sixties. But some significant signs of the press decline did exist, even in the 1960s. What might have happened without television and radio is a hypothetical question. There is little doubt that television has become the leading *entertainment* medium and it lays claim to being the leading *news* medium also; certainly many people—especially popular paper readers—think TV the leading news medium.

This latter point seems at the very least to represent a relative loss of prestige by the press. Nevertheless the press retains some strong cards: It has the bulk of British advertising expenditure. The prestige press still remains the most weighty part of the mass media. The newspaper is still the only medium (apart possibly from radio) that people literally carry around with them. Table 8 shows that much reading of the *Daily Mirror* is done at work, before work, and after work in the evening. Local newspapers and specialised magazines also remain strong.

TABLE 8

Reading the Daily Mirror (Time of day)

	All Readers %	% of Reading Time	Men %	Women %
When Newspaper Reading takes place				
Up to leaving for work or up to 9 a.m.	32	(21)	31	32
Between leaving home and starting work	5	(3)	8	2
From starting work, or from 9 a.m. up to mid-day meal time	37	(26)	43	30
During mid-day meal time/break	22	(14)	29	15
Up to leaving work or up to 5 p.m.	16	(12)	12	20
Between leaving work and getting home	2	(1)	2	1
Between getting home, or from 5 p.m. and going to sleep	36	(23)	30	44
Average number of phases read/looked at	1.5		1.55	1.44

Source: IPC Media Behaviour and opinions Studies, 1972-1973.

From Family Newspaper Company to Conglomerate Ownership

The arrival of commercial television also played a key part in radically transforming the ownership of the press. In 1955 most of the press was still controlled by family groupings; by the time the third Royal Commission on the Press reported in 1977 the bulk of the press was owned by conglomerates whose major long term interests lay in other industries (Table 9).

TABLE 9

Proportion of UK Newspaper circulation controlled by International and Conglomerate Companies 1977

Percentage of total UK circulation in category

	National Popular Dailies	National Quality Dailies	National Popular Sundays	National Quality Sundays	London Evening	Provincial Morning	Provincial Evening	Provincial Weekly + Bi-weekly
Associated Newspapers	14.7	—	—	—	54.7	3.2	14.7	4.3
Trafalgar House (Express Group)	21.7	—	20.6	—	42.6	—	—	0.2
Mirror Group Newspapers (Reed)	32.2	—	48.8	—	—	32.3	—	0.4
News International	31.0	—	30.6	—	—	—	0.6	2.8
The Observer (Atlantic Richfield)	—	—	—	23.8	—	—	—	—
S. Pearson	—	8.3	—	—	—	5.3	8.9	11.9
Scottish & Universal Investments	—	—	—	—	—	5.2	3.6	3.0
Thomson Organisation	—	14.8	—	49.2	—	18.8	16.4	3.7
Total	99.8	23.1	100.0	73.0	100.0	64.8	44.2	26.3

Source: Royal Commission on the Press (1977) *Final Report and Appendices.*

Roy Thomson and the conglomerate which bears his name played a key role in this transformation. Many of the old press families were both suspicious and disapproving of commercial television and refused the opportunity of an ownership stake; Roy Thomson, on his Canadian experience, made no such error. As owner of *The Scotsman* he went on to take an 80% interest in Scottish Television—the ITV station serving highly populated central Scotland; this was his famous 'license to print money'. In 1959 Thomson bought the Kemsley newspapers—including the *Sunday Times* and a major provincial chain. Thomson was now a major force in both television and newspapers. The next step in the sequence resulted from Thomson's unhappiness at being so heavily dependent on volatile advertising revenue. So he diversified into books and package holidays. In 1966 he bought *The Times*. And, he also diversified into North Sea Oil. This last was so successful that by 1976, when he died, the stock market already saw Thomson shares as oil shares. A press based company had become an oil based conglomerate.

Equally instructive is the transformation of the *Daily Mirror* into IPC, and then into the Reed paper-based conglomerate. The *Daily Mirror* only finally threw off its upper class readers in the late 1930s; in the war and immediately after 1945 it acquired a massive working class audience. Like Thomson, the Mirror group went into commercial television and by the late 1950s was brimming over with cash. In two years—through a series of takeovers—it bought enormous heaps of London press, especially magazine companies; these heaps of publications were then called the International Publishing Corporation. Many of IPC's properties had a poor future—not only the *Daily Herald* but also the women's magazines, and the enormous printing plant capacity. By 1970 IPC was taken over by one of its former subsidiaries, the Reed paper company.

Other press companies have gone the conglomerate way. The disparate Cowdray press interests in 1967 were re-organised into the Pearson-Longman group, itself part of a banking-based conglomerate. The old Northcliffe/Associated group—owning the *Daily Mail* and the big Northcliffe provincial chain—has also struck oil and is also seen by the stock market as an oil share. Finally in 1977 just as the Royal Commission was reporting, the Beaverbrook group—the largest and most eccentric of the remaining family firms—was bought by Trafalgar House (a shipping, construction and real estate conglomerate).

Within a decade conglomerate control had become the predominant form of press ownership in Britain. This pattern does not exist in most comparable countries, and constitutes, therefore, an important form of uniqueness in the British media. What its consquences will be also, perhaps, constitutes the greatest conundrum in the British media.

Increasing Polarisation

The wave of conglomerisation is only one part of a series of major changes which pre-dated and coincided with the 1974-77 Royal Commission on the Press. As with diversification into ITV in the mid 1950s, the oil price rises of the 1970s promised a bonanza to those who had diversified into oil, while savagely penalising those that had not. 1973 was a boom year for the British press, with advertising so plentiful that many papers could not accommodate it. But in 1974 the press was hit by mammoth rises in costs (especially of newsprint), general economic crisis, inflation and falling revenue.

These were all background factors in increasing polarisation in the British press between the prestige and popular nationals, between nationals and provincials and between newspapers and magazines. But the most dramatic foreground factor was Rupert Murdoch and *The Sun*. Murdoch having acquired the *News of the World* (in 1968) applied his techniques to *The Sun* (which he bought from IPC in 1969). *The Sun* rapidly built sales by concentrating on the old formula of sex, crime and sport; the *Daily Mirror* was forced largely to abandon its 1960s middle market pretentions. The tabloidisation of the popular dailies was completed when the *Daily Mail* (1971) and the *Daily Express* (1976) went tabloid. Behind this transformation were two significant financial facts· Firstly the high cost of paper. Secondly the decline in advertising revenue available to popular nationals (Table 10) and the decline (or disappearance) in the profitability of such advertising as existed.

In social class terms the effect is to split the national press into two nations with a vengeance. The prestige and popular national dailies in the 1970s acquired a different physical shape, different goals, different forms of revenue, and different competition. The four prestige dailies were broadsheet, the populars tabloid. The prestige dailies had a guiding goal—'prestige'; the popular dailies had a less clear goal or cluster of goals to do with entertainment, not losing money and not losing circulation.

They also had different forms of revenue. (Table 10). The populars in the 1970s became less and less dependent on advertising—as the revenue from advertising sank down to, or below, the paper and production costs of printing the advertisements. But the 'prestige' papers—with much higher advertising rates per thousand more affluent readers—were

TABLE 10

Advertising Revenue of Newspapers and Periodicals as a proportion of total revenue, 1960, 1973, 1975, and Display and Classified Advertising as a proportion of total advertising 1975.

Percentages

	Total advertising revenue as a proportion of total revenue			Display and classified advertising as proportions of total advertising in 1975	
	1960	1973	1975	Display	Classified
Newspapers					
National popular daily	45	36	27	85	15
National quality daily	73	70	58	62	38
National popular Sunday	46	38	31	91	9
National quality Sunday	79	74	66	68	32
London Evening	61	72	61	37	63
Provincial morning	58				
Provincial evening	62	67	60	39	61
Provincial Sunday	n.a.				
Provincial weekly	79	84	84	44	56
Periodicals					
General and leisure interests	46	39	37	93	7
Trade and Technical	78	64	62	71	29

Sources: 1960: Royal Commission on the Press 1961-62, 1973, 1975: national newspapers and London evenings, Royal Commission on the press 1974-77, remainder Business Monitor PQ 485.

n.a. = not available.

Source: Royal Commission on the Press 1974-7.

dependent mainly on advertising; thus their financial goal of maintaining the desired affluent readership, to deliver to advertisers, was in line with the more general 'prestige' goal. Prestige nationals had another kind of backing—subsidy. *The Guardian* has been massively subsidised ever since it began printing in London; *The Times* has been heavily subsidised since it was bought by Thomson. But again even this form of 'revenue' is consistent with a general 'prestige' goal. It is only if you make the equation 'prestige equals power' that you can't be quite sure what the goal of prestige papers is these days.

But polarisation between social classes is perhaps the most obvious consequence of this national press pattern (Table 2). In particular while many middle class people still read the *Daily Mail* or the *Daily Express* very few working class people read any of the four prestige national dailies.

A somewhat similar polarisation exists within provincial newspapers—working class evenings make profits, while mornings lose money. But a more marked polarisation exists between all provincials and all national newspapers. Because Fleet Street still brings prestige there are too many national newspapers, too little revenue and too much competition—competition which (in the TV age) is now all too real. This national press is subsidised in several cases directly by provincial chains, whose purpose is to make money some of which the nationals can then lose.

Yet another form of polarisation exists between national magazines and national newspapers. Since in Britain very few national magazines are thought to confer prestige, their fate is to make profits or to die.

The Goals of the Press

How, then, can we summarise the goals of the British press? One useful distinction may be that while magazines have single specialised and commercial goals, newspapers have a mixture of goals.

The majority of British newspapers have been in existence since before the first world war. This means that newspapers have traditions; they have printing plants and printing workers—and *production* is commercially seen as the core of the enterprise. The dominance of the production orientation is seen not only in ancient plant and practices, but also in the widespread belief that 'new technology' can solve almost any problem. Newspapers have a closely related circulation goal—the sales figure is seen by everyone, including journalists, as the single key indicator. Related to this is the advertising revenue goal; and, as Graham Cleverley has argued, selling advertising can become a goal so blindly pursued that whether it is profitable becomes a minor consideration.[8] Finally there is the general prestige goal. Some forms of journalism are aligned with one goal, others with other goals. Politics aligns with the prestige goal, subjects like fashions and motoring with the advertising goal, while subjects of ever faithful audience appeal—like crime and sport—align with the circulation goal.[9] These various goals combine together into a mixture of goals, and most battles within newspapers are to do with defining what exactly the mixture of goals is or how it should be altered.

Functionalism, Marxism and Ambiguity

Britain now has a daily press which is social class polarised to an extent probably greater than that in any other major industrial nation. Japan's newspapers, which are similarly nationally dominated are not similarly class stratified. The dominant press medium in most other industrial countries is a provincial daily press which appeals across a broad social class spectrum.

Secondly, Britain now also is an extreme example of a country whose press is predominately owned by conglomerate and multi-national companies whose main profits and concerns are in other industries. Britain has since 1960 become the leading example in the world of a pattern of ownership previously found in inter-war Germany and France and in more recent times in Latin-America and Italy.[10]

In 1960 it would have been difficult to make the case that the British press was an Ideological State Apparatus. However, the empirical facts have come much more into line with what would previously have been a Marxist caricature; this is especially so in the case of British press involvement with the international oil industry—since oil, of couse, is an industry where the state is directly and commercially involved with multi-national companies. Almost any Marxist critique of the British press would presumably assert that it is mainly under cartel control with the bulk of press profits being monopoly profits, that big business has bought up the British press in order to silence radical criticism and to control the national polictical agenda, that the affluent readers of London prestige papers like *The Times* are subsidised by working class readers of monopoly provincial papers, and the present national tabloid sales war is an illustration not only of the manufacture of false consciousness but also of the inherently self-destructive tendencies of capitalism.

The present state of the British press could, however, also be quite easily explained in functional terms. Talcott Parsons has indeed used the analogy of the commercial market in a basically optimistic view of the United States media. Parsons could point to the undoubted element of *competition* both between and within press and television in Britain. The expansion of the prestige press (and its underpinning of advertising) in recent decades can be seen as broadly benign; and while the tabloid sales war may be deplored, these papers can also be seen as relatively harmless products of mass culture which reflect the realities of popular taste, and which in any case are now only support-media to the main working class medium in Britain—the world's least worst television. As to the ownership of the press by oil companies, conglomerates and multi-nationals—this can be seen as a genuinely public-spirited act whose very overtness and obvious potential for corrupt self-interest is more likely to lead to exaggerated probity and an unusual degree of autonomy for journalists.

Marxists and functionalists can often agree on the facts. Ambiguity is especially common in the mass media content; indeed news values represent deliberate ambiguity—such as the preference for 'two sides' reporting which allows for selective audience perception, or the personality news canon which favours the building up of public figures as a preliminary to knocking them down. Thus it should not be too surprising that radically different interpretations can be attached to events in the press industry itself.

The City University, London

[1] Based on Advertising Association annual estimates.

[2] 41 per 100 population in 1976 against 39 per 100 in 1930.

[3] Alan Lee: *The Origins of the Popular Press, 1855-1914*, Croom Helm, London, 1976, p. 286.

[4] Political and Economic Planning: *Report on the British Press, P.E.P., London, 1938, pp. 59-60*

[5] J. E. Gerald: *The British Press under Government Economic Controls*, University of Minnesota Press, 1956, p. 34.

[6] op. cit. pp. 47-49.

[7] James Curran: 'The Impact of Television on the Audience for National Newspapers' in Jeremy Tunstall (ed.): *Media Sociology*, Constable, London, 1970, pp. 104-131

[8] Graham Cleverley: *The Fleet Street Disaster*, Constable, London, 1976

[9] Jeremy Tunstall: *Journalists at Work*, Constable, London, 1971.

[10] Jeremy Tunstall: *The Media Are American*, Constable, London, 1977.

Haluk Sahin and John P. Robinson examine time-use diary data in the United States and elsewhere. They note that U.S. time use in the recent past shows declines in the amount of time devoted to work, but this time, from "the realm of necessity," has been "colonized" by increased attention to television and not devoted to other leisure pursuits. Haluk Sahin is associate professor of journalism and John Robinson is professor of sociology and director of the Survey Research Center. Both are at the University of Maryland.

27

BEYOND THE REALM OF NECESSITY

Television and the Colonization of Leisure

Haluk Sahin and John P. Robinson

For ancient Greeks as well as the Romans, Sebastian De Grazia (1962: 4) has noted, the word for work was un-leisure. Leisure was the ideal state, the means to free creativity and wisdom. Work, on the other hand, was a distraction, a mundane activity better left to slaves.

In a much changed, non-slave holding world, a millenium and a half later, Adam Smith also defined leisure as man's ideal state of being. At the same time, he observed that free time was no longer *free*; the time a person devoted to work would have to be considered a price to be deducted from leisure (Avineri, 1970: 103–104). For political economy, generally, the distinction between work and leisure was quite clear-cut: labor was coercive activity, while leisure was its opposite, i.e. free and spontaneous.

Marx, refusing to see direct labor time as in the abstract antithesis to free time (Marx, 1973: 712), took issue with this categorization, arguing that labor was not naturally coercive but only appeared so because of the historical conditions under which is was performed. For Marx, the question was 'whether the work serves man as a mere means of existence or becomes the very contents of his life' (Avineri, 1970: 104). While criticizing the imposition of a coercion/spontaneity dualism between labor and leisure, Marx himself spoke of a similar division. In a rather sweeping statement, he proposed that 'in all social formations and under all possible modes of production', human activity would be comprised of a 'realm of necessity' and a 'realm of freedom'. The realm of necessity encompassed 'actual material production', the kind of labor 'which is determined by necessity and mundane considerations . . . to satisfy (man's) wants, to maintain and reproduce life'.

Marx delineated the two realms as follows:

With (man's) development, this realm of physical necessity expands as a result of his wants; but, at the same time, the forces of production which satisfy these wants also increase. Freedom in this field can consist in socialized man, the associated producers, rationally regulating their interchange with Nature, bringing it under their common control, instead of being ruled by it as by the blind forces of Nature; and achieving this with the least expenditure of energy and under conditions most favorable to, and worthy of their human nature. But it nonetheless remains a realm of necessity. *Beyond it begins that development of human energy which is an end in itself, the true realm of freedom* . . . The shortening of the working day as its basic prerequisite. (our emphasis) (Marx, 1966: 799–800).

From Haluk Sahin and John P. Robinson, "Beyond the Realm of Necessity: Television and the Colonization of Leisure," *Media, Culture and Society* 3, 1 (January 1981), pp. 85-95. Copyright © 1981 by Academic Press Inc. (London) Ltd. Reprinted by permission of the publisher and authors.

It is obvious from this passage that Marx attributed great significance to free time as the domain in which human creative potential could be liberated from the compulsions and requirements of existential needs and realized 'as an end in itself'. Elsewhere, he spoke of free time as 'time for the full development of the individual' (Marx, 1973: 711) and 'room for the development of the individual's full productive forces, hence those of society' (p. 708).

Marx did not, as can be seen from the above quote, envisage total liberation from the realm of necessity. He offered a scenario in which, with the development of technology and rational organization of production, the boundaries of this realm could be pushed back while the temporal territory of the realm of freedom expanded. He proposed a practical yardstick for measuring its scope: the length of time spent at work.

The total use of time

While time spent at work remains a meaningful indicator of the realm of necessity, it is hardly comprehensive enough to gauge the full extent of the time available for leisure. New and different kinds of demands have been placed upon the allocation of daily time as a result of the bureaucratization and impersonalization of social contacts within the urbanized and suburbanized spatial arrangements of industrial societies. This has led to empirical attempts to look at the totality of uses to which time is put in society.

How can one best examine the totality of time use? Henri Levebvre (1971: 53), for instance, has argued that the category of *compulsive time* ('the various demands other than work such as transport, official formalities, etc.') has to be added to the categories of pledged time ('professional work') before arriving at a residual time free for leisure. In Levebvre's view, compulsive time has been increasing at a faster rate than free time over the last few decades. Social scientists have introduced further refinements to clarify the concept and measurement of free time by subdividing it into its active and passive components, or its self *vs.* other orientation (e.g., DeGrazia, 1962; Szalai *et al.*, 1972). Whatever the measure, comparative time use information clearly show that the amount of time 'spared' from work in industrialized societies has generally increased since the beginning of the century, not only as manifested in the shortening of the work day or the work week, but by the lengthening of vacations and holidays as well as other kinds of paid leaves of absence.

Whether such temporal 'emancipation' has been used for the purpose of 'the full development of the individual', is a more dubious proposition. The expansion of free time has been accompanied by a large scale technological revolution which has transformed the world of free time as substantially as the technology of the Industrial Revolution transformed the world of work. In the process, and often in the name of the very forces that are in control of the realm of necessity, 'freed' time has been increasingly colonized by new technologies—the movies, radio, the phonograph, the tape recorder, and other stereo sound systems. With the large scale introduction of a new generation of technologies—cable, videotext, videotape recorders, video discs, electronic games, home computers, and computer games—the potential incursion of the technology of leisure into everyday life looms even larger. By far the most powerful colonizer of free time, however, has been the technology of television (Robinson, 1969). In very different socio-political and cultural environments, television has not only usurped time formerly spent on existing forms of mass media (particularly movies and radio), but taken time from other free time and compulsive time activities (Robinson and Converse, 1972). That seems true of no other technology of the twentieth century, including the automobile. The automobile may have reshaped the spatial landscapes of industrialized societies, but it is television that has revolutionized our temporal landscape (Robinson, 1977).

The purpose of this article is to examine the temporal structure of every day life in the United States and especially of the stretch that lies 'beyond the realm of necessity', and to elaborate on the uniquely expansionary rôle that television has assumed as a colonizer of free time in the daily lives of Americans. Without denying the importance of the ideological nexus, the article focuses on television as a time 'consumer' rather than as an ideological conduit. Although we touch upon some of the 'subjective' evaluations attached to manifold allocations of time, our primary concern is the objective structure of time use. Implicit in this approach is the contention that the observed regularities of time use not only make up the structure of daily life, but often become the very contents of it by setting priorities, imposing constraints, and establishing guiding patterns in the use of the precious personal and social resource of free time.

Earlier studies of time use

The first concerns about time use and its 'scientific' study originated in the realm of necessity. Marx himself noted that every economy is an economy of time (Garnham, 1979: 126). Early studies of time use at work, first popularized by the original efficiency expert Frederick Taylor at the beginning of the century, aimed at increasing the productivity of labor power by gaining greater control over how work was to be performed. As such, this development was another step in 'the displacement of labor as the subjective element of the (productive) processes, and its subordination to an objective element'. (Braverman, 1974: 173). The prime instrument of Taylor's time studies was the stop-watch. Frank B. Gilbreth, a student of Taylor, added the dimension of 'motion' to 'time' study. From these beginnings evolved elaborate techniques and instruments for engineering the 'human factor' in the work design.

Time-use consciousness generated by Taylorism in industrial societies soon extended into non-work time. One of the earliest sociological undertakings of this nature was a study done in Britain, aptly called *How Working Men Spend Their Spare Time* (Bevan, 1913). Similar work was carried out in the United States by sociologists, laying the groundwork for the quantitative study of time. (Lundberg *et al.*, 1934; Sorokin and Berger, 1939). Theoretical attention gradually shifted from the 'spare time' orientation to a return of the view of leisure as an end in itself by the 1950s. Many social observers saw in more creative uses of free time a potential counterweight against the standardized, engineered, and dehumanizing aspects of modern industrial work in capitalist societies. Just as time-and-motion studies in the work place were concerned about wasted time at work, leisure time studies were concerned about how the masses were squandering their free time in pursuit of unworthy activities (Riesman, 1953; DeGrazia, 1962).

The time diary

Among empirical researchers, the 'time diary' gained acceptance as the optimal way of studying time use (Converse, 1969). A time diary is an all-inclusive instrument, providing a complete accounting of daily activity for the 24 hours of the day or the 168 hours of the week. Rather than depending on the frailties of human memory in asking for estimates of how often (or how long) people have engaged in a particular activity, the diary method asks respondents to keep track of all their activities in sequence for a well-defined time period. The diary capitalizes on the fact that at any point in time 'everyone has to be somewhere'.

The diary is not without its shortcomings. Like content analysis which takes simple 'frequency of occurrence' as its basic unit of measurement, it tends to treat all time units as equal. This results in the following characterization from DeGrazia (1962):

A moment of awe in religion or ecstasy in love or orgasm in intercourse, a decisive blow to an enemy, relief in a sneeze, or death in a fall is treated as equal to a moment of riding on the bus, shovelling coal or raking leaves.

Such an unnatural levelling of time-use makes the collection of additional experiential data from respondents who keep diaries a necessary step before researchers can arrive at uneqivocal judgments about how well people are spending their time.

Nonetheless, time diaries collected from a large representative cross-section of individuals can provide a comprehensive framework for the analysis of all societal activity. Hence, this method has attracted a broad clientele of users both in the East and the West and has been utilized in a variety of ways. In the Eastern European countries where the methodology has been most widely developed, it has been used as a central tool in short-run planning. For instance, examinations of the time that working women need to spend washing clothes (and other forms of household production) has led some countries to increase their production quotas for washing machines or other household technology.

In the West, time-diary data have been mainly focused on the use of leisure for the media with the BBC in Britain and NHK in Japan being the major collectors of such data for audience research purposes. The first BBC time-use research goes back to 1939, and much of it was apparently used for wartime planning (Gershuny and Thomas, 1979). However, with the increased attention to the impact of the entry of women into the paid labor force in the last decade, Western economists have needed time-diary data to value the resulting loss of household production for the national economy. Other researchers interested in the micro-economics of the household have examined the implications of the time that parents from various social classes 'invest' in their children.

The most ambitious time-diary study done to date is the 1965–66 Multinational Time Use Study. For this study, researchers collected parallel diary data from residents of urban cities in 12 socialist as well as capitalist countries. The findings were reported in an encyclopedic work, *The Use of Time* (Szalai *et al.*, 1972). While this study did find substantial differences in the amount of free time available across societies, there were very predictable East–West *patterns* of how that free time was used.

No directly comparable cross-national time-diary studies have been conducted since 1965–66. However, both the NHK (in 1970 and 1975) and the BBC (in 1974–75) replicated their earlier data collections. The same was true in the United States, where in 1975–76 the Survey Research Center of the University of Michigan replicated its portion of the multinational collaboration of a decade earlier.

Television and changes in time use

These studies clearly indicate that television had increasingly consolidated its major thrust as a colonizer of 'freed' time across the late 1960s and early 1970s. This was especially the case for the American viewing data which rather than having reached an asymptote upon set saturation in the mid 1960s increased its share of daily activity (Robinson, 1977). While this was partly due to the increase of free time over the same decade, the expansive viewing was actually greater than the increases of total of all activities. In other words, the gains television has made as a consumer of time came as much at the expense of the realm of freedom as the realm of necessity.

Table 1. *Allocation of time in activities for persons aged 18–65 in American urban, non-farm households (in hours per week)*

	1965	1975	1965–75 change
Men in paid labor force	(N = 521)	(N = 332)	
Pledged time (work)	51.3	46.4	– 4.9
Compulsive time (household, etc.)	8.7	9.6	+ 0.9
Personal time (sleep, eat, etc.)	73.9	74.7	+ 0.8
Free time	34.1	37.3	+ 3.2
	168.0	168.0	
Women in paid labor force	(N = 342)	(N = 225)	
Pledged time	39.0	34.3	– 4.7
Compulsive time	25.4	20.8	+ 4.6
Personal time	74.3	78.8	+ 4.5
Free time	29.3	34.1	+ 4.8
	168.0	168.0	
Married women not in paid labor force	(N = 341)	(N = 141)	
Pledged time	0.5	1.1	+ 0.6
Compulsive time	50.0	44.3	– 5.7
Personal time	76.5	78.2	+ 1.7
Free time	41.0	44.4	+ 3.4
	168.0	168.0	

Table 1 shows the general shifts in time use that occurred over the 1965–1975 decade. It shows these shifts separately for the four categories of time and separately for employed men, for employed women and for women not in the paid labor force since the three groups vary widely in their uses of time. Contrary to US government estimate figures and the conventional wisdom, Table 1 first shows a declining trend in average paid work time—*for both men and women*. While more women were in the labor market in 1975, they performed more paid work in 1975 than they did in 1965. However, the average amount of work time for those women who were employed declined 4.7 hours per week; this was only slightly lower than the 4.9 hour per week decline for men. It should be noted that these average figures may be misleading in that those women who were likely to be part of the paid labor force in the 1970s were disproportionately recruited from the ranks of women who worked fewer hours. In other words, more part-time women may have joined the labor force in the 1970s bringing down the average work week for all women.

What is additionally interesting, however, is that working women also reported a 4.6 hour decline in compulsive (mainly unpaid household) work as well. Here they were joined by full-time homemakers who reported a 5.7 hour decline (from 50.0 to 44.3 hours per week). Men, on the other hand, reported a slight increase of almost an hour a week in such family care activity. Thus, it was the case that married men did spend proportionally more time doing total housework in the 1970s, although the major reason for the increase was the decline in their wives' household productive time.

Table 1 goes on to show that some of this decreased work and housework activity time was used for personal care activities for both men and women. However, most of the decrease was shifted into increased free time activities. This was the first data

Table 2. *1965–1975 differences in Americans' use of free time (in minutes per day)*

	1965	1975	1965–75 change
Men in paid labor force			
Organizations	23	31	+ 8
Social life	71	72	+ 1
Recreation	21	25	+ 4
Television	99	131	+ 32
Other media	45	28	– 17
Other (rest, travel, etc.)	37	40	+ 3
Total	296	332	+ 36
Women in paid labor force			
Organizations	18	12	– 6
Social life	81	73	– 8
Recreation	18	17	– 1
Television	62	99	+ 37
Other media	31	30	– 1
Other (rest, travel, etc.)	44	61	+ 17
Total	254	292	+ 38
Women not in paid labor force			
Organizations	27	33	+ 6
Social life	106	93	– 13
Recreation	28	35	+ 7
Television	96	157	+ 61
Other media	41	31	– 10
Other (rest, travel, etc.)	51	38	– 13
Total	349	387	+ 38

to suggest that Americans were enjoying any increase in free time during work week since the end of World War II.

How was their increased free time being used? The more specific free time activities are broken down in Table 2. According to most models of 'post-industrial' society or 'self-actualizing era' into which the US is presumably been moving (Bell, 1976; Reich, 1971), one would have expected the increased free time to be devoted to educational or organizational activity, or to increased participation in cultural participation and appreciation, or to increased physical fitness or training. Contrary to such characterizations, however, practically the entire increase in available free time in Table 2 was directed toward the television set. The change in other categories of free time activities was minimal or negative for both men and women, with significant drops in time devoted to other media in the case of men in the paid labor force and women not in the paid labor force. With the increased time devoted to television (and to resting and sleep), Tables 1 and 2 suggest the US had entered a post-industri*ous* instead of a post-industri*al* age (Robinson, 1979).

Some might attribute this increase in television viewing to improved technology and the greater selection of programs for viewing. It was clear, for example, that people with color television sets watched significantly more than those without color and the proportion of households with color rose from under 10% in the mid 1960s to almost 70% in the mid 1970s. Somewhat greater viewing was also reported in 'non-prime-time' hours for which there was expanded programming in the 1970, involving a new form of colonization. On the other hand, the availability of greater selection through cable television was not associated with significantly greater viewing. Thus, improved technology and greater choice was responsible for some of the increases of TV viewing, but not all of it. Perhaps the more relevant answers lay in the flexibility of television viewing as a free time 'activity' and various meanings and values attached to it within the overall context of the American system of broadcasting.

The increasingly pervasive and expansive features of television viewing are quite evident in time diary figures from the two years. As Table 2 shows, television has been practically the sole beneficiary of people's increased free time over the decade. Although most socio-economic differences in viewing patterns persisted in the 1970s, television's gains were found in all social groups. On the whole, the trend has been in the direction of levelling of past differences and convergence towards truly *mass* viewing.

One relatively important social disparity that endured, although again much less prominently, was the amount of viewing reported by groups with different levels of formal/completed education. Thus, adult respondents who had not completed their high school education reported almost 40% more viewing in their diaries than respondents who had completed a college degree. This reported time usage is generally in line with the evaluations people of different educational levels in the United States attach to television viewing as an activity. Whether one asks directly how much satisfaction viewers themselves derive from television (as was done in this 1975 national study) or how satisfied viewers are with the programs offered on television with the amount of time they watch television, people with less education rate television higher than people with more education.

As shown in Table 3, we can see that television is still not rated as a particularly enjoyable way of spending time. This is the case even among the less educated. The average satisfaction rating for television was also below average for most non-leisure

Table 3. *Average ratings of enjoyment/satisfaction for obligatory and free time activities*

	1975–76 ($N = 1640$) Enjoyment	
	Men	Women
Work	8.1 +	7.8 +
Cleaning house	4.8 –	5.9 –
Cooking	4.8 –	5.9 –
Household repairs	4.8 –	7.1 –
Gardening	6.3	4.4 –
Child care	8.5 +	9.1 +
Grocery shopping	3.9 –	4.8 –
Non-grocery shopping	4.4 –	6.7
Organizations	4.7 –	4.9 –
Religion	6.3	7.6
Entertainment out	6.6	6.5
Visiting, socializing	8.2 +	8.3 +
Sports/games	7.1	6.3
Television	6.3	5.9 –
Reading newspapers	7.1	6.9
Reading books/magazines	6.9	7.7
Trips/outings	7.8	8.3 +

* Respondents were asked to rate each activity on a scale from 0 (dislike a great deal) to 10 (enjoy a great deal).

  – Denotes lower than average for that group.

  + Denotes higher than average for that group.

activities, with cleaning house and shopping being the two main exceptions. Moreover, only one other free time activity in Table 3 (organizational participation) was rated lower than television. Reading, evenings out, recreational activities and religion and socializing were all rated as much more enjoyable ways of spending time. Social visiting was in fact rated at the top of the list of enjoyable activities, a point we will return to shortly.

Further insight into the human meaning of television as an everyday activity comes from the other everyday activities with which it is correlated. Because of the 'zero-sum' nature of time, the more time spent on one activity (such as television), the less must necessarily be spent on other activities. Hence, television time is generally correlated negatively with time on other activities, particularly the necessary activities of work and personal care. However, it is most negatively correlated with certain free time activities—socializing, free time travel, going to bars and parties, and religion. It will be noted that these are activities that usually occur away from one's home.

This suggests that once one is home, the television set becomes a more irresistable technology of time consumption. It does not appear to be in real competition with other media activities. An interesting finding was the *positive* correlation between television time and sleep time. Together with the low negative correlation of resting and relaxing, this suggests a distinctly sedentary character to television as an 'activity'.

This interpretation is reinforced by the persistent correlation between television viewing time and another subjective aspect of the usage of time. That question had to do with how much a person felt 'rushed' to complete everyday activities, and people who felt rushed spent much less time watching television. To be sure people who felt rushed did have less free time available to watch television. But even controlling for the actual free time that the person had available, the perception of being rushed was related to less viewing. In other words, it was as true that viewing and being rushed were related among people with under 25 hours a week of free time as among people with over 50 hours a week of free time.

This picture of television viewing as a residual 'sink' of time not usable for other purposes is further reinforced by one final set of questions asked in these national surveys to indicate the 'elasticity' of time. When asked to examine their completed diaries of daily activities and to choose from them which blocks of activities during the day of the diary they would be most likely to give up 'if something really important came up', respondents overwhelmingly nominated their TV viewing as the first choice for replacement. Once again, viewing emerges as the most expendable or least important of daily activities.

People's answers to these various subjective questions then point to a somewhat convergent picture of the meaning of television viewing in everyday American life. What emerges is the picture of an activity that is not seen as either particularly enjoyable or necessary to one's daily life. If more important activities arise, it is easily the first activity to be sacrificed. Once people are in their homes, however, the set appears to have an irresistible hold on their time.

All of this suggests that Parkinson's (1957) famous law of general time expenditure for work in bureaucracies ('Work expands so as to fill the time available for its completion'), has spread to free time in the home. The analogue here appears to be 'television time expands so as to consume all time not otherwise committed at home'. The societal consequences of this law, however, may not be so whimsical. By people's own definition, television time is not an activity which brings people particular satisfaction or significance, especially in contrast to most person-to-person encounters that occur in free time. Yet, it is this very social life that people may increasingly be sacrificing for their increased time spent viewing.

The trend toward increased viewing is not uniquely American. As noted above, both the BBC and NHK data in the 1970s showed trends toward increased viewing as well. However, in both countries, there were parallel increases in other more active uses of free time to accompany increased viewing (Gershuny and Thomas, 1979).

Institutional mechanisms of colonization

Although work and free time may be defined as temporally separated, it is often very difficult to draw a sharp line between the two in other respects. By and large, the realm of necessity casts its shadow over the realm of freedom. Much free time must be spent either recuperating from or preparing for work. Just as many social activities engaged in during free time have ramifications for work, many gratifications reportedly derived from television are directly or indirectly related to work gratifications (Blumler and Katz, 1974). The colonization of free time by commercial television, at least in the American context, represents a more direct incursion by the realm of necessity into the potential realm of freedom. In a sense, it amounts to the re-expropriation of the latter by the former.

The expansive push of television viewing as a time filler evidently characterizes other television-saturated societies besides the United States. Yet, it would be misleading to attribute this phenomenon solely to the properties of the medium or to argue that it invariably must serve the same ends everywhere. The specific form it has taken in the United States in particular is a function of the commercial American broadcasting system and various mechanisms and institutionalized practices that have evolved over the years within the framework of that system (Barnouw, 1975).

The rôle of the audience and the economic functions it performs in this system have already been investigated from both Marxist and non-Marxist viewpoints (Smythe, 1977; Owen, Beebe and Manning, 1974; Melody, 1973). Because it is the audience that is produced, marketed, and sold in the market as a commodity on a per thousand (CPM) basis, programming policy is almost totally directed towards the maximization of the aggregate audience or targeted audience groups in order that maximum profits can be realized. These market goals can be achieved by (a) acquiring new viewers by increasing the relative 'reach' (coverage area) of television broadcasts, or (b) increasing cumulative circulation (actual viewers) in areas already within 'reach', or (c) optimizing the time spent viewing television by the individual viewer. Of these, the first (relative reach) is at a virtual saturation point since practically everyone is potentially within reach (Comstock et al., 1978). Cumulative circulation offers a more expanded 'market' potential, but it is negligible given that viewing opportunity is determined by extraneous factors largely beyond the control of the broadcasting industry (Owen, Beebe and Manning, 1974).

Thus, the main viable alternative for the optimization of time spent viewing is the one that has the most elasticity, and one that allows the greatest amount of control by the broadcaster. The networks' struggle to keep the total viewing figures at the optimal level becomes more pronounced in the direction of each station competing for the largest possible share of the audience that is watching television at any given time. This requires a host of elaborate programming strategies and competitive maneuvers to grab and retain the largest chunk of the targeted audience for the longest period of time.

It is this economic rationale more than anything else that has made sequence or *flow* the main characteristic of television program planning (Williams, 1974). The 'flow' is planned in such a way that the sequence of programs parallel as closely as possible the temporal structure of daily life for the greatest number of people. This concern explains why program planners have indirectly been among the keenest students of time use. In planning the flow of viewing, discrete items are carefully interlinked so that they become inseparable parts of a larger whole. Programming tactics such as 'block programming', 'blunting', 'counter programming', and 'long forms' are designed to carry the audience through the flow for as long as possible. This means closing off possible exits, whetting appetites for what is yet to come, and transforming television viewing into a *continuous* experience.

In essence, the colonization of free time by television in the United States can be seen as another manifestation of the historical process in which free time has been turned into a commodity and re-expropriated by the forces in control of the realm of necessity. For the great majority of the people, free time has become time for television rather than 'time for higher activity', incorporating disciplined learning, practice, and exercise for the full development of the individual (Marx, 1973: 712). The extent of such colonization in other societies, specific forms it takes, functions it performs, and the institutionalized mechanisms and practices by means of which it is implemented call for diligent comparative study.

Bibliography

AVINERI. S. (1970). *The Social and Political Thought of Karl Marx*, London, Cambridge University Press

BARNOUW. E. (1975). *Tube of Plenty: The Evolution of American Television*, New York, Oxford University Press

BELL. D. (1976). *The Coming of the Post-Industrial Society*, New York, Basic Books

BEVAN. S. (1913). *How Working Men Spend Their Spare Time*, New York, Columbia

BLUMLER. J. G. and KATZ. E. (1974). *The Uses of Mass Communications: Current Perspectives on Gratifications Research*, Beverly Hills, California, Sage

BRAVERMAN. H. (1974). *Labor and Monopoly Capital*, New York, Monthly Review Press

COMSTOCK. G. *et al.* (1978). *Television and Human Behavior*, New York, Columbia

DEGRAZIA. S. (1962). *Of Time, Work and Leisure*, New York, Twentieth Century Fund

GARNHAM. N. (1979). Contribution to a political economy of mass-communication, *Media Culture and Society*, vol. 1, no. 2

GERSHUNY. J. and THOMAS. G. (1979). Changing patterns of time use, unpublished report, University of Sussex

LEVEBVRE. H. (1971). *Everyday Life in the Modern World*, New York, Harper and Row

LUNDBERG. G. *et al.* (1934). *Leisure: A Suburban Study*, New York, Columbia

MARX. K. (1966). *Capital*, vol. 3, Moscow

MARX. K. (1973). *Grundrisse*, New York, Vintage

MELODY. W. (1973). *Children's Television: The Economics of Exploitation*, New Haven, Yale

OWEN. B., BEEBE. J., and MANNING. W. Jr. (1974). *Television Economics*, Lexington, Massachusetts D. C. Health

PARKINSON. C. (1957). *Parkinson's Law*, New York, Ballantine

REICH. C. (1971). *The Greening of America*, New York, Bantam

RIESMAN. D. (1953). *The Lonely Crowd*, New York, Doubleday

ROBINSON. J. (1969), Television and leisure time: yesterday, today, and (maybe) tomorrow, *Public Opinion Quarterly*, vol. 33, Summer

ROBINSON. J. (1977). *How Americans Use Time*, New York, Praeger

ROBINSON. J. (1979). Toward a post-industrious society, *Public Opinion*, vol. 4, August/September

ROBINSON. J. and CONVERSE. P. (1972). Social change reflected in the use of time, in *The Human Meaning of Social Change*, New York, Russell Sage

SMYTHE. D. (1977). Communication: blindspot of Western Marxism, *Canadian Journal of Political and Social Theory*, vol. 1, no. 3

SOROKIN. P. and BERGER. C. (1939). *Time-Budgets of Human Behavior*, Cambridge, Harvard

SZALAI. A. *et al.* (1972). *The Use of Time*, The Hague, Mouton

WILLIAMS. R. (1974). *Television: Technology and Cultural Form*, New York, Schocken

In this essay, Simon Frith approaches leisure somewhat differently from the way other authors in this section have approached it. Taking punk rock music as a case study, Frith reviews contrasting theoretical approaches to popular-culture criticism, notably the contributions of theorists grounded in the Frankfurt School and those of followers of Walter Benjamin. His conclusion is that these contrasting approaches mirror a larger problem of contradiction in understanding the meaning of "consumption" in the study of leisure. Simon Frith is lecturer in sociology at Warwick University.

28

MUSIC FOR PLEASURE

Simon Frith

The recurring problem for cultural theorists is to relate general accounts of ideology to the structures of particular media: it is difficult, for example, to find much in studies of film or television that seems directly applicable to an assessment of the cultural significance of popular music. In this article I want to suggest that the formalism versus realism debate in film studies is relevant to the analysis of pop music, but that in looking at pop in this way we come up against a neglected concept, leisure, which is, in turn, important for the analysis of other media.

The question common to studies of all media – and at the heart of the formalism/realism dispute – concerns ideology. How do different media work ideologically? What are their ideological effects and how are they achieved? At issue here is the concept of signification: how do different media organise the meanings with which and on which they work?

'Realist' theories assume that media operate with some degree of transparency: media images represent reality as if through a window or in a mirror; they are ideological to the degree that they are false. This can be measured against non-ideological representations, against experience. The argument is common in the sociology of television: news programmes are examined for bias, for false descriptions (of industrial conflict, for example); light entertainment is examined for stereotypes, for false images (of women, blacks and so forth). The political question is posed in terms of why media distort reality, and the answer is found not in media forms (which are examined only to see how distortion works) but in their controllers. Television news is bad because it is controlled by bad people, people who, for whatever reason (professionalism, political interest) have an ideological axe to grind. There are different degrees of control – from straight censorship to the vague 'feel' that producers have for 'good television' – but all have the same ideological effect: the reproduction of a false account of how the capitalist world works. The way to change this media message is to seize the technical means of message production, to take over the machines. Ideology is a problem of content and control; the media simply communicate the knowledge that is fed into them.

'Formalist' theories concentrate, in contrast, on the formal means of signification. Their assumption is that media images don't reflect or copy reality but construct it. Media forms are structures of meaning which bind us to an ideological account of the world; the very notion that we can judge such accounts against experience is 'an ideological effect of the realist discourse'. This approach is common in film studies: films are read not as distorted pictures of an independent reality, but as complex constructions of

From Simon Frith, "Music for Pleasure," *Screen Education* 34 (1980), pp. 51-61. Reprinted by permission.

meaning which have 'a reality effect' – which makes us read them as if they were distorted pictures of an independent reality. The form has the same ideological effect whoever owns it. The political problem thus becomes not how to control a neutral process of production but how to read an ideological structure of signification; it is a question not of access, but of meaning. The ideological effect rests on the relationship between media texts and their readers.

The Problem of Pop

I have given a deliberately crude account of a familiar debate in order to emphasise the problems of applying its terms (routine, in more sophisticated forms, in discussions of literature, film, television, the press) to music.[1] There are obvious difficulties, for example, in describing musical texts in semiological terms: the theories of representation that film critics have taken from literary criticism aren't immediately available to music critics unless we reduce music to songs and songs to words. What does it mean to call a piece of music a 'classic realist text'? And, precisely because the content of music is not obvious, the question of the control of music is more confused than in, say, the politics of television. The state does seek to regulate musical communication – records are banned from radio, groups are banned from town halls – but this is a limited form of control (*Anarchy in the UK* was still a best seller) and, anyway, offence is almost always taken at the words involved. The Gang of Four, for example, were told to change the word 'rubbers' (contraceptives – a traditionally sensitive product for the BBC) to 'rubbish' in order to perform *At Home He's A Tourist* on *Top of the Pops*; the programme's producer had no other way of pinning down the subversiveness of the group's music.

It is difficult, then, to say how musical texts mean or represent, and it is difficult to isolate structures of musical creation or control. (Who owns the means of music making – the musicians? their record companies? broadcasters?) Music critics analyse pop not in terms of form and content but in terms of production and consumption: the argument is either that the ideological meaning of music lies in the way that it is commercially produced, in its commodity form; or that consumers create their own meanings out of the commodities on offer. Neither of these arguments is used in film and television studies, but the resulting disagreements do refer back to the aesthetic debates in Germany in the 1930's – the debates not about art and modernism, but about the mass media, about the political significance of cultural goods bought and sold in the market.[2]

The most convincing critique of mass culture is still that developed by the Frankfurt School. Adorno's was the original argument that the production of music as a commodity determines its cultural quality, that the standardisation of music is the source of its cultural effect. This subjection of creativity to commodity form (to 'capital discipline' in Horkheimer's words) was made possible, according to Adorno, by the technology of mass production, and he explained the popularity of mass music in psychological terms: the pleasure of mass culture is the pleasure of a particular kind of consumption – a passive, endlessly repeated confirmation of the world-as-

---

1 For a recent survey of the unresolved state of this debate in media politics (and for the inadequacy of its terms for music criticism) see Carl Gardner (ed) *Media, Politics and Culture* London, Macmillan 1979.
2 See Ernst Bloch et al *Aesthetics and Politics* London, NLB 1977 pp100-141.

it-is. The pleasure of art, in contrast, is the pleasure of imagination and involves an engagement with the world-as-it-could-be. This is a version of formalism. Adorno argued that the way a cultural text is produced (as a commodity) determines its significance. In particular, mass texts do their ideological work through their construction of an illusion of reality. Consumers 'experience' mass art as if they were grasping something for themselves but there is, in fact, no individual way into the construction of mass meaning. Subjectivity, in this context, means nothing more than market choice, and objectivity, the ability to evaluate mass culture, means nothing more than a mass of similar market choices.

The weakness of the argument lies in its account of consumption, its reduction of a complex social process to a psychological effect. Walter Benjamin's contrasting celebration of mechanical reproduction rested on the argument that because the artistic authority of cultural goods had been broken, their significance had become a matter of political dispute in which consumers did have a say: in the community of mass consumption everyone is an expert. The ideological significance of mass culture is determined, in other words, in the process of consumption itself. The grasping of particular works by particular audiences was, for Benjamin, a political rather than a psychological event; how such works got to the market was of less significance. Benjamin tended to treat the means of mass communication in technological terms, as ideologically neutral.[3]

Critical accounts of popular music still depend on the Adorno/Benjamin positions. Out of Adorno have come, however crudely, analyses of the economics of entertainment and descriptions of cultural imperialism, in which the ideological effect of commercial music making – the transformation of a creative people into a passive mass – is taken for granted. Out of Benjamin, however distantly, have come subcultural theories, descriptions of the struggle for the sign. Thus youth subcultures are said to make meanings out of records, products that have no cultural significance until they are consumed, until teenagers go to work on them.[4] These arguments are not just a matter of high theory. Adorno's analysis (mediated through Marcuse) has been important for music consumers themselves. The ideological separation of rock and pop in the Sixties rested on it. Pop was 'rubbish', 'escapist', 'vacuous' or whatever because it was 'commercial', because it was produced only for the money. Rock was superior (and potentially subversive) in as far as it was made for uncommercial reasons and remained true to the youth culture or artist's vision from which it came. The crucial struggle for Sixties rock fans was between music and money, between music as art or folk culture and music as commodity.[5]

In retrospect, now that rock is big business, the counter-cultural critique of pop seems naïve and/or dishonest, but the point is that the terms of the critique remain dominant – Leon Rosselson criticises rock, for example, in just the same way that the early rock ideologues criticised pop. The problem evaded in this approach, from Adorno onwards, is that records, pop and rock, like all cultural products, embody both use and exchange value and their ideological significance can't be reduced to exchange value alone. This explains the continued confusions in rock criticism. Rock's commodity form can't be denied (it is not a folk music, Rosselson is right), but the problem

---

3 For a more extended discussion of Adorno, Benjamin and music see S Frith *The Sociology of Rock* London, Constable 1978 pp193-6.
4 For the former argument, left orthodoxy until very recently, see, for example, Leon Rosselson's piece in Gardner op cit. For a sophisticated version of the latter argument see Dick Hebdige *Sub-Culture* London, Methuen 1979.
5 I discuss this further in *The Sociology of Rock* pp196-202.

is to what extent its commercial function determines its cultural meaning. It is with reference to this problem that music theorists can learn from the formalist/realist debates in theoretical work on other media. The subcultural solution to the problem is, without such a reference, too vague. It asserts that meanings are created out of commodities, but does not make clear how free such creation can be – what are the limits of records not as commodities but as texts, as signification structures with rules and restrictions of their own? In answering this question, subcultural studies of youth have, unfortunately, focussed more on visual than on musical signs.

This is not to say that we can take theories of the text straight from film studies to music criticism. Textual analysis, as it stands, does make the value connection – the concept of the text refers both to exchange value (a text is the result of a process of production) and to use values (the mode of representation determines 'the pleasure of the text') – but the resulting accounts of meaning tend to be ahistorical (the text is abstracted from particular readings, given an eternal value), closed (the text is given a 'real meaning', a structure that determines even the variations of individual response), and asocial (the analogy is the reader and the book – textual consumption is taken to be the interpellation of an individual [male] subject). These limitations are particularly acute for musical analysis: musical texts are volatile, contradictory and collective in their effects. This partly accounts for the deadlock in the debate about rock as commodity: meanings change so fast that both sides seem always to be right. Thus the effect of the Sex Pistols moved rapidly from shock to nostalgia; different listeners (radio programmers or youth subcultures, for example) use the same music for quite different ends; the same record can be consumed socially (as dance music) and individually (as a market choice). The meaning of musical consumption is, obviously, the result of a complex ideological process in which the significance of the text – a particular organisation of sounds – is neither static nor determinant. The textual approach, at least as it exists in film studies, lacks a convincing theory of use value, an explanation of why people like to be entertained and how they choose between entertainments. The meaning of consumption is still made to rest on psychological categories, on a biological description of human nature, on a theory of a single form of (sexual) pleasure. Something else is needed – which is where the concept of leisure comes in. But I can make this argument more clearly by applying it to recent musical history, to punk rock.

The Case of Punk

Punk is particularly important for this discussion because of its effect on cultural theorists. Before punk, popular music was rarely a matter of theoretical concern, and among organised socialists the line, in as far as there was one, tended towards folk purism. Within a few months of its public emergence in 1977, though, virtually every left paper agreed that Punk was a Good Thing. There were no doubts that it had transformed pop: it was credited with the success of Rock Against Racism and the Anti-Nazi League carnivals and, in general terms, it was argued that popular music was now being made, heard and discussed in new ways. Punk took on this extraordinary significance because it seemed to focus three different arguments.

The first was about the *audience*: punk was seen as a folk music and as a subcultural movement. The music was thus taken to represent or symbolise class consciousness – the consciousness of working class youth. The second concerned the problem of *commodity production*, in that punk seemed to challenge capitalist control of mass music. There was an emphasis on do-it-yourself, on seizing the technical means of music production. Finally, it raised questions about *meaning*, about how music works; punk seemed to involve new sounds, new forms, new texts. By combining these positions, punk was able to ease the doubts of at least some of rock's previous critics. It seemed to be different from previous mass music in terms of how it was made *and* how it was used *and* how it meant. Now, three years later, it is possible to examine the implications of these assumptions in more detail.

PUNK AS FOLK   The political argument that punk represented working class youth consciousness contained strong elements of opportunism – cultural politics often seemed to mean adopting youth styles in order to attract young people to adult issues; this was certainly an element in RAR's strategy. More important here, though, was the way that the argument drew on subcultural theory. The music was taken to articulate the values of the punk subculture and these, in turn, were read as a form of working class consciousness – 'an oblique challenge to hegemony' in Dick Hebdige's words. In many ways the punks' music, their essentially masculine styles, were not much of a departure from rock'n'roll tradition: class consciousness here meant a new variation of the established gestures of teenage bravado (gestures originally developed by teds, mods, skins and the rest). Indeed, the punk-as-folk position had to take on board an embarrassing amount of 'spontaneous' sexism and racism. The achievement of RAR in recruiting punks to the anti-racist struggle can't be over-estimated, because this was a matter of hard ideological work – RAR did not reflect some given punk consciousness. The political contradictions of punk ideology are obvious in Julie Burchill and Tony Parsons' *The Boy Looked At Johnny*: the book contained a dedication to Menachim Begin, for example, which the publishers – symptomatically, Pluto Press – felt bound to disclaim.

The left argument was that punk was a stage in the movement from class consciousness to class political consciousness: this depended on a description of punk as rank and file music, the direct expression of the way things were – a kind of realism. But even in terms of reflection theory, punk as spontaneous expression of lived experience, the argument did not make a lot of sense. The pioneering punk rockers themselves were a self-conscious, artful lot with a good understanding of both rock tradition and populist cliché; the music no more reflected directly back onto conditions in the dole queue than it emerged spontaneously from them. The musical 'realism' of punk was an effect of formal conventions, of a particular combination of sounds; more precisely, it was defined through its aural opposition to the 'unrealism' of mainstream pop and rock. The real/unreal distinction played on a series of musical connotations – ugly versus pretty, harsh versus soothing, 'raw' (lyrics constructed around simple syllables, a three-chord lack of technique, a 'primitive' beat) versus 'cooked' (rock 'poetry', virtuosity, technical complexity). These new conventions in fact drew on well known rock 'n'roll signs – often established within the original American garage band meaning of punk rock – but they now took on a rather different currency.

This shift was to a large extent achieved by the punk fanzines, which themselves had their stylistic origins (or at least parallels) in Andy Warhol's *Interview* magazine – the same 'artless' reproduction of every word spoken, the same sense of slapped together necessity, the same effect of realism as sly style.

Most of the left converts simply ignored these histories and rejected any suggestion that punk reality was *constructed*. Punk for them was simply a transparent image of a real youth condition. But even in its own terms, their account was unconvincing in that it had no basis in an independent analysis of that reality. As a result, the relationship between youth culture and youth politics, between punk ideology and socialist practice, remained extremely unclear. In this it proved even less politically developed than the attempt by the Weathermen to incorporate American street youth (and its musical tastes) into a political organisation, the RYM (Revolutionary Youth Movement), during the late Sixties. Their argument had involved two assumptions: that young people, from draftees to students, were similarly *exploited* because American capital faced a crisis of overproduction, and were similarly *oppressed* by the force of the State, whether in the army, in the classroom or on the streets.[6] Although the political strategy was a failure and the assumptions were wrong, the Weathermen did at least attempt to theorise youth mobilisation. The apologists of British punk a decade later made little attempt to analyse the effects of changing social conditions on youth, to tackle the political complexities of how (or whether) to organise punks or to understand the aesthetic conventions of the music. Based on unconsidered notions that punk described young people's reality and expressed their boredom and rage, their arguments involved not cultural analysis but a purely rhetorical optisism.

THE PROBLEM OF PRODUCTION   The punk argument about music production was drawn directly from debates in the Sixties. Punk opposed commercial music in two ways. First, it denounced multi-national record companies with a version of the assertion that 'small is beautiful' – punk music was, authentically, the product of small scale independent record and distribution companies. Secondly, punk demystified the production process itself – its message was that anyone can do it! The effect of this has been an astonishing expansion of local music making (for the results listen to John Peel's nightly show on Radio 1). In economic terms, then, punk is essentially petit-bourgeois. An important strand in its development has been a cultural version of consumerism, the idea is that record buyers have a right to maximum market choice, that record buying should involve customer expression rather than producer manipulation. Just as the hippie entrepreneurial spirit had found its expression in the shop-based Virgin Records a decade ago, so the most enterprising punk company – Rough Trade – is also, symptomatically, based on a shop. This consumerism has led to the creation of an 'alternative' production system that both parallels the established industry (alternative shops sell records made by alternative record companies and featured in the Alternative Charts) and is integrated into it. 'Independent' records, made by do-it-yourself companies, remain commodities.

---

6 For these arguments see 'You Don't Need To Be A Weatherman To Know Which Way The Wind Blows', the 1969 pamphlet reprinted in Harold Jacobs (ed) *Weathermen* San Francisco, Ramparts Press 1970.

Independence, in this context, seems to refer primarily to the question of artistic control (as in the Clash's anti-CBS records *Remote Control* and *Complete Control*). The punks, like hippie musicians before them, assume an opposition between art and business, between honesty and bureaucracy. This involves not only the Adorno argument about commodities, but also a romantic argument about creativity. Punk did not discuss the social relations of music production. Musicians were not seen as workers, as cultural employees akin to journalists, film technicians or actors: they were artists. Their music was progressive because it involved the direct expression of the people-as-artists; the punk task was to make everyone a star. Punk messages could be distorted by the process of commercial production, but only if this process was in the wrong hands (multi-national bureaucrats, boring old farts). This was the other side of punk realism and, again, the political problem is ownership. Punk truth could get through, but the means of music making had to be kept under control – by the musicians, by the kids.

THE PROBLEM OF MEANING   Although this was the most muddled strand in the argument, punk texts were clearly felt to challenge (by ridicule) pop and rock conventions of romance, beauty and ease: punk image (the safety pin) and sound (particularly of voices) had a shock effect. It soon became apparent, however, that punk was constricted by its realist claims, by its use of melodic structures and a rhythmic base which told-it-like-it-was *because* they followed rock'n'roll rules. The result of these limits to experiment was the emergence, after 1977, of a clear split: punk populism versus the punk avant-garde. The punk populists remain locked in their original position. They read teenage gestures and hear punk forms as the spontaneous expression of anti-hegemonic youth; they see the political problem as developing youth consciousness and preventing its symbols being commercialised. This is the standard left position: its clearest statements are in *Temporary Hoarding*, the RAR paper, where (usually adult) ideologists write in the populist punk style – not in reflection of a movement but in an attempt to sustain one. The punk avant-garde is more interested in musical meaning. These musicians (The Pop Group, Public Image Ltd, The Gang of Four, Scritti Politti, for example) expose textual structures in familiar ways (some of them have studied discourse theory) – by distancing themselves from their own performances and by juxtaposing terms from different genres (musical montages of rock/reggae/funk/improvisation). They undermine the populist assumptions of transparency, mocking the idea of a direct line from social experience to musical form, and expose the subjective claims deeply embedded in all rock music.

Music is a medium in which the expression of emotion, feeling and belief by performers can seem so direct (they talk straight at us) that powerful conventions of 'subjective realism', or truth to feeling, have developed. These are represented, most obviously, by the blues element in popular music – rock, for example, drew on both blues and post-Dylan singer/songwriting to develop its claims of authenticity, sincerity, depth of feeling and individuality. These terms were important for punk too; they lurk behind its realist claims, its subcultural theory and its struggle for artists' control. The avant-garde punks, in contrast, exploit 'artificial' muscial forms – pop, disco, synthesisers – and challenge their listeners to hear them without using the language of rock criticism, the terms of emotion, feeling, style. Meanwhile, the rock critics are still struggling to listen to the music of Public Image Ltd as a reflection of Johnny Rotten's 'abrasive personality'.[7]

It is therefore possible to see the contrast between avant-garde punk and traditional rock in the familiar cultural terms of the formalism/realism debate. In setting up the distinction like this, as a rock critic trying to make sense of post-punk rock texts, I am conscious of using the terms in a rather oversimplified and idiosyncratic way. 'Realism' is an especially difficult term here because in the analysis of other media (cinema, television, literature, the visual arts) it denotes both particular sets of practices within cultural production (genres) and also a mode of analysis based on an epistemological assertion about the relationship of 'text' to 'world'. The first sense doesn't apply in music – there are no classic realist musical texts – and so we have to think about the question of meaning without any of the usual critical shortcuts created by the ambivalence of 'realism'. It is in this muddled and undeveloped area that the punk avant-garde is working – along with, for example, certain schools of improvised music. Nevertheless, punk remains a commercial medium and my elevation of an 'avant-garde' is misleading – the problems of production (rock as commodity) and consumption (the rock audience) are unresolved by even the most 'objective' or 'deconstructed' musical text. The Gang of Four are still signed to EMI, for example, and they still have to work out what it means to be popular, to be consumed. Rock politics is never just a matter of meaning. This can be illustrated by one specific struggle, Rock Against Sexism, which involves three different problems. The first is the fight against sexist representation and stereotypes in rock – whether songs, images, journalism or album sleeves. This is really a question of education and propaganda, in which 'realist' assumptions are quite appropriate. Secondly, there is the need to encourage female musicians by providing places to play, gigs, contacts, workshops, and so on; this is a practical struggle in which the control of music-making institutions is a key issue. Thirdly, at the theoretical level, musical signification needs to be explored in the attempt to explain how sexual representations work musically. Although these are different forms of intervention into different forms of struggle, they are obviously related: theories of rock meaning can only be developed through rock practice, and rock practice involves a relationship between musicians and audiences in a particular cultural institution. The ideology of rock, in short, is determined not by its texts – musical forms don't have eternal sexual meanings – but by its context. Rock music is an aspect of leisure.

The Problem of Leisure

The concept of leisure provides another way of relating use and exchange value in the circulation of cultural goods and this approach has the great advantage of providing a historical and material account of needs and values. But it has been surprisingly little used by cultural theorists and it is worth making a simple point: the ideology of leisure in capitalist societies is that people (ie men) work in order to be able to enjoy their leisure – leisure is

---

7 The only rock paper critic to operate the anti-realist argument with any ease is the *New Musical Express*'s Ian Penman who draws (heavily, jokily, obscurely) on Foucault.

'free' time, when people (ie men) do what they want, realise their individual interests and abilities; even in Marxist accounts there is an assumption that leisure values are determined in a purely ideological struggle. But the freedom involved in this account of leisure is deceptive, and not only in ideological terms. Leisure is necessary for capital: it is the time when labour is replenished physically and culturally, re-creation time, and it is the time when workers consume, when surplus value is realised. 'Free' time is structured not only by ideas but also by material forces, by the availability of goods and resources, by the effects of the labour process on people's capacities and desires. Leisure involves a tension between choice and constraint; it is an aspect of the general relationship between production and consumption. Leisure, in other words, is an effect of capital accumulation and it is in this setting that the meaning of cultural goods has to be analysed. This argument has long been made by social historians, who have shown how the imposition of rational work discipline meant, necessarily, the imposition of a rational leisure discipline: traditional forms of release and riot became bound by the timed routines of the industrial labour process. It was these routines that constituted the meaning of modern leisure, and the issues discussed by historians of nineteenth century leisure remain important for the analysis of contemporary mass culture: it was then that leisure was established as a particular set of ideological and cultural relationships.[8]

The first point to make is that there is a permanent strain between the need to control leisure (hence all the licenses and licensing authorities) and the ideological importance of leisure as the time when people experience themselves as 'free' labourers – cultural conflict cannot be divided along simple class lines. Leisure commodities are not necessarily conductive to good order. Drink, for example, has been an issue of bourgeois dispite since Liberal manufacturers denounced Tory brewers, and a similar contradiction was obvious in the commercial exploitation of punk – private clubs put on the groups town halls banned, Virgin snapped up the Sex Pistols after EMI dropped them. As Marx noted, employers have quite different attitudes to their own workers, whose needs they attempt to limit, and to other people's, whose needs they attempt to extend.

Nineteenth century leisure was organised through two sorts of bourgeois enterprise. The moral entrepreneurs saw leisure as a means to the end of self-improvement. Leisure was treated as an educational institution: rational recreation was encouraged for its useful effects. The argument is well illustrated by Sir James Kay-Shuttleworth's enthusiasm for music instruction in elementary schools. Songs, he declared, were

'. . . an important means of forming an industrious, brave, loyal and religious working class. They might inspire cheerful views of industry and associate amusements . . . with duties.'[9]

This emphasis on the moral significance of leisure remains embodied in state policy – in the use of subsidies to support particular high art forms, for example. Nineteenth-century leisure was defined along moral lines for the bourgeoisie as much as for the labourer, and the assumption that middle class pleasures too must be functional lives on in the *Sunday Times* culture

---

8 This is discussed further in Tony Bennett's article on popular culture in this issue of *Screen Education*.
9 Quoted in P Bailey *Leisure and Class in Victorian England* London, RKP 1978 p46.

of joggers, gardeners and cooks. But the moral approach to leisure is complemented (and sometimes opposed) by commercial entrepreneurs churning out 'escapist' cultural commodities with reference not to their content but to their profitability. The logic of their production also puts a premium on order and routine, but through notions of professionalism, predictability and reduced commercial risk. Music hall proprietors weren't much interested in the morality of music, but they had their own concern for good order.

> 'It is one of the greatest nuisances possible to sensible people who go to places of amusement to divert their minds from politics and business alike to have the opinions of the daily papers reproduced in verse and flung at their heads by a music hall singer. Persons who go to a place of amusement to be amused, and these, we believe, form the steadily paying class, are too sensible to care to proclaim their private opinions by applauding mindless rubbish with a political meaning.'[10]

This is a familiar assertion; we hear it most often these days from radio programmers, still giving people what they *really* want.

Working class responses to the leisure provided contain their own contradictions. In working class radical traditions, leisure was equally a time for improvement, political education and disciplined consciousness. Socialists have been as much concerned to encourage the rational use of free time as bourgeois moralists (in the temperance movement, for example) and the socialist distinction between escapist and improving leisure, the socialist critiques of commercial play and 'light' entertainment, remain potent. They surface, for example, in the punk denunciation of disco as 'mindless' hedonism. There is a tension to between leisure as an individual activity (the realm of choice) and leisure as a collective activity (the realm of solidarity). State policies have always reflected a fear of public disorder – the dangers of dancing in the streets, class conspiracy, youthful anarchy. But the mass market depends on forms of collectivity, and leisure is crucially associated with the values of conviviality and comradeship. The public/private distinction has been mediated through the family: the home, as the refuge from work, has become an essential setting for most leisure consumption. Marx suggested that in capitalist social relations the worker 'feels himself at home only during his leisure', and the relationship works the other way round too – by the end of the nineteenth century workers were collecting household goods, going on family holidays and enjoying 'family entertainment'. The equation of leisure and home puts women in a double disadvantage: it is their labour which makes the home comfortable but they are excluded from the usual work/leisure distinction – women's pleasures, even more than men's, are confined to the household but this is, in fact, their place of work. The contradictions are obvious in, say, Radio 1's daytime programming – music to clean up and wash clothes by.

I have only had space here to skim the surface of the issues raised by studies of leisure, but the point I'm trying to make is that rock records aren't just commodities, they are *leisure* commodities. This is the context of their use value. To understand how leisure goods signify we have to refer them to the general meanings of leisure, meanings which have their own

---

10 *The Era*, trade paper of the licensed victuallers, November 28, 1885. Quoted in ibid p165.

processes of construction and dispute: the ideology of rock comes from a relationship between form *and* use. The pleasure of rock is not just a textual matter. It reflects those wider definitions of the leisure experience embodied in concepts like 'entertainment', 'relaxation' and 'fun', which themselves emerged from a complex cultural struggle and rest on a structure of sexual differentiation. This is the structure Rock Against Sexism has to take on. Even the simplest of rock categories – like dance music or party music – are redolent with social significance: dances and parties are historically and socially specific institutions and their ideological meanings – as breaks from work, settings for sexual contact, expressions of solidarity – are not only articulated by different types of music (disco, the Rolling Stones) but, simultaneously, determine those musics' ideological effects.

The meaning of leisure is, nevertheless, essentially contradictory. The use value of entertainment derives from its intimations of fun, irresponsibility and fulfilment – leisure is an implicit critique of work. The ideology of leisure has to strike a balance between freedom and order, and so the experience of freedom must be real (otherwise leisure goods would have no use) but not disruptive of work routines. Leisure must give pleasure, but not too much. Pleasure, in turn, is not just a psychological effect, but refers to a set of experiences rooted in the social relations of production. It is important to stress that there cannot yet be *a* theory of pleasure, if only because the concept refers to too disparate a set of events – individual and collective, active and passive, defined against different situations of displeasure/pain/reality. I am not convinced that all these experiences can be explained in terms of sexuality. And it is also in this context that the importance of the bohemian tradition in rock (as in cultural history generally) needs explaining: bohemians articulate a particular kind of leisure critique of the work ethic. They are cultural radicals not just as the source of the formalist avant-garde, but also in institutional terms.

The problem of cultural politics, in short, is not just to organise subcultural resistance, to infiltrate the means of cultural production and to open closed texts, but to do these things with reference to the contradictions that are necessarily built into cultural consumption. It is this concept of 'consumption' that remains, in cultural analysis, the most difficult to define. It is, indeed, a term in a number of quite different discourses. It may, in each case, refer to the same activity (although even this is unclear – would it mean buying a record or listening to it?) but the concept means different things according to the analytic frameworks involved: in Marxist economic theory it refers to a moment in the circulation of value, in recent literary and film theory it refers to a kind of pleasure, in historical sociology it refers to an institutional process. Cultural theories of consumption are left in a muddle – 'passive consumption', for example, is a term used by theorists of all persuasions but as a rhetorical rather than as a theoretical device. My point is that we have to clarify the different meanings of 'consumption' before we can use the term adequately in the analysis of ideology.

PART V

POLITICAL COMMUNICATION

One of the most productive hypotheses in the recent past, celebrating its tenth anniversary this year, is that of agenda-setting. Several selections are offered here commenting on it, and as was true of Volume 2, the offerings incorporate both research findings and critique of agenda-setting. As research in this area widens, skepticism of the pervasiveness of this function deepens, as Becker notes below.

However, mass communication research relevant to politics and public opinion is broader and more extensive than that which can be embraced within the agenda-setting hypothesis, and we have sought to represent that depth. The agenda-setting papers here, which may profitably be read with James Lemert's discussion in Part I of this volume, largely examine political media effects at the individual and aggregated-individual levels. Also represented here is a study by Chaffee and Choe where the unit of analysis becomes the time of voter decision in a political campaign, and, as they show, this unit becomes an important contingency in the likelihood of media influence on individuals.

At more macroscopic levels, Carlsson and his colleagues examine, employing time-series data, relationships between media presentations, economic conditions, and aggregate opinions, and Elliott argues for examination of cultural studies' concepts of ritual in explaining media presentation of news relating to threats to the social order. Finally, Blumler is concerned with development of a political philosophy for political broadcasting, one that pays attention both to recent research on mass communication effects on audiences and to research on how that broadcasting is produced.

An examination of relationships between social structure, public opinion, and media news and editorial opinion, this article suggests that in Sweden, public opinion, as indexed by support for the governing party, follows changes in social structure, as indexed by business demand for labor, and variations in editorial support for the government and number of newspaper lead articles critical of the government. Carlsson, Dahlberg, and Rosengren note that the economic indicators appear to be more direct and influential than press opinion. Gösta Carlsson is professor of macro-sociology at the Humanities and Social Sciences Research Council and the University of Stockholm; Alf Dahlberg is a research assistant and graduate student in the Department of Sociology, University of Lund; and Karl Erik Rosengren is associate professor at the University of Lund and a research fellow of the Swedish Council for Research in the Humanities and Social Sciences.

29

MASS MEDIA CONTENT, POLITICAL OPINIONS, AND SOCIAL CHANGE

Sweden, 1967-1974

Gösta Carlsson, Alf Dahlberg, and Karl Erik Rosengren

THE ROLE OF THE MASS MEDIA in connection with social change—a classic problem in the sociology of communication—has recently received increased attention among sociologists (for example, Katz and Szecskö, forthcoming). This chapter presents data on the interplay among changes in economic conditions, media content, and political opinion in Sweden during the years 1967-1974. The first section gives a theoretical background. The second section presents the data and methods used and relates them to the theoretical background. In the third section the main results are presented. The fourth and last section of the study offers a discussion of the results and some suggestions for future research in the area.

THEORETICAL BACKGROUND

For a long time mass communication research has been preoccupied with either the effects or the determinants and the more precise nature of individual mass media consumption (Liebert and Schwartzberg, 1977; Blumler and Katz, 1974). In both cases the perspective has been individualistic and the approach mainly cross-sectional. Use of the mass media has been related to hypothesized causes or consequences of that use, in or for the individuals under study. Perhaps the most important result of this type of research can be summarized as suggesting that the media act mainly as mediators and reinforcers of tendencies in society and within individuals.

From Gösta Carlsson, Alf Dahlberg, and Karl Erik Rosengren, "Mass Media Content, Political Opinions and Social Change: Sweden, 1967-1974," pp. 227-240 in Karl Erik Rosengren (ed.) *Advances in Content Analysis*, Sage Annual Reviews of Communication Research Vol. 9. Copyright © 1980 by Sage Publications, Inc.

Parallel to these broad research traditions, more or less sporadic attempts have been made to relate various aspects of media content, conceived as a macro phenomenon, directly with other macro phenomena, such as (changes in) crime rates, occupational trends, fertility, and so on (for instance, see Inglis, 1938; Davis, 1952; Middleton, 1960; Shaw, 1967; Funkhouser, 1973; Towers, 1977; Beniger, 1978). The variation necessary to establish a relationship has been obtained by means of time series data, rather than cross-sectional data. (The third possibility, regional or cross-national comparative research, seems to have been much less used; see, however, Brandner and Sistrunk, 1966). That is, instead of an individualistic perspective and a cross-sectional approach, research of this type has worked with a macro perspective and a longitudinal approach. We feel that more research of this type is needed if the problem of mass media and social change is to be better understood. (Innovative combinations of attitudinal data on a micro level with macro measurements of media content have been made by George Gerbner and Elisabeth Noelle-Neumann; see Gerbner et al., 1979, and Noelle-Neumann, 1977.)

A traditional formulation of the "mass media and social change" problem is the catchword "Molders or Mirrors?" (Brandner and Sistrunk, 1966), which suggests an either-or-approach: either media molds the social structure or the social structure determines the content of the media, so that media mirror society. Peterson (1976), treating the related but broader problem of culture and social structure, points to three rather than two possibilities: culture determines social structure (idealism); social structure determines culture (materialism); and culture and social structure are independent (autonomy). Rosengren (1978) presented four alternatives, ordered in a fourfold typology, which is applicable also to the relationship mass media content-social structure (Figure 11.1).

The typology of Figure 11.1, as can be seen, is highly abstract. It may call to mind various Marxian approaches, based upon the relationship between "base" and "superstructure." Within the Marxian tradition(s) few empirical investigations have actually been carried out in this area (see Williams, 1973). When it comes to empirical work, Figure 11.1 must be specified, conceptually and with respect to the time perspective.

The time perspective is very important in this connection. Social change may take place within days, weeks, months, years, decades, or centuries. The time scale, then, may vary with a factor of up to, for example, 100,000. It would be strange indeed if the relations between culture and social structure would be the same under those very different circumstances. It may well be that a relationship found to operate on a given time scale is not at all valid on another time scale, and vice versa (see Smith,

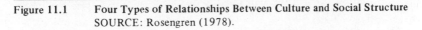

		Social structure influences culture	
		Yes	No
Culture influences social structure	Yes	Interdependence	Idealism
	No	Materialism	Autonomy

Figure 11.1   Four Types of Relationships Between Culture and Social Structure
SOURCE: Rosengren (1978).

1971). And in some cases of interdependence, the causal influence in one direction may be operating on a time scale completely different from the influence in the opposite direction. For instance, changes in social structure may affect almost immediately opinions in the population—or at least opinions among certain strata in the population—while opinion changes may affect social structure at least some aspects of social structure—only with considerable delay.

On the whole, grand theory on social change has tended to use a long time perspective, while empirical research has tended to use a short time perspective, sometimes very short indeed. The specific models demanded by the various time perspectives are all subsumable, in principle at least, under Figure 11.1. However, they may have to be rather differently structured—a difficulty which has not always been given sufficient attention.

The time perspective has other theoretical consequences as well. In a short time perspective it will seem questionable to think about relationships between base and superstructure as relationships between social structure and culture. As the time perspective narrows down to years or less, concepts like "changes in social structure" tend to be replaced by cyclical or random changes in the parameters of a social structure remaining basically the same. "Cultural change" tends to be replaced by more or less short-term fluctuations in beliefs and opinions.

METHODS AND DATA SOURCES

Our time perspective encompasses eight years. We focus on political opinions (as expressed by the population and in the press), influenced by economic changes of cyclical or quasi-cyclical character. Our main concern, then, is factors behind changes in political opinion, a problem which calls for a combination of intra- and extramedia data (Rosengren, 1979).

A natural starting point when studying the interplay among political opinion, mass media, and social structure is the political polls. In Sweden, political polls have been regularly undertaken since 1967. They are carried out by the leading Swedish polling institute, the SIFO, and sponsored by three leading newspapers. For each of the eight years under study, 1967-1974, they offer about 10 polls with a representative sample (random, weighted for missing data) of the Swedish electorate (approximately 1000 respondents).

During this period, Sweden had a one-party, social-democratic government. The opposition consisted of three bourgeois parties and one (small) communist party. The SIFO samples are asked to state their party preferences at the time of the interview; we will concentrate on the proportion favoring the government party (the Social Democrats), measured as a percentage of those expressing an opinion. The values are presented as straight averages of the polls falling within each quarter of the year. (The number of polls within each quarter varies somewhat because of the uneven time schedule of the SIFO.) These values represent our dependent variable: governmental support in the population. We have two groups of independent or intervening variables: social structure and media content.

Social structure could be measured in an infinite number of ways. We are interested mainly in economic variables which may be supposed to affect political opinion, and our final choice is managements' estimates of their need for labor in the immediate future. This need is tapped in regular surveys published quarterly as an integral part of the official system of economic analyses and forecasts. The larger the proportion who say they have a need for more people, the more favorable economic conditions are supposed to be. We will use the percentage of all firms questioned expressing a need for more unskilled labor. There is also another series not used here, on need for skilled labor. The two run parallel, and nothing seems to be gained by using both. Still other indicators could have been used, of course, but they present certain technical problems, such as breaks in the series.

It will be realized that our operational translation of "social structure" means locating the concept in the economic sphere. Furthermore, it has been stretched to cover cyclical or quasi-cyclical aspects of the economic machinery of the Swedish society rather than more or less basic changes of that machinery (see above).

Media content was measured by means of quantitative content analysis of "first-page news" and "first editorials" in a random sample of the

Swedish daily press, drawn for the purpose and weighted for circulation (ranging between some 1000 and some 600,000) and periodicity (from one to seven issues a week). The sample consists of some 1200 first-page news stories and 1200 first editorials drawn from about 1200 issues of the roughly 150 Swedish newspapers of the period—that is, about 40 news stories and 40 editorials for each of the 32 quarters studied. The newspapers were represented in the sample in proportion to their circulation (as semiofficially measured by the auditing company jointly owned by the organizations of the publishers and advertizers), and then randomly distributed over the calendar. Newspaper issues which did not appear on a day assigned to them were not included in the sample, a procedure which equals weighting for periodicity. Because of this procedure, not all Swedish newspapers are necessarily represented in the sample.

The coding was done by a graduate student of sociology specializing in content analysis. The newspaper issues sampled were coded in random order. Repeated tests of the reliability of the coding procedure were undertaken. The overall average intercoder reliability was 0.77.

The coding sheet was the same for editorials and first-page news. The leading ("first") editorial and the leading (biggest headline and similar signs of prominence) first-page news story in the sample issues were coded along some 30 variables, out of which half a dozen were elected for inspection. Our final choices were proportion of editorials with comments negative to the (Social-Democratic) government, and proportion of editorials expressing negative evaluations of the subject editorialized. (The intercoder reliability of the former variable was 0.95; of the latter, 0.70.) Substantively, the former variable is rather self-evident in this connection; the latter is less straightforward. Editorial evaluations of this type, of course, are not always partisan or political by nature. However, the point is that a high incidence of negative evaluations in the editorials of the daily press points to a general mood of pessimism, to a general feeling that conditions are getting worse, perhaps even running out of control.

These, then, are our four main variables: the state of the economy, governmental criticism in the press, general pessimism in the press, and governmental support in the population. The relationships hypothesized among the four variables are outlined in Figure 11.2. It will be seen that the relationships have been conceptualized as reciprocal. The reciprocity is subject to the restrictions imposed by the time scale used (see Section I above). Causal relationships symbolized by broken arrows are regarded as "slower" than those symbolized by full arrows.

The quarterly values of the four variables are given in Table 11.1. They will be analyzed in the next section of the paper.

TABLE 11.1   Main Variables: Quarterly Data

		% of firms needing more labor	% in favor of Soc. Dem. in polls	% of editorials critical of government	% of editorials pessimistic
1967	1	5	41.5	26	50
	2	6	42.5	18	39
	3	11	42.0	26	50
	4	9	42.3	26	56
1968	1	6	42.8	26	28
	2	9	44.5	22	32
	3	16	48.0	24	56
	4	16	51.2	18	56
1969	1	30	51.5	13	46
	2	39	51.5	17	39
	3	45	52.8	16	32
	4	43	52.3	16	42
1970	1	41	50.7	21	58
	2	42	50.0	30	64
	3	38	46.5	36	56
	4	22	44.0	19	49
1971	1	13	44.0	38	67
	2	12	43.0	17	67
	3	8	43.0	27	61
	4	5	42.5	37	58
1972	1	5	40.2	43	60
	2	11	39.0	26	51
	3	9	42.0	29	44
	4	9	41.7	32	37
1973	1	9	41.8	36	51
	2	14	40.5	22	47
	3	18	43.0	30	67
	4	16	41.5	27	49
1974	1	25	42.0	41	53
	2	28	43.5	17	43
	3	30	44.2	20	59
	4	21	44.8	15	42

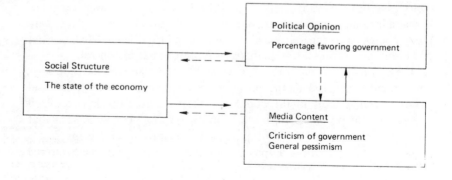

Figure 11.2   Hypothesized Relationships Between Variables under Study

RESULTS

The distribution of party sympathies according to opinion polls will here be regarded as response to events either directly felt by the public or transmitted through the media. We concentrate on the percentage favoring the Social Democratic government (see above). Figure 11.3 gives the time course of political opinion thus defined.

It is immediately striking that support for the Social Democrats oscillates in a smooth pattern, the celebrated "tides" of political life, or at least one manifestation of them. This is not an artifact due to the formation of quarterly averages, for the original series looks much the same. A convenient measure of the smoothness is the serial (auto-) correlations obtaining within the series. That is, pairs of observations are formed by taking the first and the second, the second and the third, and so forth for the serial correlation with lag 1. Similarly, the first and the third, the second and the fourth, the third and the fifth, and so on give the serial correlation for lag 2. With higher lags we proceed in an analogous manner. For 32 quarterly values the serial correlations with lags 1, 2, and 3 are 0.92, 0.79, and 0.62, respectively. A quasi-cyclical pattern, as shown by the opinion data in Figure 11.3, at the same time contains clues to the underlying forces and could obscure the true state of affairs. The series does not yield much information through direct inspection. It contains one marked peak, around 1969-1970, and a rise toward the end. This is more variability, and in that sense more information, than is contained in a series which is all trend, rising or declining. However, what we have is a far cry from 32 independent observations; rather, we have one or two swings.

There are principally two explanations of aggregate response of this type (Carlsson, 1965):

(1) Stimulus conditions likewise move smoothly with more or less identical oscillations.
(2) Response occurs with a nonnegligible degree of inertia to change in stimulus conditions.

With slow response—case 2 above—even a highly erratic, unordered series of stimulus changes could result in smooth response variations. The average length of the "cycles" will depend more on the speed of response than on the presence of any similar cycles in stimulus conditions. In that sense the response series might be quite misleading if we jump to a conclusion about underlying causes.

Let us begin, however, by looking at an explanation coming under case 1. Apart from the series of opinion data, Figure 11.3 also shows the ups

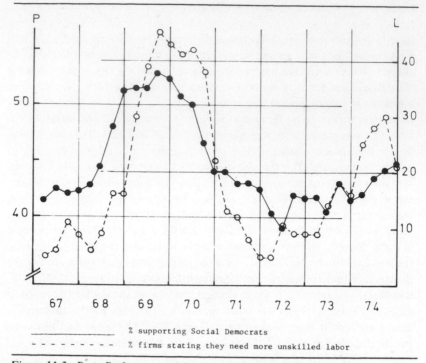

_____ % supporting Social Democrats
- - - - - - - - - % firms stating they need more unskilled labor

Figure 11.3 Party Preferences and Business Cycles 1967-1974

and downs of business conditions according to the indicator chosen, management's estimation of the need for unskilled labor in the immediate future (see above). One gets a strong impression of a close relationship between political opinion and business conditions. A period with ample job opportunities, according to the index, is also one of strong support for the governing party, the Social Democrats. Slump years, as 1971-1972, were also lean years for that party. In fact, the correlation between the two series for the 32 quarterly pairs of values 1967-1974 is + 0.79. One aspect of this is that opinion and election results (for the two generally agree closely) in the fall are predictable to some extent on the basis of business conditions in the late spring and early summer. Of course, a better predictor of later opinion is an earlier measurement of the same opinion, as witnessed by the high level of serial correlation within the series of poll data.

Seemingly, we are in the rare predicament of having succeeded all too well; not much remains to be explained about the tides of political sentiment. And it is not difficult to understand the relationship: the public holds the government (and the party it represents) responsible for bad times and gives it credit for prosperity. However, on second thought, the issue becomes a little less clear-cut.

As both response (governmental support in the population) and the alleged stimulus (economic conditions) are equally marked by a strong quasi-cyclical pattern of variation, there is much less evidence than first appears on which conclusions can be based. This fact has already been noted and need not be elaborated. Two wavelike phenomena presumably could be approximately in phase for a short period of time without any deeper significance.

Also, one would rather expect the economic series to be the leading one and the political series to lag. Of this there is little sign if the two curves are inspected; nor do correlations with lags introduced give much guidance. With the economic series leading by one-quarter, the correlation becomes + 0.68; with political data leading and the economic lagging, it is + 0.83, actually higher than before and suggesting a different kind of relationship between the two. Not much importance should be attached to these minor differences in correlation, based on rather few observations, but the possibility of alternative explanations needs to be kept in mind.

There is supporting evidence from other sources for the causal bond between economic conditions and political climate. Apart from the strong presumption from common sense and everyday experience, a study of British politics (Butler and Stokes, 1969: 417) presents a similar picture of high correlation between Labour's lead over the Conservatives and unemployment data (the Conservatives were in power at the time). In the present case it may be that we are one step removed from the economic forces affecting the voters, in that the indicator used is somewhat psychological and indirect in nature. The figures refer to an expressed need for more labor, not to a precise and direct measurement of actual employment or unemployment. Such judgments could be influenced by a general mood of optimism or pessimism. In fact, voter's reactions and employer's evaluations could be parallel responses to the stream of events (partly mediated by the mass media). This would explain a high correlation without assuming a clear-cut, unidirectional causal nexus. It is not necessary for the two responses to occur with identical lags or degrees of inertia; correlations could well be high even with moderately different speed characteristics.

To sum up, the argument for an economic explanation of shifts in party preferences is strong—strong enough to make it a rather meaningless exercise to test the hypothesis that the true correlation is zero. However, there is a difference between something being one or even one of several major determinants and that something being the only determinant. On the technical side, it should be noted that the correlation obtained from the sample (+ 0.79) could easily arise as a fluctuation in a universe with a true correlation around + 0.40 or + 0.50. A simple simulation experiment (which will not be described in detail here) shows that sample values of + 0.70 and + 0.80—as well as values close to zero—are quite common with a true value of + 0.40, if there is a marked serial correlation in the data.

In any case, there is still the question of how much of the economic realities are perceived immediately, as part and parcel of everyday experience, and how much is transmitted through media. It is here that evidence on media content is needed.

In Section II the manner of sampling media was set forth and the coding system outlined. Here only a few of many potential indicators of media content will be used. The first, and seemingly the most relevant, is the incidence of comment negative to the (Social Democratic) Government in editorials. It is an obvious choice in the context of party sympathies. The difficulties inherent in this type of analysis soon will become equally obvious. The outcome, however, is not devoid of interest.

Figure 11.4 shows the incidence of negative comment in the shape of two series, one on a quarterly and the other on a semiannual basis. Both represent the fraction of all editorials within the period coded as negative. The quarterly curve, as might be expected, is too much influenced by sampling errors to give a clear visual impression. As a rule, the total number of editorials on which the percentage of critical editorials has been computed is a little less than 40. The semiannual series is somewhat less marked by this weakness. As can be seen by comparing Figures 11.3 and 11.4, there is indeed a negative correlation between critical comment and support for the Social Democrats according to the polls. In terms of correlations the results are as follows:

Quarterly series: $r = -0.50$ (n=32);
Semiannual series: $r = -0.75$ (n=16).

Another variable tested in the analysis is the explicit evaluation of the person, institution, or event presented in the text—here again, editorials (see Section II). This indicator, however, proved less closely related to partisan attitudes or economic conditions as here measured. There is a correlation with criticism of the government, though not a strong one. (The coding reliability of this variable, it should be remembered, was fairly low.) All correlations are shown in Table 11.2.

If one bears in mind the small number of observations—for half-year data only 16—and the high level of serial correlation in the data, it is clear that any elaborate schemes of multivariate analysis of the data of Table 11.2 are out of the question. The outcome would be much too dependent on chance fluctuations. The most that can reasonably be tried is a couple of partial correlations.

The partial correlation between opinion data and editorial criticism of the government, holding constant the business-cycle indicator (demand for labor), comes out as -0.62, to be compared with the corresponding

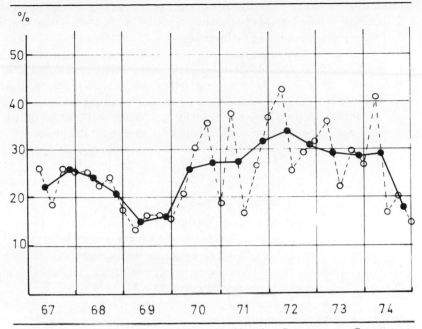

Figure 11.4 Proportion of Editorials with Negative Comment on Government:
Quarterly and Semiannual Data

TABLE 11.2 Intercorrelations of the Four Main Variables

	L	P	G	E
L	–	+ .81	– .55	– .07
P		–	– .75	– .15
G			–	+ .40
E				

L Demand for labor

P Poll data: Support for Social Democrats

G Editorial criticism of government

E Negative evaluations in editorials

zero-order correlation of – 0.75 (see Table 11.2). On the other hand, the partial correlation between business conditions and political opinions, partialing out media criticism of the government, is 0.71, to be compared with a zero-order correlation of 0.81. As far as the evidence goes, the two partial correlations provide at least tentative empirical support for the intuitively appealing notion that political opinions in the population are molded partly by economic realities in their own right (this is probably the dominating influence), partly by media content itself, and partly by economic realities as relayed by the media.

Still other indicators of media content have been considered. Where computations were carried out the results were inconclusive. In some of these series, there is hardly enough variability over time to give promise of an outcome worth the trouble. This, of course, raises the question of in what manner the press conveys, or fails to convey, real changes in the sociopolitical situation, a point which will be discussed in a moment.

DISCUSSION

The results so far presented can be called suggestive rather than definitive in their implications. There is the expected relationship between objective economic conditions and partisan attitudes. It *may* be somewhat exaggerated in strength by sampling errors in the present case, and the tides of politics may thus be more open to other influences than appears in our data. There is also the expected correlation between newspaper criticism of the government and party strength in the polls, and also a negative correlation between prosperity and criticism of the government (though somewhat weaker). None of this is sensational, but at the very least it supports the idea that newspaper content can be sampled and meaningfully measured, with the possibility of applications less restricted by common-sense assumptions.

If one reflects on the background of the data, the outcome becomes rather less predictable. It should be kept in mind that with editorial content there is seldom a question of newspapers changing from a generally critical to a generally friendly view of the government. With few exceptions, Swedish newspapers have a standing commitment, for or against, and are not likely to deviate far from the set course. Presumably what happens is that they tend to give expression to their basic and relatively fixed attitude and, hence, variations in the balance between critical and noncritical material. Editorial content, then, may convey a mood, changing only gradually and manifested often enough to be both clear to the reading public and accessible afterwards through sampling and content analysis. The data give support to such a view. (It would be quite possible to have a counterstream of positive comment in newspapers supporting the government, as opposition newspapers become more frequently and openly critical. However, there is little sign of this if one looks at the respective time series, though no detailed analysis was undertaken.)

With news items (noneditorial material) the situation is different. We may encounter difficulties with isolated but important events and with short-term fluctuations. It may well be that readers of newspapers are strongly influenced when they read about a big industrial firm closing down and many employees being laid off, or about the energy situation getting out of control. But such messages are relatively few and far between, though they have a marked impact. As too much material cannot be analyzed, *some* kind of sampling must be utilized. And with this arises the possibility of missing the rare but critical event.

Obviously, much depends on how rare such events are relative to the size of the sample and on the sensitivity of the coding system. With 40 items sampled for each quarter, one may perhaps say that content variations through time will be discovered if the true (universe) frequencies vary between 1-2 percent and 10 percent. With half-year periods and around 80 articles sampled for each half-year, one may be successful with even lower frequencies. Clearly, insufficient numbers can be compensated to some extent by changing the period of observation, but only at the price of missing information on the time pattern.

The trouble with ordinary news is the great amount of irrelevant material, chiefly crime and accidents (if by "relevant" we mean likely to influence political opinions in the population). It is reasonable to expect a rather high amount of short-run fluctuations in such material—fluctuations which may or may not result in corresponding fluctuations in the opinions of the population. To complicate matters further, these "real" fluctuations are then combined with sampling fluctuations in both the media material used and the survey sample of the population.

Since there are few realistic possibilities of ever measuring such short-term, almost day-to-day changes in population opinions for a sufficient period of time, this would point to the necessity of moving up one step in the time scale when looking for the importance of news: not monthly, quarterly, or semiannual measurements of media content, but yearly ones. This, in turn, leads to the demand for longer time series: decades or more. Since there are few opinion data available for such long periods of time, one would then have to turn to other indices of opinions in the population: debate material, letters to the editor, aggregated data on discretionary behavior, and the like. Such measurements could be more profitably undertaken if based on specific theoretical considerations.

On the methodological side, then, our attempts to combine data about social structure, population opinions, and media content have resulted in a couple of insights. To be fruitfully used in this context, news material must probably be sampled for relatively long periods of time and along dimensions suggested by a rather specific theory. Editorial material, on the other hand, may be less demanding in this respect.

Substantively, our results suggest that political opinions in the population are molded both by economic conditions and by media content, probably somewhat more by economic conditions than by media content. (The media, of course, also relay information about economic conditions.) The traditional notion of the mass media is that they mainly rely on and reinforce influences from other forces in society. Recent research, however, suggests that the mass media may be more powerful than conventional wisdom among social scientists reflects (Gerbner et al., 1978; Noelle-Neumann, 1977). With all their limitations, our data support the latter standpoint rather than the former.

REFERENCES

BENIGER, J. R. (1978). "Media content as social indicators." Communication Research 5: 437-454.
BLUMLER, J. G. and KATZ, E. [eds.] (1974). The Uses of Mass Communications. Beverly Hills, CA: Sage.
BRANDNER, L. and SISTRUNK, J. (1966). "The newspaper: Molder or mirror of community values?" Journalism Quarterly 43: 497-504.
BUTLER, D. E. and STOKES, D. (1971). Political Change in Britain. Harmondsworth: Penguin.
CARLSSON, G. (1965). "Time and continuity in mass attitude change." Public Opinion Quarterly 29: 1-15.
DAVIS, F. J. (1952). "Crime news in Colorado newspapers." American Journal of Sociology 57: 325-330.
FUNKHOUSER, G. R. (1973). "The issues of the sixties: An exploratory study in the dynamics of public opinion." Public Opinion Quarterly 37: 62-75.
GERBNER, G., GROSS, L., SIGNORIELLI, N., MORGAN, M., and JACKSON-BEECK, M. (1979). "The demonstration of power: Violence Profile No. 10." Journal of Communication, 29: 177-196.
INGLIS, R. A. (1938). "An objective approach to the relationship between fiction and society." American Sociological Review 3: 526-533.
KATZ, E. and SZECSKÖ, T. [eds.] (forthcoming). Mass Media and Social Change. A Symposium. London: Sage.
LIEBERT, R. M. and SCHWARTZBERG, N. S. (1977). "Effects of mass media." Annual Review of Psychology 28: 141-173.
MIDDLETON, R. (1960). "Fertility values in American magazine fiction." Public Opinion Quarterly 24: 139-142.
NOELLE-NEUMANN, E. (1977). "Turbulences in the climate of opinion: Methodological applications of the spiral of silence theory." Public Opinion Quarterly 41: 143-158.
PETERSON, R. A. (1976). "The production of culture." American Behavioral Scientist 19: 669-684.
ROSENGREN, K. E. (1979). "Bias in news: Methods and concepts." Studies in Broadcasting 15.
——— (1978). "Mass media and social change: Some current approaches." Lund: Dept. of Sociology. (mimeo)
SHAW, D. L. (1967). "News bias and the telegraph: A study of historical change." Journalism Quarterly 44: 3-12, 31.
SMITH, R. F. (1971). "U.S. news and Sino-Indian relations: An extra media study. Journalism Quarterly 48: 447-458, 501.
TOWERS, W. M. (1977). Reality, Pseudo-Reality and Fantasy: The Crystallization and Reinforcement of Crime as an Issue 1964-1973. University of Oklahoma. (mimeo)
WILLIAMS, R. (1973). "Base and superstructure in Marxist cultural theory." New Left Review 82: 3-16.

In this chapter, Lee B. Becker argues that agenda-setting research is at present plagued by inconsistencies and methodological problems that render statements about its pervasiveness suspect; moreover, Becker notes, assumptions in agenda-setting research have not generally been articulated, and he suggests a number of them. Becker is associate professor in the School of Journalism at Ohio State University.

30

THE MASS MEDIA AND CITIZEN ASSESSMENT OF ISSUE IMPORTANCE
A Reflection on Agenda-Setting Research

Lee B. Becker

U.S. mass communications researchers in the last decade found themselves with a striking paradox. Surrounded by a commercial media system based on the assumption that purchased space and time produce audience effects, the researchers were unable to provide convincing evidence of effects in noncommercial areas. The pervasiveness of the media argued for political and social effects that empirically could not be demonstrated.

Perhaps because of the unsettling nature of such a paradox, new formulations regarding media effects were given extraordinary attention. Supportive data were treated as a rare metal. Many were the researchers who would pursue this new idea in hopes of such a reward.

So it was with what is generally termed the agenda-setting influence of the press. In the nine years since the seminal study of McCombs and Shaw (1972) was published, a flood of manuscripts has been produced dealing with the topic. Many data have been gathered to determine the generalizability of the original finding of a similarity in the pattern of display of issues in the mass media and the concern with those issues on the part of the citizenry.

What follows is *not* an exhaustive review of this rather extensive literature. Adequate reviews already have been undertaken by Shaw and McCombs (1977), and Weaver, Graber, McCombs, and Eyal (1981). *Nor* is this an attempt to create empirical generalizations from the existing studies. Again, the two works cited

EDITORS' NOTE: This chapter was originally presented as a paper to a symposium on new approaches in the study of political communication, Swiss Society of Communication and German Association of Communications Research, Zurich, Switzerland, May 7-8, 1981.

above already have made progress in this regard. Rather what follows is an attempt to formulate in as precise fashion as possible the concepts that are important in understanding the relationship between the content of the mass média and the audience assessments of the importance of public issues. It also is an attempt to delineate the assumptions that must underlie the positing of such a relationship.

CONTROLLING LITERATURE

The early U.S. literature dealing with media effects has been reviewed in numerous articles, including those of Sears and Whitney (1973), Blumler and McLeod (1974), Becker, McCombs, and McLeod (1975), and Kepplinger (1979). A brief review of this literature, however, helps to set the stage for a discussion of the agenda-setting hypothesis.

Conceived out of a fear of international propaganda, the early research assumed that the mass media had significant impact on what was viewed as a gullible audience. To understand media effects, it was thought, one must delineate characteristics of the messages. *Message* variables, not *audience* variables, were the focus of attention.

While the Yale program of research on attitude change, viewed with hindsight, offered substantive challenge to this position by illustrating the importance of audience variables such as educational level and personality type, it was interpreted contemporaneously as supportive of massive effects. Clearly the primary thrust of the work of Hovland and his colleagues was with the capability of messages to alter audience responses (Hovland, 1957; Hovland and Janis, 1959; Rosenberg, Hovland, McGuire, Abelson, and Brehm, 1960).

It was left to the program of voting studies conducted by the Columbia University Bureau of Applied Research to present the first severe challenge to the assumption that the media were powerful determinants of audience attitudes and behavior. Perhaps no other studies have had as significant an impact on the study of mass communications as the 1940 and 1948 election studies conducted by the Columbia bureau (Lazarsfeld, Berelson, and Gaudet, 1948; Berelson, Lazarsfeld, and McPhee, 1954). Contrary to expectation, the researchers found little evidence that the media played a significant role in directly influencing voter decisions during those presidential races. Considered by the researchers to be of much greater importance was interpersonal influence, which served to mitigate any direct media effects. Klapper's (1960) *The Effects of Mass Communications* summarized these and other related findings into what is probably the most frequently cited work in the field. The media had limited effects in the real world settings, Klapper said. A similar position was taken even by Hovland (1959) in a classic article aptly titled "Reconciling Conflicting Results Derived from Experimental and Survey Studies of Attitude Change."

In general, the limited effects position enjoyed supremacy in media research for at least the decade of the 1960s. With noteworthy exceptions, such as the work of the Langs (Lang and Lang, 1968), researchers assigned to the mass media a relatively insignificant role in the formation of public attitudes and behaviors.

Perhaps nowhere was this more evident than in the area of electoral research, where mass media variables were almost totally ignored.

The 1970s represented a kind of renaissance of interest in media effects, particularly in the political area. While the specific interests of the various researchers were diverse, they coalesced around the argument that the limited effects position was simply in conflict with informal observation. Specifically, the limited effects position ignored the pervasiveness of the media (Kraus and Davis, 1976), the role of television specifically (Patterson and McClure, 1976), key findings from the data used to substantiate the position (Becker et al., 1975), and the range of potential media effects (Blumler and McLeod, 1974; Clarke and Kline, 1974; and Becker et al., 1975).

This last position—that the limited effects view ignored potential media effects of consequence—deserves additional elaboration, for it is here that the arguments of McCombs and Shaw (1972) regarding an agenda-setting effect are most appropriately classified. Historically, the focus in media effects studies has been on attitudes, and the conclusion that the media are relatively ineffective is based largely—though not entirely—on negative findings in this area. Yet what people learn from the mass media, as Clarke and Kline (1974) wrote, may be "a more rewarding topic for media effects research than attitude formation and change." Included in what we would expect people to learn from the media is much about issues, including which ones are important. Therein lies the core of the agenda-setting hypothesis.

It is worth noting, however, that this renewed interest in cognitive or informational effects of the media has not been to the exclusion of interest in other consequences. Of prime concern to Blumler and McLeod (1974), for example, were effects of the mass media on voter turnout. Other potential effects include increased use of one medium resulting from exposure to another, increased interest in politics, increased political activity in general, and increased levels of interpersonal discussion. McLeod, Durall, Ziemke, and Bybee (1979) showed the value of many of these other criterion variables in an innovative analysis of the effects of the 1976 presidential debates.

Also of importance is the observation that the increased interest in media effects has not been limited to the United States. The most striking examples of a reexamination of media effects in Europe have been the above cited work of Blumler in Britain and the work of Noelle Neumann (1974) in Germany. Nor is it true that potential attitudinal effects of the media have been ignored in this reexamination of media effects. Noelle-Neumann's work is illustrative of this point, as is the work of Robinson (1976) on the effects of U.S. television news on attitudes toward government.

EARLY AGENDA-SETTING RESEARCH

The 1972 publication by McCombs and Shaw (McCombs and Shaw, 1972) of the first empirical test of the agenda-setting hypothesis, this brief review indicates, came at a time when many researchers were willing to entertain the idea that the limited effects position was too limited. The agenda-setting hypothesis also had a certain amount of integrity resulting from the fact that this kind of an effect had been discussed by numerous earlier scholars, including Lippmann (1922), Cohen (1963), and Lang and Lang (1968). In addition, the effect matched commonsense observations. Clearly the media must have some effect on the matters people think about, if not on the specific opinions they have on those matters.

The data reported in 1972 served to encourage researchers to continue their exploration for media effects, to confirm what others had predicted in the literature, and to reinforce commonsense explanations. The data also set the pattern for numerous studies to follow, and, for that reason, it is informative to examine in more detail just what they showed.

McCombs and Shaw state the hypothesis that directed their investigation: "While the mass media may have little influence on the direction or intensity of attitudes, it is hypothesized that the mass media set the agenda for each political campaign, influencing the salience of attitudes toward the political issues." In other words, the media influence the salience of issues for individuals, and these saliences determine the campaign agenda.

To test this hypothesis, news and editorial comments appearing during a three-week period in nine media sources were content analyzed and stories related to the upcoming 1968 presidential campaign were classified according to the issue covered. During this same general period, interviews were conducted with a sample of 100 registered voters who had not yet definitely decided how to vote in the upcoming election. Included in the survey instrument was the following question: "What are you most concerned about these days? That is, regardless of what politicians say, what are the two or three main things which you think the government should concentrate on doing something about?" Responses to this question were coded according to issue mentioned and then aggregated across all 100 respondents. From this aggregation, a rank ordering of five issues was achieved, and this rank ordering was compared with the rank ordering of these same five issues summed across the various media subjected to content analysis. The result was a correlation coefficient of +.97. Correlation coefficients also were reported for the nine media sources individually, though in doing so the sample was not partitioned according to medium used or relied upon. The relationships among the issue rankings for the various media also were examined and were found to be high.

A critical assessment of this pioneering piece by McCombs and Shaw suggests that at least four distinct problems present themselves. First, the authors did not conceptually define the two key variables in the hypothesized relationship. Second, the operationalizations of these concepts suggest conceptual distinctions are needed. Third, the aggregation of data across sample respondents is an inappropriate way to test a hypothesis about individual-level media effects. And finally, potentially important methodological and conceptual issues such as the order of effects, the proper time lag for isolating effects, and the proper comparisons for evaluating effects are not addressed.

It is unfair, of course, to hold the original authors wholly responsible for each of these points. In fact, McCombs and Shaw indicated clearly that much more needed to be done in developing their idea. Yet this first study spawned numerous replications, many reflecting these same limitations. As a result, it is worth examining each problem in some detail as well as reflecting on what progress has been made toward reaching a solution.

CONCEPTUAL PROBLEMS

To say that agenda-setting research has been plagued by a high level of terminological imprecision is gross understatement. In a manuscript presented as late as 1979 McCombs (1979) speaks of the "concept of agenda-setting, which is itself a hypothesis, and . . . a larger theory of agenda-setting." Agenda-setting also is called a "metaphor" and a "macro-description" of "how people organize and structure the world around them." Nowhere is there in that discussion a conceptual definition of the message variable (the presumed cause in the hypothesis) or of the criterion, or audience response variable.

What can be gleaned from this and other writings is that the media behavior of interest is display of news about issues, which can be viewed as something called an agenda of issues. The audience response is in terms of the importance—or "salience"—ratings of issues, which, when viewed comparatively, can also be thought of as an agenda. The hypothesis is that the audience members over time have issue agendas that reflect the issue agendas of the media.

News display, of course, is not a simple phenomenon. Included in such a concept is use of copy, amount of space assigned the copy, placement of the copy in the paper and on given pages, as well as the nature of the headlines and accompanying graphics. These are print manifestations of display, of course, but the broadcast media have counterparts, such as placement of the story in the newscast, use of lead-ins and "teasers," use of photographs and film (for television) or "actualities" (for radio), and amount of time.

Before making conceptual distinctions about what is meant by display— conceptual distinctions with obvious operational consequences—it is necessary to conceptually define what is meant by an "issue." Such a definition, of course, must be sensitive to the implications of that definition for the audience variable as well. The work of Edelstein (1974) suggests that the term "issue" might well mean something quite different to a researcher from what it means to an audience member. How the mass media define issues might be something altogether different again.

The assumption must be made, then, that audience members do not treat all issues equally. Rather, it must be assumed that based on some criterion, the audience members classify issues into at least two groups: those which are high in importance and those which are not high in importance. In other words, some issues must be considered salient, i.e., conspicuous, prominent, or striking, while others are not salient. The hypothesis is that the media determine which issues are salient and which are not.

McLeod, Becker, and Byrnes (1974) argued that three different types of criterion are available to audience members in classifying issues. First, they may classify issues solely in terms of how they affect themselves. This was called an "intrapersonal" method of establishing salience. Second, audience members may classify issues in terms of how they are perceived to affect other persons or events. For example, an issue might be perceived as being important to large groups of voters or to the outcome of a campaign. This was labeled "perceived issue salience." Finally, respondents may differentiate issues in terms of how frequently they discuss them in interpersonal communication settings. This was labeled "interpersonal salience."

These conceptual distinctions suggested that, at a minimum, there are three different agenda-setting hypotheses available for assessment. The media may influence which issues are salient to individuals, which are perceived as being important in some larger context, and which are discussed. There may be some ordering of effects as well, with the most likely progression being from perceived salience to interpersonal discussion salience to individual salience. It would seem intrapersonal salience would be most resistant to media influence and more under the control of the immediate social environment within which the individual resides.

METHODOLOGICAL PROBLEMS

In the research exercise, conceptual definitions should precede operational ones. It seems clear on this case that the conceptual ambiguities of the early agenda-setting research resulted in methodological problems in the work that followed. As McCombs (1979) noted, agenda-setting research has been conducted with a variety of measures of both the media and audience agendas, resulting in problems of noncomparability of findings and placing restrictions on the generalizations that can be drawn from the existing work.

This is not to say that researchers have been entirely cavalier in their selection of measures. Efforts have been made to advance the measurement of the media agenda and to deal with different ways of measuring audience reactions. The report of the 1972 presidential election study by McCombs and his associations dealt particularly with the former (Shaw and McCombs, 1977), while the report of the 1976 election study, again by McCombs and associates (Weaver et al., 1981), addresses the latter. And Eyal's independent analyses of these same 1976 election data (Eyal, 1979) dealt specifically with issue definition. But these treatments generally have been methodological and empirical, rather than conceptual. The criterion for evaluating alternatives has, for the most part, been whether an agenda-setting effect was produced rather than how well the measures actually indexed the concept of interest. In other words, researchers have relied on what is termed construct validation at the expense of more fundamental issues of content and pragmatic validation. Construct validation, of course, is difficult and perhaps even inappropriate for research in its initial stages.

AGGREGATION OF DATA

In a certain sense, a more fundamental issues than that of operational limitations of much of the existing work has to do with the nature of the evidence presented on behalf of the agenda-setting hypothesis. Again, the initial McCombs and Shaw (1972) report had considerable and unfortunate effect here. In that study, as noted above, the crucial comparison was between the rank order of five issues in the media and the rank order of those same issues according to how frequently they were mentioned by survey respondents. In other words, the effect measure was an aggregate one, not an individual one.

The limitations of such a test were acknowledged by McCombs and Shaw (1972), who wrote that the aggregate comparison "is satisfactory as a first test of the agenda-setting hypothesis, but subsequent research must move from a broad societal level to the social psychological level." Unfortunately, that advice has not been followed; both the 1972 and 1976 election reports by McCombs and his associates relied on aggregate comparisons nearly identical in nature to those of the earlier 1968 study. The same is true for much—though not all—of the agenda-setting research conducted since that initial report.

This matter of the appropriate comparison is of such importance that some elaboration is in order. Clearly if a hypothesis is offered about the effects of the media on individual audience members, the empirical test of that hypothesis must reflect the nature of the effect offered. Aggregate comparisons fall short on this count.

This perhaps can be made most obvious by a presentation of data typical of those used in an aggregate test of the agenda-setting hypothesis. Data drawn from the 1976 election study of Weaver et al. (1981) are shown in Table 30.1 for this purpose. A simple Spearman's rho rank order correlation coefficient comparing these two sets of scores is .34, indicating some agreement in the rankings. Yet it also is clear that only 20.9% of those surveyed named foreign affairs or defense as the most important issues, despite that fact that in the newspapers that was the most important issue. In other words, almost 80% of those surveyed gave as their *most* important problem something other than what the media gave. If the top five newspaper categories are examined in a somewhat more lenient view of the data, it becomes clear that only 55% of those surveyed gave an answer treated by the media as one of the top five stories during the period. Nearly half of the sample named an issue not in the top five news categories.

This same discrepancy between media agendas and individual responses could be true for these data even if the rank order agreement was nearly perfect, as it was in the original McCombs and Shaw study. It is not possible to demonstrate just how much discrepancy there was in those original data since the actual media and audience agendas were not presented. But it is clear that rank order coefficients do not really test the hypothesis. It also is clear from the data that many people do not follow the media lead in selecting issues. In fact as is noted in Shaw and McCombs (1977: 103), nearly 40% of those surveyed in the 1972 election study failed to show anything that could remotely be judged to be an agenda-setting effect. The 1976 election study data suggest the same was true that year as well.

TABLE 1   Data form Weaver et al. Study of 1976 Presidential Election

Issue	Newspaper Agenda[a] Feb.–March		Voter Agenda[b] May	
Foreign Affairs Defense	13.0%	(1)	20.9	(1)
Government Credibility	6.8	(4)	5.2	(6)
Crime	10.9	(2)	5.2	(6)
Social Problems	9.1	(3)	5.2	(6)
General Economy	3.4	(5)	18.7	(2)
Environment and Energy	3.3	(6)	3.7	(8.5)
Government Spending and Size	1.7	(7)	3.7	(8.5)
Race Relations and Busing	1.0	(8)	3.0	(10)
Taxes	0.4	(10)	1.5	(11)
Unemployment	0.7	(9)	10.4	(4)
Inflation	0.3	(11)	14.9	(3)
TOTAL	50.6		92.4	

a. Entries are percent of 3,742 stories classified as dealing with this issue. Ranks are in parentheses.

b. Entries of percent of 134 persons surveyed in May who listed the given issue as the the most important to them personally. Ranks are in parentheses.

An adequate test of the agenda-setting hypothesis requires the researcher to move beyond these simple aggregate comparisons. The analysis must involve on an individual-by-individual basis the matching of a medium agenda with an individual agenda, as was done by McLeod, Becker, and Byrnes (1974), an issue-by-issue analysis where contrasts are presented between issues high on the media agenda and those low on the media agenda, as was done by Becker, Weaver, Graber, and McCombs (1979), or some similar technique. It is unfortunately the case that the agenda-setting hypothesis seems easier to test than it really is.

NEEDED COMPARISONS, ORDER OF EFFECTS, AND TIME LAG

Campbell (1957: 298), in his classic treatment of research designs, wrote: "The very minimum of useful scientific information involves at least one formal comparison and therefore at least two careful observations." With that particular requirement agenda-setting research has had considerable difficulty. The comparison of the agenda of the media with the audience agenda, of course, does not meet this requirement for one basic comparison. What is needed is a comparison between the agenda-to-agenda match for one group expected to show the effect and another group not expected to show the effect. Isolating two such groups has proven to be rather difficult in real world settings.

The ideal situation, of course, would be one where readers of one newspaper were compared with readers of another newspaper, the two newspapers providing opposite agendas. McLeod, Becker, and Byrnes (1974) provided a very rough approximation of this situation in their analysis of newspaper readers in Madison, Wisconsin. But the general pattern is for newspapers to have very similar agendas, making such comparisons rather fruitless.

Comparisons between different types of media, such as television and newspapers, are plagued by the fact that (1) the audiences often overlap and (2) where they do not, the people differ from each other in ways other than terms of media use. This second problem also surfaces where readers and nonreaders or viewers and nonviewers are compared. Such groups are rarely equal before they receive their cues. In addition, the relevant, controlling agenda of the nonreaders (provided they also are nonviewers and nonlisteners) is unknown.

While the ultimate solution to this problem obviously rests with experimental data-gathering designs, perhaps the most promise for nonlaboratory work is with comparisons of the sort mentioned above combined with better attempts to measure competing media agendas. Through careful measurement of selected variables and subsequent partitioning of the audience samples, initial differences in existing groups can be dealt with in a somewhat satisfactory way. In 1976, for example, comparisons between persons who watched the presidential debates and those who did not allowed for a test of the agenda-setting influence of the debate situation (Becker et al., 1979; McLeod et al., 1979). More will be said later of the results of these analysis.

The direction of effect is another problem that has confronted researchers pursuing the agenda-setting hypothesis. Obviously, it is quite possible that the media, rather than determining audience responses to issues, are reflecting those responses. Using a technique called cross-lagged correlational analysis, Shaw and McCombs (1977: 93, 94) showed that the preponderance of evidence is in favor of newspaper influence on the audience, while the reverse is true for television. The analyses are limited by the fact they result from aggregate comparisons and no attempt was made to distinguish between persons dependent on the newspapers versus those dependent on the television. This work does indicate, however, a significant concern with addressing this question of the order of the relationship.

Also given much attention, particularly by Eyal (1979) and Winter and Eyal (1980), has been the proper time lag for identifying the agenda-setting affect. Again, working with aggregate data, these researchers have found that the optimal lag differs for the media and is affected by the time constraints of the situation. Selection of time lag, of course, is a theoretical as well as a methodological issue. At this point, it is not clear theoretically just why time lag is a variable in determining the agenda-setting effect.

THEORETICAL LINKAGES IN AGENDA-SETTING

Underlying all hypotheses are assumptions about the two variables being linked and the justification for that linkage. Several different assumptions are identifiable in the literature on agenda-setting. Others are presented below because they seem to elaborate on those stated assumptions. These assumptions are:

(1) Individuals have a desire to keep themselves informed about their environment.
(2) The mass media provide a means for individuals to keep themselves informed about their environment.
(3) Because of the limitations on resources, often the mass media are the most efficient way for audience members to keep themselves informed.
(4) Included in the information provided to audience members by the mass media are materials identifiable by the audience members as dealing with something called an issue.
(5) The media provide cues as to which issues are more important through techniques of selection and display.
(6) Audience members accept the media cues regarding importance of issues and adopt them as their own.

This list of assumptions is not exhaustive. Nor is it one with which all persons doing agenda-setting research would feel comfortable. Yet it does capture the spirit of much of what has been written about this phenomenon. And as such, it provides a point of departure for examining some of the findings to date.

Clearly this formulation does not fit with the consistent findings of a match between the ranking of issues in the mass media and the ranking of issues obtained from an aggregation of responses from survey respondents. The unit of analysis or discourse for assumptions that fits these findings would have to be shifted to the macro or community level. The following assumptions are offered for comparison:

(1) Communities align themselves into groups in various ways.
(2) One such alignment is in terms of issues of concern to community members.
(3) The media, through disproportionate attention to various issues, suggest appropriate alignments.
(4) Communities divide into ,groups along the lines suggested by the issue coverage of the media, with size of group roughly proportionate to the amount of coverage given.

These assumptions are based on the belief that the order of affects is from the media to the audience members. If the reverse is true, another set of assumptions comes into play. They would probably fall along the following lines:

(1) The mass media exist to serve their audiences.

(2) One way of serving the audiences is to provide coverage of issues of concern to the audience members.

(3) Because of limitations of resources, the media must allocate their resources in covering issues.

(4) The allocation of resources is according to the size of the groups in the community concerned about given issues.

The reader can pick which of these latter sets of assumptions is most satisfactory. The assumptions are quite different from those offered at the individual level. It should be noted, however, that the final set of assumptions can be easily modified to hold regardless of the unit of discourse, since it merely posits that the media respond to their audiences.

In the remainder of this chapter, data will be examined that are appropriate to the first set of assumptions—those offered for an individual-level effect of media content on audience assessment of issue importance. The decision to limit further discussion to those studies that examine this kind of effect obviously reflects the author's biases in favor of that kind of theory about media agenda-setting.

A LIMITED REVIEW OF THE LITERATURE

One of the most obvious discrepancies between the research conducted on the individual level and the research using aggregate audience rankings has to do with the strength of the findings. For the former, findings are limited or, in some cases, nonexistent. The aggregate-level findings have replicated in numerous circumstances.

For example, McLeod, Becker, and Byrnes (1974), in their study of the 1972 presidential election, found only slight evidence of an overall effect of mass media coverage of issues on individual salience ratings of those issues. Using a measure that asked respondents to rate the importance of issues in the political campaign, these researchers found no evidence of the effect for young, first-time voters, and only slight evidence of the effect for older voters. Partitioning of the samples into subgroups did show that young voters without strong partisan predispositions were more likely to be affected by the media agenda. In general, respondents lower in political interest and motivation were more likely to show the effect.

Siune and Borre (1975) found a slight relationship between the issue focus of the media and audience assessments of issue importance in their study of the 1971 Danish general election. Respondents were asked to indicate: "Which problem do you think is the most important today, which the politicians ought to take care of?" Responses were coded on an issue-by-issue basis as either mentioning a selected issue or not mentioning such an issue, and these data were then matched with data from a content analysis of media-relayed statements by the politicians. Indeed, there was a linkage between the issue emphasis in the partisan broadcasts and the individual-level issue saliences. But a slightly stronger relationship existed between audience perceptions of issues raised by the politicians and issue saliences.

The relationship between the perception of issues raised (which might be thought of as an indicant of perceived salience) and the objective indicant of issues mentioned by the politicians was stronger than either of the other two relations examined.

Erbring, Goldenberg, and Miller (1980), using data from the 1974 national election study conducted at the University of Michigan, similarly found limited evidence of the affects of media issue coverage on issues saliences. Respondents were asked to designate the most important issues facing the country, thereby providing data for an issue-by-issue analysis of salience ratings (i.e., an issue was either mentioned or was not mentioned and could be analyzed accordingly). Consistent with the McLeod, Becker, and Byrnes analyses, Erbring and his colleagues found that the evidence of media effects on issue saliences increased when contingent conditions were examined. But unlike the McLeod, Becker, and Byrnes findings, Erbring concluded that media effects of this sort can be understood only in the context of the effects of interpersonal discussion and of prior sensitization to the issues. In other words, while the McLeod, Becker, and Byrnes findings concentrated on psychological conditions restricting and facilitating media effects, Erbring and his colleagues focused on restrictions resulting from social condition. Both analyses, however, suggest significant limitations exist on the ability of the media to influence individual assessments of issue saliences.

Such a conclusion is strengthened by the analyses of Chaffee and Izcaray (1975) who could provide no consistent evidence of an effect of the media on issue saliences in their study of residents of Barquisimeto, Venezuela. Respondents were asked to identify from a predetermined list of issues "being talked about" those that were most important and those that were next most important. Again an issue-by-issue comparison showed that use of the media did not lead to increased issue saliences even for those issues given considerable attention in the newspaper pages and on television. Social economic position of the respondent, on the other hand, did seem to play a role in determining issue salience.

The 1976 presidential election, with its series of debates between the candidates of the major parties, provided an opportunity for assessment of influence of the media on individual issue saliences. Several researchers, treating the debates as a media event expected to influence issue saliences, fielded studies allowing for pre- and postexposure comparisons. The results were almost uniformly disappointing. Atkin, Hocking, and McDermott (1979), for example, found only slight evidence that the final debate between the two presidential candidates had any effect on issues covered in the debate, a conclusion echoed by the independent research across the debates by Becker, Weaver, Graber, and McCombs (1979), McLeod, Durall, Ziemke, and Bybee (1979), and Gadziala (1980). The Gadziala analyses were perhaps the most exhaustive, examining separately each of the four debates (three involving the presidential candidates and one involving the vice presidential candidates) and using three different criterion salience measures.

Sears and Chaffee (1979), after a review of most of these debate studies examining the effects of the media on audience saliences, said that "there was in retrospect no strong reason to expect this kind of impact from the debates ... [since] the voters seem to have been searching for the candidates' positions on issues, not for issues themselves." The Sears and Chaffee position can be viewed, of course, as another statement that media influence on audience saliences is far from universal and likely to be contingent on situational and audience factors.

CONCLUDING COMMENTS

There is an important lesson lurking in the agenda-setting research literature: Be suspicious of the simple explanation of social phenomenon, no matter how promising it sounds; things are probably always more complex than they seem on first notice.

The mass media probably do have impact on how audience members assess the importance of issues. If people learn from the mass media, as we suspect (based on some solid evidence) that they do, they probably learn about issues. Part of what they probably learn is which issues are being discussed in the public arena, which issues are likely to affect public decision-making, and which issues are of concern to other citizens. These pieces of information may well affect what audience members talk about with their friends and acquaintances. And these two activities—media content and interpersonal discussion—may influence what issues are of most concern to the individual audience member.

The media probably do not act alone in providing cues to the audience members about issues, the cues probably do not affect all audience members the same way, and cues may have more influence at one point in time and for one issue than at another point in time and for another issue. In other words, the effects of the media may not be monolithic.

The first of these observations—that the media do not act alone—is underscored by a rather simple finding from an unreported study conducted during the 1980 presidential election in Ohio. Included in a survey instrument administered to 531 registered voters was a standard question on issues: What do you think is the most important problem facing the United States today? Respondents gave numerous answers, including inflation and the general lack of health of the U.S. economy. Next, respondents were asked why they had selected a particular problem as the most important one facing the country. Again, the answers were quite diverse, and they remain difficult to categorize. But what is striking is that only 5 respondents out of the 531—or just under 1%—even mentioned the mass media. While some caution is in order in interpreting these kinds of audience data, since it may have been considered by some respondents inappropriate to mention the media, it hardly seems likely that many respondents considered the media to be the sole determinant or even a very significant determinant of their selection of issues.

The McLeod, Becker, and Byrnes (1974) and the Erbring, Goldenberg, and Miller (1980) studies underscore the second observation made above: The media do not affect the issue saliences of all respondents in the same way. The uses the audience members make of the media (as noted by McLeod et al.) as well as the social situation within which the audience members reside (Erbring et al.) probably have a lot to do with how people assess issues.

Finally, times and issues differ. Economic issues, which are within the direct experience of the audience members, are less likely to be affected by media attention than international issues, which are outside the direct experience of most people. Similarly, the media may have more influence at one stage of issue development than at others. Here, too, the cycle may be different for different kinds of issues. The work of Eyal (1979) is perhaps most instructive in this area, though the data analyses themselves do not address individual-level effects.

These observations are not meant to advance the cause of those who argue that the media are insignificant in the formation of public responses to social and political issues. Rather the observations are offered as cautionary. Championing a particular effects position without a firm theoretical and empirical foundation does very little to advance our understanding of mass media impact.

One can take the point of view that the existing data are encouraging, given the low level of sophistication of much of what has been done. Researchers have paid almost no attention to the concept of "issue," which may well mean rather little to audience members. Since all measures of issue salience assume respondents have a common meaning for that term, the neglect here is rather serious. Similarly, given much less attention than would seem appropriate are operationalization of the content variables and operationalization of the effects or criterion variables. In both cases, innovation has been given more attention than replication. Serious thought about how the measure actually reflects the concepts of concern has been almost totally nonexistent.

If the existing research can be used to direct what follows, of course, it has served a very useful purpose. What must be understood is that, at present, relatively little is known. The effects of the mass media on citizen assessment of issue importance are relatively unplotted. Whether such effects take place with any regularity is still an open question.

REFERENCES

ATKIN, C., J. HOCKING, and S. McDERMOTT (1979) "Home state voter response and secondary media coverage," pp. 429-436 in S. Kraus (ed.) The Great Debates Carter vs. Ford 1976. Bloomington: Indiana University Press.

BECKER, L. B., D. H. WEAVER, D. A. GRABER, and M. E. McCOMBS (1979) "Influence on public agendas," pp. 418-428 in S. Kraus (ed.) *The Great Debates Carter vs. Ford 1976.* Bloomington: Indiana University Press.

BECKER, L. E., M. E. McCOMBS, and J. M. McLEOD (1975) "The development of political cognitions," pp. 21-63 in S. Chaffee (ed.) Political Communication. Beverly Hills: Sage Publications.

BERELSON, B., P. LAZARSFELD, and W. McPHEE (1954) Voting. Chicago: University of Chicago Press.

BLUMLER, J. G. and J. M. McLEOD (1974) "Communication and voter turnout in Britain," pp. 265-312 in T. Legatt (ed.) Sociological Theory and Survey Research. Beverly Hills: Sage Publications.

CAMPBELL, D. T. (1957) "Factors relevant to the validity of experiments in social settings." Psychological Bulletin 54: 297-312.

CHAFFEE, S. H. and F. IZCARAY (1975) "Mass communication functions in a media-rich developing society." Communication Research 2: 367-395.

CLARKE, P. and F. G. KLINE (1974) "Media effects reconsidered." Communication Research 1: 224-240.

COHEN, B. C. (1963) The Press and Foreign Policy. Princeton, NJ: Princeton University Press.

EDELSTEIN, A. (1974) The Uses of Mass Communication in Decision Making. New York: Praeger.

ERBRING, L., E. N. GOLDENBERG, and A. H. MILLER (1980) "Front-page news and real-world cues: a new look at agenda-setting by the media." American Journal of Political Science 24: 16-49.

EYAL, C. H. (1979) "Time frame in agenda-setting research," Ph.D. dissertation, Syracuse University.

GADZIALA, S. M. (1980) "A re-examination of the agenda-setting function of the 1976 debates." Ph.D. thesis, Ohio State University.

HOVLAND, C. I. (1959) "Reconciling conflicting results derived from experimental and survey studies of attitude change." American Psychologist 14: 8-17.

——— (ed.) (1957) Order of Presentation in Persuasion. New Haven, CT: Yale University Press.

——— and I. L. JANIS (eds.) (1959) Personality and Persuasibility. New Haven, CT: Yale University Press.

KEPPLINGER, H. M. (1979) "Paradigm change in communications research." Communication 4: 163-182.

KLAPPER, J. T. (1960) The Effects of Mass Communication. New York: Macmillan.

KRAUS, S. and D. DAVIS (1976) The Effects of Mass Communication on Political Behavior. University Park: Pennsylvania State University Press.

LANG, K. and G. E. LANG (1968) Politics and Television. Chicago: Quadrangle Books.

——— (1966) "The mass media and voting," pp. 455-472 in B. Berelson and M. Janowitz (eds.) Reader in Public Opinion and Communication. New York: Macmillan.

LAZARSFELD, P., B. BERELSON, and H. GAUDET (1948) The people's choice. New York: Columbia University Press.

LIPPMANN, W. (1922) Public Opinion. New York: Macmillan.

McCOMBS, M. E. (1979) "Introduction: setting the agenda for agenda-setting research." Presented to the American Association for Public Opinion Research, Buck Hill Falls, Pennsylvania.

——— and D. L. SHAW (1972) "The agenda-setting function of mass media." Public Opinion Quarterly 36: 176-187.

McLEOD, J. M., J. A. DURALL, D. A. ZIEMKE, and C. R. BYBEE (1979) "Reactions of young and older voters: expanding the context of effects," pp. 348-367 in S. Kraus (ed.) The Great Debates Carter vs. Ford 1976. Bloomington: Indiana University Press.

McLEOD, J. M., L. B. BECKER, and J. E. BYRNES (1974) "Another look at the agenda-setting function of the press." Communication Research 1: 131-166.

NOELLE-NEUMANN, E. (1974) "The spiral of silence—a theory of public opinion." Journal of Communication 24: 43-51.

PATTERSON, T. E. and R. D. McCLURE (1976) The Unseeing Eye. New York: Putnam.

ROBINSON, M. J. (1976) 'Public affairs television and the growth of political malaise: the case of 'the selling of the Pentagon.' " American Political Science Review 70: 409-32.

ROSENBERG, M. J., C. I. HOVLAND, W. J. McGUIRE, R. P. ABELSON, and J. W. BREHM (1960) Attitude Organization and Change. New Haven, CT: Yale University Press.

SEARS, D. O. and S. H. CHAFFEE (1979) "Uses and effects of the 1976 debates: an overview of empirical studies," pp. 223-261 in S. Kraus (ed.) The Great Debates Carter vs. Ford 1976. Bloomington: Indiana University Press.

SEARS, D. O. and R. E. WHITNEY (1973) "Political persuasion," pp. 253-289 in I. Pool and W. Schramm (eds.) Handbook of Communication. Chicago: Rand-McNally.

SHAW, D. L. and M. E. McCOMBS (1977) The Emergence of American Political Issues. St. Paul, MN: West.

SIUNE, K. and O. BORRE (1975) "Setting the agenda for a Danish election." Journal of Communication 25, 1: 65-73.

WEAVER, D. H., D. A. GRABER, M. E. McCOMBS, and C. H. EYAL (1981) Media Agenda-Setting in a Presidential Election: Issue, Images, Interest. New New York: Praeger.

WINTER, J. P. and C. H. EYAL (1980) "An agenda-setting time-frame for the civil rights issue 1954-1976." Presented to the International Communication Association, Acapulco, Mexico.

David Weaver here reviews results of a study of agenda-setting in the 1976 U.S. presidential election, conducted by himself and Doris Graber, Maxwell McCombs, and Chaim Eyal. In his review, he offers qualified support for the agenda-setting hypothesis and qualified rejection of an hypothesis that agenda-setting constitutes manipulation by the media. Weaver is associate professor of journalism and director of the Bureau of Media Research at Indiana University.

31

MEDIA AGENDA-SETTING AND
MEDIA MANIPULATION

David H. Weaver

I would like to deal with these questions:

(1) What is the evidence with regard to mass media agenda-setting? Or, put another way, can we conclude that the media tend to shape our perceptions of what is important and thus tell us what to think *about,* if not what to think?

(2) If media agenda-setting does exist, is it properly characterized as a form of media manipulation? How far can we go in answering this question with the available empirical evidence? What light does this evidence shed on the definition of media manipulation we have been asked to work with (the influencing of people without them being aware of the influence or the extent and nature of the influence)?

Let me tackle the question of media agenda-setting first. Is there sufficient evidence to conclude that the mass media generally set the public agenda? That is, do the media generally shape our perceptions of what to think *about,* as distinguished from our attitudes, opinions, and feelings? Does continued emphasis over time by the media on certain issues and subjects influence the perceived salience, or importance, of these subjects among citizens of the society in which the media operate?

From David H. Weaver, "Media Agenda-Setting and Media Manipulation," *Massacommunicatie,* 1981, IX, 5, pp. 213-229. Reprinted by permission of the publisher and author.

The quick and oversimplified answer to this question is, I believe, yes. But I would hasten to qualify this positive answer by saying that I mean yes only with regard to certain *groups* of people, to certain kinds of issues or subjects, to certain periods of time, to certain media, and to certain societies.

Upon what evidence do I base my qualified belief in media agenda-setting? I base it mainly upon studies of voters in the United States, although there have been some studies of media agenda-setting involving samples of general publics both inside and outside the United States.

In particular, though, I base my answer to the first question on the results of a yearlong study of the 1976 presidential election campaign in the United States, a study which involved more than 1,100 interviews with about 150 voters in three quite diverse communities, content analysis of thousands of newspaper and television news stories during the entire year, and detailed study of the daily diaries and in-depth conversations of a "core panel" of voters in one suburban Chicago community. The results of this study are reported in a just-published book entitled *Media Agenda-Setting in a Presidential Election: Issues, Images, and Interest* by myself and my three collaborators on the study, Professors Doris Graber, Maxwell McCombs, and Chaim Eyal (Weaver et al., 1981).

So, before attempting to address the second set of questions concerning media manipulation, I would like to discuss some of the major findings of this study with the hope of shedding some light, however dim, on the various qualifications to my general belief in media agenda-setting.

THE 1976 ELECTION STUDY

We conducted this study during the entire election year of 1976 because we believed a *long-term* look at media agenda-setting was needed to more precisely specify the circumstances under which such influence does and does not occur. We also felt there was a need to *expand* the focus of agenda-setting research beyond issues to political candidates, candidate image qualities, and people's general interest in politics. And, finally, we felt that a replication of earlier agenda-setting studies, especially those based on the 1968 and 1972 U.S. presidential campaigns, was needed to investigate simultaneously a number of intervening variables in the agenda-setting process suggested by these earlier studies, such as the social origins and characteristics of audience members, their media exposure patterns, and their levels of motivation to pay attention to media messages.

Assumptions

One of the most fundamental assumptions underlying this 1976 study, and previous ones, is that the press does *not* serve as a simple conduit or as a *mirror* held up to the world. In other words, the press does not *reflect* reality, but rather *filters* and *shapes* it, much as a kaleidoscope filters and shapes light. And this concentration over time on relatively few issues and subjects, and certain aspects of these subjects, out of the vast range of possible issues and subjects generally leads to the public perceiving these relatively few issues and subjects as more salient, or more important, than other issues or subjects. Thus we assumed that in covering the 1976 presidential campaign, the press, mainly newspapers and television news programs, did not simply *reflect* the campaign issues, events, and arguments but rather *selected* and *shaped* certain of these considered "newsworthy" and gave little or no coverage to those not considered "newsworthy." And we also assumed that those issues, candidates, and candidate image qualities most stressed in the coverage of newspapers and television became more salient to voters than did those not stressed.

Methods

To begin, we did not test the first assumption of press selectivity as rigorously as would be desired. We made some attempts to compare which issues were being stressed by political parties and candidates with which issues were being stressed by the press, but the main thrust of our study was in testing the second assumption, that increased media emphasis on certain subjects over time results in increased salience of these subjects among the public.

To check on the relationships of press agendas with voter agendas over time, we recruited a panel of about 50 persons in each of three communities of different sizes and from different regions of the United States in January of 1976. The panel members were purposively chosen from larger random samples of registered voters to ensure that each voter used either newspapers or television or both for political news at least "some of the time." The interviews were conducted in Evanston, Illinois, a suburban Chicago community; metropolitan Indianapolis, Indiana; and Lebanon, New Hampshire, a small New England town. Those voters not using newspapers or television for political information were eliminated from the panel because we reasoned that they could not be *directly* affected by political messages from these media. This procedure of limiting the sample to randomly selected registered voters who used newspapers and/or television for political information probably produced a sort of "elite" panel of respondents who were more politically interested and of higher socioeconomic status than would have been obtained using conventional random sampling procedures, but it also isolated those persons *most susceptible* to direct political influence from newspapers and television. Nevertheless, our findings must be construed as applying only to registered voters using newspapers and/or television for political information at least some of the time during the campaign, even though some of our panel's responses did not differ significantly from comparable responses of nationwide samples used by Gallup and Roper polls.

In exchange for a payment of $50, these voters agreed to be interviewed throughout the year. These interviews were conducted nine times—in February, March, May, July, August, September, October, November, and in late December and early January of 1977. All interviews were by telephone except for an extended face-to-face interview in July and small group meetings in December and January following the election. In addition, a "core panel" of 21 persons in

Evanston furnished taped in-depth interviews and completed daily diaries recording news stories that had come to their attention. These voters were selected in the same manner as the others in our study, but were questioned far more intensively about their past and current lifestyles and media use patterns, about their attention to specific news stories, and about their knowledge of the election and other current happenings. These "core panelists" were interviewed 10 times for an average of two hours each interview, and the average number of diary stories per person, either written or dictated to a telephone interviewer, was 533.

The data from our regular and "core panel" respondents were supplemented by content analyses of four daily newspapers and the early evening (main) news broadcasts of the three national television networks as well as the 5 p.m. NBC and 10 p.m. CBS Chicago local news broadcasts. The *Valley News* and the Chicago *Tribune,* the principal newspapers used by our panel members in Lebanon and Evanston, respectively, were analyzed on a daily basis for the entire year of 1976. In Indianapolis, it was necessary to code both the *News* and the *Star* because each serves a rather distinct portion of the city's population. For these two newspapers, every fourth issue was coded across the entire year of 1976, beginning with a random start point. Stories of three column inches or longer were classified into one, two, or three of 73 subject matter categories and into one, two, or three of 65 issue categories. More than one subject matter or issue category was used only if coders decided that a given story equally emphasized more than one issue or was about more than one subject. In all, about 13,500 stories from the *Tribune* were coded, as compared to about 3,000 each from the *Star* and *News* and about 3,500 from the *Valley News.* We used the abstracts prepared by the Vanderbilt University Library Archives for coding television network news for 1976 and we used the actual broadcasts for the local Chicago news programs. In addition to subject and issue categories, we also categorized each newspaper or television story by date, page location or order in broadcast, size or length, and other descriptive attributes.

Thus we were able to compare the ranking of various issues, candidates, candidate image attributes, and subjects over an entire year by newspapers and television with similar rankings by groups of voters. While this kind of evidence does not *prove* that media emphasis on certain subjects results in public concern over these subjects, it does provide a look at the timing of changes in media emphasis as compared to the timing of changes in public concerns. In other words, it does tell us if changes in media emphasis precede, follow, or occur simultaneously with changes in public concerns.

Findings—Issues

With regard to *issues,* our data suggest that media agenda-setting varies according to the time period of the campaign, the kind of news medium being considered, the nature of the issues, and the orientations and characteristics of the voters.

The influence of both newspapers and television on concern over issues seems to be greatest during the summer and least during the final few months of the election campaign. This suggests that the issue agenda-setting process is not static, but varies as the campaign progresses. But it should be noted that this media influence was confined mainly to those issues *least* likely to have a direct impact on voters' daily lives—those we called "unobtrusive" such as foreign affairs, government credibility, government spending and size, crime, the environment, and energy. For the more "obtrusive" economic issues such as unemployment, inflation, and taxes, we found little evidence of media agenda-setting, suggesting that personal experience is a more powerful teacher of issue salience than are the mass media when issues have a direct impact on voters' daily lives.

Our study also suggests that discussions with other persons are important in setting an agenda of issues in an election campaign. As the 1976 campaign wore on, and as political conversations increased among the voters we studied, the agendas of issues of most personal concern and those perceived to be important to other voters in the community became more similar to those discussed with others. By the last month of the campaign, these three separate issue agendas were nearly identical. Thus both direct personal experiences and conversations with other persons serve to mediate the agenda-setting influence of newspapers and television with regard to issues.

We should not belittle media influence, however. All three voter issue agendas, it must be remembered, generally became more similar over time to earlier newspaper issue agendas, suggesting that newspapers had an important influence on which issues were discussed with others and considered important by the voters in our study.

In addition, we found that the distinctions between newspapers and television as issue agenda-setters became less pronounced as the election drew nearer. During the primary elections in the spring of 1976, we found evidence of a "two-step flow" of media agenda-setting, with the newspaper issue agenda remaining very stable over time, the television agenda changing to become generally more similar to the stable newspaper agenda, and the voter agendas becoming more similar to the television issue agenda. But after the summer political party conventions, the newspaper and television issue agendas became nearly identical and changed little. Separate analyses for each community suggested that newspapers exerted an influence on the perceived importance of unobtrusive issues over a longer period of time—about two months—compared to television's influence span of about one month, supporting the idea of a "two-step flow" from newspapers to television to the voters.

As I hinted earlier, the nature of the issues was an important factor mediating the influence of media agendas on public agendas. This was particularly true in the early spring period of the campaign. During this time, the more *unobtrusive* issues, those less likely to be directly experienced by voters, were ranked by all voters combined in nearly the same order as they had been by newspapers and television during the previous two months or so, whereas the more *obtrusive* economic issues were rated considerably more important by the voters than by either newspapers or television. By the summer of 1976, the distinction between obtrusive and unobtrusive issues was less clear, however. The unobtrusive issues seemingly had become more salient after six months of rather consistent media emphasis. This seemed to make them more established concerns of the voters and less dependent upon current media emphasis.

In contrast to the declining importance of newspapers and television as issue agenda-setters and to the decreased significance of the nature of the issues later in the year, the characteristics and orientations of voters seemed to become *more* important as the election campaign drew to a close. Although levels of motivation to follow the campaign had fairly minor effects on voter issue agendas during the spring and summer seasons, this was not true during the fall period. Those voters with a high need for orientation (high interest and high uncertainty about whom to support) had issue agendas in the fall that were substantially *more similar* to the media agendas than did other voters.

Thus motivation to follow the campaign was most important in the agenda-setting process near the *end* of the race when the need for information was greatest for the still-undecided voters. And after the election, voters with a high need for orientation were more likely than other voters to cite issues as more important than either candidate images or political party affiliation in deciding for whom to vote, suggesting that they were paying more attention to the issue-related content of the media near the end of the campaign than were other voters.

In separate analyses for each community in our study, we also found that the higher educational and occupational levels of the voters in Evanston, Illinois, seemed to work *against* issue agenda-setting roles for newspapers and television, perhaps because higher status voters rely more on other sources of information, including discussion with other persons, for establishing their issue agendas than do less-educated and lower status voters.

Thus, with regard to *issues,* we found that media agenda-setting influence varies in potency according to the time period of the campaign, the kind of news medium (newspapers or television), the nature and substance of the issues, and the social characteristics (education and occupation) and motivations of voters to follow the campaign. But in spite of such variations, press influence on the salience of unobtrusive issues remains important for most of the groups of voters we studied. The voters *least* likely to be influenced by media issue agenda-setting were those with more education, higher status jobs, more prior political knowledge, and more interest in the campaign. Apparently greater knowledge and more sources of information permit greater freedom to form independent judgments about the importance of various issues. But for the majority of less well-informed voters, issue emphasis by the press, especially newspapers, seems especially significant early in a presidential campaign for determining which unobtrusive issues voters will deem most important and will discuss most often.

But, having said this, what about our first assumption that the press is not a simple conduit or conveyor belt passively reflecting the issue agendas of the political parties, interest groups, and candidates?

As I said earlier, we did not test this assumption as rigorously or systematically as we tested the second assumption concerning press influence on voters. But there is evidence from our study that not all of the issues being emphasized by the

Republican and Democratic candidates and party platforms were being heavily covered by the press. And in another major yearlong study of the 1976 election by political scientist Thomas Patterson (1980), it was found that the issues which the candidates stressed most heavily were *not* the same as those displayed most prominently in the news. Patterson found that in their campaign speeches and television political advertising, the candidates talked mostly about "diffuse" issues: broad policy proposals such as the commitment to maintain a healthy economy. In contrast, the media stressed what Colin Seymour-Ure (1974) has called "clear-cut" issues—those which neatly divide the candidates, provoke conflict, and can be stated in simple terms, usually by reference to shorthand labels such as "busing" and "detente."

One of Patterson's (1980) major conclusions regarding issues in the 1976 presidential campaign is that the issue news reflected the interests of the press more than the candidates' interests. This suggests that our initial assumption of the press as a kaleidoscope filtering and shaping reality, rather than a mirror reflecting it, has some validity, at least with respect to the issues emphasized in the 1976 U.S. presidential campaign. Still, more needs to be done to systematically compare the agendas of the various candidates, parties, and groups with press agendas.

Findings—Images

As mentioned earlier, we sought to broaden the focus of the agenda-setting idea beyond issues in our study to include candidate images and general interest in the subject of politics as one item on a larger agenda of concerns. With respect to candidate images, our study suggests that the press plays a major role in making some candidates, and certain of their characteristics, more salient than others. In fact, this aspect of agenda-setting by the press probably has more influence on the voters' early perceptions of the campaign, and the final choices available at election time, than does issue agenda-setting.

The most basic dimension of a candidate's image is name recognition, or awareness. If the voters have not heard of a candidate or do not recognize his or her name, they are not likely to have much of an image of him or her. Therefore the most fundamental *image* agenda-setting role performed by the press is simply to familiarize voters with candidates' names. In this process it is crucial how much coverage is given to the various contenders before and during the first primaries of the election campaign. Our analysis of the Chicago *Tribune*'s coverage of the candidates showed that between January 15 and June 30—three weeks after the last primary—70% of the total information referred to just three candidates—Ford, Carter, and Reagan—leaving the seven other serious contenders (Wallace, Bayh, Brown, Harris, Udall, Jackson, and Church) with a scant 30% of the coverage. And Patterson (1980) found in his study of 1,200 voters in Erie, Pennsylvania, and Los Angeles, California, that before the first primary in New Hampshire, the Democratic candidates were largely unknown to the voters, but after subsequent news coverage focused heavily on Carter; he was the sole Democrat to become dramatically more familiar to the voters. In fact, before the first primary election in New Hampshire, only 20% of Patterson's voters felt they "knew" Carter, Udall, Harris, Bayh, Brown, Church, or Jackson, but after heavy news coverage more than 80% felt they knew Carter. Comparable figures in our study of three communities were a 16% vote for Carter as front-runner in February, rising to 80% in March. In contrast, recognition levels rose by only 14% for Udall, Brown, and Jackson, by only 9% for Church, remained fairly constant for Harris, and even declined for Bayh.

And another study by Becker and McCombs (1978), using data from a study in New York, also found that from February to March, voters went from being unsure of who was leading the crowded Democratic field of candidates to placing Jimmy Carter at the top of the list—or agenda—of candidates. Based on content analysis of *Newsweek* magazine and correlations of media use patterns of voters with levels of recognition of the candidates, Becker and McCombs concluded that the media were at least partially responsible for these shifts in voter perceptions.

Thus there is evidence from the 1976 U.S. presidential election to support the conclusion that the press is a powerful influence in setting the agenda of candidates early in the primary elections by focusing coverage on only one or two perceived front-runners in each of the two major political parties. But what of the images of individual candidates? Does the press also help to set the agenda of image attributes, or qualities, for individual politicians?

In answering this question, we relied on nearly 2,000 news stories from the Chicago *Tribune* that dealt with candidate images and were specially coded in terms of various image dimensions, as well as the responses of our panels of voters. We were not able to analyze network television presentations of candidate images from the Vanderbilt University abstracts. But cross-lagged correlational analysis with the *Tribune* content data and the Illinois voter descriptions of the various candidates suggested that the *Tribune* descriptions of Carter and Ford influenced the Illinois voters rather than vice versa. These findings support the assumption that newspaper emphasis on certain image qualities of candidates can lead to increased salience of these qualities among voters.

We also found that the voters in our study thought it easier to learn about candidate images than about issues, enhancing the chance for image agenda-setting to occur. In fact, voters in our study consistently referred to images three or four times as often as issues in their descriptions of Carter and Ford. This was especially true of voters who were above average in interest in the campaign and in use of television to follow politics. In its news stories about the candidates, the press emphasized personal qualities of the candidates and campaigning activities, and the voters seemed to learn accordingly. Image attributes pertaining to personality traits and styles of the candidates were better remembered than those pertaining to job qualifications and ideology, a finding duplicated in Patterson's (1980) yearlong study.

Like issue agenda-setting, however, image agenda-setting appears to be neither simple nor direct. It varies according to a number of factors, such as media exposure patterns of voters, interpersonal communication patterns, prior knowledge and attitudes, and levels of motivation to follow the campaign. We found, for example, that prior knowledge, high interest, and high media exposure were all linked positively to learning about the personality traits and campaign styles of the candidates and, to a lesser extent, their job qualifications and ideological positions. And the more highly educated voters in our study tended to describe the candidates more in terms of their intellectual capabilities than did the less-educated voters, who described them more in terms of emotional preferences, suggesting that educational level also mediated in what kinds of image qualities were learned from those emphasized by the press. But, overall, our data suggest that the press, especially newspapers, played an important role in setting the agenda of candidates during the primary elections and the agenda of image characteristics for Carter and Ford later in the campaign. And the data from our "core panel" in Evanston suggest that both issue and image agenda-setting largely involve rather superficial learning by voters from media messages, rather than considered choices based on careful analysis of the wealth of information available in the press.

Findings—Interest

In addition to finding that the media played an important role in making certain issues, candidates, and image attributes more salient among the voters in our study, we also found that frequent use of television to follow politics during the primary elections was rather strongly related to subsequent voter interest in the 1976 presidential campaign. For the remainder of the campaign, there was a mostly reciprocal relationship between use of newspapers and television to follow politics and interest in the campaign. Thus there is evidence that exposure to the media, particularly use of television to follow politics, is most important in the spring primary period of a presidential campaign for stimulating subsequent interest in the campaign, that is, for raising the salience of politics in general on a larger public agenda. Coupled with our finding that more interested voters learned more about the personalities and styles of the candidates, this suggests that heavy press emphasis on the presidential campaign early in the year can lead, through subsequent increased interest, to more learning about the candidates in such a campaign.

CONCLUSIONS: MEDIA AGENDA-SETTING

Of course, it must be remembered that the evidence of issue and image agenda-setting supplied by our 1976 study, and by nearly every other study of agenda-setting I am aware of, is based on a comparison of media rankings of issues, or topics, with rankings of similar issues or topics by *groups* of respondents, not by individuals. Typically in such studies, randomly selected individual voters or members of the public are asked about the issues of most concern to them, and typically they mention one or two such issues. These responses from individuals are then aggregated into a ranking of issues which reflects no single individual, but rather a group, or groups, of individuals. Thus in nearly all agenda-setting studies, it is *not* accurate to speak of the media influencing individuals' agendas, but rather of the media influencing the *distribution* of the top one or two concerns among representative groups of voters or citizens. Even though this is not as dramatic an effect as some advocates of agenda-setting might hope for, it is still an important phenomenon, I believe, for it suggests that the relative amount of emphasis on various subjects by the press determines, and/or is reflective of, the size of various groups of individuals in a given community or society who are most concerned about these same subjects. And the evidence collected over time, at least in the early periods of the 1976 U.S. presidential campaign, suggests that the direction of influence is mostly from the press to the voters, rather than the reverse, a conclusion at least somewhat supported by other studies of agenda-setting across time using data from a 1972 U.S. election study (Weaver et al., 1975; Shaw and McCombs, 1977) and by another study based on the 1976 U.S. election (Eyal, 1979).

Communication researcher Lee Becker (1981), in an article reflecting on agenda-setting research, argues that because the few studies which have been conducted at the individual level have produced very limited, or nonexistent, findings of media agenda-setting (McLeod et al., 1974; Siune and Borre, 1975; Erbring et al., 1980), "the effects of the mass media on citizen assessment of issue importance are relatively unplotted." And he concludes by writing that "whether such effects take place with any regularity is still an open question." My own assessment of the agenda-setting evidence is a bit more "optimistic" than his, as I indicated earlier. I interpret the data gathered thus far as indicating some support for the proposition that media emphasis on certain subjects over time does influence the number of citizens concerned about these subjects. This is, of course, *not* the same thing as saying that the press sets an agenda of issues or subjects for the individual citizen or voter, but it comes down more on the side of a macro-level, or societal level, agenda-setting process than does Becker's (1981) conclusion. I do agree with Becker, however, that media agenda-setting is a complex process and the media probably do not act alone in providing cues to audience members about issues. I also agree that the uses made of the media, as well as the social situation within which audience members reside, have a lot to do with how people assess issues. And I agree that the media may have more influence at one stage of issue development than at others, and more influence with respect to some kinds of issues than others.

Having said all this, however, my answer to the first question of the existence of media agenda-setting is till a qualified yes. In other words, I conclude that there is evidence to suggest that media emphasis on certain issues and subjects over certain periods of time does influence which issues and subjects become of most concern to certain groups of people in an industrialized democracy such as the United States. And I agree with Katz's (1980) observation that "as a latent consequence of telling us what to think *about*, the agenda-setting effect can sometimes influence what we think." Our data from the 1976 election study suggest that by concentrating on certain attributes of candidates Carter and Ford and downplaying others, the Chicago *Tribune* did contribute to voter *evaluations* of these candidates as well as to voter images of them.

Put another way, instead of concluding, as Klapper (1960) did some 20 years ago, that "Mass communication ordinarily does not serve as a necessary and sufficient cause of audience effects but rather functions among and through a nexus of mediating functions and influences," I conclude, *with regard to public agenda-setting*, that mass communication ordinarily functions among and through a nexus of mediating functions and influences, but that it often does serve as a necessary and sufficient cause of audience effects.

MEDIA MANIPULATION

Having argued that media agenda-setting does exist in a societal- or community-level sense, if not in an individual one, is this form of media influence properly characterized as a form of media manipulation?

The quick answer to this question, it seems to me, is that "it depends." And it depends, first, on one's definition of manipulation.

Definitions of Manipulation

I have been asked to interpret the term *manipulation* to mean the influencing of people without them being aware of such influence, or without them recognizing the extent or nature of the influence. But various dictionary definitions of the term *manipulation* usually imply a kind of *unfair* use of influence for self-serving ends. For example, *The Oxford English Dictionary* (1970) defines "manipulation" as follows: "To manage by dexterous contrivance or influence; especially to treat unfairly or insidiously for one's own advantage." And *The American Heritage Dictionary of the English Language* (1976) defines manipulation as "shrewd or devious management, especially for one's own advantage."

If we take these dictionary definitions of manipulation as the proper meaning of the term, then I would argue that media agenda-setting is *not* a form of media manipulation, for I know of no systematic evidence to suggest that journalists in various media organizations generally select, consciously or subconsciously, issues and subjects for news coverage with the aim of treating audiences unfairly for the journalists' own advantage. In fact, many of the recent studies of news organizations would suggest just the opposite—that journalists are so constrained by news presentation formats and conventions, by organizational structures and ideologies, and by professional norms and values that they really have little freedom to choose what subjects to emphasize or even, in some cases, how to present these subjects to their audiences (Glasgow University Media Group, 1976, 1980; Hartmann and Husband, 1974; Cohen and Young, 1973; Hall et al., 1978; Tuchman, 1974; Golding and Elliott, 1979; Schlesinger, 1978).

In writing about the production practices of television journalists during the 1979 British general election, for example, Blumler (1980) compares such practices to coin-operated gates:

> The production practices of television journalists, then, could almost be compared to turnstiles to a zoo, which only coins of a certain size and shape will fit, such that politicians' publicity aides not only become skilled at

manufacturing the right coins of entry, but also come in some cases even to believe that the zoo keeper really knows better than anyone else what kind of food will most suit the palates of the denizens in their cages on the other side!

Although he goes on to say that he does not mean to imply that a single feature of broadcasting journalism determines the receptivity of television to political materials, and that it is all far more complex than that, this analogy nicely illustrates the point that individual journalist's motives, and those of their sources, are often subordinated to constraints in the form of news presentation practices.

Thus, there is little in these organizational studies, it seems to me, to support the kind of "conspiracy theory" notion of manipulation that is implied by the dictionary definitions. But what of some less conspiratorial definition of manipulation proposed by others? If manipulation means only that people are unaware of media influence, or unaware of the extent and nature of such influence, then is media agenda-setting a form of media manipulation? I believe the answer to this question is both yes and no: Yes, there are some *potentials* for people being influenced without being fully aware of this influence, and, no, there are some mediating factors that work against this kind of media agenda-setting influence. Let me discuss the potentials for this kind of media manipulation first.

Potentials for Manipulation

To begin, it can be argued that media emphasis on roughly the same issues, the same political candidates, the same characteristics of these candidates, and the same subjects over prolonged periods of time can result in rather uncritical audience acceptance of the importance of these things. As Katz (1980) so succinctly puts it, "Influence takes time." And, in fact, the findings from our 1976 election study and from other agenda-setting studies suggest that media emphasis over time can influence what subjects become of most concern to certain groups of people. Furthermore, the media organizational studies just referred to argue that there are constraints, both within and outside the press, that *reinforce* the stability of media agendas over time.

But are readers and viewers unaware of the extent of this influence? Here the evidence is lacking in most agenda-setting studies, simply because most such studies have failed to ask respondents *why* they think various issues or subjects are important.

In an unpublished study of 531 registered voters in Ohio, conducted by Becker (1981) during the 1980 U.S. presidential election, however, respondents were asked why they had selected a certain problem as being the most important one facing the country. Only 5 persons of the 531—or just under 1%—mentioned mass media. As Becker notes, some caution should be used in interpreting this finding because it may have been considered inappropriate by some persons to mention the media, but nevertheless, as he puts it, "it hardly seems likely that many respondents considered the media to be the sole determinant or even a very significant determinant of their selection of issues." And in our 1976 election study, we found from detailed interviews and analysis of the diaries of our "core sample" in Evanston that "both issue and image agenda-setting largely involve acts of faith by voters in media judgments, rather than considered choices based on careful analysis of the wealth of information available from the mass media" (Weaver et al., 1981: 202).

Another potential for unrecognized media agenda-setting effects stems from audience members' *dependence* upon the press for awareness of, and information about, the more "unobtrusive" issues (those that are not likely to be directly experienced, such as foreign affairs, national defense, government credibility, government spending and size, and so on). Because many persons have little or no direct experience with these subjects, and because the news consumption habits of many persons are limited to a daily newspaper and/or television news, this makes such persons particularly dependent upon these news media for their perceptions of the importance and nature of these subjects. Our 1976 election study suggested agenda-setting effects for "unobtrusive" issues, but not for "obtrusive" ones (such as inflation, taxes, and so on) with which people were more likely to have direct experience. Thus, to the extent that the subjects emphasized by the press are outside the realm of personal experience of most of the audience members, and not dealt with in different ways by other sources of information, the potential for media manipulation is increased.

And, finally, to the extent that selective processes (exposure, perception, retention) and interpersonal communication are *not* operating, the potential for media influence, and thus media manipulation, may be enhanced. As Katz (1980: 120) has argued, it seems likely that the "power" of the press "rises and falls, conceptually, as a function of the importance attributed to the intervening processes of selectivity and interpersonal relations." And our 1976 election study suggests that early in a presidential campaign is the period of greatest media influence—a time when interpersonal discussion of the campaign is relatively infrequent and perhaps when selective processes are less likely to be operating because of the relatively low level of coverage as compared to later in the campaign. Our findings from the 1976 presidential election also suggest that the characteristics and orientations of voters mattered least in the early stages of the campaign, reinforcing the notion that selective processes were not operating or were not countering media influence if operating then. And we found that some characteristics of voters that were related to lack of selectivity were positively linked to learning about candidate personalities and styles from the press, including more prior knowledge, higher interest in politics, and greater media exposure.

Undoubtedly, there are other potentials for manipulation in media agenda-setting effects, but these seem to me to be the major ones. Let me turn now to some factors which may serve to work against media manipulation.

Mediating Factors

One of the most obvious checks on the agenda-setting influence of the press, and its potential for manipulation, is *direct personal experience*. Our 1976 election study and an earlier one spanning an eight-year period by Harold Zucker (1978) suggest that the public salience of obtrusive issues, those likely to have a direct impact on many people's lives, is not much related to media emphasis. This suggests that personal experience is a more powerful teacher of the importance of subjects than the mass media. Thus, to the extent that citizens directly experience the problems and issues of the day, the potential for mass media manipulation is decreased. Of course, it can be argued that the increasing size and urbanization of many societies results in increasing isolation of members of society from more institutionalized social problems and issues, so that personal experience with or firsthand knowledge of these problems decreases (Wilkins, 1964).

But another intervening factor exists that can partially cut through the barriers of limited personal experience: *conversations with other persons* in one's family or at social gatherings of various kinds. To the extent that interpersonal discussion of various subjects increases, the potential for media manipulation probably decreases. Our 1976 study shows that as the campaign wore on, and as political conversations increased among the voters we studied, the personal concern and perceived community issue agendas became more similar to the personal discussion agendas. And Katz (1980) rightly points out that empirical research beginning with the Lazarsfeld et al. (1944) voting study has found that primary groups of family and friends are more effective than the media in influencing voting decisions and that "opinion leaders" are important filters and interpreters of media messages. Of course, much of this research is concerned with specific opinions and attitudes—what we think —rather than the subjects of those opinions and attitudes—what we think *about*. Nevertheless, there is some mixed evidence from the 1976 agenda-setting study and others that interpersonal communication agendas do not always simply reflect media agendas. It is likely, as Becker (1981) argues, that *both* media content and interpersonal discussion influence what issues are of most concern to citizens.

Yet another intervening factor to media agenda-setting and its possible manipulative effects are the *selective processes* of exposure, perception, and retention mentioned earlier. Whether stemming from psychological states, as implied in the studies of cognitive dissonance and the psychology of entertainment (Sears and Freedman, 1971; Katz, 1968; Mendelsohn, 1966; Tannenbaum, 1980), or from social origins and roles, as implied in some of the uses and gratifications research (Blumler and Katz, 1974; Johnstone, 1974; Adoni, 1979; Blumler, 1979a), such processes can work against the wholesale adoption of press agendas and thus serve to counteract possible manipulative influences of the press.

In addition, the *needs and interests* of individuals, and the resulting motives stemming from them, can be viewed as working against media manipulation in at least two senses. In the first place, such interests and felt needs can result in persons' seeking information from other sources besides newspapers and television. There is evidence from our 1976 study, for example, that those voters with more education, higher status jobs, more prior political knowledge, and more political interest were *least* likely to have issue agendas highly similar to press issue agendas, perhaps because higher status voters rely more on other sources of information, including more frequent political discussions with other persons, for establishing their issue agendas than do lower status voters.

And in the second place, the motivation to seek information from either newspapers or television implies some awareness of the possibility of media influence. In other words, the person actively seeking information from the press may often *realize* that some of the things he or she is concerned about are the result of media emphasis. In fact, even though many voters in our 1976 election study seemed to base their judgments about the importance of various issues on rather superficial learning from the press, in their final group meetings at the end of the year many of them seemed aware that the issues they had considered important and had discussed with others during the campaign had their origins in newspaper and television coverage. And several of them expressed an awareness that the relative emphasis on issues in this coverage did not necessarily reflect the actual importance of such issues in the campaign. Thus, to the extent that some media audience members are aware of an agenda-setting influence from newspapers and television, the possibility for media manipulation is decreased, at least as defined here.

And finally, the professional norms of journalism may work against media manipulation of audience members because such norms include commitments to service to the audience, the protection of the confidentiality of sources, accuracy, impartiality, and empirical evidence—values more compatible with *informing* than with manipulating readers, listeners, and viewers. As Blumler and Gurevitch (1981) have noted, "communication behavior is *normatively prescribed*, involving *legitimated* expectations and actions. This suggests that the capacity of the participants to exchange resources or exercise influence is constrained by the guidelines pertaining to the roles they perform."

In other words, journalists are not entirely free to select and disseminate whatever material they wish to with the aim of influencing audience members in a certain manner, especially not in a covert or undetected manner. To report only on subjects that favor a particular personal or political point of view would soon cost most journalists their professional reputations and would lower the credibility of their media organizations. This does not mean that media cannot have agenda-setting influences or that such influences are fully recognized by audience members, but only that such influences are not likely to be based mainly on the personal preferences and desires of journalists. Whatever agenda-setting influences exist are more likely to be based on professional norms and news values which may be shared at least somewhat by audience members and journalists.

CONCLUSIONS

In trying to distinguish between potentials for and intervening factors in media manipulation, I confess to employing a somewhat false dichotomy, especially with regard to selective processes. As Blumler (1979b) points out, it is possible for selective processes to enhance, as well as to impede, media effects. It does not always follow that just because selective processes are *not* operating, media agenda-setting influence (and other kinds of media influence) is increased, a view which Blumler (1979b) nicely summarizes in his description of the "empty vessel model." Nor does it follow that just because selective processes *are* operating that media influence will necessarily be reduced. In our 1976 election study, we found that those voters who should have been *least* selective (those with the most interest and the most prior political knowledge) tended to be least influenced by media with regard to *issue* agendas, but most influenced by media with regard to learning about candidate *images*. Thus we have an example of apparent lack of selectivity *impeding* media influence in the case of issue agendas and *facilitating* media influence with regard to the learning of images.

In addition, there is evidence from the 1976 study that those persons most motivated to follow the campaign in the press (those with most interest and most uncertainty) had issue agendas which were more similar to the media agendas by the *end* of the campaign, suggesting that those voters who were least selective were most influenced at one time during the year, but not at another. These seemingly contradictory findings reinforce Blumler's (1979b) call for an approach to media effects that emphasizes the *relevance* of media content to the circumstances and felt needs of the receiver and thus recognizes that the media can have effects even though receivers are both selective and relatively autonomous. To what extent such effects are a form of limited media manipulation, in the sense that the receiver is not aware of them or their nature, needs to be more thoroughly researched.

It does seem, though, that on the basis of the media agenda-setting evidence reviewed here, there are rather strong *potentials* for such *limited* media manipulation with regard to the perceived importance of issues and subjects which are outside the personal experience of audience members, notwithstanding the possible mediating factors of interpersonal communication, selective processes, audience members' felt needs and interests, and the professional norms of journalism.

But this conclusion should not be interpreted as suggesting that I believe that media agenda-setting studies offer evidence in support of the dictionary definition of manipulation—that is, the unfair use of influence for self-serving ends. As I said earlier, I know of no systematic evidence to suggest that journalists generally select subjects to emphasize with the aim of treating audience members unfairly for the journalists' own ends. Therefore, I reject the "conspiracy theory" notion of media manipulation, while at the same time accepting the possibility that many media audience members may not be aware of the extent of media agenda-setting influence upon them. But even this conclusion is made with hesitation, in light of the evidence from our 1976 election study that some voters were aware of, and skeptical of, media agenda-setting, and in light of the evidence from Blumler and McQuail's (1968) study of the British General Election of 1964 that suggests that many voters were wary of the manipulative potential of television.

Finally, I would suggest that the proper definition of media manipulation should include more than just the lack of awareness of influence. It should include, in addition, a high level of dependency upon media and an element of self-serving, if not unfair, influence. Otherwise the boundaries between media influence and media manipulation remain hopelessly blurred.

REFERENCES

ADONI, H. (1979) "The functions of mass media in the political socialization of adolescents." Communication Research 6: 84-106.

American Heritage Dictionary of the English Language (1976) Boston: Houghton-Mifflin.

BECKER, L. B. (1981) "The mass media and citizen assessment of issue importance: a reflection on agenda-setting research," prepared for presentation to a symposium on new approaches in the study of political communication, Zurich, Switzerland, May 7 and 8, and reprinted in this section.

BECKER, L. B. and M. E. McCOMBS (1978) "The role of the press in determining voter reactions to presidential primaries." Human Communication Research 4: 301-307.

BLUMLER, J. G. (1980) "Political communication: democratic theory and broadcast practice," Inaugural Lecture delivered by Professor Blumler on December 1 as holder of a Personal Chair in the Social and Political Aspects of Broadcasting, University of Leeds, England, and reprinted in this section.

BLUMLER, J. G. (1979a) "The role of theory in uses and gratifications studies." Communication Research 6: 9-36.

BLUMLER, J. G. (1979b) "Models of mass media effects: 'like'—but oh how different!" pp. 61-70 in 25 Jaar Televisie in Vlaanderen, Centrum Voor Communicatiewetenschappen, Katholieke Universiteit Leuven.

BLUMLER, J. G. and M. GUREVITCH (1981) "Role relationships in political communication," in D. Nimmo and K. R. Sanders (eds.) Handbook of Political Communication. Beverly Hills, CA: Sage.

BLUMLER, J. G. and E. KATZ (1974) The Uses of Mass Communication. Beverly Hills, CA: Sage.

BLUMLER, J. G. and D. McQUAIL (1968) Television in Politics: Its Uses and Influence, London: Faber and Faber Limited.

COHEN, S. and J. YOUNG (1973) The Manufacture of News: Deviance, Social Problems and the Mass Media. London: Constable.

ERBRING, L., E. N. GOLDENBERG, and A. H. MILLER (1980) "Front-page news and real-world cues: a new look at agenda-setting by the media." American Journal of Political Science 24: 16-49.

Glasgow University Media Group (1980) More Bad News. London: Routledge and Kegan Paul.

Glasgow University Media Group (1976) Bad News. London: Routledge and Kegan Paul.

GOLDING, P. and P. ELLIOTT (1979) Making the News. London: Longman.

HALL, S., C. CRITCHER, T. JEFFERSON, J. CLARKE, and B. ROBERTS (1978) Policing the Crisis: Mugging, the State, and Law and Order. New York: Macmillan.

HARTMANN, P. and C. HUSBAND (1974) Racism and the Mass Media. London: Davis-Poynter.

JOHNSTONE, J W C. (1974) "Social integration and mass media use among adolescents," in J. G. Blumler and E. Katz (eds.) The Uses of Mass Communication. Beverly Hills, CA: Sage.

KATZ, E. (1980) "On conceptualizing media effects," pp. 119-141 in E. Katz (ed.) Studies in Communications. Greenwood, CT: JAI Press.

KATZ, E. (1968) "On reopening the question of selectivity in exposure to mass communication," in A. Abelson et al. (eds.) Theories of Cognitive Consistency. Skokie, IL: Rand McNally.

KLAPPER, J. (1960) The Effects of Mass Communication. New York: Macmillan.

LAZARSFELD, P. F., B. BERELSON, and H. GAUDET (1944) The People's Choice. New York: Columbia University Press.

McLEOD, J. M., L. B. BECKER, and J. E. BYRNES (1974) "Another look at the agenda-setting function of the press." Communication Research 1: 131-166.

MENDELSOHN, H. (1966) Mass Entertainment. New Haven, CT: College and University Press.

Oxford English Dictionay (1970) Volume 6, L-M. London: Oxford University Press.

PATTERSON, T. (1980) The Media Election: How Americans Choose Their President. New York: Praeger.

SCHLESINGER, P. (1978) Putting "Reality" Together: BBC News. Beverly Hills, CA: Sage.

SEARS, D. and J. FREEDMAN (1971) "Selective exposure to information: a critical review," in W. Schramm and D. F. Roberts (eds.) The Process and Effects of Mass Communication. Urbana: University of Illinois Press.

SEYMOUR-URE, C. (1974) The Political Impact of Mass Media. Beverly Hills, CA: Sage.

SHAW, D. L. and M. E. McCOMBS (1977) The Emergence of American Political Issues: The Agenda-Setting Function of the Press. St. Paul, MN: West.

SIUNE, K. and O. BORRE (1975) "Setting the agenda for a Danish election." Journal of Communication 25(winter): 65-73.

TANNENBAUM, P. (1980) The Entertainment Functions of Television. Hillsdale, NJ: Lawrence Erlbaum.

TUCHMAN, G. (1974) The TV Establishment: Programming for Power and Profit. Englewood Cliffs, NJ: Prentice-Hall.

WEAVER, D. H., D. A. GRABER, M. E. McCOMBS, and C. EYAL (1981) Media Agenda-Setting in a Presidential Election: Issues, Images, and Interest. New York: Praeger.

WEAVER, D. H., M. E. McCOMBS, and C. SPELLMAN (1975) "Watergate and the media: a case study of agenda-setting." American Politics Quarterly 3: 458-471.

WILKINS, L. T. (1964) Social Deviance: Social Policy, Action and Research. London: Tavistock.

ZUCKER, H. G. (1978) "The variable nature of news media influence," in B. D. Ruben (ed.) Communication Yearbook II. New Brunswick, NJ: Transaction Books.

In a review of recent political communication research, Doris Graber suggests that much of it has focused all too closely on what she calls pseudo-opinion, at the expense of detailed research on what V.O. Key termed those opinions "government finds it prudent to heed." In addition, Graber calls for employment of models to which mass communication researchers have heretofore given little attention. Graber is professor of political science at the University of Illinois at Chicago Circle.

32

THE IMPACT OF MEDIA RESEARCH ON PUBLIC OPINION STUDIES

Doris A. Graber

In modern twentieth-century societies, the mass media are the primary source of political information and opinion-shaping messages at all levels of society. To understand the context in which political opinions are created, to fathom the information constraints that bind them, and to comprehend the shifts they undergo, one must know the information presented by the media and one must know the portion of that information that has been absorbed by individuals in the process of opinion formation. This interdependence of mass media content and opinion formation links mass media research and public opinion studies massively and inextricably. Consequently, major developments in public opinion theory are tied to major developments in mass media effects theory.

It is the primary purpose of this chapter to pinpoint the areas of mass media research that are most crucial for the development of public opinion theory. Before discussing what kinds of mass media research are needed to shed light on public opinion formation, the role the mass media play in the public opinion process must be delineated.

EDITORS' NOTE: This chapter was originally presented as a paper at the Fourth Annual Meeting of the International Society of Political Psychology, Mannheim, Federal Republic of Germany, June 24-27, 1981.

PUBLIC OPINION AND PUBLIC PSEUDO-OPINION

This role has to be viewed as a dual one when it comes to opinions regarding issues of actual or potential political concern. For political elites, the mass media contribute to public opinion formation. For nonelites, they assist in public pseudo-opinion formation. What do I mean by "elites" and "nonelites" and how do I distinguish "public opinion" from "public pseudo-opinion"?

By "elites," I mean political decision makers and opinion leaders in all walks of life. The latter include pressure groups, publics who are keenly attentive to selected issues, political dissidents who oppose the prevailing political ideologies, and revolutionaries pledged to the violent overthrow of existing regimes. What these elites have in common is that they pay careful attention to selected aspects of politics and seriously discuss these aspects with others, and that they are members of groups that reach consensus after discussion.

"Nonelites," with respect to particular issues, are people who do not pay serious attention to them and who discuss them only superficially, if at all. If they form an opinion, it rarely is a product of consensus reached through discussion. Most people, for most issues, belong to the nonelites. But, thanks to rising educational standards and the possibility to learn from television and radio without using literacy skills, elites have multiplied somewhat in recent decades.

"Public opinion" I define as group consensus about matters of political concern which has developed in the wake of informed discussion. This definition suggests that people have sufficient information so that they can discuss the issue in question intelligently, weighing the advantages and disadvantages of various ways to deal with it.

"Public pseudo-opinions" are politically relevant opinions expressed by various publics which lack a sound information base and the honing that comes from dialogue and debate. Pseudo-opinions result either from superficial snap judgments or from projection of past judgments retrieved from memory and adapted to fit the current setting. They may flow from reactions to the moods of the moment or they may be plagiarized from the expressed views of opinion leaders. To put it more colloquially: Pseudo-opinions are the top-of-the-head responses people make with little or no thinking or the responses they make by drawing analogies to the pasts stored in their memories. They are the answers that evolve from general moods, like pessimism or a sense that economic conditions are bad or that crime is rampant. They may also be the replies people give because a favorite opinion leader, such as a television commentator, a senator, or a respected clergyman or community leader espouses the particular view.

Opinion polls, for the most part, report public pseudo-opinions and erroneously, by my definition, label them as "public opinion." Answers to polling questions in nationwide mass surveys generally represent no consensus. Rather, they are aggregates of individual views that often are ill-considered, fleeting, and unstable. They can easily be manipulated and they shift readily as the situational context surrounding their expression changes. Their fragility has been pointed out in many recent studies that provide proof that even minor manipulations of the sequence or text of questions can bring about major shifts in the substance of expressed opinions (Bishop et al., 1978).

JOURNALISTS AS NEWS MANUFACTURERS

My views about the role that the media play in political opinion formation rest on a perception of media as active creators of political reality, rather than mere mirrors of the passing scene and transmitters of the views of others. When the *New York Times* motto claims that the *Times* publishes "all the news that's fit to print," it obviously ignores reality. Because of space and time limitations, because of the need to attract large audiences, and because of the role that media as institutions play in society, journalists must and do select and shape the news. They decide what will be covered and what will be omitted and how information will be presented. In the process, they create the information framework that sets the boundaries for political discourse and action. The journalists' freshly manufactured information product is quite different from the semi-processed product presented by the original sources. This is as true for stories involving descriptive information as for stories that express opinions and evaluations. The transformation of original messages from political figures into new products is, of course, the major source of the habitual tension between the government and the media. Each institution wants to shape the news to agree with its own vision of reality and to serve its own distinct needs. Since each institution has different goals, they disagree about what is news and about the meanings that should be conveyed.

INFORMATION PROCESSING

In American politics, it is the media-processed product rather than the government's version of reality that becomes the raw information component that goes into the public opinion process. There it serves as both foreground and background. As foreground, it conveys information about specific matters. As background, it provides the symbolic environment in which evaluative judgments are made. Elites are likely to use news as foreground, as a source of specific information, as well as using it as background. Nonelites, on the other hand, tend to ignore foreground and use news primarily as background. This background then sets the frame for their reactions to questions about their opinions (Bishop, 1981).

Let me describe what happens in a bit more detail: When the media present public issues, three types of information processing usually occur. Publics may use the media product as raw material to be combined with information and judgments stored in memory. Of course, the bulk of stored information also originated or was derived from the media. Through discussion, publics may then develop public opinion in the classical sense in which I use the term.

This genuine public opinion formation process is rare, if one considers how many issues are raised by the media. It is generally limited to what Gabriel Almond calls "attentive" publics. The process that alerts publics to issues has not been fully explored (see Lang and Lang, 1981). For the time being, we must content ourselves with Victor Hugo's vague prescription that issues catch on when "their time has come." Ripeness of time appears to be related to the saliency of issues to various publics. Saliency, in turn, depends on external conditions and the mindset of publics and on the formats into which journalists cast their presentations. For instance, at a time of soaring crime rates and widespread fears about victimization, a story about the crime problem is more likely to arouse attention if it is presented in the context of crime in the audience's neighborhood than if it is presented impersonally.

A second possibility for information processing is that publics accept media stories and the views they reflect as their own. If a variety of views about a given issue are presented by the media, publics may choose a particular one because adoption provides certain gratifications. These may range from feeling in tune with respected others to liking projected outcomes or coveting a label like "conservative" or "liberal." As agenda-setting research has shown, audiences frequently mirror media concerns to varying degrees. This should be no surprise, since the media present reality in appealing, simplified ways that make it not only comprehensible but also emotionally salient and, hence, opinion-shaping. When media personalize stories, they turn them into vicarious personal experiences for many audience members, who then identify with the stories and their conclusions.

The resulting opinions are pseudo-opinions because they lack a solid intellectual foundation. The same holds true when opinions are adopted, fully formed, from opinion leaders, whose views are apt to be heavily media-based, or when the public uses analogic reasoning, basing current opinions on past ones that appear to form a logical precedent. For instance, one may oppose public ownership of airlines in 1981 simply because one opposed public ownership of railroads forty years earlier.

A final possibility in information processing is that publics may not pay attention at all. As a result, they may have no opinions about most current political issues. This happens often in the American context, where political issues are not very salient to the average person. High percentages of "no opinion" answers on public opinion polls, even when the issues in question have received a lot of media coverage, give ample testimony to this fact.

RESEARCH METHODS

Considering the role media information plays in opinion formation, what conclusions should we draw about future research strategies? If media information flow—news, features, entertainment—furnishes the raw material and often the whole cloth for public opinion and public pseudo-opinion, the bulk of public opinion research must be conducted in combination with media research. There must be a real marriage between the two research communities, rather than the more or less casual liaisons common today. What should the focus be for the combined efforts of the marriage partners? There are several priorities.

FROM MESSAGE TO MEANING

First, we must investigate much more thoroughly than we have done what opinion-shaping information the media communicate, making the distinction between information and communication advocated by scholars like Thayer (1967) and Moles (1968). This means that we must look beyond the information presented by media content to ascertain what meanings have been conveyed. In the past we have often measured, albeit only roughly, the information flows available to the public. We have proudly displayed our quantitative skills in gathering and presenting data about the number of stories, categories of topics, story length, and the like. But we have not learned very well how to measure what is actually communicated and hence can become the basis for public opinion formation. We lack good theories about cognitive processes through which information becomes communication. Lacking such theories, we do not know how best to ask questions about the nature of learning that has taken place from exposure to media information. Therefore, we do not know the transformation factors that explain what elements of information are merged with what the receiver of information brings to the situation.

To tackle such questions, we need to develop a transactional model that incorporates the interplay of media information with audience variables. As McCombs (1981) has pointed out: "In contrast . . . to the traditional social categories approach of demographic analysis, which looks at the uniformities of behavior, a transactional model is an individual differences approach." For this type of research we need to draw much more than we have in the past on the work of cognitive psychologists. Examples are the information-integration theories of Anderson (1978) and social-psychological information-processing theories (Lachman et al., 1979). Recent work by political scientists is also promising. Iyengar and Peters (1981) at Yale University have tested the learning process in the laboratory by exposing subjects to different news telecasts and then measuring before and after attitudes toward various public policy issues. Such experiments are valuable, even though they suffer from the fact that media effects are different in natural settings than in controlled, sterile, laboratory conditions.

AGENDA-SETTING RESEARCH

We need to devote a great deal of effort to the refinement of agenda-setting research, which, basically, is public opinion formation research. Agenda-setting researchers ask people's opinions about the importance they, or people in their communities, assign to current political issues, and which issues the respondents discuss. Evaluations of the comparative importance of issues constitute opinions. They also provide evidence that some knowledge has been gained about the issues which may form the basis for further evaluation. Information about issues that have been discussed is additional evidence that an important step in the opinion-formation process has taken place. Finally, assessment of what others in the community think may provide insights into the nature of community constraints on expressions of opinions.

At present, agenda-setting research is still in its infancy, though it has grown heartily in recent years. Among recent helpful advances that should be developed further are the distinctions between obtrusive and unobtrusive issues and media impact. This research by Eyal and others (Weaver et al., 1981) has shown that the opinion-shaping powers of the mass media are sharply reduced for "obtrusive" issues. These are issues with which audience members have become familiar either because they concern matters of direct personal experience or because they involve indirect personal experiences obtained through ample media exposure, often over lengthy periods of time.

Another relatively new direction of agenda-setting research is the investigation of the time required for media information to make an impact. Depending on the issues involved, and the current political context, the time lag may range from a few hours to several months. It is, of course, essential for investigators of public opinion and pseudo-opinion to know the appropriate time when measurement is likely to show that opinions have been formed. This work, too, has been conducted primarily at Syracuse University (Eyal et al., 1981; Winter, 1981).

My own work on remembering and forgetting and the quality of political learning also needs replication and supplementation by others. It shows that opinions and pseudo-opinions and the facts and moods underlying them attenuate very rapidly. If no reminders take place through story repetition, the memory slate of facts and their attendant opinions is wiped nearly clean after six weeks. We need to learn a great deal more about this blotter effect by which steady exposure to new happenings wipes out previously acquired cognitions and opinions.

Another highly promising advance in agenda-setting research is the development of the audience-contingent effects model based on research by a group of scholars at the University of Michigan and the University of Chicago (Erbring et al., 1980; Miller et al., 1979). This model factors the experiences that people bring to media exposure and real-world events into the media agenda-setting process. It is part of the growing research efforts to specify the contingencies arising from the nature and timing of the issues and the characteristics of audience members during the agenda-setting process.

Another facet which requires much more research attention than it has received thus far is the use of media information in the discussion component of the public opinion process. This should include studies of the sources of information on which discussion is based, cultural and psychological constraints on discussion, and specific mention of the media. Studies by Kepplinger (see Kepplinger and Martin, 1980), which investigate the nature and frequency of references to the mass media during informal conversations are examples of the kind of work that needs to be done. So is the work of Noelle-Neumann (1980), who has investigated psychological aspects in discussion of public issues in her *Spiral of Silence* work. The perceptions many people have that certain views are "acceptable" to members of their community while others are not may well be cued by what the local media depict as acceptable.

I also feel very strongly that agenda-setting research should concentrate more heavily on elite opinions because of their greater impact, even if this means reduced attention to mass pseudo-opinions. There are even strategic advantages to such research. It is far easier to examine elite opinions than mass opinions because fewer individuals are involved and because their political activities, including media exposure, can usually be traced more readily. We need to study how elite opinions are shaped, how elites assess and evaluate the nature and political significance of mass opinions, and how they are able to use the media to manipulate mass opinions. When we examine mass media sources of elite opinions, we must not overlook books. Judging from the biographies of major leaders, books have often been the sources of the opinions that guided their political behavior.

INDIRECT MEDIA EFFECTS

Thus far, I have dealt with the direct impact of manifest mass media information on opinion creation. But the impact of the media on public opinion and public pseudo-opinion is often indirect. For instance, media coverage may serve to dispel public apathy and arouse interest in politics. Aroused publics may then form opinions and pseudo-opinions. Similarly, when the mass media produce the society's symbolic environment, they often imply information about the society which shapes opinions. Furthermore, the media may actually produce changes in the reality about which people form opinions. Some examples will show what I mean.

When media coverage indicates respect for the established order, as most of it does, this may legitimize the status quo in the minds of audiences. It may foster the growth of opinions supportive of the established authorities and it may retard the growth of opposition opinions. For instance, the media appear to be heavily implicated in shifts in the evaluation of key social symbols. In the early years of nuclear energy production, for example, the term "nuclear power" evoked favorable responses from most publics because the media usually presented it in the context of producing valued goods cheaply. Although nuclear power still provides needed energy at moderate costs, the term now evokes negative connotations in the public because it has become linked to the idea of life-threatening pollution. The wide publicity given to accidents in some nuclear plants accounts for the change.

This emphasis on negative aspects and the lack of emphasis on the contributions of nuclear plants to public welfare may explain the ban on the construction of nuclear energy facilities in many locations. Such a ban, in turn, spreads and strengthens the view that production of atomic energy is dangerous. For the public opinion researcher, this means that major shifts in public opinions about social phenomena cannot be understood without monitoring the symbolic environment created by the mass media.

MEDIA EFFECTS ON THE LINKAGE PROCESS

Public opinion involves more than the shifting of mental states. It also has an action component. As Key (1961) defined it, public opinion involves those opinions that "governments find it prudent to heed." The ultimate question is how public opinion at the elite and mass level affects public policy and the general welfare.

Here, too, we need more empirical work on the role that the media play in what has become known as the "linkage" process. We must investigate more carefully the extent to which decision makers use the media to gauge the substance, intensity, and pervasiveness of public opinions and then decide on appropriate political steps. Bernard Cohen at the University of Wisconsin has done some of this work in American politics, as have I (Cohen, 1973; Graber, 1980). Cohen is now working on comparative analyses of public opinion linkage factors in selected European countries. Linkage studies have shown, among other things, that media presentations are often perceived by decision makers as surrogates of public opinion. When this happens, the public opinion component in public policy, whatever it may be, is a media component.

The media also influence the perceptions of decision makers when they report the activities of various opinion-making interest groups or the results of public opinion polls. The kinds of questions raised by such polls, many of them conducted by the media establishment, and the kinds of interpretations made by newspeople are closely monitored by decision makers. This information is likely to be influential. But we do not know for sure whether and when it occurs and to what degree. We need more studies that investigate the precise impact media coverage has on linking opinions in the body politic with policies pursued by the decision makers.

Finally, we know that decision makers try to use the media to sway public opinion. We do not know to what degree and in which contexts various decision makers have been successful in manipulating the media to get publicity for stories they want from angles that suit their purposes. We do not know how often the claims, expressed or implied in media stories, that certain policies are favored by the public have become self-fulfilling prophecies. Again, much additional work is needed.

These are just some of the avenues of research that beckon us as scholars interested in the public opinion phenomenon in the mass media age. We have the skills and human resources to do the job, especially if media scholars and public opinion scholars combine forces more than they have in the past. I cannot think of any research of greater theoretical importance in a democracy than research on the public opinion process. I hope that my remarks will contribute to putting this research on the course that ought to be taken at this time in history.

REFERENCES

ALMOND, G. A. (1960) The American People and Foreign Policy. New York: Praeger.

ANDERSON, N. H. (1978) "Cognitive algebra: integration theory applied to social attribution," in L. Berkowitz (ed.) Cognitive Theories in Social Psychology. New York: Academic.

BISHOP, G. F. (1981) 'Surveys in political communication and public opinion research," in D. D. Nimmo and K. R. Sanders (eds.) Handbook of Political Communication. Beverly Hills, CA: Sage.

——— R. W. OLDENDICK, and A. J. TUCHFARBER (1978) "Effects of wording and format on political attitude consistency." Public Opinion Quarterly 42: 81-92.

——— and S. E. BENNETT (1980) "Pseudo-opinions on public affairs." Public Opinion Quarterly 44: 198-209.

BRODY, R. A. and B. PAGE (1975) "The impact of events on presidential popularity: the Johnson and Nixon administrations," in A. Wildavsky (ed.) Perspectives on the Presidency. Boston: Little, Brown.

COHEN, B. C. (1973) The Public's Impact on Foreign Policy. Boston: Little, Brown.

ERBRING, L., E. N. GOLDENBERG, and A. H. MILLER (1980) "Front-page news and real-world cues: a new look at agenda-setting by the media." American Journal of Political Science 24: 16-49.

EYAL, C., J. P. WINTER, and W. F. DeGEORGE (1981) "The concept of time for agenda-setting," in G. C. Wilhoit (ed.) Mass Communication Review Yearbook, Vol. 2. Beverly Hills, CA: Sage.

FISHMAN, M. (1980) Manufacturing the News. Austin: University of Texas Press.

GRABER, D. A. (1980) Mass Media and American Politics. Washington, DC: Congressional Quarterly Press.

——— (1968) Public Opinion, the President, and Foreign Policy. New York: Holt, Rinehart & Winston.

IYENGAR, S. and M. PETERS (1981) "Re-examining the agenda setting hypothesis: an experimental approach." Presented at the conference of the American Association for Public Opinion Research, Buck Hill Falls.

KEPPLINGER, H. M. and V. MARTIN (1980) "Functions of mass media in interpersonal communication." Mainz: Institut für Publizistik, Johannes Gutenberg-Universitaet.

KEY, V. O. (1961) Public Opinion and American Democracy. New York: Knopf.

LACHMAN, R., J. LACHMAN, and E. C. BUTTERFIELD (1979) Cognitive Psychology and Information Processing. Hillside, NJ: Erlbaum.

LANG, G. E. and K. LANG (1981) "Watergate: an exploration of the agenda-building process," in G. C. Wilhoit (ed.) Mass Communication Review Yearbook, Vol 2. Beverly Hills, CA: Sage.

LEMERT, J. B. (1981) Does Mass Communication Change Public Opinion After All? Chicago: Nelson-Hall.

McCOMBS, M. E. (1981) "The agenda-setting approach," in D. D. Nimmo and K. R. Sanders (eds.) Handbook of Political Communication. Beverly Hills, CA: Sage.

MILLER, A. H., E. N. GOLDENBERG, and L. ERBRING (1979) "Type-set politics: the impact of newspapers on public confidence." American Political Science Review 73: 67-84.

MOLES, A. (1968) Information Theory and Esthetic Perception. Urbana: University of Illinois Press.

NOELLE-NEUMANN, E. (1980) Die Schweigespirale. Muenchen: R. Piper.

SHAW, D. M. and M. E. McCOMBS (1977) The Emergence of American Political Issues: The Agenda-Setting Function of the Press. St. Paul, MN: West.

THAYER, L. [ed.] (1967) "Communication theory and research," in Proceedings of the First International Symposium on Communication Theory Research. Springfield, IL: Charles C Thomas.

WEAVER, D., M. E. McCOMBS, and C. SPELLMAN (1975) "Watergate and the media: a case study in agenda-setting." American Politics Quarterly 3: 458-472.

WEAVER, D., D. GRABER, M. E. McCOMBS, and C. EYAL (1981) Media Agenda Setting in a Presidential Election: Issues, Images, Interest. New York: Praeger.

WESTLEY, B. (1976) "Setting the political agenda: what makes it change?" Journal of Communication 26: 43-47.

WINTER, J. P. (1981) "Contingent conditions and the agenda-setting function," in G. C. Wilhoit (ed.) Mass Communication Review Yearbook, Vol. 2. Beverly Hills, CA: Sage.

ZUCKER, H. G. (1978) "The variable nature of news media influence," in B. D. Ruben (ed.) Communication Yearbook 2. New Brunswick, NJ: Transaction.

At issue in this study by Steven H. Chaffee and Sun Yuel Choe is the degree to which individuals are open to influence in political campaigns, including, of course, influence by the mass media. In this innovative study, Chaffee and Choe conclude that partisan precommitment is sufficient to preclude campaign effects, but in the absence of such precommitment, those exposed to the campaign will make their decisions on voting primarily on the basis of campaign-specific information; those who remain unexposed to campaign information make their decisions on the basis of weak cues, such as latent party identification. Chaffee is professor of communication and director of the Institute for Communication Research at Stanford University. Choe is on the faculty of the Department of Communication at Purdue University.

33

TIME OF DECISION AND MEDIA USE DURING THE FORD-CARTER CAMPAIGN

Steven H. Chaffee and Sun Yuel Choe

FALL PRESIDENTIAL election campaigns have for three decades been thought to have little impact on the vote, owing to a paradoxical relationship between media use and the time at which the voter makes his final decision. Since the pioneering work of Lazarsfeld, Berelson, and their colleagues (1944; 1954), the electorate has been pictured in terms of a dichotomous model: citizens fall into either of two possible categories, each of which is impervious to political mass communication for a quite different reason. On the one hand, there is a large group of precommitted voters. As Pool (1963) has described them, the precommitted are partisans who "are inclined to read about politics or to listen to political speeches" but who "already have strong views which are not going to be changed in the eight weeks of an election campaign." And then there are the rest of the voters, who make up their minds seemingly at the last minute. They are less opinionated and correlatively more persuasible than the early deciders, but they are also less interested and consequently pay little attention to political news. They are unaffected by the media not because of resistance, but simply because of lack of exposure (Berelson and Steiner, 1964).

There are numerous recent examples of this dichotomous analysis. For instance, Buchanan (1977) summarizes prior research as demonstrating "that relatively few people changed their opinions during a campaign and that those who did were more likely to have been influenced by primary group pressures than by the issue appeals of the candidates; . . . and that 'independent' or shifting voters were not issue-oriented in their outlook." Katz (1973) paints a similar picture: "Typically about 80 percent, or more, of the voters have made up their minds about the vote before the campaign begins, that is at least several months prior to the election. . . . The changers—those who shift from one party to another *during* the campaign—have been found to be relatively uninterested in the election and its outcome . . . [and] are not much exposed to mass communications about politics" (emphasis his). McCombs (1972) agrees: "Those who make their vote decisions . . . before the fall campaign gets underway . . . make greater use of the media than the voter who enters the campaign period uncommitted or undecided." In all of these instances, the studies of elections in the 1940s are cited as the source of empirical support for the conclusion.

Theoretical Issues

The "limited effects" or "minimal consequences" assumption that has been derived from these dichotomous contrasts can be broken down into the following causal propositions:

1. Partisan precommitment is sufficient to preclude campaign effects.

2. Partisan precommitment is necessary to produce interest in the election.

3. Interest in the election is necessary to produce exposure to the campaign.

4. Exposure to the campaign is necessary for media effects.

The first of these statements is adequate to predict limited (at most) effects for those who identify strongly with a party and who consequently decide how they will vote before the campaign begins. (While statement 1 is an obvious oversimplification, we will not digress into its merits here.) The remaining three statements comprise a chain of requirements that in the dichotomous model have been used to predict limited effects for the entire remainder of the voters—who are all presumed to lack interest because they lack partisanship (statement 2). But while statement 4 is true almost by definition, there is no clear theoretical reasoning behind statements 2 and 3. They are based upon empirical correlations that were apparently strong in the 1940s, but they are dubious as causal propositions. Given the many changes in politics and mass communication in the intervening 30 years, there is reason to consider more current evidence and the possibility of theoretical revision.

Regarding statement 2, partisanship has been steadily declining since the 1950s, both in absolute terms and in the power of party identification to predict voting behavior (Nie, et al., 1976). But the lack of corresponding evidence of a decline in political interest suggests that the two variables are not closely related in a functional sense and that the empirical correlation between them may have diminished.[1] Regarding statement 3, the emergence of television as the principal vehicle for political campaigning (Barber, 1978) has probably reduced the amount of motivation required for a person to become exposed to campaign messages. While in the 1940s it probably did require some specific effort to follow the campaign in the newspapers of Erie County (Lazarsfeld et al., 1944) and Elmira (Berelson et al., 1954), today's voter would have to go to some lengths to *avoid* exposure to the many political advertisements and newscasts that are broadcast. Such modern campaign events as televised debates are witnessed by some 80 to 90 percent of the electorate (Katz and Feldman, 1962; Sears and Chaffee, 1979). For statement 3 to remain valid in the face of this ubiquitous campaign exposure, political interest would have had to become much more widespread than was the case in the pretelevision era. While interest may be *sufficient* to stimulate added exposure, it is likely that incidental exposure also stimulates interest in the campaign. There does not seem to be a unidirectional causal process at work; recent historical evidence suggests that campaign interest and television attention have risen together (Nie et al., 1976:2).

A weakening of the presumed linkages from partisanship to campaign interest via exposure (statements 2 and 3) would imply that there has emerged a sizable voting group that is indeed interested and attentive to political content in the media, but not so partisan and precommitted as to be unaffected by the campaign and its coverage. As Katz (1973) suggests, "The combination of a low degree of [party] loyalty and yet some exposure to election communication has become

---

[1] There seems to have been a slight tendency toward lower voter turnout in recent years. The apparent decline in party identification has, however, been much more striking statistically.

a more probable combination in the era of television than ever before." The decision-making processes of such a voter would be of particular interest to students of mass communication; the amount and quality of campaign coverage by the media would be much more important factors if there are significant numbers of voters who defer their decisions until they have a chance to compare the candidates during the final months of intense campaigning.

Research Hypotheses

The purpose of this paper is to develop a model of voter decision making that involves complex relationships among partisanship, mass media use, and cognitions about candidates derived from an election campaign. Our central assumption is that vote decisions can be made on the basis of either preexisting partisan commitments *or* exposure to the campaign (or both). Empirically these two classes of voting decisions should be differentially associated with precampaign and campaign-specific cognitions, communication, and predictor variables.

Time of decision would be dependent on the class of information the voter relies upon. Precampaign decisions must be based on precampaign cognitions, such as party identification and its socioeconomic and ideological correlates. Those who lack strong precampaign decision cues must rely more on campaign-specific cognitions about the candidates and their policy positions; they should be more likely to decide *during* the campaign period when information of this type is most available. Those who lack both kinds of information—i.e., whose party identification is weak, and who lack campaign-specific information because of nonexposure—should be the most likely to remain undecided until the last days of the campaign.

The fall 1976 contest between Gerald Ford and Jimmy Carter was rich in candidate-specific information, largely because of the series of televised debates that juxtaposed the two contenders in a comparative and issue-oriented format (Chaffee, 1978; Sears and Chaffee, 1979). Given this easily accessible information, an attentive voter could have formed a fairly clear picture of the differences between the candidates after a few weeks. Many undecided voters entered the campaign period with "tentative" decisions or feelings of "leaning" toward one candidate. With heavy information flow, these decisions could be crystallized without waiting until the last minute. The Ford-Carter campaign, then, was one in which we should find a substantial group of voters who do not fit the traditional description of either group in the dichotomous model of prior electoral research.

We will call this third group Campaign Deciders and distinguish them from the other groups, which we will characterize here as Precampaign Deciders and Last-minute Deciders.

We postulate that precampaign cognitions and campaign information flow are two independent variables that lead to voting decisions made at different times. For purposes of data analysis, we will use time of decision as a sorting variable, comparing the three groups of voters for evidence of differential information-holding, communication, and decision-making processes. Strong precampaign decision cues should differentiate Precampaign Deciders from those who are undecided at the start of the campaign, and strong within-campaign decision cues should differentiate Campaign Deciders from those who remain undecided near the end of the campaign. This pattern should manifest itself in terms of both the strength of political cognitions and communication activity, and the degree to which the person's vote is predicted by precampaign vs. campaign-specific cognitions.

As in prior studies, we expect that the Precampaign Deciders will be higher than other voters in socioeconomic status. More important, we hypothesize specifically that they will exhibit greater campaign communications (mass and interpersonal) and perceived differentiation between the candidates *prior to the fall campaign*. Decisions made by the Campaign Deciders should be associated with increased communication activity, especially attention to the highly accessible information about the candidates provided by television, and with strengthened perceptions of differences between the candidates *during the campaign*.

In directional analyses of vote decisions, we hypothesize qualitative differences in the determinants of Precampaign and Campaign Deciders' choices. Decisions made prior to the campaign should be most strongly predicted by precampaign cognitions such as party identification. Within-campaign decisions, however, should be more strongly predicted by campaign-specific cognitions, such as perceived differences between the candidates in this particular election.

These hypotheses leave us with little to say about the voting decisions of the Last-minute Deciders. We expect them to be lacking in all varieties of decision cues that we have mentioned, both precampaign and campaign-specific. Consequently we should expect to account for less of the variation in their votes by the variables we have discussed here, such as party identification and differentiation between the candidates. Some writers have asserted that Last-Minute Deciders are influenced mainly by interpersonal communication rather than by the media (Berelson et al., 1954; Pool, 1963). There is no systematic data analysis to support this conclusion in the main source cited, however (Lazarsfeld et al., 1948). While we will not attempt to examine interpersonal *influence* here, our other hypotheses (above) include the prediction that the Last-minute Deciders will be the group *lowest* in interpersonal discussion both prior to and during the campaign. Prior research has shown a close association between frequency of interpersonal discussion of a topic and attention to it in the mass media (Chaffee, 1972), and most interpersonal influence attempts are directed at people who are in turn making similar influence attempts themselves (Troldahl and Van Dam, 1965; O'Keefe, 1975). In a recent study of young voters in a British election, Blumler and McLeod (1974) found that those who remained undecided late in the campaign were less interested, less attentive to the media, *and* less likely to discuss the election with their families.

Overall, then, we expect to replicate prior research that has distinguished between Precampaign and Last-minute Deciders, but to point up the possibility of significant campaign effects on a third group, who come to their decisions during the campaign period. We do not expect the Campaign Deciders to be simply waiting, but rather to be waiting for information that will come to them via the news media as the campaign progresses. We expect them to increase their communication activity to get that information, and then to use it in making their voting decisions. By contrast, we do expect the Last-minute Deciders to be uninvolved voters who have simply waited, without paying much attention to the campaign, and consequently not to make their decisions on the basis of campaign-specific information.

Design and Measurement

Our data collection design was a four-wave panel survey of a statewide random sample of Wisconsin citizens during the fall of 1976 (see Dennis and Chaffee, 1978). The first wave of interviews was conducted in the week prior to the first Ford-Carter debate (held September 23), and the second wave in the week following that debate. Wave 3 occurred following the final debate (October 23 through November 1), and the final wave following the November 2 election. All interviews were conducted by telephone, and sampling was based on a probability sample of area codes and telephone prefixes, followed by four random digits. Three callbacks were tried before a number was abandoned. Within households, adults were selected randomly according to a predetermined schedule. The panel consisted of $N = 164$ persons who were interviewed in each of the four waves. Of those who reported their votes in the postelection interview, 49.6 percent said they had voted for Carter, and 48.9 percent for Ford; these figures are quite close to the actual Wisconsin vote, of which Carter received 49.4 percent and Ford 47.8 percent.

In measuring time of final decision, we assumed that the period of heaviest campaign information flow occurred between the first and third waves of interviewing. All of the televised debates, which were the most prominent public communication events of the campaign, took place in this time period. Working back in time from the person's reported vote (Time 4), each voter was classified according to the earliest time at which he or she expressed a definite and lasting intention to vote that way.[2] Those who voted but had still not been certain of their intention even at Time 3 are the Last-minute Deciders. Those who had definitely decided by the time of the first interview, and who never expressed uncertainty in subsequent interviews, are the Precampaign Deciders. The remainder, who first said they had definitely made their voting decisions in either the Time 2 or Time 3 interview, are grouped for our analysis as Campaign Deciders.

The wording of various interview questions was standardized so that responses from one wave to another would be comparable. In each wave, we measured attention to campaign content via television, and via newspapers and magazines; discussion about the campaign; perceptions of candidates' personal qualities and abilities, or image; their own positions, and those they perceived the candidates as holding, on several issues; their party identification; and political ideology (liberal-conservative). Five-point response scales were used for all issue, image, and ideology questions. Several standard demographic measures were included, mostly in Wave 1. In Waves 2 and 3, additional questions were asked about the extent to which the debate(s) immediately preceding that interview had been watched and discussed.

Image measures consisted of the rating assigned to Ford or Carter on each of the following attributes: honesty and integrity, strength and decisiveness, capacity for effective leadership of the government, making clear his position on the issues, and ability to inspire confidence by the way he speaks. These five items were highly intercorrelated, forming a single factor; a sixth scale, friendly and pleasant, was dropped after factor analysis indicated it did not load strongly with

---

[2] Voters were classified as not yet finally decided even if they had a preference but declined in response to a probe to say they were "certain" of their intentions, or "definitely" would vote that way. We found many cases who considered themselves definite/certain at Time 1, but who were less sure in a later interview; these are classified by the final expression of definite/certain vote intention, not the first.

the other five. In the case of issues, one of the four that were included
in the questionnaire was dropped after item analyses showed it to
have extremely weak discriminating power. The deleted issue item
dealt with abortion; the three that were retained for summary
analyses had to do with government efforts to alleviate unemployment, reform of the tax system, and defense expenditures (see Dennis
et al., 1979).

Two distinct kinds of indices were constructed from the five image
and three issue items. One set of indices provides estimates of the
degree to which the respondent saw differences between the candidates; these are called *candidate discrimination* measures. Image
Discrimination was calculated by subtracting the rating of Ford on
each measure from that of Carter, and summing these absolute differences. Issue Discrimination consisted of the absolute difference
between the positions the respondent perceived Ford and Carter as
holding on each of the three issues, and summing these differences.
The image and issue discrimination indices were highly intercorrelated ($r = .61$ in the total sample), which is to say that those who saw
large differences between the candidates as individuals also tended to
perceive large policy differences.

The second set of indices based on the image and issue items were
directional measures of *candidate evaluations*. For the image items, it
was assumed that all of the attributes (honesty, strength, leadership,
etc.) were positive evaluations; separate indices of favorable ratings of
Ford and of Carter were first calculated, and then Ford's were subtracted from Carter's to create a net evaluation scale. Favorable
ratings on the issue items were assumed to be relative to the respondent's own positions. For each issue, the Ford-self and Carter-self
distances were calculated, and then the latter was subtracted from the
former to create a net score; these net distances were summed
across the three issues. These directional net evaluation measures, all
signed in the same (pro-Carter) direction, were used as predictors of
the vote in data analysis.

Party identification was measured by a conventional series of
branching questions that produced a 7-point scale ranging from
"strong Democrat" to "weak" or "leaning" or "independent"
categories, and on to "strong Republican." A 4-point measure of
partisanship was created by folding over the party identification scale
so that "strong" adherents of either party were grouped together, as
were "weak" identifiers, etc. A 5-point liberal-conservative scale was
similarly folded over, to create a 3-point measure of strength of
ideology.

Analyses and Results

Approximately 40 percent of the voters in our panel were classified as Campaign Deciders, and the remainder were almost equally divided between Precampaign Deciders and Last-minute Deciders. Different operational criteria, and a different election campaign, might have yielded fewer Campaign Deciders, but it is clear that they are a substantial group in this instance at least.

A preliminary overview of the distinctiveness of the Campaign Deciders is provided in Table 1. Here a number of precampaign and within-campaign measures are presented; all means have been converted to standard scores to facilitate comparisons between rows. No statistical tests are reported in Table 1, since we have not hypothesized univariate differences among the three groups. Before we turn to tests of our hypotheses about decided vs. undecided voters at various stages of the campaign, however, Table 1 is worth some consideration. The data are in line with most of our assumptions

Table 1. Precampaign and Within-Campaign Comparisons (Standard Scores), by Time of Decision

	Precampaign Deciders	Campaign Deciders	Last-minute Deciders
Precampaign measures (Time 1)			
Ideological strength	+15	−17	+09
Partisanship strength	+22	−13	−05
Education	+20	−04	15
Income	+14	+10	−27
Television precampaign attention	+16	−04	−04
Newspaper/magazine precampaign attention	+19	−02	−16
Discussion of campaign	+36	−04	−30
Issue discrimination	+22	−02	−18
Image discrimination	+54	−19	−28
Within-campaign measures (Time 2 and 3)			
Television campaign attention	−03	+29	−35
Newspaper/magazine campaign attention	+11	+18	−34
Discussion of campaign	+24	+06	−32
Viewing of debates	−13	+18	−34
Discussion of debates	+10	+08	−20
Issue discrimination (Time 3)	+31	−05	−23
Image discrimination (Time 3)	+42	+05	−47
	(N=41)	(N=56)	(N=42)

NOTE: For each row in this table, raw data were converted to standard scores by subtracting the mean for the total sample from each group mean, and dividing this deviation score by the overall standard deviation. Scores have been multiplied by 100 for simplicity.

about the nature of the three groups. Perhaps the most noteworthy finding is the stepped-up communication activity of the Campaign Deciders during the campaign period. The expected Time 1 differences between the Precampaign Deciders and the Last-minute Deciders, in terms of partisanship, socioeconomic status, communication, and candidate discrimination, are quite marked. These differences do not change much in magnitude during the campaign, but for campaign-related measures the standard scores at Time 3 are altered (while remaining about as far apart as before) because of changes in the Campaign Deciders.

PREDICTING DECISION TIME

To test our hypotheses about different factors in vote decisions made at different times, we performed two multiple discriminant analyses.[3] The first of these examines differences between Precampaign Deciders and all other voters in terms of the precampaign variables listed in Table 2. The second analysis then contrasts the remaining voters (Campaign Deciders vs. Last-minute Deciders) in terms of the within-campaign variables from the lower portion of Table 1.

The first multiple discriminant analysis is summarized in Table 2. Four of the nine Time 1 variables survived the stepwise selection process and this function explains 23 percent of the total group-

Table 2. Time 1 Discriminant Analysis: Precampaign Deciders vs. Others

	Function 1[a]
Image discrimination	.785
Discussion about campaign	.351
Education	.331
Partisanship	.240
Canonical correlation	.434
$\chi^2 = 28.24,\ p < .001$	
Centroids of groups in reduced space	
Precampaign deciders	−.280
All undecided at Time 1	.669

[a] Entries are standardized discriminant coefficients.

NOTE: These results represent a discriminant analysis between the Precampaign Deciders and the combined Campaign Deciders and Last-minute Deciders. The nine precampaign measures shown in Table 1 were entered in this analysis; only the significant variables are listed here.

[3] Stepwise selection starts with the best single predictor variable and combines it with each of the other predictors separately to find the pair that provides the greatest statistical separation between the groups. This pair is then combined with each remaining predictor separately to find the best triplet. This process continues until none of the remaining predictors significantly improves the discrimination between groups (Morrison, 1969, 1974; Tatsouka, 1971).

difference variance. A person's vote decision status at the beginning of the campaign is determined by the combined effect of partisanship, education, prior discussion, and image discrimination, to list them in ascending order of their importance in the discriminant function. These findings are consistent with our hypotheses and with prior research. Precampaign decisions are made predominantly by voters who are well educated, partisan, actively discussing the campaign even before the period of heaviest information flow from the media, and who already see large differences between the candidates. When these differences are taken into account, the levels of media use reported in Table 1 do not add to the discrimination between Precampaign Deciders and undecided voters.

A classification analysis was performed to check the validity of the discriminant function in Table 2. On the basis of a weighted linear combination of scores of the four predictor variables, 78 percent of our respondents were correctly classified in terms of the decision status at Time 1 ($t = 4.93, p < .01$).[4]

The second discriminant analysis, which focuses on decision making during the campaign period, is summarized in Table 3. The discriminant function in this case consists of two equally weighted variables, and explains 21 percent of the total variance between the Campaign Deciders and the Last-minute Deciders. One variable from the first discriminant function, image discrimination, is also included in this one; we should emphasize, however, that in this case it is the Time 3 image discrimination that differentiates the groups, whereas in Table 2 it was the Time 1 measure of the same variable. The other factor of importance in Table 3 is attention to the campaign via television. This

Table 3. Time 3 Discriminant Analysis: Campaign Deciders vs. Last-minute Deciders

	Function 1[a]
Attention to campaign via TV (Times 2 & 3)	.652
Image discrimination (Time 3)	.651
Canonical correlation	..415
$\chi^2 = 18.00, p < .001$	
Centroids of groups in reduced space	
Campaign deciders	.358
Last-minute deciders	-.377

[a] Entries are standardized discriminant coefficients.

NOTE: These results represent a discriminant analysis between the Campaign Deciders and the Last-minute Deciders only. The seven within-campaign measures shown in Table 1 were entered in this analysis; only the significant variables are listed here.

[4] There is an upward bias in classifying the same individuals who were used to calculate the discriminant function (Frank et al., 1965). The proportion of cases correctly classified in the sample might be greater than it would be for the true population. We were unable, however, to perform an adjustment in this analysis owing to the small sample size.

provides empirical support for our assumption that TV has become a key factor in reducing the correlation between partisanship and exposure so that a group like the Campaign Deciders would emerge in significant numbers. Classification analysis showed that 69 percent of Campaign Deciders and Late Deciders were correctly predicted on the basis of the function defined in Table 3 ($t = 3.68$, $p < .01$).

Other communication differences between the Campaign Deciders and Last-minute Deciders (see Table 1) did not add significantly to the discriminant function in Table 3. Some additional points of differentiation of the Campaign Deciders are worth noting in this connection, however. In a multiple regression analysis (Chaffee and Choe, 1978), we found a significant interaction between campaign deciders (dummy variable) and precampaign media attention, as predictors of within-campaign media attention. The within-campaign attention levels of the Campaign Deciders were the least well predicted by precampaign attention ($p < .05$) and higher than the other two groups ($p < .01$).

The robustness of this finding was tested in a multiple polynominal regression analysis (Cohen and Cohen, 1975), in which the Campaign Deciders were split into two groups, those who had decided by T_2 (after the first debate) and those who did not decide until after the last debate (T_3). This analysis produced only a significant quadratic function ($F = 5.58$, $p < .05$), among the three possible functions representing different hypothetical curves. This quadratic function corresponds to a curve that is low in media campaign attention for the Precampaign and Last-minute Deciders, and high for both groups of Campaign Deciders.

Two items regarding the televised debates further strengthen the conclusion that Campaign Deciders were particularly attentive to campaign-specific information. This group was significantly higher than the other two combined in reporting the perception that the debates had helped in understanding the candidates' positions on issues ($\chi^2 = 6.57$, $p < .05$), and that the debates were helpful in judging the abilities of the candidates ($\chi^2 = 5.21$, $p < .05$). In each case, 60 percent of the Campaign Deciders reported these reactions, compared with about 40 percent of the other groups on the average.

PREDICTING THE VOTE

Our evidence to this point establishes clear differences among the three time-of-decision groups in their communication behavior during the campaign, and in their precampaign decision cues, which are closely in accord with our hypotheses. The major empirical question remaining from those we originally raised is the extent to which these precampaign and campaign-specific cues affected the votes cast. For this analysis we turn to directional measures and limit ourselves to the major correlates of the vote: party identification (precampaign), and candidate evaluations (campaign-specific).

Table 4 summarizes the results of hierarchical regression analyses of the votes of each of the three groups. The first block of independent variables entered in this analysis is the measure of party identification. Then a second block, consisting of the Image Evaluations and Issue Evaluations of the candidates at Time 3 is added to the equation. We assume that the latter measures constitute our best evidence of information specific to the choice between Ford and Carter that a voter could have accumulated from the campaign. The hierarchical regression procedure allows us to remove the variance in these evaluations that is attributable to prior party identification, before assessing the variance in voting contributed by these campaign-specific evaluations. (We cannot rule out the influence of candidate evaluations developed prior to the fall campaign; the evidence in Tables 1 and 2 suggests that the Precampaign Deciders would have been most likely to form such perceptions earlier in the campaign year.)

Several important hypotheses are tested in Table 4. The most critical is the prediction that precampaign attachments would be more important determinants of the vote for Precampaign Deciders, whereas campaign-specific cognitions would be more important for Campaign Deciders. This contrasting set of hypotheses is definitely supported. Looking at the incremental R^2 values for each block of

Table 4. Predictors of the Vote, by Time of Decision (Hierarchical Regression)

Predictor of Vote		Precampaign Deciders	Campaign Deciders	Last-minute Deciders
Party identification (Time 1)	beta	.29**	.11	.62***
(R^2 for block)		(.55)	(.23)	(.51)
Issue evaluations (Time 3)	beta	.33**	.21*	.03
Image evaluations (Time 3)	beta	.42***	.63***	.15
(R^2 for block)		(.28)	(.49)	(.02)
(Total R^2)		(.83)	(.72)	(.53)

NOTE: R^2 values indicate incremental variance explained in successive equations in hierarchical regression analysis. Beta weights are from final equation.

$* p < .05$
$** p < .01$
$*** p < .001$

predictors, precampaign partisan ties account for 55 percent of the variance in Precampaign Deciders' votes, whereas only 28 percent can be attributed to evaluations specific to the candidates in this campaign after party identification has been controlled. For the Campaign Deciders the figures are approximately the reverse: only 23 percent attributable to party identification, but 49 percent to campaign-specific candidate evaluations. Indeed, the beta weight for party identification in the final multivariate equation is nonsignificant for the Campaign Deciders. Put in terms of proportionate variance accounted for by this set of predictors, precampaign cues account for about twice as much of the explained variance among Precampaign Deciders as they do among Campaign Deciders.

A most striking—and unanticipated—finding in Table 4 is the dominance of party identification in the voting decisions of Last-minute Deciders. This group is, as we had hypothesized, less predictable than the others, as indicated by the lower total R^2 based on our predictor variables. But almost all of this explained variance is accounted for by party identification, even though the Last-minute Deciders are *not* strongly partisan (see Table 1). Apparently when these voters finally do decide, with campaign-specific cues absent because of lack of attention to the campaign, their latent partisan predispositions are activated. This finding is contrary to the picture usually painted of Last-minute Deciders as nonpartisan. It does add to our overall stress on the importance of exposure to the campaign coupled with weak partisan ties, as a necessary set of conditions for campaign impact. The key point to be stressed again is the difference between Campaign Deciders and Last-minute Deciders, a distinction neglected in prior research.

In our data collection and in Table 4, we have adhered to the standard distinction between "image" and "issue" evaluations. But this may be more of a researcher's convention than a clearcut theoretical difference. The two indices are highly intercorrelated, and we suspect that issue positions, like party affiliations, gradually get absorbed into the more global personal images voters attribute to candidates. The relatively stronger relationships between image evaluations and various criteria in this study are likely due to lesser reliability and restricted variance of the issue-difference measures.

Discussion

A revision of the previously accepted theoretical scheme outlined at the beginning of this paper seems in order. One essential link in that limited-effects chain of reasoning appears to be incorrect as we had hypothesized. That is the presumed relationship between partisanship and exposure to the campaign, which has been thought to be mediated by interest. There is a substantial group of less partisan voters who, while not much interested prior to the campaign, pay close attention to the heavy flow of information during the campaign and vote on the basis of this information.[5] The following statements are more consonant with the current evidence:

1. Partisan precommitment is sufficient to preclude campaign effects.
2. In the absence of precommitment, those exposed to the campaign will make their decisions primarily on the basis of campaign-specific information.
3. Those who are not exposed to the campaign will make their decisions on the basis of weak cues, such as latent party identification.

The first statement here is identical to that in our earlier paraphrasing of the traditional theory. Statements 2 and 3 approximately describe the Campaign Deciders and Last-minute Deciders, respectively. The latter group, about whose voting we still understand rather little, seems to fit Ray's (1973) characterization of "low involvement" consumers, who are highly susceptible to superficial influences such as television advertising. Further research might, then, show that Last-minute Deciders are also open to media campaign effects, although not in the same way as Campaign Deciders, who utilize campaign information extensively.

Further research is necessary to determine whether these findings represent a general pattern in which many voters make their decisions during the campaign period on the basis of heavy information flow, or if this result was a peculiarity of the 1976 campaign. Several studies have shown that some voters delayed making final decisions until they could compare Ford and Carter in the debates (Sears and Chaffee, 1979). In landslide elections with less information flow (e.g., 1964, 1972) the traditional dichotomous model of early vs. late deciders might hold, as it apparently did in the era when party identification was much stronger and television not a factor (1940, 1948). In

[5] In an earlier report of this study (Chaffee and Choe, 1978) we compared the results in Table 1 with supplementary data from two other debates panel studies that were conducted in midwestern cities. While exact replication was impossible because of differing data collection designs, the findings generally coincided with the main conclusions reported here. The Precampaign Deciders were in all samples highly partisan, whereas the Campaign Deciders were distinguished mainly by heavy attention to the news media, with emphasis on debates and television, during the campaign.

1976 we were dealing with a campaign in which an unusually large number of voters were unsure of their choices, the candidates were new to presidential campaigning, and debates provided an extraordinary amount of bipartisan campaign-specific information in a highly accessible channel. After the 1960 election, when similar conditions obtained, Pool (1963) concluded that the debates had been "the decisive event" of the campaign. He treated this instance as an isolated exception to the general rule of limited effects, but it now appears that we should assume stronger potential campaign impact in future elections when those conditions recur.

References

Barber, James David (ed.)
   1978   Race for the Presidency: The Media and the Nominating Process. Englewood Cliffs, N.J.: Prentice-Hall.
Berelson, Bernard, Paul Lazarsfeld, and John McPhee
   1954   Voting. Chicago: University of Chicago Press.
Berelson, Bernard, and Gary Steiner
   1964   Human Behavior. New York: Harcourt Brace and World.
Blumler, Jay G., and Jack M. McLeod
   1974   "Communication and voter turnout in Britain." In Timothy Leggatt (ed.), Sociological Theory and Survey Research. Beverly Hills, Calif.: Sage Publications.
Buchanan, William
   1977   "American institutions and political behavior." In Donald M. Freeman (ed.), Foundation of Political Science. New York: Free Press.
Chaffee, Steven H.
   1972   "The interpersonal context of mass communication." In F. Gerald Kline and Phillip J. Tichenor (eds.), Current Perspectives in Mass Communication Research. Beverly Hills, Calif.: Sage Publications.
   1978   "Presidential debates—are they helpful to voters?" Communication Monographs. 45:330–46.
Chaffee, Steven H. and Sun Yuel Choe
   1978   "Time of decision and media use during the Ford-Carter campaign." Paper presented at the convention of the Association for Education in Journalism, Seattle.
Cohen, Jacob, and Patricia Cohen
   1975   Applied Multiple Regression/Correlation Analysis for the Behavioral Sciences. New York: Wiley.
Dennis, Jack, and Steven H. Chaffee
   1978   "Legitimation in the 1976 U.S. election campaign." Communication Research 5:371–94.
Dennis, Jack, Steven H. Chaffee, and Sun Yuel Choe
   1979   "Impact upon partisan, image, and issue voting." In Sidney Kraus (ed.), The Great Debates, 1976: Ford vs. Carter. Bloomington, Ind.: Indiana University Press.

Frank, Ronald E., William F. Massy, and Donald G. Morrison
  1965 "Bias in multiple discriminant analysis." Journal of Marketing Research 2:250–58.
Katz, Elihu
  1973 "Platforms and windows: broadcasting's role in election campaigns." Journalism Quarterly 48:304–14.
Katz, Elihu, and Jacob Feldman
  1962 "The debates in the light of research." In Sidney Kraus (ed.), The Great Debates. Bloomington: Indiana University Press.
Lazarsfeld, Paul, Bernard Berelson, and Hazel Gaudet
  1944 The People's Choice. New York: Columbia University Press.
McCombs, Maxwell
  1972 "Mass communication in political campaigns: information, gratification, and persuasion." In F. Gerald Kline and Phillip J. Tichenor (eds.), Current Perspectives in Mass Communication Research. Beverly Hills, Calif.: Sage Publications.
Morrison, Donald G.
  1969 "Interpretation of discriminant analysis." Journal of Marketing Research 4:156–63.
  1974 "Discriminant analysis." In Robert Ferber (ed.), Handbook of Marketing Research. New York: McGraw-Hill.
Nie, Norman H., Sidney Verba, and John R. Petrocik
  1976 The Changing American Voter. Cambridge: Harvard University Press.
O'Keefe, Garrett
  1975 "Political campaigns and mass communications research." In Steven Chaffee (ed.), Political Communication. Beverly Hills, Calif.: Sage Publications.
Pool, Ithiel de Sola
  1963 "The effect of communication on voting behavior." In Wilbur Schramm (ed.), The Science of Human Communication. New York: Basic Books.
Ray, Michael
  1973 "Marketing communication and the hierarchy-of-effects." In Peter Clarke (ed.), New Models for Communication Research. Beverly Hills, Calif.: Sage Publications.
Sears, David O., and Steven H. Chaffee
  1979 "Uses and effects of the debates." In Sidney Kraus (ed.), The Great Debates, 1976: Ford vs. Carter. Bloomington: Indiana University Press.
Tatsuoka, Maurice M.
  1971 Multivariate Analysis: Techniques for Educational and Psychological Research. New York: Wiley.
Troldahl, Verling C., and Robert Van Dam
  1965 "Face-to-face communication about major topics in the news." Public Opinion Quarterly 29:626–34.

Philip Elliott suggests that examination of press reports, particularly those "which reflect on the stability of the social system by showing it under threat, overcoming threat or working in a united way," show the print news media enacting ritual. This construct of ritual, moreover, helps to show that the press provides a forum in which other social institutions can maneuver and in which the public is invited to take part. Elliott is research fellow at the Centre for Mass Communication Research, University of Leicester.

34

PRESS PERFORMANCE AS
POLITICAL RITUAL[1]

Philip Elliott

Why Ritual?

Studies of ritual in modern Britain have mostly been concerned with occasions of public spectacle and ceremony.[2] In taking over the concept from social anthropologists, sociologists have mostly dealt with those contemporary rites which appeared to be directly comparable to the rites observed in primitive societies. These rites have been mainly of two types, the regular ceremonial of church and state, the coronation, investiture of the Prince of Wales and other formal establishment occasions; and the surviving rites of the life-cycle, christenings, marriages and funerals. There have also been looser applications of the concept, drawing attention to the patterned, repetitive nature of many aspects of behaviour from eating practices to the leisure activities of youth, which have built as much on common usage as on anthropology. As Nadel remarked, 'Any type of behaviour may be said to turn into a "ritual" when it is stylised or formalised and made repetitive in that form.'[3]

Not that there has been any rush to take over the concept. One reason for the lack of interest has been that a concept so widely applicable has appeared to have little analytic value. Another, the empirical one, that both the traditional types of ritual appear to be little more than historical survivals. In a sceptical if not a secular age, less and less importance is attached to either public or private ceremonial. This is not to deny that some such occasions are immensely popular. Less significance is attached to their political or personal meanings. Her Majesty's recent Jubilee for example was widely regarded as no more than an excuse for a jamboree and, in the other category, a large proportion of marriages now end in divorce rather than death.

A third reason for lack of interest in ritual as a concept has been a theoretical one. Use of the concept has implied a unitary view of society. The main paradigm for the analysis of contemporary ritual has been set out by consensus theorists of society working within the terms

From Philip Elliott, "Press Performance as Political Ritual," pp. 141-177 in Harry Christian (ed.) *The Sociology of Journalism and the Press,* Sociological Review Monograph 29, University of Keele, October 1980. Reprinted by permission of the Editorial Board of the SOCIOLOGICAL REVIEW.

of normative functionalism. In a valuable paper which marks a break with this tradition, Lukes has shown how most contemporary analyses have been set within the Durkheimian paradigm of ritual as the instrument and expression of social solidarity.[4]   Starting from the premise that 'value integration is the central aspect of the integration of a society' and that 'value consensus maintains the equilibrium of the social system', neo-Durkheimian analysts have come to the conclusion that 'political rituals play a crucial part in the integration of modern industrial societies.'[5]   This conclusion is belied by the empirical point already made, that contemporary versions of traditional rites have lost much of their original significance. It is even more doubtful on theoretical grounds, as Lukes makes clear in his paper. 'Value consensus', he argues, 'takes one very little way indeed towards solving the "the problem of order", and, insofar as it exists, itself requires explanation.'[6]

The contemporary rites selected for analysis have been precisely those which express the permanence of the political and social order, ones controlled by secular and spiritual authority, often embodied in the same person and office. The political importance of such rites is relatively transparent. It requires only a small, albeit significant, shift of focus to see them as expressions of power in society rather than expressions of consensus. Lukes's conclusion is that 'such rituals can be seen as modes of exercising, or seeking to exercise, power along the cognitive dimension'. The analysis of ritual can then be placed in 'a class-structured, conflictual and pluralistic model of society' rather than a unitary, integrated consensual one.

My aim in this paper is to show how such an account of ritual can usefully be applied to an analysis of the press and the other news media. The common usage of ritual as regular, habitual behaviour can be applied to various aspects of the press. Readers apparently experience a general sense of loss if their morning routines are broken by the non-appearance of their daily paper.[7]   Much feature content appears on a regular daily or weekly cycle and even the news columns are unpredictable only in the sense that there is no telling which of the standard repertoire of stories will break today. But my aim in this paper is less to trade on common usage than to justify the concept by showing that there is a particular class of press performances which have a clear affinity with the ritual which has been the subject of social scientific study.

Press rites are those stories which the press as a whole unite in treating as important. They are stories which reflect on the stability of the social system by showing it under threat, overcoming threat or working in a united consensual way. There is also general agreement within the press on the way they should be handled and developed. The treatment of such stories is highly predictable from one to another. They share the same formal grammar of treatment and development. In that development considerable emphasis is put on the symbolic significance or interpretation of the events. The *symbolic* as opposed to the *representational* meaning of the content is high, to borrow Gombrich's distinction, and the role of the authorities and their values visible and commended.[8] Part of the development involves reference to Bagehot's 'dignified' and 'efficient' leaders of society for comment. These leaders often provide or confirm the symbolism within which the story is treated, even if they were not directly involved in the initial incidents which produced the story. The use of 'dignified' leaders is one instance of the way in which such rituals involve 'mystical notions' in Evans Pritchard's terms.[9] Another is in the supernatural symbolism applied to the source of the threat.

The two examples on which I shall concentrate to illustrate this definition are taken from the press coverage of Northern Ireland, the Guildford pub bombings and the Balcombe Street siege trial. But before proceeding to an account of these cases it is necessary to substantiate the claim that press rites so defined are an example of the general phenomenon 'ritual'. A discussion of theoretical problems of use and definition is the subject of the next section of the paper. Then, after an account of the particular cases, the paper deals with the value of the concept for the study of social processes connected with the media The argument there will be that ritual is more than a way of characterising some types of media content. It has implications for the study of the two other divisions of the traditional mass communication triad, production and audience, particularly through its connection with the notion of performance.[10] This is best summarised as another attempt to end the use of the triad in terms of a model of linear flow and to reformulate questions about influence and effect in terms of performance and participation.

Questions of Definition

Lukes, on the basis of a brief review of the literature, extracts the following definition of ritual: 'rule-governed activity of a symbolic character which draws the attention of its participants to objects of thought or feeling which they hold to be of special significance'.[11] It is part of Lukes's purpose to argue for an extension of the traditional usage in modern society to include oppositional and sectional rituals.

The point is well made. Much writing on youth culture has referred, however obliquely, to ritual in this sense.[12] Nevertheless, it has generally been characteristic of the ritual studied in primitive societies that the symbolism and form of the ritual was laid down by established tradition and its performance involved authority figures from the society concerned. Chiefs, witch-doctors, tribal elders or mothers' brothers, all represented a mixture of secular and spiritual authority based on the organisation of the particular society. As Leach has put it, 'There is usually a "conductor", a master of ceremonies, a chief priest, a central protagonist, whose actions provide the temporal markers for everyone else'.[13]

The presence of these authority figures has not been given any special emphasis in the literature because of the general acceptance of a functional form of analysis in which ritual affirmed basic social values and the general social order. Even Gluckman's analysis of the rituals of rebellion was concerned to show how they maintained order by giving the inevitable tensions and conflicts of society ritualised expression.[14] Gluckman went on to suggest that a similar analysis might apply to some 'squabbling actions in our social life' like parliamentary debates, election campaigns and some strikes. The implication of his argument, that, whatever their intention, oppositional tactics promote order, seems less secure than Lukes's view that opposition promotes opposition. The important point is that on both analyses rituals promote something, a sense of membership and allegiance.

This sense has generally been experienced in Durkheimian terms of solidarity or group cohesion which simply stress the first sense of membership, 'togetherness'. Terms such as loyalty or allegiance, however, would stress the element of subordination which those who participate in the ritual acknowledge to be owing to those who organise it. Subordination to authority is even present in the transition phase of the rites of passage, that most cohesive, 'together' moment which has provided the basis for Turner's argument that there is another model of society to be set alongside the structural one, the 'anti-structural' based on common humanity.[15] In the liminal (transitional) phase, Turner writes, society emerges recognisably 'as an unstructured or rudimentarily structured and relatively undifferentiated comitatus, community or even communion of equal individuals who submit together to the general authority of the ritual elders'.

There is a danger that, in extending the concept of ritual to include a wider variety of repetitive, collective behaviour, this element of subordination to the authority and values expressed will become diluted, if not completely lost. May Day parades and football crowds for example seem to vary on that dimension even if they can both be taken as cases of collective, repetitive behaviour. It is not that authority rites involve subordination and oppositional rites do not. Both require participants to become parts of the whole and in both cases the whole is greater than the sum of its parts. Recognition of this element of subordination is necessary to escape the Durkheimian paradigm. It is an element which is particularly apparent in press rites, as I shall hope to show. The first addition which needs to be made to Lukes's definition therefore is this recognition that ritual itself is a structured performance in which all participants are not equal.

A second is to bring out more clearly what Lukes summarised briefly in the claim that ritual has 'a *symbolic* character' and is based on 'objects of thought or feeling' of '*special significance*'. One of the main controversies in discussions of ritual has been whether it belongs exclusively in the sacred domain. This appears to be a simple matter of terminology; whether to adopt 'ceremonial', as advocated by Wilson and Gluckman, or 'ritual', as advocated by Nadel and Goody, for the most general term to refer to elaborate conventional forms of behaviour for the expression of feeling.[16] In Wilson/Gluckman's usage, ritual is that sub-category of ceremonial which involves religious belief or 'mystical notions'; in Nadel/Goody's, ritual is the general term which may be further subdivided into such categories as magical, religious and ceremonial. The latter usage is continued in this paper. It has the advantage that it accords better with common speech. It also helps to emphasise the point that there is more to the debate than terminology. It is bound up with the attempt to distinguish between two domains, the religious and the secular or, in Durkheim's terms, the sacred and the profane.

Goody questions the distinction as applied to tribal cultures on empirical and theoretical grounds.[17] But it is a distinction which still has wide currency as a marker of different stages of development. Urban, industrial society is also secular society. Thus Gluckman, taking the narrow view of ritual as religious, argues that it is inapplicable in modern society. 'We don't have rituals in the sense that we believe that the acting of social roles will in some supernatural manner affect our prosperity and unity. But we have many ceremonials expressing unity.[18] In practice such a distinction is hard to draw. It overstates the purposive rationality of religious ritual and understates the irrationality of ceremonial. Lukes argues against restricting ritual to religious usage because of the difficulty of separating the two modes in tribal cultures but also because he is concerned with contemporary, secular rituals, 'modern, political rituals, in which the mystical or supernatural often play little or no role'.[10] In other words the two domains, interwoven in traditional society are not just separable in modern society, but separated to such an extent that the sacred and supernatural can be completely excluded. I hope to show in the account of press ritual which follows that this cannot be justified empirically. Mystical notions and supernatural agencies are apparent in at least some contemporary political rituals.

This is one of the advantages of ritual as a concept. It allows one to add an irrational dimension to rationalist accounts of ideology as reflecting interests. The notion that ritual is not rational is implicit in common as well as anthropological usage. To quote Nadel again, 'when we speak of "ritual" we have in mind first of all actions exhibiting striking or incongruous rigidity, that is, some conspicuous regularity not accounted for by the professed aims of the action'.[20] Goody goes on to build this into his definition of ritual as behaviour in which 'the relationship between the means and the end is not "intrinsic", i.e. is either irrational or non-rational'.[21] The point is summarised by Lukes in his reference to the symbolic character of ritual. But symbolism lends itself to rationalist, intentionalist analysis to find out what the symbol stands for. Often the result is to reduce the resonances of symbolism to a representational account of its meaning. In Lukes's case the symbolism of ritual *represents inter alia* particular models or political paradigms' as ways of 'exercising, or seeking to exercise, power on the cognitive dimension'.[22]

The result is a rationalist and reductionist account of ritual as 'the cognitive dimension of social control', which has little to add to the analysis of ideology.

The second necessary addition to Lukes's definition therefore is the re-introduction of Goody's point that in ritual there is no 'intrinsic' relationship between means and ends. For brevity and clarity this is best done by using Evans-Pritchard's term 'mystical notions' to side-step the problem to which Lukes points, of specifying non-contestable criteria of rationality.[23] Ritual cannot simply be reduced to the rational. It draws on what is customary, familiar and traditional in the culture. It tries to add spiritual and emotional communion to any sense of political unity, though from any single point of view it may not work. We may now proceed to the analysis of press ritual with a slightly more cumbersome definition of the basic phenomenon as follows:- *rule-governed activity of a symbolic character involving mystical notions which draws the attention of its participants to objects of thought or feeling which the leadership of the society or group hold to be of special significance.*

Two Cases of Press Ritual

Before setting out the rites an autobiographical word is in order to explain how I came to adopt this perspective while conducting a content analysis of Northern Irish news. The preoccupation of content analysis with 'isolated fragments of information' has been noted by many as a limitation of the technique. [24] Peacock has pointed to the curiosity that while mass communication research has developed techniques for studying content, there are none for studying symbolic form. [25] One advantage of such a perspective which Peacock demonstrates effectively in his study of Ludruk, a type of Javanese theatre, is its concern with the interplay between form and symbol, the social life of the participants and the social structure of society. Symbolic form is based on the cultural and social experience of the people who participate, whether they are producers, performers or audience. It breaks down those distinctions. Content analysis on the other hand suggests the creation of content by producers, in the terms set out in the traditional mass communication triad. Once separated it is difficult to relocate the creative moment in society. I attempted to resolve this problem in my study of the production of a television series by arguing that society should be regarded not only as the audience but also as the source for media productions. [26] However that formulation took no account of symbolic form, dealing almost exclusively with meaning as information.

The fact that the Guildford bombs story broke at a time when I was conducting a relatively conventional content analysis was serendipitous in alerting me to the importance of symbolic form. [27] The story was made up of the same elements as the general run of news coverage- informative reporting, propaganda from outside sources and 'interesting presentation' as shown in the personalisation of most news stories. But quantitatively and qualitatively it was a unique phenomenon. Once I had been alerted to this by the analysis, the Balcombe Street siege trial was the next story in the same line of country which showed the same qualities. Since then, in something like the same area, the story of the Lufthansa hijack and subsequent rescue at Mogadishu produced coverage of the same type. The mode of analysis is more obviously applicable to the coverage of state ceremonials like the Queen's jubilee with its proliferation of special editions and supplements devoted as much to review as to news. But as one purpose of this paper is to advocate the adoption of ritual as a perspective I shall continue to concentrate on the extended usage in the hope that if that can be made convincing, more conventional usages will follow.

The Guildford Bombings

Bombs went off in two public houses in Guildford on the evening of Saturday, October 5th, 1974. First news reports were broadcast on radio and television that evening and the story was followed up by these media on Sunday. Only the late editions of the Sunday press were able to carry the story, but on Monday all the nationals led with the story, except *The Guardian* and the *Daily Express* in which it nevertheless featured prominently on the front page.[28] By the end of the week all the national press, except the *Daily Mirror* were still carrying follow-up stories.

The Guildford bombs story which was carried during the first of two periods of content analysis of Northern Irish news was a striking exception to all the other coverage of violent incidents in the two three-week periods of the analysis.[29] It was the only account of a violent incident which became a running story in the national press even though the story of Northern Ireland was largely one of violence or its aftermath so far as the newspapers were concerned. In the six weeks covered by the analysis 50% of all Northern Irish stories in the heavy press and 65% of stories in the populars dealt with violent incidents, their aftermath or the enforcement of the law. Other incidents, however, simply appeared as the latest in a staccato procession of events. Only Guildford, the only major incident to happen on the British mainland in either period, received prolonged attention. This difference in attention can readily be explained in traditional news terms as evidence of the importance of 'proximity', even allowing for the fact that the analysis was carried out on the early Irish or Ulster editions where such were produced. One incidental result of the study was that it gave a clue to the unit of account in the apocryphal newsroom calculation—One Englishman is worth n Irishmen, (n x a large number) Europeans and (n x an even larger number) Latin Americans. In the first period twice as many people were killed in Northern Ireland as died at Guildford. The Guildford bombs, however, took up two-thirds of all the space which the British media devoted to reporting violent events. (Thus $n = 4$ in the above equation.)

But there was more to the difference in treatment than proximity. Incidents in Northern Ireland happened in a divided society. There are many senses in which Britain itself is a divided society but it is a society in which signs and symbols of unity are available, particularly in response to an external threat such as the bombs posed. In the Guildford case those which were used by the press in the follow-up can be listed as follows:-

1. reports of messages of sympathy and acts of solidarity by civic, political and religious leaders. These included the Queen, the Pope, the Prime Minister, the Leader of the Opposition, the Home Secretary and the local mayor.

2. reports of statements of condemnation by such leaders, particularly politicians, policemen and others responsible for enforcing the law. Pre-eminent among these was the then Home Secretary, Roy Jenkins, who commented that the bombings were 'a perversion of human reason which showed the dark forces of violence and terror at work'. In other words the bombings themselves symbolised society under attack from irrational, asocial forces.

3. reference of political and law enforcement issues raised by the incident to be pursued and debated by parliamentary politicians. After Guildford the issues were the reintroduction of capital punishment and the possibility that the Price sisters would be moved to a jail in Northern Ireland to serve the remainder of their sentence there. As an election campaign was in progress at the time these issues were raised by individual politicians rather than through the parliamentary forum as would usually have been the case.

4. reports of subsequent law and order activity, in particular the police hunt for those responsible. This first centred on two girls whose photo-fit pictures appeared in the papers. The suggestion that women were responsible provided a sinister counterpoint to the fact that several of the victims had been women. The girls were soon found and eliminated however. The search then became a hunt for 'the man in black', a name for the public to conjure with like the 'black panther' whom the police had been looking for earlier in connection with the kidnapping of Lesley Whittle and the murder of several sub-postmasters. The 'man in black' was linked with the attacker in another recent incident in which Colonel Pinder, an officer who had served in Northern Ireland, had been wounded. The police apparently inspired the press to make this

link even though they had earlier ruled out any 'Irish connection' in the Pinder case. The press had reported this only days before, but nonetheless resurrected the possible connection.

5. condemnatory reports of those not following the example of the leaders in 1 above by showing the appropriate solidarity and sympathy. The only sour note in the follow-up stories to Guildford were various reports that the remaining pubs were thinking twice about serving service personnel. The press clearly did not approve of this policy and carried defensive quotes and denials from publicans and brewers.

6. reports of the bombings themselves and their aftermath in human interest terms which showed them to be horrid and senseless. Most headlines emphasised the youth, feminity and innocence of the victims. Their connections with the British army were reported in terms such as 'rookies', 'trainees', 'boy and girl soldiers', which underlined that they were inappropriate and illegitimate targets. The *Daily Mail* headline, which did recognise a strategic purpose, emphasised that the strategy was a senseless outrage. 'IRA Wage War on Women'—'sinister new move in campaign of terror'. The double meaning of a word like 'senseless' used on occasions like this to mean irrational and terrible provides a good illustration of the way reportorial language comes to be overlaid with more complex meanings.

The Balcombe Street siege trial

On February 9th, 1977, the four accused of organising and taking part in various incidents in London culminating in the Balcombe Street siege of December 1975 were found guilty at the Old Bailey and on the following day sentence was passed. The press covered the early stages of the trial with a mixture of reported information, received propaganda from official sources and human interest to make the information readable. Conviction and sentence, however, were the cue for a surge in coverage in which all the papers carried lead stories and extensive inside page features reviewing the trial and the events which had led up to it. As was the case with the Guildford bombs story, the qualitative difference between this and the general run of reporting lay in the volume of the coverage, the unanimity on the development of the story and the marked use of symbolism, including in this case visual symbolism, to fill the space.

The sense of newspapers filling space for the sake of performing a rite which was apparent in some inconsistencies in the Guildford coverage, for example the linking of the 'man in black' with Colonel Pinder's attacker, was even more marked in the case of the Balcombe Street siege trial. The convicted men who were denigrated as 'so-called soldiers' and despised as 'vicious', 'ruthless', 'callous' and 'inhuman' in accounts of the final court proceedings were also credited with being 'the IRA's crack unit' in accounts of their campaign which originated from police sources. On their arrest in 1975 the four had been dismissed by the press, quoting the then Metropolitan Police Commissioner, as 'ordinary, vulgar criminals', 'low-class terrorists'. Other internal inconsistencies in the Balcombe Street coverage also suggested that on this occasion the press were more concerned with symbolic than representational meaning, getting it right according to what should have happened rather than reporting accurately what did. The Matthews, for example, the couple who had been held hostage in their Balcombe Street flat, were variously reported as being angry, bitter and still suffering from nightmares and being resigned but uncomprehending to a distant memory which now seemed unreal.

A comparison of the components of the Balcombe Street coverage with the Guildford story shows a marked formal similarity.

1. the various leaders who had expressed solidarity and condemnation in the Guildford case were replaced by one, the trial judge, who condemned the accused and their behaviour in passing sentence.

2. evidence of the industry of the law enforcement agencies was provided in retrospective reviews of the effective police 'dragnet', 'ring of steel', 'well-oiled trap', 'Operation Combo'. This also provided one of the ubiquitous visual symbols in the reports in the form of four policemen with revolvers braced and aimed at a target (the balcony of the flat) above their heads. Originally this was a news photograph from the final moments of the siege. Various versions of it were used in the trial coverage. The Guardian, for example, had the original picture heading its inside feature, the Mail and the Express had small cartoon versions as logos to mark their trial coverage and The Sun in the most complex image had the photograph flanked by pictures of destruction after a bomb and a bombing device incorporated as the crosspiece of a Celtic cross, which carried down the upright the headline 'The Bomber who came back from the dead' (Figure 1). Evidence that the image has been adopted in the culture comes from its use as the cover illustration of Paul Wilkinson's latest book on terrorism, 'Terrorism and the Liberal State'.[30]

3. condemnation of those not prepared to accept the ritual took the form of ridiculing the prisoners who refused to recognise the court and

FIGURE 1

to listen to their sentences with due humility. In an interesting sidelight on the interaction of the different participants in the performance of the same ritual, the judge, according to *The Sun*, commented on the prisoners' refusal to hear their conviction by the jury with the words 'They don't have to be here . . . They can read it in the papers afterwards'.

4. reminders of the injury suffered by society was again provided in personal terms by reviews of the victims, interviews with their relatives and with those like the Matthews who had survived. The theme of irrationality was echoed by these relatives and survivors continually putting the question 'Why?'. Perhaps the most harrowing example was Mrs. Hamilton Fairley's question in *The Sun* 'Why Gordon? His whole existence was devoted to saving lives'.

5. a difference of emphasis between the two cases was in the attention given to the origins of the assault on society. These origins which remained latent at Guildford in the form of 'sinister, dark forces' were made manifest at Balcombe Street in the four accused. The force was personalised in the form of pictures of the prisoners. A combination of four police 'mug shots' made another ubiquitous visual image. But the undercurrent of sinister, supernatural forces which could not be fully understood was maintained. Following the conviction of the accused, the *Daily Mail* led with 'The Faces of the Mass Killers' above the four 'mug shots' as if the clue was to be found in their faces, the *Daily Mirror* headlined 'Guilty! The IRA's Brethren of Blood' and the *Daily Express*, 'Faces of Evil: Bombers guilty of mass murder'. *The Sun* which led with the relatively secular headline 'Guilty: Balcombe Street Siege gang to be sentenced today' carried the complex Celtic cross image (Figure 1) as the heading for the 'three-page report by *The Sun* crime team' inside.

The Celtic cross was one of many references to Irishness. In the copy there were several examples of the impossibility that the Irish and British would ever understand each other, from the accounts of the prisoners' behaviour in the dock to comments attributed to the prisoners' parents and friends. According to *The Sun* for example Duggan's mother 'was flabbergasted. "God help us and save us," she said. "I can't believe it. My boy was a model son" '. But another mother, republican Mrs. Butler, said 'You're British. You wouldn't understand'. The same counterpoint between God-fearing, rural Ireland (Mrs. Duggan 'lives alone in a farmhouse') and unaccountably vicious and unfeeling Ireland was reproduced in the *Express* in a headline 'The victims of the "quiet country boys" ' and in the juxtaposition at the bottom of the double-page spread of two photographs illustrating 'From tranquil Ireland to the horror at Scotts restaurant—the cottage where Duggan grew up and the death scene in Mayfair'. Perhaps the *Telegraph* was nearest to resolving the conundrum in its sub-head on Docherty, 'Altar boy from Gorbals slum'. This also resonated a contemporary conventional wisdom for which the *Telegraph* usually has little time. This contrast has puzzled the British through the ages, ever since they created the two opposing stereotypes of Ireland and the Irish, Hibernia and the marauding beast.[31]

A third and equally inconclusive account of motivation appeared in various references to the gangsters and villains of fictional popular culture. 'When the Godmother said "Kill" ' headlined the *Daily Express* over its double-page feature. In the *Daily Mirror* the comparable headine was 'Mission Murder: How eight men and two women sailed to Britain with a cargo of carnage and terror . . . and 1,000 police set an ambush . . . ' The centre-piece of the spread was a comic strip providing a step-by-step account of how it was done, complete with stereotyped illustrations which would have graced an adventure comic. *The Guardian* featured a less-fictional popular memory which was also apparent to other papers. Bombs in London mean Blitz. All three of these inadequate accounts of motivation, references to the supernatural, Irishness and folk culture fitted an account in which the outcome was inevitable. Those who meddle with the supernatural do so at their peril. Confusion over Irishness is reflected in Irishmen's own confusion and errors. 'Good as it was, the unit was caught by its members' own stupidity' (*The Guardian*, attributed to police). In popular culture the police always get their man and in folk memory 'London can take it'.

6. explicit readings of the symbolism. Only the *Daily Mail* bothered to point the moral of this ritual performance in its editorial column. 'They killed without mercy. Yet they were caught without bloodshed . . . The Balcombe Street Gang slashed at the fabric of our civilisation with a callous cruelty unsurpassed even in the terrible history of urban terrorism. All they achieved is to remind us how precious that civilisation is to us.' Among all the other rhetorical devices and slogans in this short passage, 'slashed at the fabric of our civilisation' is particularly noteworthy for its echoes of holy war and biblical religion. The editorial went on to contrast the personal tragedies of the victims with the anonymity of the IRA murder gang, 'anonymous' even though

pictures of the gangs were the centre point of the paper's front page. The editorial continued with praise for the police, a reminder to the IRA that British nerve could not be broken—a reference to the Blitz without the symbol, and a final call for 'enduring vigilance'.

The Genre of Press Ritual

In the previous section I attempted in a preliminary way a formal classification of the components of these press rituals. The classification suffers from the limited number of cases but I have kept to a limited, inductive form of presentation on the grounds that even if it does not make the argument more convincing it makes it easier to follow. My purpose in this section is to move on to a discussion of press ritual as a genre. Limited data makes this an even more risky enterprise. Its importance however lies in making the case that ritual is more than a label of convenience.

1. Structure/Anti-Structure

Various authority figures played a large part in the two press rites described above. If we read the rite as ideology, then one account would concentrate on the way in which the agents of the state were shown to be effective and the hierarchy of the society made manifest. The sense of social solidarity developed in the rites is one of subordination to the authorities who can be relied on to deal with the threat posed. In spite of occasional references to IRA strategy, the threat mostly appeared as random and incomprehensible. It was less a specific common foe to be identified and beaten than a diffuse force threatening the social order which could only be tackled by the social order given ritual expression. The random, incomprehensible nature of the threat was directly stated as in Roy Jenkins's statement and also symbolised by the personalisation of society as the individual victims who had been killed and wounded. Not only were they inappropriate targets, the circumstances in which they were attacked were inappropriate—while walking to work, opening their front door, enjoying a night out, holding a reunion or celebrating a birthday party. The fatalism implicit in this emphasis on chance suggests acceptance of the situation rather than reaction to it. Rationally there is nothing to be done about it and anyway what can be done is being done. The sense of Durkheimian solidarity, 'we're all in this together', what one might call 'we-ness', was further supported by stories of lucky escapes, the irony of being in the wrong place at the wrong time and stories of bravery and heroism in minimising the effects of the outrage. But the theme of 'we-ness' is counterpoised with another— 'there but for the grace of God'. The spiritual, political and secular authorities are playing their part. Someone is looking after us after all. Little more is required of us than to participate in the performance of ritual *cauterisation* in the Guildford case or *affirmation* at the Balcombe Street trial.

Affirmation has legal and political overtones and *cauterisation* is intended as a little more complex piece of medical symbolism. It was the contrast between the coverage of Guildford and the coverage of incidents in Northern Ireland which originally suggested a medical analogy.[32] The viable British state was able to take steps to heal its wounds in a way which was not available in the divided society of Ulster. In that society the leadership could only exacerbate the conflict. Important leaders were aligned with the division and unable to rise above it symbolically. The two partisan morning papers in the province mainly quoted comments on any incident from leaders on their side. They coincided only in their use of spokesmen from the Alliance party which lacked significance because its aim was to occupy a non-existent middle ground. But cauterisation has the further significance that it is not a particularly specific or efficient remedy and certainly not a modern one which could be recommended with confidence. It is as likely to spread infection as control it.

The same, I shall argue, is true of these press rites. The ritual is much less like a rational, modern remedy for the social ills it opposes than a survival of folk medicine which has uncertain effects but is still used as a required response to sickness. The fatalistic concern with the chances that brought the individual victims to their death echoes the central question of witchcraft—'why has this happened to me now?' rather than the scientific medical interest in the nature of disease and its processes. It provides a good example of a point of inherent ambiguity in the rites which make any reading of their meaning partial.

The interpretation of the personalised, human interest aspects of the performances advanced above, that the emphasis on common humanity amounts to an assertion of solidarity within the prevailing social structure, is not one that the authorities themselves find entirely convincing. They are much more likely to interpret the reporting of suffering and disaster as a propaganda victory for the 'other side'. The same is true of the references to popular fiction and folk memory. The hyperbole involved in comparing a few home-made bombs with the Blitz exaggerates the achievement of the bombers as much as that of the authorities. Comparisons with the heroes and villains of popular culture can be read as glamourising their subject as well as denigrating them. The latest official committee to report on the troubles, the Gardiner Committee on measures to deal with terrorism in Northern Ireland, noted 'There is a tendency, which exists elsewhere, towards sensational reporting of shootings and bombing incidents which lends a spurious glamour both to the activities themselves and to the perpetrators'.[33]

The history of government-media relations in the course of the latest troubles in Northern Ireland has been a history of the government of the day repeatedly putting pressure on the media to recognise and conform to its propaganda goals.[34] As it has achieved at least partial success in this endeavour so it has become apparent that there is no limit to what may be regarded as propaganda. The case is clearest in broadcasting.[35] Continued pressure has reduced news reports to selected factual details of incidents. The broadcasting authorities have become progressively more concerned and careful about potentially sensitive aspects like attributing the cause of violence or identifying the victims. The tendency has been to select details and incidents which appeared to fit the authorities' paradigm of the conflict. Even so, reporting can still be construed as propaganda for the other side. Roy Mason, the current Secretary of State for Northern Ireland, made this clear when he called for a complete moratorium on the reporting of violent incidents.[36] Like earlier moves by his predecessors, this call was less a serious suggestion than simply the latest manifestation of continued pressure to control the flow of information. It provides striking evidence however of the limited effects of such control. Propaganda (and pari passu ideology) are inherently ambiguous in content and unpredictable in effect.

Simple broadcast accounts and human interest press reports can be regarded as propaganda victories for the opposition because to borrow Turner's distinction, they refer to 'communitas', to 'anti-structure' as well as 'structure'. The distinction is founded on Turner's account of the liminal phase in rites of passage, 'a moment in and out of time, and in and out of secular social structure, which reveals, however fleetingly, some recognition (in symbol if not always in language) of a generalised social bond.'[37] The passage of the acolyte through the rite demonstrates two fundamental forms of order in human relations. The structural model of hierarchy, roles and statuses which has been at the centre of most anthropological and sociological analysis, and anti-structure which depends on 'an essential and generic human bond without which there could be *no* society'.

The acolytes in the liminal phase of equal and undifferentiated communion submit together to the general authority of the ritual elders. But in developing the distinction and applying the concepts to more general social process Turner is concerned to emphasise the tension between the two modes of relationship. From the point of view of those maintaining social structure 'all sustained manifestations of communitas must appear dangerous and anarchical'. According to Turner, the tension is resolved over time by a continual dialectic between the pursuit of communitas and its associated spiritual modes of relationship and the pursuit of structure, which includes the economic order.

There is no space here to do justice to Turner's complex development and application of this distinction but enough has been said to show its relevance to the analysis of press ritual.[38] In the reporting of the authorities, their views and symbolism and in the presentation of human interest accounts of individual members of the society, these rites oscillated between the two poles.[39] The two modes of relationship can also be demonstrated in a difference in the language used to report the same incident. Reports of an incident on 29th March 1977 from *The Guardian* and the *Daily Mirror* show this difference of language particularly clearly as a difference between the two papers accounts (Figures 2 & 3). In *The Guardian* the terminology was that of structure—'IRA attack', 'protestant family', 'Provo gang', 'policeman's mother', 'Provisional IRA gunmen', 'reserve policemen', 'Rev. Ian Paisley, MP for North Antrim', 'Mrs. McMullen', 'Mr. McMullen', etc. The participants were continually identified with the parties to the conflict and provided with structural roles and statuses, even at the simple level of 'Mr' and 'Mrs'. The *Daily Mirror,* however, made more use of kinship terms—'wife', 'mother', 'son', 'parents', simple collectives without explicit links to the politics of the conflict—'gang', 'terrorists', 'four gunmen', and basic human categories—'woman', coming to a structural account only in the penultimate paragraph. Kinship terms, simple collectives and sexual categories can all be said to be anti-structural in the sense that their reference is to the simple experience of life rather than the business of living.

It would be idle to claim that this demonstration amounts to more than illustrated conjecture. It certainly will not bear the interpretation that the heavy press is aligned with structure, the popular with anti-structure. Nevertheless it does suggest a mode of investigation to follow

GANG SHOOT DOWN WIFE

By JOE GORROD

TERRORISTS killed a woman of sixty-three yesterday when they raked the cottage where she lived with machine-gun bullets.

Mrs. Hester McMullan was in bed in her house near Toomebridge, Co. Antrim, when the four gunmen arrived in a car.

First they ambushed her son Jim, who was driving off to work in a lorry.

They chased him, firing from the car windows until he swerved into a farmyard. He escaped with a slight bullet wound.

Then they turned and drove back to his parents' home, where they poured machine-gun bullets through the doors and windows, calmly stopping to change magazines.

Mrs. McMullan was killed instantly. Her 70-year-old husband and 21-year-old daughter Elizabeth escaped unhurt.

Police believe the gunmen's target was a second son, who is a part-time policeman.

Said a spokesman: "This was one of the most vicious attacks we have ever encountered."

FIGURE 2
Daily Mirror 29.3.77

FIGURE 3

Guardian 29.3.77

DEREK BROWN reports on the latest IRA attack on a
Protestant family

Provo gang murders policeman's mother

Provisional IRA gunmen, thwarted in their attempt to kill a reserve policeman yesterday, went to the man's house and raked it with gunfire, killing his 63-year-old mother.

It emerged later that the gang had picked the wrong man for their initial ambush. Instead of the police reservist they fired at his brother, who has no connection with the security forces.

In another display of ruthless incompetence in Belfast the IRA hijacked a petrol tanker, loaded a bomb on board and sent the vehicle into the village of Dunmurry, just outside the city. The village was evacuated as an army bomb disposal officer removed the device and detonated it.

The death of the policeman's mother, Mrs Hester McMullen, led to an angry outburst by Rev Ian Paisley, MP for North Antrim, in whose constituency the murder was committed. He announced that in protest against the Government's security policy he would not return to Parliament except to vote against the Government in vital divisions.

The McMullen family live in a farmhouse near Toomebridge. Early yesterday four or five gunmen stole a car from a neighbouring house and lay in wait near the farmhouse.

One of Mrs McMullen's sons, James, owns a lorry which he always parks overnight at the farmhouse. Yesterday he travelled as usual from his own home nearby to pick up the lorry. He had driven it only a few hundred yards when the gunmen opened fire. His windscreen was shattered but he accelerated and drove past the ambushers.

They followed him, firing from the windows of their car. But Mr McMullen, grazed by the first shots, drove into another farmyard and escaped.

Then the gunmen turned and went to the McMullen farmhouse. They surrounded it and opened fire out close range. It is not clear whether Mrs McMullen was visible to the gang, who went on firing after she had been hit.

Mrs McMullen's 73-year-old husband, and a 21-year-old daughter escaped unhurt. The son, who serves part-time with the RUC and another daughter who works for the police as a typist, were not at home.

Mr Paisley, who was quickly at the scene of the shooting, described it as a determined attempt to wipe out an entire Protestant family. He would be speaking to fellow-Unionist MPs about his partial boycott of Parliament, he said.

"If we go to Parliament and make speeches we are giving a cover to the gunmen which by its policy is destroying Northern Ireland," he said.

The petrol tanker bombing in Belfast—the third such incident in recent weeks—began in the early afternoon when the vehicle was hijacked in the Falls Road. The driver was held at gunpoint while a bomb was loaded into an empty compartment with hundreds of gallons of fuel on either side, and then ordered to take the tanker to Dunmurry.

He left the tanker outside a petrol station in the village. Police evacuated the area and diverted traffic.

It took three hours to remove the bomb and make it safe with a controlled explosion.

Dunmurry and its neighbouring suburb, Finaghy, have been the targets for a concentrated bombing campaign in recent months. One reason is that the mainly Protestant area is in the way of further expansion of Catholic West Belfast, which is crammed with refugee families intimidated out of Loyalist parts of the city.

A few hours before the petrol tanker incident another bomb in a hijacked Post Office van was planted in Finaghy. It was also defused by the army.

up the claim that press rites share a general characteristic of ritual in symbolising both types of relationship, structure and anti-structure. The caveat also needs to be entered that human interest in the press is only pseudo-communitas in the sense that one English person is worth four Ulster persons, according to the newsroom calculus noted above. To take another example, it was a greater tragedy, in terms of press attention, when Mrs. Ewart-Biggs, wife of Britain's ambassador to Ireland, was widowed than when Mr. McMullen was made a widower.[40]

2. Secular and Supernatural

Press rites display the authorities and the citizenry performing an idealised version of their secular roles. The *Daily Mirror's* cartoon version of the events leading up to Balcombe Street provided a particularly clear set of idealised stereotypes. The heroic policeman with his trusted dog calmly and effectively protecting an innocent harrassed lady from unshaven, excitable villains. But the tendency to produce an idealised version is much more ubiquitous. In the human interest accounts of incidents and their aftermath people are portrayed acting out their roles with their appropriate emotions as prescribed by the norms and traditions of the culture. Two double headines from *The Sun* illustrate the point. 'A so-cool triumph for the Yard's friendly persuaders—chat led to truce.' 'I keep asking: "Why Gordon? His whole existence was devoted to saving lives"—Agony of a widow.' One appropriate role for the ordinary citizen participating in the press rites was to pose the question 'Why?' Abnormal behaviour, in the sense of behaviour which would offend the norms, is screened out or occasionally reported critically like the Guildford publicans' attempt to introduce a ban on servicemen. The result is a process close to that which Gluckman termed 'ritualisation':—'stylized ceremonial in which persons . . . perform prescribed actions according to their secular roles'.[41]

Gluckman goes on to argue that the aim of these prescribed actions is to 'express and amend social relationships so as to secure general blessing, purification, protection and prosperity . . . in some mystical manner which is out of sensory control'. The much disputed question of the frame of reference in which ritual is seen as achieving such effects—the observer's or the participants', and in the latter case some or all of the participants—may conveniently be left aside. Instead I intend to concentrate on the evidence for contemporary press ritual working in a mystical manner, out of sensory control. The prescribed actions performed by authorities and citizenry are ranged against the opposition not as a tactical counter but as the appropriate response to dark, sinister, supernatural forces. In the rites discussed in this paper the element of the supernatural was attached most clearly to the opposing forces. Religious leaders and those whose authority straddles the two spheres did provide some of the quotes and comments. More ubiquitous however was the treatment of the origins of violence as dark, sinister, irrational and unknown. Discussion of terror as a rational strategy adopted by a political movement to achieve political ends is rare. It is not considered in those terms but taken to be irrational because it is immoral. Questions of morality have been one of the traditional concerns of religious and spiritual authority. The fact that such authorities are rarely explicitly consulted is a tribute to the extension of the political power of the modern state. It is the state which defines the morality. This decline in the separate authority and significance of religion and religious functionaries is what justified Gluckman's claim that they are no longer regarded in quasi rational terms, as effective means to achieve secular ends.

But this does not mean that such questions have lost supernatural significance and no longer involve mystical notions. One of the consequences of the equation between irrational and immoral is to exclude from social communion the perpetrators of such acts. It is this which justified the *Daily Mail's* editorial claim that the Balcombe Street gang were 'anonymous' even though their names, faces and backgrounds featured prominently on the front page. The preoccupation with the faces of the prisoners in the coverage can be seen as a throwback to the traditional notion of the face as the mirror of the soul. There is no rational, strategic explanation for their behaviour but it may be that we can come to 'know them' by looking into their souls. The quality of the pictures showed tarnished souls and, by implication, black hearts.

Edmund Leach has recently taken up this theme, pointing out that secular and religious sanctions still overlap in the contemporary responses to criminality.[42] 'In Great Britain and the United States we do not now ordinarily think of murderers and thieves as polluted sinners who have provoked the retribution of supernatural powers, but every now and again when the public is shocked by some element of horror in the crime under discussion . . . we are reminded that although, with us, some sins are not crimes, and some crimes are not sins, some crimes *are* also sins . . . Any offence which is felt to be a really major crime is a sin by another name, and, in capitalist society, the major criminal-sins are offences against the individual and against individual property.' Terrorism is another criminal-sin partly because it involves homicide and theft, crimes which are sacriligious under capitalism because they threaten the basic assumptions of social order.[43]

The terrorist goes further than the 'ordinary criminal' and selects such crimes precisely because they threaten the established order. They symbolise its intended overthrow. As an anonymous German terrorist put it in an interview in the BBC programme, *Terror International* (BBC1, 30.1.78) the aims of acts such as the kidnapping of Dr. Schleyer and the hijacking of the Lufthansa airliner to Mogadishu is 'to show the Western powers they are not God Almighty'. In his lectures Leach went on to argue that the element of sacrilege in terror tends to make vengeance and counter terror a 'religious duty' against outsiders who are no longer regarded as proper human beings. In this paper I have been concerned with another aspect of social response which shows the continuing importance of sacred, mystical notions, the presentation of the events and the response in the form of media rites. Public shock at contemporary sacrilege is not simply spontaneous but ritualised.

3. Press Ritual and Political Ritual.

The two press rites discussed above each show the press in a different relationship to other institutions in the society. In the Guildford story the press and other media provided the forum for the other participants to take part in. The various actors and commentators on the drama had no other institution in which they could all participate. Balcombe Street on the other hand was based on the report of a trial. The performance of the rite brought together a good deal of material which was only hinted at in the judge's summing up and sentencing—accounts of the police operation and reviews of the incidents—and some which was not part of the trial at all—the interviews with the relatives of the victims. But it was founded on the legal process. As Lukes has pointed out, the legal process itself is a worthy candidate for inclusion within an extended concept of ritual.[44] In short, while some press rites are run by the press itself, others are run by other social institutions, but developed and given their peculiar form by press presentation.

Not that this distinction equates with the distinction between the two rites described above. A third case, the Mogadishu rescue story was a rite of affirmation but one which was only put on through the news media. The hijack itself, involving a German aeroplane in a far country, did not prompt a rite of cauterisation in the early stages. But the dramatic rescue prompted the full treatment, extending to nine pages in the *Daily Mail.* In some cases it is more than the values and effectiveness of the national political system which is symbolised through ritual.

Not only does the press relay social ritual, it may also act as an instigator. Such an analysis can be applied to the incidents of 'bloody Sunday' in Londonderry, their reporting, the government's subsequent handling of the affair and the press reporting of that. 'Bloody Sunday' was not, as appeared, a propaganda victory for the British authorities in spite of the way it was handled in some papers.[45] Faced with a growing scandal in the press and in the political arena, the government of the day 'resorted to widgery'. The device of appointing a judge or tribunal of inquiry to deal with major threats to confidence in the political, administrative or economic machinery of the country has all the hallmarks of a political ritual. It delays resolution of the immediate crisis, subjects it to a lengthy review within the framework of strict procedure. Even if the report itself does not resolve any dispute, there is a good chance that press reporting, assisted by judicious public relations, will further obfuscate the issues. On the publication of the Widgery report 'those who read their front pages . . . would have had to have been very short-sighted to miss the PR work', commented Simon Winchester. ' "Widgery Clears Army".' they shrieked in near unison; and a relieved British public read no more—Bloody Sunday, thanks to the propaganda merchants and a half dozen lazy hacks, was now a closed book . . . '[46]

In sum the press and the media do not act alone in the performance of political ritual but in concert with other political and social institutions. Concert suggests harmony and this appears to be the more usual case but discordant press reporting may also be one of the instigators of ritual performances by other institutions. If 'our society is composed of highly fragmented and divided relationships' at an individual level, as a polity it is highly centralised with interwoven and interrelated institutions. Gluckman's account of ritual as characteristic of societies with multiplex roles and relations can be extended with the suggestion that political ritual is characteristic of multiplex polities.

4. Press Ritual as Folk Literature

The phenomenon noted above of the press drawing on popular

culture and folk memory for some of the symbolism used in the two rites is not exclusive to such ritual moments. It is a common feature of much press coverage. Helen Hughes in her account of human interest news noted that much 'news' deals with themes which are 'old in folk tales, fine literature and popular literature, so much so that many a headline tells them by using symbols like "Don Juan", "Bluebeard", "Cinderella" '.[47] Alongside accounts of the development of the press as information media, serving special interest publics with financial, economic or political reports or as partisan media recruiting support for different parties and factions needs to be set an account of their development as a form of popular literature.[48] Perennial stories and familiar plots appear in different guises from day to day. Helen Hughes quotes the case of the story of the women who kills her rich guest without realising he was her own son, a story which can be found in broadside ballad. 'When the ballads were superseded by the penny press, the story survived. But it conformed to the demands of the new medium; it purported to be a contemporary occurrence with a new name, place and data. In 1930 Alexander Woollcott and Valentine Williams, an English journalist, established the fact that substantially the same story has recurred in English, French and German newspapers about every 6 months for the last 25 years—which led them to describe it as "the perfect specimen of folklore" '.[49]

Only in a very limited sense are such stories the creation of the journalists and newspapers involved. They are reproduced from folklore and popular culture and converted into the appropriate format. The process of conversion works both ways. A familiar story is given a contemporary marker or a topical incident becomes a familiar story—'a lost child' becomes '*the* lost child' to quote another of Hughes's examples. This type of conversion is particularly apparent in press rites as in those cases it takes on overtones of obligation. To repeat the point made above, idealised accounts of secular role performance are obligatory as observances of the appropriate behaviour. Inappropriate behaviour is screened out or criticised.

But conversion in the other direction is also apparent. Stories may be conjured out of thin air to fill up gaps in the performance. To take the case of the Mogadishu hijack and rescue, ubiquitous attention was given by the press to the possibility that the hijackers were members of an international conspiracy. This produced the story in the *Daily Mail*, reproduced as Figure 4, which in substance is vacuous and speculative. It is not a report so much as an appropriate part of the ritual. So far as

FIGURE 4

Daily Mail 19.10.77

It's Terror International

TERRORISM is the world's fastest - growing multi-national business— Anarchy Amalgamated.

It has a corporate identity, it has its 'company men' (and women). Whether they are operating in Ireland, Tokio or Chile, whether they wear kaftans or blue denim, they feel that they are working for the same 'firm'.

There may be no rigidly formal bonds to a central body of terrorists, but a far-Left brotherhood does exist. It links, say, the PLO man to the IRA man in a symbiosis that produces excesses of violence.

The terrorists have their own conventions. In Belfast, in 1974, the Official Sinn Fein asked terrorists from all over the world to a grisly gathering.

Other meetings in other places have discussed ideas, tactics, strategies. They point irrefutably to a recognisable business structure with defined hierarchies and with consultants (often academics) and killers. A successful grafting between the Chamber of Horrors and the Chamber of Commerce.

Paradoxically, the anarchists have become capitalists.

Now to complete the

BY PETER STENNING

business image, the accounting principle comes into play.

In the two most recent hijackings — in Germany and in Japan — vast sums of money have figured in the ransom demands.

Who is the chairman, the brains, of the co-ordinating body? Carlos comes to mind.

Ten years ago, Carlos would have been too outrageous a figure to contemplate. Today he is as real as his entry in the files of Interpol, an assassin with the world as his beat, a man admired by every terrorist organisation.

Who is Carlos? Where does he operate from? No one on the right side of the law knows. But certainly the terrorists of this world today have an allegiance not simply to their own ghastly causes but to a supranational someone or something.

the *Mail* itself was concerned, this story might be explained simply as part of the process of keeping up with the competition. *The Times* had an 'international connections' story the day before. But so far as the press ritual as a whole was concerned the international angle was part of the way the origins of this incident were made complicated and mysterious. The symbolism of this piece in the *Mail* was particularly striking with its sustained negative analogy between multi-national corporations and international terror, culminating with a pun on supernational which reinforces the point made above. The origins are not just mysterious but mystical.

Compared with the symbols cited by Hughes, the symbols used in the rites described in this paper were strikingly contemporaneous. It is as though this form of popular literature has lost its sense of history, drawing instead on the current concerns and creations of other contemporary popular culture, films, television series and adventure novels. Again it must be emphasised that this is a two-way process. Accounts of an earlier hijack and rescue at Entebbe have already been turned into at least two feature films. Plans are in hand for similar 'spin-offs' from Mogadishu. At the time of the Balcombe Street trial a 'documentary reconstruction' of the siege and the events leading up to it was screened on ITV. Just as the media cannot be isolated from other social institutions, so the press cannot be treated in isolation from the rest of contemporary culture.

However, there are factors peculiar to the British press, its commercialism, its metropolitan concentration and the secretiveness of the state in which it operates, which suggest why it is particularly involved with other aspects of popular culture and particularly prone to the performance of national rites. In other countries, including the United States, it is easier to limit discussion of press performance to an analysis of their performance as information media. The style of journalism based on informing special publics has retained a few prestigious outlets and these have been better insulated from popular journalism than has been possible in the British national press.[50] The political and administrative authorities in the States have also been readier to accept the informative style as a constitutional duty. In Britain the safest course, if not the constitutional duty under the terms of laws such as the Official Secrets Act, is to keep silent. The presumption is against disclosure and controversy on grounds of responsibility. Although the national newspaper market in Britain may be divided into various sectors, the overall effect of having a relatively large number of newspapers based in one city and distributed through the country, has been to make all papers participate in the national culture in much the same way. Moreover, as Murdock and Golding have shown, the political economy of the British press is such that they have become part of the wider leisure industry, a complex which includes most of the other media but whose economic dynamic is the pursuit of profit wherever returns are greatest.[51] As a declining medium, the press has little economic initiative. This is paralleled by an output which has little creative initiative within contemporary popular culture. To describe press performances as ritual also draws attention to their 'striking and incongruous rigidity' in Nadel's terms, the sense of going through the motions to observe a rite, which comes from their derivative and obligatory contents.

The Significance of Ritual

The aim of this final section is to show that ritual as a perspective has a value beyond describing a particular type of press output. Nevertheless it is important to emphasise that that is the point from which this analysis started. Ritual as a perspective remains limited and focussed. It may be summarised briefly: ritual is less a communication about social reality than a customary performance giving symbolic expression to social relationships.

Lukes's attempt to avoid the Durkheimian paradigm for the analysis of ritual effectively turned it into a form of ideology, a mode of political and social control. That is the approach continued in this paper but with important modifications. Lukes does not consider the relationship between ritual and ideology but his account of ritual working through 'cognitive power' seems to miss one of the important contributions that ritual can make to the study of ideology. Ritual belongs to the idealist as well as the consensual tradition in social analysis and so there has been considerable investigation of the way it works through experience and symbolism.[52] To treat ritual performance simply as standing for political paradigms is to oversimplify. It also expresses and symbolises social relationships and so, quite literally, mystifies them.

In this section I shall develop ritual as a concept within the framework set out by Geertz in his analysis of 'ideology as a cultural system'.[53] The conceptual problems associated with ideology have led writers following Gramsci and Althusser to treat it in terms of great generality. Descriptions of ideology as 'a network of established "given" meanings' (Morley), 'the forms in which reality "presents itself' to men' (Mepham) or 'simply the "sum of what we already know" ' (Hall) have made it something of a catch-all in contemporary analysis.[54] The difficulty this creates is that the generality of ideology has to be reconciled with an account of its origins. One way in which this is done is by qualifying ideology with labels like 'bourgeois' and 'dominant' to mark out those items from the general ideological mix which can best be related to the interests of the ruling class. Another is to use the distinction between phenomenal and real in much the same way to mark out ideology as that version of reality relating to ruling interests. Both are open to Geertz's criticism that the connection is not explained but 'merely educed' by 'the crude device of placing particular symbols and particular strains (or interests) side by side in such a way that the fact that the first are derivatives of the second seems mere commonsense or at least post-Freudian, post-Marxian commonsense'.[55]

Geertz also works with a very general concept of ideology but apparently he is interested in the problem of explication for its own sake. His objective is a science of culture, symbolic behaviour. This he characterises as 'thick description', 'not an experimental science in search of law but an interpretive one in search of meaning'.[56] To develop such a science it is necessary to introduce a set of concepts which will categorise different types of symbolic behaviour and performances. This is even more essential for those who are not content to treat culture, even heuristically, as an autonomous phenomenon. Conceptual elaboration and investigation are necessary to provide the discriminatory links between ideology and power which ideology itself cannot provide because of its generality and because it is itself one of the terms of the equation. Geertz has made a particularly impressive contribution of his own in his account of the Balinese cockfight as 'deep play'. But there are relevant concepts which have received considerable attention in related fields and in other theoretical traditions which can be realigned to help show how the tricks of ideological production and effect are turned. One is propaganda, which there is no space to develop here. Another, I submit, is ritual.

This paper has mainly been concerned with presenting press ritual from the point of view of the content which appeared in the papers. Nevertheless it will be apparent from the discussion, particularly in the previous section that the press was not alone in acting out these rites. The press provided a forum in which other political and social institutions could take part and in which the public as readers were also involved. Starting from two cases there is little prospect of providing a complete taxonomy of rites in this paper. Nevertheless the two types, *cauterisation* and *affirmation* are closely related to the first and last of Van Gennep's three types or stages; separation, transition and incorporation.[58] They mark points of change in the system of social relations; in the first case, a point of crisis and in the second one of resolution. Public ceremonials, which it has been more usual to regard as rituals but which have been little discussed in this paper, bear some affinity to Van Gennep's second type, transition. They generally mark the adoption of office, the passage of time in an office or the performance of some function related to an office.

To develop this taxonomy it would be necessary to show what events, changes in the system of social relations, were ritualised. The definition of press ritual used in this paper is sufficiently restrictive to suggest that a catalogue of occurrences would show similar events of crisis, official celebration and resolution which were not ritualised, ritualised only partially or unsuccessfully, or ritualised by other institutions as in 'widgery'. One hypothesis for example would be that a crisis like Suez which is a matter of dispute between the political parties is less likely to be ritualised by the press than one like Northern Ireland which is not. In the latter case it is easier to take the conflict out of the rational, secular domain in which political, military or economic decisions have to be taken on both means and ends and to move it into a mystical, non-rational domain in which it can be left to look after itself. Successful mystification depends upon the agreement of the whole ruling class.

Such contrasts would enable the analyst to say much about the nature of British society and culture. The perspective is rather different from traditional media content analysis which has been concerned with the way press and the other news media report people and events. Such examination of media performance has produced results in terms of the general image or ideology expressed in media reports. Those who have used the term ideology have gone further in recognising that there is more to media accounts than reporting. 'Every language has its opportunity cost; evaluations are already implicit in the concepts, the language in terms of which one observes and records'.[59] Press ritual as discussed in this paper is a type of media account particularly rich in implicit and explicit values and complex layers of meaning—it is a characteristic symbolic form. It invites the development of another taxonomy, a classification of media accounts, to show the range of symbolic forms available to the press and the different occasions of their use. Content analysis has usually started from the available distinctions of journalistic practice, news versus features, verbal versus visual, popular versus quality, press versus broadcasting. The suggestion above that there are at least two modes of discourse in press reporting, the structural and the anti-structural, is an example of a type of analysis which cuts across such distinctions and concentrates instead on the implicit symbolism.

So too does the claim that in ritual performances the symbolic as opposed to the representational meaning is high. Studies of media production as well as content analysis have been concerned with the way in which journalism reports the world. This focus follows from a theory of the press as information media and has led to the investigation of bias and distortion in the production of media knowledge. But in ritual performances the inadequacy of this approach is particularly clear. They are less reports, selecting and distorting a set of events in the real world, than accounts put together after the manner of literature according to a sense of what is necessary and appropriate.

To recognise news as a form of literature is to be forced to come to terms with what Geertz has called 'the autonomous process of symbolic formation'. Concepts such as 'inferential structure' and 'media stereotypes' have made some attempt to do this by emphasising the importance of preconceptions in determining the way events are reported.[60] But they work within a framework which is still focussed on the way knowledge, not meaning, is socially determined. 'The sociology of knowledge ought to be called the sociology of meaning, for what is socially determined is not the nature of conception but the vehicles of conception.'[61] Following this approach the study of news production would involve not studies in the production of knowledge but studies in the use and development of meanings. This suggests the study of the public and private meanings available in newspaper circles and the way they feed on and feed into the meaning system of the general media culture. It also suggests the value of working above the level of the treatment of particular stories or classes of story to consider the newspaper as a vehicle for symbolic forms in which large parts are occasionally pre-empted for ritual performances or as itself a symbolic form which occasionally takes itself seriously as 'The Voice of the People' or 'The Voice of Britain'.

Geertz also has some pertinent remarks to make about studying the effectiveness of symbolism. He rejects as inadequate the two standard sociological interpretations that it 'deceives the uninformed' or 'excites the unreflective' as resting on a 'flattened view of people's mentalities'.

Accounts of media influence whether of the older stimulus-response or the more recent cognitive effect variety have tended to be of this 'all or nothing' type.[62] Either the media are influential or they are not. Either people are duped by what they read in the press or they see through it.

This is less true of some recent attempts to see media and audiences working within common, overlapping, structured sets of codes. But this work has been founded on the exposition of particular cases or classes of content. To show an effect in each case, it has usually been necessary to assume it. 'Audiences whose decodings will inevitably reflect their own material and social conditions, will not necessarily *decode* events within the same ideological structures as those in which they have been encoded. But the overall intention of "effective communication" *must*, certainly, be to "win the consent" of the audience to the preferred reading and hence to get *him* to decode within the hegemonic framework.'[63] There are compelling reasons for making this assumption but desperate problems involved in showing how what *must* happen, *does* happen to *him*, the audience as individual. The mechanism assumed is psychological and cognitive. Geertz however insists that because of the public nature of symbolism, 'human thought is a public and not, or at least not fundamentally, a private activity' (to oversimplify a complex argument).[64] The point I wish to draw out is the further possibility this suggests for trying to show how the trick of ideological effect is turned. Instead of concentrating on private processes at a particular point in time, one is directed towards the social process over time, the development, application and change of different symbols and their currency in different realms of discourse from the mediated to the interpersonal.

So far as media and audiences are concerned, this calls for an interactional approach,[65] one which would recognise such common experiences of everyday life as that people do 'talk back to their television set'. In doing so they are forced to enter into discussion with it on the terms it lays down. But on the other side the media cannot move far from the terms it is assumed their audiences will understand. Methodologically it points to an emphasis on observation and recording rather than on asking people to verbalise processes which do not happen in their heads over sufficiently short periods of time for them to be able to capture them. Concepts like role distance developed by Goffman for the study of interpersonal interaction have descriptive relevance to the relationship many people, journalists and readers, apparently have with their newspapers.[66] They direct attention towards a study of the press performances which elicit that type of response and the social circumstances under which they are made. There are various ways of distancing oneself from a newspaper and its news which have much to do with the symbolic meaning of the newspaper and its content, meaning which may change when it is read in different places and company.

There is another thread running through these various observations, and that is for audience analysis at a much more general level than has been common in media studies. By treating communicative behaviour as a social fact on the Durkheimian model it would be possible to study the interaction between social change, media performances and audience participation. Audience statistics collected on the basis of who attends to which medium remain a curiously neglected source of data. They have rarely been analysed on the basis of who attended to the various media *when*. The aim would be to relate communicative behaviour to the course of social history, not to time of day or season of the year which are among the stock in trade of audience research. The paradigm case which has received some attention is communication behaviour in crisis.[67] The focus of attention has usually been on the dissemination of news of the particular case based once more on information flow theories of the media and the analysis of their influence in terms of consensual functionalism. Nevertheless, these studies have shown the remarkable extent and intensity of communication behaviour on such occasions. Journalists have many occupational beliefs about when newspapers will sell, as for example 'wars sell papers', but they have been little investigated, particularly in the terms suggested in this paper. The point would be not just to relate events to audiences but to consider the nature of the intervening performances. If people watched television almost insatiably after the Kennedy assassination, what sort of television was it they were watching? Available evidence suggests it was heavily ritualised, but that is where we came in. Some media performances are political rites carried out on behalf of the powerful, in which the powerless are invited to take part. The nature of the British media system is such that the invitation is difficult to refuse.

Centre for Mass Communication Research,
University of Leicester.

[1] I am greatly indebted to Graham Murdock for his comments on an earlier version of this paper.

[2] For a general review see Robert Bocock: *Ritual in Industrial Society*, Allen and Unwin, London, 1974.

[3] S. F. Nadel: *Nupe Religion*, Routledge and Kegan Paul, London, 1954, p.99.

[4] S. Lukes: 'Political Ritual and Social Integration', *Sociology*, Vol. 9, No. 2, May 1975.

[5] Ibid. p. 297.

[6] Ibid.

[7] First demonstrated in Bernard Berelson's classic study: 'What "missing the newspaper" means' in P. F. Lazarsfeld and F. N. Stanton (eds): *Communications Research*, 1948-9, Duell, Sloan and Pearce, New York, 1949.

[8] 'A painting may *represent* an object of the visible world . . . , it may also *symbolise an idea.*' E. H. Gombrich: *Symbolic Images*, Phaidon, London, 1972, p. 124 (Emphasis original).

[9] 'Patterns of thought that attribute to phenomena suprasensible qualities which, or part of which, are not derived from observation or cannot be logically inferred from it, and which they do not possess.' E. E. Evans-Pritchard: *Witchcraft, Oracles and Magic among the Azande*, Clarendon Press, Oxford, 1937, p. 12.

[10] David Chaney has argued that 'performance' is to be preferred to media 'content'. It draws attention to 'symbolic expression' as well as 'the manifest symbols that constitute a particular communication' and to the 'dramatic element in mass communication which is important in understanding the sort of relationship being studied'. *Processes of Mass Communication*, Macmillan, London, 1972, p. 8.

[11] Lukes op. cit., p. 291.

[12] For example, *Resistance through Rituals; Working Papers in Cultural Studies*, Vol. 7 and 8 (Joint Issue), Summer, 1975; Paul E. Willis: *Profane Culture*, Routledge and Kegan Paul, London, 1978; Peter Marsh, Elizabeth Rosser, Rom Harre: *The Rules of Disorder*, Routledge and Kegan Paul, London, 1978. Only Peter Marsh's work explicitly develops and applies the concept of ritual.

[13] Edmund Leach: *Culture and Communication*, Cambridge University Press, Cambridge, 1976. p. 45.

[14] Max Gluckman: 'The Licence in Ritual' in *Custom and Conflict in Africa*, Basil Blackwell, Oxford, 1966.

[15] Victor W. Turner: *The Ritual Process*, Penguin, Harmondsworth, 1974. Quotation from page 82.

[16] Monica Wilson: *Rituals of Kinship Among the Nyakyusa*, Oxford University Press, Oxford, 1957; Max Gluckman: 'Les Rites de Passage', in *The Ritual of Social Relations*, Manchester University Press, Manchester, 1962; Nadel op. cit.; Jack Goody: 'Religion and Ritual: The Definitional Problem', *British Journal of Sociology*, Vol. 12, 1961, pp. 142-164.

[17] Op. cit.

[18] Gluckman (1966), op. cit., p. 135.

[19] Lukes op. cit., p. 290.

[29] Nadel, loc. cit.

[21] Goody, op. cit., p. 159.

[22] Lukes op. cit., p. 301. Original emphasis.

[23] For the definition of 'mystical notions' see note 9 above.

[24] The phrase is Merton's in 'The Sociology of Knowledge and Mass Communications', *Social Theory and Social Culture*, Collier-Macmillan, London, 1968 (revised edition).

[25] James L. Peacock: *Rites of Modernisation*, University of Chicago, London, 1968.

[26] Philip Elliott: *The Making of a Television Series*, Constable, London, 1972.

[27] For the original analysis see Philip Elliott: Reporting Northern Ireland in London, Dublin and Belfast, *The Media and Ethnicity*, UNESCO, Paris, 1977.

[28] All references to the national press in this paper exclude the *Morning Star*. It was included in the original content analysis but it differs from the other papers on the crucial point that it does not agree with the leadership of the society on the objects of thought or feeling which it holds to be of special significance and so goes out of its way not to participate in the ritual performances of the rest of the press. The *Financial Times* was not included originally, but is an interesting case as its participation in the rites discussed in this paper was nothing like so extensive as that of the rest of the press. It has remained most insulated from the general effects of competition and metropolitan centralisation in the British press providing information for a specific audience. This point is returned to below.

[29] The periods were from 23rd September to 11th October, 1974, and from 21st April to 9th May, 1975.

[30] Paul Wilkinson: *Terrorism and the Liberal State*, Macmillan, London, 1977.

[31] For discussions of this tradition see L. P. Curtis: *Anglo-Saxons and Celts*, University of Bridgeport Press, Bridgeport, Connecticut, 1968; *Apes and Angels: The Irishman in Victorian Caricature*, David Charles, Newton Abbott, 1972; P. O'Farrell: *England and Ireland Since 1800*, Oxford University Press, London, 1975.

[32] The point is elaborated in the report of the original study cited above.

[33] *Report of a Committee to consider . . . measures to deal with terrorism in Northern Ireland* (Gardiner Committee), H.M.S.O., London, Cmnd. 5847, 1975, para 76.

[34] This point is developed in Philip Elliott, 1977, op. cit.

[35] On the BBC and Northern Ireland see Philip Schlesinger: *Putting Reality Together: BBC News*, Constable, London, 1978.

[36] As reported in the *Daily Mail*, 6th January, 1977.

[37] Turner (1974) op. cit., p. 82. The following quotations are from p. 83 and p. 95.

[38] See Victor W. Turner: *Dramas, Fields and Metaphors*, Cornell University Press, 1974(b).

[39] Turner (1974(b)) also points to two other poles between which the symbolism of ritual typically oscillates, the 'orectic pole' of physiological phenomena such as blood, sex and death which carries an emotional significance and the 'normative' or 'ideological' pole of normative values and moral 'facts'. 'The drama of ritual action . . . causes an exchange between these poles in which the biological referents are ennobled and the normative referents are charged with emotional significance' p. 55. In embryo this suggests an explanation of why we have 'bad news'.

[40] Turner (1974(b)) gives patriotism as an example of pseudo-communitas.

[41] Gluckman (1962) op. cit., p. 24.

[42] Edmund Leach: *Custom, Law and Terrorist Violence*, Edinburgh University Press, Edinburgh, 1977, quotation from p. 32, emphasis original.

[43] Leach makes the point that in tribal societies founded on kin relations it was the breaking of kinship taboos like incest which were the prototypical acts of sacrilege.

[44] Lukes op. cit., especially pp. 302-3.

[45] See Simon Winchester's account of his experiences: *In Holy Terror*, Faber, London, 1974.

[46] Ibid, p. 210.

[47] Helen MacGill Hughes: 'News and the Human Interest Story' in E. W. Burgess and D. J. Bogue (eds): *Contribution to Urban Sociology*, University of Chicago Press, Chicago, 1964, p. 282.

[48] Robert Park: 'The Natural History of the Newspaper', in R. H. Turner (ed): *On Social Control and Collective Behaviour*, Chicago University Press, Chicago, 1967. See also H. M. Hughes op. cit., and *News and the Human Interest Story*, University of Chicago Press, Chicago, 1940.

[49] Hughes (1940) op. cit., pp. 195-6.

[50] This theme of why cannot British journalism be more like American runs through many of the contributions, including one by the author to a critique of the British press edited by James Curran *The British Press: A Manifesto*, Macmillan, 1978.

[51] G. Murdock and P. Golding: 'Beyond Monopoly: Mass Communication in an age of conglomerates' in Peter Beharrel and Greg Philo (ed); *Trades Unions and the Media*, Macmillan, 1977.

[52] Turner for example is an uncompromising idealist, arguing strongly that symbols are not epiphenomena but have ontological status. 'Symbolic behaviour actually "creates" society for pragmatic purposes—including in society both structure and communitas', Turner (1974(b)) op. cit., p. 56.

[53] Clifford Geertz: 'Ideology as a Cultural System', in *The Interpretation of Cultures*, London, Hutchinson, 1975.

[54] David Morley: 'Industrial Conflict and the Mass Media', *Sociological Review*, Vol. 24, No. 2, May 1976; J. Mepham: 'The Theory of Ideology in *Capital*', Working Papers in Cultural Studies, No. 6, 1974; Stuart Hall: 'Culture, the Media and the "Ideological Effect" ', in James Curran e.a. (eds); *Mass Communication and Society*, Edward Arnold, London, 1977.

[55] Geertz, op. cit., p. 207. Geertz's point is that though the device is 'crude', the analyses are usually anything but, being both impressive and compelling.

[56] 'Thick Description: Toward an Interpretive Theory of Culture' in Geertz, op. cit. Quotation from page 5.

[57] 'Deep Play: Notes on the Balinese Cockfight' in Geertz, op. cit. For another discussion of Geertz's relevance to media sociology see James Carey: 'Communication and Culture', *Communication Research*, April, 1975.

[58] For an account of Van Gennep's approach see Gluckman (1962), op. cit.

[59] D. Morley: op. cit., p. 247.

[60] See James D. Halloran, e.a.: *Demonstrations and Communication*, Penguin, Harmondsworth, 1970; The Glasgow Media Group: *Bad News*, Routledge and Kegan Paul, London, 1976.

[61] Geertz, 'Ideology . . . ' op. cit., p. 212.

[62] For a review of recent approaches see D. McQuail: 'The Influence and Effects of Mass Media', in J. Curran et al (eds.), op, cit.

[63] Hall (1977) op. cit., p. 344 (Emphasis changed).

[64] See Geertz: 'Ideology . . . ' and 'Thick Description . . . ' op. cit. Quotation from the former p. 214.

[65] Cf. the author's critique of another style of audience research which comes to a similar conclusion. Philip Elliott: 'Uses and Gratification Research; a Critique and a Sociological Alternative', in Jay G. Blumler and Elihu Katz (eds): *The Uses of Mass Communications*, Sage, London, 1974.

[66] Erving Goffman: *Encounters*, Bobbs Merrill, Indianapolis, 1961.

[67] The paradigm example of the paradigm case is the assassination of John F. Kennedy in 1963. Bradley S. Greenberg and Edwin B. Parker (eds): *The Kennedy Assassination and the American Public*, Stanford University Press, Stanford, California, 1965.

Professor Blumler, in this article, discusses the need for a political philosophy of mass communication that can stem from a considered view of political democracy. That considered view, moreover, must take into account recent research on mass communication effects and on organizational research on broadcasting, reviews of which he offers below. Jay G. Blumler is professor and director of the Centre for Television Research, University of Leeds.

35

POLITICAL COMMUNICATION
Democratic Theory and Broadcast Practice

Jay G. Blumler

Reviewing current theories of media effects a few years ago, Elihu Katz deplored "the way in which the study of mass communication has been disconnected from the study of public opinion" (Katz, 1980: 120). Latterly, a cross-disciplinary movement has been emerging, however, with Elisabeth Noelle-Neumann at its fore, which aims to forge fresh links between our understandings of mass media roles, processes of public opinion formation, and the workings of democratic institutions. Not least among the many tasks falling to scholars excited by this new spirit is a project of normative clarification. Focusing on certain deep-seated problems that have arisen in Britain and elsewhere over the place of television in politics, I outline below a twofold thesis: We lack, and urgently need to develop, what might be termed a *political philosophy of mass communication.* And we should seek its guiding principles in a *considered view of political democracy* and of what public communication should be doing for it.

By a political philosophy of mass communication I mean a body of thought that would aim coherently to explicate certain principles, incorporating both legitimate expectations and realistic possibilities, defended by appeals both to argument and to evidence, with reference back to which the role of such a major political medium as television could be more maturely assessed—that is, be justified, criticized, or

EDITORS' NOTE: This chapter was originally an inaugural lecture given by the author on assumption of a personal chair in the social and political aspects of broadcasting, University of Leeds, December 1, 1980.

From Jay G. Blumler, "Political Communication: Democratic Theory and Broadcast Practice," *University of Leeds Review* (1981). Reprinted by permission.

spurred to improvement. Although at this stage it would be premature to try to offer a fully tailored version of such a philosophy, I shall aim to make inroads into the issues involved by approaching them from four angles. Put in the form of questions, they are:

(1) How has the need to think more philosophically about political broadcasting arisen; and why has it become more urgent in recent years?

(2) What light can recent research into political communication throw on the resulting problems and needs?

(3) From what concept of democracy might we derive a basis for evaluating the role of television in politics?

(4) And to what priorities and directions of change in how political broadcasting is organized might such a view of democracy draw our attention?

I

The seeds of pressure to philosophise are ultimately traceable to the sociopolitical situation of public service broadcasting, which is inherently uneasy and unstable, and in Britain has become ever more fraught since some time in the mid-1960s. At least three features are responsible for its problematic standing. First, its purpose is thinly defined—amounting to little more than one of providing programs that will entertain, inform, and educate, serving all social interests impartially—and is therefore open to many different interpretations and expectations. Second, it is peculiarly vulnerable to criticism, more so than any other journalistic organ. That is, just because broadcasters are supposed to be impartial, avoid undue offense and in other (not very well specified) ways serve the public interest, they are correspondingly open to accusations of impropriety, bias, and neglect of duty, some sincerely voiced, others mounted to cloak the more naked pursuit of partisan and sectional advantage (Blumler, 1980). Third, broadcasting bodies are ambivalently located in the political arena, supposedly protected from its pressures, yet having to function in that arena as well to defend vital interests at stake there. Presumably that is why the late Sir Charles Curran, former Director-General of the BBC, proclaimed a need for senior broadcasters continually to engage in what he called "the politics of broadcasting." As he put it, "The broadcaster's life has to be one of continuous political ingenuity" (Curran, 1979: 319).

But talk to almost any British broadcaster who has been concerned with factual programming production, or its supervision, for some period of time, and you will soon form the impression that the resulting tensions have been much aggravated in recent years. In an address to the Royal Television Society some months ago, for example, the BBC's Director of News and Current Affairs centered the bulk of his remarks on what he first termed, "a quickening debate about the nature and role of the television medium," and then acknowledged to have become nothing less than "a crisis of confidence in television." He was thus responding to the fact that an increasing number of groups have latterly been voicing their discontent with television, ranging from standard bearers of social causes, such as racial equality and the feminist movement, to inveterate wielders of pressure, such as the major political parties, to even well-entrenched Establishment sectors, such as the police, the trade unions, and the medical profession.

What accounts for this tightening of the societal screws on broadcasters? In part, it reflects the fragmentation of what was always a rather tenuous moral, industrial, and political consensus in society and a corresponding proliferation of causes and interests, each aiming to secure the best political and publicity deal it can get out of the governmental and media powers that be. In part, it stems from the diffusion of public-relations-mindedness in previously more innocent circles, who are now determined not to be left out of the mass communication process and so give a much greater priority to the execution of planned publicity strategies. Yet more fundamentally, it reflects a growing awareness of the ultimate relativity of news judgments, even when these are made by apparently devoted journalists who conscientiously strive to serve us all. For news judgments imply criteria that are ultimately relative, in turn, to certain values, defining what events in the world are interesting and important. They can only be universal in application if there is agreement on such underlying values (Gans, 1979). And barring such an agreement, which is less likely in a more divided society, more and more groups come to regard the news as it applies to their affairs as wittingly or unwittingly politicized and therefore fit to be pressurized. In the circumstances, it would not be surprising if senior broadcasters saw themselves nowadays as if adrift on that democratic ship of state that was so magnificently, though pejoratively, portrayed in this passage of Plato's *Republic* (1955: 249-250):

> The captain is larger and stronger than any of the crew, but a bit deaf and short-sighted and doesn't know much about navigation. The crew are all quarrelling with each other about how to navigate the ship, each thinking he ought to be at the helm; they know no navigation and cannot say that anyone ever taught it to them, or that they spent any time studying it; indeed they say it can't be taught and are ready to murder anyone who says it can. They spend all their time milling round the captain and trying to get him to give them the wheel. If one faction is more successful than another, their rivals may kill them and throw them overboard, lay out the honest captain with drugs or drink, take control of the ship, help themselves to what's on board and behave as if they were on a drunken pleasure cruise.

But there is a reverse side to this coin of intensified broadcasting crisis as well; and if broadcasters are to carve a path through the mounting dilemmas, they must appreciate that they too form a *part of the problem* and are not just its inert victims. For in recent years change has been afoot inside the broadcasting organizations themselves, affecting the outlook on their work of many news and current-affairs journalists and producers. The shifts involved are numerous and complex and not easy to characterize succinctly. In essence, though, many observers, both outside and inside the broadcasting services, have noticed the increasing influence of an ethos of so-called professionalism, that is, a greater tendency for workers in television to assume the self-identity of broadcasting professionals. Although such a concept is many-sided, at least two features stand out from most accounts of what has been happening. One involves the placing of a near-supreme valuation on what experience shows television can do well. As Tom Burns (1977: 125) puts it in *The BBC: Public Institution and Private World,* since the early 1960s there has been a transition

> from an occupation dominated by the ethos of public service, in which the central concern is with quality in terms of the public good ... to one dominated by the ethos of professionalism, in which the central concern is with quality of performance in terms of standards of appraisal by fellow professionals; in brief, a shift from treating broadcasting as a means to treating broadcasting as an end.

The other feature is peer orientation, a closing of ranks, and narrowing of incentives and regard, to what one's fellow professionals can appreciate. As Lord Windlesham, who is himself the Managing Director of the Independent ATV company, has recently put it, "In the BBC and ... ITV ... the regard of fellow programme-makers for the way in which a programme fulfilled its aims became a dominating concern" (1980: 85).

Such trends may fuel the crisis I have been depicting in two ways. First, they may make it more difficult for *non*broadcasters to reach the broadcasters on some ground of shared discourse. That is, the latter may come to see themselves as commanding skills, production practices, proven program formats, styles of communicating, ways of combining words and pictures, ways of attracting and holding audiences, that nonprofessionals are inherently incapable of fathoming and appreciating.

Second, professional broadcasters may become more set in their ways, difficult to bounce out of their routines, and so lose some of their innovatory spirit and thrust. In any given topic field, then, they may increasingly behave as if they controlled a familiar and tried array of approaches, to which available materials, even when novel in themselves, should naturally be subordinated. In fact, there are signs that something like such a fate befell the British House of Commons when its debates were opened to the microphones in April 1978. So far as I and my colleagues studying this development have been able to tell, *innovatory* responses to the availability of this new facility have been few and far between, while what we have called *incorporative* ones—ones involving an adaptation of parliamentary actuality to existing program formats and styles—have predominated. Such an outlook was also reflected in the frequency with which broadcasters we interviewed described parliamentary sound to us as like an extra "tool" in their professional kit, or even like an extra "wire service," able to supplement, enliven, and bring closer to reality their characteristic patterns of parliamentary reporting, without basically changing them (Innovation in Political Communication, n.d.).

Both lines of analysis up to this point converge on a focal danger, then: that the crisis of broadcasting may degenerate into a conflict between esoteric and unyielding professional practice, on the one side, and the pressures of particular interests, on the other side, each fighting its own corner. Another way of expressing the theses mentioned at the outset of this essay is to ask whether there is some plane of democratic principle, the articulation of which would allow a more constructive dialogue to be resumed over what broadcasting should be doing for society and for its politics.

II

Now the state of affairs portrayed above might matter less if researchers into political communication could put their hands on their hearts and firmly proclaim that, according to the evidence, the political impact of mass communication generally, and television specifically, is on the whole slight, limited, and exceptional. Nowadays, however, most students of the subject would regard the metaphor recently deployed by a British political scientist—"communication is the hyphen that joins parts of the political system" (Rose, 1980: 199)—as far too bland and passive. It is true that the mass media are in a sense pigs in the political middle, buffeted and played on by external pressures, opinion climates, market forces, audience tastes, links via institutionalized reporting beats to prominent news sources, and surrounding cultural norms. And yet—in some respects, in some circumstances, on some topics, and for certain people—they must also be regarded as political forces in their own right. Of course that string of qualifications is important, and they rule out all simplistic notions of an undifferentiated, unidirectional and overridingly sweeping impact of political communication; but so too is the central thrust of the proposition they modify.

The political influence of the mass media is partly a function of how the political *arena* is organized and partly a function of how the *mass media* are organized to *present* what happens in that arena to the public. So far as the first side of that equation is concerned, a key development in recent times has been the marked decline since the early 1960s in the strength of voters' partisan loyalties and identifications—certainly in Britain and the United States, and in many other competitive democracies as well. This has created more "room" for communication effects on voters' political perceptions than existed before and has helped to transform the organization and conduct of election campaigns as well. Thus electoral volatility has increased; more cross-pressured and undecided voters have emerged to keep campaigning politicians on tenterhooks; fewer voters have sought a reinforcement of existing party preferences from political messages and have looked for other gratifications instead (voting guidance, spectator excitement, and various informational insights); it has mattered much more to politicians to reach the less rooted and more fickle electorate both during and between campaigns; television with its mass audience and credible reputation has been a prime vehicle for doing so; politicians have consequently felt obliged to adapt their messages to the demands and conventions dominant in their own countries' factual programming styles on TV and especially in television news; electioneering has become more frenetic, approximating a prize fight model of the contest in which every campaign statement, every move, every policy announcement, every news event, every gaffe, every candidate's visual appearance (ranging from cuddling a calf for thirteen minutes to driving a steamer four miles down the Mississippi River!) has to be calculated or exploited for electoral effect; and thus, paradoxically, at the very time that more people are looking to television for comparative information, structural factors are continually threatening to limit its ability to supply it in an ordered and coherent manner.

The significance of how the *mass media* are organized to report the political scene can be illustrated in two ways: first, by noting a so far little remarked common theme of the chief lines of media effects investigation that are most in vogue at present; and second, by indicating how observed features of mass media workways exert a formative pressure on politicians to address the public in certain styles than others.[1]

Perhaps four main approaches to the study of mass media effects are attracting most attention at this time. First, there is Elisabeth Noelle-Neumann's own spiral of silence theory, according to which media journalists, when spotlighting certain societal trends at the expense of others, manage to convey impressions of standpoints that are winning and losing ground to audience members, to create climates in which people feeling in the ascendant are more prepared to voice their views to others, and so to enlist the powerful engine of interpersonal communication in the molding of public opinion (Noelle-Neumann, 1980). Second, there are now many studies of the agenda-setting function of mass communication, which aim to establish whether the political issues covered most frequently and prominently in the mass media are those that audience members are also most concerned about and most want action on. A recent example in this vein, based on nine waves of interviews with samples of American electors, spanning the entirety of a presidential campaign year (February-December, 1976) provides a fascinating picture of the incidence of numerous agenda-setting effects, varying by time period, by medium, and by demographic, political, and motivational characteristics of voters themselves (Weaver, 1981). Third, a number of American scholars are examining whether certain styles of political coverage, which in concentrated bursts and doses repeatedly report instances of political conflict and failure, are generating what they term political malaise and a lack of trust in government (Robinson, 1975). Finally, there is the controversial project, based at the University of Pennsylvania Annenberg School of Communications, that purports to show how television is a prime source of reality construction for many viewers, for example, cultivating, through its fictional and factual obsessions with violence, an impression of the world as a mean and unsafe place that is more infested with crime and danger than in fact is the case (Gerbner et al., 1978). What is common to these otherwise disparate approaches is how they have shifted the research focus away from previous investigations of the impact of persuasive messages, propagated by political parties and leaders, using the media as channels for their views, toward an emphasis on how audience members' ideas might be affected by the chief reporting patterns and working methods adopted by *mass media professionals themselves.*

So what do we know about how journalists are organized to process major political events? During the British General Election of 1979, Michael Gurevitch and I were given an opportunity to observe the responses of editors and reporters of BBC Television News to the daily flow of campaign activity. At that time we were particularly impressed with the way in which certain presentation conventions that are part and parcel of the television news framework naturally dominated the election reports that were presented to British viewers night after night during the campaign. We had asked for observation facilities in the first place because we wanted to form a firsthand impression of the criteria that newsmen used when selecting passages from party press conferences and leaders' hustings speeches for inclusion in election reports.

Three points seemed to stand out from the experience. First, the selection decisions were all made back at the Television News Centre and not at the site of the political event itself. Typically, newsmen crowded around monitors relaying the event into the Centre, noticeably straining to catch quotable excerpts—bits which they would then scribble into their notebooks, together with any timing points that would help them to judge their lengths and locate them for playback later. The atmosphere of this place of decision seemed subtly but powerfully to strengthen the influence of what in my observation notes I later called "TV news presentation requirements" at the expense of what I thought of as "political significance judgments." Second, when I tried to sum up what those presentation requirements appeared to be, I noted them down as follows: need for brevity; need for crispness of expression; need for vivid and pithy phraseology; compatibility with a preconceived view of what the dominant election story or theme of the day might be; vigor of attack on the opposition; and the provision, when two or more such extracts were being taken from different party sources, of a complementary form of thrust and counterthrust or point and counterpoint. Finally, we were struck by the subordination to these criteria of other actors who might have otherwise been expected to inject more solidly political criteria into the election news selection process. For example, the BBC had a highly knowledgeable political correspondent who was supposed to write and present the totality of the election news segment in each night's bulletin. Yet, in discussing his part in selection with me, he continually played it down, treating himself as no more than one voice in a chorus, where others had at least as much right to consideration of their judgments as he himself. It was as if in working for TV news he had become socialized to its demands and accepted their legitimacy and overriding necessity. On one occasion he told me that on that particular day he had attended two party press conferences and listened to portions of a third. It struck him, he said, that the person with the clearest view of what was happening that could be newsworthy would be somebody "back here," watching the process, rather than somebody attending one of the conferences in person. At any rate, he went on, "My usual way is to try to find out what someone who has been away from the scene sees as the most interesting set of options for extraction from it."

Although this was just one experience, its findings tally with the results of similar exercises conducted by other researchers elsewhere (cf. Barber, 1978), and its implications are far-reaching. For, viewed from this standpoint, the process of political communication results from an initial conviction on the part of party publicity managers that in electoral politics "perception is the name of the game." The struggle to promote favorable perceptions then tends to be fought out largely through the television news bulletins. Consequently there is an increasing tendency for the sources of political messages, wanting to reach large audiences through the most credible outlets, to tailor and reduce them to the formats, scenarios, and styles of address characteristic of such bulletins and whatever other programs and media they wish to penetrate. The production practices of television journalists, then, could almost be compared to turnstiles to a zoo, which only coins of a certain size and shape will fit, such that politicians' publicity aides not only become skilled at manufacturing the right coins of entry, but also come in some cases even to believe that the zookeeper really knows better than anyone else what kind of food will most suit the palates of the denizens in their cages on the other side!

Perhaps this last image *was* a shade extreme. No single feature of broadcasting journalism determines the receptivity of television to political materials, and the media workways that shape political reports may vary considerably across the broadcasting systems of different societies. Nevertheless, they do matter, because they reach back, as it were, into the very quality of what the party managers and other publicists will tend to offer us as viewers and citizens. And I am bound to confess to some fear that the democratic publicity process itself, particularly at election time, may increasingly become discredited as if chiefly involving a mass response to improverished rhetoric, channeled through straitjacketed media, yielding fickle and arbitrary results.

III

Is there a view of political democracy, then, that could give us a principled platform on which to stand and resist such pressures? In tackling that question, I must confine myself to one partial though undoubtedly crucial facet of theories of democracy: what they have to say or imply about the knowledgeability of what one author recently rather charmingly called "Good Citizen Brown" (Margolis, 1979), and about the informational arrangements required to enable him to play an effective part in government and make it in some sense or other his own.

Now when you approach democratic political theory from that angle, you run into a dilemma that can be depicted in three guises. Concretely, first of all, survey evidence often suggests that Good Citizen Brown can draw upon only limited stocks of information when thinking about and reacting to political events. As Bernard Berelson and his colleagues (1954: 308) summed up the situation in the last chapter of *Voting*, their classic study of the 1948 presidential election:

The democratic citizen is expected to be well-informed. ... [But] by such standards [he] falls short. The citizen is not highly informed on details of the campaign, nor does he avoid a certain misperception of the political situation when it is to his psychological advantage to do so.

In fact, I recently learned from a colleague in Belgium that there is actually a program on television there, in which journalists ask simple questions of passersby in the street: Who is the Prime Minister? Where is such and such a country which is much spoken about? What is the 107th article of the Constitution? They then read the most funny replies and invite audience members to laugh (Thoveron, 1979).

Presumably that helps to explain why, secondly, when democratic theory tries to take account of this problem, it often seems to swing between two extremes: either comprehensively redefining the meaning of democracy to make it compatible with elitist government, or seeing mass ignorance as a transitory condition that could be dispelled by administering some appropriate remedy, from the outside as it were, through social revolution perhaps, or by instituting a new information order, or through mass education—so as to sustain an idealized vision of democracy as popular participation, involvement, discussion, interest, knowledgeability, and control.

Meanwhile, thirdly, as Carole Pateman has argued in her recent work, *The Problem of Political Obligation,* some moves in this oscillation threaten to undermine the very authority of democratic government itself. As she explains, much liberal political theory traces the citizen's duty to obey a government back to a sense in which it could be said that he or she had *consented* it be ruled by it, which in modern democracy is supposedly embodied in the act or opportunity of voting. But, she argues, that implies that citizens should "be able to ascertain what kind of commitment they are undertaking [when they vote] and whether good reasons exist for them to do so," a minimum condition that she reckons is gravely imperiled in election campaigns when "parties and candidates are 'sold' to the electorate like commodities, not for their political worth but for their commercial 'image' " (Pateman, 1979: 88).

Theorists who have wrestled with these dilemmas seem to have proposed at least five different ways of resolving them, to each of which a shorthand label may be attached in order to capture the essence of their approaches. The main contributors to this theme include, then, (1) "thoroughgoing realists," (2) "romantic collectivists," (3) "empirically minded egalitarians," (4) "technological optimists," and (5) "realistic idealists" (who pivot democracy on a division of labor between differentiated political roles). Let us look at each of these "solutions" to the informational problems of democracy in turn:

In effect, thoroughgoing realists seem to embrace the condition of mass ignorance as "natural," natural because it springs from certain traits in the common man which are quite understandable and in no way surprising: a keener interest in his personal affairs than in national or world problems; the difficulties of mastering the complexities and abstractions inherent in many civic issues; and a disregard for information that has no bearing on his immediate responsibilities. That is why, like Joseph Schumpeter, they propose a redefinition of democracy in purely procedural terms, building no expectations into it about popular knowledgeability at all, as "that institutional arrangement for arriving at political decisions in which individuals acquire the power to decide by means of a competitive struggle for the people's vote (Schumpeter, 1943: 269).

Perhaps the author who most eloquently outlined such a position, with mass media properties in mind as well, was Walter Lippmann, whose 1922 book, *Public Opinion*, rested on the assumption that, when thinking about what he called "the unseen environment," many people inevitably depended on impoverished stereotypes. In his graphic language:

> Thus, the environment with which our public opinions deal is refracted in many ways, by censorship and privacy at the source, by physical and social barriers at the other end, by scanty attention, by the poverty of language, by distraction, by unconscious constellations of feeling, by wear and tear, violence, monotony. These limitations upon our access to that environment combine with the obscurity and complexity of the facts themselves to thwart clearness and justice of perception, to substitute misleading fictions for workable ideas, and to deprive us of adequate checks upon those who consciously strive to mislead [Lippmann, 1922: 76].

What is more, in his view the mass media were unable to rescue us from this condition, because that is not the business they are in:

> The hypothesis, which seems to me the most fertile, is that news and truth are not the same thing, and must be clearly distinguished. The function of news is to signalize an event, the function of truth is to bring to light the hidden facts, to set them into relation with each other and make a picture of reality on which men can act. Only at those points where social conditions take recognizable and measurable shape, do the body of truth and the body of news coincide. That is a comparatively small part of the whole field of human interest. . . . [The press, then] is very much more frail than . . . democratic theory has yet admitted. It is too frail to carry the whole burden of popular sovereignty, to supply spontaneously the truth which democrats hoped was inborn [Lippmann, 1922: 358].

That is why when thinkers in this camp address issues about the quality of political decision-making they tend to direct their gaze upstairs, as it were, looking to the recruitment, education and organization of elites. Yet in the final analysis their realism is paradoxically incomplete. In fact, Joseph Schumpeter gave the game away by pleading for what he called "democratic self-control," or a willingness on the part of the masses to refrain from unduly influencing public policy, an insulation of decision-making from public opinion which simply cannot be sustained once democratic procedures are in operation. In short, thoroughgoing realists have no answer to Adlai Stevenson's simple yet profound observation to the effect that:

> Government (in a democracy) cannot be stronger or more tough-minded than its people. It cannot be more inflexibly committed to the task than they. It cannot be wiser than the people [Hanna et al., 1965].

What, next, about Marxist views on these issues? The question must be asked if only because in many European countries Marxists, and academics inspired by various Marxist presuppositions, have made massive contributions to mass communication scholarship since the mid-1960s. I have often personally criticized their approaches as defective in at least two major respects. First, they seem to me to propagate an essentially one-eyed view of the mass media as agencies of legitimation and social control on behalf of the status quo, without even considering the many different ways in which mass media coverage of political affairs could be undermining public support for the institutional fabric and the leaders who tend it. Second, until very recently they have neglected the task of developing a methodology for testing their theories at the crucial level of audience response. Nevertheless, Marxist-inspired analyses have added much to our understanding of the organization of mass media institutions, how they are constrained by surrounding economic and political forces and institutions, and of those systematically structured patterns of content that repeatedly appear in mass media coverage of many different topics: industrial relations developments (Glasgow University Media Group, 1976, 1980); racial conflict (Hartmann and Husband, 1974); portrayals of deviance of many varieties (Cohen and Young, 1973); social welfare issues (Golding and Middleton, 1979); and law and order problems (Hall et al., 1978)—to mention just a few that come to mind.

When it comes to the informational prerequisites of democracy, though, the Marxist cupboard is remarkably bare, and some thinkers of that persuasion openly admit it. And although their candor is welcome, it is really rather disturbing to find that, on the whole, Marxist writings still lack a principled and worked-out vision of a democratic future with a place for communication in it. Instead, present day Marxists tend to shift between a perception of modern bourgeois society as entangled in an ever-deepening crisis, to the succeeding moments of which the Left must offer suitable tactical responses, and flights into some romantic picture of an incompletely detailed near-utopian polity of the future. They know what is wrong with present-day mass media institutions and professions, the hypocrisies of which they aim at every opportunity to unmask and "deconstruct." But otherwise, it is as if they have become the prisoners of a "not to be opened before Christmas" syndrome—or as if they had bundled their preferences for future political and media arrangements into a sealed parcel with a label plastered on the outside, reading, "unknowable this side of the Revolution." It is true that many West European Marxists recognize the seriousness of the abuses of political and media power that have been perpetrated in the Soviet Union and other Communist societies. But their own alternative projections rarely go beyond a waffly populism, based on little more than slogans about rule by the people, the self-government of the working class, bringing the masses closer to the machinery of government, building a proper democratic organization of the state, keeping the masses involved in the everyday workings of the political system, uniting the working class and keeping its political consciousness at a very high pitch—and in a few cases proposing the use of television as a collective viewing medium to promote some of those ends.

Thus, it was mainly Marxists I had in mind when referring earlier to an approach of romantic collectivism to the informational predicament of democracy.

By empirically minded political egalitarians, on the other hand, I chiefly had in mind a productive Scandinavian research group, who are currently studying so-called knowledge gaps in society—or the uneven distribution of political information-holding across different levels of social stratification. The ultimate premise of their work, namely, that "information gaps are incompatible with the proper functioning of democracy" (Kjellmer, 1977: 3), may be naive, since they do not ask exactly *why* all citizens should be informationally on a par with each other, regardless of differences in their political roles and interests. But some of their findings are exceptionally interesting when related to problems of democratic philosophy.

In a sense the results of their research tend both to confirm and to challenge the bleak expectations of the thoroughgoing realists. On many topics they have found big information gaps dividing people in different social walks of life. But these were also narrowed in two significant sets of circumstances. First, the gaps were reduced, sometimes sharply, when people were questioned about issues that might affect them in their daily lives. "Relevance" is the key here, a notion that has surfaced in several other lines of research as well: to take two examples, when the gratifications that people aim to get out of following the news have been studied, and in the demonstrated ability of undecided voters to absorb useful policy information when watching televised debates between presidential candidates in the United States (Chaffee and Choe, 1980).

Second, certain compensating factors helped to counteract knowledge-gap divisions between upper and lower social levels. Organizational affiliation was one such influence, but so was personal interest in receiving information on the topic concerned. Here, too, that pattern tallies with findings from admittedly still rather scattered studies elsewhere, suggesting that people who tune in to the news with informational satisfactions in mind actually do learn more from it than do other less cognitively oriented viewers.

The standpoint of technological optimism is usefully outlined in a book entitled *Viable Democracy*, by Michael Margolis (1979). He is a political theorist who traces many of the imperfections of present-day democracy to the drastically reduced supplies of political information that are made available to Good Citizen Brown in short and sensational news reports in mass-audience-seeking communications media. He accordingly pins his hopes for the attainment of democracy, defined in terms of equal opportunities for political participation by all citizens, to the development of electronic, home-based, computerized data systems. These, he expects, would give each elector ready access to as much information as he or she might care to retrieve from large-scale data banks on whatever issues happened to concern him or her.

The underlying assumptions of this position are shaky, however, in two respects. First, the new systems of this kind that have so far been established, such as viewdata and teletext, put a high premium not on abundance, but on succinctness and brevity of information provision. This is because five three-line paragraphs are about the maximum amount of written matter that can be legibly displayed on modern television screens. Of course that constraint is "merely" technical and could be overcome by creating and selling much larger screens—a development, however, that is not on anybody's immediate horizon. Second, and more fundamentally, Margolis's concept rests on a false view of our relationship as individual voters to the world of social and political information. What we need as citizens most of all is not unprocessed data resources but a well-armed set of informational agents, able to act effectively on our behalf as mediators who can (1) scan the information environment for us; (2) reduce and relate it to a coherent view of the main issues that society faces; (3) update that agenda of main issues as required; and (4) organize a coherent dialogue about how best to tackle them.

From this survey of four very different stances toward the informational aptitude of the average man to participate in government, it is impossible to resist the conclusion that democratic theory must come to terms with inescapable divisions of political labor and prescribe for a relationship between full-time decision makers and ordinary citizens. In that case, the latter do not need to be so knowledgeable as the former. But neither should they be permanently abandoned to a realm

> Where blind and naked Ignorance
> Delivers brawling judgements, unashamed,
> On all things all day long.
>
> [Alfred, Lord Tennyson, *Merlin and Vivien*]

That is, they must be sufficiently equipped informationally to be able to hold decision makers effectively to account. Or, as John Plamenatz (1973), one of Britain's foremost political philosophers of the postwar period, put it in his latest book before his death, "There is democracy where rulers are politically responsible to their subjects."

Such a posture of realistic idealism does *not* amount to a roundabout way of espousing thorough-going realism, because insistence on a responsible relationship between rulers and ruled entails two requirements that bear directly and normatively on mass media roles. One of these was admirably stated by Plamenatz (1973: 186) himself in these words:

> If there is to be democracy, citizens when they make political choices must have intelligible, relevant and genuinely different alternatives to choose between, and the men who put the alternatives to them must have sufficient motives for putting alternatives of this kind.

In other words, since mass media workways and styles of political coverage formatively shape the messages that would-be rulers prepare for audience consumption, it is vital that public service media institutions should be so organized as to *enable and constrain politicians to address the public in as intelligible and illuminating terms as possible.*

The other requirement that stems from the concept of responsibility is that when citizens participate in politics, by voting or other means, they should be able to understand the significance of what they are doing. Such a criterion does not require all voters to become fully acquainted with all party policies on all issues of the day, which would be unreasonable. But it does suggest that a democratic test of a political communication system would be how far it *enabled people to make choices* in accord with the politics they wished to support, implying an availability of information on the basis of which they could grasp the policy goals and intentions that parties and leaders would pursue if given power.

IV

How stands political broadcasting in the light of such expectations? The point of a philosophy is not to solve practical problems but to define priorities of concern and provide a framework for principled argument over rival approaches to them. I personally see four areas of priority for discussion and action on political television arising from the view of democracy outlined above.

First, we should have the courage to redesign election campaigns on television so that voter enlightenment counts for far more than it does at present (Katz, 1971). Citizens' impressions of the possibilities of having a say and influencing political affairs in our kind of society depend heavily on the news, comments, pictures and arguments that reach them over television at election time. It is therefore disturbing that more and more people seem to be getting into a frame of mind where campaign propaganda is almost automatically expected to be off-putting. To allow such a mood to continue to grow unchecked is in nobody's interest: "Unless voters and viewers feel that there is something of value for them in the exchange that inheres in a communicator-audience member relationship, the political parties will always be fighting an uphill battle—and losing it" (Blumler and Gurevitch, 1979). There is even evidence that electoral participation itself, the readiness to stir oneself to vote on polling day, may falter as respect for political talk diminishes (Blumler and McLeod, 1974). That is why

> we cannot afford to allow [election] material to get into the schedules simply because past custom, routine convenience or stopwatch considerations let it through. More weight must be given to what voters will find interesting, informative and geared to their needs [Blumler et al., 1978: 47].

Second, far more research should be undertaken into the popular reception of television news: how its terminology is understood; what is regarded as relevant and interesting; and which conventional ways of presenting the news do and do not work for viewer comprehension. Of course, this presupposes that the news should be part of a process of civic education, to which some broadcasters might reply that news is journalism, not education for democracy or anything else. But "if that means journalism has a responsibility for telling the truth, journalists also have a responsibility for telling it in a way people can learn it" (Barber, 1979).

Third, every allegation that in some major news domain broadcasting has developed a highly structured slant that limits attention to diverse viewpoints and issues should be taken seriously, though not necessarily accepted without further investigation. But public service broadcasting should ultimately be designed to nourish the roots of citizen choice. Such a view of its purpose is not only compatible with the medium's technical capacity to combine elements from diverse quarters in a single program format, but is also consistent with its ability to serve as what one British broadcaster recently called "the national debating chamber" (Allen, 1979).

Finally, blockages to innovation in political programming should be continually identified and removed. This is important not because novelty should be valued for its own sake, but because freshness of approach is indispensable when tackling the inherently difficult tasks of making political information palatable and political argument comprehensible to large masses of voters.

NOTE

1. The expression, "mass media workways," is borrowed from an extremely insightful essay by Nelson W. Polsby (1980).

REFERENCES

ALLEN, R. (1979) "Killer satellites?" Address to Edinburgh International Television Festival, August.

BARBER, J. D. (1979) "Not the New York *Times*: what network news should be." Washington Monthly (September): 14-21.

——— [ed.] (1978) Race for the Presidency: The Media and the Nominating Process. Englewood Cliffs, NJ: Prentice-Hall.

BERELSON, M. (1979) Viable Democracy. London: Macmillan.

BLUMLER, J. G. (1980) "Mass communication research in Europe: some origins and prospects." Media, Culture and Society 2: 367-376.

——— and M. GUREVITCH (1979) "The reform of election broadcasting: a reply to Nicholas Garnham." Media, Culture and Society 1: 211-219.

BLUMLER, J. G. and J. M. McLEOD (1974) "Communication and voter turnout in Britain," in T. Leggatt (ed.) Sociological Theory and Survey Research. London: Sage Publications Ltd.

BLUMLER, J. G., M. GUREVITCH, and J. IVES (1978) The Challenge of Election Broadcasting. Leeds: Leeds University Press.

BURNS, T. (1977) The BBC: Public Institution and Private World. London: Macmillan.

CHAFFEE, S. H. and S. Y. CHOE (1980) "Time of decision and media use during the Ford-Carter campaign." Public Opinion Quarterly 44: 53-69. (reprinted in this volume)

COHEN, S. and J. YOUNG [eds.] (1973) The Manufacture of News: Deviance, Social Problems and the Mass Media. London: Constable.

CURRAN, C. (1979) A Seamless Robe: Broadcasting Philosophy and Practice. London: Collins.

GANS, H. J. (1979) Deciding What's News. New York: Pantheon.

GERBNER, G., L. GROSS, M. JACKSON-BEECK, S. JEFFRIES-FOX, and N. SIGNORIELLI (1978) "Cultural indicators: violence profile no. 9." Journal of Communication 27: 176-206.

Glasgow University Media Group (1980) More Bad News. London: Routledge & Kegan Paul.
——— (1976) Bad News. London: Routledge & Kegan Paul.
GOLDING, P. and S. MIDDLETON (1979) "Making claims: news media and the welfare state."
    Media, Culture and Society 1: 5-21.
HALL, S., C. CRITCHER, T. JEFFERSON, J. CLARKE, and B. ROBERTS (1978) Policing the
    Crisis: Mugging, the State, and Law and Order. London: Macmillan.
HANNA, E., H. HICKS, and T. KEPPEL [compilers] (1965) The Wit and Wisdom of Adlai
    Stevenson. New York: Hawthorn.
HARTMANN, P. and C. HUSBAND (1974) Racism and the Mass Media. London: Davis-
    Poynter.
Innovation in Political Communication: The Sound Broadcasting of Parliamentary Proceedings
    (n.d.) Jointly undertaken by the Centre for Television Research, University of Leeds, and
    The Hansard Society for Parliamentary Government.
KATZ, E. (1980) "On conceptualizing media effects," in T. McCormack (ed.) Studies in
    Communication, Vol. I. Greenwich, CT: JAI Press.
——— (1971) "Platforms and windows: broadcasting's role in election campaigns." Journalism
    Quarterly 48: 304-314.
KJELLMER, S. (1977) Information Gaps, Work and Social Involvement: A Summary. Sveriges
    Radio Audience and Programme Research Department No. 20, Stockholm.
LIPPMANN, W. (1922) Public Opinion. New York: Macmillan.
MARGOLIS, M. (1979) Viable Democracy. London: Macmillan.
NOELLE-NEUMANN, E. (1980) "The news media as an alternative to party in the presidential
    selection process," in R. A. Goldwin (eds.) Political Parties in the Eighties. Washington, DC:
    American Enterprise Institute.
PATEMAN, C. (1979) The Problem of Political Obligation: A Critical Analysis of Liberal
    Theory. Brisbane: John Wiley.
PLATO (1955) The Republic (H.D.P. Lee, trans.). Harmondsworth, England: Penguin.
PLAMENATZ, J. (1973) Democracy and Illusion. London: Longman.
POLSBY, N. W. (1980) "The news media as an alternative to party in the presidential selection
    process," in R. A. Goldwin (ed.) Political Parties in the Eighties. Washington, DC: American
    Enterprise Institute.
ROBINSON, M. J. (1975) "American political legitimacy in an era of electronic journalism:
    reflections on the evening news," in D. Cater and R. Adler (eds.) Television as a Social
    Force: New Approaches to TV Criticism. New York: Praeger.
ROSE, R. (1980) Politics in England: An Interpretation for the 1980s. London: Faber & Faber.
SCHUMPETER, J. (1943) Capitalism, Socialism and Democracy. London: Allen & Unwin.
THOVERON, G. (1979) "Information, culture: la pauvreté dans l'abondance." Cahiers de Clio
    60: 24-31.
WEAVER, D. H., D. GRABER, M. McCOMBS, and C. EYAL (1981) Media Agenda-Setting in a
    Presidential Election: Issues, Images, and Interest. New York: Praeger.
WINDLESHAM [Lord] (1980) Broadcasting in a Free Society. Oxford: Blackwell.

PART VI

DIALOGUE

If anything characterizes the research process, it is conflict and debate. We have added a new section to this volume to accommodate a continuation of debates begun in Volume 2 of this series.

In the first of these interchanges, Paul Hirsch critically examines the "cultivation" and "mainstreaming" hypotheses of George Gerbner and his associates at the University of Pennsylvania. When we agreed to edit this volume, we recognized immediately that inclusion of these articles would be mandatory. While Gerbner's research and commentary, and modification and expansion of it, have perhaps occupied more space than any other topic in previous volumes in this series, and while the present articles are slightly more acrimonious than one might wish, these articles and those in Volume 2 represent the most detailed and broad-ranging debate extant in the mass communication research literature in recent years. Moreover, the exchange encompasses both theoretical and methodological concerns. We do not think their importance can be underestimated. Nor do we think that these articles represent the last word on this topic, and we hope our readers will continue to follow what we expect to be a continuation of this lively exchange.

The final article in this section is a reply to a commentary, also in the most recent volume, attacking sociological and cultural approaches to bias in media studies. The original article from Volume 2, "Biasing the News: Technical Issues in 'Media Studies,' " by Digby C. Anderson and W. W. Sharrock, used as an example in critique a content analysis by Graham Murdock. Mr. Murdock replies.

The article below is Part II of a series criticizing the cultivation hypothesis suggested by Gerbner and his colleagues. More specifically, Paul Hirsch examines the "mainstreaming" and "resonance" formulations Gerbner and his associates introduced in their Violence Profile No. 11. Hirsch suggests that these constructs lack both logical adequacy and empirical support, and, moreover, that in present form the work by the University of Pennsylvania researchers is so inclusive as to be untestable. Paul M. Hirsch is associate professor of sociology in the Graduate School of Business at the University of Chicago.

36

ON NOT LEARNING FROM ONE'S OWN MISTAKES

A Reanalysis of Gerbner et al.'s Findings on Cultivation Analysis Part II

Paul M. Hirsch

A model that accommodates almost every conceivable state
of the world is an important constraint on testing it. . . .
Unless researchers attempt to produce states that can refute

AUTHOR'S NOTE: This research was generously supported by a grant from the John and Mary R. Markle Foundation to facilitate dialogue between the social

From Paul M. Hirsch, "On Not Learning from One's Own Mistakes: A Reanalysis of Gerbner et al.'s Findings on Cultivation Analysis," *Communication Research* 8, 1, pp. 3-37. Copyright © 1981 by Sage Publications, Inc.

the model . . . support will emerge by chance because of its inclusive formulation. The support may be illusory, however, for the only means of testing the model is . . . where refutation is [acknowledged as] possible.

The purpose of this examination is not to attack the authors who have worked so hard to refine theories of needs and the effects on job attitudes and behavior. Rather, it is to question the validity and value of their fundamental conceptions of needs and jobs. Second, an alternative perspective . . . is proposed.

—Salancik and Pfeffer (1977: 428, 446)

INTRODUCTION

Salancik and Pfeffer's assessment of Maslow's theory of need satisfaction is remarkably apt for reviewing the body of Violence Profiles and cultivation analyses published by Dr. George Gerbner and his associates at the University of Pennsylvania's Annenberg School of Communications. Since 1976, Gerbner et al. have reported findings which they claim show that television watching "cultivates" changes in viewers' attitudes about society and life in general. In subsequent reports, this basic contention has been markedly qualified and reformulated along three crucial lines: (1) an admission that the anticipated effects do not appear throughout the population (1980); (2) the contention that they do appear among unspecified population subgroups (1980); and (3) the apparent belief that employing different statistical strategies to analyze the same data from year to year raises no questions about the consistency and accuracy of the accompanying texts and tables (1979b). Each

---

sciences and humanities in the field of mass communication. It was initiated at the suggestion of Horace Newcomb (1978), an English professor who insisted that findings presented in support of the cultivation hypothesis by the Annenberg group were logically suspect and warranted reanalysis by the social science community. The NORC and Michigan datasets are publicly available, and the issues raised, given the prominence of the Annenberg projects, need to be formalized for discussion. For critical discussion and first-rate research assistance, I am especially indebted to Tom Panelas, and gratefully acknowledge the contributions of Sally Kilgore and Stuart Michaels.

reformulation has been announced as a "refinement" of the basic argument, rather than as a qualification or admission of earlier error and overstatement.

Two central themes throughout Parts I and II of this article are:

(1) The Annenberg group's formulation(s) is (are) so inclusive that no matter what respondents answer on survey items, it can be argued to support one or another variant of the cultivation hypothesis. This treatment makes the assertion both irrefutable and untestable, almost by definition.

(2) The detailed reanalysis presented here shows that, notwithstanding their reformulated theory's growing ambiguity and lack of precision, the data analysis reported by the Annenberg team frequently overlooks standard statistical procedures. This makes it difficult for readers to infer which version(s) of their theory (if any) is (are) supported empirically.

A basic and consistent finding in this reanalysis of the National Opinion Research Center General Social Survey data from which Gerbner et al. claim support[1] is the striking *absence* of significant or meaningful relationships between the content-analysis portion of the Violence Profiles and viewers' attitudes. The model at issue here proposes that (a) television presents a consistent set of images and messages, divined by the content analysts at the Annenberg School, and (b) these messages are salient, plausible, and clear to the viewer, such that those most exposed to them (heavy viewers) will adopt as their own attitudes and perceptions the same interpretations of television content as preferred by Gerbner et al.

Since the attitudes of heavy viewers generally show no relation to the content analysis in the Violence Profiles, four possible inferences are: (1) the categories chosen in the content analysis have no bearing on viewers' interpretation of television fare, but the anticipated effects might show up if the researchers' interpretations were brought more closely into line with those of the viewers; (2) despite the evidence from survey data that the messages adduced in the Violence Profiles are not salient, plausible, or clear to the viewing population, the content analysis they provide is a valuable tool in its own right; (3) even though the Annenberg group chose structured survey items as the arena for testing the cultivation hypothesis, alternative methods—like participant observation, community studies, depth interviews, and ethnographies—might yield more support in the direction(s) of their predictions.

A fourth possible inference is to take the evidence that shows no relation between attitudes and heavy viewing as support for the null hypothesis that attitudes and viewing are unrelated. The overall absence of this association was shown most clearly in Part I when we found no linear or monotonic relation between the amount of television viewed and respondents' answers to items tapping fear, anomia, alienation, attitude toward physical violence and suicide, and perception of the "real world" as "mean" or "scary." Over 18 relevant items, nonviewers were consistently more fearful, alienated, and favorable to suicide than light viewers; extreme viewers were less perturbed than heavy viewers. The only viewing category where respondents least often provided the "TV answer," most consistently giving the "non-television" response, was that of light viewers: There was no clear-cut pattern beyond that for respondents coded as nonviewers, medium, heavy, or extreme.[2] Where bivariate relationships of any significance did appear in the analysis by Gerbner et al., they were virtually eliminated upon the application of (almost any two) simultaneous controls in the reanalysis (see Hughes, 1980, for a report of this same finding).

The cumulative failure to locate relationships between heavy viewing and what the Annenberg group calls the "television answer" to attitude items strongly suggests that *if* viewers are affected by television program content, as they may very well be, they simply do not see as meaningful to their interpretations the categories employed by Gerbner et al. for coding characters' demographics and action sequences.

But even if these relationships do not hold across the population, might they not show up for heavy viewers within some groups, particularly those subgroups found in the Violence Profiles to be victimized most often in the world portrayed on television? Gerbner et al. have formulated three hypotheses in support of this contention:

(1) Heavy viewers from subgroups *victimized* on television should perceive the world as *more* "mean" and "scary" than light viewers from the same subgroups. Conversely, heavy viewers from subgroups *least victimized* on television should perceive the world as *less* "mean" and "scary" than light viewers from the same subgroups. This proposition follows from the text of Violence Profiles 7 through 10 (1976-1979), from which examples are provided in the next section.

(2) Heavy viewers from *unusual* subgroups (possibly including those victimized on television) may perceive the world as *less* "mean" and "scary" than light viewers from the same subgroups; they also will show less variation around these attitudes. This competing proposition is advanced as a "refinement" of the cultivation hypothesis in the most recent Violence Profile (No. 11, 1980).

(3) Heavy viewers from *unusual* subgroups (possibly including those victimized on television) may perceive the world as *more* "mean" and "scary" than light viewers from the same subgroups. (Also in Violence Profile No. 11, 1980; this is the opposite of formulation 2.)

Because Gerbner et al. fail in formulations 2 and 3 to predict or specify which subgroups' attitudes should move in either of these directions, their three versions of the "same" theory are able to account for virtually all observed difference between the percentage of heavy and light viewers. Even where there is *no* difference between the percentage of heavy and light viewers giving a "television answer," the "theory" allows one to argue that formulations 2 and 3 occurred simultaneously. In that event, the explanation offered for the absence of a relationship might be that the claimed "effects" were indeed present, but the combined upward and downward influence of television on how respondents scored on an attitude item canceled each other and, hence, cannot be shown or demonstrated. "Cultivation analysis," presented in this form, thereby precludes finding and interpreting the same results as support for the more (or equally) plausible alternative hypotheses that (1) there is *no* direct statistical relationship between number of hours viewed and attitudes, or (2) if any are found, the relationships are spurious.

In section 1 of this reanalysis, we examine evidence for the first formulation and show that heavy viewers in victimized groups do *not* perceive the world as more "mean" or "scary" than their lighter-viewing counterparts; nor do heavy viewers among the least-victimized groups perceive the world as less "mean" or "scary" than their lighter-viewing counterparts: Formulation 1 is unsupported by the data. Following that, we will consider Gerbner et al.'s concepts of "mainstreaming" (formulation 2) and "resonance" (formulation 3). Particular attention will be accorded the evidence presented as supporting these hypotheses, just as the tables and data from their earlier profiles were closely described and examined in Part I of this article. After showing why formulations 2 and 3, as presented in Violence Profile No. 11, are not stated in a testable form permitting either support or refutation, I will outline three alternative explanations, each providing a more statistically adequate and theoretically sensible interpretation of the data reported by the Annenberg group.

ABSENCE OF CULTIVATION DIFFERENTIALS AMONG VIEWERS FROM VICTIMIZED GROUPS

Measuring the ratio of risk of each group's chances for involvement also relates to the cultivation of real-life concepts.

> We may watch all kinds of characters to assess the general
> risk of involvement, but when we apply that general risk per-
> sonally, we may be especially receptive to seeing how char-
> acters *like ourselves* (male or female, young or old, black or
> white, etc.) fare in the world of television. Regardless of how
> often they do get involved in violence, if they are usually hurt
> or killed, the lesson learned may well be one of high risk.
>
> —Gerbner et al. (1978: 186; emphasis in original)

If television viewers draw inferences about the real world
from the dramatic, comic, and other fictional entertainments presented on television, there are innumerable possibilities and permutations for how this process might
unfold. For research purposes, the theory and assumptions
underlying whatever methods are chosen to test for relationships are critical and logically prior to the actual
analysis.

Questions about television's ability to shape perceptions
of the world are naturally linked to collateral issues about
viewers' personal identification with television characters.
From a universe of potential coding categories and potential
bases for viewers' cognitive and affective processing of narratives, sequences, and characterizations, the Annenberg
group has focused on and made central: sequences of violence and victimization coded in terms of demographic (age,
sex, and so on) attributes of characters on television. Instances of kindness or altruism are not coded, for example, and
we have no idea of their distribution and ratio to acts of
violence; verbal abuse is not seen as violent; individual programs are not treated as units or narrative wholes. Viewer
identification is assumed to operate one to one on the basis
of only those gross demographic characteristics which are
shared with television characters. For example, white male
viewers should identify with all white male television characters equally, across all types of plots, sequences, and
characterizations. Since individual programs are not treated
as relevant, the model equates Archie Bunker with his (dramatic foil) son-in-law on *All in the Family*, as both are

"white males"; Mary Tyler Moore with Lucille Ball, on the programs carrying their own names (both are "white women"); and the serious roles of Ben Vereen (in "Roots" and other dramas) with those of Redd Foxx (buffoon in *Sanford and Son*), as both are coded as "black men."

While the coding strategies employed in content analysis and assumptions about bases for viewer identification are clearly the prerogative of the investigator, it must be emphasized that those selected by the Annenberg team are far from the only ones available.[3] Their model imposes especially abstract sociological and demographic categories onto the interpretative mind of the viewer in a manner we will show is not supported by the NORC dataset, nor by other research in the fields of culture and communication.

The cultivation hypothesis asserts that the same "facts of life" shown on television will appear disproportionately in the attitudes and perceptions of heavy viewers, as this group is "more likely to understand social reality" (Gerbner et al., 1978: 194) in terms of the "messages" conveyed by the medium. The most salient of these "facts" and "messages," and the only aspects of behavior reported annually in the Violence Profiles, concern the ratios and rank orders in which members of various demographic groups turn up as either killers or killed, and as "violents" or victims on prime-time television.

If viewers extrapolate estimates of their own life chances from those befalling their demographic counterparts on television, as Gerbner et al. propose, heavy viewers from subgroups whose members are most often victimized or killed should appear more afraid and suspicious than light and medium viewers from the same groups. Conversely, viewers from the subgroups whose members are least often victimized or killed should reflect television's representation of their relative invulnerabilty; i.e., their levels of fear and suspicion should decline with increased viewing.

These hypotheses are easily tested, since the Violence Profiles code television characters' attributes in terms of the same standard demographic variables into which survey research sorts respondents. They follow directly from the Annenberg group's assumptions that (1) the content categories adapted in the Violence Profiles are isomorphic with the viewer's interpretation of what he/she has watched, and (2) television "cultivates" opinions about social reality which heavy viewers will "learn" from being disproportionately exposed to them: "Victims, like criminals, must learn their proper roles, and televised violence may perform the teaching function all too well" (Gerbner and Gross, 1976b: 45).

Following the content analyses reported by Gerbner et al. (1978), we examined the attitudes of three population subgroups reported to exhibit the highest frequency or probability of seeing their demographic counterparts victimized or killed on television. These are:

(1) *Women* ("Although men are more likely to enter the arena of violent contest, women carry greater risks of victimization." 1978: 187.)
(2) *Women 55 years of age and over* ("Old women are at the very bottom of the heap of both the battered and the killed." 1978: 192.)
(3) *Black women* ("Nonwhite . . . women are next in line of general victimization." 1978: 192.)

For comparison purposes, we also examined the attitudes of:

(4) *Black men* ("To be other than clearly white is similarly risky." 1978: 189);[4] and
(5) *White men*, who emerge from the Violence Profiles as dominant, insofar as they get to do more of the killing than members of most other groups and are less often victimized in television portrayals. ("The pecking order of both general mayhem and killing is dominated by men—American, white, middle class, and in the prime of life." 1978: 191.)

Table 1 shows the bivariate percentage (without controls) of viewers in each of these groups afraid to walk alone at night within a mile of their homes. If heavy viewing "culti-vates" increased fear, this should be most apparent for elderly and black women, and for all women. It should be least apparent for white males. None of the expected "culti-vation" effects obtains in any of these groups. Among black women, consistently the most fearful of all groups across viewing categories, it is the *light* viewers who are the most fearful. Their "cultivation differential" between light and heavy viewers is 15%, but in the wrong direction. The medium viewers' mean response of 63% further suggests that amount of television-viewing is unrelated to fear level, for it allows for no "trend" in either direction. (See Doob and MacDonald, 1979, who argue the proper "causal" variable here is simply whether one's neighborhood is actually safe or unsafe. In this connection, light viewers among black women could be more fearful simply because they spend more time outside their houses at night.)

In Table 1, we also see the elderly women's fear levels remain basically unchanged, as do all women's, irrespective of amount of viewing. We see consistently, in the last column, that each of the "victimized" subgroups shows a *smaller* cultivation differential between light and heavy viewers than do those groups for which the hypothesis pre-dicts lower or negative differentials, i.e., groups whose members encounter a lower level of risk when portrayed on television. The greater ratios of victimization reported for women, blacks, and white and black women in the Violence Profiles should yield *larger* differentials, and are in sharp contrast to the wider respective cultivation differentials shown for *male* respondents in each corresponding cate-gory in Table 1. A rise in fear level of black males who view more also is apparent, while the level for white males (the least fearful of all groups in each viewing category) remains stable but does not decline.

Fear of crime is more logically related to the content anal-ysis in the Violence Profiles than most of the other attitude items in the NORC dataset analyzed by Gerbner et al.

TABLE 1

Percent Afraid of Walking Alone at Night in Own Neighborhood by Television Viewing, Race, and Sex

| | Television Viewing | | | Cultivation * |
	Light (0-2 hrs.)	Medium (3 hrs.)	Heavy (4 or more hrs.)	Differential
All Men (N = 677)	22	21	28	6
All Women (N = 825)	65	61	62	-3
All Whites (N = 1328)	41	44	46	5
All Blacks (N = 174)	65	49	68	3
White Men (N = 608)	21	20	24	3
White Women (N = 720)	63	61	59	-4
Black Men (N = 69)	36	31	55	19
Black Women (N = 105)	88	63	73	-15
Women 55 and Over (N = 268)	67	68	69	2

SOURCE: NORC General Social Survey, 1977.

*Computed by subtracting the percentage of light viewers giving the "television answer" (fear of walking alone at night) from the percentage of heavy viewers. Support for the cultivation hypothesis would be indicated by large positive differentials among those groups most "victimized" on television (blacks and elderly women, white women, all women) relative to less-victimized groups (white men, all men, black men).

and/or further discussed in Part I of this article. Nevertheless, because the Annenberg team has constructed a "TV answer" for many of these additional items, we examined the answers of respondents from the same subgroups by viewing category to 18 attitude items tapping anomia, alienation, attitude toward physical violence and suicide, and perception of the "real" world as "mean" or "scary."[5] Taken as a group, the same basic finding appears across all of these variables: *Television content portraying members of these subgroups as more likely to be killed or victimized does not "cultivate" increased fears or anxieties on the part of heavy viewers from the same subgroups. The percentage differences in the responses of heavy and light viewers do not form a pattern to support claims of any relationship at all.*

Tables 2 and 3 elaborate this general finding. Here we can compare the size of the cultivation differentials shown in the last column for each subgroup, in answer to the questions:

> "Generally speaking, would you say that most people can be trusted or that you can't be too careful in dealing with people?" (Table 2)

and

> "Do you think that most people would try to take advantage of you if they got a chance, or would they try to be fair?" (Table 3)

For each of these bivariate tables, the cultivation hypothesis predicts that the magnitude of television's "effect," or size of the cultivation differential, should have a positive sign *and* be larger for victimized subgroups than for those who encounter a lower level of risk when their groups are portrayed on television. Instead, we see here that the percentage difference between light and heavy female viewers providing the "television answer" (13 and 10, respectively) is no greater than the cultivation differential for male viewers (13 and 11). For black viewers, whose differential should be larger since they are portrayed less favorably on television than are white characters, it is 13% *less* in Table 2 and about the same in Table 3. White women present a differential either the same size as white men (within 1% in Table 2) or lower (Table 3).

Black women show a smaller differential than black men in Table 2, and a larger one in Table 3. This is important to note here, for while we interpret this as evidence for no pattern, Gerbner et al.'s contradictory formulations 2 and 3 ("mainstreaming" and "resonance") assemble and interpret very similar statistics as *support* for the cultivation hypothesis, i.e., regardless of whether the cultivation differentials are larger *or* smaller. This will be discussed further in the following section.

A larger proportion of elderly female heavy viewers also provides the "television answer" to the "trust" item in Table 2, but not for the "fair" item in the following table. If one emphasizes or reports *only* those items in which victimized subgroups' differentials are in either the direction predicted by the hypothesis, or counter to it, an apparently strong, but also deceptive and false, case could be made for either interpretation. Indeed, as I showed in Part I of this article, once multiple statistical controls are applied to these items simultaneously, the cultivation differentials shrink dramatically: The amount of television viewing by members of any group is found to add nothing whatever to the small amount of variance already explained by stronger predictors like education and work status.

Summing across all of the 18 relevant attitude items,[6] Table 4 reports the number of items (out of 18) for which the cultivation differentials of victimized subgroups, compared to those of groups portrayed on television as dominant, are larger, positive, and linear, as the cultivation hypothesis proposes. This summarizes the bivariate relationships for 18 tables, including the 3 just presented and discussed. The

TABLE 2

Percent Saying that "You Can't Be Too Careful in Dealing with People" by Television Viewing, Race, and Sex

			Television Viewing		
		Light (0-2 hrs.)	Medium (3 hrs.)	Heavy (4 or more hrs.)	Cultivation* Differential
All Men	(N = 1256)	49	57	62	13
All Women	(N = 1603)	57	67	70	13
All Whites	(N = 2542)	50	60	64	14
All Blacks	(N = 307)	82	90	83	1
White Men	(N = 1113)	46	54	58	12
White Women	(N = 1429)	54	65	67	13
Black Men	(N = 133)	76	89	80	4
Black Women	(N = 174)	88	90	84	-4
Women 55 and Over	(N = 508)	59	70	73	14

SOURCE: NORC General Social Survey, 1975 and 1978.
*See note in Table 1.

TABLE 3

Percent Saying that "Most People Would Try to Take Advantage of You if They Got a Chance" by Television Viewing, Race, and Sex

| | | Television Viewing | | | Cultivation * |
		Light (0-2 hrs.)	Medium (3 hrs.)	Heavy (4 or more hrs.)	Differential
All Men	(N = 1209)	34	40	45	11
All Women	(N = 1573)	26	30	36	10
All Whites	(N = 2492)	24	33	34	10
All Blacks	(N = 290?)	64	55	66	2
White Men	(N = 1083)	25	39	41	16
White Women	(N = 1409)	23	28	31	8
Black Men	(N = 126)	73	58	66	-7
Black Women	(N = 164)	55	54	66	11
Women 55 and Over	(N = 495)	24	27	25	1

SOURCE: NORC General Social Survey, 1975 and 1978.
*See note in Table 1.

number in each cell of the table is stated as a proportion: An entry of .33 means that out of the 18 items examined, six (i.e., one-third, or .33) fell into the category described in the column heading under which that cell appears.

In looking at Table 4 we should bear in mind, once again, that multiple controls, which substantially disperse what patterns there are here, have not been added. Yet even without these controls, no consistent pattern emerges for any of the victimized subgroups which would support the cultivation hypothesis' first reformulation. To find support would require that the groups which are most victimized on television show more instances of positive "cultivation" than do less-victimized groups. For example, since women are more victimized than men on television, the proportion of items on which increased viewing is associated with their provision of "television answers" should be higher for women than for men. Instead, we find that the proportion is identical (.44). Heavy viewers from victimized groups are shown to provide "television answers" no more frequently than do heavy viewers in groups shown on television as less-often victimized. Black women, black men, and elderly women provide the "television answer" even *less* often than heavy viewers from groups portrayed as more domi-nant on television. Heavy viewers in such victimized sub-groups are no more likely than their counterparts in other groups to interpret television content in a manner consis-tent with the categories in the Violence Profiles. In sum, the general finding of no relationship is reaffirmed.

PROBLEMS WITH "MAINSTREAMING" AND "RESONANCE": AMBIGUOUS, UNTESTABLE, AND IRREFUTABLE

The definition of a need as ambiguous is, therefore, an advantage, because it permits use of the concept as an almost universal explanation for behavior. . . . The evolution of thinking about job attitudes and needs has followed a

TABLE 4

Proportional Distribution of Cultivation Patterns Among Subgroups Across 18 Items

	Patterns			
Groups	Linear Trend and Positive Cultivation Differential[1]	Negative Cultivation Differential[2]	Nonlinear Trend and Positive Cultivation Differential[3]	Cultivation Differential Stable (No Trend)[4]
All Women	(.44)	.33	.17	.06
All Men	.44	.28	.28	.00
White Women	(.44)	.28	.17	.11
White Men	.44	.28	.22	.06
Black Women	(.00)	.50	.11	.38
Black Men	.17	.39	.22	.22
Women 55 and Over	(.22)	.06	.22	.50

1. The proportions in this column, according to the cultivation hypothesis, should be largest for the most victimized groups (each female group) and smaller for each of the corresponding male groups whose proportions appear in this table.

2. The proportions in this column, according to the cultivation hypothesis, should be largest for the least victimized groups (each male group, especially white males) and smaller for each of the corresponding female groups whose proportions appear in this table. In this column, linear and nonlinear differentials are collapsed since neither supports the cultivation hypothesis.

3. Where the cultivation differential between light and heavy viewers is positive, but the percentage of "medium" viewers providing the "television answer" is greater than those for heavy viewers or less than those for light viewers, the resulting "pattern" is nonlinear. There is no trend, and the cultivation differential becomes an uninterpretable (i.e., useless) statistic. This problem is addressed in Part 1 of this article.

4. If the difference between heavy and light viewers is zero or negligible, there is no trend in either direction.

course from assumptions about the universality of humans to adopt positions that permit more and more contingencies and individual differences. The flexibility in the need-satisfaction model has been bought, however, at the cost of theoretical elegance and precision. . . . Modifications made to fit the need-satisfaction model with empirically described reality have weakened its one great strength, the intuitive appeal of its simplicity.

—Salancik and Pfeffer (1977: 437, 443)

But the lack of an overall relationship does not mean that the relationship does not hold for any specific group of respondents [sic].

—Gerbner, Gross, Morgan, and
Signorelli (1980: 19)

Like models of need-satisfaction, the cultivation hypothesis continues to be presented by its proponents in several guises. The original formulation predicted across-the-board consequences of television-viewing for all viewers. After the survey data cited as supporting this version of the hypothesis were reanalyzed by Hirsch (1980a) and Hughes (1980), the Annenberg group noted (1980: 19), "They all found that the overall association disappears when several demographic variables are controlled all at once." Gerbner et al. apparently see these findings as no reason to withdraw the original version of the hypothesis, even though propositions which contradict it appear in their own reformulations 2 and 3. In the most recent Violence Profile (1980: 14-15), they assert that the original hypothesis "still holds and provides some of the most compelling [sic] evidence for the existence of television's contributions to conceptions of social reality."

A first reformulated version of the relationship originally asserted suggests contingencies and differences to search for among subgroups where they should be most likely to appear. *Given* the absence of the claimed relationship across the population, the most logical inferences from the Annenberg team's own content analysis are that (a) heavy

viewers among those subgroups portrayed as the most victimized would reflect television's "cultivation effect" by
appearing more alienated, anomic, or "scared" than light
viewers in the same subgroups; and (b) heavy viewers
among those subgroups portrayed as more dominant and
less often victimized would also reflect television's "cultivation effect" by becoming *less* alienated, fearful, or
"scared"—or else showing no attitude change—when compared to light viewers in their own subgroups. Note that this
formulation, derived from the texts of Violence Reports 7-10
(1976-1979), specifies *in advance of the data analysis* both
a theory and predictions about (1) *which* groups will be
affected differentially, (2) *why* one should expect these patterns to emerge, and (3) *in which direction* the attitudes of
heavy viewers in particular subgroups are expected to
"move."

This version of the cultivation hypothesis is the one tested
in the preceding section of this article. Across 18 items,
including those analyzed by Gerbner et al. in the same dataset, we found no empirical support for these contingent
propositions derived from the Violence Profiles. None of the
"victimized" or "dominant" subgroups exhibited any consistency in apearing more or less "cultivated" in the directions which follow from cultivation theory in its original
version.

Undaunted in their commitment to "demonstrate" at
least some cultivation effects, the Annenberg team (1980)
has come forth with two new "refinements" and reformulations (still maintaining there is "compelling" evidence for
the original version). As in the first reformulation, the
search for relationships is confined to subgroups, with
neither claiming to find support across the general population: "Further examination of previously analyzed and new
data reveals there are substantially different patterns of
associations for different social groups between amount of
viewing and certain conceptions of social reality. . . . Therefore, a fuller understanding of television's contribution may

be achieved by paying particular attention to differences
across different subgroups" (Gerbner et al., 1980: 15; italics
added).

Unlike the first reformulation (which *we* derived from the
Violence Profiles), the Annenberg team's most recent
refinements fail to specify in advance of the data analysis
which subgroups will be affected differentially or *in what
direction* the attitudes of heavy viewers in any given subgroup are expected to "move." Perhaps anticipating or
acknowledging the results shown in the preceding
section—that the cultivation differentials between heavy
and light viewers in subgroups portrayed as victimized or
dominant do not form patterns in the respective directions
predicted by the hypothesis—the newest reformulations for
the first time drop the comparison of heavy and light viewers *within* the same subgroups. Cultivation differentials,
when displayed, are now presented in terms of *between*
(across) subgroup comparisons of heavy and light viewers.
The earlier focus on comparing cultivation differentials
across single rows for individual groups (which we have
shown fails to support the hypothesis) is simply abandoned
without explanation in Violence Profile No. 11 (1980),
which instead substitutes an entirely new method of measurement and statistical procedure.

The new method for locating cultivation effects is to (1)
calculate the percentage difference between heavy viewers
in any two (or more) subgroups on any single item and then
(2) compare it with the percentage difference between light
viewers from the same subgroups. If the size of the percentage difference between these subgroups' heavy viewers is
smaller than the corresponding difference for light viewers
in the same subgroups, then the relatively greater
"homogeneity" in outlook among the heavy viewers is
attributed to television's having cultivated "the sharing of
that commonality" among them (1980: 15). This "process"
is called "mainstreaming." It deflects attention away from
the row-by-row (light versus heavy viewers) comparison of
the cultivation differentials within subgroups utilized in pre-

vious reports, which reanalyses by others have shown fail to support the hypothesis. Instead, the "new" column-by-column (light-light versus heavy-heavy viewers) comparison of percentage differences *between* subgroups is now proposed as the methodological "refinement" by which television's "effects" on (unspecified) subgroups are really (finally?) to be found.

The "refinement" proposed here does not merely announce a switch in the method employed to seek support for the hypothesis. *It also cuts loose the search for television's effects from the content analyses in the Violence Profiles which must form the basis for any advanced predictions about which subgroups should he more likely to provide "television answers" to each of the attitude items examined.* Only by separating these two components of the project in this way can the investigator(s) claim to find an "effect" regardless of *in which direction* the attitudes of heavy viewers in different groups converge.

Gerbner et al. make this claim explicitly in Violence Profile No. 11 (1980), and provide several illustrations drawn from a battery of items tapping respondents' fears about personal safety and attitudes about crime and the likelihood of victimization. In the first illustration, they report: (1) The percentage difference between heavy and light female viewers agreeing "fear of crime is a serious personal problem" is greater than the percentage difference between heavy and light male viewers agreeing with this response. Also, the percentage difference between heavy and light viewers in cities is greater than the corresponding difference between heavy- and light-viewing suburbanites For the same item, they also report: (2) The percentage difference between heavy and light nonwhite viewers is *smaller* than the difference between heavy and light white viewers, and, similarly, that the percentage difference between heavy- and light-viewing respondents with low incomes is *smaller* than the corresponding difference between heavy and light viewers with medium and high incomes.

For this item, the first set of bivariate comparisons conforms to what one would predict from the content analyses in the Violence Profiles: Females and (presumably) city residents[7] are depicted on television as more prone to be killed or victimized than males or subordinates; if heavy viewers in each of these categories are found to agree more than light viewers that "fear of crime is a serious problem," then Gerbner et al. could claim that the responses to this item suggest television portrayals "cultivated" greater fear among the heavier viewers in these subgroups.[8] (Of course, there is ample reason to expect that these [bivariate] "effects" would disappear upon the application of multiple controls. See Part I, and the discussion to follow shortly, for elaboration and substantiation of this observation.)

The second set of comparisons, however, runs directly *counter* to what follows from the content analyses in the Violence Profiles. As we showed in the last section, in testing reformulation 1, these report low-income and nonwhite members of society are killed and/or victimized far more often in television portrayals than their white and middle-income counterparts. The prediction from this should be to specify that low-income and nonwhite respondents are the subgroups *most* likely to provide the "television answer" by exhibiting fear levels higher than those of middle-income and white viewers. The Annenberg group avoids this embarrassment only by reformulating the criterion for "finding" a cultivation effect, such that *the directionality of any percentage change where it occurs becomes immaterial.* Support is now claimed if *any* percentage difference among heavy viewers, relative to light viewers, converges "into a 'mainstream' . . . *regardless of the starting points"* (1980: 25, italics added) *and irrespective of whether or not whatever endpoint they converge on could be predicted from the content analyses in the Violence Profiles.*

"MAINSTREAMING" AND "RESONANCE"

Gerbner et al. offer two post hoc propositions to explain why the cultivation hypothesis is "supported" when heavy viewers, in subgroups whose portrayal on television yields high risk and victimization ratios, fail to provide "television answers" to attitude items tapping the anticipated "mean" and "scary" orientation to the "real world." The most peculiar of these converts the statistical artifacts of ceiling effects and regressions toward the mean (compare Campbell and Cook, 1979, and other standard texts on regression fallacies)[9] into a statement of support for findings counter to predictions from the Violence Profiles' content analyses.

"Mainstreaming" is defined (1980: 15) as "the sharing of that commonality among heavy viewers in those demographic groups whose light viewers hold divergent views." It is a "convergence" of attitudes among heavy viewers *in any two or more subgroups, at any point along any item's distribution* where the percentage divergence between the corresponding subgroups' light viewers is relatively larger. The point of convergence here varies with each item and subgroup. That is, it is not defined independently of either, with the result that there is no baseline point for any variable or for any set of subgroups which could be called (like the grand mean of a distribution) "the" mainstream. Only *after* one determines if they conform to the statistical criteria, which *are* its sole definition, is it possible to locate the "mainstream" in any subgroup comparisons. Its operational definition for a given item is simply whichever point in the distribution heavy viewers in any two or more subgroups happen to converge on. Gerbner et al. (1980) impute meaning to this joint statistical occurrence by asserting it reveals where heavy viewers in those groups selected for comparison, and so converging, share "a relative commonality of outlooks that *television* tends to cultivate" (1980: 15, italics added).

A critical feature of the mainstreaming concept is its treatment of the *direction* of this convergence as immaterial. Where heavy-viewing outliers at the high end of an item's distribution meet the criteria for "mainstreaming" and converge downward, the Annenberg team infers that their disproportionate absorption of television's messages and common symbolic universe "coaxes" them toward an apparently more benign and "relatively homogeneous" outlook: an attitude shared by all heavy viewers and closer to more "general and widespread images and norms of reality" (1980: 15, 23).

In their first illustration of this concept, described earlier, the percentage difference between heavy and light non-white viewers' responses to a "fear" item was smaller than the corresponding difference between heavy and light white viewers; and, similarly, the corresponding differences among low-income viewers was smaller than among those with higher incomes. Both findings run *counter* to the predictions about the relation of the fear levels of members of victimized groups and amount of viewing made by the original cultivation hypothesis and its first reformulation, for both of the latter anticipate a *positive* relationship. With reformulation 2—"mainstreaming"—the Annenberg team has both (a) embraced these and other findings of a *negative* association, and (b) presented them as evidence in *support* of the cultivation hypothesis in (yet) another of its guises. Our finding in Table 1 that the fear levels of black women were negatively related to television viewing and that white women's also declined slightly with increased viewing is not taken as "negative evidence" by this formulation. Rather, the absence of an association between the Violence Profiles depiction of both as victimized and their respective viewing habits is recast and transformed by the "mainstreaming" hypothesis. Even though both subgroups failed to yield support for two earlier versions of the cultivation hypothesis, they are recaptured by reformulation 2 with its unabashed reoperationalizations of the cultivation concept ("coaxing" back rather than "scaring") and substitution of a different and more forthcoming method for setting up sub-group comparisons.

Gerbner et al., as noted earlier, have nevertheless not renounced the alleged power of the hypothesis's original formulation to generate "compelling" evidence. Indeed, reformulation 3 extends it in the same illustration by attributing to television the capacity to *increase* fear levels for subgroups whose heavy viewers' responses do not vary inversely with amount of viewing. Where across-subgroup comparisons find heavy viewers in victimized groups providing "television answers" in relatively *greater* proportions than light viewers in the same groups, the authors here propose that this percentage difference increased (rather than narrowed, as in mainstreaming), because the topic of the particular item employed must have been "particularly salient" to them. Such high salience is further suggested to make television's "violent imagery" so congruent with these respondents' "real-life perceptions" that the issue becomes "amplified"; from the two (television and "real life") together, they are dealt a "double dose."

Reformulation 3, called "resonance," is said to apply, in the first illustration of Violence Profile No. 11, to the dispro-portionate agreement in attitudes expressed by women and urban residents that "fear of crime is a serious personal problem." As described earlier, the percentage differences between heavy and light viewers in these categories exceeded those between heavy and light viewers who are men and residents of smaller cities, respectively. In contrast to the "mainstreaming" illustration, in which television viewing is said to have "coaxed" *down* fear levels of low-income and nonwhite heavy viewers, formulation 3 attrib-utes the increased fear levels of heavy viewers in these two comparison subgroups to "high salience" which members of these groups place on the issue in this item.

For women, urban residents, nonwhites, and low-income earners, these post hoc explications of their scores on a single fear item raise several fascinating issues about theory-building. First, we see that whichever direction the percentage differences move in, the outcome is treated as consistent with the notion that the attitudes of respondents in all of these categories were "cultivated" by television. *There is no provision in these reformulations for theory-testing, nor is a means provided by which the cultivation hypothesis could possibly be disconfirmed.* Second, if the fear levels were exactly the reverse for all four subgroups, these concepts could just as easily provide the same post hoc speculations to "explain" the opposite results, with equal seriousness. Had nonwhites and low-income heavy viewers "mainstreamed," for example, one could easily marshall reasons from them to hold "extreme" attitudes at the starting point and then be "coaxed" downward by television content. *Since no predictions concerning (a) which groups will mainstream or resonate, or (b) what it means if they are offered in advance, one can easily adduce greater or less issue salience after the fact to "account" for any outcome.* Table 5, adapted from Gerbner et al.'s discussion of mainstreaming and resonance among low-income urban dwellers and nonwhites illustrates the combined difficulties posed for a theory of television's effects when predictions, directionality, and the possibility of disconfirmation are excluded from the discussion.

Third, while the term "mainstream" implies some knowledge of a fixed point, it is used here simply as a descriptor of the distributions of heavy and light viewers in arbitrarily selected subgroups for arbitrarily selected items. There is no search for across-item, or between-subgroup consistency, or where the mainstream appears, nor is it defined here independently of television viewing. A more theoretically sound alternative would be to take the mean of each demographic (sub)group examined, define *it* as the "mainstream," and define respondents ± one standard deviation

TABLE 5
All-Purpose Explanations for Fear of Crime by Nonwhites
in High Crime Areas (Hypothetical Example)

All-Purpose Explanations for Fear of
Crime by Non-Whites in High Crime
Areas (Hypothetical Example)

Heavy Viewers'
Fear Levels Compared
to Light Viewers'

Higher	"Resonance." Issue has "special salience." Television's violent imagery yielded a "coherent and powerful double dose."
Lower	"Mainstreaming." Television "coaxed" fear level downward, to better correspond to more "general and widespread images of social reality."
Stable	Both resonance and mainstreaming may have occurred together. Or neither might have occurred at all. If they interacted, then the effects of each remain unfound (but might have occurred); each would have cancelled the other, and give only the appearance of no cultivation effect.

away as "outliers." Cross-tabulations of these "outliers" and "mainstreamers" with their television-viewing behavior would provide a more objective and comprehensible test for any relation between the distribution of television-viewing and the distribution of responses to a given item.[10]

Absenting guidance from these reformulations of cultivation theory concerning the appropriate items for selection and what to anticipate in advance of the data analysis, we sought to find out what could be learned from a random number table. The closest approximation available in the NORC dataset is the coding of each respondent into his or her zodiac sign, according to birthday. Interestingly, in Table

Fear of Walking Alone at Night in Own Neghborhood by Television Viewing and Respondent's Zodiac Sign (in percentages)

	Television Viewing			
Astrological Sign	Light (0-2 hrs) (N 756)	Medium (3 hrs) (N 308)	Heavy (4+ hrs) (N 444)	Cultivation Differential
Aries (N 123)	53	48	41	-12
Taurus (N 114)	37	62	45	8
Gemini (N 130)	35	33	55	20
Cancer (N 121)	46	42	48	2
Leo (N 134)	38	35	51	8
Virgo (N 123)	43	35	51	13
Libra (N 153)	48	39	56	8
Scorpio (N 125)	43	35	55	12
Sagittarius (N 113)	46	55	47	1
Capricorn (N 112)	39	42	49	10
Aquarius (N 120)	41	36	48	7
Pisces (N 140)	47	56	47	0
Mean:	43	44	49	

SOURCE: NORC General Social Survey (1977).
Range among Light Viewers: 18%.
Range among Heavy Viewers: 15%.

6, we find parallels with the response patterns of other subgroups already discussed in relation to "fear" items. While the *overall* relation is weak between fear of walking alone at night and zodiac sign for light, medium, or heavy viewers, these data reveal a convergence in outlook among heavy viewers when compared with light viewers. Whereas light viewers exhibit a range of 18% across all astrological categories, the disparity narrows to 15% for heavy viewers. This convergence in the fear level of heavy viewers suggests that television serves to homogenize fear levels by moderating those of respondents under the more distant, outlying signs. Television's ability to mainstream respondents with extreme views is most impressively illustrated for viewers born under the signs of Aries and Gemini. Viewers in these subgroups are coaxed back to the mainstream as their television viewing increases. Among light viewers, Aries are considerably above the mean on fear and Geminis considerably below, but both show a convergence among heavy viewers. In a separate analysis (not shown), resonance is most clearly evidenced by respondents born under the signs of Libra and Scorpio, in their response to our item about trust in others. Their cultivation differentials, of 15% and 8%, respectively, show that for these groups, television's violent imagery clearly boosted a "mean world" view for people who already experienced the difficulty of dealing with others as a salient problem. Zodiac sign, while not consistently strong in showing the power of television to influence viewers' attitudes, remains an important indicator. It is very significantly associated ($x^2 < .01$) with the number of hours viewed by the respondents in tho NORC sample.[11]

CONCLUSION

Part I of this article presented a reanalysis of data cited by Gerbner et al. as evidence for the "cultivation hypothesis" that television viewing has positive and linear effects on individuals' feelings of fear, suspicion and alienation. We found that the relationship asserted disappears with the introduction of appropriate statistical controls. Part II reported further on the reanalysis and presented a critique of the logical adequacy of two new versions of the cultivation hypothesis proposed recently by the Annenberg researchers. We again found no consistent patterns to support the cultivation hypothesis in any of its various guises and formulations. Such negative findings call the Annenberg team's basic approach into question and invite alternative theoretical explanations for the failure to find support for the cultivation hypothesis. Although the paradigm of Gerbner et al. has dominated discussions of television content and effects for some time, it is but one among several competing frameworks which warrant the interest and attention of researchers. Rather than signaling a retreat from research into television's cultural role, disconfirmation of Gerbner et al.'s hypothesis should underscore the need to examine new approaches, including those in the humanities (see, for example, Hirsch and Carey, 1978). While a thorough treatment of the relevant theoretical and conceptual issues is beyond the scope of this article, we conclude by briefly outlining three plausible explanations for the absence of cultivation effects.

(1) No effects: patterns are random. In many respects, this is the most plausible and parsimonious explanation for the data presented, especially in view of our reanalysis. We have examined data presented by the Annenberg researchers as well as 18 of the most "relevant" survey items in the NORC dataset and have found no consistent patterns which would support the cultivation hypothesis in any of its various guises to hold up across a majority of them. We find no reason, therefore, to reject the null hypothesis of no observable effects.

(2) Differential availability. Television's heaviest viewers are disproportionately housewives, sick people, unemployed, and with low income. They are among the most alienated members of our society to begin with and are *available* to watch large amounts of television because they are confined to the home much of the time. Research indicates that alienation and isolation tend to stimulate heavy

media consumption rather than vice versa (for a summary of some of this research, see Katz and Foulkes, 1962: 379-381). (Along that line, we have also found, for example, that the number of hours one spends *listening to the radio* is positively and significantly associated with the "television answer" to several of the items which Gerbner et al. correlated with television viewing.)[12] Thus any relationship between television viewing and fear, suspicion, or alienation which emerges prior to the introduction of multiple controls may be considered an artifact of covariation with television viewing, but not an effect which television causes or "cultivates." Furthermore, the absence of high levels of personal stress among television's *heaviest* viewers—an anomaly for the cultivation hypothesis —can be explained as resulting from the arguably functional role played by television in the lives of persons who are isolated and who use it for companionship.

(3) Status inconsistency. Research on what sociologists and social psychologists have called "status inconsistency" suggests that individuals who occupy different social statuses considered mutually incongruous by others experience role strain, status ambivalence, and high anxiety (see Jackson, 1962). High-status, high-income, and high-education individuals who view television heavily can be considered status inconsistent, as can low-status, low-income, or low-education individuals who do not watch television or who watch very little. Our examination of the NORC data suggests that much of the "effects" found at both ends of the viewing spectrum are found among individuals in status-inconsistent categories.[13] This frame of reference runs contrary to that which argues for universal across-the-board effects in that it places emphasis on the mediation of television's impact by social experiences which have been found to be relevant to levels of personal stress. It likewise predicts that patterns for specific sub-groups should not emerge on the basis of simple demogra-

phic identification, but again, according to these same experiences whose nature and influence are more complex.

NOTES

1. The General Social Survey of the National Opinion Research Center is a battery of survey questions on attitudes administered annually to a national proba- bility sample of approximately 1500 respondents, aged 18 and over. The entire dataset contains nearly 500 questions, many of which are asked each year. An item on the number of hours per day respondents regularly watch television was included in the survey for the years 1975, 1977, and 1978. Combining the sam- ples for these years yields a total of 4536 respondents, who constitute the basis of much of Gerbner et al.'s analysis as well as our reanalysis. The dataset is des- cribed in greater detail in Part I of this report (Hirsch, 1980).

2. The question asked of respondents was: "On the average day, about how many hours do you personally watch television?" Gerbner et al. use the following coding scheme: light viewers, 0-2 hours; medium viewers, 3 hours; heavy viewers, 4 or more hours. In Part I of this report (Hirsch, 1980), we used the following coding scheme to analyze responses of nonviewers and extremely heavy viewers: nonviewers, 0 hours; light viewers, 1-2 hours; medium viewers, 3 hours; heavy viewers, 4-7 hours; extremely heavy viewers, 8 hours or more. In this second part of the report, we confine ourselves to the coding using by Gerbner et al.

3. A variety of other grounds upon which such personal identifications might be based include the following possibilities. Television characters are exposed to a myriad of travails, and many viewers may identify with those who appear to face adversities similar to their own. These television characters need not necessarily be of the same age, race, or sex as the viewer for such personal identification to take place (where it occurs at all). The actual dramatic setting may not be germane, so long as the television characters face conflicts, dilemmas, and challenges which are in some way analogous to those of the viewer. Alternatively, where programs utilize extensive character development, many viewers may simply feel a bond to characters whose personalities are most like their own. The importance of the cultural and historical setting may also be highly variable. Some viewers may find little to identify with in dramas which are set in cultures or historical periods other than their own. In a western or pirate movie, then, the fact that most of the violence befalls white males may be irrelevant to the white males in the audience who could scarcely imagine themselves on a pirate ship in the Caribbean or in a barroom brawl at the Last Chance Saloon. On the other hand, it is arguable that many of television's historical or exotic characters actually exhibit sensibili- ties, personality traits, and behavior designed to make them intelligible, if not clearly similar to, modern, middle-class Americans (e.g., Mork of *Mork and Mindy*). Accordingly, many viewers may find it quite easy to identify with characters whose daily lives bear little superficial resemblance to their own. Gerbner et al. sum across all such differences in order to construct a census of all television charac- ters, outside the context of the programs in which they appear. This strategy carries

an assumption that viewers watch television in a similar manner. This may or may not be warranted, for very little is known which would allow us to say anything authoritative about how and if viewers actually *do* develop identifications with television characters (Hirsch, 1980b).

4. It is impossible to break out the demographic counterparts of "good" and "bad" men and women so far as real-life respondents to the NORC (or any other) surveys are concerned. Black men are included in this section for comparison purposes even though, despite Gerbner et al.'s findings that they are at greater than average risk, they do not appear in either the top or bottom ten rankings of the Violence Profiles' "killer-killed" or "violent-victim" ratios. While "old men" rank higher than black men for both the commission of violence *and* likelihood of being killed, we cannot see how these contrary portrayals enable predicting an expected direction for the "cultivation effect." The former could reduce fear, while the latter would increase it; hence, "old men" are excluded here as one of the victimized subgroups.

5. A total of 18 items makes up this list. Each question's wording is discussed and detailed in Part I of this article.

6. See the description of these items, both earlier in this part and in Part I of this article.

7. Gerbner et al. (1980) suggest that television's violent imagery provides urban residents with a "double dose" of fear, and that crime is more "salient" for city dwellers than suburbanites. Whether television portrayals of those killed or victimized actually result in higher risk rates for urban residents, however, is not reported in their Violence Profiles. Most programs and their victims, by our estimate, are situated in urban areas. Hence, our suggestion that the higher fear levels of city residents conform to what television portrays is based on what we assume and infer would appear in the content analysis, if this variable had been coded and reported.

8. As we shall see, this explanation does appear and is subsumed under their reformulation 3, called "resonance," when television content is said to reinforce these subgroups' own predispositions, if not experience. When the direction of heavy viewers' answers is incompatible with what television portrayals of their subgroups would predict, i.e., the percentage differences *depart* from predictions based on Gerbner et al.'s content analysis, the concept of "mainstreaming" (reformulation 2) is brought forth to claim this outcome *also* supports the cultivation hypothesis.

9. Light viewers holding extreme positive views are analogous to a roll of 1 or 2 on a die. By requiring that light viewers in a subgroup start out with extreme (i.e., "divergent") attitudes in order to be selected as candidates for a "mainstreaming" table, Gerbner et al. put forth a hypothesis with an unusually high probability of being confirmed by chance. The probability that on the next throw the number will be higher is strong (.66). Conversely, light viewers holding extreme negative attitudes are analogous to a roll of 5 or 6 on a die, with a correspondingly high probability that the number will be less on the next roll.

10. For subgroups whose attitude(s) differ significantly from those of the general population, one could then formulate a testable hypothesis to learn if the attitudes of heavy viewers in that category are closer to the general population's than are those of light viewers. If so, they would be "mainstreamed" and possible

explanations for why this should be so and what it says could be adduced. Preliminary tests of such a design on the NORC dataset yield no such relationships.

11. Respondents under the signs of Cancer, Leo, and Virgo are significantly more likely to fall into the category of heavy viewers.

12. The item in the NORC dataset on respondents' daily radio listening was coded in the following way: light listeners (0-1 hour), medium listeners (2-5 hours), and heavy listeners (6 hours or more). Single controls for age, sex, and education were applied respectively in the same way Gerbner et al. did in Violence Profile No. 9 (1978). The strongest results were found between radio listening and percentage feeling that "officials running the country don't care" and percentage feeling that "most people would take advantage of you if they got a chance." The relationship was also strong for the "mean world" index, of which the latter item is a component. For these questions, nearly all "cultivation differentials" were positive and more than half the gammas are statistically significant. These results, in fact, when presented in tabular form, bear a striking resemblance to many of the tables which Gerbner et al. have reported in support of the cultivation hypothesis, the only difference being that the independent variable is radio listening rather than television viewing. Of course, we do not wish to argue on the basis of these data that radio listening "cultivates" feelings of anomia or suspicion. We report them, rather, because they illustrate very powerfully the perils of making causal inferences from the kind of correlational analysis which Gerbner et al. have done. Moreover, these findings undercut the strong assertions made by Gerbner and Gross (1976a: 174-177) as to the manifestly "unique" power of television in comparison with other mass media.

13. For example, controlling for respondents' health frequently generates interesting patterns. Although we have not examined all possible combinations, we have found that, with some regularity, affluent respondents who report their health as either "fair" or "poor" show "cultivation effects" much greater than those of other groups. Following the status-inconsistency hypothesis, one could argue that for these respondents, inability to reconcile one's dominant status (affluence and social power) with that of ill health and incapacitation produces a response of high anxiety and alienation. These responses, while associated with heavy viewing, are induced by the (prior) states of ill health and affluence. In terms of any causal model, the correlation between heavy viewing and these respondents' provision of "television answers" is spurious and cannot be interpreted as support for the hypothesis.

REFERENCES

CAMPBELL, D. T. and T. D. COOK (1979) Quasi-Experimentation: Design and Analysis Issues for Field Settings. Skokie, IL: Rand McNally.

DOOB, A. and G. E. MACDONALD (1979) "Television viewing and fear of victimization: is the relationship causal?" J. of Personality and Social Psychology 37, 2: 170-179.

GERBNER, G. and L. GROSS (1976a) "Living with television: the Violence Profile." J. of Communication 26, 2: 173-199.

————— (1976b) "The scary world of TV's heavy viewer." Psychology Today 9 (April): 41-45.

————— M. F. ELEEY, M. JACKSON-BEECK, S. JEFFRIES-FOX, and N. SIGNORIELLI (1977) "TV Violence Profile No. 8: the highlights." J. of Communication 27, 2: 171-180.

GERBNER, G., L. GROSS, M. JACKSON-BEECK, S. JEFFRIES-FOX, and N. SIGNO- RIELLI (1978) "Cultural indicators: Violence Profile No. 9." J. of Communica- tion 28, 3: 176-206.

GERBNER, G., L. GROSS, M. MORGAN, and N. SIGNORIELLI (1980) "The 'main- streaming' of America: Violence Profile No. 11." J. of Communication 30, 3: 10-29.

GERBNER, G., L. GROSS, N. SIGNORIELLI, M. MORGAN, and M. JACKSON-BEECK (1979a) "The demonstration of power: Violence Profile No. 10." J. of Communi- cation 29, 3: 177-196.

————— (1979b) Violence Profile No. 10. Philadelphia: Annenberg School of Com- munication.

HIRSCH, P. (1980a) "The 'scary world' of the nonviewer and other anomalies: a reanalysis of Gerbner et al.'s findings on cultivation analysis, part 1." Com- munication Research 7, 4: 403-456.

————— (1980b) "An organizational perspective on television (aided and abetted by models from economics, marketing and the humanities)," in S. B. Withey and R. Abeles (eds.) Television and Social Behavior: Beyond Violence and Children. Hillsdale, NJ: Lawrence Erlbaum.

————— and J. CAREY [eds.] (1978) Communication Research 5, 3. (special issue: Communication and Culture: Humanistic Models in Research)

HUGHES, M. (1980) "The fruits of cultivation analysis: a reexamination of some effects of television watching." Public Opinion Q. 44, 3: 287-302.

JACKSON, E. F. (1962) "Status consistency and symptoms of stress." Amer. Soc. Rev. 27, 4: 469-480.

KATZ, E. and D. FOULKES (1962) "On the use of mass media as 'escape': clarifica- tion of a concept." Public Opinion Q. 26, 3: 377-388.

NEWCOMB, H. (1978) "Assessing the violence profiles of Gerbner and Gross: a humanistic critique and suggestion." Communication Research 5: 262-282.

SALANCIK, G. R. and J. PFEFFER (1977) "An examination of need satisfaction models of job attitudes." Admin. Sci. Q. 22: 427-455.

In their reply to Paul Hirsch's critique, George Gerbner, Larry Gross, Michael Morgan, and Nancy Signorielli answer that Hirsch has selectively interpreted their earlier findings and that "mainstreaming" and "cultivation" are testable and are implied in the body of their work to date. George Gerbner is dean of the Annenberg School of Communications at the University of Pennsylvania, where Larry Gross is an associate professor, Michael Morgan is a research specialist, and Nancy Signorielli is research coordinator.

37

A CURIOUS JOURNEY INTO THE SCARY WORLD OF PAUL HIRSCH

George Gerbner, Larry Gross, Michael Morgan, and Nancy Signorielli

Paul Hirsch's two-part exposition (the first of which appeared in the October 1980 issue of this journal) confronts us, and the reader, with an improbable scenario. In order to take it seriously, which we intend to do, one must entertain the likelihood of a brilliant scholarly surprise attack making mincemeat out of a plodding band of academic poachers. The masterful "reanalysis" of selected data not only demolishes cumulative results of a decade of fairly massive cooperative research and theory building, along with substantial independent confirmation; it also demonstrates that the research is both worthless and stubbornly wrong-headed.

Unlikely as that dramatic coup for pure science might be we intend to demonstrate that Hirsch's analysis is flawed, incomplete, and tendentious. We believe that the data, looked at cumulatively over numerous samples (including

From George Gerbner, Larry Gross, Michael Morgan, and Nancy Signorielli, "A Curious Journey into the Scary World of Paul Hirsch," *Communication Research* 8, 1, pp. 39-72. Copyright © 1981 by Sage Publications, Inc.

the National Opinion Research Center's General Social
Survey), provide considerable evidence that television
makes a consistent independent contribution to viewers'
assumptions, outlooks, and beliefs about social reality.
Furthermore, we shall show that our two recent
refinements reflect advances which were implicity in
virtually all of our theoretical writing, rather than radical
"reformulations" of our theory.

Certain problems pervade both pieces of his "critique,"
such as overstatement, exaggeration, and inaccuracy, but
each contains its own primary flaws. The outstanding gaps
in Part I are the neglect of subgroup specifications and the
unsubstantiated claim that the overall associations are
"nonlinear." In Part II he misrepresents our recent
refinements and makes the claim that they are logically
contradictory, ambiguous, untestable, and thereby
incapable of being disproved. We shall divide this
companion piece into two sections, each focusing generally
(but not exclusively) on Hirsch's respective installments. We
believe Hirsch's work should be viewed as two independent
pieces, and we offer our two sections with this in mind.

PART I

Science is little more than a way of studying the world
that allows others to retrace your steps. Data never speak
for themselves; it is up to the consumer of research to
determine whether they support an investigator's claims.
Hirsch purports to have done just that and finds our
conclusions unjustified.

But Hirsch has come to his conclusions based upon
analysis of one dataset, the General Social Survey
conducted by the National Opinion Research Center
(GGS/NORC), incorporating some questions (e.g., the
series on suicide) which have no connection with known
data about the television world, and others which exhibit

some of the weakest associations we have ever found. Furthermore, he greatly inflates the extent to which we have relied upon GSS/NORC data, claiming that it is a "major and critical source" of "much of the empirical support" for the cultivation hypothesis, and that GSS/NORC, and the 1976 election survey from the University of Michigan (Survey Research Center) Center for Political Studies, represent the only national adult samples we have analyzed. (On the contrary, our published reports have used four others: two from Opinion Research Corporation, one from Starch, and one from Harris.) We have reported a great deal of data, including analyses which provided only peripheral or even tenuous support for our theses; but we have used many questions and many samples because all data are flawed in some way, and knowledge accumulates gradually, if not linearly, over many studies. In fact, it is the cumulative consistency of our findings that makes them most compelling.

A minor but revealing confusion begins with Hirsch's early assertion (p. 407): "Conceptually, this article begins at that point where Gerbner et al. seek to impose their categories for purposes of content analysis onto the interpretive mind of the viewer." In a footnote (p. 451), Hirsch even implies that we claim that viewers are aware of the impact of specific messages upon them. Of course, we impose neither categories nor awareness upon the "interpretive mind of the viewer," whatever that might be. We simply identify clear-cut and pervasive patterns in the world of television, such as age and sex roles, occupations, certain types of prevalent actions, and the like, and ask viewers questions that can reveal what they assume to be the facts of the real world with regard to these patterns. The questions do not mention television, and the respondents' awareness of the source of their information is irrelevant for our purposes. The relationship between amount of viewing and the tendency to respond to these questions according to the facts presented in the world of television, with other factors held constant, is what reveals television's cultivation of viewer conceptions of reality.

Amid a barrage of other accusations, Hirsch levels four primary charges against us in Part I:

(1) that our definition of "light," "medium," and "heavy" viewers varies across different samples of respondents;
(2) that when "nonviewers" and "extreme viewers" (over eight hours a day) are separated from the light and heavy viewing categories, the resulting relationships between amount of viewing and attitudes are nonlinear, with nonviewers more imbued with the "TV perspective" than light viewers, and extreme viewers less afraid/anomic than heavy viewers;
(3) that we have selectively reported findings to support our theory, overlooking other "relevant" items;
(4) that the application of multiple controls eliminates the evidence for any overall, independent contribution of television viewing to conceptions of social reality.

Although we will deal with the first three of these below, the fourth point is the most critical, and essentially identical to Hughes's (1980) reanalysis. Basically, both authors reexamined some GSS/NORC data we presented in Violence Profile No. 9 (1978) and concluded that, at least in these data, simple relationships between amount of viewing and some attitudes are wiped out when a number of control variables are held constant simultaneously. We also observed this—and more (see Gerbner et al., 1980a, 1980b).

A conclusion of "no overall relationship" is of limited value because there may be (and often are) significant, meaningful, and nonspurious associations within specific subgroups. We believe that these variations in susceptibility are critical to understanding television and are neither random nor uninterpretable. They are systematic phenomena which can usually be explained by one of two processes we call "mainstreaming" and "resonance."

"Mainstreaming" implies a convergence of outlooks among the heavy viewers in "otherwise" disparate and heterogeneous groups. Differences deriving from other factors tend to be reduced or even eliminated among heavy viewers in specific subgroups. These differential patterns may cancel each other out and thus not appear when looking only at overall relationships.

"Resonance" occurs when a given feature of the television world is most congruent with the real-life circumstances of the viewer. These are instances where specific issues have particular salience to people's everyday reality (or even perceived reality) and the combination "resonates" and amplifies cultivation.

Most of the major critiques of our work have focused on the question of controls, in one form or another.[1] Among Canadians, Doob and Macdonald (1979) controlled for neighborhood crime level and concluded that respondents' environments made any relationship between viewing and fear of crime utterly spurious. They neglected to acknowledge, however, that the relationship in question held up quite strongly for city residents—particularly those in high-crime areas.

We found parallel results in our own data (Gerbner et al., 1980a). The relationship between television viewing and fear of crime is strongest among low-income urban dwellers (who arguably are more likely to live in higher-crime areas). In addition, this association stands up under numerous controls, singly or *simultaneously*. This phenomenon is what we call "resonance"; i.e., special cases of particular salience may amplify television's impact.[2]

Hughes (1980), using some of the same GSS/NORC data as Hirsch, also added a few more controls, notably church attendance (also in Violence Profile No. 8), club membership, and hours working per week. Both Hughes and Hirsch implemented all controls simultaneously, and both convincingly demonstrate that this procedure in some cases results in either curvilinear or negative overall relationships; in most cases in the GSS/NORC dataset, the aggregate associations are reduced to trivial proportions.

But an overall aggregate relationship is simply the product of subrelationships which may tug and pull at each other in different directions and with varying intensity. Hughes's, Hirsch's, and our own reanalyses show quite clearly that for many questions—again, particularly those in 1977 GSS/NORC data—amount of viewing has no single, universal, across-the-board impact, in the same direction for all groups of respondents. To Hirsch in Part I, this seems to be the final word on the subject.

But he ignores a number of subgroup variations that almost jump out of his own tables. Also, in Table 5 he presents a problematic version of our "cultivation differential" and notes:

> A positive sign supports the cultivation hypothesis, for agreement with the "television answer" would be associated with more viewing. *A negative sign suggests there is no relationship between them* [italics in original].

Such an assertion is not only illogical, confusing, and scientifically indefensible, but it also blinds Hirsch to the more subtle aspect of the cultivation process, which we call "mainstreaming." More than anything else, and above and beyond a plethora of methodological quibbles we have yet to address, the empirical evidence leading to the concept of "mainstreaming" effectively obliterates Hirsch's "reanalysis." As we shall see below, his critique of "mainstreaming" in Part II fails to cast any doubt on the *validity of the concept,* thereby reaffirming our dismissal of Part I.

The foundations of "mainstreaming" were implicit in our early theoretical and conceptual considerations of the role of television in our society. We stressed television's central role in the mainstream of the culture, its celebration of conventional morality, and its potential for promoting homogeneity by crossing class, age, ethnic, and other boundaries. "The repetitive pattern of television's mass-produced messages and images forms the mainstream of the common symbolic environment that cultivates the most widely shared conceptions of reality'' (Gerbner et al., 1978: 178).

In the early stages of our research, the number of ''positive'' cultivation differentials in specific demographic groups led us to stress what seemed to be happening for ''most groups.'' While Hirsch was controlling for everything at once and finding no *overall* associations, we were paying closer attention to the ''exceptions.'' Signorielli (1979) found that nonwhites are more ''sexist'' as a group, but that nonwhites show a significant *negative* association between amount of viewing and expressing sex-role stereotypes. Morgan and Gross (1980) found that adolescent heavy viewers score lower on achievement tests—unless they have low IQ's; low-IQ students show a significant positive association between amount of viewing and reading comprehension scores.

In these cases, light viewers of counterpart subgroups manifest wide baseline differences, but the heavy viewers' outlooks or scores reflect a convergence. Heavy viewing thus goes with a reduction of differences attributable to other variables. This kind of homogenization is obscured in measures of overall associations.

This same principle was also found in data we had previously analyzed, including the GSS/NORC data considered by Hirsch. Education was found to be a major control illuminating ''mainstreaming.'' Less-educated people are far more likely to give ''television answers'' to ''mean world'' questions of interpersonal mistrust, alienation, and anomie; they also tend to show no relationships between expressing these views and amount of viewing. But among better-educated people—who, as light viewers, are relatively more trusting and less anomic—cultivation associations are enhanced. Most importantly, these relationships *withstand all other controls, singly or simultaneously* (Gerbner et al., 1980a). In some cases, we even found significant *negative* associations, even after controls, among extremely mistrustful groups.

Far from showing "no relationship," that "negative sign" is the key to the puzzle. While this recognition confirms our basic hypothesis—that television cultivates common conceptions of social reality—it refines, extends, and amplifies our conclusions. It also renders the remainder of Hirsch's criticisms in Part I irrelevant. Nevertheless, a few of his other points, as noted above, bear mention.

Part of his criticism is that our operational definition of light and heavy viewers varies across samples. Hirsch's charges of "shifting bases" serve only to distract attention from the larger issues. We have never implied nor argued that the terms "light" and "heavy" viewer are anything but *relative*, determined by the distribution of responses in any given sample. We approximate an even three-way split, tempered by judgment *and always clearly defined*. Any attempt to specify "absolute" levels of heavy viewing or absolute proportions of the sample is doomed to failure if these standards are applied to samples of different ages.

For example, in some of our adolescent samples, an even three-way split would require designating up to three hours a day as "light" viewing, so adjustments are made. In any case, we see self-reported viewing primarily as a useful ranking device and do not focus on specific hours of exposure. The groupings are helpful for illustrative purposes, and our increasing use of continuous data bypasses the problem completely. Unlike Hirsch, we do not take these self-reports at face value as accurate measures. We simply expect that those who report more than four hours a day do indeed consistently watch more than those who report less than two hours a day.

Hirsch has focused a major thrust of his critique on respondents in two extreme viewing categories. This analysis of "nonviewers" and "extreme viewers" in addition to the light, medium, and heavy categories and the supposed justification for it are heavy handed and unconvincing. It is a little like trying to study religion by comparing atheists and fanatic fundamentalists.

GEORGE GERBNER et al.   683

The two extreme groups together represent less than *ten percent of the GSS/NORC sample*. Moreover, since many of his reanalyses show monotonic associations among light, medium, and heavy viewers, but "nonviewers" scoring higher than "light" and "extreme" viewers scoring lower than "heavy," he has merely shown that some overall relationships *are* monotonic for over 90% of the population. Patterns of responses for these marginal groups are clearly of some interest, but they are irrelevant to cultivation theory because these groups probably differ from other viewers on uncontrolled third variables. At most, he has shown that their inclusion in our analyses means that our measures of cultivation are *underestimates* (see p. 439 of Part I).

In the case of the nonviewers, their complex and contradictory profile is even more problematic than their size. Jackson-Beeck (1977) found, and Hirsch concurs, that they constitute a bizarre and inconsistent segment. They are better educated than viewers and tend to work in higher-level careers; and yet they have significantly *lower* incomes (Jackson-Beeck, 1977) and had *higher* family incomes when they were 16 (Tankard and Harris, 1980). While they are more likely to have been raised in a "traditional," nuclear family, they tend to be unmarried and childless. They are more likely than are viewers to claim no religious preference (Jackson-Beeck, 1977); they also have a stronger view of themselves as religious but attend religious services less often (Tankard and Harris, 1980).

Hirsch insists that they are more anomic (which may not be surprising, given the above), while Tankard and Harris (1980) report that they are "happier with things in general." Measurement error may account for some of the perplexity, and factors (such as social desirability) which lead some respondents to report no viewing may color many other answers as well.

Extreme viewers are also problematic. Jackson-Beeck and Sobal (1980) examined some social and behavioral correlates of relatively extreme viewers. Their analysis is not fully comparable to Hirsch's since they defined "heavy" as over six hours a day, while Hirsch's extreme viewers report watching over eight hours a day. In any case, they pooled the 1975, 1977, and 1978 GSS/NORC samples, and found that heavy viewers (by their definition) constitute 5% of the three samples. These authors note that those who watch over six hours a day are likely to be women, young, nonwhite, homemakers, less educated, and less active socially; those who work tend to be in blue-collar occupations and have lower incomes.

Beyond these problems, his supposed demonstration of curvilinearity, based on "unexpected" findings from the small and bizarre group of "nonviewers," is utterly unsubstantiated. Let us ignore, for the moment, that some of the items he analyzes (such as approval of suicide) have no discernible basis in our TV message analyses or in any of our discussions of cultivation.

The fact is, *Hirsch's claims of nonlinearity are simply false.* In Table 1, we present the results of *tests* for linearity and nonlinearity, based on Hirsch's dependent variables *and Hirsch's viewing categories.* These are the same 18 items he discusses; we present 22 comparisons, however, because data for the 1977 and 1978 suicide questions are presented separately. Of these 22 comparisons, 17 (77%) show significant linearity beyond the .05 level. *Only one item is significantly nonlinear at the .05 level.*[3]

We know that "nonviewers" often seem to be more likely than light viewers to given "television answers." Also, it is not unreasonable to question whether they should be lumped with "light" viewers. But, given their trivial numbers, they cannot constitute grounds for claiming that relationships with viewing are nonlinear; they merely affirm that the simple relationships are indeed linear for over 90% of the population.

Hirsch then moves on to assess overall associations through Multiple Classification Analysis. (It would make more sense to begin with overall patterns and then turn to

TABLE 1

Significance of Linear and Nonlinear Trends, Based on the Simple Associations Between Hirsch's Items and Viewing Categories*

Alienation (1978)	Significance of Linearity	Significance of Non-linearity
People running country don't care	.001	.33
Rich get richer, poor get poorer	.09	.29
What you think doesn't count	.004	.23
You're left out of things	.05	.07
Powerful people take advantage of you	.004	.74
People in Washington are out of touch	.07	.48

Meanworld (1978)		
People are just looking out for themselves	.15	.55
People would take advantage of you, given chance	.0001	.37
Can't be too careful in dealing with people	.0002	.87

Approval of Suicide	(1977)	(1978)	(1977)	(1978)
If incurable disease	.44	.0008	.98	.94
If bankrupt	.0002	.0000	.38	.26
If dishonored family	.0006	.0000	.91	.74
If tired of living	.02	.03	.30	.39
Lot of average man getting worse		.0003		.05
Not fair to bring a child into world		.0002		.30
Officials not interested in average man		.0000		.08

(table continued next page)

*Nonviewers; light viewers (1-2 hrs/day); medium viewers (3 hrs/day); heavy viewers (4 to 7 hrs/day); extreme viewers (8 hrs/day and up).

TABLE 1 (Continued)

Anomia (1977)	Significance of Linearity	Significance of Non-linearity
Ability to imagine a situation in which a man punching an adult male stranger would be approved by respondent* (1978)	.0004	.53
Fear of walking alone within a mile of home at night (1977)	.07	.66

*Hirsch calls this item "actual violence."

specifications.) Importantly, he does not tell us whether the "control" variables are entered as covariates or as competing independent factors.[4]

His neglect of subgroups in Part I all but invalidates his conclusions about our so-called "unreported discrepancies," as shown for a variety of analyses *based on a variety of samples* (Gerbner et al., 1980a). It is particularly evident in his analysis of the relationship between amount of viewing and what he calls "attitudes toward actual violence."

To begin, he claims that the following two items are "comparable":

—How often is it all right to hit someone if you are mad at them for a good reason? Is it almost always all right or almost never all right?

—Are there any situations you can imagine in which you would approve of a man punching an adult male stranger?

The first question was asked of adolescents; the second comes from the 1978 GSS/NORC survey. The GSS/NORC item was "never discussed or referred to" by us for two simple reasons: (1) 1978 NORC data were not available in time for our 1978 report, and our 1979 report dealt solely with adolescents; and (2) we were suspicious of its reliability Specifically, the scale of items measuring situations in which violence might be approved is neither internally homogeneous nor unidimensional; Cronbach's alpha is only .32.

Moreover, these two questions are neither substantively nor empirically "comparable," as Hawkins and Pingree (forthcoming) note when discussing Hughes's (1980) parallel use of this question:

> Hughes' NORC questions asked people to *imagine a situation,* where Gerbner, *et al.,* asked children *how often is it all right?* Perhaps the NORC light viewers have better imaginations than heavy viewers. Hughes himself makes a similar argument about [other differences] [Hawkins and Pingree, forthcoming; italics in original].

Underscoring these contentions is Loftin and Lizotte's (1974) finding, based on GSS/NORC data, that *high-SES groups are more likely to respond affirmatively to this question.* This counterintuitive relationship also holds in the 1978 General Social Survey: those with higher occupational prestige ($r = .16$, $p = .000$), more education ($r = .20$, $p = .000$), and higher incomes ($r = .16$, $p = .000$) are more likely to be able to "imagine a situation in which they would approve of a man punching an adult male stranger." Yet, in our adolescent sample, the relationship between the supposedly comparable variable and an SES index is indeed negative ($r = -.12$, $p = .01$).

Thus, given the low reliability of the NORC question and its surprising relationship with background variables, we chose not to report or analyze its association with amount of viewing on the grounds that we cannot tell what indeed it is measuring. At the same time, even this questionable item provides evidence of mainstreaming, as seen on Table 2, which breaks down responses to this question according to Hirsch's viewing categories separately for college and non-college-educated respondents. It is worth noting the relationship is not significantly nonlinear for either group.

TABLE 2

Relationship Between Approving of a Man Punching an Adult Male
Stranger and Hirsch's Viewing Categories, by Education (NORC 1978)

| EDUCATION: | Non-Viewers | Light | Medium | Heavy | Extreme | Significance of: | |
						Linearity	Non-Linearity
No College	62.8	61.1	65.3	59.9	53.1	.43	.50
(N)	(43)	(411)	(193)	(264)	(49)		
Some College	82.9	79.3	75.6	56.7	66.7	.0002	.35
(N)	(41)	(285)	(86)	(67)	(6)		
Difference between education groups:	20.1	18.2	10.3	3.2	*		

*Too few cases in extreme viewing/high education group.

Among less-educated respondents, there is essentially no relationship. But among more educated respondents, whose light viewers (and even nonviewers) are quite likely to be able to "imagine a situation," the relationship with viewing is negative and significantly linear. Heavy viewing may thus "moderate" outlooks of "otherwise" extreme groups so that they converge into a more homogeneous "mainstream." Ignoring the college-educated "extreme" viewers (because there are only six of them), we find that the *difference* between more- and less-educated respondents *monotonically decreases at each subsequent viewing level.* The two groups of "nonviewers" are 20 points apart, while the "light" groups are 18, the "medium" groups 10, and the "heavy" groups only 3.

Further, as shown on Table 3, the relationship within the college-educated group withstands controls for sex, race, age, income, and residual variation in education itself, *either singly or all at once.* Thus, even this question, although it is fundamentally unclear what it in fact measures, provides another example where "mainstreaming" is totally masked in an overall trivial association.

If Hawkins and Pingree are correct (that light viewers are better able to "imagine a situation"), then we can conclude

TABLE 3
Simple and Partial Correlations Between Amount of Viewing
and Approving of a Man Punching an Adult Male Stranger,
Within Low and High Education Groups (NORC 1978)

	No College	Some College
Simple r	-.02	-.17[*]
Controlling for:		
Sex	-.02	-.18[*]
Age	-.03	-.17[*]
Education	-.02	-.16[*]
Income	.00	-.17[*]
Race	-.02	-.15[*]
All Controls	.00	-.14[*]
Final d.f.	887	459

[*]p < .001

that higher-educated people are also better able—*unless they are heavy viewers.* Heavy viewers in the college-educated group join those without college, resulting in a more homogeneous outlook.

In sum, Hirsch's Part I fails to demonstrate that our conclusions are unjustified. Many of the 18 items do not constitute fair or meaningful tests of the cultivation hypothesis because they are either irrelevant (with no basis in TV message analysis, as in the case of the suicide questions) or because they are of problematic reliability and validity (as with "approval of violence"). The charge that we are "shifting bases" by defining light, medium, and heavy viewers according to each sample's distribution is transparently simplistic.

Examining "nonviewers" and "extreme viewers" adds little to understanding the consequences of mass communication because both are tiny and bizarre groups.

Furthermore, Hirsch's claims of nonlinearity are statistically unsound; regardless of the inappropriateness of many items, the vast majority show significant linear trends with almost no significant deviations from linearity, across *his* five viewing groups.

Moreover, we are particularly affronted by Hirsch's insinuation that we have intentionally misreported data. He argues that, because we have used samples of different sizes and from different locations (which seems a reasonable way to help accumulate findings), and because we have used sample-relative distributions to categorize respondents' viewing patterns and have employed numerous statistical techniques, then "the question arises whether important issues covered by one or more of the samples are reported at all, and, if so, reported accurately."[5]

Above all, Hirsch's failure to consider differential patterns within subgroups and his emphasis on global associations blinds him to findings which may be more critical than any overall "effects." Our explorations of such specifications, which we analyze within the framework of "mainstreaming" and "resonance," show systematic and consistent patterns within subgroups. These concepts are considered—and rejected—by Hirsch in Part II; but as we shall show in the next section, his alleged disconfirmation is based on fundamental misconceptions.

PART II

It is sometimes assumed, either explicitly or implicitly, that there is a single correct approach to survey analysis and that approaches which deviate from this path are in error. . . . Pure hypothesis testing is a valuable research model and should be employed where appropriate, but research can be severely cramped if it is employed as the *sole* method of analysis . . . in actual practice, much survey analysis involves the hot pursuit of an idea down paths and byways which have little to do with one's original hypothesis. . . . A reluctance to follow the lead of the findings

> may stultify and abort a good deal of promising research . . . .
> Although the professional literature tends to present its
> results within the hypothesis-testing framework, the
> published report may by no means correspond to the actual
> research procedures. . . . The history of science is replete
> with . . . serendipitous discoveries. . . . It may further be
> noted that in actual research practice the contrast between
> hypothesis-testing and post-factum interpretation is not so
> great as it may appear [Rosenberg, 1968: 197-238].

The flaws in Part I of Hirsch's "reanalysis" are compounded and overshadowed by the more serious gaps, confusions, and misrepresentations which permeate his second installment. As in Part I, his reliance on one sample, further contaminated by questionable items, provides no basis whatsoever for his dismissal of our accumulated findings. In particular, in this section we will show that:

(1) Hirsch distorts and convolutes cultivation theory and pre-
    sents his erroneous straw-man extrapolations a if they
    were necessary, direct implications of our theory—only to
    refute them;
(2) contrary to these distortions and misrepresentations, "main-
    streaming" and "resonance" are neither all encompassing
    nor unfalsifiable; and
(3) far from being the drastic "reformulations" he alleges, "main-
    streaming" and "resonance" are explications of concepts
    deeply embedded in all our previous work.

We are disappointed in Hirsch's "critique" of our recent refinements. We had anticipated some challenging and novel insights into potential flaws in the conceptualization and analysis of these new ideas, and had expected careful scrutiny which might help develop theory and point toward directions for more research.

Instead, Hirsch demonstrates an astonishing ability to selectively attack limitations and ambiguities *which we explicitly acknowledge and discuss* in our work, and to present them as if he has discovered some "hidden" flaw which we are trying to obscure.

In Part II Hirsch makes the following claims:

(1) our initial hypothesis specified universal, across-the-board effects of television viewing on people's conception of social reality;

(2) growing aware of subgroup differences, we contended that real-life subgroups whose fictional counterparts are overly victimized will show the strongest cultivation patterns;

(3) finding this not to be the case, or ignoring the idea altogether, we scrambled around trying to find *post hoc* explanations for random or damaging subgroup patterns;

(4) these post hoc explanations are logically contradictory, ambiguous, and untestable, and thereby nonrefutable.

The first two claims are imaginary. They confuse clearly presented *speculations* with explicit *conclusions*. We were unable to find (and Hirsch failed to quote) any statements in our publications which assert absolute, global impact. From the earliest published cultivation analyses, the theory and the method focused on possible subgroup differences:

> All responses are related to television exposure, other media habits, and demographic characteristics. We then compare the response of light and heavy viewers controlling for sex, age, education, and other characteristics. The margin of heavy viewers over light viewers giving the "television answers" *within and across groups* is the "cultivation differential." . . . The analysis is intended to illuminate the complementary as well as the divergent roles of these sources of facts, images, beliefs, and values in the cultivation of assumptions about reality [Gerbner and Gross, 1976: 182; italics added].

Although this clearly provides for across-group comparisons, we do not, as Hirsch claims, "simply abandon without explanation" in Violence Profile No. 11 the examination of within-group cultivation differentials (a look at the tables in that report reveals that this claim is blatantly false). Moreover, Hirsch is incorrect when he states that our latest work "instead substitutes an entirely new method of measurement and statistical procedure," the "across-group" comparisons.

This is as confused and unfounded as his accusations that we have continuously "reformulated" our basic arguments and analyzed, using different techniques, "the same data from year to year." Our latest publication (Gerbner et al., 1980a) is the first time data have been reanalyzed and refinements offered to support what we believe to be an important theoretical development.[6]

In regard to point 2, while it is evident that we were aware of conditional relationships, we had not yet tested any specific hypotheses about what shapes they might take:

> The pattern of relative victimization is remarkably stable from year to year. It demonstrates an invidious (but socially functional) sense of risk and power. We do not yet know whether it also cultivates a corresponding hierarchy of fear and aggression [Gerbner and Gross, 1976: 191].

It is clear, as Hirsch notes, that we did later speculate that viewers "may be especially receptive to seeing how characters" like themselves fare in the dramatic world. But we made it equally clear in that same article that we did not offer this statement as an empirical finding:

> Television makes somewhat different contributions to the perspectives of different social groups. These differences cannot be expected to replicate the structure of power shown on television because many other factors enter into the overall determination of real-life relative powers [Gerbner et al., 1978: 206].

Yet, Hirsch asserts that our "first reformulation"—that cultivation will be most evident within the groups most victimized on television—"follows directly from the text of Violence Profiles 7 through 10." He reconstructs our theory to build in the assumption that this proposition implies that viewers will "adopt as their own attitudes and perceptions the same interpretations of television content" as we derive from message system analysis. These claims are nowhere to be found in our theory. They are *his*, not ours. It is Hirsch who "cuts loose" our message analysis from our cultivation analysis in imputing a level of conscious, isomorphic "interpretation." In clarifying a similar misconception of CBS a few years ago, we noted:

> We must repeat that the validity of a TV content indicator does not depend on viewers' conscious understanding of its meaning [Gerbner et al., 1977b: 286].

Hirsch also imputes into our theory a level of "identification" with television characters which we have never asserted. If anything, the available research (McArthur and Eisen, 1976; Miller and Reeves, 1976; Reeves and Miller, 1977) suggests that, at least for children, "identification" has far more to do with the availability and range of models presented than with one-to-one demographic correspondence between characters and viewers. Hirsch's version of our theory is symptomatic of a consistent effort to oversimplify it into a mechanical concept.

In any case, Hirsch's reformulation—that cultivation should depend upon how demographically similar characters fare in the TV world—is, although probably oversimplistic, far from uninteresting. One contribution of Hirsch's work is that it provides the first actual test of that proposition. His results suggest rejecting this hypothesis; still, we question the validity of the test, because of the small number of groups examined and the comparison of inappropriately matched groups.[7]

A more convincing test of this hypothesis (which we have begun) must be based upon a large number of groups. We report "risk-ratios" (reflecting relative likelihood of committing or suffering violence, and of killing or being killed) for five major variables which have measurable real-world demographic parallels: sex, age, race, occupation, and marital status. Each of these has two categories in our data base, except for age, which has three. This produces a total of 263 different combinations of characteristics, or 263 potentially definable groups. We are now examining the relationship between each character group's victimization likelihood and each real-life group's correlation between amount of viewing and perceptions of danger and are looking forward to determining the viability of this hypothesis.

In addition, Hirsch bases part of this analysis on the following NORC question (italics added):

—Is there *any* area right around here—that is, *within a mile*— where you would be afraid to walk alone at night? (yes, no)

and concludes that there is no evidence that television cultivates "fear." In a 1979 national probability survey conducted as part of our research by the Opinion Research Corporation, we included a question which, while similar, seems to us more focused on people's real apprehensions:

—How safe do you feel walking around in your own neighborhood *alone, at night*—very safe, somewhat safe, or not safe at all?

We found strikingly different results (see Gerbner et al., 1980a). The weak association with the NORC question may be in part due to insufficiently sensitive response categories as well as to the off-center focus of the question: Most of us could very likely think of *some* area where we would be afraid to walk alone at night; that does not mean most of us are necessarily fearful when we walk in our own neighborhoods.[8]

Still, it is worth noting that the cultivation of "fear" per se may be a "secondary" hypothesis. Our basic notion is that television should cultivate images of what "the world" is like. Since our message system analyses show over half of all leading characters involved in some kind of violence, year in and year out, we proposed the idea that television might cultivate the belief that a relatively large number of people are involved in violence. In nine out of ten samples,[9] we have found that greater television viewing (with or without multiple controls) goes with heightened estimates of the number of people involved in violence in the real world. Again, this finding represents the cultivation of a *conception of social reality*, an image of the world as a more or less violent place, and does not *necessarily* have any direct relationship to consciously experienced "fear."

By a natural extension, however, we wondered whether or not it might apply to personal projections of risk and danger. We found that, indeed, it *did* for children. For adults, using the GSS/NORC question analyzed by Hirsch (as well as by Hughes), we found *and reported* that it had a "slight tendency" to show a "weak" association with television viewing (Gerbner et al., 1978). It is hardly surprising or profound that a weak simple association disappears under simultaneous controls.

In any case, the ORC survey contains both questions—perceptions of the number of people involved in violence and level of safety in one's own neighborhood—and we have found that the two are indeed somewhat distinct concepts. The correlation between them is a relatively low .15; two-thirds (63.7%) of those who feel "very safe" in their own neighborhoods still overestimate the number of people involved in violence, despite their sense of relative security. (Conversely, 38.6% of those who inflate the proportion of people involved in violence nevertheless feel safe in their own neighborhoods.)

Even more interesting is the way each of these variables conditions the association between viewing and the other—results that reveal "mainstreaming." Figure 1 shows that the relationship between amount of viewing and exaggerating the number of people involved in violence decreases monotonically as fear of walking in one's own neighborhood increases. Those who feel "very safe" in their own neighborhoods are relatively unlikely to overestimate the proportion of people involved in violence—unless they are heavy television viewers. Similarly, light viewers who do not overestimate the proportion of people involved in violence are likely to feel "very safe" in their own neighborhoods. In both cases, the differences deriving partly from other dispositions are reduced—the proportion of the heavy viewers in these groups who give the TV answer is closer, thus reflecting a "mainstream" commonality of outlooks.

Turning to points 3 and 4, it is clear that the most important issue in Hirsch's Part II is the role of "mainstreaming" and "resonance" in cultivation theory. It is particularly difficult to respond to Hirsch's "critique" of these concepts because it is not apparent that he understands them. In his haste to manufacture "contradictions" in our position, he fails to consider rather obvious grounds for falsification and constructs an unfair and incoherent explication of their meaning.

He begins by presenting his reformulation of our "original version," and argues that it is in conflict with "mainstreaming" and "resonance." As we state in Violence Profile No. 11, cultivation is often a virtually across-the-board phenomenon. It is quite clear from our article that "mainstreaming" and "resonance" *deal with the exceptions*. The refinement which aggravates Hirsch so is simply the proposition that many (if not most) of the specifications which emerge when overall relationships disappear, as well as other systematic variations in susceptibility to cultivation, can be explained by one of these two concepts.[10]

His disregard of our observation that a majority of cultivation questions do show consistent and robust effects for most groups is based on his use of a number of problematic items from virtually one data base, which, for whatever reasons, show incongruous results. Other data of comparable quality, representativeness, and scope show dramatically different patterns. Table 4 shows within-group

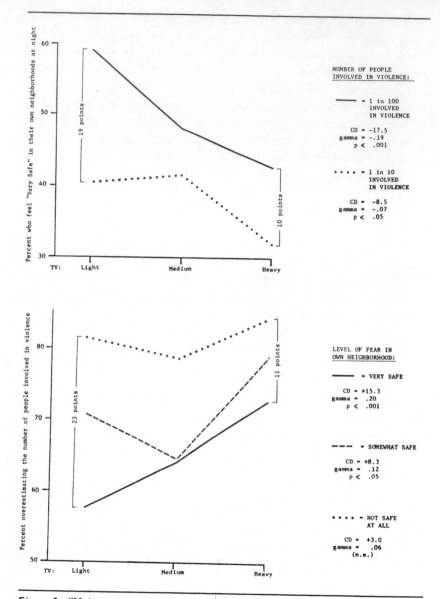

Figure 1: "Mainstreaming" in Conditional Associations Between Amount of Television Viewing, Neighborhood Fear, and Estimation of the Number of people Involved in Violence (ORC data)

TABLE 4

Within-Group Partial Correlations Between Amount of Television Viewing and an Index of Perceptions of Violence and Danger (ORC data)

	Simple r	Sex	Age	Education	Residence	Income	Race	Newspaper Reading	ALL CONTROLS	(df)
OVERALL	.17***	.16***	.17***	.14***	.18***	.15***	.16***	.17***	.11***	(4980)
AGE										
18-29	.22***	.22***	.22***	.19***	.24***	.22***	.20***	.22***	.19***	(1589)
30-54	.14***	.14***	.14***	.11***	.14***	.11***	.13***	.15***	.07***	(2049)
55+	.13***	.11***	.13***	.13***	.13***	.09***	.15***	.13***	.10***	(1320)
EDUCATION										
No College	.17***	.16***	.17***	.17***	.16***	.15***	.16***	.17***	.14***	(3467)
Some College	.12***	.11***	.12***	.10***	.12***	.10***	.11***	.12***	.08***	(1505)
NEWSPAPER READING										
Everyday	.14***	.12***	.13***	.11***	.15***	.11***	.13***	--	.09***	(3230)
Sometimes	.25***	.24***	.24***	.21***	.25***	.23***	.24***	--	.17***	(1302)
RACE										
White	.17***	.15***	.16***	.14***	.17***	.15***	--	.17***	.12***	(4405)
Non-white	.14***	.13***	.17***	.13***	.11***	.08*	--	.14***	.07 (p=.06)	(569)
RESIDENCE										
City over 250,000	.21***	.21***	.18***	.06^	--	.16***	18***	.20***	.00	(898)
City under 250,000	.22***	.23***	.23***	.17***	--	.23***	.21***	.22***	.21***	(561)
Suburb	.18***	.14***	.18***	.15***	--	.16***	.18***	.18***	.10***	(1915)
Non-metro.	.13***	.12***	.13***	.11***	--	.11***	.13***	.14***	.11***	(1583)
INCOME										
Under $10,000	.20***	.19***	.19***	.18***	.19***	.20***	.19***	.20***	.17***	(1777)
$10-25,000	.10***	.09***	.10***	.08***	.11***	.10***	.10***	.10***	.08***	(2240)
Over $25,000	.13***	.12***	.15***	12***	.15***	.15***	.16***	.15***	.08**	(946)
SEX										
Male	.16***	--	.16***	.12***	.16***	.11***	.14***	.15***	.09***	(2350)
Female	.17***	--	.16***	.14***	.17***	.15***	.16**	.17**	.13***	(2623)

*p < .05; **p < .01; ***p < .001

partial correlations between amount of viewing and scores on an index of perceptions of violence and danger drawn from questions in our ORC survey. There are seven control variables; each row presents the correlations for each subgroup, controlling for all other variables (and residual variation in the variable itself, when it is continuous), singly and simultaneously. Clearly, the associations between amount of television viewing and this index are persistent and potent.

Anticipating Hirsch's rejoinder that statistical significance is "an artifact of sample size," we would remind him that the larger the sample, the less likely the obtained coefficients are due to chance. As we have often argued, the "size" of an effect may be less important than the direction of its steady contribution.

As further confirmation of our belief that "positive" cultivation effects hold for "most groups," we present summary data from the same ORC survey in Table 5. This table summarizes the effects of single and simultaneous controls on the five variables which make up the index of perceptions of violence and danger.[11] The middle row is particularly provocative given Hirsch's claims that "practically any two" controls, when applied together, wipe out cultivation. This row represents "two controls"—in turn, each category from Table 4 is held constant along with one other variable which is partialled out—*and 483 out of 580 "double-controlled" correlations (83.3%) remain positive and significant.* In this light, our contention that "most groups" show evidence of cultivation hardly deserves Hirsch's sarcasm. But even this only tells part of the story.

Hirsch's superficial and slanted recounting of "mainstreaming" and "resonance" reflects either incomprehension or misrepresentation. The accusation that they are "all-encompassing" and nonfalsifiable reveals scanty contemplation. It does not require much effort to generate numerous conditional associations which would not support either one. He paints them as contradictory opposites (and also contradictory to our "original formulation"), and as "all-purpose" explanations, when in fact they are complementary processes which are proposed as applicable to "many" subgroup differences.

His overstated concern about specifying the conditions under which either (or neither) will occur overlooks and belies one fundamental fact—*that nonspurious and meaningful specifications do indeed exist in the very data he concludes show no associations with amount of television viewing.* By portraying them as all-encompassing (which they are not), he sidesteps the realization that certain identifiable subgroups show systematic, nonspurious, and significant cultivation patterns even

TABLE 5
Summary of Simple and Partial Within-Group Correlations Between Amount of Viewing and Perceptions of Violence and Danger (ORC data)

	Number of Correlations which are:			
	Positive and Significant	Positive and Non-Significant	Negative and Non-Significant	Negative and Significant
Within-Group Simple Correlations (N=90 r's)	77 (85.6%)	9 (10.0%)	4 (4.4%)	0 (0.0%)
Within-Group First-Order Partial Correlations (N=580 r's)	483 (83.3%)	67 (11.5%)	27 (4.7%)	3 (0.5%)
Within-Group Partial Correlations with all controls * (N=90 r's)	55 (61.1%)	24 (26.7%)	9 (10.0%)	2 (2.2%)

*"All controls" includes residual variance in the controlling variable, where contin uous; e.g., residual variance in income is held constant within any given income category, in addition to all other controls.

where overall relationships disappear. In Part II, he all but abandons data which might support or refute his conclusions. *Where are the data* to show that these conditional associations are indeed spurious or nonlinear? He argues that they are with great passion but absolutely no evidence.

Clearly, both "mainstreaming" and "resonance" are falsifiable. Figure 2 presents a variety of possible conditional associations; in these figures the amount of television viewing is the x-axis, and some assumption, belief, or conception about social reality is the y-axis. Graphs a, b, and c show examples of "mainstreaming," in

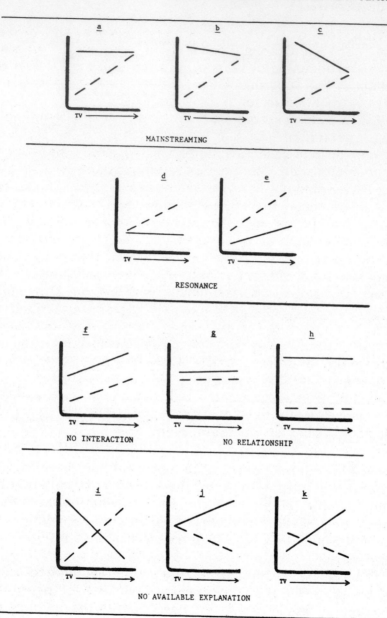

Figure 2: Hypothetical Within-Group Specifications

which the outlooks of heavy viewers are more homogeneous. Graphs d and e show "resonance," where, for some meaningful reasons, a given message is highly salient to one subgroup. The relationship may hold for both but be amplified for one, as in graph e.

The remaining six graphs show neither "mainstreaming" nor "resonance." In f, the relationship holds for both groups, despite baseline differences. In g and h, there is no relationship at all. There are clear relationships in i, j, and k, but they would not fit any available explanation. If patterns like these occur, they may indeed reflect "real" effects of television, but they would by no means be accounted for by the phenomenon of "mainstreaming" or of "resonance."

The point is that conditional patterns within subgroups may take on a wide range of forms. Given variables which have little or no overall relationship with viewing, if the bulk of the subgroup patterns fit into the shapes hypothesized in graphs g,h,i,j, or k—or many possible others not shown—it would provide unambiguous falsification of "mainstreaming" and "resonance." Hirsch's comment that we would explain the absence of within-group relationships by saying that "mainstreaming" and "resonance" are happening simultaneously and canceling each other out, while ridiculous, raises an important point.

If we were to find an unexpected within-group relationship of zero, we would not claim that "mainstreaming" and "resonance" were canceling each other out like Dr. Doolittle's "Push-Me-Pull-You." Hirsch's simplistic accusation overlooks the fact that further examination of differences within that group—controlling for additional variables—might reveal a theoretically intelligible pattern underlying the apparent lack of relationship with television viewing. A single variable would not simultaneously generate both "mainstreaming" and "resonance," but the implementation of additional controls might uncover their presence in distinct subsets of the group, just as it does in an overall association. This kind of elaboration is a fundamental task of scientific analysis—to delve ever more deeply into phenomena, to examine layers of association, with an ever-sharper focus.

The fact is that the criteria by which the constructs of "mainstreaming" and "resonance" could be falsified are painfully evident. We did not present them in a "pure hypothesis-testing framework" because they are indeed post factum interpretations. That is why they need further examination, in a broad range of cultivation issues. Our latest findings—as well as those of the California State Board of Education (1980) and Lull et al. (forthcoming)— merely suggest that stopping at the point of finding no overall associations may prevent the discovery of systematic processes which are both more subtle and more profound—and which Hirsch would bury.

These remarks should not be taken as, a reflection of Olympian smugness. We welcome critiques and find them, for the most part, helpful; they indicate a healthy scientific skepticism and often lead us to more rigor, new directions, and valuable insights.

But, we must wonder, what compels the gleeful and sarcastic hostility in Hirsch's two pieces? We are saddened by his ad hominem intimations. Surely, it is possible to reappraise our work and reach different conclusions without virulence; see Hughes (1980) for one example. Hirsch's vituperations are embarrassing, unbecoming, and serve no scientific purpose; we regret if he has provoked harsh treatment from us.

Ultimately, "mainstreaming" and "resonance" may lead to more questions. As we continue to expand the focus of our work—into the cultivation of images about sex roles, age roles, health, education, marriage and the family, occupations, science, courts and law, religion, and more— and attempt to investigate "mainstreaming" and "resonance" in this larger context, we look forward to a more even-handed and collegial scientific scrutiny and dialogue.

NOTES

1. An exception is Wober (1978), who failed to replicate our findings in Britain, but he also failed to replicate our design or our measures (Gerbner et al., 1979a; Neville, 1980).

2. Several additional instances of this concept are presented in Gerbner et al. (1980a).

3. In 19 of these comparisons (86%), the nonlinear trend does not even reach the .10 level of significance; only in two cases is the significance of linearity *not* below .10.

4. We tried it both ways for one of his items ("approval of violence") and found that which procedure is followed makes a difference. The covariate method produces a lower R^2, and stronger coefficients for television. The simultaneous independent method reveals a significant interaction between viewing and education ($p < .05$), which we discuss below.

5. It takes little effort or ability to do a hatchet-job on *any* social science research. Hirsch himself provides ambiguous or no information about which NORC datasets are used in certain analyses, beyond that they are either 1975, 1977, or 1978. For his description of the univariate distribution of television exposure, he uses all three years. Similarly, he combines all three samples when comparing his five viewing groups to background factors. But in only one analysis of the relationship between viewing and attitudes does he again use data from 1975. Further, the sample years are not specified on the tables. Some items are only in the 1977 GSS/NORC (like anomia), some are only in 1978 (like alienation), and some are in both (like suicide). He never explains which sample years are used, sometimes employing just one when two years are available.

6. In both Parts I and II, Hirsch argues that Violence Profile No. 10 (1979b) suggests that "each 'latest' statistical procedure is to supersede all previous reported results," and we find this puzzling. The only possible explanation stems from our statement in the introduction to the Technical Report that the data from previous years is summarized in each year's Technical Report, which also "presents trends for all years studied." While this statement could specify more clearly that it applies only to message analysis data, which are indeed "superseded" each year because they are included cumulatively in each subsequent report, the parallel claim of new statistical techniques appearing annually is nonsense. The only evidence we could find for this claim is in our 1978 Technical Report, in which we attempted to summarize all our previous cultivation analyses. Specifically, we presented data on individual items from ten samples (48 tables), a few of which had been reported in index form in 1977; this effort to archive results from comparable questions across samples hardly represented a "reanalysis."

7. He equates "nonwhite" characters with "black" respondents, as well as male characters who are "American, white, middle class, and in the prime of life" with respondents who are simply "white men." This further clouds the value of his test.

8. It is not likely that the difference derives simply from "house effects." Smith (1978) notes that "don't knows" and "no answers" are a common indication of such "house effects," but the proportions not answering the questions are comparable—0.7% in GSS/NORC and 0.9% in ORC. More likely, the response

categories for the GSS/NORC question are too crude to detect associations. This not only helps account for why television viewing is only weakly related to the NORC question, but may also explain why *other* variables are more strongly related to degree of neighborhood fear in the ORC data. In parallel simultaneous multiple regressions of neighborhood fear onto sex, age, income, race, and education, substantially stronger relationships were found between demographics and fear in the ORC data than in the GSS/NORC data for all predictors except sex. All betas in the ORC regression were significant beyond $p < .001$; in NORC, while most were significant, education was not. Even within the ORC data, all regression coefficients are weaker when the fear variable is dichotomized. Thus, the relatively negligible predictive power of the demographics in NORC does not establish, as Hirsch claims, a basis for rejecting the theory of cultivation; rather, it suggests that the GSS/NORC question itself is weak.

9. This relationship holds in two national probability adult samples (ORC—1974 and 1979), one national quota sample (Starch—1974), four samples of adolescents, one of college students, and one of Philadelphia adults. The one sample showing no association (also Philadelphia adults) was asked in open-ended, rather than forced-choice, questions.

10. We also note that other factors may enhance or diminish cultivation, such as absence of direct experience, parental involvement in viewing, and peer-group integration (Gerbner et al., 1980a).

11. A description of the components and their reliability can be found in Violence Profile No. 11.

REFERENCES

California State Department of Education (1980) Student Achievement in California Schools: 1979-80 Annual Report. Sacramento: California Assessment Program.

DOOB, A. N. and G. E. MACDONALD (1979) "Television viewing and fear of victimization: is the relationship causal?" J. of Personality and Social Psychology 37: 170-179.

GERBNER, G. and L. GROSS (1976) "Living with television: the Violence Profile." J. of Communication 26: 173-199.

——— M. F. ELEEY, M. JACKSON-BEECK, S. JEFFRIES-FOX, and N. SIGNORIELLI (1977a) "TV Violence Profile No. 8: the highlights." J. of Communication 27: 171-180.

——— (1977b) "The Gerbner Violence Profile: an analysis of the CBS report." J. of Broadcasting 21: 280-286.

GERBNER, G., L. GROSS, M. JACKSON-BEECK, S. JEFFRIES-FOX, and N. SIGNORIELLI (1978) "Cultural indicators: Violence Profile No. 9." J. of Communication 28: 176-206.

GERBNER, G., L. GROSS, M. MORGAN, and N. SIGNORIELLI (1980a) "The 'mainstreaming' of America: Violence Profile No. 11." J. of Communication 30: 10-27.

———— (1980b) "Some additional comments on cultivation analysis." Public Opinion Q. 44: 408-410.

———— (1979a) "On Wober's 'televised violence and paranoid perception: the view from Great Britain.'" Public Opinion Q. 43: 123-124.

GERBNER, G., L. GROSS, N. SIGNORIELLI, M. MORGAN, and M. JACKSON-BEECK (1979b) "The demonstration of power: Violence Profile No. 10." J. of Communication 29: 177-196.

HAWKINS, R. P. and S. PINGREE (forthcoming) "TV influence on constructions of social reality," in National Institute of Mental Health, Television and Behavior: Ten Years of Scientific Progress and Implications for the 80's.

HIRSCH, P. (1979) "The role of television and popular culture in contemporary society," in H. Newcomb (ed.) Television: The Critical View. New York: Oxford Univ. Press.

HUGHES, M. (1980) "The fruits of cultivation analysis: a reexamination of some effects of television watching." Public Opinion Q. 44: 287-302.

JACKSON-BEECK, M. (1977) "The nonviewers: who are they?" J. of Communication 27: 65-72.

———— and J. SOBAL (1980) "The social world of heavy television viewers." J. of Broadcasting 24: 5-11.

LOFTIN, C. and A. LIZOTTE (1974) "Violence and social structure: structural support for violence among privileged groups." Presented to the American Sociological Association, Montreal.

LULL, J., A. MULAC, and S. L. ROSEN (forthcoming) "Feminism as a predictor of mass media use." Sex Roles

McARTHUR, L. Z. and S. V. EISEN (1976) "Television and sex-role stereotyping." J. of Applied Social Psychology 6: 329-351.

MILLER, M. M. and B. REEVES (1976) "Dramatic TV content and children's sex-role stereotypes." J. of Broadcasting 20: 35-60.

MORGAN, M. and L. GROSS (1980) "Television viewing, IQ, and academic achievement." J. of Broadcasting 24: 117-133.

NEVILLE, T. (1980) "More on Wober's 'televised violence. . . .'" Public Opinion Q. 44: 116-117.

REEVES, B. and M. MILLER (1977) "A multidimensional measure of children's identification with television characters." J. of Broadcasting 22: 71-86.

ROSENBERG, M. (1968) The Logic of Survey Analysis. New York: Basic Books.

SIGNORIELLI, N. (1979) "Television's contribution to sex-role socialization." Presented at the Telecommunications Policy Research Conference, Skytop, Pennsylvania.

SMITH, T. W. (1978) "In search of house effects: a comparison of responses to various questions by different survey organizations." Public Opinion Q. 42. 443-463.

TANKARD, J. W., Jr., and M. C. HARRIS (1980) "A discriminant analysis of television viewers and nonviewers." J. of Broadcasting 24: 399-409.

WOBER, J. M. (1978) "Televised violence and paranoid perception: the view from Great Britain." Public Opinion Q. 42: 315-321.

In his reply to the Gerbner et al. comments, Paul Hirsch extends the initial dialogue by emphasizing those points on which he and they agree and suggesting areas in which they disagree. In some cases, these disagreements are theoretical, and in others, they are methodological.

38

DISTINGUISHING GOOD SPECULATION FROM BAD THEORY

Rejoinder to Gerbner et al.

Paul M. Hirsch

The number of my major points which emerge undisputed and fully intact after the preceding "Comment" is impressive and noteworthy. The Annenberg team's reply combines assertions about theory, method, and findings which I shall disentangle and divide more appropriately into separate sections for this rejoinder. Within each of these, the following analytical components of their response (in descending order of importance) will be addressed: (1) *basic issues*, on which (a) they concede, (b) we are in substantial agreement, or (c) they remain silent, despite the length of the "Comment"; (2) *areas they dispute*, but for which no new supporting information, clarifications, or data are provided; (3) *questions raised*, whose answers are already found in the text and tables of my article; (4) *additional questions* on topics which have little or nothing to do with the substance of my presentation; and (5) *suggestions* that I have committed an unconscionable (scholarly) act by holding accountable to the standards of "pure science" some glaring inadequacies in publications promoting the "cumulative

AUTHOR'S NOTE: *This project was supported generously by a grant from the John and Mary R. Markle Foundation to facilitate dialogue between the social sciences and humanities in the field of mass communication. For critical discussion and first-rate research assistance, I am especially indebted to Tom Panelas, and gratefully acknowledge the contributions of Stuart Michaels and Sally Kilgore.*

From Paul M. Hirsch, "Distinguishing Good Speculation from Bad Theory: Rejoinder to Gerbner et al.," *Communication Research* 8, 1, pp. 73-95. Copyright © 1981 by Sage Publications, Inc.

results of a decade of fairly massive cooperative research and theory building."

In the pages to follow, I will respond to the more substantive portions of the comment and leave it to the reader to judge the rest.

MAJOR FINDINGS FROM THE REANALYSIS

Let us begin by making very clear that Gerbner et al. do not dispute any of the following issues and findings:

(1) When simultaneous multiple controls were employed to test the hypothesis that heavy television viewing "cultivates" perceptions of the world as a "mean" and "scary" place, virtually no statistical support for the claimed relationship was found in the data. Gerbner et al. restate the consequences of applying this standard statistical procedure as "simple relationships between amount of viewing and some attitudes are wiped out."

(2) The amount of total variance in these attitude items explained by *all of the independent variables combined* never exceeded 18%, and more typically was less than 10%. Of the five independent variables, television viewing's relative contribution to this small percentage consistently ranked *last or next to last*. The entire search for, and debate over the extent to which television "cultivates" perceptions centers around data for which it can independently explain only a miniscule amount of variance, so small that elementary textbooks on research design suggest such "findings" are nonreportable as positive results and are better presented as *non*findings.

(3) The application of multivariate analysis to the NORC dataset yields no evidence of any consistent patterns at all, nor evidence for linearity in the relation of amount of television viewing to responses on attitude items. Gerbner et al. here acknowledge a "convincing" demonstration of either curvilinear or negative overall relationships "in some cases." (In others, there was no relationship of any kind.) They con-

tinue: "In most cases in the GSS/NORC dataset, the aggregate associations are reduced to trivial proportions."

All of the above statements hold for *both*: the (seven) items taken from the NORC dataset by Gerbner et al. and reanalyzed in the article, as well as the (eleven) new items included in the same reanalysis. They characterize *each* set of items equally well, and continue to hold up even if all the added items (such as those tapping attitude toward suicide) are excluded from the analysis altogether.[1]

(4) About 90% of the adult population views between 1 and 5 hours per day and falls within one standard deviation of the mean number of hours viewed (2.9). This is a truncated distribution from which to seek variation over a 24-hour day. Examination of respondents whose hours of viewing are furthest from the mean of the distribution found that neither nonviewers' nor extreme viewers' answers to attitude items lent support to the hypothesis that "mean" and "scary" world responses vary linearly or monotonically with amount of television viewing. While they dispute my contention that the responses of nonviewers and extreme viewers are of obvious conceptual significance for testing cultivation theory, the empirical findings are accepted by Gerbner et al., who concede that "'nonviewers' often seem [sic] to be more likely than light viewers to give 'television answers' [and that] it is not unreasonable to question whether they should be lumped together with 'light viewers.'"

At the outset, then, we discover that the Annenberg team has not disputed the empirical findings noted in 1-4 above. At the same time, Gerbner et al. contend that readers should also dismiss these for failing to raise any legitimate doubt as to the empirical value and theoretical basis for their assertions about cultivation effects. Their grounds for avoiding the obvious inferences to be drawn from these findings consist of three claims which are specious and lacking in credibility; first, these findings are based on a reanalysis of only one dataset, while they have analyzed numerous others and come to different conclusions. (The findings are "based on his use of a number of problematic items from virtually one data base, which, for whatever reasons, show incongruous results.") Second, that the *National Opinion Research Center*'s (NORC) General Social Survey is itself unreliable (it contains items which "exhibit some of the weakest associations we have ever found"); that is, the findings are unchallenged but, by implication, this entire dataset should be rejected or heavily discounted because it does not support the "theory." And finally, the reanalysis in Part I—which tests for *overall* effects and positive cultivation differentials—is rendered "irrelevant" for not paying attention to negative signs ("the key to the puzzle"); and also is "obliterated" for not appreciating sufficiently the "empirical evidence leading to the concept of 'mainstreaming.'"

It is clear from their acceptance of the main findings that the Annenberg team must succeed in their effort to discredit the data base from whence they came, in order to (1) avoid conceding the weakness of their "theory," and (2) restore their credibility in reporting results from all the other surveys from which they claim enough empirical support to assert the existence of cultivation effects. Gerbner et al. level a remarkable number of charges at NORC (and myself) in the process—some very serious, others more frivolous. These begin with the simple argument that "all data are flawed in some way" and the suggestion that their accordance of equal weight to surveys which vary widely in size, sampling design, and representativeness is not so much bad science as the "cumulative consistency" which actually makes their reported findings so persuasive, unarguable, and "most compelling." Having thus downplayed the greater reliability inherent in national probability samples, they move on from equating the NORC GSS cumulative N of 4536 (another 1500 questionnaires are now in the field) with convenience samples they have utilized with Ns as low as 116.

The second line of defense is to suggest that the reanalysis took items from NORC's dataset which are unreliable and untrustworthy. Among those with the "weakest associations we have ever found" are two questions concerning fear of walking alone and approval of using physical violence. Neither is at all central to the conclusions reached in my article, but their treatment of each warrants discussion in light of the repeated claim that these NORC data are unreliable. Of particular interest here is that nowhere in previous articles, in which Gerbner et al. marshaled the same nationally acclaimed data base in support of cultivation theory, have they expressed any doubts about its reliability.

NORC's GSS does differ from most of the surveys which the Annenberg team analyzes and derives its findings from, for it has always been available at low cost to any interested researcher. In contrast, it is unclear where one can turn to gain such easy access to reanalyze responses to the proprietary surveys which Gerbner et al. claim contradict the data in the NORC file. The organizations which conducted these surveys are not even identified in their Violence Profile No. 8.[2] After other researchers reported that those NORC data failed to support the claims of the Annenberg team, and contained seemingly relevant items whose correlates went in the "wrong" direction, Gerbner et al. quickly announced that these data are flawed. My selection, for reanalysis purposes, of the *same* "fear" item employed earlier by the Annenberg team is attacked here on the grounds that readers should realize it is misleading. The "actual violence" item which runs so contrary to expectations from the hypothesis of "across-the-board" effects is attacked on the grounds that (a) they never reported it because the item scored poorly on a test for reliability in constructing a scale; and (b) it yielded "counterintuitive" associations with the standard background variables employed in survey research. The latter "failing" constitutes reason to report, rather than suppress the finding; and its realiability in scaling has nothing to do with its value as a single item.[3]

Gerbner et al. owe the research community a far more detailed and substantiated indictment of this data base before they can be taken seriously in their efforts to undercut its reputation for reliability, careful design, and high quality. NORC's GSS is probably the most widely used and widely trusted data base employed by social scientists interested in secondary analysis. It was created by the National Science Foundation for the express purpose of permitting widespread analysis and reanalyses of items considered important by the research community. Far from being "just" one among many surveys, it (along with Michigan's CPS Survey) is the only data base utilized by the Annenberg team to which there is easy access, and which is well-known and available to all, and reanalysis of their claimed findings possible by any interested user. In light of their own documented poor performance in analyzing its contents, the burden falls on the Annenberg team to show that results they report from other, less accessible surveys have followed appropriate statistical models, assumptions, and procedures. Rather than attack NORC, they should make these other surveys available to interested researchers for reanalysis, as the GSS has been.

The third argument in the comment proposed for rejecting the damaging implications of my article is that I neglected to give proper weight or consideration to negative signs and evidence leading to the mainstreaming concept. These passages argue, in effect, that apples should be rejected for not being oranges. The "theory" tested in Part I is the "across-the-board" version of the cultivation argument, which specifies a positive sign for the cultivation differential between heavy and light viewers. When cultivation differentials either exhibit a negative sign, or fail to appear between viewing categories, *both* constitute evidence for the null hypothesis and the formulation of being tested.[4] That the explanation in Table 5 of Part I states this exact point does not mean, of course, that the article is unaware of or disinterested in contingent formulations or tests on specific subgroups. In fact, both possibilities were previewed and addressed in the introduction and conclusion of Part I, though not elaborated in detail until the hypotheses about subgroups and cultivation effects were formalized and more fully discussed in Part II. There, the Annenberg team's more recent "refinements" concerning subgroups, mainstreaming, and resonance are

considered and rejected as speculative, nonpredictive, unspecified, post hoc, and irrefutable. We shall see that it is
only the very last of these conclusions with which their
"Comment" actually takes issue.

SUBGROUPS AND REFORMULATIONS:
CULTIVATION THEORY
AND THE "WORLD OF TELEVISION"

In their comment, Gerbner et al. offer two "refinements"
of cultivation theory, which they state are intended to "deal
with the exceptions" in those (rare?) instances in which the
evidence fails to support their continued assertion that
"cultivation is often a virtually across-the-board phenomenon." Apparently these concepts, "mainstreaming"
and "resonance," need to be invoked only infrequently. In
any event, the Annenberg team suggests that if variations
in viewers' responses to attitude items fail to fit the patterns
called for in one of the "theory's" formulations, it is likely
to be compatible with either of the remaining two. As one
example, they cite viewers' responses to the NORC question
concerning approval of the use of physical violence, notwithstanding their reservations about its possible unreliability. Here, the finding that increased television viewing is
associated with *disapproval* of physical violence is not only
acknowledged as possible, albeit dubious, evidence *against*
the "across-the-board" version of the theory which predicts
the opposite, it also is presented as evidence *for* "mainstreaming"—the newer refinement which embraces findings in which response patterns can contradict those
anticipated by the more "global" formulation yet to be cited
as evidence supporting cultivation theory. This point,
stressed in Part II of my article, is only affirmed once again
in their response.[5]

Gerbner et al. correctly note that I question whether a
"theory" which exhibits such a remarkable facility for

taking as its own confirmation virtually any percentage movements in any direction by survey respondents can be treated seriously as anything more than a tautology. They see nothing peculiar about advancing "the proposition that many, if not most, of the specifications which emerge when overall relationships disappear . . . can be explained by one of these two concepts." After their "decade of theory building," they freely acknowledge that the theory of cultivation cannot anticipate in advance of the data analysis what it expects to find or which version, reformulation, or refinement of the argument will best "explain" whatever surprises or findings emerge from the data. More specifically, the authors provide no information or guidelines concerning the selection of appropriate subgroups, no predictions about whether responses by members of any subgroups to particular items will be consistent or inconsistent, or will vary positively or negatively with amount of television viewed. When explanations are offered for any findings obtained, they are ad hoc or post hoc, except for the recurring insistence that whatever emerged from the data is related somehow to the "cultivation" of respondents' perceptions by the television medium. Indeed, while my article is criticized for failing to distinguish between their own "clearly presented speculations" and "firm conclusions," it seems to me that only Gerbner et al. are able to distinguish between the latter and the former in their own work.

The only exceptions Gerbner et al. actually take to my article's critique of the concepts of "mainstreaming" and "resonance" concern (1) whether such specifications in advance are necessary or desirable, and (2) if conditions exist under which their "theory" could ever be disconfirmed or refuted. Far from being "overstated," as Gerbner et al. characterize the issue of specification, it is precisely this failure to specify the conditions under which mainstreaming and resonance will occur that makes them unacceptable in their present form as explanations for response patterns. Specification is necessary if only to avoid the appearance that these concepts represent little more than selective reporting and, for mainstreaming, the artifact of regression effects. The absence of operational procedures, for determining the point where the "mainstream" resides for the population and for the comparison of subgroups, or for predicting which items and which subgroups should exhibit mainstreaming patterns as opposed to resonance, and vice versa, demonstrates that, at best, these concepts remain at a primitive stage of development. Ideally, as pointed out in the article, the "mainstream" for an item should be defined independently of amount of television viewing. Gerbner et al. thus consistently ignore the distinction between the testing or confirmation of a hypothesis versus its generation.

They also claim to have demonstrated "clearly" that mainstreaming and resonance are indeed falsifiable. Of the six hypothetical graphs offered as examples, however, at least three also could be taken as support for one or another version of the cultivation hypothesis.[6] And, of the eleven possible outcomes, we can identify only three which could not easily be claimed as confirmation for some version of the cultivation hypothesis. Gerbner et al. have thus provided enough formulations ("specifications") of their theory to allow 73% of the patterns located to also provide support for the "theory." As stated in Part II of my article (n. 9), this "puts forth a hypothesis with an unusually high probability of being confirmed by chance." It is difficult to believe that Gerbner et al. are seriously concerned with establishing criteria for the falsification of their concepts when their own text consistently betrays a strategy of groping relentlessly to find ever new post hoc and conditional formulations for any datum that cannot be explained by any existing formulation. Indeed, nothing in their comment persuades one that where no relationship is found they would *not* propose that television's influence was "canceled out" by the interaction of variables with different subsets of the same group.[7]

A third, alternative hypothesis concerning subgroups was offered and tested in my article. This is the one-tailed extrapolation from the Violence Profiles linking the findings of "message system analysis" directly to the cultivation hypothesis. Unlike the "concepts" of mainstreaming and resonance, it formalizes a theoretical position, states predictions in advance of the data analysis, specifies the direction in which responses should "move" in order to confirm or disconfirm the hypothesis, and performs a test on items employed previously by the Annenberg team to see if there is supporting evidence for the relationships which are thus specified:

> If viewers extrapolate estimates of their own life chances from those befalling their demographic counterparts on television, as Gerbner et al. propose, heavy viewers from subgroups whose members are most often victimized or killed should appear more afraid and suspicious than light and medium viewers from the same groups. Conversely, viewers from the subgroups whose members are least often victimized or killed should reflect television's representation of their relative invulnerability; i.e., their levels of fear and suspicion should decline with increased viewing ... *Given* the absence of the claimed relationship across the population, the most logical inferences from the Annenberg team's own content analysis is that (a) heavy viewers among those subgroups protrayed as the most victimized would reflect television's "cultivation effect" by appearing more alienated, anomic, or "scared" than light viewers in the same subgroups; and (b) heavy viewers among those subgroups portrayed as more dominant and less often victimized would also reflect television's "cultivation effect" by becoming *less* alienated, fearful, or "scared"—or else showing no attitude change—when compared to light viewers in their own subgroups. Note that this formulation, derived from the texts of Violence Reports 7-10 (1976-1979), specifies *in advance of the data analysis* both a theory and predictions about (1) *which* groups will be affected differentially, (2) *why* one should expect these patterns to emerge, and (3) *in which direction* the attitudes of heavy viewers in particular subgroups are expected to "move." ... These hypotheses are easily tested, since the Violence Profiles code television characters' attributes in terms of the same standard demographic variables into which survey re-

search sorts respondents. . . . Following the content analysis reported by Gerbner et al., we examined the attitudes of
. . . population subgroups reported to exhibit the highest
frequency or probability of seeing their demographic
counterparts victimized or killed on television. . . . Across 18
items, including those analyzed by Gerbner et al. in the same
dataset, we found no empirical support for these contingent
propositions derived from the Violence Profiles. None of the
"victimized" or "dominant" subgroups exhibited any
consistency in appearing more or less "cultivated" in the
directions which follow from cultivation theory in its original
version [from Part II of Hirsch article].

Gerbner et al. assert that the failure of the audience data
to support this clearly formulated hypothesis casts no doubt
on the logic of cultivation theory. It is described as a "far
from uninteresting contribution," which is tested for the
first time in my article and has been selected by them for
testing as well; but it also is characterized simultaneously
as "probably oversimplistic," and "nowhere to be found in
our theory." It is, however, acknowledged to appear in their
own published "speculations," which is where I said it
derived from in the first place—i.e., the "text" of the
Violence Profiles. The absence of empirical support for this
formulation of the "theory" provides a suggestive (and
speculative) insight about why the Annenberg team
ventured forth with "concepts" which resist formalization,
fail to specify in advance the groups to which they apply,
and fail to predict the direction of responses by the same
subgroups to different items. That is, quite simply, because
when this *is* done, based on the results I reported, one finds
out *there simply are not consistent patterns in any direction
among the critical subgroups to which "mainstreaming"
and "resonance" are presented as most applicable.*[8] Quite
clearly, there is no advantage to be gained for asserting
cultivation effects by making the formulation testable
enough to become theoretically meaningful but also, at the
same time, falsifiable.

THE "WORLD OF TELEVISION"

An even more fundamental issue is whether cultivation analysis actually has any relation at all to the "world of television" portrayed in the "message system analysis" portions of the Violence Profiles. The original version of the cultivation hypothesis, which posited across-the-board monotonic effects, also was based on the premise that any survey item used to test the hypothesis had to have a specifiable "television answer" which could be contrasted with one that more accurately described life in the "real world." The "television answer" was derived from the content analyses of what "messages" heavy viewers have been exposed to, which are reported annually by Gerbner et al. in their Violence Profiles. This version of the hypothesis predicted that heavy viewers are more likely to give the "television answer" than light viewers, i.e., the sign of cultivation differentials should be positive. If, as we are now told, *any* difference in the responses of heavy and light viewers, whether in a positive or negative direction, is attributable to television's "cultivation" of that discrepancy, then (a) it makes no difference how members of particular subgroups are portrayed in the "world of television," since the directionality of a subgroup's response pattern is no longer specified by the knowledge of whether that group is portrayed on the screen as dominant or vulnerable. In other words, it is no longer a problem for the "theory" if a subgroup like black women, who are most likely to be seen as victims on television, exhibit a positive association between viewing and the "television answer" on one item, and a negative association on another. Also, (b) this makes even more problematic efforts to relate their acceptance of response patterns which move in either direction, to the idea of each item having a *single* television answer.

Post hoc speculations about the relative salience of *each* item to members of each subgroup, based on their responses to every item (taken singly or grouped arbitrarily) does not constitute a theory. Rather, it provides an ad hoc hypothesis, applied on a case by case basis, in place of an appropriate explanation. This is why the table presented in the article relating amount of television viewed and respondents' attitude to astrological sign is every bit as plausible (or valueless) as Gerbner et al.'s illustrations of their new "concepts" in Violence Profile No. 11.

Indeed, as the article makes clear in more detail, the "concepts" of mainstreaming and resonance, by attributing any percentage movements (including regression effects) to hours of television viewed, not only continues the practice of imposing abstract formulations about "message systems" on the interpretive mind of the viewer. They also indeed "cut loose" cultivation analysis from the content analysis portion of the Violence Profiles by adding post hoc assertions about the salience of each item for each subgroup, and by refusing to predict how respondents' attitudes will correspond to the "messages" transmitted during all the hours watched by heavy viewers.[9]

The Annenberg team's contention that the content analyses they report were *never intended* as predictive of what heavy viewers believe also is simply belied by their long-standing division of survey items of all kinds into "television" and "nontelevision" answers on the explicit assumption that larger proportions of heavy viewers would provide the latter response. Regardless of who "cut loose" each from the other, the denial that television content and viewer attitudes need be related only weakens further the logic and credibility of the entire enterprise. Without a theoretical link between them, it is a mystery how a theory of cultivation effects can even be logically possible.

CONCLUSION

In their "Comment," Gerbner et al. present a variety of tables to buttress their attack on my article. Several seek to provide evidence for mainstreaming or resonance, missing my point that it is the illogic of these concepts which the article addresses, rather than their capacity to generate mounds of printout whose relations are uninterpretable, explain practically no variance, and are subject to regression effects. Two other tables provide "tests" for linearity in order to demonstrate that for uncontrolled bivariate relationships there are patterns in the NORC dataset which show a linear trend from the lowest to the highest viewing categories. This pattern, however, which disappears when multiple controls are placed on these items, has no bearing on the conclusions reported in my article.[10]

A second methodological issue is the objection by Gerbner et al. to the inclusion of new batteries of items in Part I's reanalysis of NORC/GSS data. As noted earlier, their removal does not affect any of the major findings reported. In Part I of the article, I provided the wording of each of these items, the basis on which "television answers" were constructed, and a rationale for including them.[11]

The Annenberg team's contention that some of the items added have nothing to do with the content of television raises a larger, more interesting issue: Do the items we *both* used, and those to which they did *not* object, have anything to do with television either? While the procedure of devising "television answers" is supposedly tied to a comparison of knowledge about the relative frequencies of events in the world with their portrayal on television, there is nothing reported in their message system (content) analysis which provides a basis for designating any of the following responses as "television answers":

—"The lot of the average man is getting worse, not better."

—"It's hardly fair to bring a child into the world with the way things look for the future."

—"Most public officials are not really interested in the problems of the average man."

Indeed, little guidance is available from the variables reported in their message system analysis and overall presentation which allow for any unambiguous selection of items and "television answers" from surveys to conform to the criteria that these tie up directly to their own content analyses. As it appears throughout their formulations in general, there is a minimum of formalization, and difficulties arise for any effort seeking to follow and operationalize their own descriptions.[12]

Finally, of the three remaining questions posed about my use or abuse of appropriate methods (and criteria for evaluating their use by others), the answer to one is apparent in the tables and text of the article; a second should also be obvious to Gerbner et al., and the third is a matter of judgment.[13]

All this leads me to restate several conclusions drawn here and in my article. The first emphasizes that the theory of cultivation effects is an interesting speculation, but lacks supporting evidence to allow one to argue it is any more than that. The "theory" fails to predict in advance how television will affect audiences, claims that it has explanatory value for interpreting virtually all differences found in the attitudes of heavy versus light viewers, regardless of their direction and notwithstanding the reduction of television's contribution as an independent variable to "trivial proportions" when it is entered at the same time as other statistical controls. Second, the Annenberg team's "Comment" accepts most of the substantive findings in my reanalysis of their own work, but tries to avoid their serious implications by attacking the NORC dataset from which the items and responses were taken. This is an understandable effort to maintain credibility under duress, but it is also insulting to the national research community of social scientists who supervise the construction and administration of this prestigious annual survey, and to its many users. Significantly, if one discounts Gerbner et al.'s argument that the cumulative years of the GSS constitute merely one data base among many, and that it is less worthy than the nonpublic and unreanalyzed surveys they claim show "stronger" results, then their defense of the theory's across-the-board version—especially when based on evidence from their *own* questionable analyses—collapses.[14] Prior to the reanalyses of GSS data by Hughes and myself, empirical questions about the Annenberg team's "findings" came only when others encountered difficulty in replicating them on different samples. To find that they fail to replicate on reanalysis of the very same data from which they were reported originally poses more serious problems of confidence for Gerbner et al.'s presentation of cultivation "findings."[15]

Third, beyond questions of whether this or that item is appropriate for testing the "theory" lie two far more serious questions: Does the corpus of the Annenberg team's publication actually contain a clear, operationalizable, testable, formal theory which meaningfully explains or predicts statistical associations found in data, and which is subject to disconfirmation? If, as I propose, it does not, then many of the problems addressed in the Annenberg team's response deserve less careful attention than they have been accorded here and by communication researchers in general. A related question is whether it makes much sense at all to base our tests of television's "effects" on locating correlates of a single survey item on number of hours viewed. The assumptions that it is of no consequence which programs are seen, that they all transmit the same world view, that viewers interpret stories solely in terms of the characters' gross demographic characteristics, that single incidents are seen by viewers separate from the narrative, context, and genre in which they occur, that viewers do not distinguish what is fantasy from reality in popular entertainment, and that it is not the lifestyles and prior attitudes of individuals which account for the amount of television they view (rather than the opposite) are all untested assumptions built into the framework and rhetoric of the Annenberg team's Violence Profiles as well as the research strategies of others in this field (see Hirsch with Robinson; 1980). Research into the validity of these assumptions, and the conditions under which each may operate, is needed as much as or more than continued iterations of atheoretical efforts to locate (weak) statistical associations with hours viewed.

My article also commended the Annenberg team for its pioneer efforts to empirically investigate linkages between the content of television and its relation to viewers' perceptions and attitudes, and for assembling a vast archive of content analyses within the limited framework of its assumptions about which aspects of content should make a difference. My criticism of their work is directed not at these shared goals, but at the methodological errors and unwarranted claims about theories and findings which characterize their effort to implement and reach these common objectives.

NOTES

1. The Annenberg team has objected to items on suicide because they bear no relation to the "world of television." While this is arguable, simply on the grounds that they bear no less relation than items which they did choose (e.g., "It's hardly fair to bring a child into the world with the way things look for the future"), the important point here is that when *all* of the items which they did not take from the NORC file are excluded from the analysis, the negative findings remain. When multiple controls were placed on just the items they used, the article showed there is no stronger relationship with amount of television viewing; the amount of variance explained is no higher; and the absence of linearity remains the same. For the seven items they reported, the responses of nonviewers and extreme viewers ran counter to the direction predicted by the hypothesis in 9 of the 14 tables (64%) described in my article, while for the 11 added items, the number of tables running counter to the direction predicted by the hypothesis is 15 out of 22 (68%).

2. Gerbner et al. begin their critique by asserting that I failed to note their reliance on national probability samples other than those of NORC and the Michigan Survey Research Center. They imply that this "omission" was deliberate and exemplifies my "misrepresentation" of their procedures. A rereading of

Violence Profiles 7-10, to which Part I of my reanalysis is directed, confirms that prior to Summer 1980 no other national surveys are cited or named by the Annenberg team. Further, only in Violence Profile No. 8 does the possible utilization of alternative national surveys arise. This possibility, however, is contained only in an obscure reference (pp. 177-178) to a "quota sample" and to one "national probability sample." I mention these datasets in note 5 of Part I (p. 452) but was not able to identify their sources because they were not given. This manner of citation is hardly conducive to making information accessible to researchers wishing to reanalyze their reported results. To read that I failed to take into account their use of Harris, Starch, and ORC data is news to me, for only the Opinion Research Corporation's Survey has ever been cited by name in the Violence Profiles, and that only appears in No. 11 (1980).

3. Even if an item's reliability were questionable, the appearance of theoretically meaningful items on a dataset from which other questions are analyzed and reported naturally leads one to suspect the worst (i.e., selective reporting) when no mention is made of findings which contradict the argument made for a theory. In addition to the item on approval of "actual violence," the NORC/GSS codebook contains additional questions about crime and ownership of firearms whose response patterns run counter to predictions from the cultivation hypothesis (Hughes, 1980), are also unreported by Gerbner et al., and whose reliability they have not questioned.

4. To assert that Part I's test of the "across-the-board" variant of the hypothesis is rendered "irrelevant" by a more recent formulation which instead argues for subgroup effects (while still claiming support for the more global version) has no bearing on whether or not the first formulation is supported by data rather than mere assertion. Conceptually, because the first formulation predicts positive cultivation differentials, the one-tailed test is appropriate. The introduction of "refinements" which fail to predict directionality require that the criteria for empirical support be relaxed and that two-tailed tests be administered. These two formulations are analytically distinct and require separate tests and treatments, as provided in my article. In criticizing the first for not being the second, Gerbner et al. confound and obscure elementary canons of hypothesis testing and research design.

5. Throughout Part II of the article, the use of the term "cultivation analysis" by Gerbner et al. to embrace, take credit for, and account for contradictory patterns in the data is both highlighted and criticized. One example provided, which also speaks to the way in which Gerbner et al. used the "physical violence" item in their comment, appears early in Part II's comparison of subgroups. When the responses of black men and black women reversed from one item to the next, we interpreted this as evidence for no pattern, but continued by noting: "Gerbner et al.'s contradictory formulations 2 and 3 ('mainstreaming' and 'resonance') assemble and interpret very similar statistics as support for the cultivation hypothesis; i.e., regardless of whether the cultivation differentials are larger or smaller. This will be discussed further in the following section."

Along these same lines, it is relevant to note the Annenberg team's utilization of Morris Rosenberg's (1968) standard text. Their invocation of his injunction that "survey analysis involves the hot pursuit of an idea down paths and byways which have little to do with one's original hypothesis"; and "a reluctance to follow the lead of the findings may stultify and abort a good deal of promising research" is curious in light of my article's findings and critique. Indeed, I could not agree more with Rosenberg's observations. If high-quality social research entails going where the data take us, then we must be prepared to *relinquish* hypotheses and formulations which fail to find confirmation. This is clearly the case for the "across-the-board" version of the cultivation hypothesis. However, Gerbner et al. continue to cling to it tenaciously, even as they offer "refinements" which contradict it. Their reluctance to drop this discredited formulation, or to finally specify the conditions under which it obtains, violates Rosenberg's wise counsel more than it follows it.

6. Graph f is clearly an example of an across-the-board effect, thus conforming to the original formulation of the cultivation hypothesis and having no need for the introduction of either mainstreaming or resonance. Graph i meets the conditions for "mainstreaming," since the distance which separates heavy viewers is less than that between light viewers. Graph j is interpretable as a case of resonance, since one of the subgroups which starts out high on the dependent variable gives the television answer with increased frequency as its consumption of television increases. For graphs of this sort, taking only two subgroups, each of which can either increase, decrease, or remain the same across viewing categories, a total of nine discrete patterns can be generated, plus two additional cases where they would cross.

7. Taking two examples from their comment alone, we offer the following illustrations: (1) "further examination of differences within [a] group—controlling for additional variables—might reveal a theoretically intelligible pattern underlying the apparent lack of relationship with television viewing . . . the implementation of additional controls might uncover their presence in distinct subsets of the groups. . . . This kind of elaboration is a fundamental task of scientific analysis—to delve ever more deeply into phenomena, to examine layers of association, with an ever sharper focus." (2) "But an overall, aggregate relationship is simply the product of subrelationships which may pull at each other in different directions and with varying intensity."

The problem these statements suggest is that in light of their past performance, the Annenberg team is simply too committed to finding television effects to stop "delving" and further dividing up subgroups long enough to consider their hypothesis disconfirmed.

8. While Gerbner et al. credit my article for presenting the first test of this proposition, they nevertheless challenge the validity of its test "because of the small number of groups examined and the comparison of inappropriately matched groups." Although the Annenberg team's content analysis could perhaps generate additional subgroups for which this formulation could be tested, race, sex, and age are clearly three of the principal axes of differential victimization in the "world of television." Failure to find response patterns which correspond to those on television for racial and sexual subgroups is severely damaging to the hypothesis, even if the test is not exhaustive.

The second objection, that we examined "inappropriately matched groups," is also of dubious merit. Gerbner et al. charge, for example, that we "equate" nonwhite characters with black respondents, thus clouding the value of the test provided. But, as they are well aware, the percentage of nonwhites other than blacks in the NORC dataset (and in other probability samples) is less than 1%, not enough to make a difference in any multivariate analysis. Relatedly, we note that to confine our test to black respondents is not to "equate" them with all nonwhite characters on television. If the violence profiles indicate, as Gerbner et al. say, that to be "other than clearly white" makes one more vulnerable, then blacks (who *are* other than clearly white) should exhibit the expected response patterns when compared to whites in any event, but they did not.

9. Gerbner et al.'s assertion that I *"imply"* viewers be "conscious" of how television's role in allegedly "cultivating" misperceptions about the "real world" is unfounded and does not follow from the text (or notes) in the article.

10. Gerbner et al. readily concede that as soon as multiple controls are placed on the relation of television viewing to attitude items, the linear "pattern" found in the less appropriate, uncontrolled bivariate context is reduced to "trivial proportions." The 22 tests they report in Table 1 of the comment bear no relation to this central point for, once again, their tests are for zero-order relationships, prior to any application of even a single control. No information or citation explaining the source of either test is provided, but based on the table alone, the following points are relevant: The logic of any such test weights the proportions observed by the number of cases in each cell. Here, over 90% of the sample falls in the three middle categories; hence, because light, medium, and heavy viewers' responses to the attitude items follow a pattern of upward movement before mutiple controls are introduced, the results for the entire distribution are indeed "significantly linear."

The Annenberg team's use of this "finding" is misleading on several counts. It is *precisely the problem raised in my article*, which noted that the marked deviation of responses by nonviewers and extreme viewers is masked and obscured when they are collapsed with those of viewers in other categories (light and heavy, respectively), whose cell sizes are much larger. What is most damaging to the cultivation hypothesis conceptually—e.g., that nonviewers provide the "television answer" in larger proportions than light viewers and others—is the very issue which the Annenberg team uses these "tests" to avoid. Both tests, driven by sample size, serve to restate the obvious point that the viewing distribution is highly concentrated, with most adults reporting 1-5 hours per day. If any ambiguity surrounds the meaning of my suggestion early in Part I, that the formulation of the hypothesis as linear is challenged when respondents at both tails of the distribution fail to provide answers in the expected direction, it should be obvious from all of the text which follows that the assertion of linearity is undercut totally—for the entire distribution—as soon as multiple controls are placed on the zero-order relationships.

11. To be sure, I also questioned the theoretical logic of this whole procedure as the right way to go about linking television content to audience impact and interpretation: "There is, of course, some question about whether examining a single survey item and its correlates is adequate to this task. . . . However, accepting this presumption for the sake of argument, this article presents a reanalysis of a significant body of data on which much in the cultivation analysis reports are based."

The article noted that of all the items selected for analysis by the Annenberg team, only the question about fear of going outdoors enabled a comparison of the likelihood of victimization in the "real world," by subgroup, with the television portrayal of each subgroup's probability of being victimized. We explicitly excluded the following two items, on the grounds that "Gerbner et al.'s basis for deriving a 'television answer' for them is too obscure for us to feel comfortable in adopting it." (p. 454):

—"Do you expect the United States to fight in another war within the next ten years?"

—"Do you think it will be best for the future of this country if we take an active part in world affairs, or if we stay out of world affairs?"

The responses taken as "television answers" for items unreported by the Annenberg team were chosen on the basis of my own inferences from the text of their Violence Profiles. Except for contending that suicide items bear no relation to the "world of television," they do not take issue with these decisions on the appropriate "television answers" for the seven additional items taken from the NORC/GSS file.

12. The procedure of devising "television answers" is supposedly tied to the results of message system analysis, as in the use of questions about crime rates and the percentage of the workforce employed in law enforcement by Gerbner et al. in Violence Profile No. 8. With the questions on law enforcement officers and crime rates, the prevalence of a given phenomenon in the real world may be compared with the frequency of its appearance on television because there are operational procedures for determining both (i.e., statistical measurement). From the discrepancy between the prevalence of an event in the real world and its frequency of appearance on television, it is possible to determine which of an item's response categories is closest to the "television answer." This is only possible, however, when a phenomenon's rate of occurrence in *both* the real world and the world of television may be determined. (For example, content analysis reveals the percentage of television characters employed in law enforcement, while official statistics supply this percentage for the real world.) The researcher's inability to make *either* of these determinations for a given survey item means that that item cannot be said to have a television answer and should therefore be disqualified from use in cultivation analysis. This indeterminacy is clearly present in the anomia items above and, in our judgment, is also evident in the "mean world" items used by Gerbner et al. *and* us. Our acceptance of these items has been for argument's sake, since we continue to find their use for this purpose puzzling, at best.

In the reanalysis, my rationale for examining items tapping respondents' attitude toward suicide was included in the following summary: "Whereas a fair inference from the Violence Profiles is that television viewing 'cultivates' doubts about life's sanctity . . . we find that both television nonviewers and extreme viewers are *least likely* to see any of these circumstances as justifying the taking of one's own life" (pp. 425-426, italics in original).

In the absence of any more logical explanation for their inclusion of items which have no clearer bearing on the "world of television" than the suicide battery, it is difficult to see why Gerbner et al. so peremptorily dismiss my use of these items in their comment. Since the percentage of the total sample responding "yes" to items like "Public officials are not really interested in the problems of the average man" is as high as 62%, there is a stronger basis for asking whether perhaps *all* these items warrant exclusion than for seeking to determine only which of them is *most* inappropriate.

13. The criticism that the years and Ns for items used are unclear from my presentation is unwarranted. The article states clearly that all questions come from the surveys of 1975, 1977, and 1978 (the three years for which the item on viewing habits is available). The N provided in each table makes it easy to determine whether an item is from one, two, or three years, and I note each of the years for which every item is available when they are introduced in the text (even if each corresponding table does not restate this).

Equally uncalled for is the complaint about no explicit statement about whether the variables in the Multiple Classification Analysis (MCA) were entered as factors or covariates. Since the MCA tables provide breakdowns for all the independent variables used, it is clear that they were entered as factors, since covariates are continuous variables for which MCA yields no such discrete breakdowns. Since this is explained in all writeups of the program, and since Gerbner et al. report they have used it themselves, it seems odd that they failed to understand this.

The issue of whether it is advisable to dichotomize television viewing by breaking the sample at the median, as Gerbner et al. began doing in 1979's Violence Profile (No. 10), is a matter of judgment. In my view, this practice has two principal drawbacks which recommend against it: (1) It eliminates the category of medium viewers and makes it far more likely that any curvilinearity they represent or contribute will escape detection; and (2) it leads to a loss of comparability across samples since the categories of light and heavy viewing will be defined differently for each one.

Finally, Gerbner et al. and I agree that their statement—that each new violence profile takes precedence over those of previous years and renders the earliest reports inoperative—is also open to interpretation. I have taken it to mean, among other things, that the data analysis procedures used in the more recent profiles are considered by the Annenberg team to be improvements over those utilized in the earlier profiles, and that they view their current practice of dichotomizing television viewing as an improvement over earlier, more differentiated codings.

14. Part II of my article presented three alternative formulations to interpret findings from the GSS data. First, that heavy viewing is simply a function of more free time and availability. The demographic characteristics of heavy and extreme viewers, for example, show a disproportionate percentage of housewives and unemployed and retired people. If viewing and alienation are (weakly) associated, it could also be that heavy viewers watch more because they are alienated to begin with, rather than that television viewing makes them that way. Second, that the concept of status inconsistency offers a plausible explanation for some of the more interesting findings. It would account for higher mean scores on anomia, for example, among highly educated viewers who watch a great deal of television. Finally, since only weak relationships, where there are any, emerge from the data, the possibility that they are caused by random variation cannot be excluded or discounted. Gerbner et al. address none of these alternative formulations in their comment.

15. I am not saying here that the same findings did not appear when identical tests were conducted following the same procedures; rather, the analysis strategies were inappropriate. The former charge would be more serious, but is clearly unwarranted.

REFERENCES

HIRSCH, P. with J. ROBINSON (1980) "A research agenda for approaching the study of television." Commissioned for the Aspen Institute Conference on Proposals for a Center for the Study of Television, October. (unpublished)

HUGHES, M. (1980) "The fruits of cultivation analysis: a reexamination of some effects of television watching." Public Opinion Q. 44 (Fall): 287-302.

ROSENBERG, M. (1968) The Logic of Survey Analysis. New York: Basic Books.

In what they consider their last word in the debate, the University of Pennsylvania group focuses on questions Paul Hirsch raised in the preceding chapter.

39

FINAL REPLY TO HIRSCH

George Gerbner, Larry Gross,
Michael Morgan, and Nancy Signorielli

Hirsch's "Rejoinder" (in the January 1981 issue of this journal)—as well as his interpretation of our previous "comment" (in the same issue)—contains an impressive number of inaccuracies, errors, and convolutions of our statements and findings. His illusions about our "concessions" are particularly puzzling. He raises very few new points and seems oblivious to numerous issues we presented, choosing instead to rehash his "findings" and "conclusions" and ignoring contrary explanations and evidence.

If we do not respond here to some of his trivial points, it is not because, as he presumes, we "concede" them; rather, it is in order to prevent this discussion from bogging down in irrelevant minutiae. We will focus on the few new concerns he does present and areas which represent a markedly stepped-up attack.

ON OUR "REJECTION" OF THE GENERAL SOCIAL SURVEYS

One of the most troubling aspects of Hirsch's "rejoinder" is his imputation that we have "dismissed" the NORC

From George Gerbner, Larry Gross, Michael Morgan, and Nancy Signorielli, "Final Reply to Hirsch," *Communication Research* 8, 3, pp. 259-280. Copyright © 1981 by Sage Publications, Inc.

General Social Surveys. According to Hirsch, we have suggested that the GSS "is itself unreliable" and "is less worthy than the non-public and unreanalyzed surveys [we] claim show 'stronger' results."[1] Our so-called "attack" on the GSS has entailed "a remarkable number of charges," which imply that we believe "this entire dataset should be rejected." After Hirsch reported his "reanalysis," we "quickly announced that these data are flawed." Finally, Hirsch says that our "understandable effort to maintain credibility under duress" is "insulting to the national research community of social scientists."

Hirsch has concocted a scenario without foundation in fact. In case we have inadvertently led anyone besides Hirsch to this interpretation, let us make it clear that we acknowledge and appreciate the value and quality of the General Social Surveys. While they have not, as Hirsch claims, been the backbone of our research, we have used and are continuing to use many items from this dataset. Invoking such accolades as "nationally acclaimed" and "prestigious," Hirsch charges us with blasphemy.

The basis for his allegations is that we expressed reservations about the reliability and/or validity of *two items;* one deals with "fear," and the other with "approval of violence," and they will be discussed below. For now, let us repeat categorically that our caution about two questions should not be construed as evidence that we believe the entire dataset is flawed in some fundamental way. Only by the wildest stretch of the imagination, or by deliberate distortion, can it be said that we have "rejected" the GSS/NORC data. The fact that these controversies sparked our reassessment of the quality of these particular measures provides no grounds for complaining that we had not expressed these doubts sooner. Despite Hirsch's puzzling proclamation that greater sample size necessitates greater reliability, we do not believe that the reliability and validity of each and every item can be taken for granted. This hardly stands as a total "rejection" of GSS/NORC.

ON OUR "COVER-UP" OF DAMAGING RESULTS

The two items ("fear" and "approval of violence") about which we voiced reservations loom large in Hirsch's "re-analysis," notwithstanding the disclaimer that "neither is at all central to the conclusions reached in my article." We had reported (Gerbner et al., 1978) that when two samples of junior high school students were asked, "How often is it all right to hit someone if you are mad at them for a good reason?"[2], a significantly higher proportion of heavy than of light viewers answered, "almost always." Both adolescent and adult heavy viewers also were more likely to report being afraid to walk alone at night.[3]

Yet, Hirsch claimed to find no evidence to support our conclusions when he analyzed GSS/NORC data for adults. The GSS/NORC question asked adults, "Are there any situations that you can imagine in which you would approve of a man punching an adult male stranger?" Hirsch's results regarding this "approval of violence" item—which show adult heavy viewers *less* likely to condone the use of violence—are said to be "especially damaging to the cultivation hypothesis." In "one of the very few relationships whose statistical significance remains after the imposition of multiple controls," the sign of the association "runs directly counter" to what he claims cultivation theory would predict. Hirsch also charges us with selective reporting of this item, and with presenting only those data which are consistent with our viewpoint.

These charges, and the data regarding the relationship between television viewing and "approval of violence," deserve detailed discussion; in the process, we will address many of his other points. Strictly speaking, there is nothing in our message system analysis which implies *anything* about whether or not violence is "approved of" in the television world. We asked adolescents, "How often is it all right to hit someone if you are mad at them for a good reason?" ("almost always" or "almost never"), largely because of the commonly-voiced fear that television desensitizes young people to violence, making them more willing to use it. As we have noted, there is evidence that, for adolescents, heavy viewing tends to go with a greater likelihood of saying "it is almost always all right."

There are two critical questions here. First, why are the findings different for adults and adolescents? Second, why did we not report the results for adults from GSS/NORC?

We believe that the apparent discrepancy between the results for adolescents and those for adults do not cast doubt on our theory for two major reasons:

(1) There is substantial evidence to indicate that the GSS/NORC question asked of adults is unreliable;

(2) Regardless of whether or not the GSS/NORC question is indeed reliable, it is simply not comparable to the question we asked of adolescents.

As we noted in our previous comment, the series of questions measuring approval of violence (we have no idea why Hirsch analyzed only the lead-in question) produces a less-than-marginal estimate of reliability. Hirsch argues that an "item's reliability in scaling has nothing to do with its value as a single item." While that may be generally true, it hardly seems likely in this case. Reliability (in the sense of internal homogeneity), "accuracy" of individual responses, and random or systematic procedural biases (coding or punching errors, and so forth) are all quite different things, and Hirsch has muddled them. We feel there is reasonable doubt about the item's value as a measure of a clear and unambiguous dimension. Again, this is decidedly *not* a suggestion that we believe that lack of quality control, "cheating," or similar errors mar the General Social Surveys.

In any case, the argument that the GSS/NORC question is problematic becomes even more compelling when the lead-in question is examined in light of the follow-ups (not mentioned by Hirsch), which provide five specific situations in which the respondent might or might not "approve of a man punching an adult male stranger." We find it notable that the vast majority of all adult respondents who said "no" to the lead-in (i.e., they were unable to *imagine* a situation) answered "yes" to at least one of the follow-ups: for 1978 and 1980 combined, 985 people said "no" to the lead-in; 842, or 85.5% of the 985, subsequently cited at least one situation in which they would approve of a man punching an adult male stranger.[4] Interestingly, heavy viewers are more likely to show this discrepancy, by a difference of ten percentage points (gamma = .13, p < .0001). Thus, being unable to imagine a situation spontaneously is quite different from approving the use of violence in specific situations—especially for adult heavy viewers.

Furthermore, it seems quite likely to us that the question asked of adults taps a rather different dimension than the one we asked of young people.[5] The adolescent question asks *how often is it all right* (a value judgment about frequency of approval, not a yes/no dichotomy) to hit someone *if you are mad at them for a good reason* (providing a justification for the act, dealing with the respondents' own projected behavior, establishing some level of interpersonal familiarity between assailant and victim). The GSS/NORC question asks *are there any situations that you can imagine* (more abstract and partially dependent upon the respondent's ability to imagine) in which you would approve of *a man punching an adult male stranger* (the assailant is someone besides the respondent, and the victim is unknown to the victimizer).

We also noted in our previous comment that the GSS/NORC item shows counterintuitive relationships with background variables, with higher SES respondents more likely to be able to "imagine a situation." Hirsch rejects this reasoning, simply attempting to dismiss our contention by relegating "counterintuitive" to quotation marks, and claiming that the unexpected relationship represents "reason to report, rather than suppress the finding." This might be true if our central research interest were to determine what factors have an impact on respondents' ability to "imagine a situation." But since we are concerned with understanding the contributions of *television* to theoretically meaningful dimensions of attitudes and behaviors, such a finding is irrelevant, at best.

Finally, *our* adolescent item and various indices of "approval of violence" used by Dominick and Greenberg (1972), McLeod, et al. (1972), and McIntyre and Teevan (1972) *all* show *negative* associations with SES, while the GSS/NORC item, again, is positively associated with social class variables. Even if there were *no doubts* as to the GSS/NORC items' reliability (and there are many), this validation discrepancy suggests that different dimensions are being tapped by the respective items.

If one were either to defend the GSS/NORC item's reliability, or to argue that the adolescent and adult questions are conceptually comparable, there remain several other possible explanations for why adolescents and adults show different results. These include: (1) the question we asked of adolescents is bad; (2) our adolescent samples are bad; (3) what is true for adolescents may not be true for adults; and (4) cultivation theory is wrong. As we shall see, none of these seems to be a strong possibility.

(1) *Problems with the Adolescent Question.* This seems quite unlikely, particularly since our findings were similar to those of a number of earlier studies. Dominick and Greenberg (1972) found consistent relationships between exposure to television violence and willingness to use violence, perceived effectiveness of violence, and (for girls) suggesting violence as a solution to conflict. For boys, they also found that exposure interacts with social class and family attitudes in terms of approval of aggression. While they used more questions, our results parallel theirs.

In addition, McLeod et al. (1972) found modest positive correlations between approval of aggression and both overall viewing time and violent viewing. Particularly strong associations were found between approval of aggression and self-reported amount of violence viewed three or four

years earlier. They (1972: 265) note that "aggressive attitudes are rather closely related to both self-reported and
peer-reported aggressive behavior, and they are associated
with various viewing and family variables in a manner
similar to the measures of aggression."

Finally, McIntyre and Teevan (1972) even found that
adolescents whose favorite programs (both the single favorite and particularly the average of the four most favorite)
were more violent were more likely to approve the use of
violence. This pattern was not altered by controls for perceived realism of television violence, social class, age, and
"insulating factors" which represent strength of ties to the
social structure (e.g., aspirations, school grades, integration
into school activities, and relationships with parents and
peers). While none of these studies used precisely the same
question wording as we did, they tend to be much closer to
our than to the GSS/NORC question (except for McIntyre
and Teevan's question about adult violence, discussed
below).

(2) *Problems with the Adolescent Sample.* Hirsch chooses
to discount any findings derived from so-called "convenience" samples. We feel this is unwarranted, if only for the
paucity of national probability samples of children and
adolescents in social science research. Our panel of New
Jersey adolescents is probably one of the best of its kind,
combining six questionnaires over three years, in-depth
personal interviews, and parents' questionnaires. Hirsch
ignores our longitudinal findings completely, presumably
because they are not drawn from a national sample. In that
case, he might as well reject much research in social or
experimental psychology, and even sociology. To say that
we "equate" GSS/NORC with a "proprietary" sample of
116 New Yorkers is silly, and a facetious distortion of our
statement that our conclusions are based on consistent
patterns observed across a range of samples, while his
come from one.[6] That is not to attribute "equal weight" to
each, but to call for appropriate caution and restraint when

a large number of other samples (national probability, quota, and schoolchildren) show contrary results.

Finally, in this case, a number of different studies, which used samples of children and adolescents of different sizes and from different geographic areas, produced essentially similar results. This clearly provides added support for our samples and findings.[7]

It is also worth noting that Dominick and Greenberg (1972) found numerous interactions between violence exposure and social class in terms of willingness to use violence, approval of aggression, perceived effectiveness of violence, and so on. This takes an added import in light of the negative relationship between SES and the dependent measures: exposure to television violence is a much more predictive measure of attitudes among middle-class children than it is among lower-class children. There is less relationship with viewing for lower-class children—who have higher approval levels, regardless of viewing. This certainly fits our "mainstreaming" perspective—the association is enhanced for those otherwise less likely to share what is arguably the television perspective.

(3) *Adults and Children are Different.* It is possible that the divergence in results stems neither from problems with the adolescent sample (as Hirsch argues) nor from problems with the GSS/NORC question (which we believe we have convincingly demonstrated), but that *both* relationships are valid. One could argue that children learn that violence is an appropriate or (at least) common means of resolving conflicts or achieving goals, while adults learn that "crime does not pay," and transgressions are punished. Certainly, social class has differential implications for these attitudes for different age groups, so television could as well. Yet, given the manifest differences in demographic correlates of response patterns between the two, the likelihood of reliability problems with the GSS/NORC question, and the lack of conceptual comparability, this proposition cannot be tested.[8] It could well be that what holds for children need not hold for adults, but we do not think that this is the primary explanation for the differences.

(4) *Cultivation Theory is Wrong.* It might seem, a priori, that there is a simple reason why the opposite, "damaging" association holds in the GSS/NORC data: that the theory, which predicts that heavy viewers should be more likely to condone the use of violence, is faulty. Clearly, that is Hirsch's conclusion. He goes even further and suggests that this "damaging" negative association with television is one of the very few in GSS/NORC which persists under multiple controls.

Yet, our own reanalysis of this item over three years of the GSS (1975, 1978, and 1980; the only years where it co-occurs with the television viewing question) provides no evidence whatsoever to support his argument that heavy viewers are *less* likely to "approve of violence" under multiple controls. Controlling for sex, age, education, race, and income, the fourth-order partial correlations for each year are .02, .04, and .02, respectively (all obviously n.s.).

If, as Loftin and Lizotte (1974) suggest, "privileged groups" were more likely to respond affirmatively to the "imagine a situation" GSS/NORC question in 1973, it is not surprising that it *looks* as if heavy viewers (who tend to be of lower SES) do not. Thus, it is also not surprising that this relationship turns out to be spurious, contrary to Hirsch's superficial analysis.[9]

Thus, quite apart from the questionable characteristics of the GSS/NORC question, and the results of Dominick and Greenberg (1972) and McIntyre and Teevan (1972)—not to mention the number of other items, across many datasets, including other questions from GSS/NORC, which support cultivation—we reject his conclusion.

All this having been said about why the GSS/NORC results differ from those obtained from other samples, the question remains why we never reported these "damaging" results. The "offending" publication is Violence Profile No. 9 (Gerbner et al., 1978). While Hirsch dismisses our claims of unreliability (and turns them into a wholesale rejection of the General Social Survey) and rejects its "counterintuitive" association with background variables, he disregards the fact that (as stated in our previous comment) the 1978

GSS/NORC data were *not yet available* when we released Violence Profile No. 9. In all frankness, internal disagreement about the validity and meaning of the item led us not to report the data for 1975. The so-called "suppression" derived from conflicting viewpoints over what the item actually measured, given its clear conceptual divergence from the question asked of adolescents.

In sum, the GSS/NORC item about "approval of violence" is by no means "especially damaging" to our position. We have discussed this item extensively because it demonstrates that many of Hirsch's charges—his accusation that we "reject" the GSS, his condemnation of our other samples, our "suppression" of the results, and so forth—are tendentious and misleading and that his "reanalysis" is severely flawed.

RELATIONSHIP BETWEEN MESSAGE AND CULTIVATION ANALYSIS

Another area of confusion throughout Hirsch's discussions is the relationship between our message system and cultivation analysis. Specifically, Hirsch has charged that cultivation analysis has no manifest connection with message analysis.

A basic premise for our research is that cultivation analysis begins with the patterns found in the "world" of television drama—a world that presents coherent images of life and society. The basic question we are concerned with is how these images are reflected in viewers' assumptions and values.

We do not expect (nor have ever expected) heavy viewers to exhibit a one to one correspondence between what they see on television and what they believe or do. The television world is a fictional world in which details are selected with care and for a purpose. Its people do not live or die but are created or destroyed to tell a story. Television drama presents stories about how things work, how people behave, what is means to be a man, a woman, a child, an older person, a cop, "bad," "good," and so on. Television also conveys information about risks and power as well as information about the range of opportunities and activities that are available and acceptable for its characters. Most of what television tells us about life and people cannot be translated into discrete facts but can be construed to present potential lessons about life and society. Thus, we need not expect that viewers will specifically identify with characters who are "most like themselves" demographically.

The design is further complicated when we conduct secondary analysis of existing survey data, using questions that were specially designed to answer some *other* primary research objective. These analyses include all of our work with the GSS/NORC, the CPS election survey, and the NCOA "Myth and Reality of Aging" survey. In these cases we had no control over question design and often stretched existing response questions and response categories to meet our framework. As we noted above, the problems with the GSS/NORC questions asking respondents to "imagine a situation in which you would approve . . ." are a good example of the difficulties that one must expect in secondary analysis. Thus, a considerable portion of our research has used less than optimal questions (and response categories) for testing our ideas and/or expectations. In some cases we probably have been overly cautious in not using certain questions, while in some other cases, we probably have not been cautious enough.

Over the years we have had many graduate students and collaborators working on this project. We have tried to accommodate their interests while, at the same time, maintaining a common thread throughout the research. It is out of this variety of interests that the inclusion of the "isolationism" and "expectations for a world war" questions emerged. These items were originally included because they seemed, to some of our collaborators, to add another dimension to understanding alienation and because we saw some correspondence in message system findings (specifically, the extreme U.S. nationalism of the television world).

MAINSTREAMING AND RESONANCE

Apparently, we have not convinced Hirsch that "mainstreaming" and "resonance" are valid theoretical formulations, supported by empirical evidence and conceptual justification. Yet he does acknowledge (and in doing so contradicts himself) in Part II, that *his* "examination of the NORC data suggests that much of the 'effects' found at both ends of the viewing spectrum" hold up for "high-status, high-income, and high-education individuals who view television heavily." This sounds like "mainstreaming" to us.

We have been engaged in a long-term, ongoing, and flexible effort to develop a coherent, data-based theory of television's impact on society. There has been no similar sustained and broad-based effort. Our project has evolved and our theories developed over time. Hirsch's greatest objection seems to be that we do not define some specific problem, formulate rigid hypotheses, collect the appropriate data, determine whether they support or disconfirm the hypothesis, all in a one-shot effort, and then move on to something else. That, however, is the major shortcoming of much social research.

As Sherlock Holmes put it, "It is a capital mistake to theorize before one has data. Insensibly one begins to twist facts to suit theories, rather than twist theories to suit facts." While that sentiment rubs Hirsch the wrong way, it almost certainly captures the actual manner in which most science is conducted. Research is a continual process of interaction between theory and data, expectations and results, predictions and findings.

Hirsch makes much of what he construes as inconsistencies and contradictions in our theoretical refinements over the years. In fact, the refinements developed a steady and consistent line of theory-building, and will continue to do so. Contrary to Hirsch's implications, "mainstreaming" and "resonance" were not "dreamed up" for our response to his criticism. Passages from our earlier publications, cited in our previous response to Hirsch, suggesting that "a more refined analysis" of "differential cultivation patterns is a task of our continuing research" (Gerbner et al., 1978: 205-206) were deleted (without our knowledge or approval) from the published version of our response. Hirsch persists in confusing *his* reformulation (that cultivation will be most pronounced among the real-world counterparts of television's most victimized groups) with ours, claiming cultivation theory is disconfirmed by the failure of his (insufficient and superficial) test.

After examining the conceptual and empirical underpinnings of "mainstreaming" and "resonance," Hirsch (1981: 79) rejects them as "speculative, nonpredictive, unspecified, post hoc, and irrefutable." Let us examine these charges.

"Speculative." By "speculative," we assume that he does *not* mean "involving, based on, or constituting intellectual speculation" or "marked by questioning curiosity," because these hardly seem objectionable. "Mainstreaming" and "resonance" were indeed developed in response to "questioning curiosity," in that they reflect a paradigm designed to explain the intriguing systematic regularities we observed. Even most methodology textbooks frame theory-building as "invention, not discovery," and stress the roles of curiosity and causal observation in the development of theory.

Because these usages provide no conceivable basis for rejecting our refinements, he might mean "speculative" as in "theoretical rather than demonstrable." If so, this represents a puzzling inverse tautology, where "mainstreaming" and "resonance" are not good theory *because* they are theoretical. As to their not being "demonstrable," we can only point to the consistency with which they appear in the data, for a wide variety of cultivation topics (see, e.g., Gerbner et al., 1980b, forthcoming; Gerbner, 1980; Signorielli, 1979; Morgan and Gross, 1980; and also Hirsch's statement that "the more interesting findings" in GSS/

NORC appear primarily for high-income, high-education, high-status respondents). Strictly speaking, even his absurd interpretation of the effects of controlling for astrological sign show that they can be "demonstrated"; unlike the specifications we have presented, however, there is no theoretically intelligible reason for the resulting patterns.

Moreover, the findings that originally led us to these observations have already been supported by independent investigators.[10] In addition to the work of Dominick and Greenberg (1972), Lull et al. (forthcoming) found a significant interaction with education in the relationship between amount of viewing and feminism. In a sample of 523 Santa Barbara adults, among the highly educated, greater viewing goes with less feminism; better educated heavy viewers are more "sexist." But among those with less education (who are "otherwise" less likely to endorse feminist beliefs), the *high* feminists are the heavy viewers. As in our analysis (Signorielli, 1979), greater viewing means less sexism for the most sexist, and more sexism for the less sexist.

Impressive independent confirmation of our findings about school achievement (Morgan and Gross, 1980) comes from the California State Department of Education's (1980) massive statewide assessment program of over 510,000 sixth and tenth graders. In this study, negative relationships between amount of television viewing and scores on achievement tests of reading, written expression, and mathematics are most pronounced for high SES students, while the lowest SES students (who generally score lower) show some positive associations. Even more striking evidence for "mainstreaming" emerged under controls for English fluency. Light viewers with limited English skills score quite low, but the more television the low achievers watch, the higher their reading scores. Parental education, time spent on homework, and amount of extra-scholastic reading all produced the same results, particularly for sixth graders. Among light viewers, more parental education, more time spent doing homework, and more outside reading all go with better reading skills; among heavy viewers, these factors make almost no difference in scores.

Finally, Werner (forthcoming) reports that Norwegian adolescents' attitudes towards the United States provide evidence of "mainstreaming," in that stronger positive relationships with viewing were found in outlying areas; in central areas, attitudes were more positive regardless of viewing levels.[11]

"Nonpredictive." Whether "mainstreaming" and "resonance" are "nonpredictive" is yet to be seen. When the concepts were introduced, we (1980a: 16) stressed that they

> are still being developed and investigated. Although the number of empirical instances of each is rapidly growing, too few have been accumulated to allow for prediction of when one or the other—or neither—will occur. Nonetheless, we believe that the results we will report here suggest that these concepts merit serious consideration.

The fact that such instances *did* occur at all, always with highly plausible implications for interpretation (and *particularly* in data that Hirsch and others claimed show "no relationships"), led us to offer these concepts as new ideas worth pursuing.

Hirsch's confusions about what "mainstreaming" and "resonance" might predict in the first place underlie this issue. Not only does he persist in presenting *his* reformulation (again, that cultivation will be strongest in groups whose television counterparts are most likely to be victimized) as: (a) *our* expectations, and (b) contradictory to "mainstreaming" and "resonance," but he also asserts that the lack of support for this proposition (again, based on an inappropriate test) disconfirms "mainstreaming" and "resonance" along with the entire theory of cultivation. As with the previous charge, his argument relies on a specious inverse tautology: proposition X (which contradicts propositions Y and Z) is not borne out by the data, so propositions Y and Z should also be rejected. Specifically, Hirsch (1981: 83) claims that his test shows that *"there simply are not consistent patterns in any direction among the critical subgroups to which 'mainstreaming' and 'resonance' are presented as most applicable"* (italics in original)—in terms of a formulation which allegedly contradicts our refinements. And yet he is surprised that we "assert that the failure [sic] of the audience data to support this clearly formulated hypothesis [sic] casts no doubt on the logic of cultivation theory."

Thus, according to Hirsch, "mainstreaming" and "resonance" are "nonpredictive" because the results of his faulty test of his quite different hypothesis say so. Meanwhile, back at our ranch, the elaboration of our refinements into a predictive framework has been progressing in a variety of areas, and the shape they are taking is quite consistent with our early expectations. In Violence Profile No. 11, we suggested that "mainstreaming" is a more general process and "resonance" deals with special salience of specific issues to specific groups at certain times.

In other words, the ability of televison viewing to override or reduce the influence of demographic factors, with heavy viewers of "otherwise" divergent perspectives sharing a "television" view, reflects "mainstreaming," or the cultivation of common conceptions of social reality. When real-life experience or other dispositions increase the congruence between environmental and television messages, we should get "resonance."[12]

"Unspecified." In some ways, this charge resembles the previous one ("nonpredictive"), in that it relates to our alleged failure to "specify" which groups will show evidence of "mainstreaming" or "resonance." His criticisms which elaborate that point continue to demonstrate and affirm what we said in our previous comment: that Hirsch makes a consistent effort to oversimplify our theory into a mechanical concept. This is seen here in two ways: first, he would like to see explicit statements about which specific

groups will show these conditional patterns; second, he believes that the "mainstream" is some specific, fixed point.

As to the first, we contend that the conditional influence of other factors is not invariant across all subject areas in which we examine television's contribution to conceptions of social reality. While demographics (and particularly education) generally illuminate "mainstreaming," this need not always be the case. But the dispositions and experiences which should generate "resonance" are even more likely to vary across cultivation topics. The differential appropriateness of different controls for different analyses makes it unfeasible—even logically impossible—to set forth rules about which specific groups should "resonate." As Hornik et al. (1980) note in connection with their "distance" theory of susceptibility to media effects,[13] the "myriad of specific instances with quite varied characteristics" makes the specification of regularly vulnerable groups difficult. Our reluctance—even, refusal—to propose groups which will always show "mainstreaming" and "resonance" in all issues stems from our sensitivity to the exigencies of each analysis. What remains to be developed is a more comprehensive system of discovered specifications that *may*, in the future, suggest some dynamic *process* of specifications.

The second, and related, way in which our refinements are "unspecified" stems from the "absence of operational procedures . . . for determinig the point where the 'mainstream' resides for the population and for the comparison of subgroups." In short, the "mainstream" is *not a point*. "Mainstreaming" is a *process* of convergence, homogenization, and standardization, *in the direction of television's version of social reality*. It is this criterion which Hirsch ignores in his charge that our theory is confirmed by "whatever surprises or findings emerge from the data" and that cultivation explains "any percentage movements in any direction." The "mainstream" can *only* be identified in terms of baseline comparisons of counterpart subgroups. The "point" at which one set of (appropriately matched)

counterpart subgroups may converge need not be the same
"point" where another set of counterparts converge. The
"operational procedure" is simply the empirical identification of those groups who tend to deviate from the "mainstream" view for a particular issue or topic.

"Post Hoc." This is not too different from the preceding
"grounds for rejection" of our refinements. Again, we
explicitly introduced these constructs as having derived
from observing consistent, meaningful, conditional associations across numerous data bases and areas of analysis.
Certainly, we are aware of the potential dangers of post hoc
analysis. We can only insist that all theoretical developments are "post hoc," in the sense that they develop from
the perceived structure of regularities in phenomena. We
believe this represents reason for continued elaboration,
testing, and refinement—not rejection.

"Irrefutable" (i.e., nonrefutable). To a purist, the critical
determination of whether our refinements are "scientific"
lies in their ability to be falsified. We accept the need to
specify evidence that would constitute falsification. Furthermore, we laid out such a model in our previous comment. Yet, Hirsch "refutes" our demonstration of conditions
for falsifiability.

The only way he *can* dismiss our explanation of the
criteria by which these concepts could be falsified, however,
is by twisting what we actually said. Of the six possible
subgroup patterns *which we claimed were inconsistent
with "mainstreaming" or "resonance,"* Hirsch asserts that
three would be interpreted as evidence *supporting* them.[14] It
is bizarre to take examples presented by us as explicit
instances of contrary findings, and claim that we would
interpret them in the opposite manner.

This means that Hirsch's argument (that cultivation theory has an unusually high probability of being confirmed by
chance) is specious, because his conclusion that 73% of the
possible patterns provide support for the theory is based on
blatant distortion of what we actually said. In any case, we
doubt his assumption that all of these patterns are equally

likely outcomes (since the chance number of significant specifications would be partly determined by the number of subgroups examined), which further confuses his conclusion. And to make an additional restriction on the acceptability of supporting evidence (thus increasing the chances of falsification), we repeat that the observed specifications *must* reflect a theoretically meaningful aspect of televised social reality.

Finally, we must reiterate that Hirsch is clearly wrong, and his mistake stems from his basic misconstruction of our work, when he claims that we would interpret "no relationship" as evidence that "mainstreaming" and "resonance" cancelled each other out. Once again, his rejoinder ignores contrary explanations and evidence presented in our previous comment.

Whatever the original impetus for the critique might have been, we can only conclude that Hirsch's attack on cultivation theory and each of his reasons for rejecting the concepts of "mainstreaming" and "resonance" are unwarranted and incorrect.

NOTES

1. We are bemused that Hirsch faults us for not making these other datasets available, when during the year in which he conducted his "reanalysis," he never asked us for any information regarding our ongoing work, much less for access to other data bases.

2. We admit to a clerical error in our presentation, in Violence Profile No. 9 (Gerbner et al., 1978), of the "approval of violence" question asked of adolescents. The article erroneously states that the phrase, "for a good reason," was included in one sample (New Jersey) but not in the other (New York). A check on our original questionnaires, however, reveals that "for a good reason" was included in the questions for *both* samples. The *only* difference is that the New Jersey version reads "if you are mad at the person for a good reason" and the New York version reads "if you are mad at them for a good reason."

3. The GSS/NORC item about fear of walking alone at night has numerous problems that we detailed in our previous comment (see especially footnote 8). Since he does not address these, we need not repeat them here.

4. Two-thirds (66.6%) of those who could not "imagine a situation" said "yes" to *at least two* follow-ups.

5. This is also suggested by Hawkins and Pingree (forthcoming).

6. Despite the disappearance of our annual Technical Reports from Hirsch's library in footnote 2 and their sudden reappearance in footnote 13, these reports always contain complete sample documentation. Relatedly, we cannot fathom his allegation that we "currently" dichotomize television viewing. Except for the small samples reported in Violence Profile No. 10, we do not.

7. We surveyed 649 sixth—ninth graders in New Jersey and 113 ten-to-thirteen years-olds in New York. Dominick and Greenberg (1972) surveyed 838 fourth-sixth graders in Michigan; McLeod et al. (1972) surveyed 229 seventh graders and 244 tenth graders in Maryland, and 225 junior and senior high school students in Wisconsin; and McIntyre and Teevan (1972) surveyed 1242 senior and 1057 junior high students in Maryland.

8. McIntyre and Teevan (1972) used separate scales measuring approval of violence inflicted by adults, teenagers, and the police. The adult measure was the same as the GSS/NORC item's follow-ups; i.e., they *only* asked about approval in the specific situations, and did not include the problematic "any situations in which you can imagine" *general* version. Thus, from the data they report (again, which suggest a positive association between television and approval), we cannot unambiguously determine whether adults and children indeed show different associations with *the same measure*.

9. In our previous comment, we noted as significant specification in this relationship in 1978 among college-educated respondents. As it turns out, this is not replicated in the 1975 or 1980 data, supporting our conclusion that this association *is* essentially spurious. Examining within-group partial correlations reveals that exactly four out of 36 are significant. (The 36 correlations are obtained by multiplying the years of the GSS which include this item (three) by 12 groups, defined by sex (male/female), race (white/nonwhite), education (no college/some college), age (under 30/30-54/55 and up), and income (low/medium/high). The partials include all other demographic controls, including residual variation in the control group variable, where it is continuous.) Moreover, three out of the four significant within-group partials are in the 1978 data, accounting perhaps for his observation that this relationship holds up under multiple controls. The three that are significant (in 1978) are for males, high income respondents, and college-educated respondents—in all cases, groups who are *more* likely to be able to "imagine a situation." Thus, although this pattern does not appear in either the 1975 or 1980 data, one could argue that *when* heavier viewing *does* go with less "approval of violence," it is only within "privileged groups."

10. We had discussed these replications in our original comment. The discussion, however, was cut from our response without our knowledge or consent.

11. Note that these recent studies reflect independent confirmation *only* of our theoretical refinements. Our general findings about cultivation have been replicated by many other investigators; see Beuf (1974), Bryant et al. (1981), Elliott and Slater (1980), Freuh and McGhee (1975), Haney and Manzolati (forthcoming), Neville (1980), Tan (1979), Volgy and Schwartz (1980), Zill and Peterson (1980), and particularly the comprehensive review of this research by Hawkins and Pingree (forthcoming).

12. Analyses are in progress in two cultivation areas (conceptions of marriage and attitudes towards blacks) in which these assumptions are being implemented in an advance prediction framework. Preliminary results strongly support the validity of this framework.

13. Briefly, Hornik et al.'s (1980) concept of "distance" implies that television will be most influential when the environment is supportive of its messages, or when immediate information is low, and depending upon the "need to act" upon the issue. In some ways, this is not unlike "resonance."

14. We would agree with Hirsch that graph f illustrates an across-the-board cultivation effect; it does not, however, illustrate either "mainstreaming" or "resonance." Graph i, which was intended to be a perfect "X," does not illustrate "mainstreaming" because it does not represent the convergence of outlooks that marks the presence of "mainstreaming." Finally, graph j cannot be interpreted as an illustration of "resonance" because there are two *very different* effects of viewing. We would postulate the occurrence of "resonance" when one of the subgroups is very positively affected by viewing and the other remains static, or when one group is much more likely and the other group a little more likely to give the "television answer" (see graphs d and e). Clearly, graph j illustrates some television effect; however, since one group is much more inclined and the other group much less inclined to give the television answer, we would not explain the results as "resonance." In brief, both "resonance" and "mainstreaming" reflect the overall patterns exhibited by both (not just one) subgroups.

REFERENCES

BEUF, A. (1974) "Doctor, lawyer, household drudge." J. of Communication 24: 142-145.

BRYANT, J., R. A. CARVETH, and D. BROWN (1981) "Television viewing and anxiety: an experimental examination." J. of Communication 31: 106-119.

California State Department of Education (1980) Student Achievement in California Schools: 1979-80 Annual Report. Sacramento: California Assessment Program.

DOMINICK, J. R. and B. S. GREENBERG (1972) "Attitudes towards violence: the interaction of television exposure, family attitudes, and social class," pp. 314-335 in G. A. Comstock and E. A. Rubinstein (eds.) Television and Social Behavior, Vol. III. Washington: Government Printing Office.

ELLIOTT, W. R. and D. SLATER (1980) "Exposure, experience, and perceived TV reality for adolescents." Journalism Q. 57: 409-414, 431.

FREUH, T. and P. E. McGHEE (1975) "Traditional sex-role development and amount of time spent watching television." Child Development 11: 109.

GERBNER, G. (1980) "Sex on TV and What Viewers Learn From It." Paper presented to the National Association of Television Program Executives Annual Conference, San Francisco.

———— L. GROSS, M. JACKSON-BEECK, S. JEFFRIES-FOX, and N. SIGNORIELLI (1978) "Cultural indicators: Violence Profile No. 9." J. of Communication 28: 176-206.

GERBNER, G., L. GROSS, M. MORGAN, and N. SIGNORIELLI (1980a) "The 'mainstreaming' of America: Violence Profile No. 11." J. of Communication 30: 10-27.

———— (1980b) "Television's Contribution to Public Understanding of Science: A Pilot Project." The Annenberg School of Communications, University of Pennsylvania.

GERBNER, G., M. MORGAN, and N. SIGNORIELLI (forthcoming) "Programmng health protrayals: what viewers see, say, and do," in National Institute of Mental Health, Television and Behavior: Ten Years of Scientific Progress and Implications for the 80's.

HANEY, C. and J. MANZOLATI (forthcoming) "Television criminology: network illusions of criminal justice realities," in E. Aronson (ed.) Readings about the Social Animal. San Francisco: Freeman.

HAWKINS, R. P. and S. PINGREE (forthcoming) "TV influence on constructions of social reality," in National Institute of Mental Health, Television and Behavior: Ten Years of Scientific Progress and Implications for the 80's.

HIRSCH, P. M. (1981) "Distinguishing good speculation from bad theory: rejoinder to Gerbner et al." Communication Research 8, 1: 73-95.

HORNIK, R. C., J. GOULD, and M. GONZALEZ (1980) "Susceptibility to media effects." Presented at the International Communication Association Annual Conference, Acapulco, Mexico.

LOFTIN, C. and A. LIZOTTE (1974) "Violence and social structure: structural support for violence among privileged groups." Presented to the American Sociological Association, Montreal.

LULL, J., A. MULAC, and S. L. ROSEN (forthcoming) "Feminism as a predictor of mass media use." Sex Roles.

McINTYRE, J. J. and J. J. TEEVAN, Jr. (1972) "Television violence and deviant behavior," pp. 383-435 in G. A. Comstock and E. A. Rubinstein (eds.) Television and Social Behavior, Vol. III. Washington: Government Printing Office.

McLEOD, J. M., C. K. ATKIN, and S. H. CHAFFEE (1972) "Adolescents, parents, and television use: self-report and other-report measures from the Wisconsin sample," pp. 239-313 in G. A. Comstock and E. A. Rubinstein (eds.) Television and Social Behavior, Vol. III. Washington: Government Printing Office.

MORGAN, M. and L. GROSS (1980) "Television viewing, IQ, and academic achievement." J. of Broadcasting 24: 117-133.

NEVILLE, T. (1980) "Television viewing and the expression of interpersonal mistrust." Ph.D. dissertation, Princeton University.

SIGNORIELLI, N. (1979) "Television's contribution to sex-role socialization." Presented at the Telecommunications Policy Research Conference, Skytop, Pennsylvania.

TAN, A. (1979) "TV beauty ads and role expectations of adolescent female viewers." Journalism Q. 56: 283-288.

VOLGY, T. and J. SCHWARTZ (1980) "TV entertainment programming and sociopolitical attitudes." Journalism Q. 57: 150-155.

WERNER, A. (forthcoming) "The mainstreaming function of television: the case of attitudes to the USA among adolescents in Norway."

ZILL, N. and J. PETERSON (1980) "Television and children's inellectual develop ment: results from a national sample of youth." Presented at the Annual Conference of the American Association for Public Opinion Research, Cincinnati.

In this reply to Anderson and Sharrock's "Biasing the News: Technical Issues in 'Media Studies,'" included in Volume 2 of this series, Graham Murdock reviews recent British mass communication research in arguing that the Anderson and Sharrock reading was too narrow. Murdock also addresses a number of their criticisms of techniques of content analysis and argues, as the earlier critique did, that content-analytical answers cannot stand alone. Graham Murdock is research associate at the Centre for Mass Communication Research, University of Leicester.

40

MISREPRESENTING MEDIA SOCIOLOGY

A Reply to Anderson and Sharrock

Graham Murdock

Towards the beginning of Henry Fielding's *Tom Jones*, Tom's pompous tutors, Thwackum and Square get into an argument over religion. Thwackum, seeing he is losing ground, tries to bolster his case by narrowing the terms of the debate. 'When I mention religion' he asserts, 'I mean the Christian religion, and not only the Christian religion, but the Protestant religion, and not only the Protestant religion, but the Church of England'. In developing their critique of media sociology, Digby Anderson and Wes Sharrock (*Sociology* 13 (3) September 1979, pp. 367-85) have a good deal in common with Thwackum. When they mention media sociology, they mean exclusively British work, and not only British work but the handful of studies they happened to have come across. The result is a highly selective account which ignores whole areas of important research and seriously misrepresents the central concerns and present state of the field.

The problems begin with their general delineation of the area. Although the abstract that heads the piece promises 'a general critique of radical media/cultural studies', the first footnote clearly identifies 'media studies' with 'British sociology on the media'. Similarly, while they tend to use the general term 'media scholars' in the body of the text, almost all the studies they actually discuss are by sociologists. This slipping between terms results in major distortions. Most importantly, it tends to present 'media studies' as a more or less homogeneous field rather than the amalgam of distinctive and often antagonistic currents it actually is. In the first place, there is the long standing academic 'cold war' between sociological work and the approaches that have developed out of literary and cultural criticism, and more recently out of linguistics. Despite growing cross-disciplinary initiatives, the relationship between work centred on textual analysis and studies which focus on the social relations of production and consumption remains both institutionally uneasy and theoretically problematic. Ironically enough, studies of news (which Anderson and Sharrock single out for special attention in the first half of their paper) provide a particularly good example of these tensions.[1] On top of this, there is the whole issue of Marxism's recent revival and its incursion into cultural analysis. This cannot be adequately understood as an either/or question. Rather it is a matter of mapping the complex and shifting accommodations between the varieties of contemporary Marxism and the diverse currents within both the sociology of communications and cultural studies. Anderson and Sharrock ignore these complexities, however, and opt for a description by labelling which presents very different kinds of work as part of a composite 'radical media/cultural studies' — which is then counterposed to 'Bourgeois sociology' (p. 382) and to 'the kinds of problem that *we* would like to see

From Graham Murdock, "Misrepresenting Media Sociology: A Reply to Anderson and Sharrock," *Sociology, the Journal of the British Sociological Association* 14 (1980), pp. 457-468. Reprinted by permission of the publisher and author.

examined' (p. 371). As I shall show, had they been a little less selective in their reading and looked more carefully at the full range of recent sociological research on news, they would have noticed three things. Firstly, that sociologists interested in the area have spent a good deal of time investigating precisely the problems and issues which they claim have been ignored. Secondly, that much of this research can fairly be called 'critical' in Paul Lazarsfeld's sense of the term, which remains the usage most generally current within media sociology.[2] Thirdly, that most of this critical research (my own included) owes as much to methods and approaches developed within sociology as it does to traditions generated from within Marxism and cultural studies.[3]

　　Before taking up the major points of Anderson and Sharrock's critique in more detail, one further problem with their general presentation needs to be noted; its parochialism. It is clearly unreasonable to expect a comprehensive critical review of media sociology in the space of one article, and their decision to focus on studies of news is therefore entirely legitimate. However, their 'sociology in one country' approach prevents them from offering an adequate review of this area. Its development cannot be properly understood in splendid isolation. Here as in other fields, British work has drawn heavily on techniques and concepts developed by American researchers and they in turn have incorporated the lessons of recent British studies. To review the sociology of news without mentioning some of the more important American work is like relating the recent history of deviancy theory without mentioning Howard Becker.

　　In summary then, I want to argue that Anderson and Sharrock's highly selective reading of the field leads them to make a number of assertions which seriously misrepresent and distort both its nature and its scope. I will tackle what seem to me to be the most important of these in the order in which they appear in the original presentation.

Beyond Bias

　　Anderson and Sharrock elect to focus their general critique on the notion of bias on the grounds that this is a central and recurring theme in the academic analysis of news. This is certainly true of a number of early studies and of some more recent work. But as a general characterization of the area as a whole it is oversimple and misleading. Indeed, for the last three decades sociologists interested in news have been attempting to go beyond the restrictive notion of bias and to develop more adequate accounts of why news takes the form that it does.

　　The concept of bias is inextricably linked to a view of the news media as deliberately manipulated or managed by individuals or groups in pursuit of particular interests. This view permeates the early 'gatekeeper' studies of newsroom selection processes and the general critiques of press performance which concentrated on proprietal interventions and on the public relations and news management techniques of key sources in the political and state apparatuses and the large corporations. Clearly, bias in this sense cannot be entirely discounted. Editors do pursue their particular hobby-horses, proprietors do shape the ideological line of their papers, and organizations do attempt to engineer a favourable image of their activities. But, an analysis which focusses primarily on these kinds of specific interventions cannot explain adequately either the overall daily pattern of news coverage or the remarkable consistency of its images and rhetorics across news media and over time. As researchers recognized some time ago, this requires a detailed examination of the routine practices of news selection and processing and the working assumptions on which they rest. According to this approach then, if the news media are biased it is primarily an 'unwitting bias' which is produced by the normal organization of the news process rather than the machinations of particular editors, proprietors or sources. The *locus classicus* for this position is the Langs' study of the news coverage of Chicago's welcome parade for General MacArthur in 1951.[4] Their approach and methods were belatedly taken up in Britain in the well known study of the news media's presentation of the mass demonstration against the Vietnam War in

October 1968.[5] It particularly looked at the way that the available information and imagery was worked on and filtered on the basis of professional canons of 'news value'. However, as several commentators have since pointed out, this production-oriented approach tends to detach news organizations from the general environments in which they work.[6] Consequently, later work has been increasingly concerned with exploring the ways in which news production is constrained by the economic and ideological contexts in which it is embedded. Peter Golding and Philip Elliott's recent study, *Making the News*, for example, looks in detail at how the 'work situation' of news personnel is shaped by the 'market situation' and political position of their employing organizations.[7] They also examine the complex links between the professional ideologies of newsmen and more general social ideologies. The result does not entirely succeed in reconciling explanations in terms of action and power with explanations in terms of structures and determinations, but it does mark a decisive advance over the crude instrumentalism of the original bias approach.[8] Anderson and Sharrock, however, ignore these developments and proceed to subsume quite different concerns under the general heading of 'bias'. While sociological studies of news are certainly concerned with mapping and explaining the selective nature of news accounts of the social world, very few continue to define the problem in terms of bias.

Impartiality and Objectivity: Promise and Performance

A comparable ignorance of relevant literature and debate is also evident in their discussion of impartiality. According to Anderson and Sharrock, the notion that the news media ought to be impartial is held more or less exclusively by 'media scholars' who employ it as an imaginary standard against which to measure the performance of news organizations and find them wanting. 'Media scholars' they argue, are concerned 'to reveal that the news is biased in regard to the class struggle, against extra-parliamentary left-wingers, trade unionists, and so forth. It is far from clear to us, however, that *anyone* has ever claimed impartiality for the media in such cases' (p. 368). Well, it may not be clear to them, but it is certainly clear to television journalists.

Under the terms of the 1954 Television Act, the independent companies are under a statutory requirement to be impartial. Clause 3 subsection (c), requires 'that any news given in the programmes (in whatever form) is presented with due accuracy and impartiality'. Moreover, subsection (f) specifically extends this requirement to matters of controversy and demands 'that due impartiality is preserved on the part of the persons providing the programmes as respects matters of political or industrial controversy or relating to current public policy'. This is certainly understood as covering two of the areas mentioned by Anderson and Sharrock – trade union affairs and class conflict. The case of extra-parliamentary opposition is however, more complex.

In contrast to the ITV companies, the BBC's obligation to remain similarly impartial is not backed by statute. However, there is a long standing and binding understanding between the Corporation and the government of the day which is appended to the Licence Agreement. This takes its present form from Lord Normanbrook's letter to the then minister in 1961, in which he reaffirmed the 'Corporation's policy of treating controversial subjects with due impartiality in both the Corporation's news services and in the more general field of programmes dealing with matters of public policy'.[9] As the last Director General of the BBC, Sir Charles Curran has recently explained however, in practice this general requirement has been modified in one crucial respect. Since in his words 'the underlying assumption of the BBC is that of liberal democracy ... the whole concept of its establishment assumes its support for that system'.[10] This proviso has produced both the agreement to give electoral air time to the National Front (on the grounds that they are a properly constituted parliamentary party), and the ban on interviews with members of the IRA (on the grounds that they are enemies of liberal democracy). In this last case neutrality is indeed 'specified by relevances' in Anderson and Sharrock's phrase and not by 'a notional universal impartiality' (p. 369).

However, it is noteworthy that both decisions have generated a heated debate among journalists and other media workers as well as among academics and commentators as Jonathan Dimbleby's repeated criticisms of the BBC's coverage of Northern Ireland and the 'No Plugs for Thugs' campaign amply illustrate. In both cases argument has focussed on the meaning of impartiality and its justifiable limits, and on the gap between the television organizations' formal promises and their selective operationalization. The argument over impartiality is however only one aspect of the wider and more important debate about objectivity in news.

The canon of objectivity requires that news should offer as complete a capture of events in the world as possible, and that the presentation of these accounts should not be shaped by the personal values or commitments of the journalist involved. The ideal of objectivity then, rests on the claim that news is accurate, comprehensive and neutral, and consists of independently verifiable facts that are clearly separated from the expression of opinions or values. Consequently, news is required to eschew subjectivity and partisanship as well as partiality.[11] Although newspapers make no secret of their support for particular views and policies, they still subscribe to the ideal of objectivity in news reporting and to the consequent separation between news and editorializing. To understand why this ideal of objectivity remains central but at the same time problematic, we need to introduce an historical dimension to the analysis, a dimension which is conspicuously absent from Anderson and Sharrock's account.

As newspapers broke away from financial dependence on political groupings and became commercial institutions, subsidized by advertising, and competing for extended readerships in the market, they increasingly presented themselves as disinterested and non-partisan – a Fourth Estate of the realm operating beyond factional interests and serving the common interests of the nation and the people as a whole. The notion of objectivity was an essential bolster to this claim. It was in Gaye Tuchman's phrase a 'strategic ritual' which protected the newly professional journalist from proprietal encroachment and the press as a whole from government control and censorship.[12] From the outset however, the ideal of objectivity was challenged by counter definitions of the reporter's role. On one side there was the older notion of the journalist as man of letters, articulating his personal reactions to events of the day. On the other, there was the growth of 'muck-raking' journalism, intent on exposing abuse and graft on behalf of the poor and powerless. As Matthew Arnold complained at the time this new crusading journalism sacrificed objectivity to sensation and showed no concern whatever 'to get at the state of things as they truly are'.[13] Nevertheless, as competition for circulation increased, sensation and 'muck-raking' were useful in the struggle to get and keep readers. The result was a constant tension between the incorporation of newspapers into the entertainment business and the ideal of news as an objective record of events. This tension is still with us as notions of objectivity are once again under attack from the subjectivity of the 'new journalism' and the advocacy of which fuels much investigative reporting.[14] However, it is not, as Anderson and Sharrock would have it, that the criteria of 'attention grabbing, eyebrow raising, indignation arousing, titillating' and interest holding stories are 'vastly more important than are those of correctness, objectivity and the like' (p. 370). It is rather that news values are marked by a constant though variable tension between entertainment values and the ideal of objectivity, and that any explanation of why news assumes the forms that it does needs to take both into account. This holds for television as well as for the press.

Despite the official injunction to impartiality television news also incorporates elements of entertainment values. Indeed, as news has moved to the front line in the ratings battle, news presentations have become more and more a part of show business. This is most evident in the rise of the newsreaders as celebrities on a par with other media stars (a shift that was memorably displayed in Britain when Angela Rippon danced on the *Morecambe and Wise Christmas Show*).[15] Other commentators have pointed to the way in which the whole presentation of news bulletins – the condensed treatment of stories, the preference for dramatic visuals, the rapid cutting to sustain viewer interest – results in a highly incomplete and skewed picture of the social world. Here again, however, these criticisms have come from professional journalists like Robin Day and John Birt as well as from academic analysts.[16] The major difference is that sociologists studying news have marshalled a considerable amount of detailed empirical evidence in support of their arguments. Anderson and Sharrock, however, choose to ignore almost all of this work, or are not aware of it. As a result, their characterizations of content studies, production studies and research on audiences and impact is both ill-formed and grossly misleading.

Varieties of Textual Analysis

According to Anderson and Sharrock, within media sociology, 'the produced text' has been 'subject to little in the way of careful and detailed examination, being mainly used in illustrative service of preconceived themes. There is, thus, primarily a 'content analysis' kind of approach to those materials which examines them without any apparent concern for the form which the medium of their expression will assign them' (p. 373-4). There are several separate assertions here: (1) that most studies are content analyses; (2) that they tend to be selective and impressionistic and cursory rather than careful, systematic and detailed, and (3) that they have tended to ignore questions of form.

It is true that most major British analyses of news output have employed a version of content analysis in Berelson's sense. Recent examples include: Paul Hartmann's analysis of news about race;[17] Dave Morley, Paul Hartmann and the Glasgow Media Group on industrial relations news;[18] Philip Elliott on the coverage of Northern Ireland;[19] Peter Golding on images of welfare and scrounging;[20] and Denis McQuail's work on industrial, welfare and foreign news for the last Royal Commission on the Press.[21] To this we could add the work of Frank and others in the USA, and of Rositi and others on the Continent.[22] The one great advantage of content analysis over other methods is precisely that its selection of material is highly systematic, that its operating procedures are made explicit, and that its findings are therefore open to testing by replication. Hence, whilst the results can be criticized on a variety of grounds, content analysis certainly cannot be accused of using their material 'in illustrative service of preconceived themes'.

The claim that researchers have paid relatively scant attention to questions of form is generally correct. Although here again, a closer look at the range of recent studies would reveal several attempts to deal with 'story construction, character distribution, motive ascription, narrative flow' (p. 374).[23] Moreover, with the increasing application of linguistic techniques to media analysis, questions of form and expression are becoming more central.[24] There is in fact a growing tendency to try and combine quantitative and qualitative techniques in order to arrive at a fuller and more specific map of the way news organizes social meaning. However, textual analysis, no matter how comprehensive, can never provide a sufficient basis for a sociological account of communications. This requires an investigation of the social practices involved in their production and consumption. Contrary to Anderson and Sharrock's assertions, such investigations have in fact commanded a great deal of attention from sociologists researching in mass communication in general and news in particular.

Studying News Practices: The Ethnographic Tradition

According to Anderson and Sharrock, existing research into how news is actually produced has only involved 'very impressionistic ethnographic work at production points' (p. 372) and they cite the first volume of Bad News in support. This is a somewhat peculiar choice since Bad News is primarily a study of news output several of whose authors are on record as arguing for the primacy of textual analysis and as doubting the necessity for ethnographic studies of news making. Even had they wished to develop an adequate ethnography, however, they were unable to do so since they could not gain sustained access to the relevant news organizations. Instead, they had to fall back on brief encounters and background knowledge, with the inevitable result that the treatment of production processes is somewhat impressionistic, and has been widely criticized by other researchers on exactly these grounds. However, to present this instance as representative of production studies as a whole is a travesty. Indeed, the systematic and sustained observation of news production has been one of the major research areas in the recent sociology of mass communications. For Anderson and Sharrock to wholly ignore this substantial body of detailed work displays an intellectual myopia of a very high order.

As with other areas, work in this field is most fully developed in the United States and an adequate review of recent work would at least need to take account of the studies of Altheide, Gans, Gelles, Sigelman, and Tuchman.[25] Although British research is on an altogether more modest scale, the pioneering work of Halloran and Blumler[26] in the 'sixties has recently been supplemented by Philip Schlesinger's major ethnography of BBC news production, Michael Tracey's work on the cognate area of current affairs, and Burns' organizational study of the BBC, which deals with news in the context of the Corporation as a whole.[27] The insights into professional practices and ideologies generated by ethnographic work have been further supplemented by interview studies of journalists as an occupational group. Here again, Anderson and Sharrock cite only one example of this genre (Steve Chibnall's work on crime reporters) and ignore other central studies such as Tunstall's two monographs on specialist correspondents and the Westminster 'lobby',[28] and relevant American research by Johnstone, Rosenblum and others.[29]

All in all then, we now have a good deal of systematic empirical evidence on newsmen's professional ideologies and the way they are operationalized in a range of organizational settings and across a range of story types.

The Active Audience

To anyone with a passing acquaintance with recent research, Anderson and Sharrock's claim that: ' "The reader" does not make many appearances in the media literature as anything other than a passive dope' (p. 374) will appear positively bizarre. From the beginning of sociological research into media impact in the 1930s, researchers have been struggling to replace the image of passive consumption developed by psychologists, with an image of audience members as actively interpreting, selecting and reworking the meanings carried by media material.[30] Despite this long standing opposition however, the direct effect model still lingers on in empirical studies[31] and in certain of the general conceptions of media impact organized around the notions of reproduction or domination. At the same time, a great deal of recent British work has explicitly opposed these models and tried to develop an empirically grounded account of the ways consumers negotiate media meanings and of the limits to these negotiations. The most important of these attempts have reconnected studies of consumption to the sociology of stratification and focussed on the ways that actors' negotiations are framed by the differential access to social experience and interpretative schemas, consequent on their place in the stratified social order.

One line of analysis has taken particular areas of news coverage (race, industrial relations, welfare) and concentrated on the interplay between media imagery and situational accounts among people with differing degrees of direct experience of the social domain in question.[32] Other work has attempted to develop a more general account of variations in media consumption using Frank Parkin's model of class-based meaning systems.[33] Other researchers again have approached the question of audience negotiations through detailed ethnographic studies of particular groups.[34] As yet, these studies do not constitute a coherent body of work and they are open to criticism at a number of levels. But the one criticism that cannot be levelled against them is that they conceptualize the audience as passive dopes. On the contrary they stress the active and negotiated relationship between consumers and texts. However, negotiation is by no means the same as rejections and critique.

Commonsense Media Criticism: From Scepticism to Critique

As Anderson and Sharrock rightly point out, readers and viewers are perfectly capable of 'exercising judgement, wit, scepticism, a sense of proportion, a different conceptual scheme, an appreciation that it's only a newspaper story, or a television item' (p. 374). However, the existence of these capacities does not mean that 'the media simply cannot fulfil their hegemonic task' (p. 374).

There is certainly evidence that people have a sceptical stance towards the news media. According to the McGregor Commission's survey, for example, only around a third of the readers of all the national dailies said that their paper gave fair coverage to all points of view. Readers of the two best selling 'populars', The Sun and The Daily Mirror, were even more critical. A third agreed that their chosen paper was apt to get its facts wrong and almost two-thirds complained of sensationalism in the reporting.[35] Television news is generally seen as more accurate and impartial although even here there is considerable scepticism.[36] However, it does not follow that the press and television news 'are incapable of serving as real instruments of serious hegemonic struggle' (p. 384). The links between scepticism and critique are attenuated in a variety of ways. Firstly, and most importantly, most people do not have ready access to the alternative sources of information and interpretation on which to build a comprehensive critique, of say, the news coverage of economic affairs. They are priced out of the market for information prepared by private agencies such as stockbrokers and investment analysts, and they count themselves out of the market for specialised media such as the Financial Times and the Investor's Chronicle because they feel that they lack the competence and background to cope with the technical arguments and presentations.[37] The result, as audience surveys clearly show, is a sizeable 'information gap' which follows the contours of the more general distribution of wealth and cultural competence. This gap will almost certainly widen still further with the rise of the new privatised information technologies and the erosion of opportunities within the education system. Moreover, as the socialist press has been driven to the edges of the major newspaper markets by the spiralling costs of production, the major traditional source of critical perspectives has reached a diminishing audience with less and less frequency. In the absence of a radical meaning system to organize their criticisms, people's scepticism of the news media can co-exist quite comfortably with a ready acceptance of their dominant images and explanations. Indeed, it is exactly these ambivalences, unevennesses and contradictions in people's responses to media material that recent research has been concerned to explore.[38]

Cutting Out and Working Up

Throughout their exposition, Anderson and Sharrock proceed in precisely the way they attribute to media sociologists. They select particular cases, detach them from their relevant contexts, present them as representative, and interpret them in ways that bolster their argument but which exclude other possible readings. This technique of 'cutting out and working up' (p. 375) is well to the fore in their extended discussion of an extract from one of my articles which forms the focus of the second half of their paper.[39]

The 'cutting out' takes place at two levels. Firstly, they focus on only one page of an eleven page piece. They concede that their 'summary does no justice to the elegance of Murdock's argument' and that 'it is obviously not an adequate analysis of his presentational work' (p. 378). But they make no effort to summarize the overall argument of the article or to make clear the context in which it was presented. In fact, it began life as a speech to a conference of youth workers. It set out to summarize some of the arguments that were emerging from my ongoing research on adolescents, and to draw out their implications for youth policy. Given the non-specialist nature of the audience, I did not attempt to present the empirical results of the research or to explore the technical and theoretical issues that underpinned it. The headlines quoted were presented solely as illustrations of arguments emerging out of the more detailed analysis of the development of popular images of youth. They were not offered as demonstrations or proofs. In addition, the paper drew on my wider research in the sociology of youth and mass communications and was intended to be read as a contribution to the general arguments I have been developing in a series of publications. Anderson and Sharrock's failure to place the piece quoted in the context of my work as a whole, results in a considerable mis-characterization of my general approach and way of working.

Youth as Metaphor

In the course of their discussion, however, they do raise an important point about images of youth. The crux of their argument, 'is that the headlines (I analyse) do not attribute the qualities to youth which (I say) they do for they are not "about" youth at all' (p. 375). As Jim Schenkein points out, headlines are capable of containing a plurality of connotations and therefore present a 'referential puzzle'.[40] It is not always clear what exactly they are about. Nevertheless, I want to insist that headlines like: YOUTH FINED FOR INDECENT EXPOSURE and BOY, 16, SWIMS THE CHANNEL, are about youth. They are also about a variety of other things; including individual achievement against the odds; sexuality and its control; contrasted ways of spending spare time; the nature of conformity and deviance. However, this choice of meanings and connotations is not the case of 'either/or' which Anderson and Sharrock tend to present. On the contrary, my argument is that these general connotations are activated and expressed *through* images of youth and that it is precisely this specific mediation that invests them with much of their power and pervasiveness.[41]

Since their emergence out of the maelstrom of the Industrial and French revolutions, our modern notions of adolescence and of generations have provided a potent 'touch on the times'; a means of representing and comprehending change and conflict in culture and society. Moreover, they have been interwoven from the outset with images of class and have often been counterposed against them as everyday explanations of social division and disorder. As I have shown in detail elsewhere, these connotations cohered around the opposed images of conforming and deviant youth which crystallized in the years between 1870 and 1914 when adolescents finally emerged as a universal and problematic social category. Variants of these images permeated both academic formulations and policy debates, and were widely taken up and publicized in the emerging commercial news and entertainment media.[42] I have also attempted to show that the dominant images of youth established then, have proved remarkably resilient and still play a key role in organizing popular presentations and policy debates. My reading of the headlines I cite then, is supported by an extensive comparative investigation of images and of the ways they have developed and become institutionalized.

Even so, Anderson and Sharrock are right to insist that I make some attempt to show the extent to which my 'preferred reading' of the imagery is actually shared by media consumers. As the full text of the article they quote makes clear however, this was an integral part of the research I was drawing on. Ten lines after they break off their quotation, I explicitly point out that 'our interviews with the parents of teenagers, indicated that these stock news images provide many of the anchor points around which they organize their own perceptions of what is happening to contemporary youth'.[43] By forgetting to mention this crucial part of my work, they misrepresent both its nature and scope. My analysis of everyday conceptions is certainly limited and open to criticism. It only establishes a general homology between the overall structures and emphases of news accounts and the general structure of popular perceptions. It cannot specify the ways in which particular stories are read. Nevertheless, it does begin to unpack some of the links between media imagery and commonsense definitions of the situation. In contrast, Anderson and Sharrock offer no supporting evidence at all for their alternative readings.

Conclusion

As I have tried to indicate, this highly selective treatment of my own work is typical of their presentation of the field as a whole. The sociology of mass communications and the cognate areas of cultural and communications studies have grown rapidly over the last few years, and there is now a pressing need for a thorough-going critical review of the major areas of concern. However, this will require, at the very least, a comprehensive reading of the major studies and a secure grasp of the differing and often opposed intellectual traditions from which they spring. Anderson and Sharrock fulfil neither of these minimum requirements with the result that their presentation is more like a caricature than a critique.

Notes

1. Compare, for example, The Glasgow Media Group's *Bad News*, Routledge and Kegan Paul, 1977, and Philip Schlesinger's, *Putting 'Reality' Together: BBC News*, Constable, 1978
2. See, 'Administrative and Critical Communications Research', in Paul Lazarsfeld, *Qualitative Analysis*, Allyn and Bacon, 1972. Since Anderson and Sharrock never specify what exactly they mean by 'critical' work, it is difficult to know how far they would accept this definition.
3. I have outlined my own approach in Peter Golding and Graham Murdock, 'Theories of Communication and Theories of Society', *Communication Research*, vol. 5, no. 3, 1978, and 'Ideology and the Mass Media: the Question of Determination', in Michele Barratt, *et al.* (eds.), *Ideology and Cultural Production*, Croom Helm, 1979.
4. Cf. Kurt Lang and Gladys Lang, 'The unique perspective of television and its effects: a pilot study', *American Sociological Review*, vol. 18, no. 1, 1953.
5. James Halloran, Philip Elliott and Graham Murdock, *Demonstrations and Communication: A Case Study*, Penguin, 1970.
6. See, for example, Colin Sumner, *Reading Ideologies*, Academic Press, 1979, pp. 73-7.
7. Peter Golding and Philip Elliott, *Making the News*, Longman, 1979.
8. I have discussed the problematic relation between instrumental and structural approaches to control in, 'Class, Power and the Press: Problems of Conceptualization and Evidence', in Harry Christian (ed.), *The Sociology of the Press and Journalism*, University of Keele (in press).
9. The full text is reprinted in Anthony Smith, *British Broadcasting*, David and Charles, 1974, pp. 247-8.
10. Cf. Sir Charles Curran, *A Seamless Robe: Broadcasting Philosophy and Practice*, Collins, 1979, p. 106.

11. It is no accident that this definition of the professional journalist's role bears a strong resemblance to the ideal of sociological investigation as value free. Both emerged as professional practices at the same point in time, and both shared some of the same intellectual history.

12. Cf. Gaye Tuchman, 'Objectivity as Strategic Ritual: An Examination of Newsmen's Notions of Objectivity', *American Jl. of Sociology*, vol. 77, 1972.

13. Quoted in J. O. Baylen, ' "The New Journalism", in Late Victorian Britain', *The Australian Jl. of Politics and History*, vol. 18, no. 3, 1972, p. 367. The tension between objectivity and entertainment in the American commercial press of the period is usefully discussed in Michael Schudson, *Discovering the News*, Basic Books, 1978, chapters 2 and 3. On the career of the idea of objectivity in the British press, see, Anthony Smith, 'The long road to objectivity and back again: the kinds of truth we get in journalism', in George Boyce, *et al.* (eds.), *Newspaper History*, Constable, 1978.

14. For a discussion of the recent situation, see, Morris Janowitz, 'Professional Models in Journalism: the gatekeeper and the advocate', *Journalism Quarterly*, vol. 52, no. 4. 1975.

15. For a useful discussion of American trends see, Ron Powers, *The Newscasters: The News Business as Show Business*, St. Martin's Press, 1977.

16. Robin Day, *Day by Day*, London 1975. John Birt or Peter Jay, series of articles in *The Times*, 28 February, 30 September and 1 October 1975, and 2 and 3 October 1976.

17. Paul Hartmann, *et al.*, 'Race as News: a Study of the Handling of Race in the British National Press from 1963 to 1970', in *Race as News*, UNESCO, 1970.

18. Cf. Dave Morley, 'Industrial conflict and the Mass Media', *Sociological Review*, vol. 24, no. 2, 1976; Paul Hartmann, 'Industrial Relations in the News Media', *Industrial Relations Jl.*, vol. 6, 1975/6; Glasgow Media Group, *op. cit.*

19. Philip Elliott, 'Reporting Northern Ireland: A Study of News in Britain, Ulster and the Irish Republic', in *Media and Ethnicity*, UNESCO, 1977.

20. Peter Golding and Sue Middleton, *Information and the Welfare State*. Final report to the Nuffield Foundation, 1978, chapter 3. A fuller analysis is forthcoming in the same authors' *Images of Welfare*, Martin Robertson.

21. Denis McQuail, *Analysis of Newspaper Content* (Royal Commission on the Press, Research Series No. 4), HMSO, 1977.

22. Cf. Robert S. Frank, *Message Dimensions of Television News*, Lexington Books, 1973. Franco Rositi, 'The Television News Programme: Fragmentation and Recomposition of our Image of Society', in *News and Current Events on TV*, vol. 1, Radiotelevisione Italiana, 1976.

23. The second volume of the Glasgow Media Group's *Bad News* study deals extensively with these kind of issues. See also, Edward J. Epstein, *News from Nowhere: Television and the News*, Random House, 1973, pp. 164-80.

24. Cf. Tony Trew, ' "What the Papers Say": Linguistic Variation and Ideological Difference', in Roger Fowler, *et al*, *Language and Control*, Routledge and Kegan Paul, 1979.

25. Cf. David Altheide, *Creating Reality*, Sage Publications, 1976; Herbert J. Gans, *Deciding What's News*, Pantheon Books, 1979; Richard Gellis and Robert Faulkner, 'Time and Television News: Task Temporalization in the Assembly of Unscheduled Events', *Sociological Quarterly*, vol. 19, 1978; Lee Sigelman, 'Reporting the News: An Organizational Analysis', *American Jl. of Sociology*, vol. 75, 1973; Gaye Tuchman, *Making News*, Free Press, 1978. Although the full versions of the Gans and Tuchman studies were not available before Anderson and Sharrock submitted their piece, they were both well known from articles and conference presentations.

26. Cf. J. D. Halloran, *et al, op. cit.*, Jay Blumler, 'Producers' Attitudes towards Coverage of an

Election Campaign' in Paul Halmos (ed), *The Sociology of Mass Media Communicators*, University of Keele, 1969.

27. Philip Schlesinger, *op. cit.*; Michael Tracey, *The Production of Political Television*, Routledge and Kegan Paul, 1977; Tom Burns, *The BBC: Public Institution and Private World*, Macmillan, 1977.

28. Jeremy Tunstall, *Journalists at Work*, Constable, 1971, and *The Westminster Lobby Correspondents*, Routledge and Kegan Paul, 1970.

29. Cf. John W. Johnstone, *et al.*, *The News People: A Sociological Portrait of American Journalists and their Work*, University of Illinois Press, 1976; Barbara Resenblum, *Photographers at Work: A Sociology of Photographic Styles*, Holmes and Meier, 1978.

30. Vigorous opposition to the 'direct effects' model of media impact and the attempt to develop an active conception of audience response, is also characteristic of the 'uses and gratifications' approach developed within social psychology. For an assessment and critique of this tradition see: Philip Elliott, ' "Uses and Gratifications" Research: A Critique and a Sociological Alternative', in J. Blumler and E. Katz (eds.), *Uses and Gratifications Studies: Theories and Methods*, Sage Publications, 1974.

31. See for example, William Belson, *Television Violence and the Adolescent Boy*, Saxon House, 1978.

32. See for example, Paul Hartmann and Charles Husband, *Racism and the Mass Media*, Davis-Poynter, 1974; Paul Hartmann, *The Media and Industrial Relations*. Final report to the Leverhulme Trust, 1976, chapters 5 and 6, and, 'News and public perceptions of industrial relations', *Media, Culture and Society*, vol. 1, no. 3, 1979; Peter Golding and Sue Middleton, *op. cit.*

33. Tony Piepe, *et al*, *Mass Media and Cultural Relationships*, Saxon House, 1978.

34. See, for example, Paul Willis, *Profane Culture*, Routledge and Kegan Paul, 1978.

35. Royal Commission on the Press, *Attitudes to the Press*, HMSO, 1977, pp. 62-7.

36. According to a recent survey of viewers conducted by the IBA, for example, only 44% of those interviewed said that news and documentary programmes on industrial relations were 'most usually fair' and only 39% thought this about programmes on Northern Ireland. See, *The Need for News: Audience Attitudes Towards Nine News Topics*, Independent Broadcasting Authority, 1978, p. 25.

37. Even *The Sunday Times*, whose readers are disproportionately drawn from the highest educated strata of the population, felt it necessary to provide a guide to the technical presentations of *The Financial Times*. They introduced the feature as follows: "*The Financial Times* is not really a newspaper at all. It is a trade paper, or rather The Trade Paper. The people who read it so avidly are all professional players of the various money games running non-stop round the world, with their big tables in the City of London. Like most games, these have their own rules and language. If you do not know the jargon, *The Financial Times*, which reports the games so faithfully, does not make sense. But now you can play; here is Lifespan's ABC of the FT' (*Sunday Times Magazine*, November 25, 1979, pp. 98-9).

38. See, for example, Golding and Middleton (forthcoming), *op. cit.* This theme of the uneven and contradictory relation between 'situated' and media-relayed images and interpretative frames, has emerged independently in recent studies of workers' consciousness. Cf. Theo Nichol's 'Ideology and "Experience" ', in Theo Nichols and Peter Armstrong, *Workers Divided*, Fontana, 1976; and Howard H. Davis, *Beyond Class Images: Explorations in the Structure of Social Consciousness*, Croom Helm, 1979, especially pp. 108-9.

39. For the full text of the article see David Marsland and Michael Day, *Youth Service, Youth Work and the Future*, National Youth Bureau, 1976, pp. 15-26. The editors' introduction to

the collection clearly indicates the institutional and intellectual context of my contribution.

40. Cf. Jim Schenkein, 'The Radio Raiders Story', in George Psathas (ed.), *Everyday Language: Studies in Ethnomethodology*, Irvington Publishers, 1979, p. 191.

41. One area that has been particularly explored in recent work on the news media's presentations of youth, is the complex relationship between images of youth, and images of race and social order. See, for example, Tony Trew, *op. cit.*; Stuart Hall, *et al*, *Policing the Crisis*, Macmillan, 1978; Mark Fishman, 'Crime Waves as Ideology', *Social Problems*, vol. 25, no. 5, 1978.

42. This argument is developed in detail in Graham Murdock, *Beyond Youth Culture*, Constable (forthcoming). For a brief summary, see Graham Murdock, *Adolescent Culture and the Mass Media*, final report to the SSRC, 1979, chapter 3, and Graham Murdock and Robin McCron, 'Consciousness of Class and Consciousness of Generation', in Stuart Hall and Tony Jefferson (eds.), *Resistance Through Rituals*, Hutchinson, 1976.

43. The relevant empirical evidence is summarized in Graham Murdock, 1979, *op. cit.*, chapter 5.